THE MOST TRUSTED NAME IN TRAVEL

®

ARIZONA AND THE GRAND CANYON

20th Edition

By Gregory McNamee
and Bill Wyman

FrommerMedia LLC

Published by:
Frommer Media LLC

Frommer's Arizona and the Grand Canyon, 20th Edition
ISBN 978-1-62887-406-8 (paper), 978-1-62887-407-5 (e-book)

Editorial Director: Pauline Frommer
Editor: Holly Hughes
Production Editor: Lynn Northrup
Cartographer: Roberta Stockwell
Photo Editor: Meghan Lamb
Indexer: Maro Riofrancos
Cover Designer: Dave Riedy

For information on our other products or services, see www.frommers.com.

Frommer Media LLC also publishes its books in a variety of electronic formats. Some content that appears in print may not be available in electronic formats.

Manufactured in the United States of America

5 4 3 2 1

HOW TO CONTACT US

In researching this book, we discovered many wonderful places—hotels, restaurants, shops, and more. We're sure you'll find others. Please tell us about them, so we can share the information with your fellow travelers in upcoming editions. If you were disappointed with a recommendation, we'd love to know that, too. Please write to: Support@FrommerMedia.com.

FROMMER'S STAR RATINGS SYSTEM

Every hotel, restaurant and attraction listed in this guide has been ranked for quality and value. Here's what the stars mean:

★ Recommended
★★ Highly Recommended
★★★ A must! Don't miss!

AN IMPORTANT NOTE

The world is a dynamic place. Hotels change ownership, restaurants hike their prices, museums alter their opening hours, and buses and trains change their routings. And all of this can occur in the several months after our authors have visited, inspected, and written about these hotels, restaurants, museums, and transportation services. Though we have made valiant efforts to keep all our information fresh and up-to-date, some few changes can inevitably occur in the periods before a revised edition of this guidebook is published. So please bear with us if a tiny number of the details in this book have changed. Please also note that we have no responsibility or liability for any inaccuracy or errors or omissions, or for inconvenience, loss, damage, or expenses suffered by anyone as a result of assertions in this guide.

CONTENTS

LIST OF MAPS

ABOUT THE AUTHORS

The author of *Tortillas, Tiswin, and T-Bones: A Food History of the Southwest,* **Gregory McNamee** was the first writer to document the Sonoran hot dog, which has since become an international sensation. He has also written *The Ancient Southwest: A Guide to Archaeological Sites; Monumental Places: Arizona's National Parks and Monuments;* and many other books. He has lived in Tucson since 1975. Visit him at www.gregorymcnamee.com.

Bill Wyman is a former assistant managing editor of National Public Radio in Washington, where he oversaw the network's arts, digital, and media coverage across its signature news shows. He was a senior editor at Salon, the pioneering Internet magazine. His work has been published in *The New York Times, The New Yorker, New York* magazine, and other publications. He grew up in Arizona and currently lives in Phoenix.

THE BEST OF ARIZONA

1

It's even on the license plate, so there's no getting away from the Grand Canyon when you're in the Grand Canyon State. But anyone's who has seen magnificent Monument Valley, or the exquisite Canyon de Chelly, or the unique cactus forests in Saguaro National Park, knows that the state's wonders merely begin there. The sunburst colors of Antelope Canyon, the desolate landscape around Four Corners, the towering red-rock buttes of Sedona, and on a smaller scale, wonders like the Meteor Crater or southern Arizona's Kartchner Caverns—there's so much here to intrigue and delight visitors and residents alike. It's not just natural wonders, either: Both Phoenix and Tucson are distinctive cities with top-tier restaurants and resorts, lively nightlife scenes, and museums, galleries, and parks bursting with art.

THE best PLACES TO DISCOVER THE OLD WEST

- **Rodeos:** Any rodeo, and this state has plenty, will give you a glimpse of the Old West, but the rodeos in Prescott (p. 170) and Payson (p. 335) both claim to be the oldest in the country. Whichever rodeo you attend, you'll see plenty of bronco busting, bull riding, and beer drinking.
- **Guest Ranches:** On guest ranches all over the state, the Old West lives on, and wranglers lead city slickers on horseback rides through desert scrub and mountain meadows. Campfires, cookouts, and cattle are all part of the experience. See "Where to Stay" choices throughout this book.
- **Monument Valley:** If you've ever seen a shot of John Wayne riding a horse against a sweeping backdrop of massive buttes, you've seen Monument Valley. The starkly beautiful and fantastically shaped buttes and mesas of this valley are the quintessential western landscape. See p. 318.
- **Old Tucson Studios:** Originally constructed as a movie set, this back lot and amusement park provides visitors with a glimpse of

Monument Valley, the quintessential Western movie backdrop.

the most familiar Old West—the Hollywood West. Sure, the shootouts and cancan revues are silly, but it's all in good fun. See p. 365.

- **Cowboy Poetry Festivals:** From heroes on horseback to poets on the prairie, it's been a long, lonesome ride for the American cowboy. At several events around the state, you can hear how some cowboys deal with the hardships and happiness of the cowboy life. See "Arizona Calendar of Events" on p. 30.
- **Tombstone:** Unlike Old Tucson—the *reel* Old West—Tombstone is a genuine historic town, the *real* Old West. However, "the town too tough to die" was reincarnated long ago as a tourist attraction, with gunslingers in the streets, stagecoach rides, and shootouts at the O.K. Corral. See p. 454.

THE best NATIVE AMERICAN RUINS & ROCK ART

- **Tonto National Monument:** Reached via the Apache Trail scenic road, this archaeological site east of Phoenix has one of Arizona's few easily accessible cliff dwellings, where visitors can walk around inside the ruins, under the watchful eye of a ranger. See p. 161.
- **Besh-Ba-Gowah Archaeological Park:** Reconstructed to look the way they might have appeared 700 years ago, these Phoenix-area ruins provide a bit more cultural context you'll get at others in the state, making them especially good for kids. See p. 161.
- **Casa Grande Ruins National Monument:** While most of Arizona's ruins are built of stone, this massive structure south of Phoenix is built of packed desert soil. Inscrutable and perplexing, Casa Grande seems to rise from nowhere. See p. 162.

- **Montezuma Castle National Monument:** Located just off I-17 south of Sedona, this is one of Arizona's best preserved cliff dwellings, its adobe surface still intact. Nearby Montezuma Well also has some small ruins. See p. 185.
- **Canyon de Chelly National Monument:** Small cliff dwellings up and down the stunning length of Canyon de Chelly can be viewed from overlooks; even better, take a tour into the canyon itself to see some ruins up close. See p. 310.
- **Wupatki National Monument:** North of Flagstaff, visitors can walk around several Sinagua village ruins, including a three-story, 100-room pueblo with a ball court. See p. 263.
- **V Bar V Heritage Site:** The extensive petroglyphs at this national forest site near Sedona have an intriguing astronomical connection: At different times of the year, shadows fall on different images on the rock wall. See p. 195.
- **Rock Art Ranch:** Set in a remote canyon southeast of Winslow, this private historic site preserves one of the most extensive collections of petroglyphs in the state. You can visit only by reservation; if you're lucky, you'll have the place all to yourself. See p. 290.

THE most offbeat TRAVEL EXPERIENCES

- **Taking a Vortex Tour in Sedona:** Crystals and pyramids are nothing compared to the power of the Sedona vortexes, which just happen to be in the middle of some gorgeous scenery. Organized tours shuttle believers from one vortex to the next. If you offer it, they will come. See p. 193.
- **Gazing at the Stars:** Stargazers will find plenty to keep them sleepless in the desert as they peer at the stars through telescopes at Lowell Observatory in Flagstaff (p. 261) or Kitt Peak National Observatory near Tucson (p. 360). North of Flagstaff, you can even stay at a B&B that doubles as an astronomical observatory.
- **Marveling at a Meteorite Crater:** West of the town of Winslow, you can visit the world's best-preserved meteorite impact crater, 2½ miles in circumference and 550 feet deep. In the 1960s, NASA even used the crater to train moon-bound astronauts. See p. 290.
- **Sleeping in a Wigwam:** Back in the heyday of Route 66, the Wigwam Motel in Holbrook lured passing motorists with its unusual architecture: concrete, wigwam-shaped cabins. Today, this little motel is still a must for anyone on a Route 66 pilgrimage. See p. 305.
- **Exploring the Titan Missile Museum:** Want to find out what it feels like to have your finger on "the button"? At this former ICBM missile silo, now decommissioned and open to the public, you can find out—in a blast-protected control room more than 100 feet underground. See p. 374.

You can still spend a night in the Wigwam Motel, a classic Route 66 experience.

- **Stopping to Smell the Rose Tree:** The town of Tombstone in southeastern Arizona is best known as the site of the shootout at the O.K. Corral, but the "town too tough to die" also boasts the world's largest rose tree. See p. 457.

THE best ACTIVE VACATIONS

- **Rafting the Grand Canyon:** Whether you go for 3 days or 2 weeks, nothing else comes even remotely close to the excitement of a rafting trip through the Grand Canyon. Sure, the river is crowded with groups in the summer, but the grandeur of the canyon more than makes up for that. See p. 241.
- **Hiking into the Grand Canyon or Havasu Canyon:** Not for the unfit or the faint of heart, a hike down into the Grand Canyon or Havasu Canyon is a journey through millions of years set in stone. This strenuous trip takes plenty of advance planning. There's both a campground and a lodge at the bottom of each canyon, so you can choose to make this trip with either a fully loaded backpack or just a light daypack. See p. 235 and 276.
- **Riding the Range at a Guest Ranch:** Yes, there are still cowboys in Arizona. They ride ranges all over the state, and so can you if you book a stay at one of Arizona's guest ranches (once known as dude ranches). You might even get to drive some cattle down the trail. After a long (or short) day in the saddle, you might opt to soak in a hot tub, go for a swim, or play tennis before chowing down. See chapters 5, 9, and 10.
- **Staying at a Golf or Tennis Resort:** The Phoenix/Scottsdale area has one of the nation's greatest concentrations of resorts, and Sedona and Tucson add many more options to the mix. There's something very satisfying about swinging a racket or club with the state's spectacular scenery in the

background, and the climate means you can play practically year-round. See chapters 4, 5, and 9.

- **Mountain Biking in Sedona:** Forget fighting for trail space in Moab—among the red rocks of Sedona you can escape the crowds and pedal through awesome scenery on some of the most memorable single-track trails in the Southwest. There's even plenty of slickrock for that Canyonlands experience. See p. 202.

THE best DAY HIKES & NATURE WALKS

- **Camelback Mountain:** For many Phoenicians, the trail to the top of Camelback Mountain, the city's highest peak, is a ritual, a Phoenix institution. Even halfway up offers striking views. See p. 90.
- **Peralta Trail:** This moderately difficult trail through the rugged Superstition Mountains, east of Phoenix, will lead you to one of the most astonishing views in the state. Hike the trail on a weekday to avoid the crowds. See p. 92.
- **Picacho Peak State Park:** A short but strenuous hike to the top of this central Arizona landmark leads to superb views out over the desert. The best time is in spring, when the peak is painted with wildflowers. It's 60 miles southeast of Phoenix, just off I-10. See p. 162.
- **Bell Rock/Courthouse Butte Loop Trail:** There's no better introduction to Sedona's myriad red-rock hiking opportunities than this easy 4-mile loop hike. Views, views, views! Unfortunately, there are plenty of other hikers, too. See p. 200.
- **The South Kalbab Trail:** Forget the popular Bright Angel Trail, which, near its start, is a human highway. Grand Canyon's South Kaibab Trail offers better views to day hikers and is the preferred downhill route from the South Rim to Phantom Ranch. It's a strenuous hike, even if you go only a mile down the trail. Remember, the trip back is all uphill. See p. 235.
- **The White House Ruins Trail:** There's only one Canyon de Chelly hike that the general public can take without a Navajo guide, and that's the 2.5-mile trail to the White House Ruins, once inhabited by Ancestral Puebloans. The trail leads from the canyon rim across bare sandstone, through a tunnel, and down to the floor of the canyon. See p. 313.
- **The Wildcat Trail:** Similarly, there's only one trail at Monument Valley you can hike without a guide. This easy 3.2-mile trail looping around West Mitten Butte gives you a close-up of one of the most photographed rock formations in the West. Don't miss this hike. See p. 320.
- **Betatakin:** In the Navajo National Monument, most people just marvel at this impressive cliff dwelling from a distance. A ranger-led 5-mile hike through remote Tsegi Canyon to the ruins will give you an infinitely better understanding of the Ancestral Puebloan people who once lived here. See p. 317.

- **Antelope Canyon:** More a slow walk of reverence than a hike, this short trail near Lake Powell leads through a picture-perfect sandstone slot canyon, only a few feet wide in some places. See p. 327.
- **The Seven Falls Trail:** There is something irresistible about waterfalls in the desert, and on this trail in Tucson's Sabino Canyon you get more than enough falls to cool you off on a hot desert day. See p. 375.
- **The Heart of Rocks Trail:** Chiricahua National Monument, down in the southeast corner of the state, quietly lays claim to some of the most spectacular scenery in Arizona. On this trail, you'll hike through a wonderland of rocks. See p. 469.

THE best SCENIC DRIVES

- **The Apache Trail:** Much of this winding road, which passes just north of the Superstition Mountains, is unpaved (sometimes precariously so) and follows a rugged route once traveled by Apaches. This is some of the most remote country in the Phoenix area, with far-reaching desert vistas and lots to see and do along the way. See p. 159.
- **Desert View Drive:** While everyone else is crowding through the Grand Canyon's southern entrance, take the lesser-used east entrance to the South Rim and cruise along forested 25-mile-long Desert View Drive to Grand Canyon Village. There are just a few overlooks, but they deliver some of the park's most awesome views. See p. 233.
- **Oak Creek Canyon:** Slicing down from the pine country outside Flagstaff to the red rocks of Sedona, Oak Creek Canyon is a cool oasis—with a scenic highway leading right through it, from the overlook at the top of the canyon to swimming holes and hiking trails at the bottom. See p. 190.
- **Monument Valley Navajo Tribal Park:** Countless movies, TV shows, and commercials have made this valley of sandstone buttes and mesas familiar to people all over the world. A 17-mile dirt road winds through the park, giving visitors close-up views of such landmarks as Elephant Butte, the Mittens, and Totem Pole. See p. 318.
- **Mount Lemmon:** Rising some 7,000 feet above Tucson, this massive peak has some impressive rock formations, an incongruous mountain town at the top, and in winter, lots of snow. Drive up the Catalina Highway from the east side of town to see it all. See p. 382.

THE best PLACES TO COMMUNE WITH CACTUS

- **Desert Botanical Garden:** There's no better place in the state to learn about the plants of Arizona's Sonoran Desert. Displays at this Phoenix botanical garden explain plant adaptations and how indigenous tribes once used many of this region's wild plants. See p. 59.
- **Boyce Thompson Arboretum:** East of Phoenix, just outside the town of Superior, this was the nation's first desert botanical garden. Set in a small

A horseback ride through Saguaro National Park winds through majestic stands of cactus.

canyon framed by cliffs, it has desert plantings from all over the world—a fascinating educational stroll in the desert. See p. 162.

- **Saguaro National Park:** With units both east and west of Tucson, this national park preserves "forests" of saguaro cacti. It's the very essence of the desert as so many imagine it. You can hike it, bike it, or drive it. See p. 366.
- **Tohono Chul Park:** Although not that large, this Tucson park packs a lot of desert scenery into its modest space. Impressive plantings of cacti are the star attractions, but there are also delightful wildflower displays in spring. See p. 376.
- **Organ Pipe Cactus National Monument:** A smaller, multi-trunked relative of the giant saguaro, the organ pipe cactus lives only along the Mexican border in southern Arizona, about 100 miles west of Tucson. This remote preserve has hiking trails and a couple of scenic drives. See p. 427.

THE best GOLF COURSES

- **Troon North Golf Club** (Scottsdale): Designed by Tom Weiskopf and Jay Morrish, this semiprivate, desert-style course is named for the famous Scottish links overlooking the Firth of Forth and the Firth of Clyde—but the similarities end there. Troon North has two 18-hole layouts; the original Monument Course is still the favorite. See p. 86.
- **The Gold Course at the Wigwam Golf Resort & Spa** (Litchfield Park, near Phoenix): Are you a traditionalist who eschews those cactus-filled desert target courses? Reserve a tee time on the Wigwam's 7,100-yard resort-style Gold Course, a longtime Arizona legend. See p. 87.

- **Gold Canyon Golf Resort** (Apache Junction, east of Phoenix): This resort offers superb golf at the foot of the Superstition Mountains. The 2nd, 3rd, and 4th holes on the Dinosaur Mountain Course are truly memorable, crossing the foot of Dinosaur Mountain. See p. 112.
- **We-Ko-Pa Golf Club** (northeast of Scottsdale): Located on the Yavapai Nation, this top-rated golf club has two challenging 18-hole courses bounded by open desert and stupendous views. See p. 88.
- **Sedona Golf Resort** (Sedona): Not all of Arizona's best courses are in the Phoenix and Tucson areas. Up in red-rock country, at the mouth of Oak Creek Canyon, the Sedona Golf Resort boasts a traditional course with terrific red-rock views. See p. 202.
- **Lake Powell National Golf Course** (Page): One of the most scenic golf courses in the state, its fairways wrap around the base of the red sandstone bluff Page sits on, walls of eroded sandstone come right down to the greens, and one tee box is on top of the bluff. Stunning. See p. 329.
- **Ventana Canyon Golf and Racquet Club** (Tucson): Two Tom Fazio–designed desert-style courses, the Canyon and the Mountain, play through some of the state's most stunning scenery. If I had to choose between them, I'd play the Mountain Course. See p. 379.
- **Omni Tucson National Resort** (Tucson): With wide expanses of grass on 18 holes and an additional 9 holes of desert-style golf, this course, once the site of the PGA Tour's Tucson Open, is both challenging and forgiving. The 18th hole was considered one of the toughest finishing holes on the tour. See p. 380.

THE best FAMILY EXPERIENCES

- **Grand Canyon National Park:** It's an iconic family vacation destination, and for good reason: Breathtaking views aside, you've got trails to hike, mules to ride down into the canyon (if your kids are old enough), rafting trips both wild and tame, and even a train ride to and from the canyon. See chapter 6.
- **Kartchner Caverns:** Visiting this living cave in southern Arizona is an adventure in itself, as you traverse airlocks down into a spectacular underground world with strange and rare cave formations. See p. 448.
- **Arizona–Sonora Desert Museum:** No dusty museum, this is actually a zoo featuring the animals of the Sonoran Desert. Exhibits include rooms full of snakes, a prairie-dog town, enclosures with bighorn sheep and mountain lions, and an aviary full of hummingbirds. Both kids and adults love this place. See p. 361.
- **Old Tucson Studios:** Cowboy shootouts, cancan girls, and horseback rides make this old movie-studio set loads of fun for the family. You might even get to see a movie or commercial being filmed. See p. 365.

Tombstone shamelessly exploits its Wild West history with staged gunfights and bawdy saloons—but it's still undeniably fun.

- **The O.K. Corral:** Tombstone may be "the town too tough to die," but poor Ike Clanton and his buddies the McLaury boys have to die over and over again in continual reenactments of the town's iconic gunfight. See p. 455.
- **Dude Ranches:** Ride off into the sunset with your family at one of Arizona's many guest ranches. Most have lots of kid-oriented activities. You'll find several around Wickenburg (p. 164), Tucson (p. 382), and Cochise County (p. 473).
- **Floating on a Houseboat:** Renting a floating vacation home on Lake Powell (p. 330) or Lake Mead (p. 483) is a summer tradition for many Arizona families. With a houseboat, you aren't tied to one spot and can cruise from one scenic beach to the next.

THE best MUSEUMS

- **Heard Museum:** One of the nation's premier museums devoted to Native American cultures, this Phoenix institution has not only historical exhibits (including a huge kachina doll collection) but also an excellent museum store, annual exhibits of contemporary Native American art, and frequent dance performances and demonstrations of traditional skills. See p. 59.
- **Musical Instrument Museum:** Housing thousands of musical instruments from all over the world, this huge Phoenix museum has galleries organized by countries and continents, as well as exhibits of such rare instruments as the first Steinway piano ever made and the Steinway piano on which John Lennon composed "Imagine." See p. 151.
- **Phoenix Art Museum:** This large art museum has acres of wall space and houses an outstanding collection of contemporary art as well as a fascinating exhibit of miniature rooms. See p. 67.

- **Western Spirit: Scottsdale's Museum of the West:** The Phoenix area's newest museum is a major endeavor: Two vast floors of Western art and artifacts in a striking building in the heart of downtown Scottsdale. See p. 62.
- **Desert Caballeros Western Museum:** In the Wild West town of Wickenburg, this museum celebrates all things Western, from cowboy art to the trappings of the American West. See p. 167.
- **Phippen Museum:** Devoted exclusively to Western art, this museum in Prescott features works by members of the prestigious Cowboy Artists of America. See p. 173.
- **Museum of Northern Arizona:** Geology, ethnography, and archaeology are all explored in fascinating detail at this Flagstaff museum. Throughout the year, excellent special exhibits and festivals focus on the region's tribes. See p. 261.
- **The University of Arizona Museum of Art:** This Tucson collection ranges from the Renaissance to the present. Georgia O'Keeffe and Pablo Picasso are among the artists whose works are on display here. See p. 371.
- **Amerind Foundation Museum:** Located in the remote southeastern corner of the state, this museum and research center houses a superb collection of Native American artifacts. Displays focus on tribes of the Southwest, but other tribes are also represented. See p. 468.

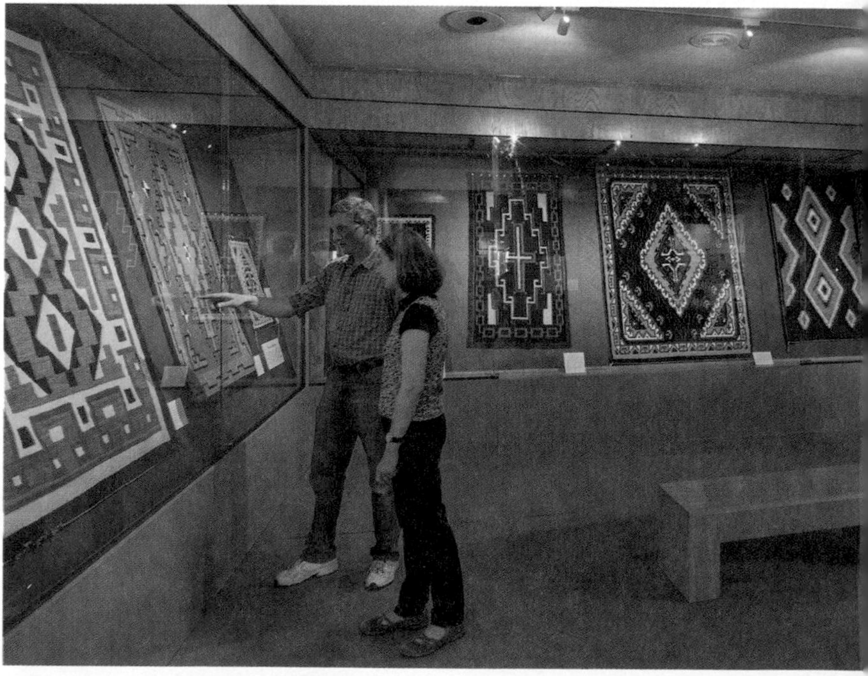

In Flagstaff's Museum of Northern Arizona, visitors learn the ethnological significance of colorful Navajo rugs.

THE best PLACES TO SAVOR SOUTHWEST FLAVORS

- **Cowboy Ciao:** Scottsdale may not have many real cowboys anymore, but it has great cowboy chow. Forget burned steaks and chili; this place serves the likes of buffalo carpaccio and wild-boar meatballs. See p. 116.
- **Vincent on Camelback:** Phoenix chef Vincent Guerithault has made a career of merging classic French culinary techniques with the robust flavors of the Southwest. The results, for many years, have been absolutely unforgettable. See p. 124.
- **Fry Bread House:** Ever had a fry-bread taco? This stick-to-your-ribs dish is a staple on Indian reservations throughout Arizona; the fry-bread tacos at this Phoenix restaurant are among the best I've had anywhere in the state. See p. 130.
- **Barrio Cafe:** Chef and owner Silvana Salcida Esparza conjures up alluring dishes using traditional Mexican ingredients and her own mind-expanding experiments with chilis. (No tacos and tostadas here.) A must stop for foodies in Phoenix. See p. 125.
- **The Turquoise Room:** Dishes at this Winslow restaurant incorporate both Mexican and Native American influences, while conjuring up the days when the wealthy still traveled by railroad. Rarely will you find such superb meals in such an off-the-beaten-path locale. See p. 291.
- **Café Poca Cosa:** Forget gloppy melted cheese and flavorless red sauces. This Tucson eatery treats south-of-the-border ingredients with the respect they deserve. It's Mexican food the likes of which you'll never find at your local Mexican joint. See p. 400.
- **El Charro Café:** Nothing sums up Tucson-style Mexican food quite like the *carne seca* at this, the oldest family-run Mexican restaurant in Tucson. *Carne seca,* which is a bit like shredded beef jerky in a spicy sauce, is made from strips of beef air-dried on the restaurant's roof. See p. 401.
- **El Guero Canelo:** Ever had a Mexican hot dog? No? Well, here's your chance. Wrapped in bacon, topped with beans and salsa, and known locally as Sonoran dogs, the pups served at this big Mexican fast-food joint in Tucson are legendary. See p. 404.

ARIZONA IN CONTEXT

2

Despite the searing summer temperatures, the desolate deserts, and the lack of water, people have been drawn to Arizona for hundreds of years. In the 16th century, the Spanish came looking for gold, but settled on saving souls. In the 19th century, despite frightful tales of spiny cactus forests, ranchers drove their cattle into the region and discovered that a few corners of the state actually had lush grasslands. At the same time, sidetracked forty-niners were scouring the hills for gold (and found more than the Spanish did). However, boomtowns—both cattle and mining—soon went bust. Despite occasional big strikes, mining didn't prove itself until the early 20th century, and even then, the mother lode was neither gold nor silver, but copper, which Arizona has in such abundance that it is known as the Copper State.

In the 1920s and 1930s, Arizona struck a new source of gold: sunshine. The railroads had made travel to the state easy, and word of the mild winter climate spread to colder corners of the nation. Among the first "vacationers" were people suffering from tuberculosis. These "lungers," as they were known, rested and recuperated in the dry desert air. It didn't take long for the perfectly healthy to realize that they, too, could avail themselves of Arizona's sunshine, and wintering in the desert soon became fashionable with wealthy Northerners.

ARIZONA TODAY

Today, the golden sun still lures people to Arizona; Scottsdale, Phoenix, Tucson, and Sedona are home to some of the most luxurious resorts in the country. Then there are those who come to Arizona on vacation and decide to make the move permanent, or at least *semi*-permanent. In the past half-century, the state has seen a massive influx of retirees, some of whom stay year-round in the pockets of Arizona where the climate is perfect year-round, and many thousands of others—the "snowbirds"—who leave the cold winters back east for 3 or 4 months in the state's sunshine.

The big population growth has at once changed and not changed the state. Everything's bigger, of course—Maricopa County, home to Phoenix, boasts more than 4 million people, more than half the state's total. But in a way that has just translated into more of the same suburban malls, freeways, chain stores, and the like, and—in the upscale desert hills outside Phoenix and Tucson—more of the very pricey homes stretching out into the distance. More people means more cars, so there's more pollution, too. The once-healthful air of Phoenix now rivals that of Los Angeles for its thick smog. Allergy sufferers are plagued by pollen from non-desert plants that were introduced to make this desert region look more lush and inviting.

Until the economic downturn of 2008, the state's economy was growing quite rapidly. Then came the 2008 recession, which hit Phoenix real estate as hard as anywhere in the country. During the same time period, anti-Mexican actions from elected officials playing to the dark side of the state's psyche damaged Arizona's image nationally. The state suffered for years.

Today, much of that is behind us. After a lull of more than 5 years, the Valley of the Sun at last is blossoming again. Downtown Phoenix, particularly, is unrecognizable. A clanging light rail rumbles past an immense new ASU campus, which has spurred the construction of untold thousands of new housing units—just the sort of "infill" development decaying downtowns need. These in turn have spawned nightlife, restaurants, and shops. A few high-tech companies have located in Arizona, too. And finally, the large Latino population, a sleeping giant, is slowly making itself felt politically and culturally.

LOOKING BACK AT ARIZONA

EARLY HISTORY Arizona is the site of North America's oldest cultures and one of the two longest continuously inhabited settlements in the United States—the Hopi village of Oraibi, which has had inhabitants for roughly 1,000 years. However, the region's human habitation dates back more than 11,000 years, to the time when Paleo-Indians known as the Clovis people inhabited southeastern Arizona. Stone tools and arrowheads of the type credited to the Clovis have been found in southeastern Arizona, and a mammoth-kill site has become an important source of information about these people, who were among the earliest inhabitants of North America.

Few records exist of the next 9,000 years of Arizona's prehistory, but by about A.D. 200, wandering bands of hunter-gatherers took up residence in **Canyon de Chelly** (p. 310) in the northern part of the state. Today these early Arizonans are known as the Ancestral Puebloans. The earliest Ancestral Puebloan period, stretching from A.D. 200 to 700, is defined as the **Basket Maker period** because of the large number of baskets that have been found in ruins from this era. During the Basket Maker period, the Ancestral Puebloans gave up hunting and gathering and took up agriculture, growing corn, beans, squash, and cotton on the canyon floors.

During the **Pueblo period** (700–1300), the Ancestral Puebloans began building multistory pueblos and cliff dwellings. Despite decades of research,

Relics of Ancestral Puebloan culture are found all over Arizona, such as these petroglyphs in Canyon de Chelly National Monument.

it is still not clear why the Ancestral Puebloans began living in niches and caves high on the cliff walls of the region's canyons. It may have been to conserve farmland as their population grew and required larger harvests, or for protection from flash floods. Whatever the reason for their construction, the cliff dwellings were all abandoned by 1300. It's unclear why the villages were abandoned, but a study of tree rings indicates that there was a severe drought in the region between 1276 and 1299; perhaps the Ancestral Puebloans left in search of more fertile farmland. Keet Seel and Betatakin, at **Navajo National Monument** (p. 316), as well as the many ruins in Canyon de Chelly, are Arizona's best-preserved Ancestral Puebloan sites.

During the Ancestral Puebloan Basket Maker period, the **Sinagua culture** began to develop in the fertile plateau northeast of present-day Flagstaff and southward into the Verde River valley. The Sinagua, whose name is Spanish for "without water," built their stone pueblos primarily on hills and mesas such as those at **Tuzigoot** (p. 187) near Clarkdale and **Wupatki** (p. 263) near Flagstaff, both now preserved as national monuments. They also built cliff dwellings in places such as **Walnut Canyon** (p. 262) and **Montezuma Castle** (p. 185), both also national monuments. By the mid-13th century, Wupatki had been abandoned, and by the early 15th century, Walnut Canyon and pueblos in the lower Verde Valley region had also been deserted.

As early as A.D. 450, the **Hohokam culture,** from which the Sinagua most likely learned irrigation, had begun to farm the Gila and Salt River valleys between Phoenix and Casa Grande. Over a period of 1,000 years, they constructed a 600-mile network of irrigation canals, some of which can still be seen today. Because the Hohokam built their homes of earth, few structures exist from this period, one exception being the **Casa Grande** ruin (p. 162), a well-preserved massive earth-walled building that is now a national monument. Many Hohokam petroglyph (rock art) sites remain as well, a lasting record of the people who first made the desert flourish. By the 1450s, however, the Hohokam had abandoned their villages; many archaeologists believe that the irrigation of desert soil over hundreds of years eventually left a thick crust of alkali in fields, which would have made further farming impossible. The very name Hohokam, in the language of today's Tohono O'odham people, means "the people who have vanished."

HISPANIC SETTLEMENT The first Europeans to visit the region may have been a motley crew of shipwrecked Spaniards, among whom was an enslaved black African man named Estévan de Dorantes. This unfortunate group spent 8 years wandering across the Southwest, and when they arrived back in Spanish territory, they told a fantastic story of having seen seven cities so rich that the inhabitants even decorated their doorways with jewels. No one is sure whether they actually passed through Arizona, but in 1539 their story convinced the viceroy of New Spain (Mexico) to send a small expedition, led by Father Marcos de Niza and de Dorantes, into the region. Father de Niza's report of finding the fabled Seven Cities of Cíbola inspired **Don Francisco Vásquez de Coronado** to set off in search of wealth in 1540. Instead of fabulously wealthy cities, however, Coronado found only pueblos of stone and mud. A subordinate expedition led by Garcia Lopez de Cárdenas stumbled upon the Grand Canyon, while another group of Coronado's men, led by Don Pedro de Tovar, visited the Hopi mesas.

Over the next 150 years, however, only a handful of Spanish explorers, friars, and settlers visited Arizona. In the 1580s and 1600s, Antonio de Espejo and Juan de Oñate explored northern and central Arizona and found indications of mineral riches in the region. In the 1670s, the Franciscans founded several missions among the Hopi pueblos, but the **Pueblo Revolt of 1680** (see "Indian Conflicts," below) obliterated this small Spanish presence. In 1687, Father Eusebio Francisco Kino, a German-educated Italian Jesuit, began establishing missions in the Sonoran Desert region. In 1691, he visited the Pima village of **Tumacácori** (p. 433), where he planted fruit trees, taught the Natives European farming techniques, and gave them cattle, sheep, and goats to raise. In 1692, Father Kino first visited the **Tucson** area (see chapter 9); by 1700 he had laid foundations for the first church at the mission of **San Xavier del Bac** (p. 364), although it wasn't until 1783 that construction began on the present church, known as the White Dove of the Desert.

The Spanish began settling in the area around Tumacácori and nearby Tubac (p. 430), calling it Pimeria Alta. In 1775, a group of settlers led by Juan

Traditional dancers at a heritage festival in Phoenix. Arizona was once part of Mexico, and Hispanic cultural ties still run deep.

Bautista de Anza set out from Tubac to find an overland route to California; in 1776, they founded the city of San Francisco. That same year, the Tubac presidio was moved to Tucson. In 1821, Mexico won its independence from Spain, and Tucson, with only 65 inhabitants, became part of Mexico, which at that time extended all the way to Northern California.

INDIAN CONFLICTS At the time the Spanish arrived in Arizona, the tribes living in the southern lowland deserts were peaceful farmers, but in the mountains of the east lived the **Apache,** a hunting-and-gathering tribe that frequently raided neighboring tribes. In the north, the **Navajo,** relatively recent immigrants to the region, fought over land with the neighboring **Ute** and **Hopi** (who were also fighting among themselves).

Coronado's expedition through Arizona and into New Mexico and Kansas was to seek gold. To that end he attacked one pueblo, killed the inhabitants of another, and forced still others to abandon their villages. Spanish-Indian relations were never to improve, and the Spanish were forced to occupy their new lands with a strong military presence. Around 1600, 300 Spanish settlers moved into the **Four Corners region** (see chapter 7), which at the time supported a large population of Navajos. The Spanish raided Navajo villages to take slaves, and angry Navajos responded by stealing Spanish horses and cattle.

For several decades in the mid-1600s, missionaries were tolerated in the Hopi pueblos, but the Pueblo tribes revolted in 1680, killing the missionaries and destroying the missions. Throughout the 1700s, others native peoples followed suit, pushing back against European settlement. Encroachment by farmers and miners moving into the Santa Cruz Valley in the south caused the **Pima people** to stage a similar uprising in 1751, attacking and burning the mission at Tubac. A presidio was soon established at Tubac to protect Spanish settlers; after the military garrison moved to Tucson in 1776, Tubac was quickly abandoned due to frequent Apache raids. In 1781, the **Yuman tribe,** whose land at the confluence of the Colorado and Gila rivers had become a Spanish settlement, staged a similar uprising, wiping out that first Yuma settlement.

By the time Arizona became part of the United States, it was the Navajos and Apaches who were most resistant to white settlers. In 1863, the U.S. Army, under the leadership of Col. Kit Carson, forced the Navajo to surrender by destroying their winter food supplies. The survivors were marched to an internment camp in New Mexico; the Navajo refer to this as **the Long Walk.** Conditions at the camp in New Mexico were deplorable, and within 5 years the Navajo were returned to their land, although they were forced to live on a reservation.

The Apaches resisted white settlement 20 years longer than the Navajo did. Under the leadership of **Geronimo** and **Cochise,** the Apaches, skillful guerrilla fighters, attacked settlers, forts, and towns despite the presence of U.S. Army troops. Cochise eventually died in his Chiricahua Mountains homeland. After Geronimo finally surrendered in 1886, he and many of his followers were relocated to Florida by the U.S. government. Open conflicts between whites and Indians finally came to an end.

TERRITORIAL DAYS In 1846, the United States went to war with Mexico, which at the time extended all the way to Northern California and included parts of Colorado, Wyoming, and New Mexico. When the war ended, the United States claimed almost all the land extending from Texas to Northern California. This newly acquired land, called the **New Mexico Territory,** had its capital at Santa Fe, New Mexico. (The land south of the Gila River, which included Tucson, wasn't included at first; after surveys determined that this land was the best route for a railroad from Mississippi to California, in 1853 the U.S. government negotiated the **Gadsden Purchase** and the current Arizona-Mexico border was set.)

When the California gold rush began in 1849, many hopeful miners from the east crossed Arizona en route to the gold fields, and some stayed to seek mineral riches in Arizona. However, despite ever-growing numbers of settlers, the U.S. Congress refused to create a separate Arizona Territory. When the Civil War broke out, Arizonans, angered by Congress's inaction, sided with the Confederacy, and in 1862, Arizona was proclaimed the **Confederate Territory of Arizona.** Although Union troops easily defeated the Confederate troops occupying Tucson, this dissension finally convinced Congress, in 1863, to create the **Arizona Territory.**

The capital of the new territory was temporarily established at Fort Whipple near **Prescott** (p. 170); later the same year it was moved to Prescott itself. In

1867 the capital moved again, this time to Tucson. Ten years later, Prescott again became the capital, which it remained for another 12 years before the seat of government finally moved to **Phoenix,** which remains Arizona's capital to this day.

During this period, mining flourished, and although small amounts of gold and silver were discovered, copper became the source of Arizona's economic wealth. With each mineral strike, a new mining town would boom, and when the ore ran out, the town would be abandoned. These towns were infamous for their gambling halls, bordellos, saloons, and shootouts. **Tombstone** (p. 454) and **Bisbee** (p. 459) became the largest towns in the state and were known as the wildest towns between New Orleans and San Francisco.

> **Name Game**
>
> *As the mythical phoenix rose reborn from its ashes, so shall a great civilization rise here on the ashes of a past civilization. I name thee Phoenix.*
>
> —"Lord" Bryan Phillip Darrell Duppa, the British settler who named Phoenix

In 1867, farmers in the newly founded town of Phoenix began irrigating their fields using canals that had been dug centuries earlier by the Hohokam. In the 1870s, ranching became another important source of revenue in the territory, particularly in the southeastern and northwestern parts of the state. In the 1880s, the **railroads** finally arrived, and life in Arizona changed drastically. Suddenly the region's mineral resources and cattle were accessible to the east.

STATEHOOD & THE EARLY 20TH CENTURY By the beginning of the 20th century, Arizonans were trying to convince Congress to make the territory a state. Congress balked at the requests, but finally in 1910 allowed the territorial government to draw up a state constitution. Territorial legislators were progressive thinkers, and their draft included clauses for the recall of elected officials—provisions that made President William Howard Taft, an opponent of recalling judges, veto the bill. Arizona politicians removed the controversial clause, and on **February 14, 1912,** Arizona became the 48th state. One of the new state legislature's first acts was to reinstate the clause providing for the recall of judges.

Much of Washington's opposition to Arizona's statehood had been based on the belief that Arizona could never support economic development. This belief was changed in 1911 by one of the most important events in state history—the completion of the Salt River's **Roosevelt Dam** (later to be renamed the Theodore Roosevelt Dam). The dam not only provided irrigation water to the Phoenix area, but it also tamed the river's violent floods. The introduction of water to the heart of Arizona's vast desert enabled large-scale agriculture and industry. Over the next decades, more dams were built throughout Arizona, and, in 1936, the **Hoover Dam** on the Colorado River became the largest concrete dam in the Western Hemisphere. This dam also created the largest man-made reservoir in North America, **Lake Mead** (p. 478). Arizona's dams would eventually provide not only water and electricity, but also the state's most popular recreation areas.

Despite labor problems, copper mining increased throughout the 1920s and 1930s, and with the onset of World War II, the mines boomed as military munitions manufacturing increased the demand for copper. However, within a few years after the war, many mines were shut down. Today, Arizona is littered with old mining ghost towns that boomed and then went bust. A few towns, such as **Jerome** (p. 179) and **Bisbee** (p. 459), managed to hang on and were eventually rediscovered by artists, writers, and retirees.

World War II created a demand for beef, leather, and cotton, and Arizona farmers and ranchers stepped in to meet the need. Cotton, which was used in the manufacture of tires, quickly became the state's most important crop. Goodyear planted huge fields of it, and a far west suburb sprang up bearing the company name. During the war, Arizona's clear desert skies also provided ideal conditions for training pilots, and several military bases were established in the state, helping to double Phoenix's population. When peace finally arrived, many veterans returned with their families, although it wasn't until air-conditioning was invented that major population growth truly came to the desert.

THE POSTWAR YEARS During the postwar years, Arizona attracted a number of large manufacturing industries and slowly moved away from its agricultural economic base. Today aerospace engineering remains a major industry, and tech-industry growth is slow but steady.

But the economy of the state still relies heavily (too heavily, some say) on real estate, and of course, tourism. The **Grand Canyon** (p. 220), which had been luring visitors since the days when they had to get there by stagecoach, was declared a national park in 1919, and by the 1920s, Arizona had become a winter destination for the wealthy. The clear, dry air also attracted people suffering from allergies and lung ailments, and Arizona came to be known as a healthful place. With the immense popularity of Hollywood Westerns, dude ranches began to spring up across the state. From the 1960s on, the rustic guest ranches of the 1930s began to give way to luxurious golf resorts, and "snowbirds" played an increasing role in the state's economy.

Continued population growth throughout the 20th century resulted in an ever-increasing demand for water. Yet, despite the damming of nearly all of Arizona's rivers, the state still suffered from insufficient water supplies in the population centers of Phoenix and Tucson. It took the construction of the controversial and expensive **Central Arizona Project** (CAP) aqueduct to carry water from the Colorado River over mountains and deserts, and deliver it where it was wanted. Construction on the CAP began in 1974, and in 1985 water from the project finally began irrigating fields near Phoenix. In 1992, the CAP reached Tucson. However, a drought that began in the mid-1990s has left Phoenix and Tucson once again pondering where they will come up with water to fuel future growth.

ARIZONA IN POP CULTURE

Books

HISTORY Marshall Trimble's *Roadside History of Arizona* is an ideal book to take along on a driving tour of the state. Covering the state road by road, its discusses events that happened in each area. To learn more about the infamous shootout at the O.K. Corral, read Paula Mitchell Marks's *And Die in the West: The Story of the O.K. Corral Gunfight,* an objective, non-Hollywood look at the most glorified and glamorized shootout in western history. For a somewhat dystopian view on Phoenix's future, try *Bird on Fire: Lessons from the World's Least Sustainable City*, by Andrew Ross.

THE GRAND CANYON & THE COLORADO RIVER John Wesley Powell's diary produced the first published account (1869) of traveling through the Grand Canyon. Today, his writings still provide a fascinating glimpse into the canyon. *Exploration of the Colorado River and Its Canyons,* with an introduction by Wallace Stegner, is a republishing of Powell's writings. Alternatively, read Stegner's *Beyond the Hundredth Meridian: John Wesley Powell and the Second Opening of the West,* an in-depth biography of Powell. Stephen J. Pyne's *How the Canyon Became Grand* explores the recent human history of the canyon, while *Grand Canyon: True Stories of Life Below the Rim* provides a wide range of perspectives on the Grand Canyon experience. For a slightly macabre look at the canyon, read *Over the Edge: Death in Grand Canyon* by Thomas M. Myers and Michael P. Ghiglieri, a look at the many ways people have died in the Grand Canyon.

NATURAL HISTORY & THE OUTDOORS Anyone curious about the plants and animals of the Sonoran Desert should pick up *A Natural History of the Sonoran Desert.* Cacti, wildflowers, tarantulas, roadrunners—they're all here and described in very readable detail. Two handy books to keep in the car are Halka Chronic's *Roadside Geology of Arizona* and *Geology Underfoot in Northern Arizona,* by Lon Abbott and Terri Cook. Hikers will find Scott S. Warren's *100 Classic Hikes in Arizona* invaluable.

FICTION The murder mysteries of **Tony Hillerman** are almost all set on the Navajo Reservation in the Four Corners area of the state. **Barbara Kingsolver,** a biologist and social activist, has set several novels either partly or entirely in Arizona: *The Bean Trees, Pigs in Heaven,* and *Animal Dreams* are quirky, humorous narratives that provide insights into Arizona's cultural mélange. **Edward Abbey**'s *The Monkey Wrench Gang* and *Hayduke Lives!* are tales of an unlikely gang of "eco-warriors" determined to preserve the wildernesses of the Southwest. **Zane Grey** spent many years living in north-central Arizona and set many of his Western novels there, including *Riders of the Purple Sage, The Vanishing American, Call of the Canyon,* and *The Arizona Clan.*

Film

Spectacular landscapes, rugged deserts, ghost towns, and its cowboy mystique have, over the years, made Arizona the location for hundreds of films, from obscure B Westerns to the seminal works of John Ford. This state has become so associated with the Old West that fans come from halfway around the world to walk in the footsteps of John Wayne and Clint Eastwood.

In 1939, a set was built in Tucson for the filming of the movie *Arizona,* and when the shooting was done, the set was left to be used in other productions. Today, visitors can enjoy this mock-Western town, known as **Old Tucson** (p. 365), which is still used for film and video productions. Movies that have been filmed here include *Tombstone;* Clint Eastwood's *The Outlaw Josey Wales;* Kirk Douglas's *Gunfight at the O.K. Corral;* and Paul Newman's *The Life and Times of Judge Roy Bean.*

John Ford made the otherworldly landscape of **Monument Valley** (p. 318) a trademark of his filmmaking, using it as the backdrop for such movies as *Stagecoach, She Wore a Yellow Ribbon, My Darling Clementine, Rio Grande,* and *The Searchers.* The valley has also starred in such non-Western films as *Back to the Future III, Thelma and Louise,* and *Forrest Gump.*

The red rocks of **Sedona** and nearby **Oak Creek Canyon** (p. 190) have also attracted filmmakers, from the silent film *The Call of the Canyon* (1923) to *The Riders of the Purple Sage* (1941) and the 1957 version of *3:10 to Yuma.* The area around **Patagonia** (p. 441) in southeastern Arizona has served as backdrop for quite a few films, including *Oklahoma!, Red River, McClintock, Broken Lance,* and the Barbra Streisand version of *A Star Is Born.* TV shows such as *Little House on the Prairie, The Young Riders,* and *Red Badge of Courage* have been filmed in this part of southern Arizona, too.

In 1987, the Coen Brothers produced *Raising Arizona,* one of the most offbeat films ever shot in that state. Other offbeat and non-Western films filmed here include *Days of Thunder* (starring Tom Cruise), *Traffic* (with Michael Douglas and Catherine Zeta-Jones), and the toy-inspired *Transformers.*

Music

Arizona has a soundtrack—the sound of **Native American flute music.** You hear it in hotel lobbies and gift shops, in restaurants and national park visitor centers; its haunting melodies are the perfect accompaniment to a long drive across the wide-open spaces of Arizona. R. Carlos Nakai, who was born in Flagstaff and is of Navajo and Ute heritage, is considered the preeminent Native American flutist; you'll find his music for sale in gift shops all over the state.

Tucson is called the **mariachi capital** of America; year-round you can hear this lively south-of-the-border music in Mexican restaurants. Also in Tucson, you can sometimes catch a bit of indigenous ***waila*** music, the music of southern Arizona's Tohono O'odham tribe: It's a mix of polka, waltz, and various Mexican influences.

In the **pop world,** the state's favorite sons and daughters, adopted and native alike, include Link Wray, Waylon Jennings, Glen Campbell, Alice Cooper, Stevie Nicks, Giant Sand, Calexico, the Gin Blossoms, and Linda Ronstadt, among many others.

EATING & DRINKING IN ARIZONA

Arizona is such a mélange of cultures—Anglo, Hispanic, Native American—it's no surprise that its culinary scene is equally diverse. Along with restaurants following the latest trends, you'll find Native American foods little changed in hundreds of years, and an astonishingly wide variety of Mexican food, from Baja-style fish tacos to Nuevo Latino preparations.

We're particularly fond of the state's **Southwestern** restaurants. Although many of these can be expensive, the flavors, which combine the spices of Mexico with the fruit-and-meat pairings of nouvelle cuisine, are distinctive and flavor-packed. Don't worry, Southwestern cooking is not all about fiery peppers. Expect pistachio-crusted meats, fruit salsas, cream sauces made with smoky chipotle peppers, and creative mash-ups such as duck tamales or cassoulet made with indigenous tepary beans.

At the other end of the culinary spectrum is the simple fare favored by Arizona's Native Americans. On reservations throughout the state, you'll usually find **fry bread** on the menu: deep-fried disks of dough, similar to that county-fair staple, the elephant ear (only without sugar and cinnamon). Fry bread is eaten as a side or is used to make fry-bread tacos (called Navajo tacos on the Navajo Reservation), made by piling shredded lettuce, ground beef, pinto beans, and cheese on top of a circle of fry bread. The best fry-bread tacos are in Phoenix at the Fry Bread House (p. 130).

A uniquely Arizona culinary mash-up: the fry-bread taco, made with Mexican taco toppings on deep-fried Navajo fry bread.

Desert Wines: Defying Expectations

You may never have thought of the desert as wine country, but Arizona has lately been producing some decent wines, particularly big reds. Wineries can be found in southern Arizona, near **Sonoita** (p. 441) and **Willcox** (p. 467), and in central Arizona in the **Verde Valley** (p. 183 and 184) and around **Sedona** (p. 205). Top wineries in the state include Callaghan Vineyards (p. 444), Caduceus Cellars (p. 183), Alcantara Vineyard (p. 184), and Page Springs Cellars (p. 206).

Other than fry-bread tacos, authentic **Native American fare** is hard to come by in Arizona. At the Ch'ihootso Indian Market (see "Eat Local, Shop Local" in chapter 7, p. 310), in the Navajo Nation capital of Window Rock, you can sample such traditional dishes as mutton stew and steam corn (a soup made with whole corn kernels). If you happen to see a roadside sign for kneel-down bread, be sure to buy some—it's traditional Navajo corn bread, similar to a tamale, only sweeter. Wherever you sample Navajo food, ask for Navajo tea as well, a mild herbal tea made from a plant that grows only in northern Arizona. On the Hopi Reservation, at the Hopi Cultural Center (p. 294), you can sample traditional Hopi stew (hominy, green chilies, and lamb). In the Tucson area, you can often find Native food stalls in the parking lot of Mission San Xavier del Bac (p. 364).

No discussion of Arizona cuisine would be complete without mentioning **Mexican food.** Yes, I know Mexican food is available all over the U.S., but Arizona Mexican restaurants have far more to offer than the same old, same old. It comes in several variations—New Mexico Mexican at Richardson's in Phoenix (p. 123), Mexico City Mexican at Gallo Blanco in Phoenix (p. 131), high Mexican cuisine at sister restaurants Barrio Café and Gran Reserva in Phoenix (p. 125), and, in Tucson, the flavorful and creative dishes concocted by chef Suzana Davila at Café Poca Cosa (p. 400). Margaritas are among the most popular cocktails in the state, and they come in a wide range of flavors, including prickly pear. Prepared with a syrup made from the fruit of the prickly pear cactus, they're shockingly pink and surprisingly good.

THE LAY OF THE LAND

Although the very mention of Arizona may cause some people to turn the air-conditioning on full blast, this state is much more than a searing landscape of cacti and mesquite trees. From the baking shores of the lower Colorado River to the snowcapped heights of the San Francisco Peaks, Arizona encompasses virtually every North American climatic zone. Cactus flowers bloom in spring and mountain wildflowers in summer. In autumn, aspens color the White Mountains golden, and in winter, snows blanket higher elevations from the Grand Canyon North Rim to the Mexican border.

But it's the Sonoran Desert, with its massive saguaro cacti, that most people associate with Arizona, with the state's two largest cities—Phoenix and

Tucson—planted in its heart. Relatively plentiful rains make the Sonoran Desert one of the world's greenest and most biologically diverse deserts. In Arizona, rain falls both in winter and in late summer; the summer rainy season, when clamorous thunderstorms send flash floods surging down arroyos, is known as the monsoon season and is the most dramatic time of year in the desert. Desert sunsets are unforgettable, but so, too, are the heat and humidity.

> **The River Wild**
>
> *We are three-quarters of a mile in the depths of the earth, and the great river shrinks into insignificance as it dashes its angry waves against the walls and cliffs that rise to the world above.*
>
> —John Wesley Powell, leader of the first river trip through the Grand Canyon

Before the introduction of dams and deep wells, many Arizona rivers and streams flowed year-round and nurtured a surprising variety of plants and animals. Today, however, only a few rivers and creeks still flow unaltered through the desert—Sonoita and Aravaipa creeks (see chapter 10) and the San Pedro, Verde, and Hassayampa rivers (see chapter 5). Rare cottonwood-willow forests thrive in the green **riparian areas** along these watercourses, serving as magnets for wildlife, harboring rare birds as well as fish species unique to Arizona. Preserves near Prescott (p. 170), Patagonia (p. 441), and Sierra Vista (p. 446) protect the last few riparian forests.

Outside the desert regions, there is great diversity as well. In the southern part of the state, small mountain ranges rise abruptly from the desert floor, creating so-called **sky islands,** refuges for plants and animals that require cooler climates. The greatest varieties of bird species in the continental United States can be seen here (see box, p. 27).

Although rugged mountain ranges crisscross the state, only a few rise to such heights that they support actual forests. Among these are the Santa Catalinas outside Tucson, the White Mountains along the state's eastern border, and the San Francisco Peaks north of Flagstaff. However, it's atop the Mogollon Rim and the Kaibab Plateau that the **ponderosa pine forests** cover the greatest areas. The Mogollon Rim, a 2,000-foot-high escarpment that stretches from central Arizona all the way into New Mexico, supports the largest ponderosa pine forest in the world, dotted with lakes well known for their fishing. Sedona (p. 190) is a great base for exploring the Rim. At more than 8,000 feet in elevation, the Kaibab Plateau is even higher than the Mogollon Rim, yet it is through the Kaibab Plateau that the Grand Canyon cuts its mighty chasm (see chapter 8).

Arizona Flora & Fauna

SAGUAROS & THEIR SPINY FRIENDS

From the diminutive hedgehog to the stately saguaro, the cacti of the Sonoran Desert display a fascinating variety of shapes and sizes. In spring, their large, waxy flowers paint the desert with splashes of color. May is probably the best all-around month for seeing cactus flowers, but you can also see them in April and June.

SAGUARO CACTUS The saguaro (pronounced sa-*hwah*-ro) is the largest cactus of Arizona's Sonoran Desert and grows nowhere else on earth. (Saguaro throughout the state are protected by law.) Reaching heights of as much as 50 feet, saguaros are the redwoods of the desert, and often grow in dense stands that resemble forests. Saguaros grow slowly; a 6-inch-tall cactus might be 10 years old, and it can take 75 years for a saguaro to sprout its first branch. The oldest-known saguaros are around 200 years old; some have more than 40 arms.

To support their great size in such an arid environment, saguaros have a highly efficient root system, as large as 100 feet in diameter. These roots soak up water quickly and store it in the cactus' spongy interior. After a rainstorm, a mature saguaro can weigh as much as 7 tons and survive for up to 2 years without another drop of water. Supporting this great mass is an internal framework of sturdy ribs, while the pleated exterior of the cactus expands and contracts as it takes in or loses water.

Each spring, waxy white flowers sprout from the tips of saguaro arms. These flowers are pollinated by white-winged doves and lesser long-nosed bats, which come from hundreds of miles away in Mexico just for saguaro flowering season. Other animals that rely on saguaros include Gila woodpeckers and elf owls, which nest in holes in saguaro trunks.

The Tohono O'odham people, natives of the Sonoran Desert, have long relied on saguaro cactus fruit as an important food source, even making a traditional ceremonial wine from the red, seedy pulp. So important is the saguaro harvest that the Tohono O'odham consider it the start of a new year.

ORGAN PIPE CACTUS This close relative of the saguaro is named for its many trunks, which resemble the pipes of a church organ. Even more frost-sensitive than the saguaro, these cacti live in only one place: an area 100 miles west of Tucson, straddling the Mexican border, today protected as the Organ Pipe Cactus National Monument (p. 427).

BARREL CACTUS Mature barrel cacti, with their stout keg-shaped trunks, can be confused with young saguaros. You can tell them apart by their fish-hook-shaped spines, usually yellow or red. For years, barrel cacti have been touted as a source of life-giving water to anyone lost in the desert; in fact, the liquid in their spongy interiors is quite bitter and foul-tasting. Cook the spongy pulp in sugar water, however, and it becomes delicious.

CHOLLA CACTUS The cholla (pronounced *choi*-yah) is the most dreaded of all the Arizona cacti, with its many long, sharp, brittle spines—brush up against a cholla and you'll feel certain pain, so beware. Arizona has several species of cholla, most of which look like small trees. Their names are delightfully descriptive: Jumping cholla is said to throw pieces of its spiny branches at unwary passersby; teddy bear cholla has so many spines that it looks fuzzy; chain fruit cholla displays its fruit in fragile, spiny chains. Cactus wrens and doves love to nest in chollas.

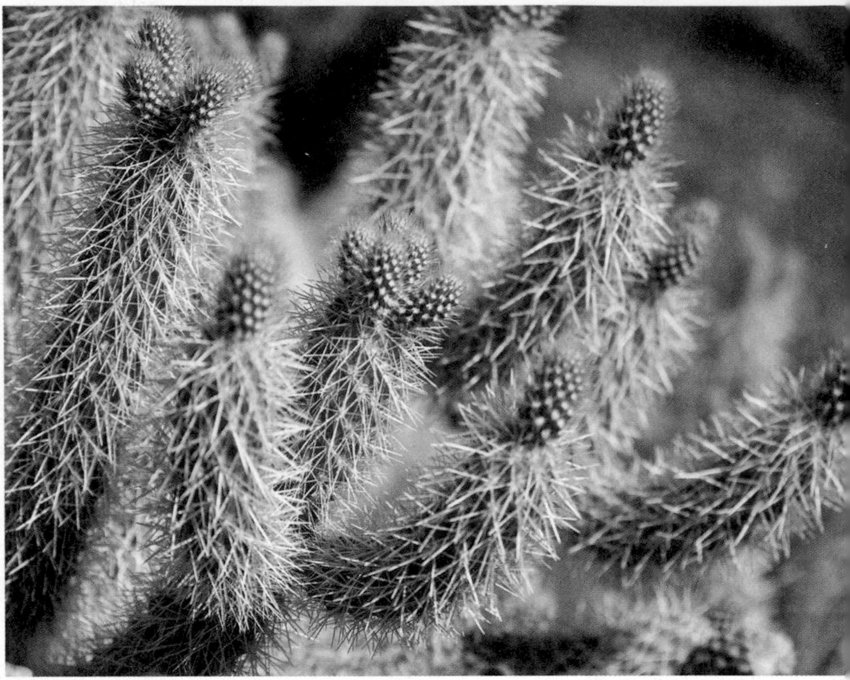

Beware of touching the sharp, fine spines of a teddy bear cholla cactus, no matter how soft and fuzzy it appears.

PRICKLY-PEAR CACTUS One of the largest and most widespread families of cacti, prickly pears can be found throughout the U.S., not just in the desert. The flat stems or pads (*nopales* in Spanish) of one species are used in Mexican cooking; you can find them both fresh and canned in Arizona markets. The fruit of the prickly pear is also relished by both humans and animals. In Arizona shops, look for not only prickly-pear jams and jellies, but also prickly-pear ice cream and even margaritas.

ROADRUNNER, COYOTE & OTHER DESERT DENIZENS

Just as cacti have adapted to the desert, so too have the animals that live here. Many spend the sweltering daytime in burrows and venture out only in the cooler night.

GREATER ROADRUNNER The largest North American member of the cuckoo family, a real roadrunner (not the cartoon one) darts around the desert at speeds up to 15 mph, hunting snakes and lizards (not hapless coyotes). They can fly, but they rarely do.

COYOTE No creature better symbolizes the desert Southwest than the coyote. Celebrated as the Trickster in Native American lore, coyotes are curious animals that have adapted well to life amid Arizona's ever-expanding cities and towns. They can be seen boldly strolling across stretches of

A Birder's Bonanza

Bird-watchers tend to agree: Arizona has probably the best bird-watching in the country. In its southeastern corner, many species found primarily south of the border reach the northern limits of their ranges, and mountains that rise like islands from the desert provide appropriate habitat for hundreds of species.

Birding hot spots include **Ramsey Canyon Preserve** (p. 449, known for its many species of hummingbirds); **Cave Creek Canyon** (p. 471, nesting site for elegant trogons); **Patagonia–Sonoita Creek Sanctuary** (p. 441, home to 22 species of flycatchers, kingbirds, phoebes, and Montezuma quails); **Madera Canyon** (p. 379, another "mountain island" hot spot with many of the same species as Ramsey Canyon and Sonoita Creek); **Buenos Aires National Wildlife Refuge** (p. 430, home to masked bobwhite quails and gray hawks); and the sewage ponds outside the town of **Willcox** (p. 471, known for avocets and sandhill cranes). To find out which birds have been spotted lately or to join a bird-watching field trip, call the **Tucson Audubon Society's Rare Bird Alert line** (www.tucsonaudubon.org; ✆ **520/629-0510,** ext. 3).

highway; they prowl residential streets and alleys even in the central cities. Nothing captures the essence of the desert quite like the crazy cackling of coyotes at sunset.

GILA MONSTER Despite the fearful name, this is actually just a lizard, albeit a large, ugly, and poisonous one. (Gila monsters are one of only two poisonous lizards in the world.) With their mottled black-and-pink coloring, warty-looking scales, and fat, stubby tails, these slow-moving lizards are indeed a monstrous sight. ***Creepy fact:*** Those scales are caused by osteoderms, bony plates common among dinosaurs but rare in modern reptiles.

CALIFORNIA CONDOR With a wingspan of 9 feet, the largest of any North American bird, California condors were once nearly extinct—in 1987, only 22 were left on earth, all of them captured to be bred in captivity. Today, there are nearly 300 of the huge birds, many of them living in Grand Canyon National Park and Vermilion Cliffs National Monument. They're spotted in the vicinity of Grand Canyon Village on the South Rim (p. 228).

COLLARED PECCARY Known in Arizona as javelinas (pronounced hav-uh-*lee*-nuhs), these strange creatures look a bit like long-haired, neckless pigs. Javelinas are so well adapted to life in the desert they can even eat prickly pear cactus—spines and all. They're not normally aggressive, but they're so nearsighted that, rushing to get away from you, they might run straight at you, not realizing where you're standing.

TARANTULA Okay, I know these giant arachnids, with 2-inch bodies and 4-inch-long legs, are about as creepy as a crawly thing can be, but actually they're neither aggressive nor particularly poisonous. After summer rainstorms, you may see a male tarantula wandering across a road in search of a mate. After mating, the male usually dies within a few months; female tarantulas can live for 25 years or more.

WHEN TO GO

While Arizona is a year-round destination, people head to different parts of the state at different times of year. In Phoenix, Tucson, and other parts of the desert, high season runs from October to mid-May, with the highest hotel rates January to April. At the Grand Canyon, summer is the busy season.

The all-around best times to visit are spring and autumn, when temperatures are cool in the mountains and warm in the desert. May and September are excellent times to visit, with low summer rates still in effect at the desert resorts and the Grand Canyon relatively uncrowded. In spring, you may catch great wildflower displays, which begin in March and last until May, with the tops of saguaro cacti covered with waxy white blooms. Be aware that even in May and September it can be extremely hot in Phoenix; however, if you don't *mind* three-digit temperatures, you can get some of the best hotel deals in the nation then, at the Valley's top resorts.

One thing to keep in mind: Sedona and the Red Rocks region is just high enough that it actually gets cold in the winter—sometimes it even snows. So if you're looking for sunshine and time by the pool, book your Sedona vacation for a time other than winter.

Weather

The first thing you should know is that the desert can be cold as well as hot. Although winter is the prime tourist season in Phoenix and Tucson, night temperatures can occasionally dip below freezing and days may sometimes be too cold for sunning or swimming. In January and February, there can be stretches of cool, cloudy, and even rainy weather. On the whole, however, winters in the state's two largest cities are positively delightful. In higher-elevation areas, of course, you'll find traditional winter weather. Don't be surprised to see snow as late as Memorial Day in the mountains.

In the deserts in winter, temperatures average in the high 60s (low 20s Celsius) by day (it gets even warmer in Yuma). In summer, when desert temperatures top 110°F (43°C), the mountains of eastern and northern Arizona are pleasantly warm, with daytime averages in the low 80s (high 20s Celsius). Prescott and Sierra Vista, in the 4,000- to 6,000-foot elevation range, claim temperate climates that are just about ideal.

Monsoons—in Arizona?

There are summer rains in the Arizona's southern deserts, including over the cities of Phoenix and Tucson. And once in a while you'll witness a dust storm—a big dust storm. Under circumstances that aren't quite clear, in the 1980s and 1990s it became fashionable to call those thunderstorms "monsoons," a term traditionally associated with the Far East. From there it was just one more step of nonsense meteorology to calling dust storms "haboobs." Don't be surprised to hear local weathercasters use this exotic nomenclature for these ordinary local phenomena.

Arizona Weird

Looking for something out of the ordinary? Here are three of Arizona's more offbeat festivals:

Ostrich Festival, Chandler. These unusual (and brief!) races are something you should see at least once in your life. www.ostrichfestival.com. Mid-March.

Welcome Back Buzzards, Superior. This annual event welcomes back the turkey vultures (buzzards) that roost in eucalyptus trees and on volcanic cliffs at the Boyce Thompson Arboretum. azstateparks.com. Mid- to late March.

Sidewalk Egg Fry Contest, Oatman. In the ghost town of Oatman, located near one of the hottest places on earth, contestants compete to fry an egg in 15 minutes. www.oatmangoldroad.org. July 4 at high noon.

If you happen to be visiting the desert in July or August, be prepared for sudden thunderstorms and dust storms. Storms often cause flash floods that make many roads briefly impassable. Looks for signs warning motorists not to enter low areas when flooded, and take them seriously.

Also, *don't even think about* venturing into narrow slot canyons, such as Antelope Canyon near Page (p. 327) or the West Fork of Oak Creek Canyon (p. 190), if there's any chance of a storm anywhere in the region. Rain falling miles away can send flash floods roaring down narrow canyons with no warning.

Average Temperatures & Days of Rain

PHOENIX

	JAN	FEB	MAR	APR	MAY	JUNE	JULY	AUG	SEPT	OCT	NOV	DEC
Avg. High (°F)	67	71	77	85	95	104	106	104	100	89	76	66
Avg. High (°C)	19	22	25	29	35	40	41	40	38	32	24	19
Avg. Low (°F)	46	49	54	60	70	78	84	83	77	65	53	45
Avg. Low (°C)	8	9	12	15	21	25	29	28	25	18	12	7
Days of Rain	4	4	4	2	1	1	4	5	3	3	3	4

FLAGSTAFF

	JAN	FEB	MAR	APR	MAY	JUNE	JULY	AUG	SEPT	OCT	NOV	DEC
Avg. High (°F)	43	45	50	58	67	78	82	78	73	63	51	43
Avg. High (°C)	6	7	10	14	19	25	22	26	23	18	11	7
Avg. Low (°F)	12	14	20	25	30	37	46	47	37	20	19	12
Avg. Low (°C)	–11	–10	–7	–4	–1	2	8	8	3	–3	–8	–12
Days of Rain	8	7	9	6	5	3	11	11	6	5	5	6

Holidays

Banks, government offices, post offices, and many stores, restaurants, and museums are closed on the following legal national holidays: January 1 (New Year's Day), the third Monday in January (Martin Luther King, Jr., Day), the third Monday in February (Presidents' Day), the last Monday in May (Memorial Day), July 4 (Independence Day), the first Monday in September (Labor Day), the second Monday in October (Columbus Day), November 11 (Veterans' Day/Armistice Day), the fourth Thursday in November (Thanksgiving Day), and December 25 (Christmas).

Arizona Calendar of Events

The major annual events below are all worth checking out; they're also worth knowing about because they may impact local hotel costs and traffic congestion. As the Valley of the Sun grows, its event schedule gets more and more crowded. Walk-up tickets to many of these events are a thing of the past. If anything in the Phoenix area appeals to you, buy tickets as far in advance as possible.

JANUARY

Barrett-Jackson Collector Car Auction, Scottsdale. This premier car show and auction draws attendance of over 250,000, with competing auctions nearby. www.barrett-jackson.com. Mid-January.

Rock 'n' Roll Arizona Marathon, Phoenix/Scottsdale/Tempe. www.runrocknroll.com/arizona. Mid-January.

Wings over Willcox Birding & Nature Festival, Willcox. Birders flock here for tours, workshops, and, of course, watching tens of thousands of sandhill cranes gather in the Sulphur Springs Valley. www.wingsoverwillcox.com. Mid-January.

Fiesta Bowl, University of Phoenix Stadium, Glendale. This college bowl game usually sells out nearly a year in advance. There's also a parade. www.fiestabowl.org. Late January.

Waste Management Phoenix Open Golf Tournament, Scottsdale. This prestigious PGA golf tournament is held at the Tournament Players Club. www.wmphoenixopen.com. Late January–early February.

FEBRUARY

Renaissance Fest. Patterned after a 16th-century English country fair, this festival features costumed participants and tournament jousting at fairgrounds 40 miles east of downtown Phoenix. Renfestinfo.com. Weekends mid-February–early April.

Parada del Sol, Scottsdale. The city's annual Western parade is nearly 70 years old. paradadelsolparade-trailsend.com. Early February.

Tubac Festival of the Arts, Tubac. North American artists and craftspeople display their work. www.tubacaz.com/festival. Early February.

World Championship Hoop Dance Contest, Phoenix. Native American dancers from around the nation take part in this colorful competition at the Heard Museum. www.heard.org. Early February.

Arabian Horse Show, Scottsdale. Ten days of equestrian events and displays. www.scottsdaleshow.com. Mid-February.

Tucson Gem and Mineral Show, Tucson Convention Center. With seminars, museum displays, and hundreds of dealers, this huge show takes over Tucson. More than 30 smaller shows occur in the weeks beforehand (visit www.tucsonshowguide.com for info on these). www.tgms.org. Mid-February.

Cochise Cowboy Poetry & Music Gathering, Sierra Vista. More than 50 cowboy poets, singers, and musicians gather in Sierra Vista for a weekend of Wild West poetry and music. www.cowboypoets.com. Early February.

Cowboy Days & O'odham Tash, Casa Grande. At one of the largest annual Native American festivals in the country, dozens of tribes participate in rodeos, arts-and-crafts exhibits, and dance performances. Mid-February.

La Fiesta de los Vaqueros, Tucson Rodeo Grounds. This cowboy festival and rodeo includes the Tucson Rodeo Parade, the world's longest nonmotorized parade. www.tucsonrodeo.com. Late February.

Sedona International Film Festival, Sedona. View various new indie features, documentaries, and animated films before they get picked up for wider distribution. www.sedonafilmfestival.com. Late February.

Devour, Phoenix. Expect crowds at this massive food fest featuring top Valley chefs, held on the grounds of the Phoenix Art Museum; dedicated foodies should consider buying early-admission VIP tickets. classic.devourphoenix.com. Late February.

Spring Training. The so-called Cactus League brings more than a dozen professional baseball teams—the Chicago Cubs,

SF Giants, etc.—to play 200 games at small stadiums across the Valley. Madness. www.cactusleague.com. Late February–late March.

MARCH

Heard Museum Guild Indian Fair & Market, Phoenix. Indian cultural and dance presentations and one of the largest selections of Native American crafts in the Southwest make this a fascinating festival. Go early to avoid the crowds. www.heard.org. First weekend in March.

Highland Games, Phoenix. This highly enjoyable Scottish festival features feats of strength—the hammer throw, stone put, etc.—and a bagpipe army. Steele Indian School Park, early March.

McDowell Mountain Music Fest, Phoenix. Top-flight acts play for 3 days of music in Downtown Phoenix. www.m3ffest.com. Mid-March.

Melrose Street Fair, Phoenix. 7th Ave. north of Indian School Rd. is closed off for a street fest in one of the city's hipper, and gayer, neighborhoods. www.m7streetfair.com. March.

Scottsdale Arts Festival, Scottsdale Mall. Concerts, an art fair, and children's events give a lively taste of the visual and performing arts. www.scottsdaleartsfestival.org. Early March.

Wa:k Pow Wow, Tucson. At Mission San Xavier del Bac, this Tohono O'odham celebration features many Southwestern Native American groups. www.facebook.com/walpowwow. Second weekend in March.

Art Detour, Phoenix. The city's annual art festival stretches across a weekend on Roosevelt Row, Grand Avenue, and around town. www.artlinkphx.org. Mid-March.

APRIL

Pride Week, Phoenix. Events culminate in a 2-day festival at Steele Indian School Park, with a Sunday parade running up Third St. www.phoenixpride.org. Early April.

Phoenix Film Festival, Phoenix. Ten days of films and seminars are held at the Harkin's Scottsdale 101 Theatre. www.phoenixfilmfestival.com. April.

Tucson International Mariachi Conference, Tuscon. Mariachi bands from all over the world come to compete before standing-room-only crowds. www.tucsonmariachi.org. Late April.

Arab American Festival, Phoenix. Arab food, music, and events fill Steele Indian School Park downtown. www.arabamericanfestival.org. Late April.

MAY

Cinco de Mayo, Phoenix and other cities. Celebrating the Mexican victory over the French in a famous 1862 battle, this holiday is commemorated with food, music, and dancing. Check local newspapers for area festivities. Around May 5.

Route 66 Fun Run, Kingman area. Classic hot rods hit the road for 3 days of roaring up and down historic Route 66. www.azrt66.com. First weekend in May.

Arizona Restaurant Week (Spring), Scores of fine restaurants offer three-course prix-fixe menus around the state. www.arizonarestaurantweek.com. Mid May.

FORM, Mayer. Live music from big stars accompanies camping and desert art installations at Arcosanti, an hour north of Phoenix. www.experienceform.com. May.

Phippen Museum Western Art Show & Sale, Prescott. This is the state's premier Western-art sale. www.phippenartmuseum.org. Memorial Day weekend.

Wyatt Earp Days, Tombstone. Gunfights are reenacted in memory of the shootout at the O.K. Corral. www.wyattearpdays.com. Memorial Day weekend.

JUNE

Prescott Frontier Days/World's Oldest Rodeo, Prescott. This is one of two Arizona rodeos claiming to be the nation's oldest. www.worldsoldestrodeo.com. Late June to July 4.

JULY

Hopi Festival of Arts and Culture, Flagstaff. This exhibition and sale, held at the Museum of Northern Arizona, includes crafts vendors and demonstrations, music, dancing, Hopi foods, and other cultural events. www.musnaz.org. Early July.

AUGUST

Navajo Festival of Arts and Culture, Flagstaff. This exhibition and sale at the Museum of Northern Arizona includes rug-weaving demonstrations, hoop dances, crafts vendors, and cultural events. www.musnaz.org. Early August.

Southwest Wings Birding and Nature Festival, Sierra Vista. Participants attend lectures and join field trips throughout southeastern Arizona. www.swwings.org. Early August.

August Doins Rodeo, Payson. This rodeo also claims to be the country's oldest. www.paysonrimcountry.com. Third weekend in August.

Grand Canyon Music Festival, Grand Canyon Village. For more than a quarter of a century, this festival has been bringing classical music to the South Rim of the Grand Canyon. www.grandcanyonmusicfest.org. Late August–early September.

SEPTEMBER

Navajo Nation Fair, Window Rock. Traditional music and dancing, a Miss Navajo contest, and more fill the Navajo Nation's capital. www.navajonationfair.org. Early September.

Arizona Restaurant Week (Fall), Scores of fine restaurants offer three-course prix-fixe menus around the state. www.arizonarestaurantweek.com. Late September.

OCTOBER

Sedona Arts Festival, Sedona. Exhibits and entertainment draw art lovers to one of the top arts festivals in the state. www.sedonaartsfestival.org. Early–mid-October.

Arizona Exposition & State Fair, Phoenix. A little bit trashy, a little bit guilty pleasure. Farm animals, a rodeo, and lots of triple-fried food and midway rides. Check the concert schedule; several big-name acts play in the fairgrounds' cavernous Veterans Coliseum. www.azstatefair.com. Mid-October–early November.

Bisbee 1000, Bisbee. Runners compete up and down 1,000 steps in this old mining town. www.bisbee1000.org. Third weekend in October.

Helldorado Days, Tombstone. Festivalgoers can check out an 1880s fashion show, beard contest, reenactments, and street entertainment. www.tombstonehelldoradodays.com. Third full weekend in October.

Lost Lake Festival, Phoenix. Top-name pop, rock, and hip-hop acts perform at Steele Indian School Park. www.lostlakefestival.com. October.

NOVEMBER

Scottsdale Film Festival, Scottsdale. scottsdalefilmfestival.com. Early November.

DECEMBER

Festival of Lights, Sedona. Thousands of luminarias are lit at dusk at the Tlaquepaque Arts and Crafts Village. www.tlaq.com. Mid-December.

Electric Light Parade, Phoenix. Central Ave. north of Camelback Rd. is kept dark and the floats all have lights. Neighborhood oriented. Early December.

Pueblo Grande Museum Indian Market, Phoenix. The largest market of its kind in the state features more than 250 Native American artisans. www.pueblogrande.com. Second weekend in December.

ZooLights, Phoenix Zoo. Hundreds of light sculptures on the grounds create this kid-friendly (and crowded) holiday tradition. Buy tickets in advance. www.phoenixzoo.org. Late November–mid-January.

SUGGESTED ARIZONA ITINERARIES

3

You could spend a lifetime exploring Arizona—an important fact to keep in mind when planning a trip to this vast and astonishingly diverse corner of the American Southwest. Maps just don't convey how big this state is. It's roughly 400 miles from north to south (about as far as from New York City to Raleigh, North Carolina; or Brussels, Belgium, to Bern, Switzerland), and 300 miles from east to west (think New York to Richmond, Virginia; or Paris to London). It's also incredibly mountainous: If Arizona were flattened out, it's said, it would be the size of the entire continental United States. Seeing any sizable chunk of territory will mean being behind the wheel for sizable chunks of time. Thankfully, most Arizona roads have generous speed limits. Just don't speed in 15mph school zones: Tickets are a cash cow for towns from Yuma to Window Rock.

Where should you go? What should you see? What's the best route? This chapter helps you answer those questions. Reading through these itineraries, you'll notice a bit of overlap: Some attractions just should not be missed on any visit to the state. Still, try to think of these as general ideas. Because Phoenix and Tucson are less than 2 hours apart, for example, you could easily swap time in bustling Phoenix for time in laid-back Tucson (or vice versa) and not add too much extra driving to your vacation.

REGIONS IN BRIEF

PHOENIX, SCOTTSDALE & THE VALLEY OF THE SUN

The sprawling metropolitan Phoenix area covers more than 400 square miles and includes more than 20 cities and communities, all surrounded by mountain ranges. It's the economic and population center of the state, and Arizona's main winter and spring vacation destination. Here you'll find the greatest concentrations of resorts and golf courses—along with the worst traffic and highest lodging rates.

Arizona
UTAH
NEVADA
NEVADA
CALIF.
60 mi
60 km
Four Corners
Navajo Tribal Park
Navajo National Monument
Monument Valley
Navajo Tribal Park
Kayenta
Canyon de Chelly National Monument
Chinle
Window Rock
Ganado
NAVAJO
INDIAN
RESERVATION
HOPI INDIAN RESERVATION
Glen Canyon National Recreation Area
Lake Powell
Page
Tuba City
Cameron
Vermilion Cliffs National Monument
THE GRAND CANYON
Grand Canyon Village
Grand Canyon North Rim
KAIBAB NATIONAL FOREST
Grand Canyon National Park
HAVASUPAI INDIAN RESERVATION
HUALAPAI INDIAN RESERVATION
Grand Canyon - Parashant National Monument
River
Colorado
Temple Bar
Grand Canyon West
Lake Mead National Recreation Area
Lake Mead
Las Vegas
Hoover Dam
Lake Mohave
Laughlin
Bullhead City
Kingman
Needles
Lake Havasu City
Lake Havasu
Seligman
Williams
San Francisco Peaks
Humphreys Peak
Wupatki National Monument
Flagstaff
Meteor Crater
Winslow
PAINTED
DESERT
Petrified Forest National Park
Holbrook
St. Johns
APACHE-SITGREAVES NATIONAL FORESTS
COCONINO NATIONAL FOREST
Sedona
Camp Verde
Jerome
PRESCOTT NATIONAL FOREST
Prescott
15
59
389
89
ALT 89
67
64
180
40
66
93
68
95
17
179
279
69
260
87
377
77
61
191
160
98
264

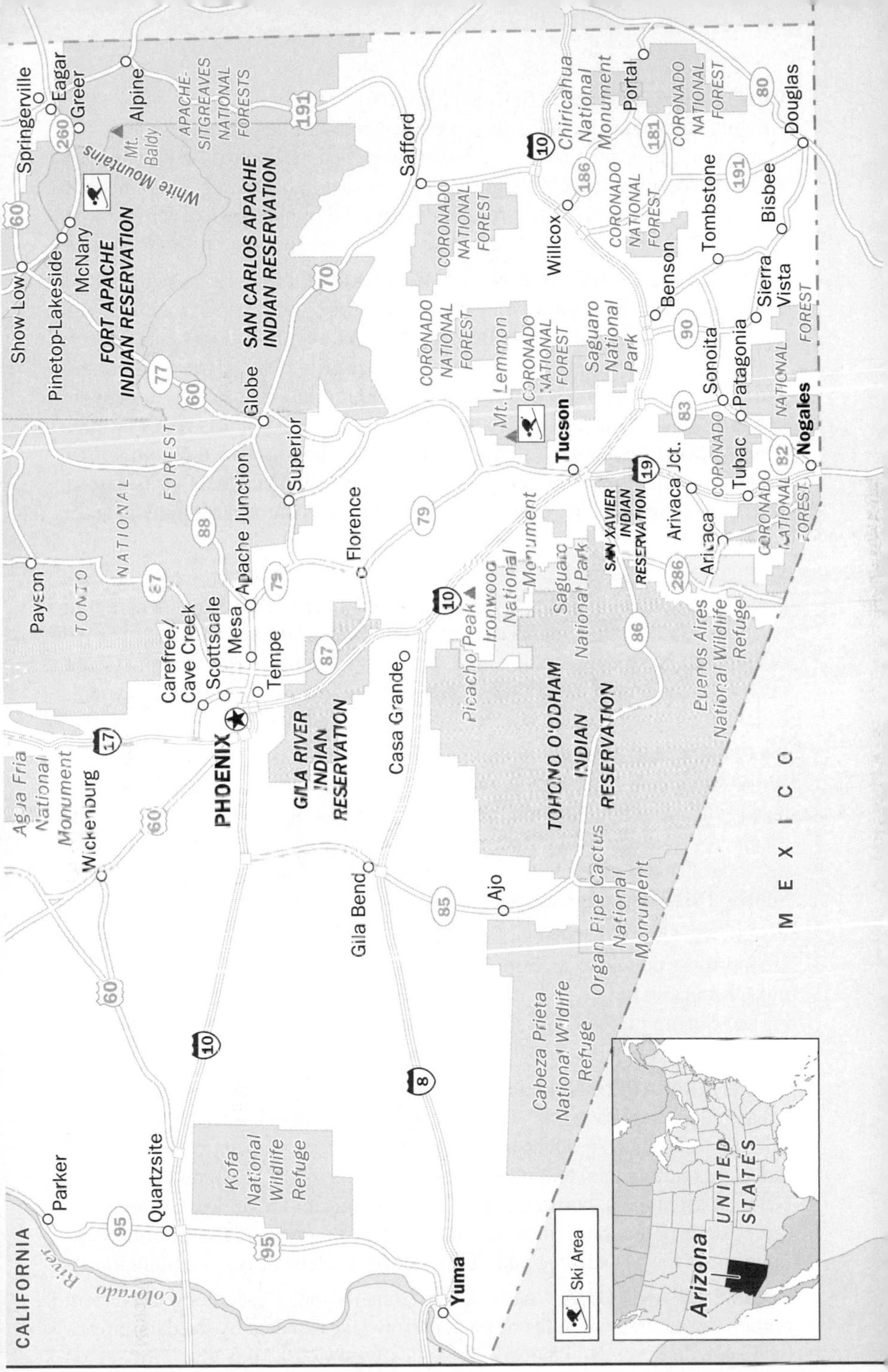

CALIFORNIA
Colorado River
Parker
Quartzsite
Kofa National Wildlife Refuge
Yuma
Wickenburg
Agua Fria National Monument
PHOENIX
Carefree/ Cave Creek
Scottsdale
Mesa
Tempe
Apache Junction
Payson
TONTO NATIONAL FOREST
Show Low
Pinetop-Lakeside
McNary
Springerville
Eagar
Greer
Alpine
Mt. Baldy
White Mountains
APACHE-SITGREAVES NATIONAL FORESTS
FORT APACHE INDIAN RESERVATION
SAN CARLOS APACHE INDIAN RESERVATION
Globe
Superior
Florence
Safford
GILA RIVER INDIAN RESERVATION
Casa Grande
Gila Bend
Ajo
Picacho Peak
Ironwood National Monument
Saguaro National Park
TOHONO O'ODHAM INDIAN RESERVATION
Organ Pipe Cactus National Monument
Cabeza Prieta National Wildlife Refuge
Mt. Lemmon
Tucson
CORONADO NATIONAL FOREST
SAN XAVIER INDIAN RESERVATION
Arivaca Jct.
Arivaca
Buenos Aires National Wildlife Refuge
Tubac
Nogales
Patagonia
Sonoita
Sierra Vista
Benson
Willcox
Tombstone
Bisbee
Douglas
Portal
Chiricahua National Monument
MEXICO
Ski Area
Arizona
UNITED STATES

CENTRAL ARIZONA Between Phoenix and the high country of northern Arizona, this region includes the rugged red-rock country around Sedona, one of the state's most popular tourist destinations. Sedona abounds in art galleries, recreation options, and excellent lodgings. Also within this region are historic Prescott (once Arizona's territorial capital); the old mining town of Jerome, now an artists' community; and several Native American ruins and petroglyph sites.

THE GRAND CANYON & NORTHERN ARIZONA Home to the Grand Canyon, one of the natural wonders of the world, northern Arizona is a vast and sparsely populated region, Because Grand Canyon National Park attracts millions of visitors each year, the city of Flagstaff and the towns of Williams and Tusayan abound in accommodations and restaurants catering to canyon-bound travelers. The famous Route 66 (or what's left of it) also runs through here. North of the Grand Canyon lies a remote and untraveled region known as the Arizona Strip, with Vermilion Cliffs National Monument at its eastern end, and the inaccessible Grand Canyon–Parashant National Monument at the western end.

THE FOUR CORNERS The point where Arizona, Utah, Colorado, and New Mexico come together is the only place in the United States where four states share a common boundary. The region is also almost entirely composed of Hopi and Navajo reservation land. Amid its spectacular canyons and towering mesas and buttes you'll find such famous natural attractions as Canyon de Chelly, the Painted Desert, the Petrified Forest, and Monument Valley.

EASTERN ARIZONA Comprising the Mogollon Rim region and the White Mountains, this high country is covered with ponderosa pine forests, laced with trout streams, and dotted with fishing lakes. It's a summertime escape for residents of the lowland desert areas, abounding in mountain cabins, lodges, and summer homes. It also has the best winter ski area in the state: Sunrise Park Resort, on the White Mountain Apache Indian Reservation.

TUCSON More than 100 miles southeast of Phoenix, Tucson is Arizona's second-most populous metropolitan area, with plenty of resorts and attractions. Mountain ranges rise in all directions, making it a good base for exploring the Sonoran Desert; Tucson also displays its Hispanic, Native American, and pioneer roots more than Phoenix does.

SOUTHERN ARIZONA From desert lowlands to mountain "islands" to vast grassy plains, this is a region of contrasting landscapes and relatively few towns. Mile-high elevations produce a surprisingly temperate climate, which brings in rare birds (and birders) and supports a small wine industry. Organ Pipe Cactus National Monument, bordering the Tohono O'odham Indian Reservation, preserves some of the state's most spectacular desert scenery. A couple of interesting historic towns—Bisbee and Tubac—have become artists' communities.

WESTERN ARIZONA Although Arizona is landlocked, along its western border are hundreds of miles of long, narrow lakes created by the damming of the Colorado River. Nicknamed "Arizona's West Coast," this low-lying region is one of the state's hottest places in the state in summer (and the warmest in winter). College students and families come here for water-skiing, fishing, and other watersports.

ARIZONA IN 1 WEEK

Arizona is a big state, so don't expect to see it all in 7 days. If you want to take in some of my favorite spots in just a week, you'll need to do a lot of driving and get up early. (You'll be rewarded with absolutely awe-inspiring sunrises, however.) This itinerary is best from fall through spring—Phoenix is just too hot for hanging out in the summer (unless you swim at night and tee off at dawn). During the hot months, you might prefer to head straight to Sedona after landing in Phoenix; if your return flight isn't too early, you can even spend your last night in Sedona or Prescott and still have a fairly short drive to the Phoenix airport. ***Note:*** Make reservations as far ahead as possible for in-park lodgings at the Grand Canyon (see p. 244 and 255). Otherwise you'll have to stay in forgettable accommodations outside the park.

Days 1 & 2: Phoenix ★★

Head straight for the pool at your resort—after all, lounging in the sun is one of the main reasons to be here. If you've got time, visit the **Desert Botanical Garden** (p. 59) around sunset to admire its amazing variety of cacti; it's an excellent introduction to the Arizona desert. Head to Scottsdale for dinner, and, if it happens to be a Thursday night, check out some art galleries, many of which stay open late on Thursday.

The next morning, if you're a golfer, hopefully you've made a reservation well in advance for an early round of golf (see p. 85 for courses). Otherwise, visit the **Heard Museum** (p. 59), one of the nation's premier museums of Native American art and culture. Grab a bite to eat at the museum's excellent cafe and then stroll down to **Heritage Square** (p. 66) to see what's left of Phoenix's historic core. Be sure to leave by at least 4pm for the 2-hour drive north to Sedona so you can catch your first glimpse of red-rock country by sunset.

Day 3: Sedona ★★★

Sedona may be touristy, but the red-rock cliffs, buttes, and mesas that surround the city make it one of the most beautiful places in America. To get out amid the red rocks, take a **jeep tour** (p. 199) or hike the 4- to 5-mile loop trail around **Bell Rock** and **Courthouse Butte.** Although this trail sees a lot of hikers, it is just about the best trek in the area. Head to **Crescent Moon Picnic Area** or **Airport Mesa** for the sunset. Enjoy a Mexican or Southwestern meal at one of Sedona's excellent restaurants (p. 214).

Day 4: Grand Canyon ★★★

With a 3-hour drive ahead of you, get an early start. Drive north to **Flagstaff** by way of scenic **Oak Creek Canyon** (p. 190), then take U.S. 89

Arizona in 1 Week

Arizona in 2 Weeks

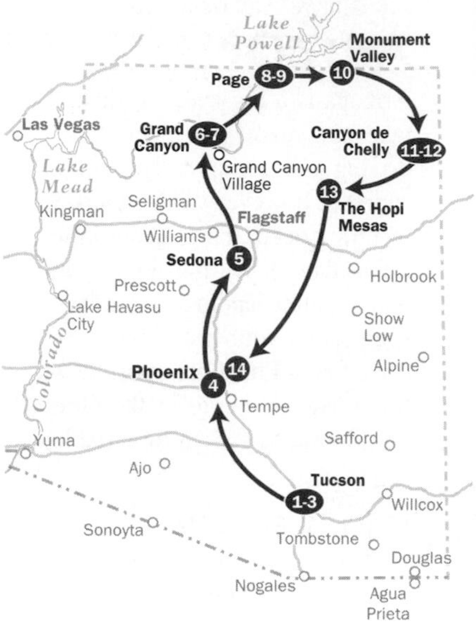

Arizona for Families

A Sojourn in Southeastern Arizona

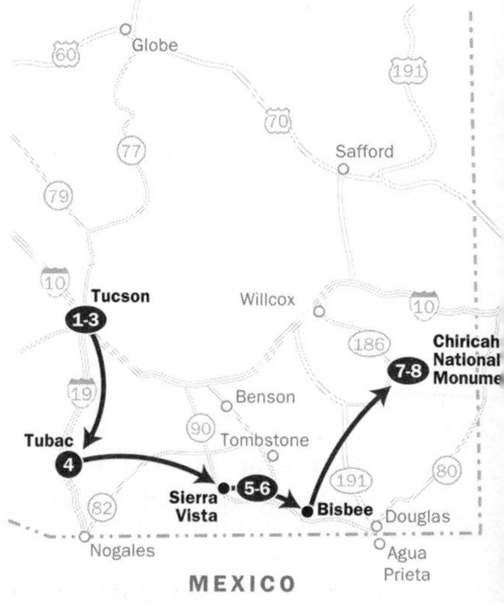

from Flagstaff to the east entrance of Grand Canyon National Park. Stop en route at the **Cameron Trading Post** (p. 243) to see the gallery of Native American artifacts in the historic old trading post; grab lunch at the cafe here (try the fry-bread tacos). Entering Grand Canyon National Park, stop at **Desert View,** just inside the entrance, and also **Lipan Point.** Once you reach Grand Canyon Village, take a short hike along the rim or down into the canyon (remember, you have to hike uphill to return!). Catch the sunset over the Grand Canyon, then settle into your hotel. (If you couldn't get in-park reservations, stay in **Tusayan** [p. 246], just outside the park's south entrance.) Inside or outside the park, dining options tend to be modest.

Day 5: The Painted Desert & Petrified Forest ★

The next day, get up early to catch the sunrise, then retrace your drive to Flagstaff and on east on I-40. (**Winslow**, p. 288, makes a good lunch stop.) An hour's drive east of Winslow, spend your afternoon tramping around the one-of-a-kind landscape of the **Petrified Forest National Park** (p. 302), which preserves both the petrified forest and parts of the Painted Desert. Drive north to Chinle, on the Navajo Nation reservation, to stay overnight.

Day 6: Canyon de Chelly ★★★

Staying in Chinle, you'll be ready first thing in the morning to visit **Canyon de Chelly National Monument** (p. 310), with its amazing ruins of ancient pueblos. Make reservations in advance for one of the **truck tours** (p. 314) of the canyon or to hire a Navajo guide to take you into the canyon by jeep or on horseback. Alternatively, drive the **South Rim Drive** (p. 312), which provides an opportunity to hike down into the canyon on the **White House Ruins Trail** (p. 313). Drive back to either Holbrook or Winslow to spend the night.

Day 7: Return to Phoenix ★★

From either Holbrook or Winslow, it's about 3 hours' drive back to Phoenix, passing through the Apache National Forest, a green contrast to the deserts, mesas, and canyons you've been visiting. Stop off in Camp Verde to see more cliff dwellings at **Montezuma Castle National Monument** (p. 185), then shoot down I-17 to reach your Phoenix hotel for your last night. After this whirlwind tour of Arizona's highlights, you'll probably want to park yourself by the pool for the rest of the day!

ARIZONA IN 2 WEEKS

Plan on spending 2 weeks in Arizona, and you'll get a much better sense of this state's diverse landscapes. You can spend more time at the Grand Canyon, marvel at massive saguaro cacti in the desert lowlands, have a bit more time to lounge at a resort, and visit one or more of the state's picturesque artists' communities. Just remember that Arizona's size makes for lots of what locals call "windshield time" going from one place to another.

Days 1, 2 & 3: Tucson ★★

To get yourself in vacation mode, head straight for the pool at your resort. If you're a hiker, try one of the trails in the foothills of the Santa Catalina Mountains. **Sabino Canyon** (p. 375), with its trams and network of trails, is just about the best place in the city for a quick hike. On Day 2, go west to the **Arizona–Sonora Desert Museum** (p. 361), the state's single-best introduction to the Sonoran Desert. (Despite the name, this is more zoo than museum.) By the way, there's a great cafe here. After you've hung out with the desert critters, drive a few miles farther west to the west unit of **Saguaro National Park** (p. 366), full of impressive stands of the saguaro cacti for which the park is named. Be sure to check out the petroglyphs at Signal Hill. On Day 3, drive south to **Mission San Xavier del Bac** (p. 364), a Spanish mission church that is known as the "White Dove of the Desert," then on south to the historic arts community of **Tubac** (p. 430). Check out the art galleries, **Tubac Center of the Arts,** and **Tubac Presidio State Historic Park** (p. 432), and then head a few miles south to **Tumacácori National Historical Park** (p. 433), which preserves the ruins of another Spanish mission church. Finish the day on the Mexican border in **Nogales,** with dinner at Zula's (p. 440), southern Arizona's favorite Greek-Mexican restaurant. It's an hour's drive back to Tucson from here.

Day 4: Phoenix & Scottsdale ★★

Drive north on I-10, exiting in Tempe to head first to downtown Scottsdale, where you can take the **Old Scottsdale walking tour** (p. 73). After lunch, go west to downtown Phoenix, where you should definitely stop to visit the **Heard Museum** (p. 59), the state's best introduction to Native American cultures. Stroll down to **Heritage Square** (p. 66) to see what's left of Phoenix's historic core. Your stay in Phoenix will be brief, so don't book a pricy resort, where you'll pay for amenities you won't have time to use; stay downtown or in the Camelback corridor (see p. 97 for options).

Day 5: Sedona ★★★

Take the scenic route to Sedona via Wickenburg and Prescott. Stop at Wickenburg's **Desert Caballeros Western Museum** (p. 167) for the cowboy perspective on the Wild West. The back road, U.S. 89A, is slow and vertiginous, but the Verde Valley views are worth it. Once in Sedona, take a **jeep tour** (p. 199) or hike the 4- to 5-mile loop trail around **Bell Rock** and **Courthouse Butte** (p. 200). When the sun sets, be sure you're either at the **Crescent Moon Picnic Area** (p. 197) or atop **Airport Mesa.**

Days 6 & 7: Grand Canyon ★★★

Drive north to **Flagstaff** through scenic **Oak Creek Canyon** (p. 190), then take U.S. 89 to the east entrance of Grand Canyon National Park. Stop en route at the **Cameron Trading Post** (p. 243), to see the gallery of Native American artifacts in the historic old trading post; grab lunch at the cafe here (try the fry-bread tacos). Entering Grand Canyon National Park, stop at **Desert View,** just inside the entrance, and also **Lipan Point.** Once you reach Grand Canyon Village, hike along the rim to catch the sunset over the Grand Canyon. Settle into your hotel for the night (reserve well in advance for in-park lodging, or stay in **Tusayan,** just outside the park).

On Day 7, get up early to catch the sunrise, then do a day hike or mule ride down into the canyon. (You must reserve far in advance for the mule ride—see p. 239.) If you're not a hiker, spend the day exploring the viewpoints along **Hermit Road** (p. 230). In cool weather, it's a treat to spend time sitting by the fire at **Hermit's Rest,** a fascinating little building designed by Mary Elizabeth Jane Colter, who designed several of the most attractive buildings on the South Rim.

Days 8 & 9: Page & Lake Powell ★★

From the Grand Canyon, go northeast to the town of Page, which sits atop a mesa overlooking **Glen Canyon National Recreation Area** (p. 325) and **Lake Powell,** the reservoir created by Glen Canyon Dam. This reservoir is the most astonishing body of water in the West, a vast miragelike lake flanked by red-rock canyon walls. You can tour the massive dam and rent a variety of boats for exploring the lake. Just outside Page, take a guided tour of **Antelope Canyon** (p. 327), one of the most renowned slot canyons in the Southwest. On Day 9, take a boat tour up the lake to **Rainbow Bridge National Monument** (p. 326).

Day 10: Monument Valley ★★★

From Page, head to **Monument Valley Navajo Tribal Park** (p. 318), a 2-hour drive west through the Navajo Nation reservation. On the way, visit the **Navajo National Monument** (p. 316), where a 1-mile hike will take you to an overlook viewing the Betatakin cliff dwellings. Just be sure you arrive at Monument Valley early enough in the afternoon to do a jeep tour of the valley with a Navajo guide. Stick around to take pictures of the sunset on the Mitten Buttes. Stay overnight in Kayenta.

Days 11 & 12: Canyon de Chelly ★★★

The next day, perhaps after a horseback ride or jeep tour in Monument Valley (whichever you didn't do the day before), drive to **Canyon de Chelly National Monument** (p. 310). Cruise around the rim drives to get an overview of this extraordinary canyon, where the Navajo have been living for centuries. On Day 12, take a **truck tour** (p. 314) of the canyon, or hire a Navajo guide to take you into the canyon by jeep or on horseback.

Day 13: The Hopi Mesas ★★

After leaving Canyon de Chelly, drive south to Ganado and visit the historic **Hubbell Trading Post National Historic Site** (p. 306). Then head west across the Hopi Reservation, stopping in the village of **Walpi** (p. 293) on First Mesa, where you can take a guided tour of this ancient mesa-top pueblo. On Second Mesa, visit the **Hopi Cultural Center** (p. 294) and check out **Tsakurshovi** (p. 297), a tiny crafts shop specializing in traditional Hopi *katsina* (kachina) dolls. Continue south to Winslow and stay at the historic **La Posada** hotel (p. 291), with its renowned Turquoise Room as your preferred dining spot.

Day 14: Phoenix ★★

On your way back to Phoenix to catch a plane home, stop at **Meteor Crater** (p. 290), 20 miles east of Winslow. Once you're back in Phoenix, if you have a later flight, try to fit in a visit to the **Pueblo Grande Archaeological Park** (p. 70) near the airport for one last taste of Southwest Native American culture.

ARIZONA FOR FAMILIES

With the exception of the Grand Canyon and a few other mountainous areas, Arizona may be too hot in the summer for your family to enjoy themselves. Spring break, however, is ideal: The weather is usually just warm enough in Tucson and Phoenix, and not too cold or snowy at the Grand Canyon. A bit of time by the pool, a little culture, the grandest of canyons—this one should keep everyone happy.

Days 1, 2 & 3: Tucson ★★

In Tucson, the kids can pet snakes and tarantulas at the **Arizona–Sonora Desert Museum** (p. 361), which is actually more of a zoo than a museum. After lunch, explore the cactus forests of **Saguaro National Park** (p. 366). On Day 2, visit **Old Tucson Studios** (p. 365), a storied movie set that's now a sort of Wild West amusement park (minus the thrill rides), with plenty to keep kids and adults entertained. Your kids might also enjoy visiting the **Mini-Time Machine Museum of Miniatures** (p. 377). On one of your nights in town, have dinner at **Pinnacle Peak Steakhouse** (p. 411), a family-oriented cowboy steakhouse. On Day 3, take a day trip to **Tombstone** (p. 454), where Wyatt Earp and Doc Holliday shot it out with the Clantons at the O.K. Corral. On the way to or from Tombstone, visit **Kartchner Caverns State Park** (p. 448), a wonderland of underworld rock formations.

Day 4: Sedona ★★★

From Tucson, drive north to Sedona. It's a long drive (about 4 hours in good traffic), so start early and break up the trip with a few stops. In the hamlet of Picacho, not far north of Tucson, the kids can feed ostriches at the **Rooster Cogburn Ostrich Ranch** (p. 163). North of Phoenix in the town of Rock Springs, stop for lunch (and great pie) at the **Rock Springs Café** (p. 163). Older kids might be fascinated by the futuristic **Arcosanti** development (p. 163). If you get to Sedona early enough, take the kids on **Pink Jeep Tours'** (p. 199) gnarly Broken Arrow tour—four-wheeling at its most rugged. At sunset, head to **Crescent Moon Picnic Area** (p. 197), where the kids can splash in Oak Creek while you marvel at the sunset light show on Cathedral Rock.

Days 5 & 6: Grand Canyon ★★★

Leave Sedona and head up scenic **Oak Creek Canyon** (p. 190) to Flagstaff. If it's a hot day, take a cooling swim in the creek at **Slide Rock State Park** (p. 198). From Flagstaff, continue north on U.S. 89 to the east entrance of **Grand Canyon National Park** (chapter 6); it's worth the slightly longer drive to avoid the backed-up south entrance's waiting time. Check out the views from Desert View Drive's many overlooks as you head west to Grand Canyon Village. You can dawdle along the way, but be sure you make it to the Grand Canyon in time for sunset. Spend the next day hiking into the canyon, riding a mule along the rim, or exploring along **Hermit Road** (p. 230). If the weather's chilly, the historic Hermit's Rest is a good place to get cocoa and hang out by a fire.

Days 7 & 8: Phoenix ★★

From the Grand Canyon, head back south to **Phoenix.** On Ariz. 64, you may want to stop at the **Planes of Fame Air Museum** (p. 273) in Valle, or the **Grand Canyon Deer Farm** (p. 273) near Williams. Once back in Phoenix, spend a couple of days chilling out at one of the city's big resorts—many have water parks with slides and other features aimed specifically at keeping kids happy. If you can pry the kids away from the pool, take them to the **Heard Museum** (p. 59) to expose them to a little Native American culture. If you haven't yet had enough of Wild West towns, head east of the city to Apache Junction and **Goldfield Ghost Town** (p. 79)—not a real ghost town, but loads of fun—or south to **Rawhide** (p. 80), a mock-up of an old cowtown next to the Wild Horse Pass Casino. For more kid-friendly Phoenix suggestions, see p. 80.

A SOJOURN IN SOUTHEASTERN ARIZONA

Tombstone, Wyatt Earp, Doc Holliday, Geronimo, Cochise, the O.K. Corral—these legendary names all live on in southeastern Arizona. This corner of the state may not have major natural attractions, but it does have loads of Wild West history and plenty of natural beauty, not to mention being one of the best bird-watching regions in the country. With the exception of the Tucson area, the climate here is mild year-round, too.

Days 1, 2 & 3: Tucson ★★

Spend your first few days exploring Tucson and, if the weather is warm, lounging by the pool. On Day 1, check out the **Arizona–Sonora Desert Museum** (p. 361), the state's best introduction to the flora and fauna of the Sonoran Desert. It's just a few miles from the west unit of **Saguaro National Park** (p. 366), where you can hike or take a scenic drive to get up close to some gigantic saguaro cacti. On Day 2, visit the **Tucson Museum of Art** (p. 368) and wander around downtown Tucson's historic neighborhoods to get a feel for the city's mix of Spanish, Mexican, and Anglo history. If your timing is right, take a guided tour of one of the museum's historic homes. On Day 3, hike, bike, birdwatch, or swim in a swimming hole at **Sabino Canyon Recreation Area** (p. 375).

Day 4: Tubac ★★

Drive south of Tucson to get more of the area's Hispanic flavor. Your first stop should be **Mission San Xavier del Bac** (p. 364), a historic Spanish mission church on the Tohono O'odham reservation, known as the "White Dove of the Desert." This is a good place to try Indian fry-bread tacos; there's a walk-up food window in the plaza across the parking lot, and Native Americans often sell food from stalls in the parking lot. Continue south to the historic town of **Tubac,** founded by the Spanish 2 centuries ago, which is now full of art galleries. Just south of Tubac at **Tumacácori National Historical Park** (p. 433), you can see the ruins of another mission church. Spend the night at the **Tubac Golf Resort & Spa** (p. 435).

Days 5 & 6: Bisbee or Sierra Vista ★★

From Tubac, drive down to the border town of **Nogales** and then head east to **Patagonia** (p. 441), a small town known for great bird-watching, and **Sonoita** (p. 441), wide-open ranch country with an ever-growing cache of wineries (Callaghan Vineyards is my favorite, but several other good producers have tasting rooms here). Birders should make a beeline for **Patagonia Lake State Park/Sonoita Creek State Natural Area** (p. 443), the Nature Conservancy's **Patagonia–Sonoita Creek Preserve** (p. 441), and the **Paton Center** (p. 442). Try to time things for lunch at Patagonia's **Velvet Elvis Pizza Company** (p. 445). If you're a birder, you'll want to stay at one of the inns south of Sierra Vista that cater specifically to birders so you can spend Day 6 at hummingbird haven **Ramsey Canyon Preserve** (p. 449) and the birding hot spot **San Pedro Riparian National Conservation Area** (p. 450). If you're not a birder, continue to the funky historic town of **Bisbee** (p. 459), a former copper-mining town; countercultural types have turned this into the most interesting small town in Arizona. Be sure to eat dinner at **Cafe Roka** (p. 465). On Day 6, visit **Coronado National Memorial** (p. 448) to learn about the Spanish explorer who passed through this region between 1540 and 1542. From either Bisbee or Sierra Vista, it's a half-hour drive to **Tombstone** (p. 454), home of the famous shootout at the O.K. Corral.

Days 7 & 8: The Chiricahuas ★★

From Bisbee or Sierra Vista, head northeast to **Chiricahua National Monument** (p. 469), in the Coronado National Forest. Hike part or all of the **Heart of Rocks Trail,** one of the most memorable hikes in the state. Not far away, you can also visit **Fort Bowie National Historic Site** (p. 470), where a 3-mile round-trip hike will have you communing with the ghosts of Apaches, soldiers, and stagecoach travelers. Stay overnight in Pearce or Willcox. On Day 8, visit the **Amerind Foundation Museum** (p. 468), set amid huge granite boulders in Texas Canyon, which has an outstanding collection of Native American artifacts. On your way back to Tucson on I-10, detour south from Benson to **Kartchner Caverns State Park** (p. 448), among the most spectacular caverns in the Southwest.

NATIVE TRAILS OF ARIZONA

People have lived in Arizona for thousands of years, drawn to the region by its abundance of plant and animal life—and doubtless, even then, for its beauty as well. Down near the present-day San Pedro River, archaeologists discovered a mammoth kill site that proves humans were living in Arizona more than 10,000 years ago. All across Arizona you'll find signs of those who have come before—cliff dwellings, pueblo ruins, and petroglyphs galore. This itinerary will lead you to outstanding remains of Arizona's Native American cultures, both past and present, along with museums that focus on Native American art, artifacts, and heritage.

Days 1, 2 & 3: Phoenix ★★

The best "trail head" for an exploration of Arizona's Native trails is Phoenix. Start off at the superb **Heard Museum** (p. 59) to learn all about the tribes of the region and see samples of their traditional arts and crafts. Have lunch at the nearby **Fry Bread House** (p. 130) to try fry-bread tacos, a staple on reservations across the state. Near Skyharbor airport, at **Pueblo Grande Museum and Archaeological Park** (p. 70), you can visit the remains of a Hohokam village and learn about the people who once built an extensive network of canals here in the middle of the desert. On Day 2, visit the model Hohokam village in the **Arizona Museum of Natural History** (p. 72), check out the **Desert Botanical Garden** (p. 59) to see desert plants used by ancient Sonoran natives, then drive north to Cave Creek and hike to the **Sears Kay Ruins** (p. 91). On Day 3, head northeast of town to visit the reconstructions at **Besh-Ba-Gowah Archaeological Park** (p. 161), and then **Tonto National Monument** (p. 161), the southernmost cliff dwelling in the state. Unless you suffer from acrophobia, return to Phoenix on the winding, gravel **Apache Trail** route (p. 159), which is spectacular but scary.

Native Trails of Arizona

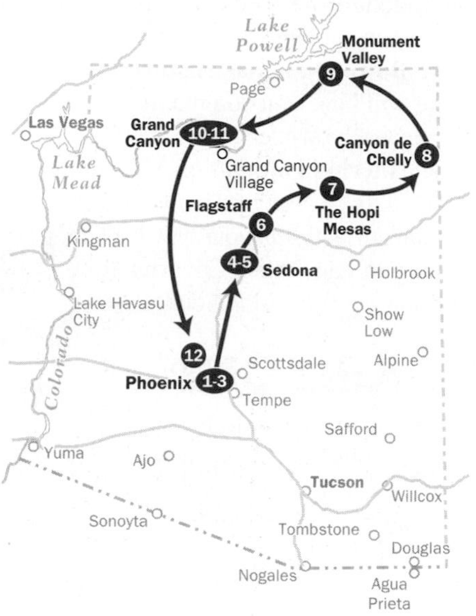

Arizona in the Winter

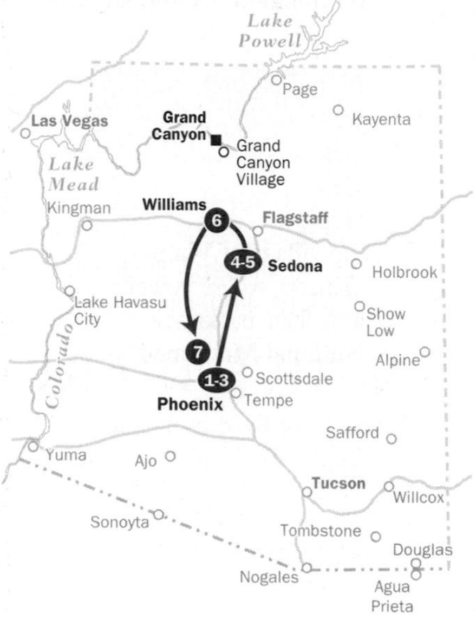

Days 4 & 5: Sedona ★★★

From Phoenix, journey north to Sedona on I-17, making three stops en route. At Camp Verde, detour to Cottonwood to visit the reconstructed hilltop ruins of **Tuzigoot National Monument** (p. 187). Head back to I-17 and continue north to **Montezuma Castle National Monument** (p. 185), another well-preserved cliff dwelling. At the Ariz. 179 exit for Sedona, get off I-17, but turn away from Sedona, not toward it, to reach the **V Bar V Heritage Site** (p. 195), one of the state's most impressive petroglyph sites. On Day 5, after you've spent some time ogling the red rocks, head west of town to **Palatki Heritage Site** (p. 197), where you can see the ruins of Sinagua cliff dwellings. While you're out this way, hike up **Boynton Canyon,** where you may spot some of the canyon's small ruin sites.

Day 6: Flagstaff ★★

It's barely an hour's drive from Sedona to Flagstaff, and the first place to visit there is the **Museum of Northern Arizona** (p. 261), which has outstanding exhibits on the Native cultures of the Colorado Plateau. Outside of town, two national monuments preserve old ruin sites. The more impressive of the two, **Wupatki National Monument** (p. 263) contains several Sinagua pueblo sites; at the main pueblo of Wupatki, you'll find both a ball court similar to those found in Mexico and a fascinating "blowhole." Closer to Flagstaff, you can explore small Sinagua cliff dwellings at **Walnut Canyon National Monument** (p. 262).

Day 7: The Hopi Mesas ★★

From Flagstaff, head east to the villages of the Hopi mesas. Along the way, you'll pass numerous shops selling Hopi silver overlay jewelry, as well as *katsina* dolls, pottery, and baskets. Stop at the **Hopi Cultural Center** (p. 294) to tour the small museum and have a lunch of traditional Hopi stew. At First Mesa, you can take a guided tour of the ancient cliff-top village of **Walpi** (p. 293). Continue east to the Navajo community of Ganado, where you can tour the historic **Hubbell Trading Post** (p. 306), and then backtrack a few miles to head north to **Canyon de Chelly National Monument** (p. 310).

Day 8: Canyon de Chelly National Monument ★★★

Do a "shake-and-bake" truck tour of Canyon de Chelly. Riding in rugged military surplus trucks, you'll head deep into the canyon to places you can't visit without a Navajo guide, stopping at numerous ruin sites and well-preserved pictographs. You may even encounter Navajo farmers and shepherds, who still live in the canyon every summer. See p. 314.

Day 9: Monument Valley Navajo Tribal Park ★★★

Monument Valley Navajo Tribal Park (p. 318) is really a landscape attraction and not a cultural attraction, but you can't visit this park without meeting a few Navajos. Local families operate jeep tours, horseback tours, and hiking tours. Take a **jeep tour** (p. 314), and you'll see some interesting petroglyphs, along with some of the most memorable landscapes in the desert Southwest, made famous in several classic Western movies.

Days 10 & 11: Grand Canyon ★★★

En route to the Grand Canyon from Monument Valley, visit **Navajo National Monument** (p. 316), where you can take a 1-mile walk to a viewpoint overlooking the large Betatakin cliff dwelling. (If you have an extra day, try to get a space on one of the guided hikes to the ruins.) All through the **Grand Canyon** (chapter 6) there are caves, cliff dwellings, and pueblo sites—Native Americans have lived in and near here for millennia—but most of them are far from established trails; the park service doesn't really want the public to know these sites exist, hoping to preserve them for scientific study. You can, however, visit the **Tusayan Museum** (p. 234) just outside the park, built on the site of an Ancestral Puebloan (Anasazi) ruin. Spend Day 11 in Grand Canyon National Park exploring along the park's rim drives or hiking down into the canyon.

Day 12: Phoenix ★★

Head back to Phoenix by taking Ariz. 64 south to U.S. 180 to Flagstaff, where you'll pick up I-17. Once you reach Phoenix, check into your hotel, pull up a lounge chair by the pool, and meditate on all that you've seen as you've followed the Native trails of Arizona.

ARIZONA IN THE WINTER

Sure, you can go to the Grand Canyon in winter, when it's at its least crowded, but it will be very cold, and snow often makes the area's roads impassable. In the lower elevations of Phoenix, Tucson, Yuma, and Sierra Vista, however, winter means golf, hiking, desert explorations, and enough sunshine to help you forget all about shoveling snow out of your driveway back home.

Days 1, 2 & 3: Phoenix ★★

You'll be forgiven if you decide to spend your first day or two in the big city hanging out by the pool of an elegant resort. But once you've relaxed for a bit, it's time for some peak bagging. On Day 2, if you've got lots of energy, hike up **Camelback Mountain** (p. 90) or **Piestewa Peak** (p. 90) for incomparable views of the valley. Outdoor-minded locals also recommend **McDowell Sonoran Preserve** (p. 92), northeast of Scottsdale, with its incomparable views of the lower Verde River Valley, and **North Mountain Park** (p. 91), which lies northwest of the Phoenix Mountains Preserve. Head to Scottsdale or downtown Phoenix for dinner. On Day 3, play a round of golf or some tennis in the morning; in the afternoon, get some culture at the **Heard Museum** (p. 59) or the **Phoenix Art Museum** (p. 67). Around sunset, visit the **Desert Botanical Garden** (p. 59) in Scottsdale.

Days 4 & 5: Sedona ★★★

Drive north on I-17 to **Sedona** (p. 190), which has good reason to claim the most beautiful setting of any town in the West. Your best introduction to the surrounding red-rock country is a **jeep tour** (p. 199). Just make sure that by sunset you're atop **Airport Mesa** (p. 196) to take in the natural light show. On Day 5, in the morning, visit the **V Bar V Heritage Site** (p. 195), one of the most impressive petroglyph sites in the state; it's at its photogenic best before the sun hits the rocks in early afternoon. Then do some hiking or mountain biking—Sedona is surrounded by national forest, and there are dozens of miles of easily accessed trails. Hiking the **Boynton Canyon Trail** (p. 196) or the **Vultee Arch Trail** (p. 201) will put you close to **Palatki Heritage Site** (p. 197), a small Sinagua cliff dwelling. You'll also end the day not far from **Crescent Moon Picnic Area** (p. 197), where you can watch sunset light up Cathedral Rock as the waters of Oak Creek flow by.

Day 6: Route 66 ★★

Drive north to Flagstaff on Ariz. 89 through **Oak Creek Canyon** (p. 190). Flagstaff's downtown (p. 258) is built along old Route 66, America's vintage coast-to-coast highway, famous in story and song.

When the interstates were built, they bypassed Route 66, but pop culture refused to let the old highway die. To see the largest surviving section of Route 66, head west on I-40 through **Williams** (p. 272), which has lots of Route 66-themed shops and cafes; turn off exit 139 west of Williams for a fun joyride on the Mother Road. Of course, you can always scrap this jaunt if you've got golf tee times or spa appointments in Sedona.

Day 7: Phoenix ★★

Head back to Phoenix by way of the former mining town of **Jerome** (p. 179), once almost a ghost town, now an artists' community. Browse its galleries and sample surprisingly good Verde Valley wines in its tasting rooms. Then head south to Phoenix—if you time it right, you can get in one last swim at your resort before flying back to winter the next morning.

PHOENIX, SCOTTSDALE & THE VALLEY OF THE SUN

4

Phoenix—once a sleepy Sun Belt also-ran—is now a bustling mini-metropolis of some 1.6 million people. It's the center of the sprawling Valley of the Sun, which, with 4.6 million people, has become the 12th-largest metropolitan area in the U.S. A revitalized Phoenix downtown, a new light-rail system that stretches across the Valley, and a rebounding economy after a crippling recession have created something that, if you squint a little, might be a new go-go era for both residents and tourists. Golf and resorts, sure, but also a bustling art scene, creative restaurateurs, and hopping nightlife. It's all a lot of fun—at least, during those 8 months of the year when the average temperature is less than 100 degrees.

First settled in 1867, Phoenix was named capital of the Arizona Territory only a few years later, in 1889. Back then the Salt River, now a dry waterbed, was a real river, and the town began on the river's north side, roughly where downtown is now. In 1912, when Arizona became a state—the last entrant into the Union before Alaska and Hawaii, in 1959—Phoenix remained the capital. A population boom after World War II transformed the Valley as the Sun Belt era dawned. Once air-conditioning became widely available (and a permanent water source was found from the Colorado River), Phoenix and its surrounding towns grew rapidly. Phoenix proper now stretches some 50 miles north to south, and the Valley is nearly that wide.

The still-growing East Valley includes the booming 'burbs of Mesa, Chandler, Gilbert, and a few other towns, tucked away southeast of Phoenix. (Mesa is the state's third-largest city, after Tucson, and is catching up fast.) Due east of Phoenix lies Scottsdale, which was first settled in 1888. (It was originally called Orangedale for its citrus groves.) Scottsdale was not officially incorporated until 1951, but during the Depression, it developed a reputation as a haven for artistic types, including the influential architect Frank Lloyd

Wright. Today it's a somewhat glitzy town—and the area's wealthiest, after tiny, residential Paradise Valley—but still has an artsy vibe. Just south of Scottsdale, Tempe is home to large Arizona State University, descended from Arizona Territory's first college, founded in 1885. ASU lived under a "party school" stigma for decades, but an ambitious new president plans to transform it into what is said will be the "New American University." Stay tuned.

ESSENTIALS

Arriving

BY PLANE **Sky Harbor International Airport,** 3400 E. Sky Harbor Blvd. (www.phxskyharbor.com; ✆ **602/273-3300**), is just a few minutes from downtown Phoenix, 20 minutes from Scottsdale. There are three terminals; running west to east, they are 2, 3, and 4. (Terminal 1 is gone.) Four, the newest, is a major hub for Southwest and American and has the best restaurants (including satellite versions of local favorites) and shops. Sky Harbor has a rep as a friendly airport, and it is. ***One warning:*** After scores of visits to the airport, I can say with certainty that the Wi-Fi service, by Boingo, is glitchy and can hijack your phone (and not send important texts and e-mails).

A sleek automated people mover, the **SkyTrain** ferries passengers from the terminals to long-term parking and a passenger drop-off station at 44th and Washington streets. That last is supposed to save people from having to negotiate the airport proper to drop off passengers. But SkyTrain is poorly designed, and there's an awful lot of walking involved. If you're traveling with kids, lots of baggage, or seniors, opt for being dropped off at your terminal. An extension that will take the SkyTrain to the big car-rental facility west of the airport is scheduled to open in 2020.

There are two entrances to Sky Harbor, east and west. The west entrance is convenient to downtown Phoenix and points west; it's accessed by I-10 or 24th Street. Scottsdale and points northeast and southeast use the east entrance via the Hohokam Expressway (Ariz. 143), the Red Mountain Freeway (Ariz. 202), or 44th Street. The routing at Sky Harbor is complex and signage is hit-or-miss. If you're driving in or out, remember that 24th Street is the west entrance (for downtown Phoenix) and 44th Street the east entrance (for Scottsdale). Keep an eye out for the sometimes hard-to-find signs and you should end up where you want to be.

There is also now an alternative airport on the east side of the Valley. The **Phoenix-Mesa Gateway Airport,** 6033 S. Sossaman Rd., Mesa (www.gatewayairport.com; ✆ **480/988-7600**) is served by **Allegiant Airlines** (www.allegiantair.com; ✆ **702/505-8888**), which has service from small cities in the Northwest and Midwest. Mesa is a southeast suburb, south of the Ariz. 202 Loop at the Power Road exit.

FROM THE AIRPORT TO YOUR LODGINGS

SuperShuttle (www.supershuttle.com; ✆ **800/258-3826** or 602/244-9000) offers 24-hour door-to-door van service between Sky Harbor Airport and resorts, hotels, and homes throughout the Valley. Per-person shared-ride fares average $12 to $14 to the downtown and Tempe area, $16 to downtown Scottsdale, and $24 to $31 to north Scottsdale.

Taxis can be found outside all three terminals and cost only slightly more than shuttle vans. You can also call **AAA/Yellow Cab** (✆ **602/888-8888**), **Apache Taxi** (✆ **480/557-7000**), or **Mayflower Cab** (www.discountcab.com; ✆ **602/955-1355**). All taxis from the airport charge $5 for turning on the meter, $2.30 per mile, and a minimum fare of $15. Traffic delays are $23 an hour. There's a flat fee of $17 to downtown Phoenix. A taxi from the airport to central Scottsdale is $30 and up in light traffic.

Both Uber and Lyft operate in the Valley; there's a big savings over cab rates, but the drivers don't know the city as well as professional cabbies.

Valley Metro Rail (www.valleymetro.org; ✆ **602/253-5000**), generally referred to as "the light rail," is a key part of the city's transformation. The airport is at the middle of a single 25-mile-long route running from northwest Phoenix to downtown, and then east past the airport to Tempe and Mesa. Metro runs daily every 12 to 20 minutes, between about 5am and 11pm (until 1:40am on weekends). At Sky Harbor, the SkyTrain will take you to the light-rail station at the corner of Washington and 44th streets. The ride to or from downtown or Tempe takes about 15 minutes and costs $2. There is no light rail service to Scottsdale. The Valley has an extensive bus system but it's not designed to serve the airport; for the record, the 1, 13, 32, and 44 lines will get you there.

BY CAR Phoenix is connected to Los Angeles and Tucson by I-10 and to Flagstaff via I-17. If you're headed to the resorts in north Scottsdale, the easiest route is to take the Red Mountain Freeway (Ariz. 202) east to U.S. 101 N. (If you're headed to central Scottsdale from the airport, you might ask the driver to take McDowell Road east through the beautiful Papago Buttes.) The Superstition Freeway (U.S. 60) leads east to Tempe, Mesa, and Chandler.

BY TRAIN Time was a train trip from LA to Chicago took you through Phoenix; no more. Today there is no Amtrak service to Phoenix. If you're tied to the magic of travel by rail, take **Amtrak** (www.amtrak.com; ✆ **800/872-7245**) to Tucson or Flagstaff and make your way to Phoenix via **Arizona Shuttle** (www.arizonashuttle.com; ✆ **877/226-8060** or 928/226-8060). There is a closer stop to Phoenix, in the far south community of Maricopa, but you'll then have to take your chances on a 45-minute drive with Uber or Lyft.

Visitor Information

You'll find **tourist information desks** with helpful folks in purple jackets in all three terminals at Sky Harbor Airport. The city's main visitor center, the **Greater Phoenix Convention & Visitors Bureau,** is at 125 N. Second St., Ste. 120 (www.visitphoenix.com; ✆ **877/225-5749;** Monday–Friday 8am–5pm), across from the main entrance of the Hyatt Regency in downtown Phoenix.

If you're staying in Scottsdale, you can get information at the Scottsdale **Tourist Information Center** (www.experiencescottsdale.com; ✆ **800/782-1117;** Monday–Saturday 9am–6pm, Sunday 10am–5pm), located in the food court of Scottsdale Fashion Square, the mall on the northwest corner of Camelback and Scottsdale roads.

City Layout

Some Phoenix residents grouse about L.A.-style traffic, but in reality there are only a few terrible times and places to be out on the freeway here. Most of the time you'll find trips even to the far corners of the Valley reasonably efficient. Ditto for the main east-west arteries, though of course they get more crowded during rush hour.

MAIN ARTERIES & STREETS **I-10** runs to Phoenix from LA and then heads southeast to Tucson. The I-10 is not pleasant during rush hour; don't, for example, stick your kids in the car in Scottsdale and head for Los Angeles at 4pm. But otherwise traffic moves well. **Ariz. 51 (Piestewa Fwy.), "the 51,"** heads north from I-10 through the center of east Phoenix to U.S. Loop 101 and is the best north-south route in the city. **Ariz. 202 (Red Mountain Fwy.)** shoots off east from I-10 and the 51 and is the quickest route to south Scottsdale, Tempe and Mesa, and points southeast, the burgeoning "East Valley."

U.S. Loop 101 circles the top half of the Valley. It can get slow at rush hour over its many miles, but is your best route to the north Scottsdale resorts, Cave Creek, and Carefree. **I-17 (Black Canyon Fwy.), "the 17,"** runs up the west side of town, connecting Phoenix with Flagstaff, Sedona, and the Grand Canyon. It's an older truck route and feels narrow and chaotic until you get north of U.S. 101. Residents take the 51 if they can. East of the airport, little-used **Ariz. 143 (Hohokam Expwy.)** connects Ariz. 202 with I-10.

The vast majority of the Valley's tourist attractions and major hotels are on the east side of the city, which is to say east of Central Avenue (which runs north from the heart of downtown) in the direction of Scottsdale.

Phoenix and virtually all of its surrounding cities are based on a grid system. On the Scottsdale side of town (east), numbered *streets* run north and south; on the Phoenix side (west), you have numbered *avenues*. Every eight streets is a mile—and every mile you have a big street (16th Street, 24th Street, etc.) with only a few exceptions. Scottsdale's main commercial artery,

A Name Change

In 2003, the official name of Phoenix's Squaw Peak was changed to Piestewa Peak (pronounced Pee-*ESS*-twa) to honor Pfc. Lori Ann Piestewa, a member of the Hopi tribe and the first female soldier killed in the Iraq War. The peak in north Phoenix has long been a popular hiking destination. If you hear people referring to both Squaw Peak and Piestewa Peak, it's one and the same place. Ditto for the Squaw Peak Parkway, Ariz. 51, which is now Piestewa Freeway.

Scottsdale Road, is where 72nd Street should be. On the west side, the arteries are odd-numbered but on the same eight-street grid: 19th Avenue, 27th Avenue, etc. Two other major arteries are **7th Street** and **7th Avenue** in central Phoenix, which are respectively a half-mile east and west of Central. ***Please note:*** Both use the center turn lane as an extra traffic lane during rush hour—south in the morning, north in the evening. This can be a little nerve-wracking, particularly during winter months when the sun sets early. Left-hand turns at most major intersections are not allowed during these times.

The main east-west commercial arteries in central Phoenix are set a mile apart too: Getting more upscale as you go north, they are **McDowell, Thomas, Indian School,** and **Camelback** roads. The city's major shopping thoroughfare, **East Camelback Road,** begins at Central with a cluster of stores and nice restaurants, heads east to the tony shopping districts of Biltmore and Arcadia, then curves around its namesake Camelback Mountain to the intersection of Scottsdale Road in central Scottsdale, home to the ever-expanding Scottsdale Fashion Square mall and many other shopping destinations.

An important note for drivers: The high-end suburb of Paradise Valley, centered in the valley behind Camelback Mountain in east Phoenix, has two main through streets, **Lincoln Avenue** and **Tatum Boulevard,** which is where 48th Street should be. Traffic laws in this small ritzy community are implacably enforced with a network of cameras, and tickets are pricey. Follow the locals, who drive no more than 5 miles over the speed limit.

In the East Valley, a well-laid-out grid system of freeways will get you where you want to go. Secondary highways in the Valley include the **Beeline Highway (Ariz. 87),** which starts at the east end of Ariz. 202 (Red Mountain Fwy.) in Mesa; it's the scenic route to Payson and the Mogollon Rim (see p. 335), and ultimately the Petrified Forest National Monument (p. 300) and other sites in the state's northeast corner. **Grand Avenue (U.S. 60),** just about the only diagonal street in the entire Valley, starts downtown and heads due northwest to Sun City, Wickenburg, and ultimately, Las Vegas.

FINDING AN ADDRESS **Central Avenue,** which runs north to south through downtown Phoenix, is the starting point for all east-and-west street numbering. **Washington Street,** also in downtown Phoenix, is the starting point for north and south numbering. ***The key thing to remember:*** North-to-south numbered *streets* are to be found on the east side of the city, while north-to-south numbered *avenues* will be found on the west. In other words, W. Camelback Road will intersect with numbered *avenues*, while E. Camelback Road will intersect with numbered *streets*. Odd-numbered addresses are on the south and east sides of streets, while even-numbered addresses are on the north and west sides of streets.

Most tourist sites are on the north and east sides of town, so in practice you're going to be dealing mostly with streets. Keep an eye out for addresses with a numbered avenue or a "west" street name, and make sure you're going in the right direction. For example, the Arizona Cardinals football stadium and

The sprawl of metropolitan Phoenix encompasses several distinct desert communities.

the attached malls are at *West* Glendale Avenue and 91st *Avenue* on the far west side of town. That's a long way from 91st *Street*!

Neighborhoods in Brief

The Valley of the Sun (or just "the Valley") encompasses Phoenix and a metropolitan area of more than 20 cities. Phoenix has some 1.6 million residents (more than Philadelphia, fewer than Houston); the whole metropolitan area has a population of 4.6 million. Besides Tempe and Scottsdale, there are now genuine downtown "scenes" in cities like Gilbert. Still, much of the Valley will come across as undifferentiated suburb to those from just about anywhere other than the Sun Belt. You have to remember that great restaurants or shops are often found in an unprepossessing strip mall.

DOWNTOWN PHOENIX

While residents of the outer city and the suburbs often use this term to refer to central Phoenix generally, the actual **Downtown,** with its high-rise office towers, is clustered around Central Avenue and Washington Street and stretches from 7th Street to 7th Avenue. (The state government complex is a mile west.) Here you'll find Arizona State University's ever-expanding downtown Phoenix campus, as well as the Arizona Diamondbacks' Chase Field and the Phoenix Suns' Talking Stick Resort Arena**.** Several major performing arts venues and museums are located close by, and there's a big convention center.

Heading north on Central, the area around the intersection of Indian School Rd. is called **Midtown.** The intersection of Central Avenue and Camelback Road a mile north is **Uptown,** which has several good restaurants and even—heavens!—actual pedestrians. From there, Central Avenue continues north through miles of expensive homes.

BILTMORE DISTRICT

"The Biltmore," as it's called, 3 miles east of Uptown on the **Camelback Corridor,** centers on Camelback Road between 24th and 40th streets. You'll find upscale shopping, a few residential and office towers, and local landmarks like the Arizona Biltmore Hotel, the Wrigley Mansion, and the chi-chi Biltmore Fashion Park shopping mall, at 24th Street and Camelback Road.

ARCADIA

Just east of the Biltmore, Arcadia includes the intersection of Camelback and 44th Street, a cluster of upscale stores and restaurants, and some very expensive homes stretching east toward Scottsdale and creeping up the sides of Camelback Mountain. Indian School Road, a mile south of Camelback, has become a strip of lively restaurants as well.

SCOTTSDALE

Scottsdale, a narrow city of 250,000, forms the east border of Phoenix. It extends from Tempe in the south up past Carefree in the north, a distance of some 30 miles. Downtown Scottsdale includes Old Town (Western-themed galleries and shops), the Waterfront (upscale shopping and restaurants next to a canal), the swanky Scottsdale Fashion Square mall, and a raucous nightlife quarter. North Scottsdale has miles and miles of shopping and restaurants along Scottsdale and Hayden roads.

TEMPE

The home of huge Arizona State University, Tempe has lots of nightclubs and bars and all the other trappings of a university town. **Mill Avenue,** with dozens of interesting shops along a 6-block stretch, is the center of activity both day and night.

PARADISE VALLEY

This 15-square-mile residential enclave, surrounded by Phoenix and Scottsdale, is largely nestled between Camelback and Mummy mountains north of the Biltmore. Multi-acre desert lots with expensive homes are ringed by gazillion-dollar mountainside manses. The town is spotted with topline resorts as well.

MESA

This fast-growing eastern suburb, home to some tech activity and an extravagant Mormon Temple, is marked by large shopping malls, numerous chain motels, and the beautiful Mesa Arts Center.

GILBERT

A welcome respite from the somewhat bland East Valley, charming downtown Gilbert is a few blocks of two-story buildings fronting N. Gilbert Road a few miles south of route 60. It has several restaurants and an old-fashioned water tower that stands over a fun splash pad for kids.

GLENDALE

The Valley's major northwest suburb has a semi-historic downtown, with dozens of antiques shops. A few miles west of that is an enormous sports, entertainment, and shopping complex, which includes the University of Phoenix Stadium, where the Arizona Cardinals play football, and the Gila River Arena, home of the Phoenix Coyotes hockey team. A casino is under construction just to the north.

CAREFREE & CAVE CREEK

These sister cities lie about 20 miles north of central Scottsdale. Carefree is predominantly large desert homes surrounding a low-key shopping and dining plaza. Just to the west, Cave Creek plays up its Western heritage with a 2-mile strip of saloons, restaurants, and shops selling Western crafts and other gifts.

GETTING AROUND

By Car

Phoenix is a sprawling Sun Belt metropolis; if you're not bunking at ASU or sequestered downtown on a business trip, you need to make transportation plans. Uber and Lyft can take care of incidental needs, but if you are planning to poke around at some of the Valley's major attractions, a rental car might be your most cost-effective option.

Outside downtown Phoenix and the ASU campus, there's almost always plenty of free parking. Winter can get busier; during the tourist season, some of the newer restaurants have even resorted to that newfangled valet parking, which is generally free, but of course you want to tip the valets.

Renting a car isn't hard, but just be aware that published daily rates nearly double once taxes and fees are added in. Expect to pay a bit more than you would in most mid-American cities—$300 or more a week in the winter, less in the desultory summer. See p. 506 for general tips on car rentals.

At Sky Harbor, all the major rental-car companies have desks at a big but efficient Rental Car Center just outside the airport, with free buses to ferry you on the quick trip to and from. I wouldn't advise going there without an advance reservation in the high season; you can get hit with very high last-minute rates. There are also individual car-rental outlets scattered around town, though not that many in downtown proper. You can probably save a bit on your rental by picking up your car someplace other than the airport.

By Public Transportation

Valley Metro (www.valleymetro.org; ✆ **602/253-5000**) runs the buses and the light rail. The Phoenix public bus system does its best, but this is a big city with arteries a mile apart; it is not very useful to tourists. Fares on buses and the light rail are $2, $1 for seniors and kids. The **Valley Metro light-rail system** starts in the northwest part of the city and then runs along Central Avenue, through downtown Phoenix, and from there east to Tempe and Mesa. Attractions along or fairly close to the line include Uptown, the Heard Museum, Phoenix Art Museum, Historic Heritage Square, Arizona Science Center, Pueblo Grande Museum and Archaeological Park, the airport, Tempe's Mill Avenue shopping district, ASU, even the old Mormon Temple in Mesa. But be aware that "served by" in Phoenix Speak can mean "within a half-mile or a mile walk in 90-plus-degree heat," and that the Metro does not run as frequently as a big city subway system does. Midmorning on a weekday, trains should come every 12 minutes, about every 15 minutes on Saturdays, and 20 on Sundays. The Metro's 44th Street/Washington Street stop connects to the SkyTrain to the airport.

Of slightly more value to visitors is the Metro's free **Downtown Area Circulator (DASH),** which goes up and down Central Avenue and 1st Avenue and then swings out to the State Capitol complex a mile west of downtown. It runs Monday through Friday from 6:30am to 6:30pm. There's a transit hub close to the center of downtown, at Central Avenue and Van Buren Street. In Tempe, **FLASH** buses provide a similar service on a loop around Arizona State University, including Mill Avenue and Sun Devil Stadium, Monday through Friday from 7am to 6pm. The Tempe Transit Center is at Veterans and College avenues. Buses run every 10 or 12 minutes. For information on both DASH and FLASH, visit www.valleymetro.org or call ✆ **602/253-5000.**

In Scottsdale, **Scottsdale Trolley** (www.scottsdaletrolley.com; ✆ **480/421-1004**) shuttle buses run between Scottsdale Fashion Square, the Fifth Avenue shops, the Main Street Arts district, and the Old Town district. These buses run daily from 11am to 9pm, with service every 10 minutes.

By Taxi or Uber

Phoenix's sprawl can make the price of an ordinary taxi ride quite high. **AAA Yellow Cab** (www.yellowcabaz.com; ✆ **602/252-5252**) charges $2.75 for the first mile and $2.20 per mile thereafter. Lyft and Uber serve the Valley as well, and they are generally a lot cheaper than cabs; my only complaint is that the newer drivers sometimes lack basic knowledge of the city. It's smart to make sure both you and the driver agree on where you're going before you get into traffic.

[Fast FACTS] PHOENIX

Dentist Call the **Dental Referral Service** (www.dentalreferral.com; ✆ **877/423-1702**).

Doctor There are now urgent-care centers in strip malls throughout the Valley.

Emergencies For police, fire, or medical emergencies, phone ✆ **911.**

Hospitals The **Banner University Medical Center Phoenix,** which Phoenicians refer to by its old name, Good Samaritan or "Good Sam," is closest to downtown. It's at 1111 E. McDowell Rd. (www.bannerhealth.com; ✆ **602/839-2000**). In Scottsdale, the **HonorHealth Scottsdale Osborn Medical Center,** 7400 E. Osborn Rd. (✆ **480/882-4000**) is right on the edge of downtown.

Lost Property If you lose something at the airport, call ✆ **602/273-3333** or e-mail lostandfound@phoenix.gov; for anything that was lost on a Valley Metro bus or the light rail, call ✆ **602/534-5053.**

Newspapers & Magazines The ***Arizona Republic*** (azcentral.com) is Phoenix's daily newspaper. ***New Times*** (phoenixnewtimes.com) is the alternative weekly with a long history of investigative reporting and provocative articles; it can be found downtown in street boxes and in the hipper restaurants and cafes. Neither website is particularly user-friendly, but poke around and you can often find interesting things to do.

Pharmacies **Walgreens** and **CVS** outlets dot the city. In downtown Phoenix there's a big CVS (pharmacy ✆ **602/296-7611**) in the far southwest corner of the mall at CitySpace center, on the corner of 1st Ave. and W. Jefferson St., open 6am–10pm.

Post Office The Phoenix Downtown Post Office, 522 N. Central Ave. (✆ **602/253-9648**) is open Monday–Friday 9am–5pm. In Scottsdale, the Scottsdale Post Office, 1776 N. Scottsdale Rd. (✆ **480/948-1448**) is open Monday–Friday 8:30am–4:30pm and Saturday 9am–3:30pm.

Safety Crime isn't a terrible problem in Phoenix; the number of property and violent crimes has been dropping for decades, even as the city's population has grown. Downtown and the Central Corridor are among the safest areas of the city. That said, there's little reason to walk into sparsely populated and unknown areas day or night. Rental cars are targets, so don't leave phones, laptops, or valuables in them. Once in a while, a road-rage incident is reported. Drive sensibly and let aggressive drivers have their way. Here's the most important safety tip I can give you: Look twice before stepping out onto just about any street, driveway, parking lot, or intersection, and that goes double if you're on a bike. This is a car town; pedestrians in general and bike lanes in particular are new phenomena in much of the Valley.

Taxes Local taxes are about 9% in total on most but not all goods. Gas is far cheaper—like, $1 a gallon cheaper—here than in Nevada or California, so fill up before you cross the border. Hotel room taxes vary by city but are mostly between 12% and 15%. Car rental taxes bite: Expect to pay 50% over the daily rate.

EXPLORING PHOENIX & SCOTTSDALE

Phoenix is a big city now, and as such it has plenty of attractions—art galleries, museums, and the like—beyond the desert scenery. A few are in fact world class, and anyone with an interest in the various strains of desert culture will find a lot to gawk at and learn about. Families will find a number of places that will fill at least a day of sightseeing, the Musical Instrument Museum, OdySea, and the Desert Botanical Garden among them. They are all open year-round, although outdoor sites like the botanical gardens and the zoo are a little more enjoyable when the temperature is less than 90 degrees.

Have any architecture geeks in your group? Phoenix is a home of midcentury modernism—the sleek and unadorned style of desert architecture you might associate with 1960s-era movie-star manses in Palm Springs—and has an architectural scene more vibrant than you might expect. The **Phoenix Art Museum** and the **ASU Art Museum** both hold annual architectural tours that can get you into some of the Valley's most distinctive homes. Check the organizations' respective sites for details. A local group called **Modern Phoenix** (http://modernphoenix.net) holds various programs throughout the year and an annual festival of talks and neighborhood tours. (Those tours tend to sell out immediately; check the website for dates and be ready to buy tickets online as soon as they go on sale.) Or if you just like poking around, turn up some of the streets around Camelback or Mummy Mountain, or take a slow drive along Tom Darlington Drive in Carefree, to ooh and aah at some extraordinary residences built into the hillsides.

Top Attractions in the Valley of the Sun

Desert Botanical Garden ★★★ GARDENS In Papago Park adjacent to the Phoenix Zoo (p. 69), this botanic garden is a beautiful and restful place, displaying more than 20,000 desert plants from around the world. The walk called Plants and People of the Sonoran Desert Trail is the state's best introduction to southwestern ethnobotany (human use of plants). Along this trail you can make your own yucca-fiber brush and practice grinding corn as Native Americans once did. On the Desert Wildflower Trail, you'll find colorful wildflowers throughout much of the year. Each spring, there's usually a butterfly pavilion filled with live butterflies. If you come late in the day, you can stay until after dark and see night-blooming flowers and dramatically lit cacti. A cafe on the grounds makes a great lunch spot. During the cooler months, concerts are held in the garden and there are movie nights, too. In December, during Las Noches de las Luminarias, the gardens are lit at night by luminarias (candles inside small bags).

In Papago Park, 1201 N. Galvin Pkwy., Phoenix. www.dbg.org. ✆ **480/941-1225.** $25 adults, $13 kids 3–17, free for kids 2 and under. Oct–Apr daily 8am–8pm; May–Sept daily 7am–8pm. Closed July 4, Thanksgiving, and Christmas. Check website for occasional early closings. Bus: 1 or 3. METRO: Priest Dr./Washington St.

Heard Museum ★★★ MUSEUM One of the nation's finest museums dealing exclusively with Native American cultures, the Heard is an ideal introduction to the indigenous peoples of Arizona. The heart and soul of the museum is the permanent exhibit **Home: Native People in the Southwest,** which examines the culture of each of the major tribes of the region. Included

Agua Fria National Monument **1**
Arcosanti **1**
Arizona Biltmore **11**
Arizona Capitol Museum **5**
Arizona Commemorative Air Force Museum **19**
Arizona Heritage Center at Papago Park **22**
Arizona Museum of Natural History **28**
Arizona Science Center **6**
Arizona State University Art Museum **26**
Burton Barr Library **4**
Children's Museum of Phoenix **8**
Desert Botanical Garden **20**
Hall of Flame Firefighting Museum **23**
Heard Museum **2**
Historic Heritage Square **7**
I.d.e.a. Museum **27**
McCormick-Stillman Railroad Park **16**
Musical Instrument Museum **12**
Mystery Castle **10**
OdySea Aquarium **15**
Phoenix Art Museum **3**
Phoenix Zoo **21**
Pueblo Grande Museum and Archaeological Park **25**
Scottsdale Museum of Contemporary Art **18**
Skyspace: Air Apparent **26**
Taliesin West **14**
Tovrea Castle **24**
Western Spirit: Scottsdale's Museum of the West **17**
Wildlife World Zoo & Aquarium **9**
Wrigley Mansion **12**

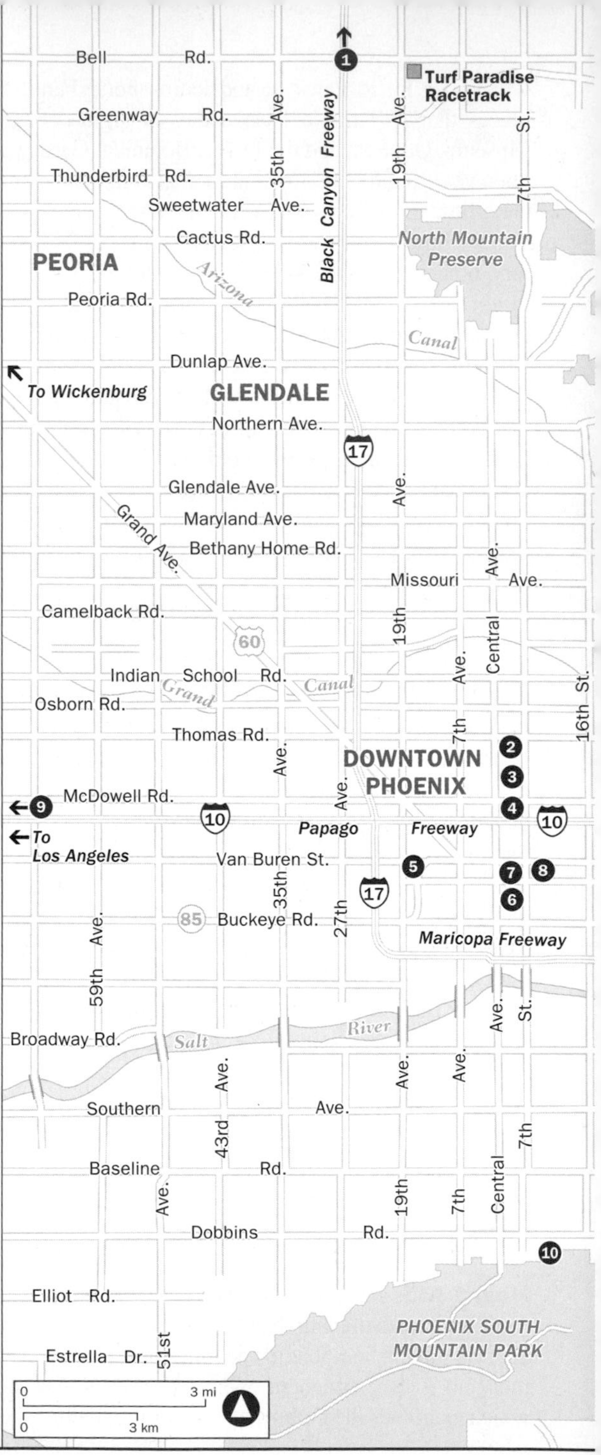

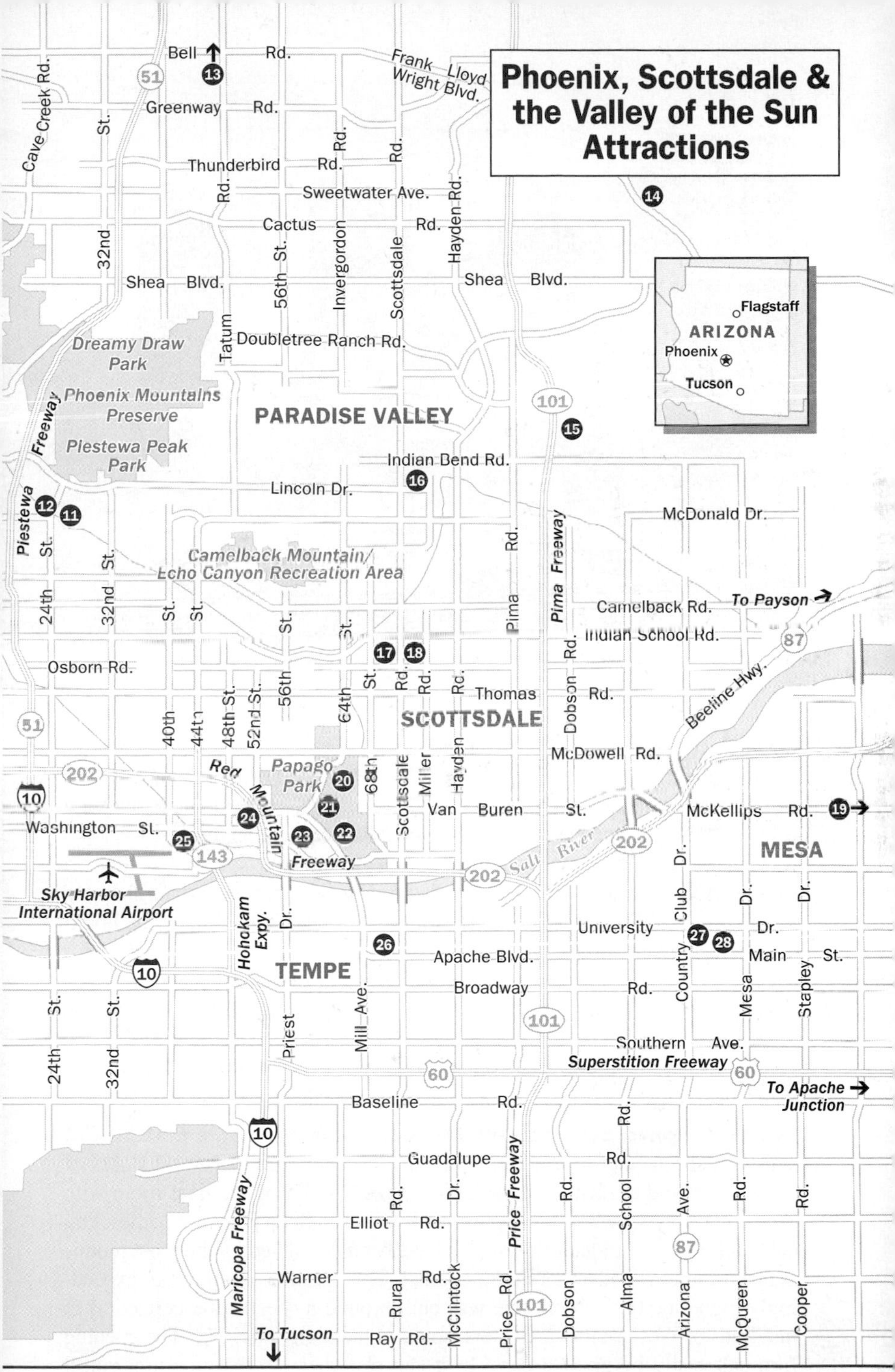
Phoenix, Scottsdale & the Valley of the Sun Attractions
ARIZONA
Flagstaff
Phoenix
Tucson
PARADISE VALLEY
SCOTTSDALE
TEMPE
MESA
Dreamy Draw Park
Phoenix Mountains Preserve
Piestewa Peak Park
Camelback Mountain/ Echo Canyon Recreation Area
Papago Park
Sky Harbor International Airport
Salt River
Bell Rd.
Greenway Rd.
Thunderbird Rd.
Sweetwater Ave.
Cactus Rd.
Shea Blvd.
Doubletree Ranch Rd.
Indian Bend Rd.
Lincoln Dr.
McDonald Dr.
Camelback Rd.
Indian School Rd.
Osborn Rd.
Thomas Rd.
McDowell Rd.
Van Buren St.
Washington St.
McKellips Rd.
University Dr.
Apache Blvd.
Main St.
Broadway Rd.
Southern Ave.
Baseline Rd.
Guadalupe Rd.
Elliot Rd.
Warner Rd.
Ray Rd.
Frank Lloyd Wright Blvd.
Cave Creek Rd.
Tatum Rd.
Piestewa Freeway
Pima Freeway
Pima Rd.
Beeline Hwy.
Red Mountain Freeway
Hohokam Expy.
Superstition Freeway
Maricopa Freeway
Price Freeway
To Payson
To Apache Junction
To Tucson
24th St.
32nd St.
40th St.
44th St.
48th St.
52nd St.
56th St.
64th St.
68th St.
Invergordon Rd.
Scottsdale Rd.
Hayden Rd.
Miller Rd.
Dobson Rd.
Country Club Dr.
Mesa Dr.
Stapley Dr.
Priest Dr.
Mill Ave.
Rural Rd.
McClintock Dr.
Price Rd.
School Rd.
Alma
Arizona Ave.
McQueen Rd.
Cooper Rd.
51
202
10
143
101
87
60
11
12
13
14
15
16
17
18
19
20
21
22
23
24
25
26
27
28

The Heard Museum in downtown Phoenix digs deep into the culture of Arizona's native peoples.

in this exhibit are more than 400 Pueblo kachina dolls (in art circles generally now called *katsina* dolls), with fascinating explication of the ideas embedded in them and the ingenuity that goes into their creation. The Heard also shows a lot of spectacular contemporary Native American art. Guided tours are offered daily. The annual **Indian Fair and Market,** held on the first weekend in March, includes traditional dances in the museum's grand dance circle on Central Avenue, along with the world's top Native American artists showing off their wares. The museum's cafe is a good place for lunch, and the bookstore is a sprawling affair with a superior collection of Native American art for sale. (A branch of the Heard in north Scottsdale closed in 2014.)

2301 N. Central Ave., Phoenix. www.heard.org. ✆ **602/252-8848.** $18 adults, $13.50 seniors, $7.50 students and kids 6–12. Mon–Sat 9:30am–5pm; Sun 11am–5pm. Open 6–10pm First Friday. Closed Easter, July 4, Thanksgiving, and Christmas. Bus: O. METRO: Encanto Blvd./Central Ave.

Western Spirit: Scottsdale's Museum of the West ★★ MUSEUM This is a spectacular new addition to the city arts scene—two vast floors of Western art and artifacts in an impressive facility. There's a giant room with Western artifacts, swimmingly presented, from saddlebags to faro games. You can get lost in the art galleries, which have been populated by the most prominent Western art collectors in the country. The exhibitions are of an exceedingly high quality; a recent one was built around a spectacular collection of hundreds of Western movie posters, some of them gigantic. ***Tip:*** The opening film can easily be given a pass. In it and elsewhere in the museum, you'll sense a romanticized view of cowboys and Indians that says too little about the realities of that era.

3830 N. Marshall Way. E. Main St., Mesa. www.scottsdalemuseumwest.org. ✆ **480/686-9539.** $15 adults, $13 seniors and military, $8 students and children, free for kids 5 and under. Tues–Sat 9:30am–5pm, Sun 11am–5pm (Nov–Apr open till 9pm Thurs). Closed major holidays. Bus: 30.

Musical Instrument Museum ★★ MUSEUM The MIM, less than 10 years old, lives in a gorgeous sandstone monolith on a sprawling campus just south of the 101 in north Phoenix. Vast halls, broken down by continent, showcase an astonishing variety of musical instruments—some 6,000 on display at a time—from all over the world. Not only will you see countless unfamiliar instruments, but you'll get to watch videos of them being played in their countries of origin. (The museum has done a great job with the technology of its audio guides, which are a must here.) Among the many displays are the first Steinway piano ever made (built in 1836 in the Steinweg family's kitchen in Seesen, Germany); the tools brought to America in 1833 by guitar-maker C. F. Martin; and the piano Taylor Swift played on her Red Tour. One room that is especially popular with children has instruments you can play yourself. And music fans should look at the MIM's concert calendar; just about anyone's worth seeing in its jewel of a theater.

4725 E. Mayo Blvd. (at N. Tatum Blvd.), Phoenix. www.themim.org. ✆ **480/478-6000.** $20 adults, $15 teens and seniors, $10 ages 4–12, free for kids 3 and under. Open 9am–5pm. Closed Thanksgiving and Christmas.

OdySea Aquarium ★★ AQUARIUM The big new tourist destination in the Valley is this large complex, which boasts not only one of the largest aquariums in North America, but also a big butterfly habitat, a dolphin building, and several other attractions, along with a two-story mini-mall of shops and restaurants. It's easy to spend a good part of an enjoyable day here. The aquarium itself has a slightly odd industrial feel inside, but there are lots and lots of stops for everything from an otter tank to a low-slung pool that lets kids stroke manta rays as they glide by. A big room with round aquariums hanging from the ceiling is a stunner, as is the escalator that descends right down through the big shark tank. The big attraction is a wild revolving theater at the center of a giant donut of tanks; you revolve a quarter-turn and get a new show, sometimes with divers in the tanks with the various spectacular fish, including sharks. If you're taking kids, it's kinda fun not to let them know this is coming. Enlightening information in the exhibits points out how the aquarium's populations will be affected by climate change. The butterflies and dolphins require separate admissions; all of the attractions allow same-day re-entry.

9500 Via de la Ventura, Scottsdale. www.odyseaaquarium.com. ✆ **480/291-8000.** $38 adults, $28 ages 2–12, free for kids under 2. Daily 9am–8pm (closes at 6pm Sun); check website for occasional early closings due to private events.

Taliesin West ★★★ HISTORIC HOME Frank Lloyd Wright loved the Arizona desert and, in 1937, built Taliesin West as a winter camp that served

Famed architect Frank Lloyd Wright designed his winter home, Taliesen, to blend into its desert surroundings.

as his home, office, and school. Today, the buildings of Taliesin West, perched on a foothill in far-east Scottsdale, are the headquarters of the Frank Lloyd Wright Foundation and School of Architecture. Wright believed in using local materials in his designs, and this is much in evidence at Taliesin West, where local stone was used for building foundations. With its glass-walled buildings and patio areas, Taliesin West also showcases Wright's ability to integrate indoor and outdoor spaces. Tours include a general introduction to Wright and his theories of architecture, and also explain the campus buildings. A variety of tours (see website for full details) range from 90 minutes to 3 hours. If you have anything other than a passing interest in Wright, shell out for the Behind the Scenes 3-hour tour, which includes tea and snacks and costs $75. And if you have an evening free, the Night Lights tour ($45) is a treat. Reservations are required, and kids under 13 are discouraged, on all but the basic tour. It's smart to make a reservation for that one, too; it's a long drive out there and there's not much to see besides the gift shop if you're not on a tour. ***Tip:*** The first tour of the day, at 8:45am, is discounted.

12621 Frank Lloyd Wright Blvd. (entrance at intersection of E. Cactus Rd. and N. Frank Lloyd Wright Blvd.), Scottsdale. www.franklloydwright.org. ✆ **888/516-0811.** Basic tours start at $35, $25 students, $18 kids 6–12. No kids under 6. Prices go up Fri–Sun. Other tours more expensive. Daily 8:45am–4pm. Closed Easter, Thanksgiving, Christmas, and for occasional special events.

Downtown Phoenix Attractions

See also the **Heard Museum ★★★**, p. 59.

On the first Friday of each month, from 6pm to 10pm, arts comes alive in downtown Phoenix with **First Friday,** centered on the Roosevelt Arts District (E. Roosevelt Road, between Central Avenue and 7th Street, also Grand Avenue south of Roosevelt Road). Street musicians and vendors vie for the attention of highly un-Phoenix-like throngs of pedestrians, and the diverse collection of local art galleries and museums in this area remain open late for browsing. Check **artlinkphx.org** for accompanying events and details on the First Friday shuttle, which stops at the Phoenix Art Museum. There are sometimes crowds (parking can be tough—we recommend you use light rail instead) but it's a highly enjoyable mix of people and art.

Arizona Capitol Museum/Wesley Bolin Memorial Park ★ HISTORIC SITE A mile due west of downtown, the state's original 19th-century territorial capitol building sits at the center of a new complex of buildings housing the state legislature; inside it, over four floors, are rooms of artifacts, photos, and changing displays on various aspects of the state's history and culture. You can see schoolchildren on tours in the original House chamber and even sit in the chamber's upstairs visitors gallery. There's a restored four-story atrium, too, along with a small museum store and a Starbucks. Just to the east of the state government buildings is a large but somehow unlovely park named for Wesley Bolin, who was Arizona's governor for 5 months, the shortest term of any Arizona governor. (Having been Arizona's secretary of state for 28 years, he ascended to the office after a previous governor resigned, only to die himself soon thereafter. Talk about luck!) Anyway, this has become the state's go-to place for memorials and statues; there's a hodgepodge of more than a dozen here, many of them military, others of less import, like the one for police dogs that died in the line of duty.

1700 W. Washington St. www.azlibrary.gov/azcm. ✆ **602/926-3620.** Free admission. Mon–Fri 9am–4pm. Closed state holidays. Bus: 1 or DASH downtown shuttle.

Arizona Science Center ★ MUSEUM The kids can spend the afternoon pushing buttons, turning knobs, and interacting with all kinds of cool science exhibits at this downtown complex. (I say afternoon advisedly; mornings tend to be filled with kids on field trips.) In the end, they might even learn something in spite of all the fun they have. The science center includes a planetarium and a big-screen theater, and generally has a special exhibition or two going on, all of which carry additional charges.

600 E. Washington St. www.azscience.org. ✆ **602/716-2000.** $18 adults, $13 seniors and ages 3–17; free for kids 2 and under. Day pass (includes museum, planetarium, film, and special exhibits): $43 adults, $35 ages 3–17; free for kids 2 and under. Daily 10am–5pm. Closed Thanksgiving and Christmas. Bus: 0 or DASH downtown shuttle. METRO: 3rd St./Washington and 3rd St./Jefferson stations.

Burton Barr Library ★ ARCHITECTURE The most daring piece of public architecture in the city is this downtown public library, designed by local architect Will Bruder. The five-story cube is partially clad in enough ribbed copper sheeting to produce roughly 17.5 million pennies. The design makes use of the desert's plentiful sunshine to provide light for reading, but also incorporates computer-controlled louvers and shade sails to reduce heat and glare. Architecture mavens in town for the summer solstice, June 21, should check the library schedule; most years the architect gives a talk at noon

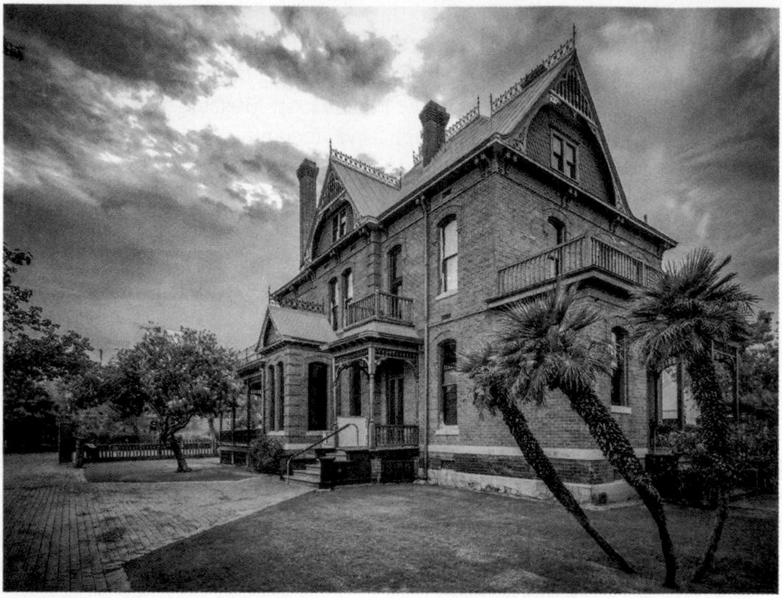

Rosson House, an elegant Victorian mansion, is one of several historic houses set around Heritage Square.

on that day, when a set of skylights is designed to create a shadow dance on the walls.

1221 N. Central Ave. www.phoenixpubliclibrary.org. ✆ **602/262-4636.** Free admission Mon and Fri–Sat 9am–5pm; Tues–Thurs 9am–9pm; Sun 1–5pm. Bus: 0. METRO: McDowell Rd./Central Ave.

Historic Heritage Square/Heritage and Science Park ★ HISTORIC SITE The city of Phoenix was founded in 1870, but today few of the city's early homes remain. If you want a glimpse of how Phoenix once looked, stroll around this collection of historic homes on the original town site. Although most of the houses are modest buildings from the early 20th century, there is one impressive Victorian home that dates to 1895. Today, the buildings house museums, restaurants, and gift shops. The typically over-the-top Queen Anne **Rosson House** (www.rossonhousemuseum.org; ✆ **602/262-5070**), furnished with period antiques, is open for tours. The Silva House is now home to

The Flying Net/Jellyfish/Cloud

It hovers over a small park at the corner of Taylor Street and Central Avenue downtown. It's . . . well, you decide what it is. It's a massive piece of public art by artist Janet Echelman. (The title, "Her Secret Is Patience," is a quote from Emerson.) It is made of polyester netting and suspended from three poles more than 100 feet high. While during the day the effect of the work is a bit blah, at night colored lights projected on the net bring it alive, and you can see it in all its mysterious glory. Whatever it is.

Cool Phoenix

As the Valley has grown, the **Central Corridor** has become the closest thing in the state to hip. There are fine coffee shops, nice clubs, and see-and-be-seen hipster museum events.

An afternoon coffee at **Lux Central** (4402 N. Central Ave.; www.luxcoffee.com; ✆ **602/327-1396**) universally known as Lux, is de rigueur; ASU profs, designers, and entrepreneurs cluster from 6am on every day in its warren of rooms. At night it serves dinner with a full bar and mixologists on hand. **The Valley Bar,** 130 N. Central Ave. (✆ **602/368-3121**), accessible only via a steep set of stairs in an alley on the southwest corner of Central and Monroe (just walk down the alley and you'll see the illuminated sign), is a wonderful place for a quiet drink and fairly good bar food in the afternoon and early evening; later on, things get noisier. An ingenious mobile above the bartenders is engineered to cast shadows of figures on a vellum screen; ask your bartender about the (lurid) tale they tell. There's a small concert room to the side, too, sometimes with nationally known artists. In late evening it goes full-on nightclub.

Check the schedule at the **Phoenix Art Museum** (below) for evening events there. The museum is free after 3pm Wednesdays and from 6pm or 10pm on First Fridays, and on the Second Saturday and Sunday of the month.

Roosevelt Row—that's Roosevelt Road, a half-mile north of the center of downtown, just east of Central Avenue—has become a major ASU hang and has cool restaurants and shops. This is ground zero for the First Friday gallery walk, when the city's artistic community comes out in force. Third Friday is a toned-down version.

The **Found:Re Hotel** (1100 N. Central Ave.; ✆ **602/875-8000**), on Central Avenue just around the corner from Roosevelt Row, is a swellegant remodeled hipster boutique hotel with its own curated art gallery—and the convivial sprawling lounge bar and restaurant don't hurt, either. Coolest feature: An art installation right inside the front door projects groovy moving designs onto the lobby floor—projections that somehow move and puddle when guests walk across them. Finally, there's **Food Truck Friday,** when a cluster of the Valley's finest gather for lunch at Civic Space Park—that's the park with the big net sculpture above it, 424 N. Central Ave. at Taylor St. The trucks gather from 11am to 1:30pm every Friday until the weather gets too hot.

the **Rose & Thorn** pub. In the Teeter House, you'll find **Nobuo at Teeter House** (p. 128). The old Baird Machine Shop contains **Pizzeria Bianco** (p. 129), with the Thomas House home to its sister operation, **Bar Bianco.**

115 N. 6th St. (at Monroe St.). www.heritagesquarephx.org. ✆ **602/261-8063.** Rosson House tours $9 adults, $8 seniors, $4 kids; Wed–Sat 10am–4pm, Sun noon–4pm, last tour 3pm. Closed on major holidays. Bus: Red 0, 1, or DASH downtown shuttle. METRO: 3rd St./Washington.

Phoenix Art Museum ★ MUSEUM An ambitious reimagining in 2007 doubled the size of this once-sleepy institution and spring-boarded a contemporary art collection. Recent curators have given long-overdue recognition to local artists, particularly Latinos, as well. (For Western and so-called cowboy art, turn to **Western Spirit: Scottsdale's Museum of the West,** p. 62.) The museum's modern works and its notable costume collection are worth

Arizona Luxury, Circa 1929

Tucked away at the top of the Biltmore district, the **Arizona Biltmore ★** hotel (2400 E. Missouri Ave.; ✆ **602/955-6600**), built in 1929, wasn't designed by Frank Lloyd Wright, but he did consult on this magnificent endeavor designed by one of his former students, Albert Chase McArthur. You can see the famed architect's hand in its distinctive cast-cement blocks; it also displays sculptures, furniture, and stained glass designed by Wright. The best way to soak up the ambience of this exclusive resort (if you aren't staying here) is over dinner, a cocktail, or tea, but 90-minute tours ($10) are given Tuesday, Thursday, and Saturday at 10am; there's also a happy hour tour Fridays at 6pm; $20 gets you a shorter tour and two cocktails.

On a hilltop adjacent to the Arizona Biltmore, elegant **Wrigley Mansion ★** (2501 E. Telawa Tr.; www.wrigleymansionclub.com; ✆ **602/955-4079**) was built between 1929 and 1931 by the resort's owner, chewing-gum magnate William Wrigley, Jr., as a present for his wife, Ada. Now a National Historic Landmark, this Spanish Colonial–style mansion has been restored to its original grandeur and turned into a high-end event space with **Geordie's Restaurant** (p. 122), an adjoining bar, and a swellegant premium wine bar. A sunset drink here is a wonderful experience. Guided tours, offered daily except Mondays, give a fascinating glimpse into the lives of the Wrigleys; reservations are required. Tours cost $15; Tuesday through Saturday, they're at 10am, noon, 2pm, and 4pm; there's also a Sunday tour at 2pm.

checking out. It's not the Whitney or LACMA, but even sophisticated art mavens won't feel they've wasted their time. Families in particular shouldn't miss the permanent Yayoi Kusama installation, known colloquially as "Fireflies." The cafe here is a good spot for lunch. The museum is free from 3pm to 9pm on Wednesdays, on First Fridays from 6pm to 10 pm, and all day on the second Saturday and Sunday of the month.

1625 N. Central Ave. (at McDowell Rd.), Phoenix. www.phxart.org. ✆ **602/257-1222.** $23 adults, $20 seniors, $18 students, $14 kids 17 and under; $5 discount when various galleries are closed. Free admission Wed 3–9pm, 1st Fri of month, and 2nd Sat & Sun of month. Open Tues–Sat 10am–5pm, until 9pm Wed; Sun noon–5pm. Also 6–10pm 1st Fri of month. Closed major holidays. Bus: O. METRO: McDowell Rd./Central Ave.

Papago Park & Nearby

See also the **Desert Botanical Gardens ★★★**, p. 59.

Arizona Heritage Center at Papago Park ★ MUSEUM Technically called the Centennial Museum, this is the headquarters of the Arizona Historical Society, and its well-designed exhibits present a serious and sometimes whimsical look at the history of central Arizona—how settlers made it through, how folks lived, and what they were interested in. An interesting permanent exhibit features life-size statues of everyday people from Arizona's past (a Mexican miner, a Chinese laborer, and so on).

1300 N. College Ave. (just N. of Curry Rd.), Tempe. www.arizonahistoricalsociety.org. ✆ **480/929-9499.** $12 adults, $10 seniors, $8 ages 7–17, free for kids 6 and under. Two-for-one admission 1st Tues of month. Mon–Thurs 10am–5pm, Fri-Sat 10am–4pm.

The Hole-in-the-Rock natural geological formation is visible from across one of Papago Park's ponds.

Hall of Flame Firefighting Museum ★ MUSEUM This is a great place to stop after a morning at the nearby Phoenix Zoo (see below)—the nation's largest firefighting museum, which houses a fascinating collection of vintage firetrucks. The displays date from a 1725 English hand pumper to several classic engines from the 20th century. All are beautifully restored and, mostly, fire-engine red. In all, more than 90 vehicles are on display.

At Papago Park, 6101 E. Van Buren St. www.hallofflame.org. ✆ **602/275-3473.** $10 adults, $8 seniors, $8 students 6–17, $4 ages 3–5, free for kids 2 and under. Mon–Sat 9am–5pm; Sun noon–4pm. Closed New Year's Day, Thanksgiving, and Christmas. Bus: 1 or 3. METRO: Priest Dr./Washington St.

Phoenix Zoo ★ ZOO It can get toasty in spring and summer, but all in all this is a respectable Sun Belt zoo. The African savannah exhibit, as you might imagine, feels the best. You can also ride a camel, check out a komodo dragon, and take the younger kids to a big petting zoo. All animals are kept in naturalistic enclosures, and what with all the palm trees and tropical vegetation, the zoo sometimes manages to make you forget you're in the desert; still, you'll enjoy this better if you get everyone up early and hit the zoo when it opens at 9am, 7am in summer. (Indeed, one of the advertised advantages of zoo membership is that you can get in an hour earlier!) **Zoolights,** an after-hours holiday-light display, is held late November to early January and is a fine

Hunt's Tomb: The Great Pyramid of Phoenix

If you're driving through Papago Park on your way to the Desert Botanical Garden or the zoo and see a shimmering white pyramid on a hilltop, it's not a heat-induced hallucination. The pyramid is real. It is the tomb of Gov. George W. P. Hunt, who was governor on and off through much of Arizona's first 20 years as a state. He died in 1934. The tomb is accessible from a road leading north out of the parking area of the zoo.

diversion for families, but get your tickets early and be prepared for crowds headed by bristling phalanxes of strollers. You can save $2 per ticket by buying online.

In Papago Park, 455 N. Galvin Pkwy. www.phoenixzoo.org. ✆ **602/286-3800.** $25 adults, $15 ages 3–12, free for kids 2 and under. Open 9am–5pm. Closes 4pm Nov–mid-Jan and at 2pm Jun–Aug. Closed Christmas. Bus: 1 or 3. METRO: Priest Dr./Washington St.

Pueblo Grande Museum and Archaeological Park ★★ OUTDOOR MUSEUM Located near Sky Harbor Airport and downtown Phoenix, the Pueblo Grande Museum and Archaeological Park houses the ruins of an ancient Hohokam village, one of several villages along the Salt River between A.D. 300 and 1400. Sometime around 1450, these villages were mysteriously abandoned, perhaps because drought and a buildup of salts from irrigation

A reconstructed pithouse at the Pueblo Grande Archaeological Park evokes daily life in an ancient Hohokam village.

water reduced the soil's fertility and forced the people to seek better growing conditions elsewhere. The small museum here displays many artifacts that were dug up at the site. These exhibits are actually more interesting than the ruins themselves, although some furnished replicas of Hohokam-style houses give a good idea of how the Hohokam lived. The museum sponsors interesting workshops, demonstrations, and tours (including petroglyph hikes). The **Pueblo Grande Indian Market,** held in mid-December, is one of the largest of its kind in the state and features more than 250 Native American artisans.

4619 E. Washington St. www.pueblogrande.com. ✆ **602/495-0901.** $6 adults, $5 seniors, $3 ages 6–17. Oct–Apr Mon–Sat 9am–4:45pm, Sun 1–4:45pm; May–Sept Tues–Sat 9am–4:45pm. Closed major holidays. Bus: 1. METRO: 44th St./Washington St.

Scottsdale

See also **OdySea Aquarium ★★** (p. 63), **Taliesin West ★★★** (p. 63), and the walking tour of **Old Scottsdale** (p. 73).

Scottsdale Museum of Contemporary Art ★ MUSEUM Highly eclectic and ambitious changing exhibitions fill the three large galleries of this modern structure, designed by Will Bruder, who did the Burton Barr Library downtown (p. 65). The visionary artist James Turrell has contributed his "skyspace" *Knight Rise,* accessed from a patio off the museum shop, which you can visit without paying museum admission. There's an imaginatively stocked gift shop (and an equally imaginative and even bigger one next door at the **Scottsdale Center for the Arts,** right across the way). It's open until 9pm (and free after 5pm) Thursday through Saturday, making this a great place to stop by after dinner in Old Town Scottsdale.

7374 E. 2nd St., Scottsdale. www.smoca.org. ✆ **480/874-4666.** $10 adults, $7 students, free for kids 15 and under, free for all Thurs and Fri–Sat 5–9pm. Sun, Tues, Wed noon–5pm; Thurs–Sat noon–9pm. Closed Mon. Closed major holidays. Bus: 41, 50, or 72. Also accessible via Scottsdale Trolley shuttle bus.

Mesa

See also **Western Spirit: Scottsdale's Museum of the West ★★**, p. 62.

Arizona Commemorative Air Force Museum ★ MUSEUM Fans of World War II bombers: This museum is home to *Sentimental Journey,* a B-17G bomber that was built in 1944 and is still flying today. It's housed with a variety of other refurbished aircraft in a couple of big hangars, where you can watch mechanics working on the planes, on the edge of Falcon Field, a small airport in Mesa. The museum also has a B-25, a couple of Russian MiGs, and an F4 Phantom. Flights in *Sentimental Journey* and a couple of other aircraft can be arranged here, with tour prices ranging from $275 to $425 per person.

Falcon Field, 2017 N. Greenfield Rd., Mesa. www.arizonawingcaf.com. ✆ **480/924-1940.** $15 adults, $12 seniors, $5 kids 5–12, free for kids 4 and under. Oct–May 10am–4pm daily, Jun–Sept Wed–Sun 9am–3pm. Closed New Year's Day, Thanksgiving, and Christmas. Bus: 136.

Gay Phoenix

Arizona remains a red state, and anti-gay rhetoric—sometimes coded, sometimes explicit—can still be heard from actual elected officials. The good news is that central Phoenix, Scottsdale, and Tempe, well protected from such talk, are explicitly gay-friendly enclaves. Gay Phoenix is centered in the **Melrose**—7th Avenue between Indian School and Camelback. Don't expect some desert version of the Castro, though; there are basically just a bunch of bars and shops, nothing terribly upscale, that come alive Thursday, Friday, and Saturday nights. Look for ***Echo*** magazine, which keeps up with events on the scene month to month, in downtown hotel lobbies and restaurants. In reality, just about all of the bars and restaurants in the central core—7th Street to 7th Avenue, from downtown to uptown—are part of the gay scene. The burgeoning strip of restaurants on 7th Street north of Missouri Avenue are gay-friendly, too.

Arizona Museum of Natural History ★★ MUSEUM Don't expect anything like the endeavors of the same name in New York or Chicago, but this is one of the best museums in the Valley, and its wide variety of exhibits appeals to people with a range of interests. There are some animated dinosaurs on Dinosaur Mountain, complete with roaring waterfall, and lots of dinosaur skeletons, too. Also of interest are an exhibit on Mesoamerican cultures, a display on Arizona mammoth kill sites, some old jail cells, and a walk-through mine mock-up with exhibits on the Lost Dutchman Mine, the legendary mine in the nearby Superstition Mountains that tantalizes fortune-seekers to this day. There's also a Hohokam village.

53 N. MacDonald St. (at 1st St.), Mesa. www.azmnh.org. ✆ **480/644-2230.** $10 adults, $9 seniors, $8 students, $6 children 3–12. Tues–Fri 10am–5pm; Sat 11am–5pm; Sun 1–5pm. Closed major holidays. Bus: 30.

Tempe

Arizona State University Art Museum ★★ MUSEUM Housed in a concrete faux-Mayan ziggurat just north of the landmark Grady Gammage Auditorium on the ASU campus, the museum is accessed down a flight of stairs that leads to a cool underground plaza area. Inside are ascending galleries for crafts, prints, contemporary art, and Latin American art, along with outdoor sculpture courts and a gift shop. The affiliated **Ceramics Research Center,** a vibrant gallery that showcases the university's extensive collection of fine-art ceramics, is 2 blocks north at the Brickyard Center, 699 S. Mill Ave. Check the schedules for both for speakers, special events, and lively exhibition openings, a/k/a parties.

10th St. and Mill Ave., Tempe. asuartmuseum.asu.edu. ✆ **480/965-2787.** Free admission. Tues–Sat 11am–5pm (during academic year, Thurs until 8pm). Closed major holidays. Bus: 66. METRO: Mill Ave./Third St.

Skyspace: Air Apparent ★★ PUBLIC ART On the edge of the ASU campus, this outdoor structure is more of the work of artist James Turrell, known for his large public constructions that play with space and color. It's basically a giant open-air cabana with a roof suspended above it—a roof with a large square opening in the middle. Inside the cabana, the walls are lined with benches. The idea is that you sit, look up, and watch—here's the catch—either sunrise or sunset through the giant square skylight, which is enhanced with subtly shifting lights, which in turn manage to change the color of the sky beyond. The schlep there at sunrise or sunset is slightly inconvenient, but it's a great experience.

Rural Rd. at S. Terrance Rd., just S of University Dr., Tempe. skyspace.asu.edu. No phone. Free admission. Open 24 hours. METRO: University Dr./Rural Rd.

West Valley

Wildlife World Zoo & Aquarium ★ ZOO This place specializes in your more colorful animals, from meerkats and porcupines to cheetahs and warthogs. (Some color*less* ones, too, like the albino alligator.) There are also lions, zebra, and giraffes. You can get really close to some of these and even feed a few; there are also informative animal shows, including parrot feedings, throughout the day. The aquarium isn't as big as the new OdySea (p. 63), but there are sharks, stingrays, piranhas, and that albino alligator. Take I-10 west to Ariz. 303 (exit 124) and drive north 6 miles to Northern Ave. eastbound; or take Ariz. 101 west to Northern Ave. (exit 101) and continue west for 8 miles.

16501 W. Northern Ave., Litchfield Park. www.wildlifeworld.com. ✆ **623/935-9453.** Zoo and Aquarium $40 plus tax adults, $20 plus tax ages 3–12, free for kids 2 and under; Aquarium only (evenings only) $17 adults, $9 ages 3–12, free for kids 2 and under. Zoo daily 9am–6pm (last admission 4:30pm). Aquarium daily 9am–7pm.

WALKING TOUR: OLD TOWN SCOTTSDALE

START:	**Scottsdale Historical Museum.**
FINISH:	**Scottsdale Waterfront.**
TIME:	**2 hours (not including shopping and visiting the museums).**
BEST TIMES:	**Thursdays, when the Scottsdale Museum of Contemporary Art waives its usual admission charge and art galleries stay open late.**
WORST TIMES:	**Mondays, when galleries and the Scottsdale Museum of Contemporary Art are closed, and summer, when it's just too hot to do any walking.**

Downtown Scottsdale is a curious place. Yes, it's a tourist magnet with a lot of tacky souvenir shops, but it's also a legitimate art destination and a lovely city in its own right, with civic adornments—not to mention a lot of nice restaurants—to be proud of. With half a dozen distinct shopping districts around the area, it's easy to miss many of the highlights. This walking tour leads you past the best downtown Scottsdale has to offer.

Make it easy on yourself and park in the convenient garage at the south end of old town, just above E. 2nd St. on N. Wells Fargo Ave. Go to the northwest corner of the garage where, at 7333 E. Scottsdale Mall, you will find the:

1 Scottsdale Historical Museum

This little museum, housed in a little red schoolhouse that was built in 1909, is free, and a great place to get some quick historic background before you start exploring modern Scottsdale's heart.

Turn right as you leave the museum and take a stroll around the:

2 Scottsdale Civic Center Mall

As you walk east, the mall opens wide, and you'll see a big green space circled by restaurants, civic buildings, and lots of sculpture. (Scottsdale has an active department of public art.) There are often public events in the winter months. As you walk west to where the major sculptures are, poke your head into the gift shop at the **Scottsdale Center for the Performing Arts** (7380 E. 2nd St.).

Just past the performing arts center, you'll find the city's most beloved sculpture:

3 Robert Indiana's *Love*

With its iconic canted letter *O,* this image got international attention when it appeared on a U.S. postage stamp in 1973.

Savor the fountains and trees and keep heading east to:

4 Louise Nevelson's *Windows to the West*

This monumental piece by the celebrated sculptor anchors the east edge of the mall in front of a large fountain; **Scottsdale City Hall** is right next door.

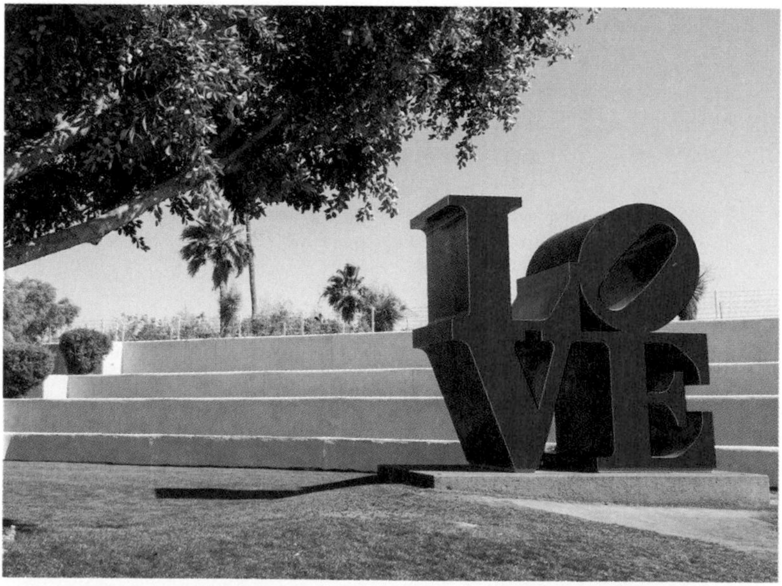

An enduring icon on the Scottsdale Civic Center Mall: Robert Indiana's *Love* sculpture.

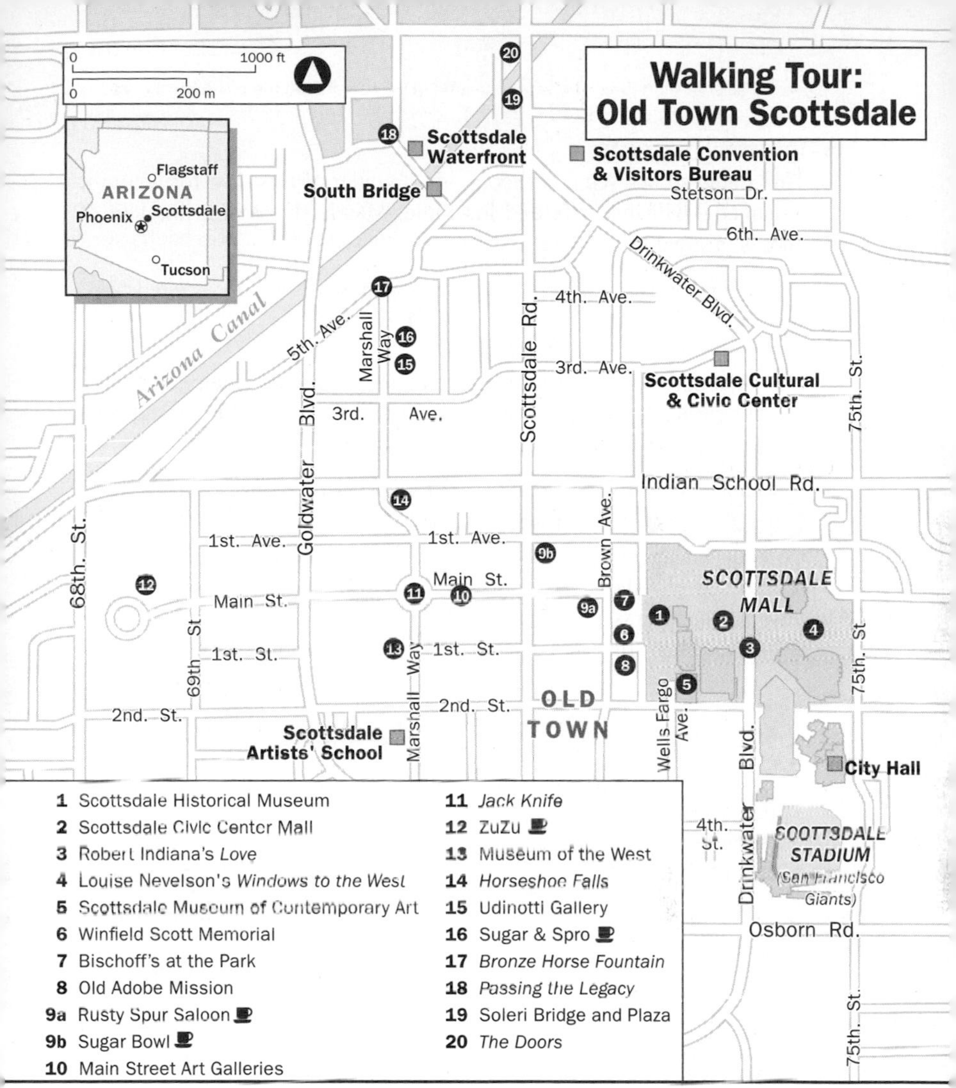

Turn around and head back to the central part of the mall, looking for any other art pieces that catch your eye. Then head to the southwest corner of the main plaza, where you'll find:

5 Scottsdale Museum of Contemporary Art

SMOCA, as it's called, generally has a different innovative show in each of its three ever-changing galleries, and admission is always free. Check the schedule for any special events or openings, the latter of which are fun parties, and free. See p. 71 for more details.

Head back out of the mall the way you came in by way of the little red schoolhouse, and you will see a statue of:

6 Winfield Scott

This statue shows Winfield Scott—the founder of this city, for whom it is named—with his wife and his mule, Maude. It's set on the site of Scott's original homestead.

To the left as you exit the mall, at 3925 N. Brown Ave., you'll find an ivy-covered building called:

7 Bischoff's at the Park

This is about as good as it gets for Native American jewelry and other southwestern arts and crafts. The affiliated Bischoff's Shades of the West across the street is a lower-end souvenir shop.

Turn left when you come out of Bischoff's and walk a block and a half south to the:

8 Old Adobe Mission

On your left as you walk, it's easy to miss a cluster of metal sculptures behind some bushes and trees. A block down, you'll see the recently restored small mission church, built in 1933 by Hispanic and Yaqui Indian families. Inside, you'll usually find someone ready to answer

main street SHOPPING & GALLERY HOPPING

Just south of Main Street on Scottsdale Road, you'll find **Gilbert Ortega Galleries & Museum** (p. 143), which has one of the best selections of Native American jewelry in Scottsdale, as well as museum-quality displays of Native artifacts. On the same side of the street, down half a block, check out **AzTex Hat Company** (p. 143), a high-end purveyor of cowboy hats, fedoras, and custom hats of any conception.

East of Scottsdale Road, E. Main Street becomes the realm of serious art galleries. At 7164 Main Street, you'll find one of my favorite antiques shops, the cluttered and cramped **Bishop Gallery for Art & Antiques** (p. 138), full of rare and unusual antiques from around the world as well as original works of art. Next door, **Gebert Contemporary** (p. 139) is probably the most serious remaining Scottsdale gallery for modern art, representing several of the most important local artists and sculptors. A few doors down, at 7149 Main Street, **Arizona West Galleries** (✆ **480/990-1834**) has antique cowboy gear and the trappings of the American West, along with prints and all sorts of books.

At 7100 E. Main Street, **Faust Gallery** (p. 142) deals in collector-quality old Native American baskets and ceramics and Navajo rugs. Right next door, **Territorial Indian Arts & Antiques** (www.territorialindianarts.com; ✆ **480/945-5432**) is the oldest Indian arts-and-crafts shop on Main Street, with a good selection of Hopi *katsina* (kachina) dolls, Zuni fetishes, and Navajo silver jewelry. At 7056 E. Main Street, **Knox Artifacts Gallery** (p. 138) is filled with an intriguing mix of pre-Columbian artifacts and antiquities from ancient Greece, Rome, and Egypt. Finally, at 7033 E. Main Street, the **River Trading Post** (p. 143) is a trove of ancient southwestern pottery, Navajo rugs, and reasonably priced Native American crafts.

questions about the building. On the corner across the street is a small group of colorful sculptures by Elizabeth Conner.

Walk back north on Brown Ave. to Main St. and turn left. On this block, you'll find lots of souvenir shops and stores selling Native American jewelry. In the middle of the block, you'll find a longtime favorite Scottsdale watering hole.

9a Rusty Spur Saloon

For many years, Scottsdale billed itself as the West's most Western town, and at the **Rusty Spur Saloon,** 7245 E. Main St., the West lives on with country bands playing throughout the day and couples dancing and drinking the night (and day) away. If you're a cowboy or cowgirl at heart, you owe it to yourself to stop in for a beer.

9b The Sugar Bowl

Not the saloon type? Go to the corner and turn right, and you'll see the bright pink facade of the **Sugar Bowl,** the Valley's most venerable family ice-cream joint. You can grab just a sandwich and coffee if you want; good luck resisting the shakes, parfaits, or extravagant sundaes, often deranged concoctions that involve cream puffs, fudge, and brownies.

And right there on the corner of Main St. and busy Scottsdale Rd., you'll see the:

10 Main Street Art Galleries

We've now reached the heart of the Old Scottsdale gallery district. See the "Main Street Shopping & Gallery Hopping" box above for suggestions on which to visit, according to your particular interests.

Continue on East Main St. until it meets Marshall Way at a roundabout. In the middle of it, you'll see Ed Mell's sculpture:

11 *Jack Knife*

This kinetic, evocative work—Mell's first large-scale sculpture—is a masterpiece of modern equestrian statuary.

Looking for another break? Go straight ahead another block and a half and you'll be in the lobby of the swellegant confines of the Hotel Valley Ho. Make your way to:

12 ZuZu

Chill out in comfy retro midcentury modern interiors. You'll find creative cocktailing available, and some nice snacks, too, amid a casual and sophisticated crowd.

Head back to the roundabout, and take a right. You'll immediately notice a magnificent copper-clad new building:

13 Western Spirit: Scottsdale's Museum of the West

This is a gorgeous place, a major museum with two vast floors of spectacular art and exhibits. In the permanent collection room there are innumerable Western artifacts; you can lose yourselves in the galleries, taking in the landscapes and portraits. See p. 62 for more details.

Head north into what's called Fifth Avenue or the Waterfront: Walk up Marshall Way to the major thoroughfare of Indian School Rd. You'll notice another piece of public art:

14 *Horseshoe Falls*

The columns of Michael Maglich's sculpture are actually stacks of horseshoes arranged in the shape of a horseshoe. Mist periodically rises from the ground beneath the statute.

Cross Indian School Rd. and head north. Major galleries used to mark this section of Marshall Way; they're now gone, but there are nice shops and a few quirky endeavors, like at 4215 N. Marshall Way:

15 Udinotti Gallery

A highly eclectic selection of art, photography, and sculpture, not the least of which is the unmistakable work of the proprietor, Agnese Udinotti, whose peculiar elongated metal figures ooze out of everything.

Unlike me, you may be able to resist a different sort of art next door, at 4225 N. Marshall Way:

16 Sugar & Spro

These guys make elegant little truffles, each a masterpiece in its own right, in both the culinary and aesthetic sense of the word. Bananas Foster, Piedmont Sunrise, Framboise au Poivre . . . even the names are delicious. There's coffee, too.

In the middle of the roundabout at the intersection of North Marshall Way and East Fifth Ave., you'll see Bob Parks':

17 *Bronze Horse Fountain*

The four life-size bronze horse statues thundering away from this fountain have long been a symbol of the Fifth Avenue shopping district.

From the roundabout, walk a block up Stetson Dr. to the pedestrian bridge over the canal. At the north end of the bridge, you'll come to yet another horse sculpture, Herb Mignery's:

18 *Passing the Legacy*

This classic Western bronze statue shows two Pony Express riders passing the mail at a full gallop. One sculpture is meant to represent cowboys of the past, while the other represents cowboys of the present.

Head 2 blocks east along the north bank of the Arizona Canal, a pleasant walk next to high-rise condominiums. The busy Scottsdale public art office often sponsors extravagant art pieces using the canal, so keep an eye out for those. Just before the canal reaches Scottsdale Rd., you'll find:

19 Soleri Bridge & Plaza

Arizona-based architect Paolo Soleri, known for his futuristic city Arcosanti and his bronze wind bells (p. 163), designed this bridge, dedicated in late 2010, three years before his death at 93. The bridge is anchored by a 64-foot pylon with massive bronze wind bells suspended from it. Each day at solar noon, sunlight shines through the bridge pylon onto a red stripe on the bridge deck. ***Note:*** Solar noon is different from noon on your watch.

Have time for one more piece of massive public art? Still on the north side of the bridge, continue a few steps to the corner of Scottsdale and Camelback rds., where you'll find Donald Lipski's unusual sculpture:

20 *The Doors*

From the outside, this sculpture looks like three huge colonial doors leaning against each other, but step inside the doors, and you'll find yourself inside a giant mirrored kaleidoscope.

Still have more energy? Go back over the Soleri Bridge into the Waterfront District, where Stetson Drive has yet more shops and restaurants. Or cross busy Camelback Road and dive into the scores of stores and restaurants in the giant Scottsdale Fashion Square mall.

Outlying Attractions: Wild West Theme Towns

The Valley's Western culture is fading fast, but if you poke around at the outer edges of the Valley, you'll find a couple of Hollywood-style cowtowns. These are basically tourist traps, but, hey, if you've got the kids along, you owe it to them to visit at least one of these places.

Cave Creek, founded as a gold-mining camp in the 1870s, still has a Wild West facade, a mile or two of cowboy saloons, Western art galleries, restaurants, souvenir shops, and the like, about 20 miles due north of downtown Scottsdale. By day, anyone can park, poke into the stores (don't miss **The Dump,** a gigantic indoor-and-outdoor purveyor of crazy Western statuary and related ornamentations), and grab a bite at one of the local burger joints, Mexican restaurants, or cafes. Tourist ground zero is **Frontier Town,** 6245 E. Cave Creek Rd. (www.frontiertownaz.com; ✆ **480/488-3317**), a sort of mock cowtown with lots of little shops, a restaurant, and a saloon. By night, things get wilder, with a cluster of cavernous Western watering holes—the Buffalo Chip, the Horny Toad—offering everything from local country bands to bull-machine riding, along with endless bars and large-portion bar food. To learn more about the history of this area, stop in at the **Cave Creek Museum,** at Skyline Drive and Basin Road (www.cavecreekmuseum.org; ✆ **480/488-2764**), open from October to May on Wednesday through Sunday from 1 to 4:30pm (on Fridays it opens earlier, at 10am). Admission is $7 for adults, $5 for seniors and students 12 and older, and free for kids 11 and under.

On the east side of the Valley, just 4 miles northeast of Apache Junction on Ariz. 88, **Goldfield Ghost Town** (4650 N. Mammoth Mine Rd.; www.goldfieldghosttown.com; ✆ **480/983-0333**) is a reconstructed 1890s gold-mining town—more or less a tourist trap, with gift shops, an ice-cream parlor, and the like. **Goldfield's Historic Museum** (✆ **480/677-6463**) does have some interesting exhibits on the history of the area, particularly the exhibit on the Lost Dutchman gold mine, the famous lost gold mine that may or may not exist. Museum admission is $4 adults, $3 seniors, $1 ages 5–12. **Goldfield Mine Tours** provides guided tours of the gold mine beneath the town for $9 adults,

$8 seniors, $6 ages 6–12. You can pan for gold, watch a gunfight, and ride the **Superstition Narrow Gauge Railroad** that circles the town (train rides $9 adults, $8 seniors, $6 children 5–12). If you're here at lunchtime, you can get a meal at the steakhouse/saloon. The town is open daily (except Christmas) from 10am–5pm; museum, tour, and ride hours vary.

Sadly, the beloved longtime attraction **Rawhide at Wild Horse Pass** (5700 W. North Loop Rd., Chandler) is open now only for special events and on certain holidays, like Thanksgiving, when in addition to a buffet meal you can see the site's Western accouterments, try the amusement-park rides, and so forth. Check the site's website, **www.rawhide.com**, for any upcoming openings.

Especially for Kids

In addition to the museums listed below, kids are likely to enjoy the **Arizona Science Center** (p. 65), the **Arizona Museum of Natural History** (p. 72), the **Hall of Flame Firefighting Museum** (p. 69), and the **Phoenix Zoo** (p. 69).

Children's Museum of Phoenix ★ ACTIVITY CENTER Housed in a large downtown Phoenix building that was once a school, this children's museum makes learning fun for the little ones. Hands-on, interactive exhibits include an art studio, a cool climbing structure, a noodle forest, a giant room full of balls, and a place for toddlers. In one exhibit, kids can learn about the flora and fauna of the Sonoran Desert.

215 N. 7th St. www.childrensmuseumofphoenix.org. ✆ **602/253-0501.** $15 adults and kids, $14 seniors, free for children under 1; free for all 1st Fri of month. Tues–Sun 9am–4pm. Closed New Year's Day, Thanksgiving, and Christmas. Bus: DASH downtown shuttle. METRO: 3rd St./Washington station.

I.d.e.a. Museum ★ ACTIVITY CENTER This used to be called the Museum for Youth; it's since expanded to include a more technical bent along with its commitment to participatory activities that allows kids to explore the fine arts and their own creativity. It's housed in a refurbished grocery store, and the highlight is Artville, an arts-driven kid-size town. Exhibits are geared mainly toward toddlers through 12-year-olds, but all ages can work together to experience the activities.

#150 W. Pepper Pl. (at Robson Rd.), Mesa. www.ideamuseum.org. ✆ **480/644-2468.** $9 adults and kids, free for children under 1. Tues–Sat 10am–4pm, until 6pm on Fri; Sun noon–4pm. Closed Mon and major holidays.

McCormick-Stillman Railroad Park ★ OUTDOOR MUSEUM This 30-acre park is a blast for train lovers of all ages. There are restored railroad cars and engines, two old railway depots, model railroad layouts, and, best of all, a 5/12-scale model railroad that takes visitors around the park. Exhibits in the Scottsdale Railroad Museum delve more deeply into train history. A 1929 carousel and a general store round out the attractions.

7301 E. Indian Bend Rd. (at Scottsdale Rd.), Scottsdale. www.therailroadpark.com. ✆ **480/312-2312.** Free admission to park; train rides $2; carousel rides $2; museum admission $2 adults, free for children 12 and under. Hours vary; call for schedule. Closed Thanksgiving and Christmas (museum closed June–Sept). Bus: 72.

Now That's a Fountain

Arizona loves its water features. Reservoirs, canals, pools, fountains—they're everywhere in the desert. (You'd never think that water is in short supply.) One of the most unusual water features is in the aptly named town of Fountain Hills, 10 miles east of Scottsdale on Shea Blvd. (turn left on N. Saguaro Blvd.). The bubbler in the town's Fountain Park is one of the tallest fountains in the world, with three pumps shooting water 560 feet into the air. Most days, however, the fountain operates on only two pumps, with the plume reaching a mere 330 feet. Unless there are high winds, the fountain operates for 15 minutes, every hour on the hour, daily 9am to 9pm.

Parks & Gardens

Beyond the beauties of the **Desert Botanic Garden** (p. 59), there are few parks in central Phoenix, and to be honest there's not much to write home about in any of them. With average temperatures pushing 90 degrees 7 months of the year, they wouldn't get much use even if they were better. **Steele Indian School Park,** at the northeast corner of Indian School Road and Central Avenue (✆ **602/495-0739**), surrounds what was once a school for Native American children; some exhibits in the buildings are still standing, and the city has recently added fountains, gardens, and interpretive displays. Where I-10 cuts through central Phoenix, the city built **Margaret Hance Park** (67 W. Culver St.; ✆ **602/534-2406**); there are plans to make Hance a showcase, but those are years off. Still, check local listings for fairs or festivals at either of these centrally located expanses. Big-name rock acts appear at the McDowell Mountain Music Festival in Hance Park, generally in April, and all manner of ethnic, beer, taco, and other fests pop up at Steele Indian School Park. In an upscale neighborhood slightly west of downtown, gorgeous **Encanto Park** (2605 N. 15th Ave.; ✆ **602/261-8991**) has a small amusement park, a golf course, and a big lake. For information on these and other parks, go to **www.phoenix.gov/parks**.

More enjoyable is **Tempe Town Lake,** 620 N. Mill Ave., Tempe (www.tempe.gov/lake; ✆ **480/350-8625**), which was created in 1999 by damming the Salt River with inflatable dams. With parks and bike paths lining both the north and south shores, this 2-mile-long lake is a good place to stretch your legs, picnic, let kids run around, or just hang out. There's no swimming, however. The best lake access is at Tempe Town Beach, at the foot of the Mill Avenue Bridge.

The major parks in the rest of the valley are desert preserves. Stretching across the middle of the Valley is the **Phoenix Mountains Preserve** (site of Piestewa Peak), **North Mountain Preserve, North Mountain Recreation Area, Camelback Mountain–Echo Canyon Recreation Area,** and **Phoenix South Mountain Park,** which bills itself as the largest municipal park in the U.S. For more info on these parks, see "Outdoor Activities," p. 84.

ORGANIZED TOURS

If you don't want to spend your time driving, a guided tour is a good option. As the Valley grows, wackier options—from serene balloon rides to the decidedly less serene Hummer treks in the desert—abound.

BUS TOURS **Open Road Tours** (www.openroadtoursusa.com; ✆ **855/563-8830** or 602-997-6474) will pick you up at most Valley hotels for a long but lively day up through Sedona to the Grand Canyon for $180, $120 for kids. There's also a half-day tour of the Valley's highlights, including some mountain views and an hour for shopping in Old Town Scottsdale ($65 adults, $45 kids). Honesty compels me to say that some may find the ratio of "time spent driving around" to "actual things to see" a little out of whack. For an only-in-Arizona excursion, try the company's run up into the Superstition Mountains for a boat cruise on one of the Salt River lakes ($125 adults, $65 kids). Among other more elaborate tours, **Detours** (www.detoursofthewest.com; ✆ **866/438-6877**) boasts of its buses' comfy reclining "individual leather captain's chairs"; the company offers half-day tours of the Valley ($89 adults/$69 kids), Superstitions excursions ($139/$109), and even a day run to Antelope Canyon, the spectacular crimson canyon in the north of the state ($370/$300).

GLIDER RIDES The Valley's calm winds were made for rides like this. **Arizona Soaring,** 22548 N. Sailport Way, Maricopa (www.azsoaring.com; ✆ **520/568-2318**), operating since 1986, offers four options, ranging from a 20-minute, 3,000-foot-high gentle sail over the Estrella Mountains southwest of the Valley to a 40-minute, mile-high acrobatics run for daredevils. Prices range from $160 to $350—one person per ride—and there's not much red tape. To reach the airstrip, take I-10 E to exit 164 (Queen Creek Rd.), go 15 miles west on Queen Creek Rd. (which becomes Maricopa Rd./Ariz. 347), turn right on Ariz. 238, and continue 6½ miles. On the north side of the Valley, there's **NWSkySports,** 51623 W. Alvin Rd., Aguila (www.nwskysports.com; ✆ **602/284-9977**), an hour northwest of central Phoenix and west of Wickenburg. You can ride two to a glider here, with views of the Valley's rugged northwest terrain. Prices range from $150 for a 15- to 30-minute one-passenger flight to $300 for an hour-long two-passenger flight.

Top Gun

Ever wanted to be a fighter pilot? Well, at **Fighter Combat International** (www.fightercombat.com; ✆ **866/359-4273**) you can find out if you've got the right stuff. This company, operating out of the Phoenix-Mesa Gateway Airport in Mesa, offers a variety of exciting aerobatic flights, including mock dogfights. Best of all, on some flights, you get to learn how to do loops, rolls, spins, and other aerobatic moves. A half-day introduction to "air combat maneuvering" starts at $1,195; there's also a day-long one ($1,495) and a two-day "squadron wingman program" ($2,245).

Off-Beat in the Valley

Want to get a taste of a local dining scene? Take a food tour with **Arizona Food Tours** (www.arizonafoodtours.com) and you'll wander the streets of Old Town Scottsdale and downtown Tempe visiting local restaurants and tasting some of their most popular dishes.

While no one was looking, Roller Derby became a thing again! Now it's wholesome and packed with girl-power messages. Phoenix has an enthusiastic team, the **Arizona Derby Dames,** who play throughout the fall and winter months on a banked track about 2 miles west of downtown. For details and a schedule, visit www.arizonaderbydames.com.

For those looking for serenity, movement, the open air, and a heady mix of art and reflection, check out the **Museum of Walking.** This group, led by ASU art professor Angela Ellsworth, organizes a sophisticated crowd in silent walks in area parks each full moon. Details at www.museumofwalking.org.

Finally, Marshall Shore, the self-styled **Hip Historian,** offers periodic bus tours of Phoenix on such varied topics as Winnie Ruth Judd, the notorious murderess; the city in movies; and Haunted Phoenix. Details at marshallshore.blogspot.com.

HOT-AIR BALLOON RIDES The Phoenix climate is great for ballooning, and there are lots of operators to choose from, and a variety of experiences. **Aerogelic Ballooning** (www.aerogelicballooning.com; ✆ **866/359-8329**) offers everything from a sunrise flight for $169 per person to an $899-per-couple full-moon night cruise from four different sites around the Valley. And everyone gets champagne and hors d'oeuvres on landing. **Float Balloon Tours** (floatballoontours.com; ✆ **480/256-8695**) start at $235 per adult; they make the trip an event, with a professional photographer on hand and a gourmet champagne breakfast or dinner at the end of each sunrise or sunset flight. **Rainbow Ryders** (www.rainbowryders.com; ✆ **877/771-0776**) offer sunrise and sunset rides, $179 adults, $99 kids. The sunset rides sell out weeks in advance, so book early.

JEEP TOURS After spending a few days in Scottsdale, you'll likely start wondering where the desert is. Well, it's out there, and the easiest way to explore it is to book a jeep tour. Most will pick you up at your hotel, take you off through the desert, and maybe let you pan for gold or shoot a six-gun. Depending on how many people are in your party and where you're staying, expect to pay $65 to $100 per person for a 3-hour tour. Companies include **360 Adventures** (www.360-adventures.com; ✆ **481/418-3866**), **Apache Trail Tours** (www.apachetrailtours.com; ✆ **480/982-7661**), and **Wild West Jeep Tours** (www.wildwestjeeptours.com; ✆ **480/922-0144**).

Or how about a Hummer tour? **Arizona Hummer Tours** (www.azhummertours.com; ✆ **602/692-7124**) and **Stellar Adventures** (stellaradventures.com; ✆ **602/402-0584**) can take care of you; they run from $100 to $165 per person, less for kids.

If rumbling through the desert on a Hummer isn't rugged enough for you, then you might be a candidate for a Tomcar—little open-sided buggies that you drive yourself and let you get covered with desert dust as you four-wheel past cactus and creosote bushes. If this sounds like your kind of outing, contact **Desert Wolf Tours** (www.desertwolftours.com; ✆ **877/613-9653**), which charges $165 for a half-day tour and, among other variations, will even include some machine-gun shooting starting at $314 per person. There's also **Green Zebra Adventures** (www.gogreenzebra.com; ✆ **480/214-4435**), which charges $99 for a 1-hour ride ($59 ages 12 and under) and $149 for a 2-hour ride ($89 ages 12 and under).

SCENIC FLIGHTS **360 Adventures**' helicopter tours (www.360-adventures.com; ✆ **481/418-3866**) start at $250 for one person, $150 per person for two or more, for a 15-minute ride. The folks at **Westwind Scenic Air Tours,** 732 W. Deer Valley Rd., Phoenix (www.westwindairservice.com; ✆ **480/991-5557**) do air tours that range from a 7-hour journey to the Grand Canyon ($559) to 45-minute jaunts over the Valley ($229 per person).

WALKING TOURS **Phoenix Rising** (www.phxtours.com; ✆ **480/710-1006**) does history tours, mural tours, even ghost tours, based in downtown.

OUTDOOR ACTIVITIES

Bicycling

As we've said elsewhere, be a bit careful whenever you're out on the street. This is a car town slowly coming to terms with alternative means of transportation—and here that means anything that isn't a car, and sometimes anything that isn't a big car. The city's nice and flat, which is great for biking, but outside the city center, the Valley's grid street system means that even on calm side streets, you'll hit a large artery or intersection every mile or so, so casual bike riding isn't all that relaxing. That said, bike lanes are cropping up, and both Phoenix and Scottsdale have ambitious grab-and-go city bike programs, which you will find all over the downtown areas and beyond. Prices vary from $1 per half-hour to $1 per hour, with discounts if you buy more in advance. Right now the main bike-share companies in the Valley are **Grid Bike Share, Spin Bikeshare, Lime Bike,** and **Ofo.** Download their respective apps and off you go. The only complaint I have is that the yellow Ofo bikes in Scottsdale take your money in $10 doses—and keep it if you haven't used up your rides when you leave town.

Visit **azmag.gov/bike** for a map of the city's bike-friendly streets; the maps will also direct you to the closest of the city's sprawling mountain parks, which have miles of trails, paved and not, to ride on. These are desert areas; don't forget to take water and a phone and let someone know where you're going. Among the best mountain-biking spots in the city are amid the gorgeous buttes at **Papago Park** (Van Buren St. and Galvin Pkwy.), or the more challenging routes at **South Mountain Park** (use the entrance off Baseline Rd. on 48th St.), and the **North Mountain Preserve** (access off 7th St. between Dunlap Ave. and Thunderbird Rd., or off Northern Ave. just east of the I-51).

Looking for something more leisurely? Just south of downtown, at the north side of Central Avenue and the Salt River, a new park called the **Rio Solado Habitat Restoration Area** is a wonderful place with paved paths for a walk, a run, or a bike ride, with all sort of revivified animal and plant areas. (Rio Solado mean "Salt River.") Over in Scottsdale, the **Indian Bend Wash greenbelt** is a paved path that extends for more than 10 miles along Hayden Road—from north of Shea Blvd. all the way down to Tempe Town Lake, the Mill Avenue shopping district, and bike-friendly ASU. You can access it virtually anywhere along the way. Finally, **the canals** that cross Phoenix have leveled and sometimes paved paths beside them that many walkers and cyclists use. I recommend the newly restored paths along the grand arc made by the **Arizona Canal** from North Central Avenue. You can get on it on any street divided by four on the east side of town. It goes east to the Biltmore Hotel and then across to the Scottsdale Waterfront, a 10-mile ride across town. From there it hooks up with Indian Bend Wash. There are lots of places to grab a bite or a cup of coffee along the way.

BIKE RENTALS In Scottsdale, **Arizona Outback Adventures,** 16447 N. 91st St., Ste. 101 (www.azoutbackadventures.com; ✆ **866/455-1601** or 480/945-2881), tucked away at the far northeast curve of Hwy. 101 in north Scottsdale, is the place to start for mountain-bike riding in the nearby McDowell Mountains. Prices for basic bikes start at $35 for 4 hours; high-performance bikes start at $95, with full-day rates just $15 or $20 more. They will help you with maps to local trails, too. On the southern end of the city, **Cactus Adventures** (www.cactusadventures.com; ✆ **480/688-4743**) is based near the east end of South Mountain; call and they will meet you at the nearby Arizona Grand Resort with bikes, helmets, water, and maps. **Sonoran Outdoor Adventures** (sonoranoutdooradventures.com; ✆ **602/668-7995**) offers "fat tire" bike tours and rentals ($65 a day), and even delivers. If you have a group and are feeling adventurous, **360 Adventures** (www.360-adventures.com; ✆ **602/795-1877**) can set you up with guided hiking or biking tours of any difficulty throughout the state.

Golf

Phoenix is golf nirvana. Sunshine, nice views, and desert flora and fauna can make playing a round of golf here memorable. All in all, there are close to 300 courses, public, private, and executive, in the Valley of the Sun; **Visit Phoenix**

Always Keep In Mind . . .

Whenever you're doing anything outdoors here, remember that this is a very warm environment. Even in April and October, the *average* high temperature is close to 90 degrees. Take plenty of water with you, apply sunscreen, and wear sun-protective clothing. Dehydration is a genuine danger, even in winter; in March of 2017 a dehydrated hiker was taken off Camelback Mountain by helicopter and died after 3 days in a hospital.

(formerly the Greater Phoenix Convention & Visitors Bureau) maintains a pretty good guide to them online at www.visitphoenix.com/things-to-do/golf.

Desert-style golf layouts, like this course in Scottsdale, are designed with cacti and other native plants edging the green fairways.

Golf is a huge draw for the crowds that flock here in winter, and it can be difficult to get an ideal tee time at the more popular courses, especially from February to April. If you're staying at a resort with a course during the high season, make your tee-time reservations at the same time you make your room reservations. If you're staying elsewhere but yearn to play at one of the resort courses, you might still be able to snag a last-minute tee time. (See "The Pick of the Resort Courses" box, below.) To avoid the hassle of booking tee times yourself, contact **Golf Now** (www.golfnow.com), **Golf Arizona** (www.golfarizona.com), or **Golf Xpress** (www.azgolfxpress.com), which can often make reservations further in advance than you could on your own, and can sometimes get you lower greens fees as well.

There's often sticker shock, however. Greens fees during high season at most public and resort courses range from $100 to $200, with the top courses often charging $300 or more. Many courses here are on the cutting edge of dynamic pricing when it comes to online reservations, and prices for desirable tee times skyrocket to the highest the market will bear. In theory, this means that prices get lower for less desirable times, which in practice is early and mid-afternoon. In summer, of course, even the top courses practically start giving tee times away.

PUBLIC GOLF CLUBS

The Valley's most celebrated public courses are probably the ones at **Troon North Golf Club ★★★**, 10320 E. Dynamite Blvd., Scottsdale (www.troonnorthgolf.com; ✆ **480/585-7700**). Particularly when the light is right, there are crazy beautiful vistas here. With five tee boxes on each hole, golfers of all levels can enjoy the game. Greens fees in winter and spring are $245 to $295 ($120–$145 for twilight play). Beware, Troon also has a tacky 5% "water fee" that gets added to your bill. (What's next—a "grass fee"?)

If you want to swing where the pros do, beg, borrow, or steal a tee time on the Tom Weiskopf and Jay Morrish–designed Stadium Course at the **Tournament Players Club (TPC) of Scottsdale ★★**, 17020 N. Hayden Rd. (www.tpc.com/scottsdale; ✆ **888/400-4001** or 480/585-4334), site of the PGA's Phoenix Open. The 18th hole has standing room for 40,000 spectators, but

THE PICK OF THE resort COURSES

The many resort courses are the favored fairways of Valley visitors. For spectacular scenery, you just can't beat the two Jay Morrish–designed 18-hole courses at the **Boulders ★★★**, 34631 N. Tom Darlington Dr., Carefree (www.bouldersclub.com; ✆ **480/488-9028**). Given the option, play the South Course, set amid the striking rock formations that give the resort its name. Tee times for non-guests are very limited in winter and spring. Non-guests will pay at least $220 to $250 for a round in winter.

The big news in resortland is the entirely new 18-hole course at the **Phoenician Golf Club,** 6000 E. Camelback Rd. (www.thephoenician.com; ✆ **800/888-8234** or 480/423-2449), part of the ritzy Phoenician resort, set right in town at the base of Camelback Mountain. An expensive 2-year rebuild-from-scratch turned the former 27 holes into 18, designed to create "a natural rhythm and flow in the routing." Rates range from $179–$249, $89–$179 at twilight. You can reserve 45 days in advance.

At Litchfield Park, on the far west side of the Valley, the **Wigwam Golf Resort & Spa ★**, 300 Wigwam Blvd. (www.wigwamgolf.com; ✆ **623/935-3811**) has three championship 18-hole courses. The Gold Course is legendary, but even the Blue and Red courses are worth playing. These are traditional courses, with vast expanses of green rather than cacti and boulders. In high season, greens fees are $119 to $139 on any of the three courses.

On the east side of the Valley at the foot of the Superstition Mountains, the **Gold Canyon Golf Resort ★★**, 6100 S. Kings Ranch Rd., Gold Canyon (www.gcgr.com; ✆ **480/982-9449**) is well worth the 35-mile drive from downtown Phoenix or Scottsdale. The top-rated Dinosaur Mountain Course, frequently referred to as a roller-coaster ride complete with breathtaking scenery, has three of the state's best holes: the 2nd, 3rd, and 4th. Greens fees on this course range from $135 to $210 in winter. For the more traditional and less dramatic Sidewinder Course, greens fees are lower, $79 to $89 in winter. You can make online reservations some weeks in advance. (The club says 90 days, but that's not always the case.)

For a traditional course that's been played by presidents and celebrities, try for a round at the **Arizona Biltmore Golf Club,** 2400 E. Missouri Ave. (www.azbiltmoregc.com; ✆ **602/955-9655**). The Adobe Course is a spectrum of wide fairways covered in a green lushness that belies the desert around it; the more desert-y Links Course stretches up and around toward the nearby Phoenix Mountain preserve. Both are more relaxing than challenging. Greens fees are $185 in winter and spring, $99 after 2pm. Non-guests can make reservations up to 30 days in advance.

The Camelback Golf Club, 7847 N. Mockingbird Lane (www.camelbackinn.com; ✆ **480/596-7050**) is part of the fabled Camelback Inn in Paradise Valley, although it's 4 or 5 miles northeast of the resort. The tree-shaded Padre Course ($179 in winter, $99 for twilight play) is more challenging, while the Ambiente Course ($219, $129 for twilight play) is a links-style course with great mountain views and lots of water hazards.

hopefully there won't be that many around the day you double-bogey this hole. The TPC's second 18, the Champions Course, is actually a municipal course. While Stadium Course fees top out at $299 in winter ($194 for twilight play), Champions Course fees are somewhat more reasonable: $137 in winter, $97 for twilight play.

On the Fort McDowell Yavapai Nation, in the far northeast corner of the Valley, **We-Ko-Pa Golf Club,** 18200 E. Toh Vee Circle, Fort McDowell (www.wekopa.com; ✆ **866/660-7700** or 480/836-9000) is as pure a set of desert courses as can be found—the links stretch over an area nearly a mile and a half square, with nary a luxury home to be seen. Greens fees are $175 to $195 in winter, and reservations are taken up to 90 days in advance. It's located off the Beeline Highway (Ariz. 87).

The **Kierland Golf Club,** 15636 N. Clubgate Dr., Scottsdale (www.kierlandgolf.com; ✆ **480/922-9283**) was designed by Scott Miller as three 9-hole courses that can be played in various combinations. This is one of the prettiest courses in the Valley, and the amenities are a cut above, right down to the carts, which boast videos screens and AC units that blow while you're driving. Greens fees are $190 to $210 in winter ($140 to $160 for twilight play).

On the north side of the Valley, **Dove Valley Ranch Golf Club,** 33750 N. Dove Lakes Dr., Cave Creek (www.dovevalleyranch.com; ✆ **480/488-0009**), designed by Robert Trent Jones, Jr., blends desert and traditional styles. Greens fees are $90 to $120 in winter ($45 to $60 for twilight play). Nearby **Rancho Mañana Golf Club,** 5734 E. Rancho Mañana Blvd., Cave Creek (www.ranchomanana.com; ✆ **480/488-0398**) isn't as challenging, but greens fees are $139 in winter ($59 for twilight play). And I have friends who say the **500 Club Golf Course,** 4707 W. Pinnacle Peak Rd., Glendale (www.the500club.com; ✆ **623/492-9500**), tucked away behind desert foothills on the northwest side of town, is the most underrated course in the Valley.

MUNICIPAL COURSES

Phoenix has a half-dozen municipal courses; note that non-residents need to buy a $100 card to reserve tee times, and that golf carts cost extra. **Papago Golf Course,** 5595 E. Moreland St. (www.papagogolfcourse.net; ✆ **602/275-8428**), at the foot of the red sandstone Papago Buttes, offers fine views and a killer 17th hole. Greens fees are $49 to $129 in the winter/spring high season. The third-oldest course in Arizona, **Encanto Golf Course,** 2775 N. 15th Ave. (✆ **602/253-3963**), just a mile or two northwest of downtown, is very forgiving, with wide fairways, a lack of hazards, and nice downtown views. **Cave Creek Golf Course,** 15202 N. 19th Ave. (✆ **602/866-8076**), in north Phoenix, is another good, economical choice; it was built atop a former landfill. **Aguila Golf Course,** 8440 S. 35th Ave., Laveen (✆ **602/237-9601**), although a bit inconveniently located in the southwest corner of the Valley, was designed by Gary Panks. In winter, greens fees at Encanto, Cave Creek, and Aguila are $25 to $57. For details, contact **Phoenix Golf** (✆ **602-534-4653)** for reservations or visit www.phoenix.gov/parks/golf.

On the south side of Papago Park, with up-close-and-personal views of the Papago Buttes' rocky red moonscape, Tempe's **Rolling Hills Golf Course,** 1415 N. Mill Ave., Tempe (www.tempe.gov/golf; ✆ **480/350-5275**) is a good little municipal outfit with two executive 9-hole courses. Its cool-season greens fee is a very reasonable $24 for 18 holes; a golf cart will cost you another $22. Reservations can be made a week in advance.

Hiking

All of the regional governments do a great job with park information online, and at just about every trail I mention here, you'll find maps posted at the trail heads and often paper copies to carry with you. As you look up the trails online, remember that there are different jurisdictions involved—Phoenix, Scottsdale, Maricopa County, the state, etc. If you can't find a particular trail, you may be on the wrong governmental site.

Want a guide? There are lots to choose from. **Arizona Outback Adventures** (www.aoa-adventures.com; ✆ **866/455-1601**) does half-day hikes from the Gateway Trailhead, starting at $150 for two people. Guided hikes with all sorts of variations are available from **360 Adventures** (www.360-adventures.com; ✆ **602/418-3866**) and **Cactus Adventures** (www.cactusadventures.com; ✆ **480/688-4743**).

Finally, I've said it before and I'll say it again: Phoenix is a hot city; temperatures can reach the 90s in winter and the 100s in spring. **Take water along for desert hikes.**

SOUTH OF PHOENIX

Let's start with the turgidly titled **South Mountain Park/Preserve** ★ (www.phoenix.gov/parks; ✆ **602/495-0222**), a 16,000-acre preserve that encompasses a low mountain range; it's said to be the largest city park in the world, and it has 50-something miles of hiking, mountain biking, and horseback-riding trails. Views of town from the crest give you an unusual look at the Valley from the south; sunset is worth staying for if you're not too far from your car. The park's main entrance is at the foot of Central Avenue, 5 miles

Hikers savor the views from Dobbins Lookout on South Mountain.

south of downtown. Follow Central Avenue up to the ridge's Summit Road; turn left, and go 3 or 4 miles to the Dobson Lookout, which features a few large concrete cabanas to hang out in. Just to the south of this you can hook up with the park's **National Trail,** an incredible walk along the ridge; it crosses most of the park's other trails. If you hike east on this trail for 2 miles, you'll come to an unusual little natural tunnel that makes a good turnaround point. The **Holbert Trail,** a 5-mile round-trip hike that passes numerous petroglyphs, is another of my favorite trails here. To access this trail, turn left at the activity complex just inside the Central Avenue gate and drive to the last covered picnic area near the restrooms.

CENTRAL PHOENIX

Papago Park, at Galvin Pkwy. and McDowell Road (www.phoenix.gov/parks; ✆ **602/261-8318**) features a magnificent pair of red-rock buttes that are great to hike around, with caves and natural insets, and **Hole in the Rock,** a big natural bridge topping one of the buttes. There are both paved and dirt trails within the park; the most popular hikes are around the buttes (park on W. Park Drive) and up onto the rocks at Hole in the Rock (park past the zoo at the information center). The Desert Botanical Garden and the Phoenix Zoo are right next door.

NORTH OF DOWNTOWN

The city's most iconic feature is **Camelback Mountain ★**, technically part of the **Echo Canyon Recreation Area** (www.phoenix.gov/parks; ✆ **602/261-8318**), which has popular trails on the west and east ends. The western one, **Summit Trail,** will take you about 3 hours there and back; it's tough toward the top but just about anyone can hike its earlier stretches. The trail head is on the mountain's northwest flank, off McDonald Drive; turn south on East Echo Canyon Pkwy. and drive up the hill to the parking lot. If it's full you're out of luck, so go as early as you can. At the far east end of the mountain, the **Cholla Trail** is an easier hike, although also steep near the top and a bit longer; access it on Cholla Road west of Invergordon Road. Parking here is even more annoying; there's no lot, and the ritzy neighborhood has pulled strings to keep hiker parking limited to Invergordon Road. Be prepared to walk a half-mile or more through the neighborhood just to get the trail head. (If I sound churlish it's because these parks encompass many square miles of land; there's ample room to provide parking to allow the public to enjoy them.) The resort and golf course you're looking down on is the Phoenician, one of the Valley's fanciest. If you're determined to reach the summit, remember that while the city is spread out before you, these are desert mountains, trail signs are scarce, and all those fellow hikers can quickly disappear. Use caution and bring lots of water.

In the **Dreamy Draw Recreation Area** (www.phoenix.gov/parks; ✆ **602/262-7901**), the **Piestewa Peak** trail offers another aerobic workout with spectacular views at the end. It is 1.2 miles to the summit, and the trail gains almost 1,200 feet. Even a walk partway up is fun—there are periodic saddles in the mountain where you can stop, take a breath, and enjoy the views. Trail

Hiking with History

Want to stretch your legs, take in some fresh desert mountain air, and see something you won't see back home? The **Sears-Kay Ruins,** 15 miles northeast of Cave Creek, are worth searching out (head northeast from Carefree on Cave Creek Road, which becomes first Seven Springs Road and then Forest Service Road 24). It's an easy 1-mile round-trip hike to this hilltop Hohokam pueblo ruin, with interpretive plaques along the way explaining aspects of Hohokam culture. The pueblo, which dates to between 1050 and 1500, once consisted of 40 rooms in four compounds. What's left are low stone walls tracing the rooms, on the crest of a hillside with magnificent views. For more information, contact the Tonto National Forest's Cave Creek Ranger District (www.fs.usda.gov/tonto; ✆ **480/595-3300**).

On the south side of the Superstition Mountains, near the Gold Canyon Resort, a relatively short hike takes you to **Hieroglyphic Canyon,** a rock-art site reached via a 1.1-mile trail up a gentle slope through dense stands of cactus. To reach the trail head, drive east from Phoenix on U.S. 60 to Gold Canyon. Turn north on King's Ranch Road and be prepared to meander a bit. Follow this road to a right turn onto Baseline Road. Then turn left on Mohican Road, left again on Valley View Drive, and right on Cloudview Avenue, which leads into the trail head parking lot. The trail head parking lot fills up quickly, so go early if you're interested. For more info, contact the Tonto National Forest's Mesa Ranger District (www.fs.usda.gov/tonto; ✆ **480/610-3300**).

access is on Squaw Peak Drive, off Lincoln Drive between 22nd and 23rd streets. Another section of this park, with much easier trails, can be reached by taking the Northern Avenue exit off Ariz. 51 and then driving east into Dreamy Draw Park.

For a nice view of the city from a lower altitude, try **North Mountain Park** (www.phoenix.gov/parks; ✆ **602/262-6862**), in North Mountain Preserve, located on either side of Seventh Street between Dunlap Avenue and Thunderbird Road. There's an easy paved walk to a small butte on the west side of Seventh Street, which you can do in an hour to get the blood going.

NORTH SCOTTSDALE

Of all the mountain trails in the Phoenix area, the trail through **Pinnacle Peak Park ★★★**, 26802 N. 102nd Way (www.scottsdaleaz.gov/parks/pinnacle; ✆ **480/312-0990**), in north Scottsdale, is my favorite. Pinnacle Peak is a distinctive and picturesque destination, with a pencil eraser of a rock formation at the top. It can be as long as 3.5 miles round-trip—that's up, down, out to the west edge of the park, then back the way you came—but you can also navigate the switchbacks to the top and hang out there for a while if you just want an hour-long trek. There's a cozy information kiosk and informative flora and fauna signs along the way. The parking lot fills up by 9am on weekends. November through April, there are guided hikes on Wednesdays, Fridays, and Sundays at 10am; there are also full-moon hikes and astronomy evenings (check website for details).

Another great place for a desert hike is north Scottsdale's **McDowell Sonoran Preserve** (www.mcdowellsonoran.org; ✆ **480/312-5000**), where you'll find miles of relatively easy and uncrowded trails over an extravagant landscape. The preserve's main access is at the Gateway Trailhead, 18333 N. Thompson Peak Pkwy. The 2.5-mile **Ringtail Loop Trail** is a good choice for an hour's hike. At the **Brown's Ranch Trailhead,** 30301 N. Alma School Rd., about 2 miles north of Pinnacle Peak, there's a large welcome center and helpful volunteer guides. The hikes here are largely level, and there are a couple of low, distinctively shaped hills to scale.

CAVE CREEK AREA

North of Scottsdale, in the town of Cave Creek, you'll find a couple of my favorite hikes. The uncrowded 1-mile **Black Mountain Trail** ★★ leads to the summit of Black Mountain; from the top you can gaze out over all of Cave Creek and Carefree—and some of the crazy mountainside mansions. Keep an eye out for lizards lounging on the rocks at the summit. To find the trail head, take N. Schoolhouse Road south from Cave Creek Road for ¼ mile and park beside the road at the end of the pavement. The hike starts on the road that seems to lead straight up the mountain and then veers off onto a narrow trail.

EAST VALLEY

Way out on the east side of the Valley in the impossibly steep and jagged Superstition Mountains, the **Peralta Trail** ★★★ just might be my favorite hike in the entire state. Unfortunately, a lot of other people feel the same way, and on weekends, it's almost always packed. However, if you come early on a weekday, you can have this trail almost all to yourself. The route climbs steadily, though not too steeply, past huge old saguaros to a saddle with a view that will take your breath away—an in-your-face look at Weaver's Needle, the Superstition Mountains' most famous pinnacle. The hike to the view at Fremont Saddle is 4.6 miles round-trip. To reach the trail head, drive 8 miles north on Peralta Road from U.S. 60. For info, contact the **Tonto National Forest's Mesa Ranger District** (www.fs.usda.gov/tonto; ✆ **480/610-3300**).

Horseback Riding

There are plenty of places around the Valley to saddle up your palomino. The stables will make sure you're hydrated on the trail, but don't forget the sunscreen and a hat. The prices given are generally for group rides at scheduled times, so definitely make reservations. Most outfits will arrange private rides for a higher price, and most offer all sorts of variants to meet your tastes.

In north Scottsdale, **Cave Creek Outfitters,** 31313 N. 144th St., Scottsdale (www.cavecreekoutfitters.com; ✆ **480/471-4635**) offers 1- and 2-hour rides throughout the day from September through May, at $49 and $75 per person respectively, in the McDowell Sonoran Preserve and Tonto National Forest. For $20 more you can include lunch and "cowboy games" like horseshoe tossing and archery. In summer months they do just one ride in the morning and evening.

MacDonald's Ranch, 26540 N. Scottsdale Rd., Scottsdale (www.macdonaldsranch.com; ✆ **480/585-0239**) has a big operation that includes horseback rides, stagecoach rides, hayrides, a petting zoo, and more. Horseback rides are in a large tract of undeveloped land next to the ranch, not in the national forest. One-hour rides start at $48; moonlight rides start at $85.

On the south side of the city, **Ponderosa Stables,** 10215 S. Central Ave. (www.arizona-horses.com; ✆ **602/268-1261**) leads rides into South Mountain Park, charging $40 for a 1-hour ride, additional hours are $20 each. These stables also offer dinner rides ($55) to the T-Bone Steakhouse (p. 129) for a Western dinner in the middle of the ride. They will also arrange desert cookouts. Mid-October through mid-April, you can ride through Cave Creek Regional Park with **Cave Creek Trail Rides** (www.cavecreektrailrides.com; ✆ **623/742-6700**). A 1-hour ride costs $46 for adults and $41 for children 6 to 12. Longer rides are also offered, including sunset rides starting at $56. The park is off Carefree Highway (Ariz. 74) at 32nd St. There's a $7 park admission fee.

On the east side of the Valley, on the southern slopes of the imposing Superstitions, **OK Corral Horseback Riding Stables,** 5470 E. Apache Trail, Apache Junction (www.okcorrals.com; ✆ **480/982-4040**), has a half-hour ride for $35 and an hour ride for $45. They also scale up into 4-hour and daylong rides for experienced riders, some of it through challenging terrain.

Tennis

Most major hotels in the area have tennis courts, and there are several tennis resorts around the Valley. If you're staying someplace without a court, try the **Phoenix Tennis Center,** 6330. 21st Ave. (www.phoenixtenniscenter.net; ✆ **602/249-3712**). Fees start at $4 per person plus a $5 court fee. In Scottsdale, there's the **Scottsdale Ranch Park & Tennis Center,** 10400 E. Via Linda (www.scottsdaleaz.gov/parks/scottsdale-ranch; ✆ **480/312-7774**). Court fees start at $5 per person, $8 at night, for 90 minutes. You can reserve 1 day ahead.

Water Parks

These are open only during the summer months and skew their appeal to families and teens, but anyone would find them a refreshing respite from the summer heat. ***Essential tip:*** Get there when the park opens and claim some chairs and lounges under a cabana or umbrella. Latecomers get left out in the sun.

The classic venue **Big Surf,** 1500 N. McClintock Rd., Tempe (www.bigsurffun.com; ✆ **480/994-2297**) has been around for 50 years. At its opening it made headlines for its large man-made lake with a novel wave-making mechanism. Over the years it's added massive slides, too. Still it has a homey, mom 'n' pop feel and it's great for kids. Admission is $33, $23 for kids under 48" tall. Hunt around on the web for discount admission; it's not hard to find 30% or 50% off vouchers. Out in the East Valley, the newer **Mesa Golfland Sunsplash,** 155 W. Hampton Ave., Mesa (www.golfland.com; ✆ **480/834-8319**) has a wave pool and a big ol' lazy river, where you can relax in an inflated tube and let the current take you around and around. Lots of water slides, too. This park is generally open from Memorial Day weekend to Labor Day weekend (call for hours) and charges $26 for anyone taller than 48", $20 for seniors and anyone under 48", $3 for kids 2 and under. There's a big **Wet 'n' Wild** park up in the northwest part of town, but its myriad money-gouging extras (like a $13 parking fee) and poor upkeep (like the reeking banks of toilets last time I was there) make it impossible to recommend.

White-Water Rafting & Tubing

Up in the mountains to the northeast of Phoenix, the **Upper Salt River** flows wild and free. Most years from about late February to late May, snowmelt from the White Mountains floods the river and fills it with Class III and IV rapids (sometimes, however, there just isn't enough water). Companies operating full-day, overnight, and multi-day rafting trips on the Upper Salt River (conditions permitting) include **Wilderness Aware Rafting** (www.inaraft.com; ✆ **800/462-7238**), **Canyon Rio Rafting** (www.canyonrio.com; ✆ **800/272-3353**), and **Mild to Wild Rafting** (www.mild2wildrafting.com; ✆ **800/567-6745**). Prices start at $71 per person.

For tamer river trips, check out **Salt River Tubing and Recreation** (www.saltrivertubing.com; ✆ **480/984-3305**), headquartered 20 miles northeast of Phoenix on Power Road (at Usery Pass Road) in the Tonto National Forest. The company rents large inner tubes for $18 and transports riders upriver for a float back down. Some will find the clientele a little party-oriented, and you may experience crowds, long waits, and rowdy behavior; probably not best for families. The inner-tubing season runs from May to September.

SPAS

Resort spas are a big business in the Valley of the Sun. The top-tier ones have their own hair and nail salons, men's and women's locker rooms, daily yoga and fitness classes, whirlpools, and the like. You start with massages and wraps and quickly ramp up to hot-stone therapies, hydrofacials, body treatments, and more. In other words, all the pampering and indulgence you could want.

Most resorts open their spas to the public, and for the cost of a body treatment or massage, you can spend the day doing yoga or lounging in the sauna or by the (often luxurious) pools. Rates plummet in the summer, but they're sometimes higher on Fridays, Saturdays, and Sundays. Most of the top spas add on a 20% service charge for tips.

Well & Being Spa ★★★, at the Fairmont Scottsdale Princess (p. 104), is the current champion in the resort spa arms race. It's about as beautiful a place as you can imagine, more than 44,000 square feet, recently rebuilt into an experience that combines palatial surroundings with alluring tranquility. Over three floors, with a pool on the roof, the spa has everything from fitness classes to all the massages and treatments you could want. It's a place worth spending the day at; there's a towering waterfall bath in the grotto, and a secret garden reached via a path down from the pool. Wellness coaches are on hand for consultations. Because this is one of the largest spas in the Valley, you stand a better chance of getting last-minute reservations. Most 60-minute treatments cost $169 to $189. There are also several options for couples.

Sitting right at the foot of Mummy Mountain in Scottsdale, the **Spa at Camelback Inn ★★★** (www.camelbackspa.com; ✆ **800/922-2635** or 480/596-7040) has long been one of the Valley's premier spas. It's easy to get to and park at, the views are fabulous, and the setting is tranquil. For the cost of a single 1-hour treatment—between $130 and $175—you can use all the facilities, which include a fitness center and a lushly landscaped spa-only pool. There's a healthy and friendly cafe, too. Among the treatments available are the Bindi Herbal Body Treatment, which will leave your skin feeling like silk, and the Sonoran Rose facial, perfect for making sure you come back from vacation looking like you were actually on one. Also everything from hair and nails to waxing. Packages run from $190 to $360.

A walk through lush gardens and romantic passageways is restful just making your way to the **Alvadora Spa at Royal Palms**, 5200 E. Camelback Rd. (p. 107). Inside, a Mediterranean ambience prevails. The citrus ritual and orange-blossom body buff are two of the spa's signature treatments. Most 60-minute treatments cost $135, and packages run $232 to $380.

For truly spectacular surroundings, head north to the Boulders Resort and the **Spa at the Boulders ★**, 34631 N. Tom Darlington Dr., Carefree (p. 104), where a 2017 renovation retains an extravagant list of ayurvedic and Native American–inspired treatments, like bindi balancing and a Yuzu sage splash. Massages start at $155 and packages run $800.

One of the Valley's most elegant spas, the **Phoenician Spa ★★** (www.centreforwellbeing.com; ✆ **480/423-2452**) sits at the foot of the vast hill at Scottsdale's Phoenician resort (p. 101) in a new extravagant building that holds the resort's multi-tiered pools. Massages start at $165; leave time to choose and mix the essential oils you'd like to use beforehand. But that's just the start of a kaleidoscope of treatments, classes, and other things on tap here, from daily yoga classes to a gemstone healing facial to a Kalahari hydration wrap to a session with an astrologer. Prices top out at $600.

The **Spa Biltmore ★** at the Arizona Biltmore, 2400 E. Missouri Ave. (p. 106) is as luscious as its resort surroundings. The spa menu includes a variety of massages, body scrubs, facials, and specialties like the Organic Super Fruit Hydration Wrap or a Volcanic Clay body scrub. Purchase of a basic 50-minute treatment ($145 to $360) allows you to use all of the spa's facilities, including saunas, fitness classes, and tennis courts, for the rest of the day.

At **Joya Spa ★★**, 4949 E. Lincoln Dr., Paradise Valley (www.joyaspa.com; ✆ **480/627-3020**), in the Omni Scottsdale Resort & Spa at Montelucia (p. 100), you'll find the most romantic, and perhaps the largest, spa in the Valley. The spa's signature treatment is the *hammam* ritual ($59), which involves relaxing in a warming room, then a scrub followed by an herbal steam bath, whirlpool, sauna, and cold deluge. Things get a little more elaborate with the Orroccan Orange Blossom Ritual, which includes a sugar rub, a Rhassoul clay mask, and a foot treatment; that's about $250. Most 50-minute massages run $145 to $165, and there are various packages that let you choose two or three treatments, which have a top price of $430.

Spa Avania (www.spaavania.com; ✆ **480/444-1234**), at the Hyatt Regency Scottsdale Resort & Spa at Gainey Ranch (p. 97), takes its name from the Greek work for "tranquil." It's an appropriately sprawling place for this sprawling resort, with nearly a dozen treatment rooms, a mineral pool, a lotus pond, and more. One-hour treatments run $165 to $225, while packages cost anywhere from $300 to $850.

WHERE TO STAY

Hotel rates in the Valley spike up in the winter and crater in the summer. Still, there's a lot of competition for the tourist dollar even in the high season; that, and the rise of Airbnb and similar alternative lodging sites, ameliorate the pain somewhat.

There aren't a lot of traditional urban four-star hotels in Phoenix, although recently downtown Phoenix has seen an influx of tony brands, like the high-rise Westin (p. 110) and Palomar (p. 110). Outside of downtown proper, however, accommodations are invariably branded "resorts." Some of these, truth be told, stretch the generally accepted meaning of the term, but anything with a four-star designation will at least have a pretty nice pool and some other amenities, and most will be set on spacious grounds. The high-end ones are comfortably among the best in the country, with top-flight golf courses, large and pricey spas, multiple pools and restaurants, and more than enough things to keep kids occupied. There are oodles of each group to choose from, particularly on the east side of town. And while you'll pay a surcharge, rooms with mountain views—particularly at the Paradise Valley resorts—are worth asking for.

SEASONAL RATES March and April are baseball's spring training season, and baseball fans from all over the world converge on the Valley, driving the rates higher and higher. It can sometimes be hard to find the room you want where you want, so book early during those times. The good news is that rates are fairly reasonable at other times, and given the competitive environment there are bargains to be had, so shop around. And if you *want* to experience Phoenix in the hot season, from June to September, you'll find rates at $100 a night or lower at some highly desirable locations, and all sorts of other crazy offers, like food credits and upgrades.

Most resorts offer a variety of weekend, golf, and tennis packages, as well as off-season discounts and corporate rates (which you can often get just by asking). And of course you can find discounts online (p. 508). Poke around for spa deals as well.

RESORT FEES I know it's a lost consumers' cause at this point, but for the record, the practice of adding "hotel fees" or "resort fees" of $20 and $30 a day to the bill remains a racket. If you're paying to stay at a resort, why is there a "resort fee" on top? When you go to the grocery store you don't get hit with a "grocery fee" as you leave! (And don't get me started on the places that have begun calling rooms "casitas.") The fees are not optional, and in effect just allow the hotels to advertise prices that don't exist. If any of the amenities included in the fee aren't up to snuff, by all means call the front desk and get them removed from the bill. (Some, for example, limit the "free Wi-Fi" to two devices, which is not nearly enough for a traveling couple.) In any case, don't forget to do the mental math as you browse prices; they don't go away, even on those discounted summer deals.

Finally, pay parking used to be extremely rare in Phoenix. These days, the downtown hotels charge for parking in the garages below, and most of the four-and five-star resorts will hit you up for valet parking as well. Often, however, this is included in the resort fee.

Scottsdale & Paradise Valley

There are more self-described resorts in Scottsdale and the swanky suburb of PV than you can count. Some line Scottsdale Road heading north out of the center of the city, meaning you get the benefits of the close-by nightlife. If you want mountain views, go for the high-end PV resorts or look at the north Scottsdale section below.

EXPENSIVE

Hyatt Regency Scottsdale Resort & Spa at Gainey Ranch ★★★ From the colonnades of palm trees to the lobby walls that slide away, this luxurious resort is designed to impress, and it continues to be my favorite Scottsdale resort. It's relatively close to downtown Scottsdale and has interesting architecture, beautiful grounds, and a large spa. What's not to love? A 2½-acre water playground serves as the resort's focal point, an extravagant complex of swimming pools that includes a water slide, sand beach, and huge whirlpool spa. Guest rooms are just as luxurious as the surroundings would suggest. The resort's **Alto ristorante e bar** features after-dinner gondola rides, and the Native American and Environmental Learning Center provides a glimpse into Sonoran Desert culture and ecology. Children's programs make this a super choice for families.

7500 E. Doubletree Ranch Rd., Scottsdale. www.hyatt.com. ✆ **480/444-1234.** 493 units. High season $587–$677 double, from $727 suite; summer $171–$201 double, $311–$521 suite. $29 daily resort fee. $33 valet parking; $21 self-parking. Pets accepted. **Amenities:** 5 restaurants; 3 lounges; babysitting; bikes; children's programs; concierge; 27-hole golf course; health club & spa; 4 Jacuzzis; 10 pools; room service; 4 tennis courts; Wi-Fi (included in resort fee).

JW Marriott Camelback Inn Resort & Spa ★ The Camelback Inn, which for some 80 years has represented the epitome of resort luxury in the Valley, runs from Lincoln Avenue in Paradise Valley a full half-mile up to the base of Mummy Mountain; its views of Mummy and Camelback mountains are spectacular. There's lots of southwestern character here, in what is really

Aloft Tempe **30**
Arizona Biltmore Resort & Spa **17**
Arizona Grand Resort **31**
Best Western InnSuites Phoenix **2**
Best Western Plus Sundial Resort **28**
The Boulders Resort **12**
The Camby **24**
The Clarendon Hotel **4**
Crowne Plaza San Marcos Golf Resort **34**
Dobson Ranch Inn Resort **32**
Embassy Suites Biltmore **25**
Embassy Suites Scottsdale **28**
Extended Stay America Phoenix Biltmore **3**
Fairmont Scottsdale Princess **10**
Found:Re Hotel **6**
Four Seasons Resort Scottsdale at Troon North **11**
Gold Canyon Golf Resort **33**
The Hermosa Inn **26**
Hotel Valley Ho **27**
Hyatt Regency Scottsdale Resort & Spa at Gainey Ranch **14**
Inn at Eagle Mountain **15**
Omni Scottsdale Resort & Spa at Montelucia **20**
JW Marriott Camelback Inn Resort & Spa **18**
JW Marriott Desert Ridge Resort & Spa **13**
Magnuson Hotel Papago Inn **29**
Mountain Shadows **18**
The Palomar **7**
The Phoenician **23**
Pointe Hilton Squaw Peak Resort **16**
Pointe Hilton Tapatio Cliffs Resort **1**
Royal Palms Resort and Spa **22**
Sanctuary on Camelback Mountain **19**
The Scott Resort & Spa **28**
Sheraton Wild Horse Pass Resort & Spa **36**
Tempe Mission Palms Hotel **31**
Westin Kierland Resort & Spa **9**
Westin Phoenix Downtown **5**
Wigwam Golf Resort & Spa **8**

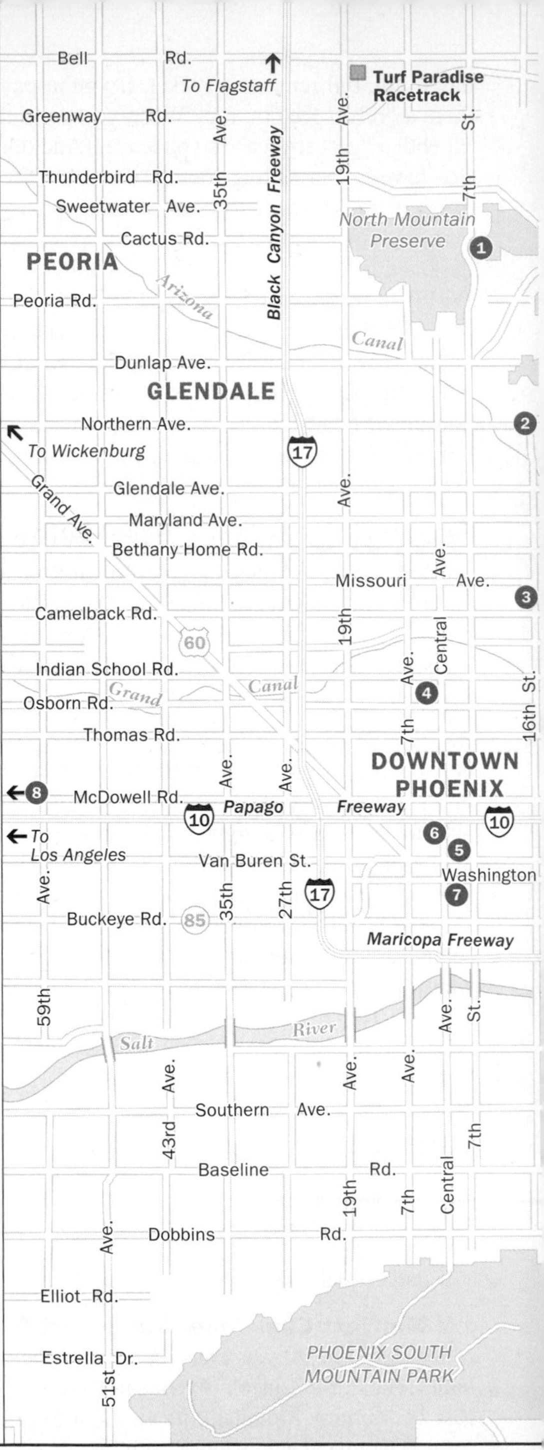

Phoenix, Scottsdale & the Valley of the Sun Hotels

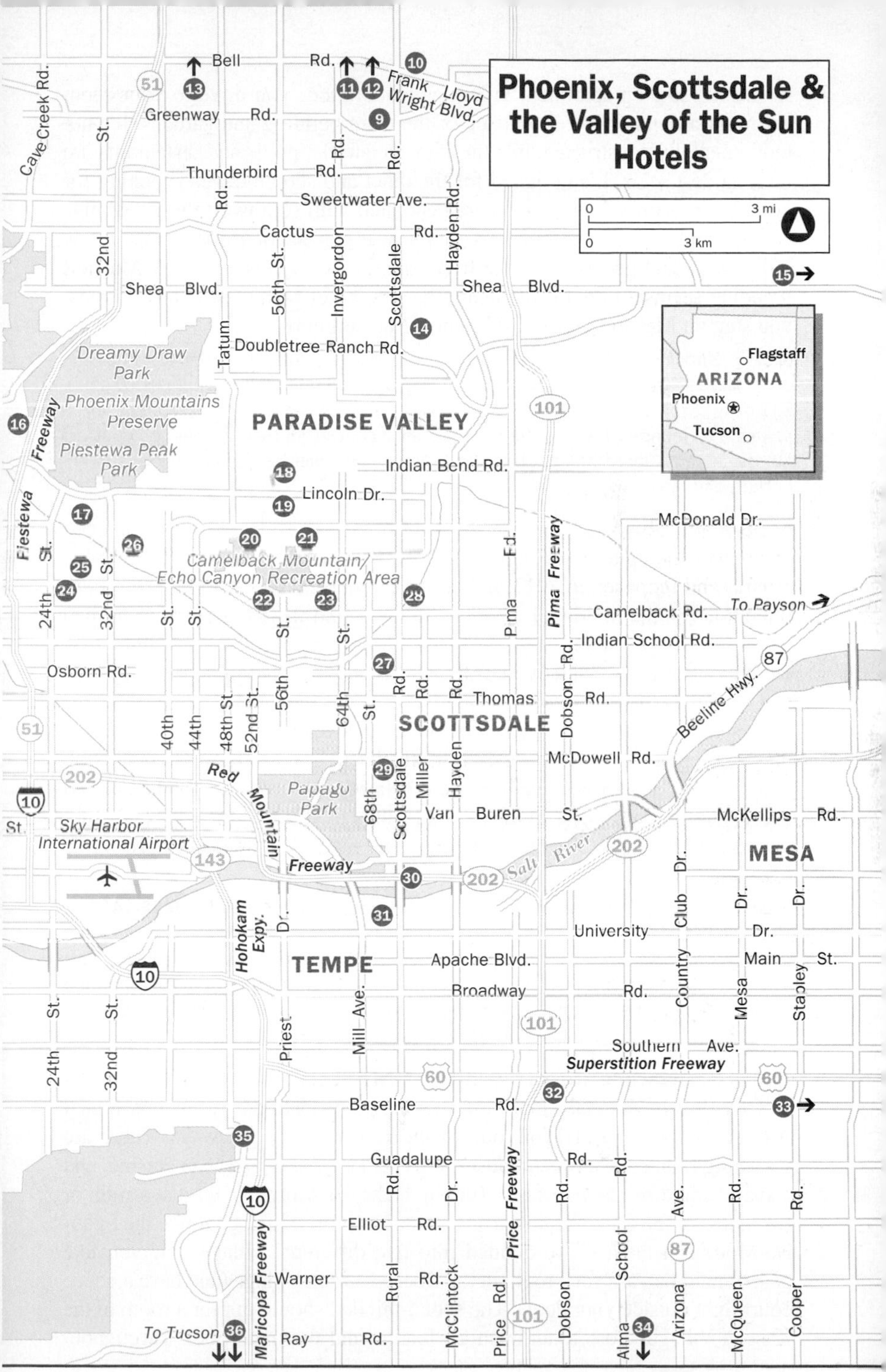

something like an apartment village neighborhood; you drive to your room and walk around on streets outside of the main building and gardens. It's not monumentally constructed, like the Phoenician; the pools and restaurants are on a modest scale. It's designed for the quiet and serene traveler looking for good basic luxury. Guest rooms are decorated with southwestern furnishings and art, and all have balconies or patios. You golf at the resort's links a few miles away and get back and forth via shuttle. To my taste, the JW Marriott branding seems a little overdone at a historic hotel with these kinds of rates; you stay on Marriott Drive, drink out of Marriott cups, etc.

5402 E. Lincoln Dr., Paradise Valley. www.camelbackinn.com. ✆ **480/948-1700.** 453 units. High season $335 double, $725–$1200 suite; summer $109 double, $300 suite. $35 daily resort fee includes valet parking. Pets accepted ($250 fee). **Amenities:** 5 restaurants; lounges; bikes; children's programs; concierge; two 18-hole golf courses; fitness center; 3 Jacuzzis; 4 pools; room service; full-service spa; 6 tennis courts; Wi-Fi (included in resort fee).

Mountain Shadows ★ In the 1960s and '70s this evocatively named resort was the epitome of midcentury modern desert opulence. Torn down, rebuilt, and reopened in 2017, it's now a thoroughly modern mid-sized boutique hotel in the middle of Paradise Valley. I find the front entrance a mystery—with no fountains and no fancy plaza, it looks like an employees' entrance. But once inside, you're treated to picture-window mountain vistas and all the latest luxury conveniencs. The rooms have polished cement ceilings, spacious bathrooms, and even bathtub alcoves tucked next to the balconies where you can soak and gaze at Camelback. The property caters to a hip young crowd, with a sleek but not overwhelming party vibe on weekends, and a free shuttle takes guests to the spa and tennis facilities at the adjacent Sanctuary on Camelback Mountain (below). The main restaurant, **Hearth 61,** is excellent.

5700 E. McDonald Dr., Paradise Valley. www.sanctuaryaz.com. ✆ **855/485-1417** or 480/948-2100. 183 units. High season $389–$529 double, $689–$2,899 suite; summer $129–$259 double, $299–$1,999 suite. $32 daily resort fee includes valet parking. Pets accepted. **Amenities:** 2 restaurants; 2 lounges; bikes; concierge; exercise room and access to nearby health club; Jacuzzi; pools; room service; sauna; shuttle to spa and tennis courts; Wi-Fi (included in resort fee).

Omni Scottsdale Resort & Spa at Montelucia ★★ The red rocks of Camelback Mountain loom over architecture inspired by Spain's fabled Alhambra at the Montelucia, one of the newer Valley getaways. There are splashing fountains, a restaurant serving excellent Mediterranean cuisine, and a spa inspired by the *hammams* (public baths) of Morocco, all just a mile or two north of the Camelback Corridor. Guest rooms, which continue the Spanish/Moroccan themes, are divided into five different "villages." If you like peace and quiet, ask for a room in the Bocce Garden Village (and have a bocce court right outside your door). The social-minded should opt for a room in the Kasbah Village, close to an open-air lounge and the main pool. Throughout the property you'll see fascinating Spanish antiquities, including two giant amphorae in the entry courtyard and huge wooden doors that lead to the resort's ballroom.

4949 E. Lincoln Dr., Paradise Valley. www.omnihotels.com. ✆ **888/627-3010** or 480/627-3200. 293 units. Jan–Apr $395–$845 double, $695–$4,000 suite; May–mid-June and mid-Sept–Dec $245–$625 double, $545–$3,000 suite; mid-June–mid-Sept $145–$425 double, $345–$2,000 suite. $24 daily resort fee. Children 18 and under stay free in parent's room. Valet parking $19. Pets accepted ($100 fee). **Amenities:** 5 restaurants; snack bar; 2 lounges; babysitting; bikes; children's programs; concierge; exercise room and access to nearby health club; 2 Jacuzzis; 3 pools; room service; full-service spa; Wi-Fi ($13 per day).

The Phoenician ★★★ Situated on 250 acres nestled right up against Camelback Mountain, this palatial getaway—recently given a spectacular complete makeover—is the model of a world-class resort. The expansive grounds are dotted with magnificent Native American sculptures; two giant works by Allan Houser frame the main lobby entrance. The massive pools, on three levels, plus a waterpark for kids, are everything you could ask for, and the overall scale, from the lobby to the rooms, is big enough to impress without being overwhelming. The spa—now a three-story behemoth—is first-class, and there are innumerable activities every day, starting with morning yoga in front of magnificent Camelback Mountain, continuing with afternoon tea, and ending with a late-evening fun room for kids—the "Fun!ician"—get it? There are also 18 holes of golf (p. 87) on a course completely rebuilt in 2018. The luxurious guest rooms have large patios and sunken tubs for two. And even the resort's second restaurant, **Mobray & Cotton,** has a first-class chef. Don't miss the gorgeous and extensive cactus garden and its accompanying trails, tucked between the back of the resort and the mountain. If you're staying here you probably aren't worried about money, but be aware the charges add up— with a resort fee, valet fee, and tips, it's possible to drop nearly $75 before you unpack!

6000 E. Camelback Rd., Scottsdale. www.thephoenician.com. ✆ **800/888-8234** or 480/941-8200. 645 units. High season $459–$629 double, $869–$1,499 suite; summer $179–$299 double, $379–$699 suite. Children 17 and under stay free in parent's room. $35 daily resort fee. Valet parking $33. Pets accepted (under 40 lbs.; $175 fee). **Amenities:** 9 restaurants, snack bars/cafes; 2 lounges; babysitting; bikes; children's programs; concierge; executive-level rooms; 18-hole golf course; health club and spa; 3 Jacuzzis; 8 pools; room service; 11 tennis courts; Wi-Fi (included in resort fee).

Sanctuary on Camelback Mountain ★★ This visually breathtaking place was the Valley's first hip resort, and I still like the contemporary rooms here better than those at other hip hotels around town—and so do the celebrities who stay here. Located high on the back (i.e., northern) flanks of Camelback Mountain, the lushly landscaped property has unforgettable views across Paradise Valley, especially from its restaurant and two bars. The extremely spacious guest rooms are divided between conservative deluxe casitas and boldly contemporary spa casitas, which are absolutely stunning, with dyed-cement floors,

L-shaped couches, and streamline-modern cabinetry. Bathrooms are huge, and some have private outdoor soaking tubs. The resort's spa is gorgeous.

5700 E. McDonald Dr., Paradise Valley. www.sanctuaryaz.com. ✆ **855/245-2051.** 116 units. High season $599–$899 double, $759–$999 suite; summer $209–$379 double, $309–$479 suite. $36 daily resort fee includes valet parking. Pets accepted ($100 fee). **Amenities:** Restaurant; lounge; bikes; full-service fitness facility; Jacuzzi; 4 pools; room service; full-service spa; 5 tennis courts; Wi-Fi (included in resort fee).

Westin Kierland Resort & Spa ★★★ This is about as good as it gets for an upscale family resort. There's lots for kids to do, but the place is spread out enough that you don't get a Disney feel at all. A slew of events each day—from desert-animal demonstrations to a bagpiper at sunset—give the place a lively vibe, but it's also easy to find your own space, whether at the cowboy bar, the "Scotch library," etc. A giant pool with a lazy river keeps families occupied, while the extra-large "adults pool" stays serene. You're right next door to the Kierland Commons open-air mall, which has a variety of high-end shops, restaurants, and novelties like a Tesla store, and the upscale Scottsdale Quarter right across the street from that, which has, among other things, a ritzy iPic movie house. So this is an unbeatable place for those who want to hole up and take it easy but not get bored by the surroundings. Guest rooms all have balconies or patios; be sure to request a room overlooking the golf course and the mountains to the north. The best of the in-house restaurants, **deseo** (p. 121), is one of the best hotel restaurants in the Valley.

6902 E. Greenway Pkwy., Scottsdale. www.kierlandresort.com. ✆ **800-354-5892** or 480/624-1000. 732 units. High season $449–$509 double; $559–$619 suite; summer $146–$194 double, $269–$319 suite. $35 daily resort fee. Valet parking $31. Pets accepted ($20 fee). **Amenities:** 10 restaurants; 2 lounges; babysitting; children's programs; concierge; 27-hole golf course; health club and full-service spa; 3 Jacuzzis; 2 pools and water park; room service; 2 tennis courts; Wi-Fi (included in resort fee).

MODERATE

Hotel Valley Ho ★★★ This Scottsdale landmark does hip right—and brings midcentury modern into the 21st century. It's as close as Scottsdale gets to Palm Springs, with highly elegant stylings throughout and a whiff of retro camp that makes this a fun place to hang—I recommend the bar at Café ZuZu—or stay. The jazzily appointed suites are cool enough to host a dinner party in; regular rooms are smaller, but all are quite stylish. The pool, a magnet for guests, has a relaxed feel and is surrounded by palm trees.

6850 E. Main St., Scottsdale, AZ 85251. www.hotelvalleyho.com. ✆ **480/248-2000.** 241 units. High season $299–$499 double, $499–$1,799 suite; summer $129–$199 double, $269–$949 suite. Valet parking $18. Pets accepted. **Amenities:** Restaurant; lounge; bikes; concierge; exercise room ; Jacuzzi; 2 pools; room service; full-service spa; free Wi-Fi.

The Scott Resort & Spa ★ With an exceptional location, just on the northern edge of the downtown Scottsdale shopping district, the Scott has dramatic southwestern contemporary styling (the focal point of the lobby is an impressive sandstone fireplace). Now, this isn't a big resort; it has a pretty small footprint, but it makes an impression. There's a lushly landscaped lagoon-style pool, complete with sand beach and waterfall, and a second pool with flame-topped columnar waterfalls. The guest rooms are quite comfortable, and there's a pretty little spa on the premises.

4925 N. Scottsdale Rd., Scottsdale. www.thescottresort.com. ✆ **800/528-7867** or 480/945-7666. 204 units. Jan–mid-Apr $189 double, $599 suite; mid-Apr–May $159 double, $499 suite; June–Aug $109 double, $325 suite; Sept–Dec $159 double, $499 suite. Children 18 and under stay free in parent's room. Pets accepted. **Amenities:** Restaurant; lounge; concierge; exercise room and access to nearby health club; Jacuzzi; 2 pools; room service; full-service spa; Wi-Fi ($10 per day).

INEXPENSIVE

There are a few relatively inexpensive chain motels scattered throughout Scottsdale. Still, they will be pricier than you would expect in winter months, and spike even more during spring training. For location alone—it's right next to Scottsdale Fashion Square and you can walk to just about all the shopping and nightlife downtown Scottsdale has to offer—your best choice would be the **Motel 6 Scottsdale**, 6848 E. Camelback Rd. (www.motel6.com; ✆ **480/946-2280**), which has doubles in the $140 area during the high season.

Best Western Plus Sundial Resort ★ Throw away any preconceived ideas you have about Best Western hotels—this conveniently located little resort boasts bold contemporary styling in its guest rooms, with black granite counters and wall-hung TVs. A wide variety of room types provide plenty of options. There are suites with sunrooms and large patios, and high-ceilinged "bungalow"-style rooms. The location is just west of Scottsdale Road, on Camelback; all of downtown Scottsdale is a short walk away.

7320 E. Camelback Rd., Scottsdale. www.bestwestern.com. ✆ **480/994-4170.** 54 units. High season $149 double, $179 suite. Rates include full breakfast. Pets accepted ($25 per night). **Amenities:** Concierge; exercise room and access to nearby health club; Jacuzzi; outdoor pool; free Wi-Fi.

Embassy Suites Scottsdale ★ The full name—Embassy Suites by Hilton Scottsdale Resort—is another example of how the word "resort" is overused by some Scottsdale hotels. It does have a very pleasant pool area in a palm-shaded courtyard, and rooms were redone in a sort of Spanish colonial style a few years ago. It's a good choice if you are looking for a budget suite close to Old Town Scottsdale.

5001 N. Scottsdale Rd., Scottsdale. www.embassysuites.com. ✆ **480/949-1414.** 211 units. Jan–Apr $100–$200 double, $180–$230 suite; May–Dec $55–$120 double, $110–$150 suite. Children 17 and under stay free in parent's room. Pets accepted ($250 deposit plus $25 per night). **Amenities:** Restaurant; lounge; fitness room; Jacuzzi; outdoor pool; room service; free Wi-Fi.

Magnuson Hotel Papago Inn ★ This older hotel used to call itself a "resort"; now it's styled as a boutique hotel. It has some nice architectural touches, but it's basically a Best Western, which is what it used to be. Located just east of Scottsdale Road in south Scottsdale, it's a few miles from the swanky area. While it may not be fancy, a pretty courtyard with green lawns creates a secluded feeling you wouldn't expect with a busy four-lane road out front. It is currently in the last half of an extensive years-long remodel.

7017 E. McDowell Rd., Scottsdale. www.bestwestern.com. ✆ **480/947-7335.** 58 units. High season $178–$209 double; summer $65 double. **Amenities:** Restaurant; lounge; exercise room; outdoor pool, free Wi-Fi.

North Scottsdale, Carefree & Cave Creek

With great golf courses, superb restaurants, rugged desert scenery, and a bit of Western character, this area gets my vote for best place to get away from it all, soak up some sun, and get to know the desert. Remember that you're 20 or 30 minutes away from downtown Scottsdale.

EXPENSIVE

The Boulders Resort ★★ Set aside the towering jumble of giant boulders that gave the place its name, the adobe buildings of this luxury golf resort blend unobtrusively into the desert, on the southern edge of Carefree about 30 minutes north of downtown Scottsdale. Its two golf courses epitomize the desert golf course experience, and when not golfing, you can lounge by the small pool, play tennis, relax at the resort's Golden Door Spa, or even try rock climbing. The lobby is in a Santa Fe–style building with tree-trunk pillars and a flagstone floor, and guest rooms continue the pueblo styling, with beehive fireplaces and beamed ceilings. For the best views, ask for one of the second-floor units. Bathrooms are large and luxuriously appointed, with tubs for two and separate showers. The restaurants emphasize organic ingredients.

34631 N. Tom Darlington Dr., Carefree. www.theboulders.com. ✆ **888/579-2631** or 480/488-9009. 222 units. High season $459 casita, $700 villa; summer $139 casita, $325 villa. $30 daily resort fee includes self-parking. Valet parking $25. **Amenities:** 5 restaurants; 2 lounges; bikes; concierge; two 18-hole golf courses; health club and full-service spa; 4 Jacuzzis; 4 pools; room service; 8 tennis courts; Wi-Fi (included in resort fee).

Fairmont Scottsdale Princess ★★★ This faux Moorish palace, with its royal palms, tiled fountains, and waterfalls—and most of all, a maze of buildings over some 60 acres—offers an exotic and sprawling place to relax and have fun. An extravagant water playground (with two large water slides) and dedicated kids center—not to mention those spacious grounds with hidden treasures that reward explorers—make this resort a hit with families. The nearby TPC golf course is top-notch, guest rooms are done in contemporary southwestern style, and bathrooms have double vanities and separate showers and tubs. All units have private balconies. For stepped-up amenities, opt for a double-sized room in the recently upgraded Gold wing. There's also what is probably the best spa in the Valley, **Well & Being** (p. 94), the Hacienda bar with its 240 kinds of tequila . . . and did I mention the Friday night fireworks? Finally, this is probably the best resort in the Valley to spend Christmas; it's redone in holiday splendor from Thanksgiving to New Year's, with wall-to-wall family activities.

7575 E. Princess Dr., Scottsdale. www.fairmont.com/scottsdale. ✆ **480/585-4848.** 750 units. High season $719 double, $849 suite. Summer $189 double, $369 suite. $32 daily resort fee. Valet parking $24; self-parking $8. Pets accepted ($25 per night). **Amenities:** 4 restaurants; 4 lounges; babysitting; bikes; children's programs; two 18-hole golf courses; exercise room; 2 Jacuzzis; 6 pools; room service; full-service spa; 7 tennis courts; Wi-Fi (included in resort fee).

Four Seasons Resort Scottsdale at Troon North ★★★ Dazzlingly set next to Pinnacle Peak, north Scottsdale's most distinctive mountain landmark, this super-luxurious resort is more intimate than the nearby Boulders. Casita accommodations are scattered across a boulder-strewn hillside and curled around three pools. There are two restaurants, including a high-end Spanish steakhouse, **Talavera,** along with a cozy lounge dubbed **Onyx** (this with a patio boasting terrific views of faraway Camelback Mountain and Piestwa Peak), and an enjoyable Western saloon-like affair called **Proof.** Guests get golf privileges at the nearby Troon North golf course (p. 86). This is a great place for those who want to explore the desert on foot: You can walk to nearby Pinnacle Peak Park (p. 91), or get a lift from the resort to nearby trail heads into the Sonoran Reserve. Guest rooms and suites are lavish; the priciest ones include a private plunge pool and an outdoor shower. Daily activities range from exercise and yoga to kids' stuff. ***Note:*** There are lots of stairs and inclines here; make sure to ask for a ground-level room if that's a problem.

10600 E. Crescent Moon Dr., Scottsdale. www.fourseasons.com/scottsdale. ✆ **888/207-9696** or 480/515-5700. 210 units. High season $499–$1,079 double, $868–$2,809 suite; summer $209–$699 double, $499–$1,799 suite. $35 daily resort fee includes self-parking. Valet parking $35. Pets accepted. **Amenities:** 3 restaurants; 2 lounges; children's programs; concierge; 2 18-hole golf courses; health club and spa; Jacuzzi; 3 pools; room service; 2 tennis courts; free Wi-Fi.

MODERATE

Inn at Eagle Mountain ★ While the location is a bit out of the way—15 minutes east of U.S. 101 and just off Shea Boulevard near the town of Fountain Hills—a hillside setting, valley views, spacious accommodations, and adjacent golf course make this secluded, residential-style hotel a good choice. Rooms, of which there are several styles and sizes, have simple southwestern-inspired furniture; all have gas fireplaces and large bathrooms with Jacuzzi tubs, and several have balconies and patios. The pool overlooks a small lake on the golf course. There's a desert preserve with hiking trails nearby, but it's at least a 15-minute drive to good restaurants. The restaurant serves dinner, but for breakfast and lunch you'll have to make do with the golf club restaurant.

9800 N. Summer Hill Blvd., Fountain Hills. www.innateaglemountain.com. ✆ **855/988-4745** or 602/842-7529. 38 units. High season $150–$200 double, $225–$275 suite; summer $75–$110 double, $110–$125 suite. Free parking. Pets $25 per day (max. $75). **Amenities:** Restaurant; lounge; concierge; 18-hole golf course; access to nearby health club; Jacuzzi; outdoor pool; free Wi-Fi.

Central Phoenix & the Camelback Corridor

This area includes the newly revitalized downtown and points directly north, and then the shopping areas along Camelback Road running east from Central Avenue. Big as it is, Sky Harbor Airport, which is just a few miles southeast of downtown, has relatively few hotels around it. A number of serviceable midline chain outlets are clustered along 44th Street just north of the airport, and a few more scattered to the south. The most engaging of these is probably **Aloft** (4450 E. Washington Ave.; www.aloftphoenixairport.com; © **602/275-6300**). None are in particularly attractive surroundings, however.

EXPENSIVE

Arizona Biltmore ★★★ For more than 80 years, this resort has been the favored Phoenix address of celebrities, politicians, and old money. The architect was Albert Chase McArthur, with an assist from Frank Lloyd Wright, whose influence across this striking expanse is plain. It has a lot of history—presidents have been staying here since the 1940s—and swellegance; a breathtaking lobby, wide, hushed hallways, serene outdoor walkways, etc. There are two golf courses, a swanky spa, an extravagant pool complete with an ornate waterfall and slide for kids, great food available everywhere you turn, and high-end shops. You're just a mile from the Biltmore Fashion Park mall, with lots of shops and additional restaurants.

2400 E. Missouri Ave., Phoenix. www.arizonabiltmore.com. © **602/955-6600.** 740 units. High season $359 double, $599 suite; summer $145 double, $275–$474 suite. $28 daily resort fee. Valet parking $28; self-parking $12. Pets accepted ($100 deposit). **Amenities:** 4 restaurants; lounge; bikes; children's programs; concierge; 2 18-hole golf courses; health club; full-service spa; Jacuzzi; 8 pools; room service; saunas; 7 tennis courts; Wi-Fi (included in resort fee).

The Camby ★★ A relatively new high-end boutique operation, this 11-story tower (itself fairly unusual for Phoenix) occupies the site of the former Ritz-Carlton, looking out on the bustling intersection of 24th Street and Camelback Road, the Biltmore Fashion Park mall, and a gorgeous vista of mountains beyond. You're as centrally located as you can get in the Valley. The interior has been successfully redone in high postmodern hip. It's lots of fun to stay here; there are absurdist touches everywhere, like the large cow-skull light on the wall of your room that projects the word "moo" on the wall below it, a giant topiary hummingbird by the pool, and a gym called "JIM." The bar and restaurant are great hangs, and the hotel offers free loans of record players, old-fashioned LP records, and even some Gretsch guitars for retro listening, or playing, in your room.

2401 E. Camelback Rd., Phoenix. www.thecamby.com. © **602/468-0700.** 227 units. High season $299–$499 double, $459–$699 suite; summer $119–$219 double, $279–$429 suite. No resort fee; valet parking $27; self-parking $12. Pets accepted ($100 fee). **Amenities:** Restaurant; 2 lounges; bikes; concierge; fitness center; spa; pool; room service; free Wi-Fi.

The Hermosa Inn ★★ The 1930s adobe home of cowboy artist Lon Megargee sits in the center of this boutique desert hideaway, technically in Paradise Valley but just a half-mile off the Camelback Corridor. There's not a golf course in sight, and it's not a resort, though there's a pleasant pool. But if you are looking for a) luxury and b) a quiet place to chill in the evenings, this is for you. There are 35 rooms on just 6 acres, set amid quiet walkways, cactus gardens, towering mesquites, and fountains. Most of the rooms were redone in 2015; they are spacious, with arching wood skylights, big bathrooms with large walk-in showers and deep bathtubs, and patios right outside. (I've stayed in boutique hotel rooms in NYC smaller than the patios—or the bathrooms, for that matter!) The setting, amid sprawling desert mansions, is a great place for a morning bike ride, and the restaurant, **Lon's** (p. 123), will take care of you.

5532 N. Palo Cristi Rd., Paradise Valley. www.hermosainn.com. ✆ **800/241-1210** or 602/955-8614. 43 units. High season $429–$519 double, $559–$659 suite; summer $149–$299 double, $259–$349 suite. Pets accepted ($75 each). $30 daily resort fee includes parking. **Amenities:** Restaurant; lounge; babysitting; bikes; concierge; fitness center; 2 Jacuzzis; outdoor pool; room service; Wi-Fi (included in resort fee).

Royal Palms Resort and Spa ★★★ Constructed more than 80 years ago by Cunard Steamship executive Delos Cooke, the Royal Palms is done in Spanish Mission style; it's full of winding, tree-covered paths, arches, narrow walkways, gardens, and antique fountains, creating the tranquil feel of a Mediterranean monastery. The denseness landscaping belies its relatively small footprint on Camelback Road in Arcadia. The most memorable guest rooms are the designer casitas, each with a distinctive decor ranging from opulent contemporary to classic European, but all the rooms are beautiful, with super-plush beds. **T. Cook's** restaurant (p. 123) is one of the best in the city.

5200 E. Camelback Rd., Phoenix. www.royalpalmsresortandspa.com. ✆ **800/672-6011** or 602/840-3610. 119 units. High season $526–$566 double, $576–$1,026 suite; summer $169–$174 double, $394 suite. $25 daily service fee. Pets accepted (50 lbs. max). **Amenities:** 2 restaurants; 2 lounges; babysitting; concierge; exercise room; Jacuzzi; outdoor pool w/cabanas; room service; full-service spa; free Wi-Fi.

MODERATE

Embassy Suites Biltmore ★ If you can sleep better with a Saks next door, this is for you. This hotel is just west of the ritzy Biltmore Fashion Park; there are some fine restaurants just steps away, and a Hillstone steakhouse in the parking lot. The atrium is filled with interesting tile work, tropical greenery, waterfalls, and ponds filled with koi; here you'll also find a romantic lounge with huge banquettes shaded by palm trees. All in all, this hotel is a fairly good value, with a catch or two. There's no resort fee and you get a free full breakfast and afternoon drinks. But you'll pay for parking and Wi-Fi.

2630 E. Camelback Rd., Phoenix. www.phoenixbiltmore.embassysuites.com. ✆ **800/362-2779** or 602/955-3992. 232 suites. High season $199–$309; low season $109–$159. Rates include full breakfast and afternoon drinks. Parking $12. Pets accepted ($40 fee).

Amenities: Restaurant; lounge; babysitting; bikes; concierge; exercise room; Jacuzzi; outdoor pool; room service; Wi-Fi ($10 per day).

INEXPENSIVE

Extended Stay America Phoenix-Biltmore ★ Billing itself as a "temporary residence," this hotel just north of Camelback Road (not far from Biltmore Fashion Park) consists of studio-style apartments; discounts kick in for stays of 7 days or more. Maid service is once a week, though fresh towels are always available. While it's designed primarily for corporate business travelers in town for long projects, this lodging makes a good choice for families as well. All units have full kitchens, big bathrooms, and separate sitting areas, and there's a laundry available.

5235 N. 16th St., Phoenix. www.extendedstaydeluxe.com. ✆ **800/804-3724** or 602/265-6800. 112 units. High season $140 double, summer $65 double. Rates include continental breakfast. Pets accepted ($25 per night, $150 max). **Amenities:** Exercise room; Jacuzzi; outdoor pool; free Wi-Fi.

North Phoenix

Some of the Valley's best scenery is in north Phoenix; the mountains of the Tonto National Forest north of the city present an impressive vista. Lots of parks and preserves, and you're close to Lake Pleasant, too. But the Valley's best shopping and dining, as well as most major attractions, are all at least a 20-minute drive away.

MODERATE

JW Marriott Desert Ridge Resort & Spa ★ At this monumentally proportioned resort with two golf courses, convention groups, families, and golf fanatics wander through a towering lobby, which sits, airport-terminal style, at the hub of several large room wings. (There are nearly 1,000 rooms, comfortably if conventionally furnished.) The lobby looks out into an extravagant pool area, with all sorts of different places to sunbathe and a long lazy river for the kids to float around endlessly. There's a shopping mall nearby, with a collection of chain restaurants next to it, and the Musical Instrument Museum (p. 151) is close, but other major shopping or dining areas are 15 or 20 minutes away.

5350 E. Marriott Blvd., Phoenix. www.jwdesertridgeresort.com. ✆ **800/835-6206** or 480/293-5000. 950 units. High season $299–$499 double, $499–$699 suite; summer $159–$199 double, $359–$399 suite. $35 daily resort fee. Valet parking $29; self-parking $10. **Amenities:** 7 restaurants; 4 lounges; babysitting; bikes; children's programs; concierge; 2 18-hole golf courses; health club and full-service spa; 2 Jacuzzis; 5 pools; room service; 8 tennis courts; Wi-Fi (included in resort fee).

Pointe Hilton Squaw Peak Resort ★★ At the foot of the Phoenix Mountains, this lushly landscaped midline resort makes a big splash with its 4-acre Hole-in-the-Wall River Ranch aquatic playground, which features a lazy river, a water slide, a waterfall, a sports pool, and a lagoon pool. Lots of kids programs, too. The resort is done in a Spanish villa style, and most of the accommodations are large two-room suites. For a family vacation, this place is hard to beat. Also check out its sister resort nearby, the Pointe Hilton Tapatio Cliffs Resort (below); guests in each have access to the other's facilities.

7677 N. 16th St., Phoenix. www.squawpeakhilton.com. © **800/947-9784** or 602/997-2626. 563 suites. High season $293–$386 suite, $417–$709 casita; summer $133–$169 suite, $203–$662 casita. $28 daily resort fee includes Wi-Fi. Valet $10. Pets accepted ($75 fee). **Amenities:** 3 restaurants; 2 snack bars; 5 lounges; babysitting; children's programs; concierge; health club and small full-service spa; 7 Jacuzzis; 8 pools; room service; 3 tennis courts; Wi-Fi (included in resort fee).

Pointe Hilton Tapatio Cliffs Resort ★ If you love to lounge by the pool, then this resort is a great choice. The Falls, a 3½-acre water playground, includes two pools, a 138-foot water slide, 40-foot cascades, and a whirlpool tucked into an artificial grotto. There's also a miniature golf course. If you're a hiker, you can head out on the trails of the adjacent North Mountain Recreation Area. All rooms are spacious suites with southwest-inspired furnishings; corner units are particularly bright. This resort has steep walkways, so you need to be in good shape to stay here. At the top of the property is **Different Pointe of View,** a continental restaurant with one of the finest views in the city. This resort is more adult-oriented than the Pointe Hilton Squaw Peak Resort (see above), but otherwise is similar.

11111 N. 7th St., Phoenix. www.pointehilton.com. © **800/876-4683** or 602/866-7500. 563 suites. High season $179–$359 suite; summer $129–$239 suite. $28 daily resort fee includes valet parking. Pets accepted ($75 fee). **Amenities:** 3 restaurants; lounge; children's programs; concierge; 18-hole golf course; exercise room; 4 Jacuzzis; 5 pools; room service; full-service spa; 2 tennis courts; Wi-Fi (included in resort fee).

INEXPENSIVE

Best Western InnSuites Phoenix ★ It's not in the center of things, but it is just a block off Ariz. 51, which puts you on the Camelback Corridor in 3 minutes and downtown in 10. The Dreamy Draw Recreation Area, Piestewa Peak, and the Phoenix Mountain preserves are all basically next door, too (see "Hiking," p. 89). Rooms are modern, attractively furnished, and have plush, pillowtop beds—and I give this hotel props, too, for taking out the "Biltmore" it used to have in its name. (It's a long way from the Biltmore.) With its breakfast buffet, evening snacks, and large rooms, this is a fairly economical place to stay with the kids.

1615 E. Northern Ave. www.bestwestern.com/phoenix. © **602/997-6285.** 111 units. High season up to $200 double, summer $65 double. Rates include full breakfast and evening social hour. Pets accepted ($20 per night). **Amenities:** Exercise room; Jacuzzi; outdoor pool, free Wi-Fi.

Downtown, South Phoenix & the Airport Area

Phoenix's downtown has exploded in the last 10 years. ASU, the light rail, sport facilities, and all manner of new clubs have contributed to make it a decent place to hang out for a few days—and finally, there are a couple of nice hotels to experience it all from. There are a few midline hotels around the airport, but nothing special. And there are a few fun places to stay in south Phoenix and points south.

EXPENSIVE

Palomar ★★ This Kimpton hotel is as hip as downtown Phoenix gets—a high-rise four-star hotel, and all part of a mixed-use downtown redevelopment that includes stores, restaurants, clubs, and more. The rooms are contemporary and stylish with a midcentury modern feel. The hotel's **Blue Hound** restaurant—it calls itself "an American gastro-lounge with a southern twist"—is a worthy destination dining spot in its own right, and the attached bar is a lively but not overwhelming hang. The lounge on the roof, **Lustre,** is where you go for real high energy.

2 E. Jefferson St., in the CityScape development. hwww.hotelpalomar-phoenix.com. ✆ **877/488-1908** or 602/253-6633. 242 units. High season $338 double, $387 suite; summer $220 double; $232 suite. Valet parking $32, self-parking $25. Pets accepted. **Amenities:** 2 restaurants; 2 lounges; bikes; concierge; fitness center; pool; room service; free Wi-Fi.

Westin Phoenix Downtown ★★ You know what a Westin is, and this is a classic Westin. Calm, reliable, professional. There are not many high-rise hotels in Phoenix; this one gives you great views to the north. You're right at the heart of downtown and you can walk to everything from the sports stadiums to Roosevelt Row. **Province,** the restaurant, is as classy and reserved as the hotel.

333 N. Central Ave. www.westinphoenixdowntown.com. ✆ **602/429-3500.** High season $380–$450 double, $480–$550 suite; summer $78–$118 double; $198–$269 suite. Valet parking $32. Pets accepted. **Amenities:** 2 restaurants; lounge; children's programs; concierge; fitness center; Jacuzzi; pool; room service; Wi-Fi ($10 per day).

MODERATE

Arizona Grand Resort ★★ This sprawling resort, which renovated all of its rooms 2 years ago, abuts the 17,000-acre South Mountain Park and is one of the best choices in the Valley for families. These guys win the Water Park Wars: If I were a 12-year-old, I would beg my parents to stay here and spend every day playing in the wave pool, a lazy river, a towering water slide, and two free-fall–style water slides. There are also numerous children's programs. The guest rooms, all suites, feature contemporary southwestern furnishings and lots of space. **Rustler's Rooste** (p. 153), the resort's fun cowboy steakhouse, serves rattlesnake appetizers and is a favorite with families.

8000 S. Arizona Grand Pkwy., Phoenix. www.arizonagrandresort.com. ✆ **877/800-4888** or 602/438-9000. 744 units. High season $303–$533 suite; summer $160–$269 suite. $50 daily resort fee. **Amenities:** 5 restaurants; 3 lounges; babysitting; bikes; children's programs; concierge; 18-hole golf course; health club and full-service spa; 9 Jacuzzis; 7 outdoor pools (including 7-acre water park); room service; Wi-Fi (included in resort fee).

Sheraton Wild Horse Pass Resort & Spa ★ Attached to the Indian casino south of Phoenix on the way to Tucson, this resort is owned by the

Maricopa and Pima tribes, who go out of their way to share their culture with resort guests. The back of the casino looks off onto miles of undeveloped reservation land, so from certain perspectives it has a remote feel. Throw in horseback riding, a full-service spa featuring desert-inspired treatments, two golf courses, a nature trail along a 2½-mile-long artificial river, a pool with a water slide, and of course the casino, and you'll find plenty to keep you busy. Guest rooms have great beds, small patios, and large bathrooms. The menu in **Kai** (p. 134), the main dining room, focuses on indigenous Southwestern flavors.

5594 W. Wild Horse Pass Blvd., Chandler. www.wildhorsepassresort.com. ✆ **602/225-0100.** 500 units. High season $250–$300 double, $429–$629 suite; summer $175–$200 double; $325–$425 suite. Valet parking $22. Pets accepted. **Amenities:** 5 restaurants; 4 lounges; children's programs; concierge; 2 18-hole golf courses; health club and full-service spa; 5 Jacuzzis; 4 outdoor pools; room service; 2 tennis courts; Wi-Fi ($12 per day).

INEXPENSIVE

The Clarendon Hotel ★ This is the hip place to stay on the Central Corridor, favored by sophisticated travelers, traveling rock bands, and the like. Guest rooms are done in a sort of budget contemporary that will appeal to the young and artistic. The center courtyard boasts a giant hot tub and a gorgeous pool with gold- and platinum-coated tiles, dozens of fountains that spray water into the pool, and underwater speakers. Definitely a see-and-be-seen pool scene. The restaurant and cocktail bar are designed to appeal to young night-clubbers and fashionistas, and there's a rooftop lounge for sunset cocktails. It's been constantly upgraded over the past decade and now even has a spa.

401 W. Clarendon Ave., Phoenix. www.goclarendon.com. ✆ **602/252-7363.** 105 units. High season $150–$190 double, $250–$275 suite; summer $84–$104 double, $104–$150 suite. $20 daily resort fee, $10 parking fee. Pets free. **Amenities:** Restaurant; lounge; concierge; exercise room; Jacuzzi; outdoor pool; room service; Wi-Fi (included in resort fee).

Tempe, Mesa & the East Valley

Tempe, just southeast of the airport, is home to giant Arizona State University and has the nightlife scene you'd expect, centered on Mill Avenue just south of the Salt River in the northwest part of town. Tempe is also convenient to Papago Park, home to the Phoenix Zoo, the Desert Botanical Garden, a municipal golf course, and hiking and mountain-biking trails. And central Scottsdale is just a few miles up the road.

MODERATE

Aloft Tempe ★ At the Aloft chain, a budget wing of über-hip W hotels, you get a high-ceilinged room with big windows and modern decor. It's tucked in between the north bank of the Gila River and the 202 highway on the far eastern edge of ASU proper, so you're not going to be walking to any ASU meetings, and remember that parking at ASU is something of a hassle.

But it is the most interesting place to stay if you're doing work at the university's research park, SkySong, 2 miles north up Scottsdale Road. Aloft has a LEED certification and offers special amenities for kids (goodie bags, special kid bedding, a splash pool).

951 E. Playa del Norte Dr., Tempe. www.alofthotels.com/tempe. ✆ **877/462-5638** or 480/621-3300. 136 units. High season $140–$159; summer $99–$109. Pets accepted. **Amenities:** Concierge; exercise room; outdoor pool; free Wi-Fi.

Crowne Plaza San Marcos Golf Resort ★ Built in 1912, the San Marcos is the oldest golf resort in Arizona, with a classic Mission-revival styling that looks great after a recent upgrade. I love the timeless feel of this resort's palm-shaded courtyards. Guest rooms are simply furnished and nothing special, but they've been kept up to date. You'll want to spend your time splashing around in the pool when you aren't playing tennis or golf. Downtown Chandler, where the San Marcos is located, has been undergoing a renaissance in recent years. There are now art galleries and some decent restaurants on the blocks north and south of the hotel.

1 San Marcos Place, Chandler. www.sanmarcosresort.com. ✆ **800/528-8071** or 480/812-0900. 263 units. High season $145–$177 double; summer $91–$117. $15 daily resort fee. Pets accepted ($25 fee). **Amenities:** 2 restaurants; 2 lounges; concierge; 18-hole golf course; exercise room; Jacuzzi; outdoor pool; room service; 2 tennis courts; Wi-Fi (included in resort fee).

Gold Canyon Golf Resort ★ Golfers willing to stay way out on the eastern outskirts of the Valley of the Sun (a 30- to 45-minute drive from the airport) will be thrilled by the economical room rates and great golf at this resort. At the foot of the Superstition Mountains, Gold Canyon is a favorite of golfers for its exceedingly scenic holes. The spacious guest rooms are housed in pueblo-inspired buildings; some have fireplaces, while others have whirlpools. The deluxe golf-course rooms are definitely worth the higher rates. If you're here primarily to play golf and don't have a fortune to spend, this is *the* place to stay.

6100 S. Kings Ranch Rd., Gold Canyon. www.gcgr.com. ✆ **480/982-9090.** 85 units. High season $260 double, $300 suite; summer $115 double, $200 suite. $16 daily resort fee. Children 18 and under stay free in parent's room. Dogs accepted ($25 per day, max. $75). **Amenities:** Restaurant; lounge; concierge; 2 18-hole golf courses; exercise room; Jacuzzi; pool; full-service spa; Wi-Fi (included in resort fee).

Tempe Mission Palms Hotel ★ With a great location just off Tempe's lively Mill Avenue, and guest rooms decorated in shades of beige and brown, this is the perfect choice for a fun-filled weekend in Tempe. It works for business travelers (there are ergonomic desk chairs), but with a rooftop pool, tennis court, and nightlife right outside the front door, it's also a great choice for active travelers. It's also the best hotel within walking distance of ASU.

60 E. 5th St., Tempe. www.missionpalms.com. ✆ **800/547-8705** or 480/894-1400. 303 units. High season $149–$299 double, $269–$399 suite; summer $99–$109 double, $219–$239 suite. $17 daily resort fee includes valet parking. Pets accepted ($100 deposit, $25 per day). **Amenities:** Restaurant; lounge; concierge; fitness room; 2 Jacuzzis; outdoor pool; room service, Wi-Fi (included in resort fee).

INEXPENSIVE

Apache Boulevard in Tempe running east becomes Main Street in Mesa, and along this stretch of road there are numerous old motels charging some of the lowest rates in the Valley. However, these motels are very hit-or-miss. If you're intent on staying at non-chain motels, you might want to cruise this strip and check out a few places. Otherwise, look for the chain motels that dot the East Valley, particularly near the numerous freeway off-ramps.

Dobson Ranch Inn Resort ★ This aging budget resort isn't luxurious, but it has just about everything a sun-starved winter visitor could ask for—green lawns, flower gardens, palm trees, and a big pool surrounded by lounge chairs. The location, right off U.S. 60 at the junction with U.S. 101, makes this resort convenient for exploring the Valley; downtown Scottsdale is 10 minutes away. Guest rooms are simply furnished yet quite modern, and although they are more functional than fancy, the grounds more than make up for unremarkable rooms.

1666 S. Dobson Rd., Mesa. www.dobsonranchinnresort.com. ✆ **480/831-7000.** 213 units. $51–$120 double. Rates include full breakfast. Pets accepted ($50 deposit). **Amenities:** Restaurant; lounge; exercise room; 2 Jacuzzis; outdoor pool; room service; free Wi-Fi.

West Valley

EXPENSIVE

The Wigwam Golf Resort & Spa ★★ Located 20 minutes west of downtown Phoenix and more than twice that far from Scottsdale, this property, which opened its doors to the public in 1929, is a sleeper among the nation's premier golf resorts. It's a classic, old-money sort of place that makes a great golf getaway; its lower prices reflect the fact that it's inconveniently located for anyone planning on visiting museums and galleries or eating out. With its green lawns, tall palms, flower gardens, and Santa Fe–style buildings, the resort is a neatly manicured world unto itself. Guest rooms are spacious and feature southwestern furniture and plush beds, and some units have fireplaces. The traditional-style golf courses here are the main attraction, and the rooms to request are those along the fairways. In addition to the golf courses, there's the enormous LeMonds–Aveda Salon.

300 E. Wigwam Blvd., Litchfield Park. www.wigwamarizona.com. ✆ **800/327-0396** or 623/935-3811. 331 units. High season $241–$309 double, $334 suite; summer $110–$140 double, $150 suite. $30 daily resort fee includes valet parking. Pets accepted ($25 per day per pet). **Amenities:** 3 restaurants; poolside snack bar; 4 lounges; babysitting; children's programs; concierge; 3 18-hole golf courses; health club and full-service spa; 3 Jacuzzis; 3 pools; room service; 9 tennis courts; Wi-Fi (included in resort fee).

WHERE TO EAT

Phoenix is growing up, and there are decent-to-excellent restaurants throughout the Valley. The big story in the restaurant scene here is the recent mini-explosion of **mid-priced locally owned eateries:** There are dozens popping up everywhere, sometimes with sister operations overseen by the same chef

Alo Cafe **34**
Arcadia Farms **34**
Barrio Café Gran Reserva **7**
Binkley's **37**
Bourbon Steak **16**
Bryan's Black Mountain Barbecue **20**
Caffe Boa **40**
Café Lalibela **43**
Chelsea's Kitchen **29**
The Chuckbox **42**
Compass Arizona Grill **11**
Cowboy Ciao Wine **33**
Delux **25**
Deseo **18**
El Chorro Lodge **21**
Elements at Sanctuary Camelback Mountain **23**
English Rose Tea Room **19**
The Farm Kitchen **39**
FnB **33**
Frank & Lupe's **34**
Fry Bread House **5**
Gallo Blanco **9**
Geordie's **26**
Guedo's Taco Shop **47**
House of Tricks **41**
Joe's Farm Grill **47**
Joe's Real BBQ **48**
Kai **46**
Khyber Halal **36**
La Grande Orange Pizzeria **31**
Lo-Lo's Chicken & Waffles **13**
Lon's at the Hermosa **24**
Los Dos Molinos **15**
Malee's Thai Bistro **34**
Marcellino's **33**
The Mission **35**
Nobuo at Teeter House **12**
Old Town Tortilla Factory **34**
Organ Stop Pizza **45**
The Original Blue Adobe Grille **44**
The Parlor **27**
Phoenix Public Market **10**
Pizzeria Bianco **12**
Quiessence at the Farm **39**
Rancho Pinot **22**
Red Thai **1**
Richardson's **2**
Southern Rail **3**
The Stand **30**
St. Francis **4**
The Stockyards Restaurant **38**
T Bone Steakhouse **14**
T. Cook's **32**
Tuck Shop **8**
Vincent on Camelback **28**
Vincent Market Bistro **28**
Woody's Macayo **6**
Zinc Bistro **17**

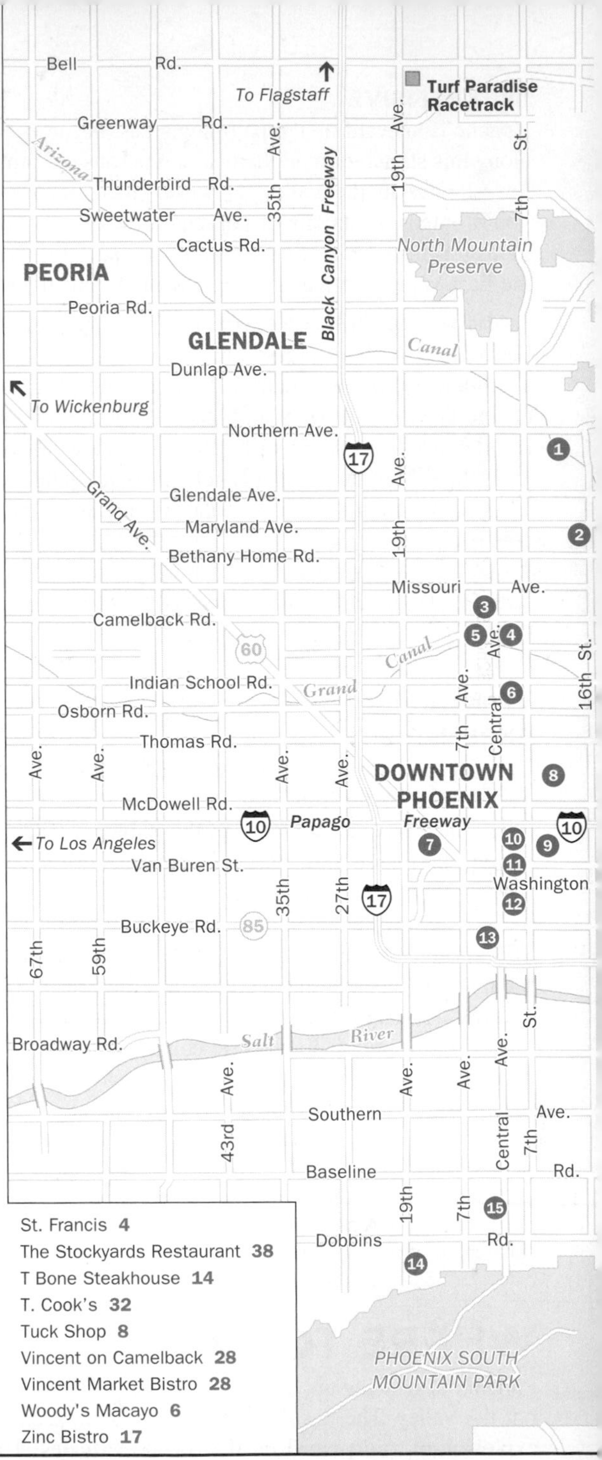

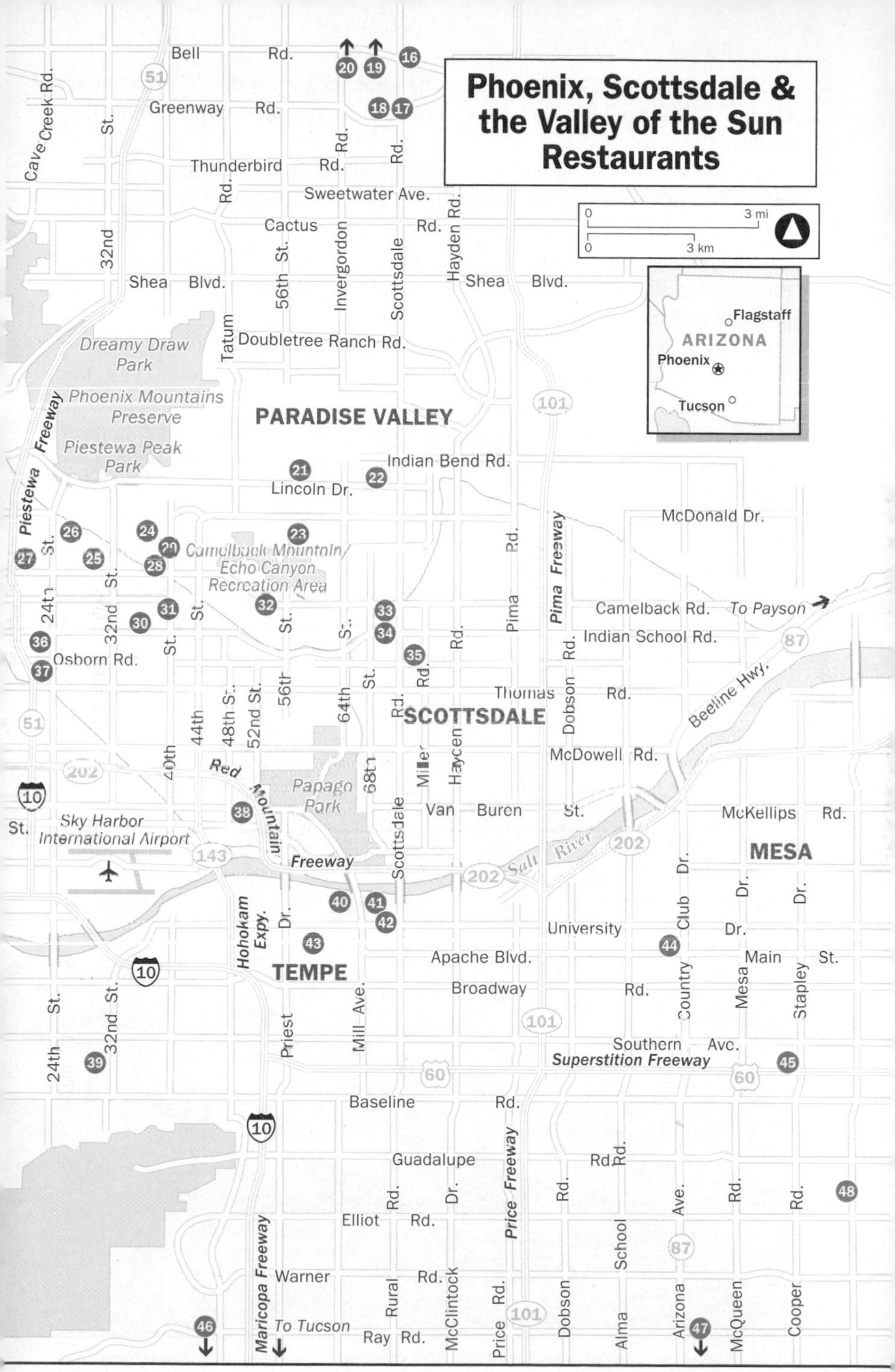
Phoenix, Scottsdale & the Valley of the Sun Restaurants
0 3 mi
0 3 km
Flagstaff
ARIZONA
Phoenix
Tucson
Bell Rd.
Greenway Rd.
Thunderbird Rd.
Sweetwater Ave.
Cactus Rd.
Shea Blvd.
Doubletree Ranch Rd.
Cave Creek Rd.
32nd St.
Tatum Rd.
56th St.
Invergordon Rd.
Scottsdale Rd.
Hayden Rd.
Dreamy Draw Park
Phoenix Mountains Preserve
Piestewa Peak Park
Piestewa Freeway
PARADISE VALLEY
Indian Bend Rd.
Lincoln Dr.
McDonald Dr.
Camelback Mountain/ Echo Canyon Recreation Area
Camelback Rd.
To Payson
Indian School Rd.
Osborn Rd.
Thomas Rd.
SCOTTSDALE
McDowell Rd.
Beeline Hwy.
Pima Rd.
Pima Freeway
Dobson Rd.
24th St.
40th St.
44th St.
48th St.
52nd St.
64th St.
68th St.
Miller Rd.
Hayden Rd.
Red Mountain Freeway
Papago Park
Van Buren St.
McKellips Rd.
Sky Harbor International Airport
Salt River
MESA
University Dr.
Country Club Dr.
Mesa Dr.
Stapley Dr.
Hohokam Expy.
Priest Dr.
Apache Blvd.
Main St.
TEMPE
Broadway Rd.
Mill Ave.
Southern Ave.
Superstition Freeway
Baseline Rd.
Guadalupe Rd.
Elliot Rd.
Warner Rd.
Ray Rd.
To Tucson
Maricopa Freeway
Rural Rd.
McClintock Dr.
Price Freeway
Price Rd.
Dobson Rd.
Alma School Rd.
Arizona Ave.
McQueen Rd.
Cooper Rd.

or local organization, or clustered in the same area. (See the "Camelback & Central: Mid-Priced Menus Galore" box, p. 124, for an example of how this plays out.)

On the upscale restaurant front, a major player these days is a company called **Fox** (which insists on calling its restaurants "concepts," but don't hold that against them). They've got a cottage industry of top-end eateries, each with its own approach and theme, but united in never-miss food, good value for the price, and a highly professional staff. See "The Fox Connection" box, p. 119, for details.

One final note: Some of the more conscientious restaurants devoted to healthy eating offer reasonably sized portions; but it's not uncommon in the Valley to be served an entrée big enough for two or even three people. If you're not interested in having a gigantic meal, ask your waiter about portion sizes; from many area restaurants, couples can emerge well fed splitting a single entree.

Scottsdale

EXPENSIVE

Cowboy Ciao ★★ SOUTHWESTERN/NEW AMERICAN A fun cowboy-chic atmosphere and delicious food with a global influence marks this longtime Scottsdale favorite. Your group has to start with the Stetson chopped

Postino's wine bar is one of several local mini-chains thriving in the casual, mid-priced dining niche.

salad, with its uncanny ingredients—couscous, corn, tomatoes, salmon, lots more—laid out in stripes across the generously sized bowl. Big wine list, lively bar.

7133 E. Stetson Dr. (at 6th Ave.). www.cowboyciao.com. ✆ **480/946-3111.** Reservations recommended. Main courses $13–$15 lunch, $27–$39 dinner. Daily 11:30am–2:30pm and 5–10pm.

El Chorro Lodge ★ NEW AMERICAN This Arizona landmark has been a restaurant for 80 years—back when everything around it was desert—and is set up to display the splendor of Camelback and Mummy mountains as well as any eatery in Paradise Valley. (Despite the name, it's not a hotel.) Weekend brunches are among the most popular meals here, partly due to the meltingly warm sticky buns served with every order. The dinner menu is classic American, done with brio—trout almandine, steaks, beef stroganoff, rack of lamb and the like—with a nod or two to non-carnivores, like seafood pasta and a polenta-and-vegetable Napoleon.

5550 E. Lincoln Dr., Paradise Valley. www.elchorro.com. ✆ **480/948-5170.** Reservations recommended. Main courses $25–$21 lunch, $25–$45 dinner. Mon–Fri 11am–2pm and 5–10pm; Sat 11am–3pm and 5–10pm; Sun 9am–3pm and 5–10pm.

Elements at Sanctuary Camelback Mountain ★★ NEW AMERICAN The view here from the north side of Camelback Mountain is delicious, and the food is as well, a high-end handling of some basic dishes, with a sophisticated Asian patina (seven spice marlin, Kurobuta pork chop with a hoisin glaze). Make sure you make your reservation for sunset time. If you'll be eating inside, try to get one of the lower-level booths.

At Sanctuary Camelback Mountain Resort, 5700 E. McDonald Dr., Paradise Valley. www.sanctuaryoncamelback.com. ✆ **800/245-2051** or 480/948-2100. Reservations recommended. Main courses $11–$23 lunch, $39–$68 dinner. Breakfast 7–11am, lunch 11:30am–2pm, dinner 5:30–9:30pm (until 10pm Fri–Sat); Sun brunch 7am–2pm.

FnB ★★ NEW AMERICAN This is about as good as Valley dining gets—fresh and adventurous ingredients, locally sourced, with a devotion to Arizona wines that has opened up palates across the Valley. Chef Charlene Badman has a way of transforming the familiar into the fabulous, allowing each vegetable and fruit to stand up and take a turn in the spotlight. The menu—which changes constantly, depending on what Badman finds—mixes standards like chicken or Brussels sprouts or blueberries or shrimp—with unusual herbs, seasonings, and sauces. It's not a meat 'n' potatoes kind of place. Anyone interested in what one of the state's best chefs is doing on any particular evening is urged to check it out.

7133 E. Stetson Dr. www.fnbrestaurant.com. ✆ **480/284-4777.** Reservations recommended. Main courses $22–$33. Tues–Sat 5–10pm, Sun 5–9pm. Closed Mon–Wed June-Aug.

Marcellino ★ ITALIAN Forget trendy or hip—this is pure Italian, from Chef Marcellino Verzino, who now and again is noted as one of the Valley chefs who do Italian best. Verzino and his wife Sima made their rep drawing fans to an indifferent corner of north Phoenix; in 2010 they were induced down to the tony Waterfront in Scottsdale and provide some much-needed culinary seriousness. The staff can deliver some knockout wines—red, Italians, of course—to go with the meals. Don't overthink things: Get any of Marcellino's pastas and you'll be fine. Wife Sima sings with a jazz trio Thursdays and Friday; she's great but it's not conducive for a quiet conversation, so ask to sit outside if that's what you need.

7114 E. Stetson Dr., Scottsdale www.marcellinoristorante.com. ✆ **480/990-9500.** Reservations recommended. Main courses $22–$38. Mon–Sat 11am–11pm; Sun noon–10pm.

The Mission ★ NUEVO LATINO With its Spanish colonial decor and back-lit wall of salt blocks, this downtown Scottsdale restaurant melds old-world decor and cuisine with a modern aesthetic. Taking its name from the historic adobe church next door, the Mission is best for a light graze. I like to get a few appetizers and a drink and call it a meal. Try the duck *carnitas empanadas,* the pineapple-glazed pork shoulder tacos, or the Peruvian clam stew. The fries here should not be missed. The bar emphasizes its extensive tequila selection and makes a great margarita. If the weather is good, get a seat on the small patio out front.

3815 N. Brown Ave. www.themissionaz.com. ✆ **480/636-5005.** Reservations recommended. Main courses $12–$18 lunch, $22–$36 dinner. Sun–Thurs 11am–10pm; Fri–Sat 11am–10:30pm.

Rancho Pinot ★★ NEW AMERICAN Rancho Pinot, tucked away in a shopping center at Scottsdale Road and Lincoln Avenue, combines a homey cowboy-chic decor with contemporary American cuisine, and has long been a favorite with the moneyed locals of North Scottsdale and Paradise Valley. Its secret is owner-chef Chrysa Robertson, who seems to be making comfort food—like the must-try Nonni's Sunday Chicken—but is really delivering comfort *cuisine,* using local products and putting them all together with grace and a lack of pretense.

In Lincoln Village Shops, 6208 N. Scottsdale Rd. (SW corner Scottsdale Rd. and Lincoln Dr.). www.ranchopinot.com. ✆ **480/367-8030.** Reservations recommended. Main courses $22–$36. Daily 5:30–9pm (closed Mon–Tues Jun-Aug).

Zinc Bistro ★ FRENCH In one of those not-quite-clear-on-the-concept Phoenix things, Zinc refers to itself as "a true New York–style Parisian bistro." I'm not sure what that means, but Zinc does have a French flair, from the zinc bar to the sidewalk cafe seating to the hooks under the bar for ladies' purses. Try the *moules marinieres* or the crab-and-truffle omelet, both of which come with addictive shoestring potatoes. Steak eaters should be sure to try the melt-in-your-mouth *sous vide* steak, which is cooked for hours in a vacuum bag. For dessert, there is decadent chocolate soufflé.

In Kierland Commons, 15034 N. Scottsdale Rd. www.zincbistroaz.com. ✆ **480/603-0922.** Reservations recommended. Main courses $14–$25 lunch, $18–$42 dinner. Daily 11am–10pm.

The Fox Connection

The local restaurant company Fox has developed winners all over the Valley. There's **Olive & Ivy** (p. 152) at the Scottsdale Fashion Square mall, which offers hip fine dining; **North** (www.northitaliarestaurant.com; ✆ **480/948-2055**), a decent casual Italian restaurant at the Kierland Mall; **Culinary Dropout** (www.culinarydropout.com; ✆ **602/680-4040**), an upbeat, more raucous joint for classic American burgers and the like, ideal for groups looking for a good time; and several more. Bottom line is that these are all very safe bets if, say, you're in a group with some folks who are hard to please. You can check them all out at **www.foxrc.com**.

MODERATE

Arcadia Farms ★ NEW AMERICAN Long a favorite of the Scottsdale ladies-who-breakfast-and-lunch crowd, this Old Town restaurant features well-prepared contemporary fare. Try the delicious raspberry goat cheese salad with jicama and candied pecans, or the warm mushroom, spinach, and goat-cheese tart. Ask for a seat on the shady patio.

7014 E. 1st Ave. www.arcadiafarmscafe.com. ✆ **480/941-5665.** Reservations recommended. Main courses $12–$15. Breakfast Mon–Fri 7–11am, Sat–Sun 7–11:30am. Lunch Mon–Fri 11:30am–2:30pm, Sat–Sun noon–2:30pm.

Malee's Thai Bistro ★ THAI While there are now upscale Asian restaurants all over the Valley, this was one of the first to move the spicy flavors of Asia out from under fluorescent lights and into a setting that would impress a date. The decor is not as over-the-top as at the nearby P.F. Chang's (which got its start here in Scottsdale), but it is certainly elegant for a Thai restaurant, an ideal place for lunch or dinner during a day of gallery hopping. Start with the creamy *tom ka gai,* then be sure to try the spicy crispy fish or the tropical pineapple dish (seafood and chicken curry served in a half-pineapple).

7131 E. Main St. www.maleesthaibistro.com. ✆ **480/947-6042.** Reservations recommended. Main courses $12–$22. Mon–Sat 11am–9am; Sun 4:30–9pm.

Old Town Tortilla Factory ★ MEXICAN Located in an old house surrounded by attractive patios and citrus trees that bloom winter and spring, this Mexican restaurant has great atmosphere, good food, and a lively bar scene (with more than 120 premium tequilas). As you enter the restaurant grounds, you might even see someone making fresh tortillas, which come in two dozen different flavors. Rich tortilla soup and the tequila-lime salad make good starters. For an entree, try pork chops crusted with ancho chili powder and raspberry sauce.

6910 E. Main St. www.oldtowntortillafactory.com. ✆ **480/945-4567.** No reservations. Main courses $14–$29. Sun–Thurs 5–9pm; Fri–Sat 5–10pm.

INEXPENSIVE

Alo Cafe ★ EUROPEAN This little cafe tucked in a courtyard down the street from the Hotel Valley Ho (p. 102) is one of my favorite places for coffee,

We All Scream for Ice Cream

If you have kids, you have to make a stop at Scottsdale's **Sugar Bowl,** 4005 N. Scottsdale Rd. (www.sugarbowlscottsdale.com; ✆ **480/946-0051**), in the heart of Old Town Scottsdale. You can't miss it; the pink facade is visible from a block away, and you feel a bit like you're walking into a cotton-candy machine. But this venerable Valley outfit, made famous in local Bil Keane's "Family Circus" cartoons many decades ago, makes for a fun visit for ice cream lovers of all ages.

Another longtime Phoenix outfit is **Mary Coyle,** recently moved to 5823 N. Seventh St. (www.marycoyle.net; ✆ **602/626-5996**), which makes its own ice cream and has been in business for more than 50 years. The hip gelato hangout **Gelato Spot,** 3164 E. Camelback Rd. (www.gelatospot.com; ✆ **602/957-8040**) serves both Arcadia and the Biltmore.

The best ice cream in town, however, is at **Sweet Republic:** Its deep texture and clever flavors (from all the basics to flights of fancy like Peaberry Espresso and Honey Lavender) have gotten national attention. Each day's flavors are kept up-to-date on the website. Sweet Republic (www.sweetrepublic.com) has two shops, in Scottsdale (9160 E. Shea Blvd.; ✆ **480/248-6979**) and Phoenix (6054 N. 16th St.; ✆ **602/535-5990**). Both places look pretty utilitarian; once you taste the ice cream, you won't care.

breakfast, or a quick bite removed from Scottsdale's tourist crowds. The Estonian owners named the cafe after Estonian composer Alo Mattiissen. There's not a lot of exotica here, just many delicious things to eat, from the interesting to the basic, from yummy breakfast dishes (corn-flake–crusted French toast, Estonian dessert bread, omelets) to a variety of lunch sandwiches.

6950 E. 1st St. www.alcafeaz.com. ✆ **480/878-4172.** Main courses $7.50–$13.50. Daily 7am–2pm.

Frank & Lupe's ★ MEXICAN On the same street as some of Scottsdale's top contemporary art galleries, this casual Mexican joint is a welcome throwback to the days when Scottsdale was still a real cowtown. It's a family place, with all the chilis grown in New Mexico. If possible, eat on the back patio; it feels so much like a restaurant patio in Mexico that you'll be shocked to find you're still in Scottsdale at the end of your meal.

4121 N. Marshall Way. www.frankandlupes.com. ✆ **480/990-9844.** No reservations. Main courses $9–$16. Daily 11am–9pm.

North Scottsdale, Carefree & Cave Creek

EXPENSIVE

Bourbon Steak ★★★ STEAK One of celebrated chef Michael Mina's steakhouses, this posh place is a top resort eatery and worth visiting even if you're not staying at the Fairmont. If you've never had beef tartare, this is the place to try it, and for a delicious twist on an old favorite, try the lobster pot pie—at a market price that can get close to $100. Everything's good, like the *jidori* chicken with roman gnocchi and kohlrabi, and the crab tortelloni. Obviously, however, steaks are the thing here. Keep in mind that the steaks are served a la carte, and there are lots of tempting side dishes and accompaniments.

At the Fairmont Scottsdale, 7575 E. Princess Dr. (12 mi N of downtown Scottsdale). www.scottsdaleprincess.com. ✆ **480-585-2694.** Reservations highly recommended. Main courses $35–$160. Open daily 5:30–9pm (Fri–Sat until 9:30pm).

deseo ★★★ NUEVO LATINO Never mind that this is a hotel restaurant (in a big Westin): The menu and overall experience makes it worth dining here whether you're staying at the hotel or not (and worth walking over to if you're in the Kierland Commons Mall next door). Get ready for a heady mix of Asian and Mexican. You enter down a hushed stairwell with Japanese lanterns lighting your way; the luscious, crimson-drenched dining room surrounds an open kitchen with seating around it. It feels like . . . a sushi bar, really, but the specialty here is ceviche, a kaleidoscopic list of which, all delectable, is one of the high points of the menu. The meat and seafood dishes are all done with verve—like the 24 Hour Wagyu Shortrib with black garlic lacquer, jalepeño chimichurri, and crispy Brussels sprouts. For dessert, get the Oasis—a medley of tropical flavors served in a mischievous glass terrarium.

Westin Kierland Resort, 6902 E. Greenway Pkwy. www.kierlandresort.com. ✆ **480/624-1202.** Reservations recommended. Main courses $27–$36. Wed–Sun 6–10pm.

MODERATE

English Rose Tea Room ★ BRITISH Decorated right to the point of the absurd—all that's missing is the queen's corgis—the English Rose attracts a great crowd, particularly on weekends, when ladies arrive in their big hats. The secret? Serving up both authenticity and surprisingly good food. The tea trappings—from the $28 Duchess of Bedford selection of petit fours, sandwiches, and scones, on down—will delight those aching to feel like they're in the London Ritz. The ham-and-cheese bread pudding or the salmon quiche will satisfy those wanting something more substantive. Do they have tea? Oh, my crumpets, do they have tea!

201 Easy St., Carefree. www.carefreetea.com. ✆ **480/488-4812.** Lunch $13–$18. Daily 11am–4pm.

INEXPENSIVE

Bryan's Black Mountain Barbecue ★ BARBECUE Cave Creek loves to play up its cowboy character, and nothing says "cowboy grub" quite like smoked meats. This little barbecue joint gets you in the cowboy mood with Western movie posters and old Hollywood Western movies projected on the wall. There's even a guitar on the wall with a sign that says play me. Just don't pick up the guitar until you're done with your half-rack of pork ribs or ribs and beef brisket combo. Don't despair if there's a vegetarian in your group; Bryan's has a "pulled" squash sandwich on the menu.

6130 E. Cave Creek Rd., Cave Creek. www.bryansbarbecue.com. ✆ **480/575-7155.** No reservations. Sandwiches $8.50–$12.50. Main courses $10–$23. Tues–Sat 11am–8pm.

Pizza, Phoenix-Style

Phoenix has become quite a decent pizza town. Some Chicago-style thick-crust interlopers have moved in—there's a Lou Malnati's at Central and Camelback in Uptown, and a Gino's East and a Giordano's or two as well. However, I recommend the homegrown, delectably chewy experiments some local chefs have produced in the realm of the thin crust.

The gold standard is, of course, **Pizzeria Bianco,** where Chef Chris Bianco has established a national reputation with his perfect crust and discriminating ingredients. There's often a wait at the main branch, downtown at Heritage Square (p. 152). There's also a highly enjoyable, more upscale Bianco location in the courtyard of the Town and Country Mall, 4743 N 20th St. (✆ **602/368-3273**), at the southeast corner of 20th Street and Camelback Road.

But there are more players these days. Kitty-corner from Town and Country, at 19th Street and Camelback, the upscale casual **Parlor** (p. 126) serves delectably sweet crusts in a converted midcentury modern building. On Central Avenue just 2 blocks north of Camelback Road, **Federal Pizza,** 5210 N. Central Ave. (✆ **602/795-2520**) serves another thin variant with toppings that pop. (Try the Big Star, with local sausage and peppers, or the Brussel Sprout, with pancetta and lemon zest.)

Downtown, for atmosphere and quality, you can't beat **Cibo,** 603 N. Fifth Ave. (✆ **602/441-2697**), set in an old downtown bungalow. Full bar, too. This is a great place for a romantic dinner in the glittering garden. And over in Arcadia, **La Grande Orange Pizzeria** (p. 126), the beating heart of Arcadia, produces an enjoyable thin crust—and in vegan and gluten-free forms as well.

Central Phoenix & the Camelback Corridor

EXPENSIVE

Binkley's ★★★ NEW AMERICAN Foodies up on the latest trends in molecular gastronomy will want to make sure they visit this little restaurant in a nondescript part of central Phoenix, where the Valley's most outlandish culinary wizard casts his thunderbolts. Chef Kevin Binkley, an eminence of the scene for years with several restaurants, has consolidated them all in this one very expensive one-of-a-kind dining experience. There is one seating per night for the restaurant's 20-something tables. Each course is announced and described; the number of courses can run into the dozens and may include trips to the kitchen to visit with Chef himself. It's a prix-fixe affair, lasting close to 4 hours, $180 per person, paid in advance; wine flights and add-ons like caviar can double that and more, and there's a 22% service charge, too. The restaurant says it can accommodate most dietary restrictions.

2320 E. Osborn Rd. www.binkleysrestaurant.com. ✆ **602/388-4874.** Reservations required. Prix-fixe $180; wine pairings $98–$200. Wed–Sat at 6:30pm.

Geordie's Restaurant ★★ FRENCH This previously inconsistent operation at an unbeatable locale—the enormous Wrigley Mansion, impressively perched on a hill high above the Biltmore—is now a must-visit. Chef Christopher Gross, known for his excellent restaurant Christopher's in the Biltmore Fashion Square, has taken over the food operation at the mansion and is in the midst of renovations, which among other things will include a new tasting restaurant to open sometime in 2019. For now, his classic French cooking and the massive mansion, with its various bars and porches and gardens, combine for an unmatchable evening. Foie gras is a must, as is the duck confit. De rigueur: The soufflés, which are generally Grand Marnier or chocolate; they take 30 minutes to prepare, so order them when your entrees arrive. ***Tip:*** Make a reservation for whenever sunset is, and arrive an hour earlier for drinks at the bar. Hang out on the porch and take in terrific Valley views as the sun says its goodbye. Then go in and see what Christopher has in store.

2501 E. Telawa Trail. www.wrigleymansion.com. ✆ **602/955-4079.** Tues–Sat 11am–9pm; Sun 10am–2pm; closed Mon (call for summer hours).

Lon's at the Hermosa ★ NEW AMERICAN This beautiful old adobe hacienda, built by cowboy artist Lon Megargee at his Hermosa Inn, is, along with El Chorro Lodge (p. 117), about as classically Arizona as you can get in its tranquil desert elegance. The spacious patio, protected by a giant mesquite, is a lovely place to dine or drink in the winter months, from brunch to dinner. The restaurant proper and its intimate, dark bar are cozy and romantic. Dishes often include herbs grown in the restaurant's own garden, and other ingredients are, as much as possible, from ecologically sound sources.

At the Hermosa Inn, 5532 N. Palo Cristi Rd. www.lons.com. ✆ **602/955-7878.** Reservations recommended. Main courses $10–$17 lunch, $26–$36 dinner. Mon–Fri 7–10am, 11am–2pm, and 5–10pm; Sat–Sun 7am–2pm and 5–10pm.

Richardson's ★★ NEW MEXICAN Restaurateur Richardson Browne is a Phoenix iconoclast. One of his restaurants doesn't even have a sign. (Called Dick's Hideaway, it's highly recommended for serious drinkers.) Another is called, for some reason, Rokerij—and Phoenix isn't a town that likes furrin-sounding names. Anyway, Richardson's flagship, just across the parking lot from Rokerij, has a no-nonsense name for a sensational experience, perfect for anyone who wants to explore the dark and dusky flavors of New Mexico Mexican food. Start with the New Mexico *con queso*, a cheese dip with spinach, onions, and chorizo. Someone in your party needs to get the roasted pork *mole*, that classic Mexican sauce with a base of chilis, allspice, and cloves that lends itself to extraordinary culinary experiments. Then poke around in the rest of the menu, with delightful interpretations of classic meals, like chicken cordon bleu with green chili and jalapeno hollandaise. It's lots of fun for brunch and lunch, which it serves daily. Some dishes are quite hot; the kitchen suggests you ask for a taste in advance if you're unsure whether you can take the heat. Richardson's Rule, as articulated on the menu: "You order it, you own it."

6335 N. 16th St. (at Maryland). www.richardsonsnm.com. ✆ **602/265-5886.** Reservations highly recommended. Main dinner courses $17–$44. Open Mon–Thurs 10am–10pm, Fri 10am–midnight, Sat 8am–midnight, Sun 8am–10pm.

T. Cook's ★★★ MEDITERRANEAN Resort dining is generally hit and miss, but this gracious, exquisitely operated restaurant combines a unique setting with first-rate food. Located within the Mediterranean-inspired Royal Palms Resort on Camelback Road, with that street's namesake mountain looming overhead, T. Cook's is surrounded by decades-old gardens—there are even palm trees growing through the roof of the romantic, ravishingly comfortable dining room. The menu—variants on Spanish food including a delectable paella and meticulously prepared seafood—is sublime. Desserts (including an insane aggregation of pistachio gelato, dark chocolate, and brandied cherries, or a Catalan-style crème bruleé) are heart-attack-inducing, and the service—in a town where, even at the best restaurants, waiters interrupt conversations, proudly present wine in glass decanters, and snatch dishes away the second you put down your fork—is the soul of discretion and tact.

At the Royal Palms Resort, 5200 E. Camelback Rd. www.royalpalmshotel.com. ✆ **602/808-0766.** Reservations highly recommended. Main courses $11–$16 lunch, $29–$52 dinner. Daily 6:30–10:30am, 11am–2pm, and 5:30–9:30pm (brunch Sun 6–10am).

Vincent on Camelback ★ FRENCH Vincent is a sui generis product of Phoenix. The chef—he goes by one name—is classically trained, but in his early years in the Valley began to explore southwestern ingredients. The menu is largely French traditional, but there are wonderful surprises in the starters, like a must-try duck tamale or the Anaheim chili stuffed with mushrooms and lobster. He's got an attached casual cafe, Vincent Market Bistro (p. 127), and on Saturday mornings in winter hosts an open-air French market, serving

Camelback & Central: Mid-Priced Menus Galore

In central Phoenix, at the uptown intersection of Camelback Road and Central Avenue, there's a profusion of mid-range dining options that would have been unthinkable 10 years ago. You can't miss with Chef Aaron Chamberlin's **St. Francis** (p. 126), an upscale boite with terrific food. Chamberlin also started the **Phoenix Public Market** (p. 129), probably your best eating bet around the ASU downtown campus, a few miles south, at Central and McKinley avenues. Also at Central and Camelback, in the Uptown Plaza strip mall, you'll find **Flower Child** (✆ **480/212-0180**), a vegetarian- and vegan-friendly upscale cafe; **Lou Malnati's** (✆ **602/892-9998**), deep-dish pizza imported from Chicago; a spacious breakfast joint called **Elly's** (✆ **602/603-9600**); and more.

Just a long block west from Camelback and Central, in an innovative complex called The Newton, you can find a cool new Cajun-y place called **Southern Rail** (below), next to the big independent bookstore Changing Hands; you can't go wrong with the gumbo or jambalaya here.

A quarter-mile north of Central and Camelback, there's a cluster of four restaurants at Central and Colter avenues from a local company called Upward: **JoyRide** (yummy tacos and Mexican, ✆ **602/274-8226**); **Federal Pizza** (yummy pizza and accompanying pasta dishes, p. 122); the **Windsor** (yummy American food, ✆ **602/279-1111**); and **Postino** (wine bar with food, ✆ **602/274-5144**). Park at the northeast corner of Central Avenue and Colter and take your pick—and then hit **Churn** (✆ **602/279-8024**), next door to the Windsor, for some homemade ice cream.

exquisite omelets and all manner of other fare, perfect if you're looking for a fun alternative to a stuffy brunch.

3930 E. Camelback Rd. vincentsoncamelback.com. ✆ **602/224-0225.** Reservations recommended. Main courses $32–$36 dinner. Tues–Sat 5–10pm.

MODERATE

Barrio Café Gran Reserva ★★★ HAUTE MEXICAN Chef Silvana Salcido Esparza is as distinctive a figure as the Phoenix food scene has produced, a deeply thoughtful impresario of Mexican cooking. She has basically created a new high Mexican cuisine, by refusing to traffic in tacos and tamales and so forth, instead focusing on the ingredients and flavors that move her. You have two venues to try. One is her original Barrio Cafe, 2814 North 16th Street. (www.barriocafe.com; ✆ **602/636-0240;** no reservations), where she made her name, turning a once-marginal neighborhood into a culinary must-visit. Here she mixes various meats and vegetables with flavorful chili-based sauces—like a poblano stuffed with pear, apple, apricot, and pecans, and finished with cilantro and pomegranate. To go even deeper into Silvana's World, however, try the smaller and more formal **Gran Reserva,** a tiny triangle space alongside the hip art galleries on Grand Avenue. You can get some Barrio dishes here on the a la carte menu, but trust me—go with the $44 tasting menu, where her chefs treat you to six-plus courses of delicacies, each exquisitely presented, like a luscious single scallop soaked in chili and lime. This may be the single most mouthwatering culinary deal in the Valley. Wine aficionados will swoon to the accompanying wine pairing. Call in advance to reserve seats at the (two-person) bar at the kitchen for personal service and the chance to talk to the chefs about what they're preparing.

1301 W Grand Ave. www.barriocafe.com. ✆ **602/252-2777.** Reservations recommended. Small courses $15–$35. Tues–Sat 5–10:30pm; Sun 5–9pm. Closed June–Sept.

Chelsea's Kitchen ★ NEW AMERICAN An upscale offshoot of the La Grande Orange (below), Chelsea's Kitchen serves its upscale Arcadia clientele—friends, couples of all persuasions, families, seniors—with comfort and confidence in a big dining room (with spacious booths) and an expansive patio. This place works hard to make gluten-free variants of its meals, too. The bar's a great place to hang on a sultry afternoon. The menu is familiar comfort foods, nothing more. Seasonal salads are usually a good choice, as are the fish tacos. Be sure to try the fried chicken and the short ribs. Highly kid-friendly.

5040 N. 40th St. www.chelseaskitchenaz.com. ✆ **602/957-2555.** Main courses $12–$27. Mon–Sat 11am–10pm; Sun 10am–9pm.

Southern Rail ★ SOUTHERN An offshoot of longtime Phoenix favorite, Becket's Table, this newish Cajun place does just about everything right, from the red beans and rice to the cornbread, from the collard greens to the smoked chicken and andouille sausage gumbo ya ya. It's a big airy room, and there's a spacious patio, too. Highly recommended for weekend brunch.

300 W. Camelback Rd. www.southernrailaz.com. ✆ **602/200-0085.** Reservations recommended. Main courses $14–$29. Mon–Fri 11am–10pm, Sat 10am–10pm, Sun 10am–9pm.

St. Francis ★★ NEW AMERICAN One of central Phoenix's best restaurants, it calls itself a neighborhood gathering place, part of the vision of chef Aaron Chamberlin, who also runs the Phoenix Public Market (p. 129). With its brick walls, loft dining room, and exposed-beam ceiling, the emphasis is on the food, locally sourced and adventurous without getting out of touch. The forbidden rice bowl and the salmon superfood dish are light and healthful, and there are also nicely prepared steaks, plus delicious unexpected offerings like the pork chile verde or Moroccan meatballs. Recommended for brunch.

111 E. Camelback Rd. www.stfrancisaz.com. ✆ **602/200-8111.** Reservations recommended. Main courses $15–$34. Mon–Thurs 4–10pm; Fri 4–11pm; Sat 9am–3pm, 4–11pm; Sun 9am–3pm, 4–9pm.

INEXPENSIVE

Delux ★ AMERICAN With sleek and stylish decor and a big selection of draft beers, this is the ultimate ultra-hip burger-and-beer joint. It stays open very late—till 2am, every night—and has an extensive sushi bar, too. The gourmet burgers are top-end, and these guys also know how to do fries (served in mini shopping carts), but here in swanky health-conscious Arcadia, the menu also has turkey and veggie burgers and a yummy mahi sandwich. Like many of the top restaurants along the Camelback Corridor, very gay-friendly.

In the Biltmore Plaza, 3146 E. Camelback Rd. www.deluxburger.com. ✆ **602/522-2288.** No reservations. Main courses $10–$17. Daily 11am–2am.

Khyber Halal ★ AFGHAN At this family-owned affair, you start with the *mantoo*, Afghani dumplings with meat and onions inside, served with a yogurt sauce. Someone has to get the Qabuli Pulaw, the country's national dish, which is a gigantic skewer of beef, served with cucumber salad and rice with carrots and raisins. (There's also an Uzbek Pulaw, with lamb.) Then you're on your own. Portions are large at this casual, delicious, and friendly place. "Halal" is the rough equivalent of "kosher," incidentally, and just means permissible foods for Muslims to eat. So no pork, and no alcohol.

4030 N. 24th St. (at Indian School Rd., SW corner). www.khyberhalalfood.com. ✆ **602/954-5290.** No reservations. Main courses $10–$15. Mon–Sat 11am–8:30pm.

La Grande Orange Pizzeria ★ PIZZA With the Postino wine bar next door and a bustling market churning out breakfast, salads, and sandwiches in addition to the wide selection of pizza, LGO, as it's known, has put itself at the center of the upscale Arcadia neighborhood. (It's a half-mile south of the Camelback Corridor.) You can't go wrong with the pizza at the bar or at the roomy, first-come, first-served tables. It's highly kid-friendly and doubles as a coffee shop, from breakfast on, for a relaxing hang and people-watching. The market's good for high-end picnic fixin's, too.

4410 N. 40th St. (at Campbell Ave.). www.lagrandeorangepizzeria.com. ✆ **602/840-7777.** No reservations. Main courses $11–$14. Daily 6:30am–10pm.

The Parlor ★ PIZZA I love this bustling pizza parlor both for its tasty pizzas and for its hip setting (a midcentury modern shell of a onetime beauty parlor). Vegetable and herb gardens line the sidewalk as you approach the front door, and lots of recycled wood has been used in the interior decor. You can assemble your own dream pizza from such ingredients as wild mushrooms, goat cheese, roasted chicken, calamari, and cilantro, or order one of the house pizzas. My favorite is the *salsiccia* (sausage) pizza, prepared with a local sausage that's custom-made for the Parlor. There are also a few sandwiches and some great salads, including a steak salad and one made with roasted beets.

1916 E. Camelback Rd. www.theparlor.us. ✆ **602/248-2480.** No reservations. Main courses $9–$22. Mon–Thurs 11am–10pm; Fri–Sat 11am–11pm; Sun 11am–9pm.

Red Thai ★ ASIAN FUSION The latest outfit from enterprising restaurateur Jonny Chu is a bit out of the way, at 12th Street and Northern Avenue, but it's worth hitting if you're interested in consistently delicious big-tasting Asian fusion fare, from wok-fried sensations to pho noodle dishes. Adventuresome kids will love the ultra-hip setting: The main dining room has a row of booths paralleling a bar that seems to go on forever, backed by gigantic video screens showing Asian cartoons.

7822 N. 12th St. www.redthaiphx.com. ✆ **602/870-3015.** No reservations. Main courses $11–$15. Lunch Tues–Fri 11am–3pm; dinner Sun and Tues–Thurs 5–9pm; Fri–Sat 5–10pm.

The Stand ★ BURGERS The Stand does burgers, it does fries, and it does shakes. Aside from soft drinks and lemonade, that's the menu. I know what you're thinking. Are the burgers succulent and even better with bacon, jalapeño, and onions? Are the shakes frosty? Are the fries hand-cut and salty? Yes, yes, and yes. And it's all in a retro roadside stand with a neon sign outside in south Arcadia.

3538 E. Indian School Rd. www.thestandbnt.com. ✆ **602/314-5259.** Basic burger $6; fries $3; shakes $5. Daily 11am–9pm; drive-thru until 10pm (11pm Fri–Sat).

Vincent Market Bistro ★★ FRENCH This casual French outfit located right behind chef Vincent's formal dining room (p. 124) does a respectable job of conjuring up a casual back-street bistro in Paris. It gets packed on winter Saturday mornings when Vincent's farmer's market attracts crowds of shoppers in search of gourmet snacks and fresh produce. Be sure to order the coq au vin or the smoked salmon quesadilla. You can also get great dinners to go.

3930 E. Camelback Rd. www.vincentsoncamelback.com. ✆ **602/224-3727.** Main courses $7–$16. Mon–Fri 11am–8pm; Sat 5–8pm; Sun 9am–2pm. Open Sat 9am–1pm for brunch with open-air market Oct–May.

Woody's Macayo ★ MEXICAN Macayo's is a Valley Mexican chain of some 7 decades' standing, with locations from Tucson to Vegas; this one-off outlet is slightly different. Named after its founder, it's downtown-specific, with a distinctive light take on this sometimes heavy food. Ignore the rest of the menu, and look over the *platos especiales.* Choose your form—taco, burrito, enchilada, bowl. Then you chose your meat (you can't go wrong with the green chili pork) and the particular sauce (go for the tomatillo). Macayo's does the rest.

3815 N. Central Ave. www.macayo.com. ✆ **602/264-6141.** Main dishes $11–$14. Mon–Wed 8am–10pm. Thurs–Fri 8am–midnight, Sun 10am–10pm.

Downtown, South Phoenix & the Airport Area

EXPENSIVE

Compass Arizona Grill ★AMERICAN In the heady days of the city's original Sun Belt growth, the Hyatt Regency was the signature hotel downtown, and the revolving restaurant atop it a premier event-dining destination. It was moribund for years, but has now been reopened and reimagined. Start with the pork carnitas fry bread and maybe the calamari, and then look over the menu, which has some strong a la carte meat dishes and crowd pleasers like scallops, salmon, and venison shanks. Everything's prepared and presented with a lot more verve that you'd expect. The views are great, and the overall experience of rotating 360 degrees 300 feet up is a lot of fun. Go an hour before sunset, of course. There's validated parking in the Hyatt garage just south of the hotel.

122 N. 2nd St. www.hyatt.com. ✆ **602/252-1234.** Reservations recommended. Main courses $20–$50. Daily 5:30–10pm.

Nobuo at Teeter House ★★★ JAPANESE In this little Craftsman bungalow on downtown Phoenix's Heritage Square, James Beard–award-winner Nobuo Fukuda serves his distinctive style of Japanese food. The menu lists barely more than a dozen dishes, and not one can really be considered sushi, so don't show up expecting to get a California roll. Instead, try less well-known Japanese specialties like *shiromi* (white-fish) carpaccio, house-cured salmon, or *okonomiyaki* (a savory pancake made with pork and seafood). While Nobuo has long been known for his wine pairings, here he also features rare Japanese microbrews.

Heritage Sq., 622 E. Adams St. www.nobuofukuda.com. ✆ **602/254-0600.** No reservations. Small plates $8–$30. Tues–Sun 11am–2pm, 5:30pm–closing (9–10pm).

Quiessence at the Farm ★★ NEW AMERICAN Set at the back of a shady pecan grove not far from South Mountain Park, Quiessence is surrounded by organic vegetable gardens, which make this place the epitome of "farm to table." The menu changes often, and the food is often wonderful, from the vegetables to the meats (trout, strip steak, guinea hen). For the full Quiessence experience, get one of the tasting menus (four, five, or six courses, running $79–$99, with $35–$55 wine pairings). ***One caveat:*** Things move slowly at the Farm. Nudges to the waitstaff produce knowledgeable but somewhat long-winded details about how the place operates—and no discernable change in the pace of the meal. Not the place for high-metabolism types.

6106 S. 32nd St. www.qatthefarm.com. ✆ **602/276-0601.** Reservations recommended; children discouraged. Main courses $23–$32 dinner; prix-fixe menu $75–$95 ($120–$140 with wine). Tues–Sat 5pm–closing (about 11pm). Closed July–early Aug.

Cowboy Steakhouses

I have some bad news to share with you: The fabled Phoenix cowboy steakhouse of yore is fading off into a desert sunset. The Reata Pass and Greasewood Flats, two sprawling cowboy eateries out near Pinnacle Peak, are gone. Bill Johnson's Big Apple, along with its 70-foot neon sign on Van Buren, is gone as well. Rawhide, the Western town, is open now only for special events. But there are a couple of places left. **The Stockyards,** 5009 E. Washington St. (www.stockyardssteakhouse.com; ✆ **602/273-7378**), which dates back to the time when there were stockyards in central Phoenix, was restored in 2004 and continues to offer top-tier meats (entrees run $36–$70). For something a little more casual for the family, drive to the **T-Bone Steakhouse,** 10037 S. 19th Ave. (www.tbonesteakhouseaz.com; ✆ **602/276-0945**), which lives on, high up South Mountain at the southern foot of 19th Avenue, on the west side of town. The history of this place goes back to the 1920s, and it still offers reasonably priced cowboy fixin's with sweeping views of the valley below.

MODERATE

Phoenix Public Market ★★ AMERICAN Chef Aaron Chamberlin's casual spot, just a block or two north of the center of downtown, sits off a Central Avenue parking lot devoted to a large farmer's market Wednesdays and Saturdays. Inside, you'll find an adult ASU crowd enjoying a variety of imaginative salads and a reliable lineup of comfort food with a Southwestern flavor, like pork chili pot pie. A casual bar and great coffee are available as well. Recommended breakfast stop, too. There's a variant, the **Tempe Public Market,** at 8749 S Rural Rd., Tempe (✆ **480/629-5120**).

14 E. Pierce St. (at Central Ave.). www.phxpublicmarket.com. ✆ **602/253-2700.** Main dishes $10–$19. Daily 7am–10pm.

Pizzeria Bianco ★★ PIZZA It's not often that a pizza place ranks as one of the most famous restaurants in a city, but this little downtown hole in the wall is exactly that. Chef/owner Chris Bianco has a huge reputation both here in the Valley and across the nation. The good news is that there's no longer the 2-hour wait. You can judge for yourself whether the rustic, brick oven pizzas are worthy of their rep. (I think so.) Bianco's signature pizza might be the Rosa, with red onion, Parmesan, rosemary, and crushed pistachios.

Heritage Sq., 623 E. Adams St. www.pizzeriabianco.com. ✆ **602/258-8300.** Reservations accepted for 6–10 people. Pizzas $14–$19. Daily 11am–9pm, Sun 11am–7pm.

Tuck Shop ★ AMERICAN Housed in a 1950s building and decorated in vintage Scandinavian modern style, Tuck Shop feels both hip and casual. You can show up in jeans and just have a drink and some appetizers, or get dressed up and make a night of it. The menu leans toward small plates and shareable dishes, with lots of comfort foods, including macaroni and cheese with prosciutto and a delicious citrus-brined fried chicken served with cheddar-cheese waffles. The Medjool dates stuffed with local chorizo sausage should not be

Coffee Culture

In the last 10 years, the Valley has come of age coffee-wise. Premium roasters can be found everywhere. In central Phoenix, **Lux Coffee** (4400 N. Central Ave.; luxcoffee.com) is the place where, from 6am on, artists and businesspeople meet up, and earnest writers, designers, and other "creatives" sip coffee, eat breakfast, and sit for hours in a virtually unmarked building on Central Avenue south of Camelback Road. There's sometimes a line, but you can generally find a place to sit. In the evening, there's a decent dinner menu, and wine and drinks come to the fore, courtesy of some talented resident mixologists, until midnight daily and till 2am on weekends. Farther downtown, try **Lola Coffee** (1001 N. 3rd Ave.; lolacoffeebar.com), another favorite of activists, business folks, ASU profs, students, and the like. **Press Coffee** (1616 N. Central; presscoffee.com) does amazing things with coffee beans at a swanky new shop and cafe at Central and McDowell, right across the street from the Phoenix Art Museum. I find the prices a bit high for the Valley—$20-plus a pound? Yikes!—but boy it's good. **Cartel Coffee Lab** (1 N. 1st St.; cartelcoffeelab.com) does careful slow drips and is the best place for great coffee in the heart of downtown.

In Scottsdale: Downtown has its own **Cartel** (7124 E. 5th Ave.; cartelcoffeelab.com) amid the 5th Avenue Shops. Up in north Scottsdale, visit the original **Press** in the tony Scottsdale Quarter shopping center (15147 N. Scottsdale Rd.; presscoaffee.com). In south Scottsdale, near the Phoenix city line, is **Echo Coffee** (2902 N. 68th St.; www.echocoffee.com), one of the best local micro-roasters and purveyor of some of the best slow drip in town, all in an airy environment highly conducive to creativity.

missed. There's an afternoon tea on Saturdays noon to 3pm, which requires reservations.

2245 N. 12th St. www.tuckinphx.com. ✆ **602/354-2980.** Reservations accepted for 6 or more. Main courses $16–$19. Tues–Sat 5–10pm; weekend brunch Sat–Sun 9am–2pm.

INEXPENSIVE

The Farm Kitchen ★ LIGHT FARE Another element of the restaurant complex at the Farm at South Mountain (pricy Quiessence, p. 128, is inside), this rustic outbuilding has been converted to a casual counter-service lunch restaurant, where you can order a filling sandwich or a delicious pecan turkey Waldorf salad. The grassy lawn, shaded by pecan trees, is ideal for a picnic if the sun's not beating down too harshly; you can let the kids run all over and play lawn games while you enjoy your salad or sandwich. At the back of the farm, you'll also find the **Morning Glory Café** (✆ **602/276-8804**), a cozy little breakfast place.

6106 S. 32nd St. www.thefarmatsouthmountain.com. ✆ **602/276-6545.** Sandwiches and salads $10. Daily 10am–3pm (closed late May–late Sept).

Fry Bread House ★ NATIVE AMERICAN Fry bread is just what it sounds like—fried bread—and it's a mainstay on Indian reservations throughout the West. Although you can eat these thick, chewy slabs of fried bread plain, salted, or with honey, they also serve as the wrappers for Indian tacos, filled with meat, beans, and lettuce. If you've already visited the Four Corners region (see chapter 7), then you've probably had an Indian taco or two. Forget them—the ones here are the best in the state (especially those with green chili). For dessert? Fry bread with chocolate and butter, of course.

4140 N. 7th Ave. ✆ **602/351-2345.** No reservations. Main courses $4.25–$7.75. Mon–Thurs 10am–8pm; Fri–Sat 10am–9pm.

Gallo Blanco ★★★ MEXICAN When I have friends in town, I take them here first. This is Mexico City Mexican food, done up by a formally trained chef and served in an airy, hip environment. It's a lot different from the sloppy tostadas and refried beans of a normal Mexican restaurant. Start with the guacamole, tangy with lime, with warm tortilla chips, or the delicious *elote callejero,* a wood-grilled ear of corn with cheese and paprika sprinkled on it. Then start ordering tacos, which are about $3 each; two are enough, but you'll wish you'd ordered three. There's a selection, but try the carne asada and the *al pastor* (pork marinated with alluring *achiote* spice); there's also shrimp, fish, and *verduros de temporada* (seasonal vegetables). Then hit the rest of the menu. For dessert, you have to get the deep-fried churros, which are basically donut sticks that come with three sweet thick dipping bowls: sweetened condensed milk, caramel, and chocolate. Yum.

928 E. Pierce St. www.galloblancocafe.com. ✆ **602/327-0880.** No reservations. Main courses $9–$15. Tues–Thurs 11am–10pm, Fri 11am–midnight, Sat 8am–midnight, Sun 8am–10pm.

Lo-Lo's Chicken & Waffles ★ SOUL FOOD What part of "chicken & waffles" do you not understand? This is a south Phoenix perennial, now expanded to seven locations. The original is just a mile or two below downtown and just a mile or so west of Sky Harbor's car rental return. It's a great place to start or end your trip to the Valley—highly enjoyable, if you can handle very casual, with huge comfy booths, a great staff, and a very-un-Phoenix-like diverse clientele. Someone in your group has to order the "Double-D," two large and crispy chicken breasts atop a large circular waffle with syrup. But others should try the chicken gizzards, and I recommend an order of catfish beignets and fried pickles for the table. For dessert, try the "banana puddin'." ***Note:*** The portions are not small.

1220 S. Central Ave. www.loloschickenandwaffles.com. ✆ **602/340-1304.** All items $8–$17. Mon–Thurs 9am–10pm; Fri–Sat 8am–11pm; Sun 8am–6pm.

Los Dos Molinos ★ MEXICAN With the development of south Phoenix, Dos Molinos doesn't have the remote feel it used to (silent-era Western star Tom Mix lived here, lifetimes ago). This is just casual Mexican food, but as serious (and as hot) as it gets, prepared by many generations of its family owners. The place has long been favored by discriminating locals for its warm tortilla chips, different types of zesty salsas, an eye-opening mole, and a sprawling menu with all the usual elements—tacos, enchiladas, tortas, chimichangas, etc. There are additional locations in Uptown (1044 E. Camelback Rd.; ✆ **602/528-3535**) and Mesa (260 S. Alma School Rd.; ✆ **480/969-7475**).

8646 S. Central Ave. www.losdosmolinosphoenix.com. ✆ **602/243-9113.** Main courses $7–$17. Tues–Sat 11am–9pm.

Tempe & Mesa

Tempe, despite the massive presence of ASU, has not yet emerged as a dining destination, but there are a few places to check out if you're there for a stay.

MODERATE

Caffe Boa ★ EUROPEAN Biodynamic, Organic, Artisanal—that's apparently where the name Boa comes from. That tells only half the story, though, because it doesn't capture how good the food is. Classy but not stuffy, this is the place to go for a perfect pasta or seafood dinner. Everything's organic and local, and all the pasta is made in house. Lots and lots of wines, and also "rakija tastings" of Serbo-Croation liqueurs made from fermented fruit. Note that the website is spelled slightly differently from the restaurant's actual name.

398 S. Mill Ave., Tempe. www.cafeboa.com. ✆ **480/968-9112.** Lunch $16–$21, dinner $16–$32. Mon–Wed 11am–10pm, Thurs–Sat 11am–11pm.

House of Tricks ★ NEW AMERICAN Downtown Tempe's favorite decent restaurant, housed in a pair of old Craftsman bungalows surrounded by a shady garden, this romantic spot seems a world away from the bustle on nearby Mill Avenue. A garlicky Caesar salad or house-smoked salmon with avocado, capers, red onion, and lemon cream are good bets for starters. Entrees change regularly, on a menu inspired by the Mediterranean and the Southwest. Try for a seat on the grape-arbor-covered patio.

114 E. 7th St., Tempe. www.houseoftricks.com. ✆ **480/968-1114.** Main courses $12–$14 lunch, $24–$36 dinner. Mon–Sat 11am–10pm. Closed July.

An Unexpected Ethnic Enclave

Everyone knows Mesa is lily white and mostly Mormon, right? So what explains the Mekong Grocery and its companion operation, the AZ International Marketplace? They are about a half-mile from each other on Dobson Road a few miles south of I-60. The Asian-themed **Mekong Plaza** (66 S. Dobson Rd., at W. Main; www.mekongplaza.com; ✆ **602/833-0095**) is a strip mall with an incongruous pagoda-like roof. A variety of Chinese and Vietnamese shops and eateries face the parking lot; behind them is a very large, crammed-to-the-rafters Asian market. Every manner of Asian food and packaged goods, only some with English translations, can be found here, along with a wall of live fish tanks. A bit south on the other side of the street is the **AZ International Marketplace** (1920 W. Broadway Rd., at S. Dobson; ✆ **602/633-6296**), a gigantic Walmart-sized operation with a similar phalanx of casual Asian food operations in front. Both are open daily from 9am to 9pm.

The Original Blue Adobe Grille ★★ MEXICAN This restaurant looks like the sort of place you should drive right past. Don't! Despite appearances, this New Mexican–style restaurant serves deliciously creative Southwestern fare at very economical prices. To get an idea of what the food is all about, try the Cruz Kitchen combination plate (a tenderloin *relleno* and a smoked-pork tamale) or lobster tamales with mango salsa and raspberry chipotle sauce. Of course, there are great Chicago margaritas, but there's also a surprisingly good wine list. It's a good dinner stop on the way back from driving the Apache Trail (p. 159).

144 N. Country Club Dr., Mesa. www.originalblueadobe.com. ✆ **480/962-1000.** Reservations recommended. Main courses $8–$20. Mon–Thurs 11am–9pm; Fri–Sat 11am–10pm; Sun noon–8pm.

INEXPENSIVE

Café Lalibela ★★ ETHIOPIAN/VEGETARIAN Ethiopian food consists of savory stews, many of which are quite spicy, scooped up with pieces of a traditional Ethiopian crepe-like bread called *injera.* No utensils allowed! For the best introduction to this flavorful cuisine, try the Lalibela Exclusive platter, which feeds three and comes with a dozen different dishes. There are lots of meatless dishes on the menu, so this is a good choice for vegetarians.

849 W. University Dr., Tempe. www.cafelalibela.com. ✆ **480/829-1939.** Reservations recommended on weekends. Main courses $6–$16. Mon–Thurs 11am–9pm; Fri 11am–10pm; Sat noon–10pm; Sun noon–9pm.

The Chuckbox ★ BURGERS . . . and just about nothing but burgers. They grill 'em, you eat 'em in this weird little bungalow abutting the ASU campus on University Drive, where students have chowed down on Big Ones, Great Big Ones, Double Big Ones, etc.—all cooked over mesquite charcoal—for almost 50 years. In belated recognition of the 21st century, chicken burgers and veggie burgers are now available as well.

202 E. University Dr., Tempe. www.thechuckbox.com. ✆ **480/968-4712.** Burgers $5–$10. Mon–Sat 10:30am–11pm; Sun 10:30am–8pm.

Organ Stop Pizza ★ PIZZA The pizza here may not be the best in town, but the mighty Wurlitzer theater organ, possibly the largest in the world, sure is memorable. This massive instrument, which in addition to its gigantic playing console includes more than 5,500 pipes, has four turbine blowers to provide the wind to create the sound, and with 40-foot ceilings in the restaurant, the acoustics are great. Kids will love all the mechanical sound-effect gadgets on the walls. Groups sit on long tables and watch the agreeable organist field requests and play everything from pop classics to currents hits to—by request, once a set, forever and ever amen—"Let It Go," from *Frozen*.

1149 E. Southern Ave. (at Stapley Dr.), Mesa. www.organstoppizza.com. ✆ **480/813-5700.** Reservations for large groups only. Pizzas and pastas $5.50–$19. No credit cards. Mon–Thurs 4–9pm, Fri 4–10pm, Sat 3–10pm, Sun 3–9pm. Doors open 1 hr. later mid-April–Thanksgiving.

Chandler & Gilbert

EXPENSIVE

Kai ★★★ NEW AMERICAN With ingredients sourced from Native American tribes around the country, the food at Kai is as adventurous and alluring as any you'll find in Arizona. It's all highly conceptual—courses are billed as "birth," "the beginning," "the journey," etc.—and wildly creative, from the melon-and-crab appetizer to the Msickquatash, a braised lamb shoulder with succotash, to buffalo tenderloin with saguaro-blossom syrup. Only Binkley's (p. 122) can match Kai's 13-course tasting menu. These are some of the most exotic flavors in the Southwest. Add service that is second to none and, if you're lucky, a big-sky sunset, and you have an unforgettable meal.

At Sheraton Wild Horse Pass Resort & Spa, 5594 W. Wild Horse Pass Blvd., Chandler. www.wildhorsepassresort.com. ✆ **602/225-0100.** Reservations highly recommended. Main courses $45–$62; tasting menus $145 and $245 ($250–$375 with wine). Tues–Thurs 5:30–9pm; Fri–Sat 5:30–9:30pm.

INEXPENSIVE

Guedo's Taco Shop ★ MEXICAN Taco stands are a peso a dozen around the greater Phoenix metro area, but few have the cult following of Guedo's. The food is simple yet fresh and bursting with flavor. Order two or three tacos (I like the fish and shrimp tacos), and then load them with toppings from the salsa bar. Accompany your meal with a cold beer or a margarita, and you just might forget you're still in the States. So beloved is this place that a former customer took it over when the original owner decided to bow out. It was moved to a location in nearby Gilbert.

3107 S. Gilbert Blvd., Gilbert. ✆ **480/621-8280.** Main dishes $2–$6.50. No credit cards. Tues–Sat 11am–9pm, Sun 11am–8pm.

Breakfast & Brunch

For years, lovers of the eggs, omelets, scrambles, and griddlecakes at **Matt's Big Breakfast,** 801 N. 1st St. (www.mattsbigbreakfast.com; ✆ **602/254-1074**), had to line up outside a tiny operation just off Roosevelt Row downtown. Now there's a bigger operation where the Biltmore meets Arcadia, at 32nd Street and Camelback Road (3118 E. Camelback Rd.; ✆ **602/840-3450**), and another tucked away in a new cluster of office buildings on the south side of Tempe Town Lake (400 E. Rio Salado Pkwy.; ✆ **480/967-5156**). For casual outdoor breakfasting in a bucolic farm setting, there's **Morning Glory Café,** 6106 S. 32nd St. (www.thefarmatsouthmountain.com; ✆ **602/276-8804**), part of the Farm complex, which also includes the celebrated Quiessence restaurant. (***Note:*** It's closed June through August.) In Arcadia, you can get great breakfasts and hearty coffee, among the locals who populate this place in droves, at hotspot **La Grande Orange** (p. 126). For a high-end brunch, you can't go wrong amid the desert mountain views at **El Chorro Lodge** (p. 117), or **Lon's at the Hermosa** (p. 123). However, for a unique experience, make a brunch reservation at **Geordie's Restaurant at the Wrigley Mansion** (Sundays only 10am–2pm; $64, $32 kids 5–12), served in the historic mansion that chewing gum built.

Joe's Farm Grill ★ AMERICAN Designed to resemble a 1950s burger stand and set in the middle of a farm that's part of the Agritopia housing development, Joe's serves creative comfort food: big salads with various toppings, barbecued ribs, chicken sandwiches, pizzas, and, best of all, burgers that are among the best in the Valley. It's a huge hit with families. As much as possible, produce comes from the surrounding Agritopia farm. After a meal, walk next door to the **Coffee Shop** (✆ **480/279-3144**) for a pastry.

3000 E. Ray Rd., Gilbert. www.joesfarmgrill.com. ✆ **480/563-4745.** Main dishes $6–$20. Daily 8am–9pm.

Joe's Real BBQ ★ BARBECUE Just how "real" is this restaurant? Well, the service is cafeteria style, and should you forget whence your veggies came, there's a huge John Deere tractor in middle of the dining room. Portions are as huge as that tractor: piles of barbecued ribs, chopped brisket, and pulled pork, all smoked over pecan wood, and served with a choice of one or two sides. There's a sunroom dining area and a shady side yard that's the perfect place to eat on warm days.

301 N. Gilbert Rd., Gilbert. www.joesrealbbq.com. ✆ **480/503-3805.** No reservations. Main courses $10–$20. Daily 11am–9pm.

VALLEY OF THE SUN SHOPPING

High-end shopping in the Valley comes in the shape of a big backward L. It begins 4 miles north of the heart of downtown Phoenix with the hip and trendy boutiques at Central Avenue and Camelback Road. Follow **Camelback Road** (the first leg of the L) east 2 miles and you'll pass more juicy shopping stops, including the Camelback Esplanade, the Town and Country Shopping Center, and swanky Biltmore Fashion Park. Another 6 miles due east of that, the intersection of Scottsdale and Camelback roads is ground zero for Scottsdale shopping, with the gigantic Scottsdale Fashion Square and many, many surrounding blocks of art galleries, boutiques, jewelry stores, Native American craft stores, and Western shops, all collectively known as downtown Scottsdale. Old Town Scottsdale, the city's main tourist destination (see walking tour, p. 73), is a couple miles south of here.

For the other leg of the L, head north on **Scottsdale Road,** though 10 miles of ever-swankier shopping territory with high-end strip malls on both sides of the street. You'll also find some shopping areas on parallel Hayden and Pima roads. Kierland Commons and Scottsdale Quarter, two major malls with high-end retailers, are 8 or 9 miles north of downtown Scottsdale.

Malls & Shopping Centers

The traditional suburban malls you'd find in any big city ring the Valley; two worth noting are the **Desert Ridge Marketplace** (at Tatum and the 101, in north Phoenix) and the **Tempe Marketplace** (at McClintock Road and the 202, in north Tempe), both open-air affairs with lots of chain restaurants and a big movie multiplex. The most distinctive shopping areas are listed below.

Biltmore Fashion Park/Esplanade ★ The premier shopping destination in Phoenix proper, high-toned Biltmore Fashion Park is an open-air shopping center with a Saks, Macy's, Apple Store, Lauren, Pottery Barn, etc., along with some cool coffee places and a variety of casual-to-upscale restaurants. A pedestrian tunnel under Camelback Road takes you to the Esplanade, a recently renovated group of shops and restaurants in an office complex. There's also a decent AMC multiplex with reserved seats and a full menu. 2502 E. Camelback Rd. (at 24th St.). www.shopbiltmore.com. ✆ **602/955-8400.**

Kierland Commons/Scottsdale Quarter ★★ Here's one of the Valley's more pleasant shopping experiences. Kierland is a massive complex that includes everything from a Westin resort to an extensive Main Street–style shopping mall with residences upstairs; it's all pretty novel for the Valley. There are pleasant shaded streets to walk down as you pop in and out of Crate & Barrel, Coach, and some local specialty stores like the Queen Creek Olive Mill Marketplace. (No large anchor stores, however.) Right across Scottsdale Road to the east, Scottsdale Quarter is a similar but sleeker endeavor with its own attractions: shops (including an Apple Store and the high-end furniture outfit Design Within Reach), good restaurants (True Food and the enjoyable and spacious eatery Bice) and a swanky reserved-seat movie multiplex, iPic. Kierland: 15205 N. Scottsdale Rd. www.kierlandcommons.com. ✆ **480/348-1577.** Scottsdale Quarter: 15059 N Scottsdale Rd. www.scottsdalequarter.com. ✆ **480/270-8123.**

The upscale Scottsdale Quarter mall, lit up for night shopping.

Scottsdale Fashion Square ★★★ Scottsdale's iconic mall has had its ups and downs; a much-ballyhooed Barneys New York came and went. Now it's regained its footing with a seemingly never-ending construction boom and teeming crowds after a full interior revamp in 2018. Nordstrom, Dillard's, Neiman Marcus, and Macy's are the anchors; Cartier and Jimmy Choo outlets can be found among scores of others, along with oodles of eateries and a next-generation art-movie complex, complete with restaurant and bar. 7014–590 E. Camelback Rd. (at Scottsdale Rd.), Scottsdale. www.fashionsquare.com. ✆ **480/941-2140.**

The Shops Gainey Village ★ This ultra-upscale strip mall has a dense concentration of chi-chi women's clothing stores and a variety of pricey eateries where locals gather. 8777–8989 N. Scottsdale Rd. (at Doubletree Ranch Rd.). www.theshopsgaineyvillage.com. ✆ **602/953-6150.**

OUTLET MALLS

Outlets at Anthem ★ Anthem is a planned development on the northern outskirts of Phoenix, 20 miles up I-17 from downtown. And just north of Anthem is the newest Valley outlet mall, featuring all the usual fashion suspects. 4250 W Anthem Way, Phoenix. www.outletsanthem.com. ✆ **623/465-9500.**

Phoenix Premium Outlets ★ This is a Simon outlet mall, just north of the Wild Horse Pass Casino complex, about 15 miles south from downtown Phoenix or Scottsdale. 4976 Premium Outlets Way, Chandler. www.premiumoutlets.com/outlet/phoenix. ✆ **480/639-1766.**

Tanger Outlets Westgate ★ In Glendale, 15 miles NW of downtown Phoenix, the massive Westgate complex includes a football stadium and arena and the Westgate Entertainment District, which bills itself as a mall but is really just a mass of chain restaurants to serve the sports facilities before games. The outlet mall is just west of all that, sporting Saks Off 5th, Kate Spade, Coach, and scores of others. 6800 N. 95th Ave., Glendale. www.tangeroutlet.com/glendale. No phone.

Shopping A to Z

ANTIQUES & COLLECTIBLES

Downtown Glendale (a suburb northwest of downtown Phoenix) is the Valley's main antiques district, with a great concentration of dealers on Glendale Avenue between 56th and 59th avenues, plus a few more in the blocks just north. The **Melrose District,** close to downtown Phoenix on 7th Avenue between Indian School and Camelback roads, has a dozen or more vintage, collectible, and furniture stores of highly variable quality, with the emphasis on midcentury modern furnishings.

Antique Trove ★ More than 100 dealers show their wares in this very large showroom on Scottsdale Rd., a mile or so south of downtown Scottsdale. 2020 N. Scottsdale Rd., Scottsdale. www.antiquetrove.com. ✆ **480/947-6074.**

Arizona West Galleries ★★ Nowhere else in Scottsdale will you find such a fab collection of cowboy collectibles and Western antiques—antique saddles and chaps, old rifles and six-shooters, sheriffs' badges, spurs, and the like. 7149 E. Main St., Scottsdale. www.facebook.com/arizonawestgalleries. ✆ **480/994-3752.**

Bishop Gallery for Art & Antiques ★ This cramped shop is wonderfully eclectic, with everything from Asian antiques to unusual original art. Definitely worth a browse. 7164 E. Main St., Scottsdale. www.bishopgallery.net. ✆ **480/949-9062.**

Femme Fatales & Fantasies ★ It's also known as FFF Movie Posters, because that what this Scottsdale shop is all about. Lots of gorgeous old posters for sale, and lots of rare selections from the owner's collection on display. 7013 E. Main St., Scottsdale. www.fffmovieposters.com. ✆ **480/429-6800.**

Knox Artifacts Gallery ★★ Ancient ceramics pieces from around the Southwest are among the specialties at this store. There are lots of other pre-Columbian artifacts, as well as Roman, Greek, and Egyptian pieces—museum-quality artifacts with prices to prove it. 7056 E. Main St., Ste. B, Scottsdale. www.fortknoxartifacts.com. ✆ **480/874-1007.**

ART

The Valley's unexpectedly strong and active arts scene is most visibly manifested in the **First Friday gallery walk,** which centers on Roosevelt Row, right off Central Avenue just north of downtown. There are big crowds but it's a great diversion for interested families, students, singles, and art lovers, who will appreciate being exposed to the Valley's most venturesome underground artists and its up-and-coming stars. (**Third Fridays** are a quieter alternative.)

Downtown Scottsdale has its own **Thursday ArtWalk** every Thursday even in summer, from 7pm to 9pm, centered on Main Street just south of Indian School Road, but also stretching up Marshall Way to Fifth Avenue. A little more genteel, it focuses on established commercial galleries—from cowboy to contemporary, from the garish to the sublime. It's a great time to mingle with other art lovers in a casual atmosphere, meet some artists and craftspeople, and even grab a cup of wine or two.

Some of the most important contemporary arts galleries from Scottsdale have moved to downtown Phoenix; see the Bentley Gallery and Lisa Sette Gallery, below.

Art One ★ This gallery specializes in works by art students, from high school to universities, and other area cutting-edge artists. The works can be surprisingly good, and prices are very reasonable. 4130 N. Marshall Way, Scottsdale. www.artonegalleryinc.com. ✆ **480/946-5076.**

Bentley Gallery ★ Housed in a huge old warehouse south of Chase Field in downtown Phoenix, this massive gallery is one of the city's most exciting

Up-and-Comers on Roosevelt Row

Just off Central Avenue, stretching along Roosevelt Road almost to 7th Street, a dozen or more locally owned art galleries are devoted to finding the next generation of Phoenix artists. Quality, of course, varies greatly, and the upheaval wrought by ASU's expansion means it's changing all the time. But you'll definitely find interesting work to check out at **Monorchid, Modified Arts** and the **Eye Lounge,** each within a block of the intersection of 3rd Street and Roosevelt Road. There's a good guide at **rooseveltrow.org**.

contemporary-art spaces. A second gallery is in Scottsdale at 4161 N. Marshall Way (✆ **480/946-6060**). 215 E. Grant St., Phoenix. www.bentleygallery.com. ✆ **602/340-9200.**

Cattle Track Artist Compound ★ In this venerable desert spread, a dozen or so artists, sculptors, and jewelry makers have collected over the years to craft and show their work. It's worth a visit by serious arts folks. Check the website for artist or author talks, sales, or other events. 6105 N. Cattle Track Rd., Scottsdale. www.cattletrack.org. No phone.

Gebert Contemporary ★ Gebert has a pair of sister galleries in Santa Fe; its Scottsdale operation shows the finest southwest contemporary artists, and is probably the most serious contemporary art operation left in Scottsdale. 7160 Main St., Scottsdale. www.gebertartaz.com. ✆ **480/429-0711.**

Lisa Sette Gallery ★ The valley's premier contemporary art gallery is now in midtown, housed in a half-subterranean building by midcentury modern architect Al Beadle. Sette shows works by significant artists with local and international reputations. 4142 N. Marshall Way, Scottsdale. www.lisasettegallery.com. ✆ **480/990-7342.**

Riva Yares Gallery ★ One of Scottsdale's largest and most respected contemporary-art galleries, with a second location in Santa Fe, Riva Yares favors monumental sculptures; if you're lucky you might stumble on a show by the likes of Milton Avery or Frank Stella. 3625 Bishop Lane, Scottsdale. www.rivayaresgallery.com. ✆ **480/947-3251.**

Xanadu Gallery ★ Featuring glass art, colorful and graphic two-dimensional works, and the fun Wild West collages and paintings of Dave Newman, this gallery always seems to show art that's distinctly different from that at most of other Main Street galleries. 7039 E. Main St., Ste. 101, Scottsdale. www.xanadugallery.com. ✆ **866/483-1306** or 480/368-9929.

BOOKS

There aren't too many big-chain bookstores left; what remain are a few large **Barnes & Noble** locations in some of the suburban malls ringing the Valley. The one closest to tourist areas is at 10500 N. 90th St., Scottsdale (✆ **480/391-0048**). In Phoenix, there's also a **Bookmans,** a sprawling operation with vast selections of used books, DVDs, and pop collectibles (8034 N. 19th Ave.; www.bookmans.com; ✆ **602/433-0255**); there's one in Mesa, too.

Book Gallery ★ The best traditional used bookstore in the Valley, Book Gallery purveys rare and collectible books, plus a substantial selection of used tomes across the spectrum. 3643 E. Indian School Rd., Phoenix. ✆ **602/508-0280.**

Changing Hands ★★ This vibrant independent bookstore has two locations; one a bit far afield in south Tempe (6428 S McClintock Dr., Tempe; ✆ **480/730-0205**), and this newer uptown location, just west of Camelback Road and Central Avenue. Both have exceptional staffs, many author appearances, and lots of other events for book lovers and families. The Phoenix location also has a lively and spacious bar and cafe, a must-stop for any book lover or weary traveler in search of a respite in civilized surroundings. 300 W. Camelback Rd., Phoenix. www.changinghands.com. ✆ **602/274-0067.**

Guidon Books ★ Old Town Scottsdale used to have an array of shops for rare books, stamps and coins, and the like; now they are all gone. This longtime downtown denizen, however, has moved to north Scottsdale—it's worth the trip if you're interested in books about the West, Native Americans, and the Civil War. 7380 E. Redfield Rd., Scottsdale. www.guidon.com. ✆ **480/945-8811.**

The Poisoned Pen ★★ This whodunnit and mystery specialty shop has thrived with a great selection, a sharp staff, and lots of author events; mystery lovers should check its online schedule to see who's in town. Lots of collectible first editions and books signed by the authors. 4014 N. Goldwater Blvd., Ste. 101, Scottsdale. www.poisonedpen.com. ✆ **888/560-9919** or 480/947-2974.

CHOCOLATE

Cerreta Candy Company ★ Want to feel like a kid in Willy Wonka's candy factory? Head west to Glendale and the Cerreta Candy Company factory, which is open for tours Monday through Friday at 10am and 1pm (shopping hours are longer). The store here is packed with all kinds of sweet treats. 5345 W. Glendale Ave., Glendale. www.cerreta.com. ✆ **623/930-9000.**

Sugar & Spro ★ In Scottsdale's Waterfront district, this candy boutique crafts elegant little truffles that combine curious and surprising flavors, such as the Silk Road (Morello cherry, pistachio, cardamom, chocolate), and the Jasmine Night (berry pate, jasmine, chocolate)—with hallucinatory designs that live up to their names. 4225 N. Marshall Way, www.facebook.com/sugarandspro scottsdale. ✆ **602/885-4673.**

FASHION

For cowboy and cowgirl attire, see "Western Wear," below.

Frances ★ This lovely uptown boutique has tastefully selected women's clothes and equally tasteful local designer jewelry. 10 W. Camelback Rd., Phoenix. francesvintage.com. ✆ **602/279-5467.**

Muse ★ Stocking upscale casual wrap dresses, skirts, and tops, with flowing fabrics and summer colors, this boutique is tucked next to the Flower Child restaurant at Uptown Plaza. 100 E. Camelback Rd., Phoenix. http://shopatmuse.myshopify.com. ✆ **602/749-8880.**

My Sister's Closet ★ Upscale Valley women favor this high-end resale shop, both to unload last season's fashions and to shop for slightly used designer clothing. This branch is the swankiest, but there's good stuff at the other locations, too: in the Town & Country shopping plaza, 4869 N. 20th St., Phoenix (✆ **602/954-6080**), and at Lincoln Village, 6204 N. Scottsdale Rd., Scottsdale (✆ **480/443-4575**). Men's variants, called **Well Suited,** are in the same plazas. At Desert Village, 23269 N. Pima Rd., Scottsdale. www.mysisterscloset.com. ✆ **480/419-6242.**

Nouvelle Armoire ★ Well loved by its clientele, this upscale neighborhood clothing operation is tucked away in the Camelback Village Center at the northeast corner of Camelback Rd. and 44th St. 4424 E. Camelback Rd., Phoenix. ✆ **602/954-1221.**

Objects ★ Creatively curated, this store sells all sorts of apparel and accessories, from independent designers both local and not. Call to see if any trunk shows are in the offing. 6560 N. Scottsdale Rd., Scottsdale. www.objectsaz.com. ✆ **480/878-5343.**

Stefan Mann ★ El Pedregal, the shopping center close to the Boulders Resort, seems to be in a transitional period and is largely empty. Fortunately, this extravagant leather shop remains, offering gorgeous leather purses, wallets, and luggage. It's been in business for more than 25 years. 34505 N. Scottsdale Rd., Ste. J-6, Scottsdale. www.stefanmann.com. ✆ **480/488-3371.**

GIFTS & SOUVENIRS

Bischoff's Shades of the West ★ A one-stop shop for all things southwestern, from T-shirts to regional foodstuffs, this sprawling store has it all, with good selections of candles, Mexican crafts, and wrought-iron cabinet hardware that can give your kitchen a Western look. 7247 Main St., Scottsdale. www.shadesofthewest.com. ✆ **888/239-5872.**

Sphinx Date Ranch ★ Dates—love 'em or hate 'em, there's no denying the connection these supersweet little palm fruits have to the desert. At this old-fashioned shop—more than 60 years old—just south of Old Town Scottsdale, you can buy all kinds of dates and date products. 3039 N. Scottsdale Rd., Scottsdale. www.sphinxdateranch.com. ✆ **480/941-2261.**

The Store @ Scottsdale Center for the Performing Arts ★ This gift shop in the downtown Scottsdale mall has a wonderful selection of fun, contemporary, and artistic gifts, including lots of jewelry. There's another gift shop next door at the Scottsdale Museum of Contemporary Art. 7380 E. 2nd St., Scottsdale. www.scottsdaleperformingarts.com. ✆ **480/874-4644.**

Two Plates Full ★ Inside, this store looks as if a piñata exploded—if it had been filled with colorful art and crafts, home accessories, and jewelry. You can't miss the turquoise exterior amid the maze of strip malls on the southeast corner of Scottsdale Road and Shea Blvd. 10337 N. Scottsdale Rd., Scottsdale. www.twoplatesfull.com. ✆ **480/443-3241.**

JEWELRY

Cornelis Hollander ★ Although this shop is much smaller and not nearly as dramatic as the nearby Jewelry by Gauthier (below), the designs are just as hip. Whether you're looking for classic chic or trendy modern designs, you'll find plenty to interest you. 4151 N. Marshall Way, Scottsdale. www.cornelishollander.com. ✆ **480/423-5000.**

French Designer Jeweler ★ One of the more interesting jewelry stores on Scottsdale's Main Street, this highly curated selection of artisan designers is the creation of metalsmith French Thompson. (His name just happens to be French.) 7148 E. Main St., Scottsdale. www.frenchonmain.com. ✆ **480/994-4717.**

Jewelry by Gauthier ★ This elegant store sells the designs of the phenomenally talented Scott Gauthier, stylishly modern pieces that use precious stones and are miniature works of art. A second, much smaller shop is in Kierland Commons, 15034 N. Scottsdale Rd., Ste. 120 (✆ **480/443-4030**). 6378 N. Scottsdale Rd., Scottsdale. www.jewelrybygauthier.com. ✆ **480/941-1707.**

Molina Fine Jewelers ★ If you can spend as much on a necklace as you can on a Mercedes, then this is *the* place to shop for your baubles. By appointment only, for personalized service as you peruse the classically styled jewelry. 3134 E. Camelback Rd., Phoenix. www.molinafinejewelers.com. ✆ **602/955-2055.**

Sami ★ Northeast of Scottsdale in the city of Fountain Hills, this little jewelry store specializes in amethyst from a mine in the nearby Four Peaks Mountains, which has been producing gemstones since Spanish colonial times. The very best of the stones wind up at this shop. You'll also find Arizona peridot and "anthill" garnet jewelry here. 16704 Ave. of the Fountains, Ste. 100, Fountain Hills. www.samifinejewelry.com. ✆ **480/712-7193.**

NATIVE AMERICAN ARTS, CRAFTS & JEWELRY

Bischoff's at the Park ★★ Affiliated with the other Bischoff's right across the street (above), this very large and packed store and gallery carries higher-end jewelry, Western-style home furnishings, and clothing, ceramics, sculptures, contemporary paintings, and books and music with a regional theme. 3925 N. Brown Ave., Scottsdale. www.shadesofthewest.com. ✆ **480/946-6155.**

Faust Gallery ★ Old Native American baskets and pottery, as well as old and new Navajo rugs, are the specialties at this interesting shop. It also sells Native American and southwestern art, including ceramics, paintings, bronzes, and unusual sculptures. 7100 E. Main St., Ste. 3, Scottsdale. www.faustgallery.com. ✆ **480/200-4290.**

Gilbert Ortega Gallery & Museum ★ You'll find Gilbert Ortega shops all over the Valley, but this is the biggest and best. As the name implies, there are museum displays throughout the store. Jewelry is the main attraction, but there are also baskets, sculptures, pottery, rugs, paintings, and *katsina* dolls. 3925 N. Scottsdale Rd., Scottsdale. www.gilbertorteganativeamericangalleries.com. ✆ **480/990-1808.**

Heard Museum Gift Shop ★★ The Heard Museum (p. 59) has a top-tier collection of well-crafted Native American jewelry, art, and crafts of all kinds. This is the best place in the Valley to shop for Native American arts and crafts; you can be absolutely assured of the quality. Because the store doesn't have to charge sales tax, you'll also save a bit of money. Also be sure to check out the affiliated Berlin Gallery, which features contemporary Native American art. At the Heard Museum, 2301 N. Central Ave., Phoenix. www.heard.org. ✆ **602/252-8344.**

John C. Hill Antique Indian Art ★★ While shops selling Native American art and artifacts abound in Scottsdale, few offer the high quality available in this tiny shop. The store has one of the finest selections of Navajo rugs in the Valley, including quite a few older rugs; there are also *katsina* dolls, superb pieces of Navajo and Zuni silver-and-turquoise jewelry, baskets, and pottery. 6962 E. 1st Ave., Ste. 104, Scottsdale. www.johnhillgallery.com. ✆ **480/946-2910.**

Old Territorial Shop ★★ Owned and operated by Alston and Deborah Neal, this is the oldest Indian arts-and-crafts store on Main Street, and it offers good values on jewelry, concho belts, *katsina* dolls, fetishes, pottery, and Navajo rugs. 7100 E. Main St., Scottsdale. www.oldterritorialshop.com. ✆ **480/945-5432.**

River Trading Post ★ Interested in getting into collecting Native American art or artifacts? This is a good place to get in on the ground floor—quality is high and prices are relatively low. Not only are there fine Navajo rugs, but there are also museum-quality pieces of ancient southwestern pottery. 7033 E. Main St., Scottsdale. www.rivertradingpost.com. ✆ **480/444-0001.**

WESTERN WEAR

Az Tex Hat Company ★ Cowboy hat central. This small shop in Old Scottsdale offers custom shaping and fitting of both felt and woven hats. They can ship your purchase home, too; a lot of their creations don't fit in most suitcases. 3903 N. Scottsdale Rd., Scottsdale. www.aztexhats.com. ✆ **800/972-2116.**

Cave Creek Cowboy Co. ★ All the fashions the modern cowboy and cowgirl needs, at a big shop in the center of downtown Cave Creek. 6137 E. Cave Creek Road, Cave Creek. www.cavecreekcowboycompany.com. ✆ **480/575-3130.**

Saba's Western Stores ★ Since 1927, these family-owned stores have been outfitting Scottsdale's cowboys and cowgirls, visiting dude ranchers, and anyone else who wants to adopt the look of the Wild West. Lots of fun to look around at both locations. The Main Street store features boots galore; the other, across the street at 3965 N. Brown Ave. (✆ **480/947-7664**), has a full selection of Western clothes. 7254 Main St., Scottsdale. www.sabaswesternwear.com. ✆ **877/342-1835** or 480/949-7404.

Wild West Mercantile ★ This big, big place in Mesa, with a wide selection of Western wear, specializes in getting local Western groups suited up. 7302 E. Main St., Mesa. www.wwmerc.com. ✆ **480/218-1181.**

ENTERTAINMENT & NIGHTLIFE

As downtown Phoenix has revitalized itself and the whole Valley has begun to shrug off the effects of extended downturns, fun places to hang out at night are popping up all over. Although much of the nightlife scene is centered on downtown Scottsdale, Tempe's Mill Avenue, and downtown Phoenix, you'll find things going on all over.

Tickets to many concerts, theater performances, and sporting events are available through **Ticketmaster** (www.ticketmaster.com; ✆ **866/448-7849** or 800/745-3000), but smaller, hipper venues use other services like **Ticketfly** (www.ticketfly.com; ✆ **877/987-6487**). Venue websites will direct you to the right place.

The Performing Arts

Although things get quiet in summer, you'll generally find the Phoenix Symphony, the Arizona Opera Company, and Ballet Arizona offering full seasons in downtown Phoenix through the fall and winter. And as the Valley has grown, new state-of-the-art performing arts centers have appeared in the suburbs. Aficionados should check all the listings—it's not uncommon these days to find acts like Yo-Yo Ma, Alvin Ailey, or high-end rock singer-songwriters performing out in the 'burbs.

While you'll find box-office phone numbers listed below, you can also purchase most performing arts tickets through **Ticketmaster** (www.ticketmaster.com; ✆ **800/745-3000**); just about everyone adds on those exorbitant "ticket fees" these days. For sold-out shows, check with your hotel concierge, or try the biggest local scalping operation, **Tickets Unlimited** (www.ticketsunlimited.com; ✆ **800/289-8497** or 480/388-3888), or **StubHub** (www.stubhub.com), which is owned by Ticketmaster.

MAJOR PERFORMING ARTS CENTERS

Built in the early 1970s, **Symphony Hall,** 75 N. Second St. (www.phoenixconventioncenter.com/symphonyhall; ✆ **602/262-7272**) is an austere and impressive place to see just about anything downtown. It is home to the **Phoenix Symphony, Ballet Arizona,** and the **Arizona Opera Company,** and also hosts touring Broadway shows and various other concerts and theatrical productions. Also downtown is the **Comerica Theatre,** 400 W. Washington St. (www.livenation.com; ✆ **602/379-2800** or 602/379-2888), a 5,000-capacity modern pop- and rock-concert hall presenting prestige acts from all genres of entertainment. A splendid piece of Spanish baroque Revival, built downtown in 1929 and successfully restored in the 1990s, the **Orpheum Theatre,** 203

The sleek Tempe Center for the Arts presents a varied bill of music and theater.

W. Adams St. (www.phoenixconventioncenter.com/orpheum-theater; ✆ **602/262-7272**) hosts a variety of cultural events and some rock concerts.

A few miles east of downtown, **Celebrity Theatre,** 440 N. 32nd St. (www.celebritytheatre.com; ✆ **602/267-1600**) is a Phoenix classic. Outside it's a big round building with almost Brutalist architecture; inside there's a vast room with a revolving stage in the middle, making for pretty good sightlines for everyone—for half the show, anyway. It's definitely worth going there if an act you like is appearing. The lineup is crazy eclectic, from Latino stars to country to comedy to classic-rock acts.

On the Arizona State University campus in Tempe, **Grady Gammage Memorial Auditorium** (1200 S. Forest Ave.; www.asugammage.com; ✆ **480/965-3434**) is a spectacular Frank Lloyd Wright work (completed after his death). Top-name acts and touring Broadway shows, from Wilco to *Hamilton*, are the mainstays at this 3,000-seater. Just about anything is fun to see there, but this is now a very old building; a run to the restrooms is quite a trek! A quick walk over the Mill Avenue Bridge from Tempe's downtown, the **Marquee,** 730 N. Mill Ave. (www.marqueetheatreaz.com; ✆ **480/829-0607**), is a 2,500-capacity music venue featuring lots of mid-level touring rock, hip-hop, and pop artists amid local bands and tribute acts. Also in Tempe, on the shore of Tempe Town Lake, the **Tempe Center for the Arts,** 700 W. Rio Salado Pkwy. (www.tempe.gov/TCA; ✆ **480/350-2822**) has water views out its big wall of glass. Its two performance halls present frequent jazz concerts, as well as performances by the Tempe Symphony, Tempe Little Theatre, and Childsplay, a local children's theater company.

The **Scottsdale Center for the Arts,** 7380 E. Second St., Scottsdale (www.scottsdaleperformingarts.org; ✆ **480/994-2787**), has become one of the Valley's preeminent venues for dance, classical, jazz, and public-radio events like *This American Life*. It's set among restaurants and nightspots ringing the gracious Scottsdale Civic Center Mall.

The beautiful **Mesa Arts Center,** 1 E. Main St. (www.mesaartscenter.com; ✆ **480/644-6500**) is part of a spectacular plaza with canopies, sculptures, and water features; the big names it books are often worth the 15-mile trip from downtown Phoenix.

A testament to the East Valley's explosive growth, the **Chandler Center for the Arts,** 250 N. Arizona Ave., Chandler (chandlercenter.org; ✆ **480/782-2680**) often hosts top-tier names in dance, pop, country, and the performing arts in its gorgeous theater.

OUTDOOR VENUES & SERIES

Ak-Chin Pavilion, 2121 N. 83rd Ave., Phoenix (www.ticketmaster.com; ✆ **602/254-7200**), about 10 miles due west of downtown with corporate branding from a local Indian community, is a somewhat faded concert "shed," tending to the rowdy end of top-name stars (Kid Rock, Kendrick Lamar) with a lot of variety throughout the year, from country to metal to classic rock. Beware lawn seats in all but the winter months.

The relatively small **Mesa Amphitheater,** 263 N. Center St., Mesa (www.mesaamp.com; ✆ **480/644-2560**) holds an idiosyncratic variety of concerts in spring and summer, and sometimes hosts the Phoenix Symphony.

Throughout the year, the Scottsdale Center for the Performing Arts, 7380 E. Second St., Scottsdale (www.scottsdaleperformingarts.org; ✆ **480/994-2787**) stages outdoor performances in the adjacent **Scottsdale Amphitheater** on the Scottsdale Civic Center Mall. The Sunday A'fair series runs from January to April, with free concerts from noon to 4pm on selected Sundays of each month. Performances range from acoustic blues to zydeco.

On Sundays from February to May, Music in the Garden concerts are held at the **Desert Botanical Garden,** 1201 N. Galvin Pkwy. in Papago Park (www.dbg.org; ✆ **480/941-1225** or 480/481-8188). The season always includes an eclectic array of musical styles. Tickets are $30; garden admission is included.

Lunch and a Show

At downtown Phoenix's **Herberger Theater Center** (www.herbergertheater.org; ✆ **602/254-7399**), lunch break means the actors hit the stage while the audience grabs sandwiches for Lunch Time Theater. (It's in a small theater around the corner from the main entrance, at 3rd Ave. and Van Buren St.) Through much of the year, 30- to 45-minute plays are staged at noon Tuesday through Thursday. Tickets are $7, and inexpensive boxed salads, sandwiches, and pasta salads can be ordered in advance.

CLASSICAL MUSIC, OPERA & DANCE

None of the main performing-arts organizations in town are second-rate, but **Ballet Arizona** (www.balletaz.org; ✆ **602/381-1096**) stands out. Under impresario Ib Andersen, a principal dancer for Balanchine in the early 1980s, the ensemble delivers superior presentations. (I'm not joking; if during the holidays you're in the mood for a ravishing Nutcracker, for example, you won't be disappointed.) The 2019 schedule includes an all-Balanchine program the first weekend in May. The group performs at both the Orpheum Theatre (p. 144) and Symphony Hall (p. 144); tickets typically run $35 to $150. The **Center Dance Ensemble** (www.centerdance.com; ✆ **602/252-8497**), the city's contemporary dance company, stages several productions a year at the Herberger Center (below). Tickets cost $28 with discounts for seniors and students.

The **Phoenix Symphony** (www.phoenixsymphony.org; ✆ **800/776-9080** or 602/495-1999), the Southwest's leading symphony orchestra, performs at Symphony Hall (p. 144); most tickets run $25 to $100. Programs run from the standard repertoire to the creative pops-oriented programming many such orchestras rely on to keep the keisters in the seats. It's worth checking the schedule out if you're staying downtown and feel like walking over for a show.

The **Arizona Opera** (www.azopera.org; ✆ **602/266-7464**) enthusiastically delivers the warhorses you'd expect in Symphony Hall (p. 144), and more experimental works (like *Charlie Parker's Yardbird*) at the smaller Herberger Center up the street (below). A highlight of the 2019 season is the Pulitzer Prize–winning *Silent Night*, set during the 1914 Christmas truce on the front lines of World War I. The company puts on shows in Tucson as well. Tickets cost $25 to $100.

THEATER

Phoenix isn't a major theater center, but it does get some touring shows, and there are a couple of respectable local operations, in addition to some plucky local troupes.

The city's main venue for live theater, the **Herberger Theater Center,** which vaguely resembles a Spanish colonial church, is located downtown at 222 E. Monroe St. (www.herbergertheater.org; ✆ **602/254-7399**). Its two Broadway-style theaters together host hundreds of performances each year, including productions by the state theater company, **Arizona Theatre Company** (www.aztheatreco.org; ✆ **602/256-6995**). ATC splits its performances between Phoenix and Tucson. Tickets run $40 to $110.

Phoenix Theatre, 100 E. McDowell Rd. (www.phoenixtheatre.net; ✆ **602/254-2151**) shares a building with the Phoenix Art Museum on the corner of McDowell Rd. and Central Ave. It has a strong artistic director and delivers credible work across the spectrum, including rousing musicals. Tickets to most shows are $29 to $79; be aware of a dispiriting $7 ticket fee if you buy online.

Author! Author!

Arizona State University has an enormous number of events in any given week, including author appearances in a dizzying number of fields. It's a bit difficult to find out about them, but it's worth looking at the school's events web page at **asuevents.asu.edu**. Current-events junkies should search for events at the law and journalism schools, both in downtown Phoenix. Fiction fans should take note of the **Virginia G. Piper Center for Creative Writing** (piper.asu.edu/events/upcoming), on the Tempe campus, which has an ongoing schedule of author appearances. **The Poisoned Pen** (p. 140) has a bursting schedule of crime and mystery writers, and the Valley's major independent bookstore, **Changing Hands** (p. 140), has a full schedule of appearances by authors major and minor, and many family and kids' events. Finally, the **Desert Foothills Library** in Cave Creek, 38443 N. Schoolhouse Rd. (www.fdla.org; ✆ **480/488-2286**) has a surprising number of free author events each month.

For touring Broadway productions, you have two choices. Downtown, the **Theater League** (www.theaterleague.com; ✆ **800/776-7469** or 602/262-7272) brings shows to the restored Orpheum Theatre (p. 144); tickets range from $50 to $60. In Tempe, **Broadway Across America–Arizona** (www.broadwayacrossamerica.com/tempe; ✆ **480/965-3434**) brings shows to ASU's gorgeous Gammage Auditorium (p. 145); tickets usually cost between $50 and $150, more for blockbusters like *The Book of Mormon*, which will be there in the fall of 2019.

If you're looking for something to do with the whole family, the **Scottsdale Desert Stages Theatre,** 4720 N. Scottsdale Rd. (www.desertstages.org; ✆ **480/483-1664**) stages primarily musicals and children's theater productions in new digs at the upscale Scottsdale Fashion Square mall. Tickets range from $22 to $28, less for teen productions.

One of the more enterprising—and longest-lasting—underground-y outfits, **Nearly Naked** (100 E. McDowell Rd. www.nearlynakedtheatre.org; ✆ **602/254-2151**) aims for the edgier side of the spectrum. The group puts on shows on one of the small stages at Phoenix Theater (above).

In a comfortable, intimate 150-seat theater a mile or so east of downtown, **The Black Theater Troupe,** 1333 E. Washington Ave. (www.blacktheatretroupe.net; ✆ **602/258-8129**) puts on ambitious programming throughout the year. You can't go wrong if they're staging a musical, from the popular (*The Wiz*) to unearthed obscurities (*The Three Sistahs*).

The Club & Music Scene

As most denizens of any urban nightlife scene know, clubs come and go. I wish I could say there was a nightlife bible to consult here, but there's isn't. But poke around the *Phoenix New Times* website (**phoenixnewtimes.com**) and the *Arizona Republic* website (**azcentral.com**) and you should be able to get some leads on the latest openings.

COUNTRY MUSIC

The best country band in Phoenix is the **Pat James Band;** James, a fine figure of a man in a ten-gallon hat, delivers country ballads, rollicking two-steps, and some unexpected covers with a crack band. Check his website (www.pat james.net) to see where he's playing.

Buffalo Chip Saloon & Steakhouse ★ Come for the mayhem, stay for the (live) bull-riding. Lots of food, drinks, and music available—everything for the visiting cowpoke. There's live music Tuesday through Thursday, with free two-step lessons at 7pm on Mondays, Tuesdays, Thursdays, and Sundays. The bull-riding starts at 7pm Wednesdays and Fridays. Kids are allowed in with parents. The Chip, once owned by Green Bay Packers hall-of-famer Max McGee, is a home-away-from-home for Wisconsinites; head here to watch Packers and Badgers football with kindred souls. 6823 E. Cave Creek Rd., Cave Creek. www.buffalochipsaloon.com. ✆ **480/488-9118.** No cover.

Handlebar J ★★ This Scottsdale landmark has a history that goes back to the early 1960s, when the now busy intersection of Shea Blvd. and Scottsdale Road was basically desert. The Herndon Brothers Band plays most Thursdays, Fridays, and Saturdays. There are free dance lessons on Thursdays; it's closed Mondays. 7116 Becker Lane, Scottsdale. www.handlebarj.com. ✆ **480/948-0110.** $5 cover weekends in tourist season.

The Valley's Nightlife Hubs

If you're looking for big ol' Scottsdale bars with a vaguely Western theme, head over to the city's rather blandly titled **Entertainment District.** The name doesn't do justice to the 4 or 5 sprawling blocks of drinking holes, centered on an extended cul-de-sac just east of the intersection of Camelback and Scottsdale roads. The lineup includes Dierks Bentley's Whiskey Row, Bottled Blonde, Maya Day and Night Club, and the like. If recent history holds, the names may have changed by the time you get there, but the boisterous action will live on. It's all right next to the W Hotel.

Five miles north, at the intersection of Scottsdale Road and Shea Blvd., you'll find some slightly more authentic country joints, like **Handlebar J** (above) on the northwest corner and **Ernie's** (www.erniesscottsdale.com; ✆ **480/948-4433**), on the southwest corner, where you can karaoke to your heart's content with other cowpokes-for-the-night.

Mill Avenue in Tempe is a good place to wander around in search of your favorite type of music; the bars and clubs here are mostly within walking distance of one another. Because Tempe is a college town, the crowd tends to be young and occasionally rowdy. The best venue for touring acts is the **Marquee,** 730 N. Mill Ave., Tempe (www.marquee theatreaz.com; ✆ **480/829-0607**), a half-mile walk north over the Mill Avenue Bridge.

Downtown Phoenix has a growing number of live music venues—the **Van Buren,** the **Crescent,** the **Valley Bar** (all below)—and some dance clubs. It is also home to Symphony Hall (p. 144) and the Herberger Theater Center (p. 147). However, much of the action revolves around sports events and concerts at US Airways Center and Chase Field, which of course are surrounded by sports bars for pre- and post-game drinking.

Rusty Spur Saloon ★ A small, rowdy, drinkin'-and-dancin' place frequented by tourists, this bar claims to be the oldest saloon in Old Town Scottsdale. It's loads of fun, with peanut shells all over the floor, dollar bills stapled to the walls, and live country-music afternoons and evenings. If you're a cowboy or cowgirl at heart, this is the place to party in Scottsdale. 7245 E. Main St., Scottsdale. www.rustyspursaloon.com. ✆ **480/425-7787.** No cover.

DANCE CLUBS & DISCOS

Bar Smith ★ Often packed, this downtown Phoenix nightclub serves up music on two floors—sometimes house and hip-hop, sometimes indie and EDM. 130 E. Washington St., Phoenix. www.barsmithphoenix.com. ✆ **602/456-1991.** Cover $10.

Cirq ★★ Hot-hot Scottsdale nightclubs are always in a state of churn. The latest is Cirq, a self-styled circus-themed club on the southern edge of the Entertainment District. On a given weekend night you may indeed see stilt-walkers or acrobats among the beautiful people gathered here. 7340 E. Stetson Dr., Scottsdale. www.cirqnightclub.com. ✆ **480/828-0347.**

Club Dwntwn ★ This downtown Latino dance club has a good side and a bad side. There are sometimes long lines and service isn't always great; various promoters rule on different nights, and the quality of the entertainment varies accordingly. But when things are hopping, it's the place to be. 702 N. Central Ave., Phoenix. www.clubdwntwn.com. No phone. Cover $10.

Wasted Grain ★ Across the street from Cirq (above), Wasted Grain offers two floors of nightlife fun, plus an outdoor deck. In the concert room, tribute bands play songs from the '80s and '90s; in the 100 Proof Lounge, DJs play the latest sounds. Decent bar food is available, too. 7295 340 E. Indian Plaza, Scottsdale. www.wastedgrain.com. ✆ **480/970-1112.**

ROCK, BLUES & JAZZ

Char's Has the Blues ★ A recurring lineup of steamy soul, r&b, and funk bands pack this uptown club, incongruously occupying a cottage on 7th Avenue, a few blocks south of Camelback Road. There's live music 7 nights a week. 4631 N. 7th Ave., Phoenix. www.charshastheblues.com. ✆ **602/230-0205.** $6 cover Thurs–Sun.

Crescent Ballroom ★ The hang of the moment in downtown Phoenix, this 500-capacity showroom with an accompanying restaurant offers all manner of entertainment, from occasional national touring acts to trivia nights, flamenco dancing, and comedy. The street cafe, **Cocina 10,** was created by two of the Valley's coolest chefs, Chris Bianco (of Pizzeria Bianco, p. 129) and Doug Robeson (of Gallo Blanco, p. 131). Keep an eye out for the Crescent's tribute nights, in which some of the scene's best artists share the stage playing music of this or that songwriter. 308 N. 2nd Ave., Phoenix. www.crescentphx.com. ✆ **602/716-2222.** Cover to showroom varies.

Musical Instrument Museum ★ The MIM has a jewel of a theater, with maybe 400 seats, and books a colorful array of world, jazz, and rock performers—a show almost every night. Music fans contemplating a Valley visit should check out the schedule in advance. If there's a performer you've always wanted to see, or even someone you're curious about, by all means buy tickets online and go; you won't ever experience them in a more intimate setting. The MIM's just south of the 101 in north Phoenix, 15 or 20 minutes from downtown Phoenix or Scottsdale. 4725 E. Mayo Blvd., Phoenix. www.mim.org. ✆ **480/478-6000.**

The Rhythm Room ★ Hardy, homey, and friendly, this downtown club leans toward the blues and Americana. There are regular local bluesmen and national acts once or twice a week. 1019 E. Indian School Rd., Phoenix. www.rhythmroom.com. ✆ **602/265-4842.** Cover $7–$35.

Valley Bar ★ If you're in downtown Phoenix, definitely check this out, as laid-back cool as Phoenix gets. You enter off an alley at the southwest corner of Monroe and Central, in the heart of downtown. Descend a flight of (steep) stairs, and you're in an expansive bar with some decent flatbreads and other food to munch on. It's especially calm for an hour or two after it opens (4pm weekdays, 6pm weekends). An adjoining music room has some strong bookings; on weekends there's generally a late-night DJ. 130 N. Central Ave., Phoenix. www.valleybarphx.com. ✆ **602/368-3121.** No cover; for live shows tickets vary.

The Van Buren ★ Another recent entrant to the downtown music scene, this big (nearly 2,000 capacity) venue, just a few blocks west of the center of downtown, presents everything from Sting to Courtney Barnett. 401 W. Van Buren Ave., Phoenix. www.thevanburenphx.com. ✆ **480/659-1641.** Cover $7–$35.

The Bar & Pub Scene

Lots to choose from. As in other cities, trivia nights are available across the valley, generally on weeknights.

SCOTTSDALE & TEMPE

AZ88 ★ Just steps from the Scottsdale Center for the Arts, this sophisticated bar/restaurant has a hip, contemporary ambience marked by ever-changing extravagant art installations. It's favored by a classy arts crowd, particularly for the convivial patio area. 7353 Scottsdale Mall, Scottsdale. www.az88.com. ✆ **480/994-5576.**

Coach House ★ At this open-air, all-day, every day (that's including Thanksgiving and Christmas) drinking establishment—some would say dive bar—you can check your Scottsdale pretentions at the door. In business for more than 50 years, the place glows at night, particularly during the holiday season, with thousands of stringed lights. 7011 E. Indian School Rd., Scottsdale. www.coachhousescottsdale.com. ✆ **480/990-3433.**

Don & Charlie's ★ Although this is primarily a steakhouse, it also has the best sports bar in Scottsdale. What makes Don & Charlie's such a great sports bar is not the size or number of its TVs, but rather all the sports memorabilia on the walls. 7501 E. Camelback Rd., Scottsdale. www.donandcharlies.com. ✆ **480/990-0900.**

Dos Gringos ★ For young partiers who don't feel like getting dressed up to go out on the town, this is a great choice in south Tempe. With its open-air bar, Dos Gringos is patterned after Mexican beach bars and can be loads of fun on a Saturday night. Locations in Mesa (1958 S. Greenfield Rd.; ✆ **480/633-5525**) and Chandler, too (1361 N. Alma School Rd.; ✆ **480/855-3303**). Open till 2am every night. 8000 S. Priest St., Tempe. www.dosgringosaz.com. ✆ **480/753-4577.**

Hyatt Regency Scottsdale Lobby Bar ★★ The open-air lounge just below the main lobby of this posh Scottsdale resort sets a romantic stage for nightly live music (often flamenco or Caribbean steel drum music). Wood fires burn in patio fire pits, and the terraced gardens offer plenty of spots to sit and chat. 7500 E. Doubletree Ranch Rd., Scottsdale. www.hyatt.com. ✆ **480/444-1234.**

Kazimierz World Wine Bar ★ There's a wine-cellar feel at this sophisticated boite, with a big selection of wines. It's next door to its sister Cowboy Ciao restaurant (p. 116) on the Scottsdale Waterfront, but you enter around back through a big wooden door with a sign that says THE TRUTH IS INSIDE. There's groovy live music for dancing every night except Monday, when it's closed. 7137 E. Stetson Dr., Scottsdale. www.kazbar.net. ✆ **480/946-3004.**

Olive & Ivy ★ At one of the Fox company's most enduring Valley operations, a big bar scene spills out onto a huge patio right on the canal on the Scottsdale Waterfront. (The ostensible address on Camelback Road is misleading—the restaurant is at Marshall Way and the Canal, a quarter-mile south of Camelback Rd. on the far southern tip of the Scottsdale Fashion Square complex.) There are more than 45 wines available by the glass, and the bartenders mix decent drinks, too. Be sure to dress the part. 7135 E. Camelback Rd., Ste. 195, Scottsdale. www.foxrestaurantconcepts.com. ✆ **480/751-2200.**

Papago Brewing ★ Brewing some of the best beers in the valley and serving lots of great beers from other breweries, this pub in south Scottsdale is a beer geek's nirvana, offering a changing lineup of 30 varieties on tap at any one time, plus 500 others by the bottle. 7107 E. McDowell Rd., Scottsdale. www.papagobrewing.com. ✆ **480/425-7439.**

PHOENIX

Bar Bianco ★ Located downtown on Heritage Square, this little wine bar in a restored historic home is affiliated with Pizzeria Bianco (p. 122), the tiny and ever-popular designer-pizza place next door. It's a very romantic spot for a drink. 609 E. Adams St. www.pizzeriabianco.com. ✆ **602/528-3699.**

Cocktails with a View

The Valley of the Sun has more than its fair share of spectacular views. Unfortunately, most of them are from expensive restaurants. All these restaurants have lounges, though, where, for the price of a drink (and perhaps valet parking), you can sit back and ogle a crimson sunset and the purple mountains' majesty. Among the best choices are the **Terrace Room at Different Pointe of View,** at the Pointe Hilton Tapatio Cliffs Resort (p. 109); **Rustler's Rooste,** at the Arizona Grand Resort (p. 110); and the swanky **Jade Bar,** at the Sanctuary on Camelback Mountain (p. 101). The **Thirsty Camel,** the central lounge of the top-tier Phoenician resort (p. 101) boasts some particularly wonderful views. ***Tip:*** To avoid the pricey valet fee, tell the folks at the front gate you want to self-park; you'll be directed to the underground parking garage and the lounge will validate.

It's hard to think of a more spectacular setting in all the Valley than the Wrigley Mansion, sitting on a hill high atop the Biltmore neighborhood a mile north of Camelback Road. It's harder still to think why any casual Valley visitor wouldn't want to go at least once for a drink on the terrace at sunset. Adjoining **Geordie's Restaurant** (p. 122), there's a first-class wine bar, **Jamie's ★**, where you can do just that. It's worth paying for the valet at the top of the hill; it's a steep climb from the self-parking area.

The Bikini Lounge ★★ If the Venn diagram of your perfect bar includes "tiki," "uber-hip," and "right on the edge of skanky," this is your place. The Bikini Lounge has been around since the 1940s; it sits at the top of the Grand Avenue arts district, secure in its distinctive mix of retro and artsy, with some neighbors in the mix to prop up the working-class bona fides. DJs show up most nights, many playing vinyl. Tropical drinks galore, but it's a place for serious drinkers, too. 1502 Grand Ave. www.thebikinilounge.com. ✆ **602/252-0472.**

Bitter & Twisted Cocktail Parlour ★ One of the newest cocktail haunts downtown conjures up extravagantly cockamamie libations in a small but ravishing spot in a redeveloped classic building (it proudly occupies the onetime home of the Arizona Prohibition Commission). The cocktail menu is highly creative, offering fantastical concoctions in everything from plastic honey dispensers to a vintage teacup to—I'm not making this up—a bathtub gin punch served in a small porcelain bathtub, complete with miniature rubber duckies. 1 W. Jefferson St. www.bitterandtwistedaz.com. ✆ **602/340-1924.**

Durant's ★★ As throwbacky as Phoenix gets, this is one of those old-time high-end, enter-through-the-kitchen steakhouses, with a luxe interior and a waitstaff that rocks it old-school. No place in town classier for a late-night drink. 2611 N. Central Ave. www.durantsfinefoods.com. ✆ **602/264-5967.**

Hidden Track Bottle Shop ★ If you're into wine, this small shop on the ground floor of a downtown high-rise is a must-stop. The name is a reference to a "hidden track" on an album or CD; the proprietors pride themselves on finding overlooked wines to share. There's a cafe next door, and wine tastings twice a week. Check the website for the schedule for those, as well as occasional "pop-up dinners" for wine aficionados. 111 W. Monroe St. www.hiddentrackcafe.com. ✆ **602/566-7932.**

Majerle's Sports Grill ★ Phoenix Suns fans won't want to miss this outfit, owed by onetime Suns star Dan Majerle, located just a block north of the Talking Stick Resort Arena, where the Suns play. Drenched in Suns memorabilia. 24 N. 2nd St. www.majerles.com. ✆ **602/253-0118.**

The Mix Up Bar ★★ If you can't make dinner at the exquisite T. Cook's at the Royal Palm (p. 123), try this bar next door—it has the same romantic gentility, but adds a wide range of drink concoctions. You can come late (it's open until 11pm) or come early for some of the best happy-hour deals in town. At the Royal Palms Resort and Spa, 5200 E. Camelback Rd. www.royalpalmshotel.com. ✆ **602/840-3610.**

Postino ★ This popular wine bar—or "industrial wine cafe," as the owners put it—is in the heart of the Arcadia neighborhood behind La Grande Orange (p. 126), a half-mile south of Camelback Road. Casual yet stylish, the bar has an affable staff and garage-style doors that roll up to open the restaurant to the outdoors. Choose from a great selection of wines by the glass and a nice menu of sandwiches and brioches. Postino has become one of the most successful restaurants in the Valley; there's another on N. Central Avenue, just north of Camelback (5144 N. Central Ave.; ✆ **602/274-5144**). Check the website for additional locations in north Scottsdale, central Scottsdale, Tempe, and Gilbert. 3939 E. Campbell Ave. www.postinowinecafe.com. ✆ **602/852-3939.**

The Rose and Crown Pub ★ In a historic Craftsman bungalow on downtown's Heritage Square, this place does a very respectable job of replicating an English pub. The only real difference is that when you sit out on the front porch with your pint of beer, the air is balmy, not damp. I'll drink to that. 628 E. Adams St. www.theroseandcrownaz.com. ✆ **602/256-0223.**

Sun Up Brewing ★ This excellent little brewpub is a bit hard to spot as you drive down busy Camelback Road in central Phoenix, but keep an eye out on the north side of the road and you'll find it. There are usually more than a half-dozen beers on tap, and the seasonal brew can be quite distinctive. 322 E. Camelback Rd. www.sunupbrewing.com. ✆ **602/279-8909.**

The Womack ★★ A very suave hang, the Womack captures the lingering cool of '70s soul. Slide into one of the big circular leather booths and consult with the mixologists at the bar for their latest creations. In late afternoon and early evening, it's dark and quiet; later there are DJs and, on Thursdays, Fridays, and Saturdays, live music, generally groovy soul, blues, or jazz. Open until 2am; closed on Mondays. 5749 N. 7th St. www.thewomack.us. ✆ **602/283-5232.**

IN TEMPE & CHANDLER

Four Peaks Brewing Company ★ Named after a distinctive lineup of mountains in the Superstitions east of Phoenix, this Tempe establishment is consistently voted the best brewpub in Phoenix. Housed in a former creamery, it brews good beers and serves decent pub grub. Serious beer aficionados should check out the once-a-week tasting room opening; call ✆ **480/634-2976** for details. There's a second Four Peaks in north Scottsdale at 15745 N. Hayden Rd. (✆ **480/991-1795**). 1340 E. 8th St., Tempe. www.fourpeaks.com. ✆ **480/303-9967.**

Rula Bula ★ Every college nightlife strip worth its name has a good Irish pub; this is Tempe's version. Rula Bula has such an authentic feel that it's easy to imagine that it's damp and dreary outside. The pub stays packed, primarily with college students. 401 S. Mill Ave., Tempe. www.rulabula.com. ✆ **480/929-9500.**

San Tan Brewing Company ★ This brewpub is another of the reasons I like to hang out in downtown Chandler. With good beer, live music, and walls that roll back to let the warm Arizona air inside, San Tan Brewing is a fun place to cool off on a hot day. 8 S. San Marcos Plaza, Chandler. www.santanbrewing.com. ✆ **480/917-8700.**

Gay & Lesbian Bars & Clubs

The heart of gay Phoenix is **the Melrose**—that's 7th Avenue north of Indian School Road. There's a jog in 7th Avenue—known as "the Curve"—where a distinctive arch has been constructed over the street to celebrate Melrose. (Here's a free barstool conversation starter: Ask if anyone knows why the Curve is there at all. The answer: It was created when surveyors building the 7th Avenue canal crossing just a few blocks north discovered that the street had been inaccurately surveyed heading north from downtown, and was actually tilting northwest! It had to be wrenched back to due north.)

There are also gay- and lesbian-friendly bars dotting the northeast quadrant of the Valley—but note that outside of the Melrose, gay bars don't generally advertise themselves as such. (In fact, if you see a place with a somewhat generic name and no other information, you can pretty much assume it's a gay bar!) In a lot of the hipper clubs and restaurants on Central and 7th avenues you can find a magazine called ***Echo*** that can guide you into the scene and any gay-related events that month.

Anvil ★ This raucous leather bar specializes in good-natured theme nights—"High Heels & Harness," "Fur-i-day," get it?—and karaoke on Thursdays. 2424 E. Thomas Rd., Phoenix. anvilbaraz.com. ✆ **602/334-1462.**

BS West ★ Scottsdale's premier gay bar has a 2pm–8pm happy hour in which your second drink is $1. Friday nights feature the long-running Elements drag show. Sunday is Drunk Karaoke. 7125 E. 5th Ave., Scottsdale. www.bswest.com. ✆ **480/945-9028.** No cover–$3.

VALLEY CASINOS GO FOR THE jackpot

With reservations ringing much of the Valley, casinos are becoming an ever-bigger attraction. And as the sites get bigger, so do the accouterments, including concert facilities, spas, and family activities.

Casino Arizona at Talking Stick Resort ★ The area's lushest casino resort has an unmissable high-rise hotel, conveniently located in the Salt River Pima–Maricopa Indian Community lands just east of north Scottsdale. You can find top-name talent in the theater and all the slot machines and card games you could want. There's a sister casino, Casino Arizona at Salt River, 10 miles south on U.S. 101. U.S. 101 and Indian Bend Rd. *www.talkingstickresort.com.* ✆ **480/850-7777.**

Desert Diamond Casino ★ Currently this is a small casino, on the western edge of the Valley in Glendale, but a larger version is under construction, scheduled to open at the end of 2019. 9431 W. Northern Ave., Glendale. *www.ddcaz.com/west-valley.* ✆ **623/877-7777.**

Fort McDowell Casino ★ Located about 45 minutes northeast of downtown Scottsdale, this is the oldest Indian casino in the state, offering slot machines, poker, keno, bingo, and free shuttles from hotels around the Valley. There's also a very attractive resort hotel here and a big RV park. You'll notice a lot of construction—the casino is replacing itself with a new and even bigger facility next door, slated to open in 2020. 10424 N. Fort McDowell Rd., Fort McDowell (off Ariz. 87, 2 mi NE of Shea Blvd.). *www.fortmcdowellcasino.com.* ✆ **800/843-3678.**

Wild Horse Pass Casino ★ The other large-scale casino and resort in the Valley, Wild Horse Pass is about 15 miles south of downtown Phoenix or Scottsdale, with a full slate of gaming, along with several restaurants, a nightclub, and a concert venue. 5040 Wild Horse Pass Blvd., Chandler. *www.wingilariver.com.* ✆ **800/946-4452.**

The Cash Nightclub & Lounge ★ The most casual lesbian bar in town might be Cash, a few miles east of downtown. The sign outside reads "Cash Inn Country," and it leans a bit to the wannabe cowgirl, with line-dancing and two-step lessons on Tuesdays; a variety of music is played on other nights. Open until midnight weekdays, 2am weekends. 2140 E. McDowell Rd., Phoenix. www.thecashnightclub.com. ✆ **602/244-9943.**

Charlie's ★ The biggest and loudest gay cowboy bar in the city is right around the corner from the top of the Melrose, on Camelback Road just west of 7th Avenue. Besides the usual drag shows and dancing, there's occasional craziness like Foam Parties—and country dance lessons Wednesday, Thursday, and Saturday nights. Looking for late-night fun? On Fridays and Saturdays, the club is open until 4am. 727 W. Camelback Rd., Phoenix. www.charliesphoenix.com. ✆ **602/265-0224.** No cover–$3.

Cruisin' 7th ★ This veteran bar—which is on 7th Street, not 7th Avenue—has everything from drag shows to transsexual pole dancers to comedy. Happy hour starts at 6am—that's *6am*—daily, and the club stays open until 2am. Some nights there's a modest cover. 3702 N. 7th St. www.cruisin7th.com. ✆ **602/212-9888.**

Downtown's Chase Field, home to Arizona Diamondbacks baseball.

Spectator Sports

Phoenix is a decent sport town, albeit one where a lot of visitors and transplants retain loyalty to the home teams back east. Some barely notice, but the Valley has pro franchises in the big four sports: baseball, basketball, football, and hockey. Add to this baseball's spring training Cactus League, golf and tennis tournaments, the annual Fiesta Bowl college football classic, and any number of ASU sports, and you'll generally be able to find a game going on any time of year. **Ticketmaster** (www.ticketmaster.com; ✆ **866/448-7849** or 800/745-3000) sells tickets to most events; for sold-out games, try **Stubhub.com**. ASU collegiate sports tix can be found at www.thesundevils.com.

AUTO RACING At the **ISM Raceway** (formerly Phoenix International), 7602 S. Avondale Blvd. at Baseline Rd., Avondale (www.ismraceway.com; ✆ **866/408-7223**), there's NASCAR and Indy Car racing on the world's fastest 1-mile oval. Tickets generally range from around $10 to $120.

BASEBALL The **Arizona Diamondbacks** (www.diamondbacks.com; ✆ **888/777-4664** or 602/462-6500) have a devoted fan base and regularly pack downtown Phoenix's impressive Chase Field, opened in 1998. The ballpark's retractable roof allows for comfortable play during the blistering summers; it's one of only a few enclosed baseball stadiums with natural grass. Tickets are sold through Ticketmaster, MLB.com, and the Chase Field box office. For some games you can get in for as little as $15; top tickets can be $175-plus. There are three guided tours a day, the last one starting at 12:30pm. Tours cost $7 for adults, $5 for seniors, and $3 for kids 4 to 6.

Cactus League spring training games, which involve more than a dozen major-league baseball teams, have become a huge draw in March and April;

more than 200 games are played at 10 mini-stadiums spread across the entire Valley. Prices start at reasonable—you can get lawn tickets for less than $10—up to as much as $80 for the hottest seats, and of course pricey VIP packages are available. Buy tickets early, particularly for weekend games, if you have your heart set on perennial favorites like the Cubbies or the Giants. While all the teams have their "home" stadiums, they also play a lot of "away" games. So if you're a Cleveland Indians fan, "home" is in Goodyear, in the far west Valley, but the team may also play games at a stadium 20 or 30 miles away—peruse the schedule a bit to figure out where to stay. None of the stadiums are close to downtown Phoenix; there's one in central Scottsdale, however. Check the Cactus League website (www.cactusleague.com) for maps, schedules, and tickets.

BASKETBALL The NBA's **Phoenix Suns** play at the Talking Stick Resort Arena, 201 E. Jefferson St. (www.suns.com; ✆ **800/462-2849** or 602/379-7867). Most tickets cost between $10 and $275. Suns games usually sell out. Buy long in advance or hit the resale sites. Phoenix's WNBA team, the **Phoenix Mercury** (mercury.wnba.com; ✆ **602/252-9622** or 602/514-8331), plays at the same arena between May and August. Tickets cost $10 to $200-plus.

FOOTBALL The **Arizona Cardinals** (www.azcardinals.com; ✆ **800/999-1402** or 602/379-0102) play at the 65,000-seat state-of-the-art University of Phoenix Stadium in the west Valley city of Glendale. This stadium has a retractable roof made of translucent fabric—and a movable 2-acre playing field, which is rolled out into the sun outside the stadium during rock concerts and other uses. Ticket prices range from $50 to $445; single-game tickets for the entire season go on sale in late July.

GOLF TOURNAMENTS Late January's **Waste Management Phoenix Open Golf Tournament** (www.wastemanagementphoenixopen.com; ✆ **602/870-0163**) is the golf event of the year. Held at the Tournament Players Club (TPC) of Scottsdale, it attracts more spectators than any other golf tournament in the world (usually more than 500,000 each year). The 18th hole has standing room for 40,000. Tickets start at $25.

HOCKEY The NHL's **Phoenix Coyotes** (www.phoenixcoyotes.com; ✆ **480/563-7825**) plays at the state-of-the-art Jobing.com Arena in Glendale (northwest of downtown Phoenix). Tickets cost $36 to $354.

HORSE RACING **Turf Paradise,** 1501 W. Bell Rd., Phoenix (www.turfparadise.com; ✆ **602/942-1101**) offers racing from early October to early May, generally Saturdays through Wednesdays. Tickets are $3, free Mondays through Wednesdays; reserved clubhouse seats are $5.

RODEOS, POLO & HORSE SHOWS There's no real Phoenix rodeo, but there is a rodeo with Scottsdale's annual Western parade, the **Parada del Sol,** in early March (www.paradadelsol.net), held at WestWorld of Scottsdale, 16601 N. Pima Rd., Scottsdale (www.westworldaz.com; ✆ **480/312-6802**). WestWorld also hosts the annual massive **Arabian horse show** in the second week of February each year. The American Quarter Horse Association's **Ari-**

Thoroughbreds have been racing at Turf Paradise since 1956.

zona **Sun Circuit** of shows is very popular (for info, go to www.sun circuit.com). Farther north, Prescott hosts **Prescott Frontier Days** at the end of June each year (for info, go to www.worldsoldestrodeo.com), and Wickenburg hosts all manner of **roping events;** check www.arizonateamroping.com.

A SIDE TRIP FROM PHOENIX: THE APACHE TRAIL ★

There isn't a whole lot of desert or history left in Phoenix, but only an hour's drive to the east, you'll find quite a bit of both. The **Apache Trail,** a narrow, winding, partially gravel road that snakes its way around the north side of the mysterious and beautiful Superstition Mountains, offers some of the most scenic desert driving in central Arizona. Along the way are ghost towns and ancient ruins, saguaros and century plants, reservoirs and hiking trails. You could easily spend a couple days traveling this route, though most people make it a day trip.

One thing you should know: The Apache Trail is a real trail, following the Salt River on the side of a mountain, and there aren't guardrails. After about Canyon Lake, the paved road turns into dirt. It's well graded—and you'll see, particularly on weekends, a lot of folks tow pleasure boats up the thing. But be prepared to navigate cliffs on the road heading up, and be particularly mindful coming down, when you'll be on the cliff side of the road.

To start this drive, head east on U.S. 60 to the town of **Apache Junction** (officially named Ariz. 88) on the eastern edge of the valley, then go north on Ariz. 88. About 4 miles out of town is **Goldfield Ghost Town,** a reconstructed gold-mining town (p. 79). Allow plenty of time if you plan to stop here.

Not far from Goldfield is **Lost Dutchman State Park,** 6109 N. Apache Trail (www.azstateparks.com; ✆ **480/982-4485**), where you can hike into the rugged Superstition Mountains and see what the region's gold seekers were up against. (The hike to the top of the jagged, rugged Flatiron is tough going, but a keeper.) Springtime wildflower displays here can be absolutely gorgeous. Park admission is $7 per vehicle; the campground charges $15 to $17 per site.

Continuing northeast over 10 miles of winding road, you'll reach **Canyon Lake,** set in a deep canyon flanked by colorful cliffs and rugged rock formations. This is the first of three reservoirs you'll pass on this drive; together the three lakes provide much of Phoenix's drinking water. (The other big source of water is the Colorado River on the state's western border.) At Canyon Lake, you can swim at the **Acacia Picnic Area** or the nearby **Boulder Creek Picnic Area,** in a pretty side cove. You can also take a 90-minute cruise on the reproduction paddle-wheeler ***Dolly* steamboat** (www.dollysteamboat.com; ✆ **480/827-9144**); it costs $25 for adults, $23 seniors, $15 ages 5 to 12, and $6 for kids 1 to 4. A Saturday dinner cruise ($68 adults, $40 children) is also available, and once a month, there is a twilight astronomy cruise. There's also a lakeside restaurant at the boat landing.

But hold out for **Tortilla Flat** (www.tortillaflataz.com; ✆ **480/984-1776**), an old stagecoach stop with a restaurant, saloon, and general store, 3 miles up the road. The ceiling and interior walls of this funky old place are plastered with thousands of dollar bills left by previous customers. If it's hot out, stop in at the general store for some prickly-pear ice cream (guaranteed spineless).

Past Tortilla Flat, the asphalt ends. Drive carefully, but check out the truly spectacular desert scenery. Among the rocky ridges, arroyos, and canyons on this stretch of road, you'll see saguaro cacti and century plants (a type of agave that dies after sending up its flower stalk, which can be as high as 15 feet tall). After 15 miles of sometimes treacherous road you'll come to **Apache Lake,** which is not nearly as spectacular as Canyon Lake, but a much bigger and busier operation, including the **Apache Lake Marina and Resort** (www.apachelake.com; ✆ **928/467-2511**), with a motel, restaurant, and general store. Rooms run $90 to $120; in summer there are 2-night minimums on weekends, 3-night minimums on holiday weekends.

Shortly before reaching pavement again, you'll see **Theodore Roosevelt Dam.** This dam, built in 1911, the year before Arizona became a state, forms Roosevelt Lake; despite its concrete face, it's the largest masonry dam in the world and was quite an achievement in its day. Roosevelt Lake is four or five times as big as the other lakes along the Salt, but I have to say it's not as picturesque, aside from the beautiful arched bridge near the dam.

Right here you have a choice. You can go north over the bridge, if you're in the mood for more highways winding through desert mountains. From there you'll go northwest on Ariz. 188 for another 30 miles; there are a few restaurants to stop at along the way. Ultimately, you'll hit Ariz. 87. Take a left, go south, and in another 35 or 40 minutes you'll be back in the town of Fountain Hills, where you can get a cold drink and head another 10 minutes into north Scottsdale.

Going the other direction is a little more interesting. Staying on Ariz. 88, you'll next come to **Tonto National Monument** ★ (www.nps.gov/tont; ✆ **928/467-2241**), which preserves some of the southernmost cliff dwellings in Arizona. Occupied between about 1300 and 1450 by the Salado people, these pueblos are some of the few remaining traces of this tribe, which once cultivated lands now flooded by Roosevelt Lake. The lower ruins, open daily year-round, are a half-mile up a steep trail from the visitor center. The upper ruins are reached by a 3-mile round-trip trek, and can only be visited on a guided hike on weekends. Call the number above to make a reservation; space is limited. The park is open daily (except Christmas) from 8am to 5pm (you must begin the lower ruin trail by 4pm); admission is $7.

Thirty miles along on Ariz. 88, you'll come to the copper-mining town of **Globe.** Although you can't see the mines themselves, the tailings (remains of rock removed from the copper ore) can be seen, piled high all around the town. Be sure to visit **Besh-Ba-Gowah Archaeological Park** ★ (www.globeaz.gov/visitors/besh-ba-gowah; ✆ **928/425-0320**), on the eastern outskirts of town, a partially reconstructed Salado Indian pueblo site with several rooms set up to reflect how they might have looked when occupied, about 700 years ago. They're among the most fascinating ruins in the state. Besh-Ba-Gowah is

A highlight of the Apache Trail drive: the pueblo ruins at Besh-Ba-Gowah Archaeological Park.

open daily 9am to 4:30pm (closed New Year's Day, Thanksgiving, and Christmas); admission is $5 adults, $4 seniors, and free for kids 12 and under. To get there, head out of Globe on South Broad St. to Jesse Hayes Rd.

From Globe, head west on U.S. 60. Three miles west of Superior, you'll come to the 320-acre **Boyce Thompson Arboretum ★★**, 37615 U.S. 60 (arboretum.ag.arizona.edu; ✆ **602/287-3000**). Dedicated to researching and propagating desert plants, this was the nation's first botanical garden established in the desert; it's set in two small, rugged canyons. From the impressive cactus gardens, you can gaze up at sunbaked cliffs before ducking into a forest of eucalyptus trees that grow along a stream. As you hike the nature trails, watch for the two bizarre boojum trees. September through April, the arboretum is open daily 8am to 4pm; May through August, it's open 6am to 3pm. Admission is $7.50 adults, $3 for ages 5 to 12. There are regularly scheduled guided tours of the garden; call for the schedule.

EN ROUTE TO TUCSON

The drive to Tucson from Phoenix is 90 minutes or so on I-10, where you'll find the attractions below. For a slightly meandering alternative, take Ariz. 60 east past Apache Junction to Ariz. 79 south. You'll have an hour or two of undeveloped desert vistas on the way to Tucson; you can stop in **Florence,** which has a historical downtown, and pay your respects at the death marker of Tom Mix, the Western star of the silent movie era, who lost his life in a car accident there in 1940. (That's 17 miles south of Florence on Ariz.79.)

Casa Grande Ruins National Monument ★★ ANCIENT SITE This spectacular ruin is 12 miles east of I-10 and its namesake town of Casa Grande. *Casa grande*, of course, means "big house," and that's exactly what you'll find here, the dramatic ruins of an earth-walled adobe structure built 650 years ago by the Hohokam people. Towering four stories high, it is protected from the elements by an even more towering ramada roof designed by Frederick Law Olmsted. The visitor center exhibits and tours are fascinating; they provide a glimpse into the lives of the somewhat mysterious Hohokam people, who lived in the region for thousands of years before abruptly disappearing in the 1400s.

1100 W. Ruins Dr., Coolidge (Ariz. 87, 1 mi N of Coolidge). www.nps.gov/cagr. ✆ **520/723-3172.** $10 adults; free for kids 15 and under. Daily 9am–5pm (closes at 4pm May–Sept). Closed Fourth of July, Thanksgiving, and Christmas.

Picacho Peak State Park ★★ PARK You can't miss Picacho Peak, a wizard's cap of rock rising 1,500 feet above the desert, just before you hit the outskirts of Tucson. Hiking trails lead around the lower slopes of the peak and up to the summit; these trails are especially alluring in spring, when the wildflowers bloom. Campsites cost $30 ($25 in summer).

Exit 219 off I-10. www.azstateparks.com/picacho. ✆ **520/466-3183.** $7 per car. Daily 5am–10pm.

Rooster Cogburn Ostrich Ranch ★ WILDLIFE VIEWING A goofy but enjoyable novelty roadside attraction: an offbeat petting zoo, with ostriches, miniature deer and goats, lorakeets, and other animals to feed and pet (though don't try to pet the ostriches!). ***Note:*** In summer it's open only from Fridays through Mondays.

Exit 219 (Picacho Peak exit) off I-10. www.roostercogburn.com. ✆ **520/466-3658.** $10 admission includes feed for the animals. Free for children 5 and under. Nov–Apr daily 9am–5pm; May–Oct Fri–Mon 9am–5pm.

EN ROUTE TO NORTHERN ARIZONA

Just as you leave the Phoenix city limits on I-17, there's a big outlet mall: the **Outlets at Anthem,** 4250 W. Anthem Way (www.outletsanthem.com; ✆ **623/465-9500**). Among the offerings are Ann Taylor, Polo Ralph Lauren, and Levi's. Take exit 229 (Anthem Way).

Some 10 miles farther north, just before you hit the town of Black Canyon City, exit 242 is a mandatory stop for pie lovers. Follow the signs to the **Rock Springs Café,** 35769 S. Old Black Canyon Hwy., Rock Springs (www.rockspringscafe.com; ✆ **623/374-5794**). In business since 1918, it's a fine family restaurant that has made its name selling a delectable array of pies.

One of Arizona's most interesting cultural figures is **Paolo Soleri,** an Italian architect who came to the Valley in 1956 and lived here until his death, at 93, in 2013. Soleri was an architectural utopian who envisioned a grand futuristic city—or "bio-climatic architectural environment"—in the desert. His masterwork is **Arcosanti** (www.arcosanti.org; ✆ **928/632-7135**), an array of concrete buildings an hour north of Phoenix, built on ecological principles atop a natural desert canyon. It has slowly been expanded by generations of students since 1970; to help finance the construction, the foundation casts and sells distinctive Soleri-designed bronze wind bells, available at the gift shop. Arcosanti is open daily from 9am to 5pm except on national holidays. There's no admission per se; tours are held hourly (except at noon) from 10am-4pm with a $10 suggested donation. Most weekday mornings you can see the foundry in action; call after 9am weekdays to see when the bells will be poured that day. If you'd like to stay overnight, basic accommodations ($35–$100 double) are available by reservation. There's also a cafe. Take the Arcosanti Rd. exit off I-17, 1 mile north of the junction with Ariz. 69.

Between Black Canyon City and Cordes Junction lies **Agua Fria National Monument** (www.blm.gov/visit/agua-fria), a large tract of land running for miles on both sides of I-17. Within it lies a vast network of prehistoric Native American ruin sites, which date from between 1250 and 1450. ***Note:*** There is very limited access to the monument, and there are no facilities for visitors. If you have a high-clearance vehicle, preferably four-wheel-drive, you can enter the monument from I-17 at the Badger Springs exit (exit 256) or the Bloody Basin Road exit (exit 259).

CENTRAL ARIZONA

5

It's easy—you fly into Phoenix, drive north, and in 4 or 5 hours you're at the Grand Canyon. Nothing to see in between, right?

Between Phoenix and the Grand Canyon lies one of the most beautiful landscapes on earth, the red-rock country of Sedona and Oak Creek Canyon. It's one of those places where, when you see it for the first time, it's almost as if a tympani beats a fanfare. That's reason enough to allot some extra time on the trip to the Grand Canyon.

But there's more. Central Arizona also has the former territorial capital of Prescott, historic sites, ancient Indian ruins, an old mining town turned artists' community in Jerome, and even a few good old-fashioned dude ranches (and some recently-in-the-news rehabilitation clinics) out Wickenburg way. Lately, central Arizona has even begun to become somewhat of a wine region.

People have been drawn here for hundreds of years. The Hohokam nation farmed the fertile Verde Valley as long ago as A.D. 600, followed later by the Sinagua. By the time the first white settlers arrived in the 1860s, Apache and Yavapai tribes inhabited the area, and the U.S. Army established Fort Verde, now in the town of Camp Verde, in 1871, beginning decades of bloodshed and suppression of the native peoples. The mining industry brought prosperity to the region—that is, until the mines gave out, leaving ghost towns in their wake. Layers of history are piled deep in this stunning landscape.

WICKENBURG ★

53 miles NW of Phoenix; 61 miles S of Prescott; 128 miles SE of Kingman

Known a half-century ago as the dude-ranch capital of the world, Wickenburg still has a handful of dude (or guest) ranches, ranging from rustic to luxurious, where you can ride horses and throw a horseshoe or two. A growing sprawl—miles and miles of nice houses are now visible on the road from Phoenix—surrounds a small town with an old-time downtown and a few cowboy activities still to be seen. (Wickenburg calls itself the team roping capital of the world—see box, p. 168.) It's also home to a number of rehab centers, including the Meadows, where a number of scandal-shamed celebrities have found themselves in recent years.

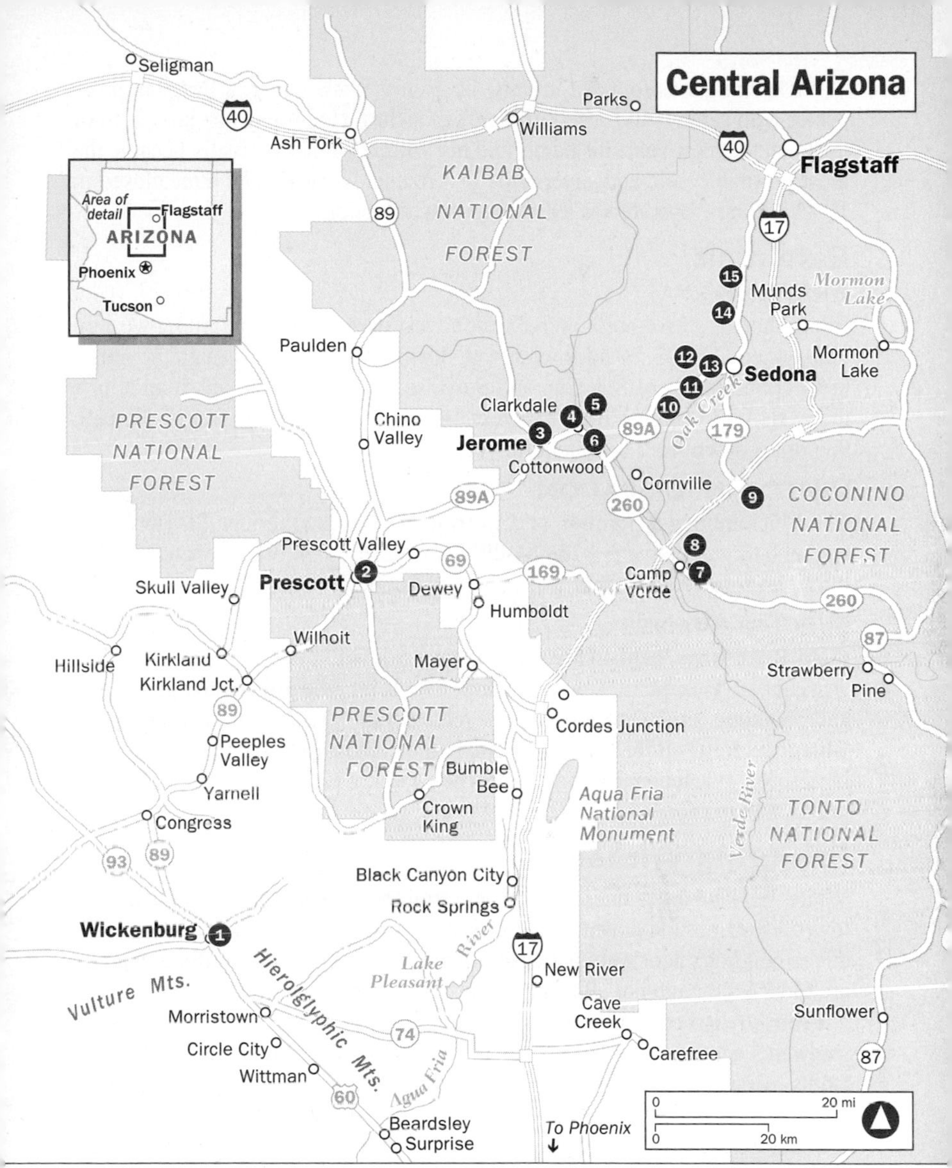

Boynton Canyon **13**
Camp Verde **7**
Clarkdale **4**
Cottonwood **6**
Crescent Moon Picnic Area **11**
Jerome **3**
Montezuma Castle National Monument **8**
Oak Creek Canyon **15**
Palatki Heritage Site **12**
Prescott **2**
Red Rock State Park **10**
Slide Rock State Park **14**
Tuzigoot National Monument **5**
V Bar V Heritage Site **9**
Wickenburg **1**

Wickenburg was founded in 1863 by Henry Wickenburg, a Prussian prospector who came to the desert in search of riches. He hit pay dirt just south of the town that now bears his name, and his Vulture Mine eventually became the most profitable gold and silver mine in Arizona. Although the mine closed in 1942, it is now operated as a minor tourist attraction.

Essentials

ARRIVING

From Phoenix, drive north on I-17, then west on Ariz. 74, continuing west on U.S. 60, or take U.S. 60 northwest from downtown, passing through the retirement communities of Sun City and Surprise. Either way, it's about an hour's drive. If you're coming from the west, take U.S. 60 northeast from I-10. U.S. 93 comes down from I-40 in northwestern Arizona.

VISITOR INFORMATION

The **Wickenburg Chamber of Commerce,** 216 N. Frontier St. (www.outwickenburgway.com; ✆ **928/684-0977** or 928/684-5479) is open Monday through Friday 9am to 5pm, Saturday and Sunday 10am to 2pm.

SPECIAL EVENTS

Gold Rush Days, held on the second full weekend in February for more than 70 years, is Wickenburg's biggest party; events include gold panning, a rodeo, and shootouts in the streets. On the second full weekend in November, the **Bluegrass Festival** features fiddle and banjo contests. On the first weekend in December, Wickenburg's annual **Cowboy Poetry Gathering** features lots of poetry and music.

Exploring Wickenburg

While Wickenburg's main attractions remain the guest ranches outside of town, a walk around downtown also provides a glimpse of the Old West. Most of the buildings here were built between 1890 and the 1920s (although a few are older), although not all of them look their age.

Frontier Street is preserved as it looked in the early 1900s. The covered sidewalks and false fronts are characteristic of frontier architecture; the false fronts often disguised older adobe buildings that were considered "uncivilized" by settlers from back east. Stop by the old Santa Fe train station on Frontier Street, now the **Wickenburg Chamber of Commerce** (see above), to pick up a map that tells the history of the town's buildings. The brick post office, almost across the street from the train station, once had a ride-up window providing service to people on horseback. **The Garcia Little Red Schoolhouse,** 245 N. Tegner St. (www.wco.org; ✆ **928/684-7473**), open Tuesday through Saturday 10am to 2pm, is another of the town's old-timey sights.

Two of the town's most unusual attractions aren't buildings at all. The **Jail Tree,** behind the convenience store at the corner of Wickenburg Way and Tegner Street, is an old mesquite tree that served as the local hoosegow.

Wickenburg cherishes its cowboy heritage, with guest ranches, cowboy poetry readings, and its status as "team roping capital of the world."

Outlaws were simply chained to the tree. Their families would often come to visit and have a picnic in the tree's shade. Then there's the **Wishing Well,** standing beside the bridge over the Hassayampa. Legend has it that anyone who drinks from the Hassayampa River will never tell the truth again. How the well adjacent to the river became a wishing well is unclear.

Desert Caballeros Western Museum ★ MUSEUM Inside this museum, an outstanding collection of Western art depicts life on the range, including works by Albert Bierstadt, Thomas Moran, Charles Russell, Frederic Remington, Maynard Dixon, and other members of the Cowboy Artists of America. The impressive "Spirit of the Cowboy" collection of historical cowboy gear alone makes this museum worth a stop.

21 N. Frontier St. www.westernmuseum.org. ✆ **928/684-2272.** $12 adults, $10 seniors, free for ages 17 and under. Mon–Sat 10am–5pm; Sun noon–4pm. Closed Mon June–Aug and on major holidays.

Hassayampa River Preserve ★ NATURE PRESERVE At one time, the Arizona desert was laced with rivers that flowed for most, if not all, of the year. In the past century, however, these rivers, and the riparian forests they once supported, have disappeared at an alarming rate as rivers are dammed and wells lower the water tables. Riparian areas support trees and plants that require more water than is usually available in the desert, and this lush growth provides food and shelter for hundreds of species of birds, mammals, and reptiles. Today, the riparian cottonwood-willow forests of the desert

The Team Roping Capital of the World

Team roping is when two cowpokes on horses chase a calf across an arena and get points for how fast they immobilize it. Wickenburg's large rodeo facility, the **Everett Bowman Rodeo Grounds,** 935 Constellation Rd. (www.ci.wickenburg.az.us/69/Rodeo-Grounds), is a mile or two northeast of the town center; another popular roping venue, **Rancho Rio,** is north of downtown at 1325 N. Tegner St. (ranchorioaz.com). From November through April there are team roping events there and at several other venues. For an event calendar, go to outwickenburgway.com or call the Chamber of Commerce at ✆ **928/684-0977.**

Southwest are considered the country's most endangered forest type. The Nature Conservancy, a nonprofit organization dedicated to purchasing and preserving threatened habitats, and the Maricopa County Parks Department work together to manage the Hassayampa River Preserve. It's an important bird-watching site—280 species of birds have been spotted here. Nature trails lead along the river beneath cottonwoods and willows, and past spring-fed Palm Lake. On-site are a visitor center and bookshop. On the Maricopa County parks website, www.maricopacountyparks.net, under "programs and events" you can find a schedule of nature walks and other activities at this preserve; private guided tours are available as well.

49614 N. U.S. 60 (milepost 114, 3 mi SE of Wickenburg). www.maricopacountyparks.net. ✆ **928/684-2772.** $5, free for kids 12 and under. Oct–Apr Wed–Sun 8am–5pm; May–Oct Wed–Sun 7am–4pm. Closed Mon–Tues. Closed Thanksgiving, day after Thanksgiving, Christmas Eve, Christmas Day, New Year's Eve, and New Year's Day.

The Vulture Mine ★ HISTORIC SITE Lying at the base of Vulture Peak (the most visible natural landmark in the Wickenburg area, about 12 miles south of the town proper), the Vulture Mine was first staked by Henry Wickenburg in 1863, fueling the small gold rush that helped populate this part of the Arizona desert. Today, the Vulture Mine feels like a ghost town. You can't go down into the old mine itself, but you can wander around the aboveground shacks and mine structures, either on tours or, in summer, by yourself. It's interesting for Western history buffs, and fun for kids.

36610 N. 355 Ave. (12 mi S of U.S. 60 W via Vulture Mine Rd.). www.vultureminetours. $15; free for kids under 6. Cash only. Check website for hours, which vary. No guided tours in summer. Closed Thanksgiving and Christmas.

Outdoor Activities

If you'd rather explore the desert backcountry by jeep than on horseback, call **B.C. Jeep Tours** (www.bcjeeptours.com; ✆ **928/684-7901**), which charges $75 per person with a two-person minimum. If you've got time for only one jeep tour on your Arizona vacation, however, make it in Sedona.

Los Caballeros Golf Club ★★, 1551 S. Vulture Mine Rd. (www.loscaballerosgolf.com; ✆ **928/684-2704**) has been rated one of the best courses in the state. Greens fees range $85 to $125 in the cooler months.

Southwest of town at the end of Vulture Mine Rd. (off U.S. 60), hikers can hit the trails around **Vulture Peak,** which include a steep but rewarding climb best done in the cooler months. The views from up top (or even just the saddle near the top) are well worth the effort. There are sometimes spectacular wildflower displays here in the spring.

Where to Stay in Wickenburg

Flying E Ranch ★ This is a working cattle ranch with 20,000 high, wide, and handsome acres for you and the cattle to roam. In business since 1946, the Flying E attracts plenty of repeat business; families find it a particularly appealing place. Accommodations vary in size, but all have Western-style furnishings and either twin or king-size beds. Three family-style meals are served in the wood-paneled dining room; there's no bar (you'll need to bring your own liquor). Guests like to gather by the fireplace in the main lodge's spacious lounge. Breakfast cookouts, lunch rides, hayrides, and evening chuck-wagon dinners are organized. Horseback riding costs an additional $40 to $60 per person per day.

2801 W. Wickenburg Way (4 mi W of town on U.S. 60). www.flyingeranch.com. ✆ **928/684-2690.** 17 units. $360 double, $720 4-person cabin. Rates include all meals. Closed May–Oct. **Amenities:** Dining room; exercise room; Jacuzzi; outdoor pool; sauna; tennis court; free Wi-Fi.

Kay El Bar Guest Ranch ★ This is the smallest and oldest of the Wickenburg guest ranches, and its adobe buildings, built between 1914 and 1925, are listed on the National Register of Historic Places. The well-maintained ranch is quintessentially Wild West in style—the lobby is Westerned up to within an inch of its life—and the setting, on the shady banks of the Hassayampa River (usually dry), is surprisingly lush compared with the arid surrounding landscape. While the Homestead House and the Casa Grande are the most spacious, smaller rooms in the adobe main lodge have original Monterey-style furnishings and other classic 1950s dude-ranch decor. I like this place because it's so small you feel like you're on a friend's ranch. Guests can go out horseback riding twice a day, except on Sunday when there's a long morning ride followed by lunch on a hilltop. There are also cookouts, cowboy poetry nights, and other Western activities.

2655 S. Kay El Bar Rd. (take S. Rincon Rd. N from U.S. 93). www.kayelbar.com. ✆ **928/684-7593.** 11 units. $55–$610 double; $1,194 cottage (sleeps 4). Rates include all meals and horseback riding. 2- to 4-night minimum stay. Closed May–mid-Oct. **Amenities:** Dining room; lounge; Jacuzzi; outdoor pool.

Rancho de los Caballeros ★★ A few miles south of town on Vulture Mine Road, this quiet, sprawling resort-cum-dude-ranch offers lots of opportunity for horseback riding, golf on a ravishingly beautiful adjoining golf course, or pampering treatments in the classy spa. There's also trap and skeet shooting and guided nature walks. The main lodge, with its flagstone floor, copper fireplace, and colorfully painted furniture, has a very southwestern feel. Peace and quiet are the keynotes of a visit here. Guest rooms have

En Route to Prescott

Between Wickenburg and Prescott, as Ariz. 89 climbs out of the desert, the town of **Yarnell** lies at the top of a steep stretch of road. The landscape around Yarnell is a jumble of weather-worn granite boulders, giving the town a unique look; in recent years it's become a favored getaway for Phoenix types. Several crafts and antiques shops here are worth a stop. However, the town's main claim to fame is the **Shrine of St. Joseph of the Mountains** (✆ **928/778-5229**), a beautiful path set on the side of the mountain with carved stone sculptures marking the Stations of the Cross. Watch for the sign to the shrine off Ariz. 89 on the north end of town.

handcrafted furnishings, exposed-beam ceilings, Indian rugs, and, in some, tile floors and fireplaces. Most have small kitchens, which you don't need because the food here, created and prepared by real chefs, is so good; the layouts for breakfast and lunch—with custom omelet-making and meat-carving tables and the like—seem to go on forever. And the pies! (The biggest complaint you hear here is that there's too much food.) Dinner, which is served formally, with proper attire required, is even better.

1551 S. Vulture Mine Rd. (S off U.S. 60 west of town). www.ranchodeloscaballeros.com. ✆ **800/684-5030** or 928/684-5484. 79 units. $200–$400 double. 15% gratuity charge. Rates include all meals. Closed May–Nov. **Amenities:** Dining room; lounge; children's programs; concierge; 18-hole golf course; pool; full-service spa; 4 tennis courts; free Wi-Fi.

Where to Eat in Wickenburg

If you'll be staying at a guest ranch, all your meals will be provided. In town, it's almost obligatory to stop in at the **Rancho Bar 7,** 111 E. Wickenburg Way (www.ranchobar7.com; ✆ **928/684-2492**), which has a big ol' bar, a decent menu, and cowboy statues outside. Across the street, there's a friendly sports bar, the **Mecca,** 163 E. Wickenburg Way (✆ **928/684-35270**), with a big patio and decent bar food. Want something homier? **Nana's Sandwich Shop,** 48 N. Tegner St. (✆ **928/684-5539**) is just around the corner.

PRESCOTT ★★

100 miles N of Phoenix; 66 miles SW of Sedona; 87 miles SW of Flagstaff

Prescott is an Arizona anomaly, a unique mixture of mountain town and western town. It doesn't seem like the Southwest at all. With its stately courthouse on a tree-shaded square, two-story 19th-century buildings fronting most of it, and wooded mountains surrounding the town, Prescott still has the air of the rugged territorial capital it once was. The obligatory stroll around Courthouse Plaza is a delight, passing restored saloons, hotels and souvenir and antique shops—and, these days, decent cafes and restaurants, too. Add to this several small museums, a couple of historic hotels, the strange and beautiful landscape of the Granite Dells, and nearby Prescott National Forest, and you have a town that appeals to a wide range of visitors.

Prescott's pioneer history dates from 1863, when the Walker party discovered gold in the mountains of central Arizona. Soon miners were flocking to the area to seek their own fortunes. A year later, Arizona became a U.S. territory, and the new town of Prescott, located right in the center of Arizona, was made the territorial capital. It would eventually lose that title to Tucson and then to Phoenix, but for part of the late 19th century, Prescott was the most important city in Arizona. Wealthy merchants and legislators transformed this pioneer outpost into a beautiful town filled with stately Victorian homes.

Today Prescott has become an upscale retirement community, with the housing prices to prove it. In summer, Prescott is a popular weekend getaway for Phoenicians; it is usually 20° cooler here than in Phoenix (and most winters even see some snow).

Essentials

ARRIVING

Prescott lies at the junction of Ariz. 89 and Ariz. 69. If you're coming from Phoenix, take the Cordes Junction exit (exit 262) from I-17 onto Ariz. 69 and drive northwest for 25 miles (traffic is sometimes slow-going). The trip from Phoenix takes a little under 2 hours. From Flagstaff, the most direct route is I-17 to Ariz. 169 to Ariz. 69; there's also a more picturesque but significantly slower route, Ariz. 89A, through Sedona and Cottonwood.

From Sky Harbor Airport, **Arizona Shuttle** (www.arizonashuttle.com; ✆ **520/795-6771**) provides service to Prescott for $39 one-way.

VISITOR INFORMATION

The **Prescott Chamber of Commerce** is at 117 W. Goodwin St. (www.visit-prescott.com; ✆ **800/266-7534** or 928/445-2000), on the south side of Courthouse Plaza. It's open Monday through Friday 9am to 5pm, and Saturday and Sunday 10am to 2pm.

CITY LAYOUT

Prescott Valley has grown explosively; the stretch of Ariz. 69 from I-17 is now lined with shopping malls and housing (there's even a Trader Joe's!). Prescott's main drag is **Gurley Street,** which ultimately forms the north side of Courthouse Plaza. Ariz. 89, heading north from Wickenburg, eventually becomes **Montezuma Street,** also known as Whiskey Row, which forms the west side of the plaza.

SPECIAL EVENTS

In early June, **Territorial Days** features special art exhibits, performances, tournaments, races, and lots of food and free entertainment. Prescott's biggest annual event is the **World's Oldest Rodeo** (www.worldsoldestrodeo.com; ✆ **928/445-3103**), generally held during the week leading up to the Fourth of July. In mid-July, the Sharlot Hall Museum (see below) hosts the **Prescott Indian Art Market.**

The stately Yavapai County Courthouse in Prescott recalls the city's heyday as capital of the Arizona territory.

Exploring Prescott

A walk around **Courthouse Plaza** should be your first introduction to Prescott. The stately old courthouse in the middle of the tree-shaded plaza sets the tone for the whole town. If it seems far too large for a small regional town, it is—it was built in the days when Prescott was capital of the Arizona territory. Under the big shade trees, you'll see several bronze statues, including a striking one dedicated to Teddy Roosevelt's Rough Riders, a group of Spanish-American War volunteers who headed off from the plaza in 1898. I really like the historical timeline painted into one of the walks.

Surrounding the courthouse and extending north for a block or so is Prescott's historic business district. Stroll around admiring the brick buildings, and you'll realize that Prescott was once a very important place. On Montezuma Street facing the plaza is **The Palace,** an old-time saloon where parts of the Steve McQueen film *Junior Bonner* were filmed, as a giant poster for the movie on the wall attests. Looking for antiques? **Cortez Street** is lined with almost a dozen big antique stores. Duck into an old saloon or the lobby of one of the historic hotels, and you'll understand that the town was also part of the Wild West.

Fort Whipple Museum ★ MUSEUM North of town off Ariz. 89, on the grounds of what is now a Veterans Affairs hospital, this small museum tells the history of Fort Whipple, which was active from 1863 to 1922. You can learn about activities of the Buffalo Soldiers in the state; there's even a cameo from legendary NY Mayor Fiorello LaGuardia. Many stately officers' homes still stand on the grounds. The museum is overseen by the Sharlot Hall Museum (see below).

Veterans Affairs campus, Bldg. 11, 500 N. Ariz. 89. ✆ **928/445-3122.** Free admission. Thurs–Sat 10am–4pm. Closed New Year's Day, Thanksgiving, and Christmas.

Phippen Museum ★ MUSEUM Named after the first president of the prestigious Cowboy Artists of America organization, the Phippen exhibits works by both established Western artists and newcomers. Also on display are artifacts and photos that help place the artwork in the context of the region's history. The long-running **Western Art Show & Sale** is held each year over Memorial Day weekend, including Monday.

4701 Ariz. 89 N. www.phippenartmuseum.org. ✆ **928/778-1385.** $7 adults, $5 students, free for kids 12 and under. Tues–Sat 10am–4pm; Sun 1–4pm.

Sharlot Hall Museum ★ MUSEUM Two blocks west of Courthouse Plaza, this fascinating museum of Arizona and frontier history opened in 1928 in a log home that was once the governor's mansion of the Arizona territory. The museum was founded by Sharlot Hall, an early activist who fought to preserve Native American artifacts; she played a part in Arizona statehood as well, successfully arguing that Arizona be admitted to the Union as a separate state, not as part of New Mexico. (She then served as territorial historian from 1909 to 1911.) In addition to the governor's "mansion," which is furnished much as it originally might have been, several other interesting buildings can be toured. With its traditional wood-frame construction, the **Frémont House,** built in 1875 for the fifth territorial governor, shows how quickly Prescott grew from a remote logging and mining camp into a civilized town. The 1877 **Bashford House** reflects the Victorian architecture that was popular throughout the country in the late 19th century. The **Sharlot Hall Building** houses exhibits on Native American cultures and territorial Arizona. Every year in early summer, artisans, craftspeople, and costumed exhibitors participate in the museum's **Folk Arts Fair.**

415 W. Gurley St. www.sharlot.org. ✆ **928/445-3122.** $9 adults, $8 seniors, $6 students, $5 ages 13–17, free for kids 12 and under. May–Sept Mon–Sat 10am–5pm, Sun

A Big Little Collection

Prescott is home to Embry-Riddle Aeronautical University, and in the university library, you can marvel at the world's largest collection of miniature airplanes. The **Kalusa Miniature Airplane Collection** includes more than 5,500 hand-carved and hand-painted miniature airplanes, created by John W. Kalusa over a period of more than 50 years. The planes are built to a consistent scale of 1⁄18th inch to 1 foot, so you can see how their sizes compare with each other—some are barely an inch across, while others, like Howard Hughes's famed *Spruce Goose*, are much larger. The collection is displayed on the first and second floors of the Christine and Steven F. Udvar-Hazy Library and Learning Center, Embry-Riddle Aeronautical University, 3700 Willow Creek Rd. (hazylibrary.erau.edu/kalusa-collection; ✆ **928/777-3811**). Hours vary with the university's schedule.

noon–4pm; Oct–Apr Mon–Sat 10am–4pm, Sun noon–4pm. Closed New Year's Day, Thanksgiving, and Christmas.

The Smoki Museum ★ MUSEUM Set in a historic stone building, this interesting collection of Native American artifacts is named for the fictitious Smoki tribe, which was dreamed up in 1921 by a group of non-Native Americans who wanted to inject new life into Prescott's July 4th celebrations. Despite its phony origins, the museum contains genuine artifacts and basketry from many different tribes, mainly southwestern. The museum also sponsors interesting lectures on Native American topics.

147 N. Arizona Ave. www.smokimuseum.org. ✆ **928/445-1230.** $7 adults, $6 seniors, $5 students, free for kids 12 and under. Mon–Sat 10am–4pm; Sun 1–4pm. Closed Thanksgiving and Christmas.

Outdoor Activities

Prescott is situated on the edge of a wide expanse of high plains, with the pine forests of **Prescott National Forest** at its back. Within the national forest are lakes, campgrounds, and many miles of hiking and mountain-biking trails. For maps and information on hikes and bike rides in the area, stop by the **Bradshaw Ranger Station,** 344 S. Cortez St. (www.fs.fed.us/r3/prescott; ✆ **928/443-8000**).

My favorite hiking and biking areas in the national forest are Thumb Butte (west of town) and the Granite Mountain Wilderness (northwest of town). **Thumb Butte,** a rocky outcropping that towers over the forest just west of town, is Prescott's most easily recognizable natural landmark. A 1.2-mile trail leads nearly to the top of this butte, and from the saddle near the summit, there's a panoramic vista of the entire region. The trail is very steep but paved much of the way. The summit of the butte is a popular rock-climbing spot. An alternative return trail makes a loop hike possible. To reach the trail head, drive west out of town on Gurley St. for about 4 miles (it becomes Thumb Butte Rd.). Past the National Forest signs, you'll find a parking lot, picnic area, and trail head. The parking fee is $5.

The Granite Basin Recreation Area provides access to the **Granite Mountain Wilderness.** Trails lead beneath the cliffs of Granite Mountain, where you might spot peregrine falcons. For the best views, hike 1.5 miles to Blair Pass and then on up the Granite Mountain trail as far as you feel like going. To reach this area, follow Iron Springs Rd. northwest out of town to the signed road for the Granite Basin Recreation Area (less than 8 miles from downtown). There is a $5 parking fee here.

Both of the above areas also offer **mountain-biking** trails. Although the scenery isn't as spectacular as in the Sedona area, the trails are great. You can rent a bike and get maps and trail recommendations at **Ironclad Bicycles,** 710 White Spar Rd. (www.ironcladbicycles.com; ✆ **928/776-1755**), which charges $24 to $48 per day for mountain bikes.

Want to explore the area on horseback? A half-hour drive southeast of Prescott, **Foothills Ranch,** at Finley Rd. and Ariz. 69 in Mayer (www.foothills-ranch.

EXPLORING THE granite dells

Five miles north of Prescott on Ariz. 89, jumbled hills of rounded granite suddenly jut from the landscape, creating a maze of huge boulders and smooth rock known as the **Granite Dells ★★**. In the middle of this dramatic landscape lies **Watson Lake,** its waters pushing in among the boulders to create one of the prettiest lakes in the state. On the highway side of the lake, **Watson Lake Park,** 3101 Watson Lake Rd. (www.cityofprescott.net; ✆ **928/777-1122;** $3 parking fee) has picnic tables and great views. Spring through fall (weather permitting), you can rent canoes and kayaks at the lake ($15–$20 for the first hour, $10–$15 per hour after that) Friday through Sunday 8am to 4pm. Reservations aren't accepted, but you can call **Prescott Outdoors** (www.prescottoutdoors.com; ✆ **928/925-1410**) to make sure they'll be at the lake with their boats.

For hiking in the Watson Lake area, I recommend the scenic **Peavine Trail ★★**, one of the most gratifying easy hikes in the state. To find the trail head, turn east onto Prescott Lake Parkway, between Prescott and the Granite Dells, and then left onto Sun Dog Ranch Road. (There's a $3 parking fee at the trail head.) This rails-to-trails path, extending several miles through the middle of the Granite Dells, is the best way to fully appreciate their unique beauty (you'll be away from both people and the highway). The trail also makes a great easy mountain bike ride that can be extended 7.5 miles on the **Iron King Trail.** Also accessible from the same trail head, the **Watson Woods Riparian Preserve** has some short trails through the wetlands and riparian zone along Granite Creek.

A couple of miles west of Watson Lake you can hike in **Willow Lake Park,** 1497 Heritage Park Rd. (www.cityofprescott.net; ✆ **928/777-1122**). Parking areas on Willow Creek Road provide access to several miles of trails that lead through grasslands and groves of huge cottonwood trees adjacent to Willow Lake. The trails eventually lead to the edge of the Granite Dells. There's fine bird-watching in the trees in this park, and there are great blue heron and cormorant rookeries. The trail head on Heritage Park Road also provides access to the **Willow Dells Trails** network, which meander through the jumbled boulders of the Granite Dells; they're some of the most fascinating trails in the state. There's a $3 parking fee at all park trail heads.

com; ✆ **928/379-0260**), offers guided trail rides in the Prescott National Forest. A 1-hour ride is $50; longer outings include brunch or lunch.

Reasonably priced golf is available at the 36-hole **Antelope Hills Golf Course,** 1 Perkins Dr. (www.antelopehillsgolf.com; ✆ **928/776-7888**). Greens fees start at $40.

Prescott Shopping

Downtown Prescott is the best place in Arizona for antiques shopping. For Native American crafts and Old West memorabilia, stop in at **Ogg's Hogan,** 111 N. Cortez St. (✆ **928/443-9856**).

In the Hotel St. Michael's shopping arcade, **Hotel Trading,** 110 S. Montezuma St. (✆ **928/778-7276**) carries some genuine Native American artifacts at reasonable prices. Owner Ernie Lister also makes silver jewelry in the

19th-century Navajo style. In this same arcade, the **Old Sage Bookshop,** 110 S. Montezuma St. (✆ **928/776-1136**) is a wonderful used-book store selling primarily hardback editions. On the same block, you'll find the **Arts Prescott Gallery,** 134 S. Montezuma St. (www.artsprescott.com; ✆ **928/776-7717**), a cooperative of local artists; **Van Gogh's Ear,** 156B S. Montezuma St. (www.vgegallery.com; ✆ **928/776-1080**), which was founded by a splinter group from the co-op; and the **Newman Gallery,** 106-A S. Montezuma St. (www.newmangallery.net; ✆ **928/442-9167**), which features the colorful Western-inspired pop-culture imagery of artist Dave Newman.

Want to sample some local wine while you're in the area? Head north of Prescott to **Granite Creek Vineyards,** 2515 Rd. 1 E., Chino Valley (www.granitecreekvineyards.com; ✆ **928/636-2003**), which produces organic, sulfite-free wines that are surprisingly good. The winery is open Friday through Sunday 1 to 5pm. Call for directions. And right in town, at the top of Courthouse Plaza, is **Superstition Meadery,** 120 W. Gurley St. (www.superstitionmeadery.com; ✆ **928/458-4256**), which brews mead (made with honey) and ciders.

Where to Stay in Prescott

MODERATE

Hassayampa Inn ★ This is the most fun and beautiful place to stay in Prescott. The stately Hassayampa, designed in a slightly incongruous Italianate style, was built as a civic undertaking in 1927 to give the town a first-class hotel worthy of its status as the bustling territorial capital. (The hotel remains on the National Register of Historic Places.) The lobby is all exposed ceiling beams, wrought-iron chandeliers, and arched doorways; the elevator, an original part of the hotel, is stately, too, by which I mean slow. There's a quite good restaurant in the **Peacock Room,** which has been redone with Art Deco touches, and the adjoining **Glass Bar** is a comfortable place to unwind, whether you're staying at the hotel or not. The rooms have been restored as well, with some original furnishings or antiques, but they can be small and oddly configured. Solo travelers will be fine, but couples should ask in advance about what exactly they are getting.

> **Haunted Hotels**
>
> Jerome may be the region's top ghost town, but in Prescott, three hotels claim to be haunted: The Hassayampa Inn, Hotel St. Michael, and Hotel Vendome are all said to have resident ghosts.

122 E. Gurley St. www.hassayampainn.com. ✆ **928/778-9434.** 67 units. $79–$199 double. Pets accepted ($10 per night). **Amenities:** Restaurant; lounge; exercise room; room service; free Wi-Fi.

INEXPENSIVE

Hotel St. Michael ★ Located right on Whiskey Row, this hotel has a resident ghost and the oldest elevator in Prescott, and also a self-described "historic ambience"—meaning narrow hallways and small rooms in all manner of configurations. Ask what you're reserving. Some rooms have tubs but no showers. Its restaurant, the casual **Caffe St. Michael,** overlooks Courthouse

Plaza, and there's a charming attached cobblestone-paved mini-mall of shops, including a decent bookstore (p. 175).

205 W. Gurley St. www.stmichaelhotel.com. ✆ **928/776-1999.** 70 units. $79–$189 double; $119–$149 suite. Rates include full breakfast. **Amenities:** Restaurant; free Wi-Fi.

Hotel Vendome ★ Not quite as luxurious as the Hassayampa, yet not as basic as the St. Michael, the Vendome is a good middle-price choice for those who want to stay in a historic hotel. Built in 1917 as a lodging house, the restored brick building is only 2 blocks from the action of Whiskey Row, but far enough away that you can get a good night's sleep. Guest rooms are outfitted with modern furnishings, although some bathrooms still have original claw-foot tubs. Two-bedroom units with an interconnected bathroom are ideal for families. There's an in-house bar open all day and evening; next door is a welcoming gastropub, and on the other side is a groovy coffee shop (**Cuppers,** see below). And yes, like a couple of other Prescott hotels, the Vendome has a resident ghost.

230 S. Cortez St. www.vendomehotel.com. ✆ **928/776-0900.** 20 units. $99–$149 double; $149–$299 suite. Rates include continental breakfast. **Amenities:** Lounge; concierge; free Wi-Fi.

The Motor Lodge ★ Originally opened in 1937 as a collection of summer cabins, this vintage getaway has been revived as a midcentury modern motor court. Rooms are decorated with retro furnishings—more Scottsdale hip than Prescott country, but if you want to stay someplace with a cool aesthetic, this is about your only choice in town. Keep in mind that this is budget hip; rooms vary in size and amenities.

503 S. Montezuma St. www.themotorlodge.com. ✆ **928/717-0157.** 13 units. $109–$179 double. **Amenities:** Free Wi-Fi.

Where to Eat in Prescott

For delicious baked goods and coffee, try the airy, friendly **Wild Iris Coffee Shop,** 124 S. Granite St. (www.wildiriscoffee.com; ✆ **928/778-5155**); the coffee's great, and all baked goods are made from scratch on premises. It's 2 short blocks west of Whiskey Row. **Cuppers,** 226 S. Cortez St. (www.cupperscoffee.com; ✆ **928/445-1636**) is a genteel place to stop for a cup, right next to the Hotel Vendome just south of Courthouse Plaza.

EXPENSIVE

Murphy's ★ AMERICAN Prescott's high-end steakhouse, Murphy's is housed in an 1890 mercantile building that's on the National Register of Historic Places; it's long been one of Prescott's favorite special-occasion restaurants. Sparkling leaded-glass doors usher diners into a high-ceilinged room with fans revolving slowly overhead. Many of the shop's original shelves can still be seen in the lounge area, and the restaurant does a good job of creating a historical ambience. The best bets on the menu are the mesquite-grilled meats, but the fish specials can also be good.

201 N. Cortez St. www.murphysprescott.com. ✆ **928/445-4044.** Main courses $19–$49. Daily 11am–10pm. Brunch Sun 11am–3pm.

MODERATE

El Gato Azul ★ MEDITERRANEAN This casual but careful creekside restaurant in downtown Prescott is a great choice. By careful I mean that they are serious about food. You can have as few or as many tapas (small plates) as you and your group want—try the green chili carnitas, the fried artichokes, or the sticky chicken.

316 W. Goodwin St. www.elgatoazulprescott.com. ✆ **928/445-1070.** Main courses $8–$12 lunch, $12–$21 dinner; tapas $6–$13. Daily 11am–9pm.

INEXPENSIVE

Dinner Bell Café ★ AMERICAN A big hit with local students and other people in the know, this casual little breakfast-and-lunch place has a split personality. Up front there's a classic old diner, in business since 1939, while in back is a colorful modern space with walls that roll up in good weather. Regulars order either the waffles (served with a variety of toppings) or the thick, juicy burgers. (The waffles are available at lunch, but I don't think you can get the burger at breakfast.) The setting, a block off Whiskey Row, makes this a great hideaway for a quick meal; kids will enjoy wandering along the adjacent creekside path.

321 W. Gurley St. ✆ **928/445-9888.** Main courses $9–$11. No credit cards. Mon–Fri 6:30am–2pm; Sat–Sun 7am–2pm.

Prescott Entertainment & Nightlife

PERFORMING ARTS

The **Yavapai College Performing Arts Center** (www.ycpac.com; ✆ **928/776-2000**) hosts a wide range of shows, from Cowboy Poet gatherings to national acts of some repute. Check the center's schedule to see who's in town. The **Prescott Fine Arts Association,** 208 N. Marina St. (www.pfaa.net; ✆ **928/445-3286**) puts on plays and musicals in the 1891 Sacred Heart Church, which is on the National Register of Historic Places. A block away, you'll find the **Prescott Elks Theater,** 117 E. Gurley St. (www.prescottelkstheater.com; ✆ **928/777-1370**), a renovated theater, built in 1905, that hosts everything from jazz nights (on the second Monday of the month) to touring artists to movie nights.

BARS & SALOONS

Back in the days when Prescott was the territorial capital and a booming mining town, it supported dozens of rowdy saloons, most of them along Montezuma Street on the west side of Courthouse Plaza, which became known as Whiskey Row. Legend has it there was a tunnel from the courthouse to one of the saloons so lawmakers wouldn't be seen ducking into the saloons during business hours. On July 14, 1900, a fire consumed most of Whiskey Row, although cowboys and miners managed to drag the tremendously heavy bar of the Palace saloon to safety across the street before it was damaged.

Whiskey Row is no longer a place where respectable women shouldn't be seen, but it still has a few noisy saloons with genuine Wild West flavor. Some feature live country music on weekends and are dark and dank enough to provide solace to a cowboy (or a construction worker) after a long day's work. And within a few blocks of Whiskey Row, you can hear country, folk, jazz, and rock at a surprisingly diverse assortment of bars, restaurants, and clubs. In fact, Prescott has one of the densest concentrations of live-music clubs in the state.

To see what this street's saloons looked like back in the old days, drop by the **Palace,** 120 S. Montezuma St. (www.historicpalace.com; ✆ **928/541-1996**), which still has that classic bar up front. These days, the Palace is more of a restaurant than a saloon, but there's live music on weekends and, a couple times a month, dinner-theater performances—generally tribute bands to this or that country-rock artist, but occasionally an evening of historical tales and music. Call to find out if anything is happening while you're in town.

If you want to drink where the ranchers drink and not where the hired hands carouse, head upstairs to the **Jersey Lilly Saloon,** 116 S. Montezuma St. (www.jerseylillysaloon.com; ✆ **928/541-7854**), which attracts a more well-heeled clientele than the street-level saloons. A block away, the **Raven Café,** 142 N. Cortez St. (www.ravencafe.com, ✆ **928/717-0009**) is the most artsy nightlife venue in town: It has the best beer list (with an emphasis on Belgian beers and American microbrews) and an entertainment lineup that ranges from Monday-night movies to live jazz and bluegrass on weekends. As the town becomes more upscale, you'll also find joints like the **Point Bar & Lounge** (www.prescottbrewingcompany.com; ✆ **928/237-9027**), which boasts of organic ingredients in its craft cocktails and some 150 different whiskeys, and the **Prescott Brewing Company,** 130 W. Gurley St. (www.prescottbrewingcompany.com; ✆ **928/771-2795**), which brews and serves its own tasty microbrews.

JEROME ★★★ & THE VERDE VALLEY

35 miles NE of Prescott; 28 miles W of Sedona; 130 miles N of Phoenix

I'll put it simply: You *have* to go to Jerome. Few towns anywhere in Arizona make more of an impression on visitors than this historic mining town, clinging to the slopes of Cleopatra Hill 2,000 feet above the Verde Valley.

On a clear day, the view from Jerome is stupendous—it's possible to see for more than 50 miles, with the red rocks of Sedona (p. 190), the Mogollon Rim (p. 197), and the San Francisco Peaks (p. 257) all visible in the distance. What's more, in the past decade this iconoclastic arts enclave has come into its own; there are galleries, good restaurants, engrossing museums, and a new wine industry that should intrigue oenophiles of any stripe. Families, couples, and singles will all enjoy maneuvering the streets, which are rugged without being annoyingly so.

Once called the billion-dollar copper camp, Jerome was founded in 1883 and by the 1920s was the fourth-largest city in Arizona. In the early years, Jerome's ore was mined using an 88-mile-long network of underground railroads. But the town's (and the mining industry's) biggest nemesis those days were fires: Jerome burned down with some regularity, and fires in the mines smouldered uncontrollably. Eventually, the mining companies were forced to abandon the tunnels in favor of open-pit mining.

Northeast of Jerome, the Verde Valley is so named by early Spanish explorers, impressed by the sight of such a verdant valley in an otherwise brown desert landscape. Cottonwood and Clarkdale, the valley's two largest towns, are old copper-smelting centers, while Camp Verde was an army post during the Indian Wars. Most visitors here focus on the valley's two national monuments—Tuzigoot and Montezuma Castle, both remarkable Native American ruins, preserving the vestiges of Sinagua villages that date from long before the first European explorers entered the Verde Valley. By the time the first pioneers began settling in this region, the Sinaguas had long since moved on, and Apaches had claimed the valley as part of their territory; Fort Verde, now a state park, was established to deal with settlers' conflicts with the Apaches. Between this state park and the two national monuments, hundreds of years of Verde Valley history and prehistory can be explored.

Jail Brakes?

One unforeseen hazard of open-pit mining next to a town built on a 30-degree slope was the effect dynamiting would have on Jerome. Mine explosions would regularly rock Jerome's world, and eventually buildings in town began sliding downhill. Even the town jail broke loose. With no brakes to stop it, the jail slid 225 feet downhill. (Now that's a jailbreak.)

Between 1883 and 1953, Jerome experienced an economic roller-coaster ride as the price of copper rose and fell. By the early 1950s, it was no longer profitable to mine the copper ore of Cleopatra Hill, and the last mining company shut down operations. Almost everyone left town. By the early 1960s, Jerome was on its way to becoming just another ghost town. But then artists discovered the phenomenal views and dirt-cheap rents and began moving in; slowly the near-ghost town developed a reputation as an artists' community. Soon tourists began visiting to see and buy the artwork being created in Jerome, and old storefronts turned into galleries.

As the state has pulled out of the recession of the late 2000s, Jerome has blossomed. On summer weekends its streets are packed with visitors browsing the galleries and crafts shops. The ghost town image lingers, but only in a string of shops playing up the haunted theme.

Essentials

ARRIVING

Jerome is on Ariz. 89A roughly halfway between Sedona and Prescott, about an hour's drive (sometimes less) from either. Coming from Phoenix, it's a 2-hour drive via I-17 and Ariz. 260, which will take you northwest through Camp Verde, Cottonwood, and Clarkdale before reaching Jerome.

VISITOR INFORMATION

The **Jerome Chamber of Commerce** (www.jeromechamber.com; © **928/634-2900**) runs a charming visitor center, about the size of two shoeboxes stacked on top of each other, at the bottom of town, at Hull Street and 1st Avenue. The chamber's website is a good place to check for art walks, home tours, and the like. Also check out the websites of the **Cottonwood Chamber of Commerce,** 1010 S. Main St., Cottonwood (www.cottonwoodchamberaz.org; ✆ **928/634-7593**) and the **Sedona Verde Valley Tourism Council** (www.sedonaverdevalley.org).

FESTIVALS

Avid birders may want to plan their visit to coincide with the annual **Verde Valley Birding & Nature Festival** (www.birdyverde.org; ✆ **928/282-2202**), which is held the last weekend in April.

Exploring Jerome

That same remote and rugged setting that once made it so expensive to mine copper is now one of Jerome's main attractions. Because it's literally built on the side of a mountain, its streets switch back from one level of houses to the next, with narrow alleys and stairways connecting the different levels of town. All these winding streets, alleys, and stairways are lined with old brick and wood-frame buildings—some businesses, some private residences—clinging precariously to their perch. The entire town has been designated a National Historic Landmark, and today, homes, studios, wine-tasting rooms, and galleries stand side by side, looking (externally, anyway) much as they did when Jerome was an active mining town.

Jerome is an interesting enough place that you won't regret spending half an hour or so before you hit the town proper at the **Jerome State Historic Park,** off Ariz. 89A at the end of Douglas Road in the lower section of town (www.azstateparks.com; ✆ **928/634-5381**). It's a bit tricky to get here: Watch for signs and be ready to veer right onto Douglas Road as you approach the mountain; Douglas Road curves alongside the mountain for about a mile. It's called a park but it's really a museum, occupying the one-time home of mining magnate "Rawhide Jimmy" Douglas. Here you'll find wonderful photos and artifacts of the town's colorful history, along with an amazing view: the crazy constructions of Jerome on one side, and sweeping Verde Valley vistas on the other. The mansion, constructed of adobe bricks made on-site, once boasted a wine cellar, billiards room, marble shower, steam heat, and central

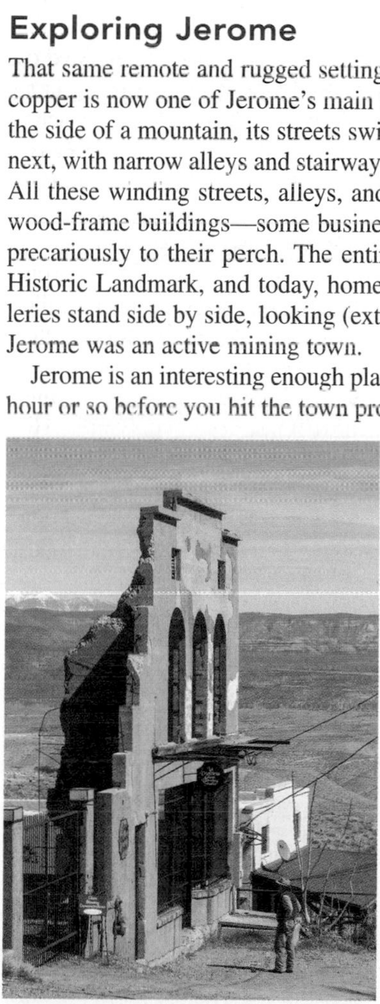

Jerome, once nearly a ghost town, preserves even the most crumbling relics of its copper-mining boom days.

vacuum system. The park is open Thursday through Monday 8:30am to 5pm; admission is $7 adults, $4 for ages 7 to 13.

Returning to Ariz. 89A, drive the last quarter-mile into town; park in one of the gravel lots in the first block or two. You'll enjoy your time in Jerome a lot more if you're walking back down to your car at the end of your visit rather than up.

For more local history, visit the **Jerome Historical Society's Mine Museum,** 200 Main St. (www.jeromehistoricalsociety.org; ✆ **928/634-5477**) to see some great panoramic pictures of Jerome in the old days; the museum also has a fun little dark mine passageway, which among other things will answer your questions about how and where miners went to the bathroom. It's open daily 9am to 5pm; admission is $2 adults, $1 seniors, free for kids 12 and under. Still haven't gotten enough? You can take a 1-hour **Jerome History Tour** (jeromehistorytours.com; ✆ **928/592-3768**) for $15 ($10 for kids). For something a bit more irreverent, **Ghost Town Tours,** 403 N. Clark St. (ghosttowntours.org; ✆ **928/635-6118**) offers a variety of ghost and history tours from $30 to $65 (half price for kids); you can probably get a discount by stopping by the store.

As you walk along Main Street, you'll notice some surprises among the shops and the overgrown residential gardens. Look for a small inlet with one of the mine's old blast furnaces; a sign explains that it was fueled by coke brought to Arizona from Wales, UK. Just to the left of that, a concrete stairway will take you to a hidden park right above it, shaded and with a picnic table and swing set for the kids.

Once you get to the final switchback, Clark Street, you have two choices. The first is to drop into **Wicked City Brew,** 403 Clark St. (✆ **928/351-7940**) for some locally brewed craft beers (all on tap with old horseshoes and such on the tap handles) and a selection of Arizona wines. The second is to press on up Clark Street, past the **Haunted Hamburger** restaurant (p. 189), to Hill Street, which veers up to the right. If you follow this road for about a quarter-mile over rather steep gravel, you'll reach the wonderful **Grand Hotel** (p. 188), the most prominent building in the town, and its restaurant, the **Asylum.** Views here are as good as they get. It's a great place to stop for a drink or a bite to eat before heading back down the mountain.

The Jerome Grand Hotel, originally a hospital, crowns its steep hillside of switchback streets.

Sipping the Local Vintages: Jerome

Central Arizona is working hard to develop worthy wineries; right now, Jerome is ground zero for finding out whether they are on to something. Most of the new shops in town have deals for tastings; some offer small plates of food, too, and they'll generally throw in the cost of the tasting if you end up buying a few bottles. **Caduceus Cellars,** 158 Main St. (www.caduceus.org; ✆ **928/639-9463**) drew attention originally because it was started by a member of the rock band Tool; it is now the most respected winemaker in the state. **Bitter Creek Winery,** 240 Hull St. (www.bittercreekwinery.com; ✆ **928/634-7033**), at the north end of Hull Street, has some nice views of the Verde Valley to contemplate while you sip. Another respected company markets two wines, Passion and Salvatore, in a swanky shop called **Cabal,** 417 Hull St. (www.passioncellars.com; ✆ **928/649-9800**).

JEROME SHOPPING

Artists have made Jerome's name in the 21st century. By all means, stop at the **Jerome Artists Cooperative Gallery,** 502 Main St. (www.jeromeartistscoop.com; ✆ **928/639-4276**), on the west side of the street where Hull Avenue and Main Street fork as you come uphill into town. It's a bright and airy place with room after room of respectable art and craftwork. Don't miss the eclectic offerings—everything from surplus Russian army and navy uniforms to feather boas—at the **House of Joy,** 416 N. Hull Ave. (www.jeromesfinest.com; ✆ **928/634-5339**), which styles itself as a "brothel boutique" after the business that occupied the space in the bad old days. For more tastefully curated women's wear, visit **Threads on Main,** 367 Main St. (www.threadsjerome.com; ✆ **928/649-9502**). **Arizona Discoveries,** 317 Main St. (✆ **928/634-5716**) is probably the best of the shops selling tchotchkes and such. Where else can you get vintage spittoons—for the man, or woman, who has everything? (Whatever you do, though, don't ask the proprietor if you can take photos—I found that out the hard way.) Someone's going to want to stop in at **Copper Country Fudge,** 337 Main St. (✆ **928/634-4040**).

A little farther up the road, the **Raku Gallery,** 250 Hull Ave. (www.rakugallery.com; ✆ **928/639-0239**) has gallery space on two floors and walls of glass across the back, with views of the red rocks of Sedona in the distance. Don't miss **Nellie Bly,** 136 Main St. (www.nellieblyscopes.com; ✆ **928/634-0255**), a shop full of handmade kaleidoscopes. A couple of doors away you'll find **Pura Vida Gallery,** 501 School St. (www.puravidagalleryjerome.com; ✆ **928/634-0937**), which has a fascinating and eclectic selection of fine art, jewelry, and unusual Southwest-inspired furniture and fashions.

Exploring the Verde Valley

In **Clarkdale,** 5 miles northeast of Jerome on Ariz. 260, the small **Clarkdale Arizona Historical Society Museum,** 900 First North St. (www.clarkdalemuseum.org; ✆ **928/649-1198;** free admission), has a lot of interesting information on the grand copper smelters that once dominated the region's economy. And right down the street is something special: the **Arizona Copper Art Museum ★**, 849 Main St. (www.copperartmuseum.com; ✆ **928/649-1858**), an extraordinary collection of some 5,000 works of art made from copper. The glow alone is unforgettable. It's open daily 10am–5pm; adult tickets are $9, with discounts for seniors and kids.

Cottonwood, 4 miles or so southeast of Clarkdale, isn't nearly as atmospheric as Jerome, but in its Old Town district, where one side of Main Street has an old-fashioned covered sidewalk, you'll find quite a few interesting shops, galleries, and cafes. I could point you, for example, to **Adventures Unlimited Books,** 1020 N. Main St. (www.adventuresunlimitedpress.com; ✆ **928/639-1664**). Just a normal bookstore, right? But look around a bit and you'll start to hear the theme from *The X-Files.* You'll find everything you ever need to know on aliens, sightings, chemtrail, conspiracy theories, antigravity machines, mystical phenomena, and many other things. Farther down the street is an iconoclastic purveyor of sculpture, a shop that calls itself **The Most Interesting Store in the World,** 909 N. Main St. (✆ **928/821-0313**), which is only somewhat hyperbolic.

A half-hour's drive southeast on Ariz. 260, **Camp Verde** is the closest town for Montezuma Castle and Fort Verde State Park. Here you'll also find **Cliff Castle Casino,** 555 Middle Verde Rd. (www.cliffcastlecasino.net; ✆ **800/381-7568**

Sipping the Local Vintages: Verde Valley

About halfway between Camp Verde and Cottonwood, **Alcantara Vineyards,** 3445 S. Grapevine Way, Verde Valley (www.alcantaravineyard.com; ✆ **888/569-0756** or 928/649-8463) is far and away the most beautiful winery in Arizona, with terraced vineyards overlooking limestone cliffs and a bend of the Verde River. There are tours on Friday and Saturday at 11:30am. The tasting room is open daily 11am to 5pm; there is an $10 per person tasting fee.

In Cottonwood, wine-tasting rooms are popping up all over. At the **Pillsbury Wine Company,** 1012 N. Main St. (www.pillsburywine.com; ✆ **928/639-0646**), you can choose from among more than a dozen wines. Wines here are produced by several area wineries, which makes this one of the best places in the region to get an idea of the breadth of the local productions. For $12 to $16, you can taste five wines (additional tastes are $2 each). The tasting room is open Monday through Thursday 11am to 6pm, Friday and Saturday 11am to 9pm, and Sunday noon to 6pm. Across the street, **Arizona Stronghold Winery,** 1023 Main St. (www.azstronghold.com; ✆ **928/639-2789**) is a joint operation of Page Spring Cellars' Eric Glomski and Caduceus Cellars' Maynard Keenan, which says it's "the expression of the fierce and wild Arizona terrain." (Keenan has some renown as the lead singer of the rock band Tool.) The tasting room is open Monday, Thursday, and Sunday noon to 7pm, Tuesday and Wednesday noon to 5pm, and Friday and Saturday noon to 9pm. (There's live music on weekend evenings, too.) The tasting fee is $9.

Want to dig deeper into Arizona wines? The **Verde Valley Wine Trail** is a promotional site that is an efficient guide to most of the local wineries, and can offer some helpful maps for touring the territory. Check it out at www.vvwinetrail.com.

or 928/567-7900), at exit 289 off I-17. There's a brand-new $30-million hotel attached, too.

Dead Horse Ranch State Park ★ PARK On the north outskirts of Cottonwood, not far from Tuzigoot National Monument, this state park on the banks of the Verde River offers picnicking, fishing, swimming, hiking, mountain biking, and camping. Trails winding through the riparian forests along the riverbanks visit marshes that offer good bird-watching; they also lead into the adjacent national forest, so you can get in many miles of scenic hiking and mountain biking. (The ranch was named in the 1940s, when the children of a family looking to buy a ranch told their parents they wanted to buy the place with the dead horse by the side of the road.) For a guided horseback ride in the park, contact **Trail Horse Adventures** (www.trailhorseadventures.com; ✆ **928/634-5276**). A 1-hour ride costs $64 and a 3-hour lunch ride costs $125.

675 Dead Horse Ranch Rd., Cottonwood (from Main St., drive north on N. 10th St.). www.azstateparks.com. ✆ **928/634-5283.** Entry $7 per car. Visitor center daily 8am–5pm. Closed Christmas.

Fort Verde State Historic Park ★ HISTORIC SITE Just south of Montezuma Castle (see below) in the town of Camp Verde, this park preserves the remains of Fort Verde, established in 1871 as the third military post in the Verde Valley. The military first came to the Verde Valley in 1865 at the request of settlers who wanted protection from the local Tonto Apache and Yavapai; the tribes had been raiding farms for food after their normal economy was disrupted by the sudden influx of settlers. Between 1873 and 1875, most Indians in the area were rounded up and forced to live on various reservations. An uprising in 1882 led to the last clash between local tribes and Fort Verde's soldiers; in 1891, Fort Verde was closed down, having accomplished its purpose. The 10-acre park preserves three officers' quarters, an administration building, and some ruins. The restored buildings house exhibits on the history of the fort and what life was like here in the 19th century. With their gables, white picket fences, and shake-shingle roofs, the buildings of Fort Verde suggest that life at this remote post was not so bad, at least for officers. The park does a great job with events, from horseback riding displays to a vintage baseball game in tribute to the Buffalo Soldiers. Fort Verde Days, a weekend of events, takes place in October; call for details.

125 E. Hollaman St., Camp Verde. www.azstateparks.com. ✆ **928/567-3275.** $7 adults, $4 ages 7–13, free for kids 6 and under. Thurs–Mon 8am–5pm. Closed Christmas.

Montezuma Castle National Monument ★★ ANCIENT SITE This isn't a castle and it has nothing to do with Montezuma, but at this point no one even talks about renaming it. This Sinagua ruin is, however, one of the best-preserved cliff dwellings in Arizona. The site in fact has two impressive stone pueblos that were, for unknown reasons, abandoned by the Sinagua people in the early 14th century. The more intriguing of the two is set in a shallow cave 100 feet up a cliff overlooking Beaver Creek. Construction on this five-story,

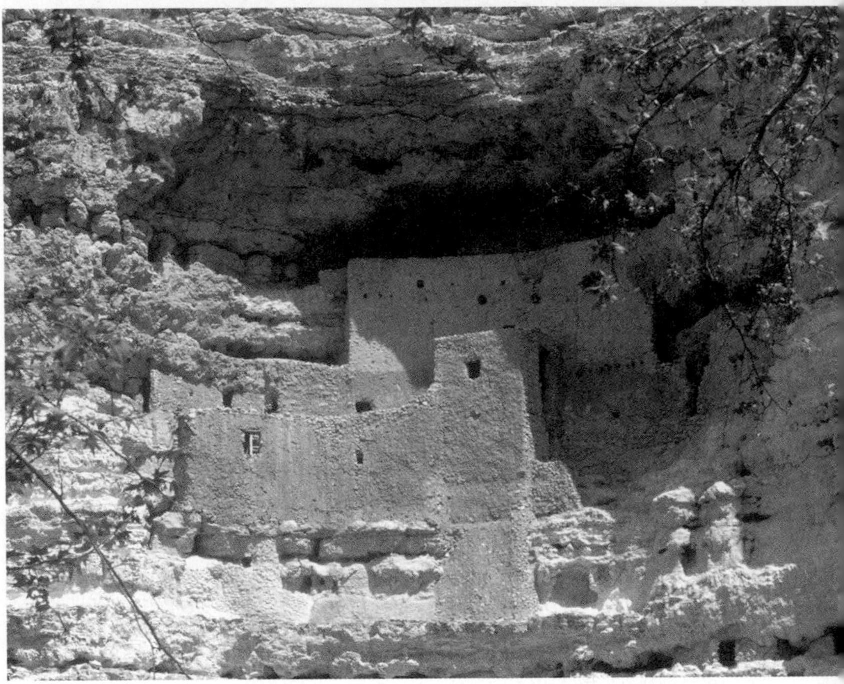

Set in a dramatic cliff face, the Sinagua ruin known as Montezuma Castle is amazingly intact.

20-room village began sometime in the early 12th century. Because it has been protected from the elements by the cave's overhanging roof, the original adobe mud that was used to plaster over the stone walls of the dwelling is still intact. Another structure, containing 45 rooms on six levels, stands at the base of the cliff; it has been subjected to rains and floods over the years and is not nearly as well-preserved as the cliff dwelling. In the visitor center, you'll see artifacts unearthed from the two ruins. Eleven miles north (although still part of the national monument), **Montezuma Well** is a spring-fed sinkhole that was, for the Native peoples of this desert, a genuine oasis. This sunken pond was formed when a cavern in the area's porous limestone bedrock collapsed. Underground springs quickly filled the sinkhole, which today contains a pond measuring more than 360 feet across and 65 feet deep. Over the centuries, the presence of year-round water attracted first the Hohokam and later the Sinagua people, who built irrigation canals to use the water for growing crops. Some of these channels can still be seen. Sinagua structures and an excavated Hohokam pit house built around 1100 are clustered in and near the sinkhole. To reach Montezuma Well, you have to get back on I-17 and go north; take exit 293.

Exit 289 off I-17. www.nps.gov/moca. ✆ **928/567-3322.** $10 adults, free for kids 15 and under (combined entry with Tuzigoot National Monument, below); no charge to visit Montezuma Well. Daily 8am–5pm. Closed Christmas and New Year's.

Out of Africa Wildlife Park ★ WILDLIFE VIEWING Lions and tigers and bears, oh my. And zebras and giraffes and wildebeests, oh yes. That's what you'll encounter at this sprawling wildlife park between Camp Verde and Cottonwood. The park includes both a "wildlife preserve" of large fenced predator enclosures, home to numerous lions, tigers, wolves, panthers, and hyenas, and an "African Bush Safari" area, where you ride on a rugged safari vehicle through a vast enclosure populated by giraffes, zebras, ostriches, wildebeests, and other African animals. You may even get to feed a giraffe or zebra. The carnivores are fed on Sunday, Wednesday, and Friday at 3pm, and following the feeders is one of the highlights of a visit to the park. One of the park's most popular attractions, especially with kids, is the Tiger Splash, in which big cats and their caretakers demonstrate predator-prey interactions in a large pool.

3505 W. Ariz. 260 (at Verde Valley Justice Rd.), Camp Verde. www.outofafricapark.com. ✆ **928/567-2840.** $34 adults, $32 seniors, $19 ages 3–12, free for kids 2 and under. Daily 9:30am–5pm. Closed Thanksgiving and Christmas.

Tuzigoot National Monument ★ ANCIENT SITE Perched atop a hill overlooking the Verde River, this network of stone-walled rooms, of which a large system of walls of various heights remain, was built by the Sinagua people and inhabited between 1125 and 1400. The Sinagua, whose name is Spanish for "without water," were traditionally dry-land farmers relying entirely on rainfall to water their crops. When the Hohokam, who had been living in the Verde Valley since A.D. 600, moved on to more fertile land around 1100, the Sinagua moved in. Their buildings progressed from individual homes called pit houses to the type of communal pueblo seen here at Tuzigoot. ("Tuzigoot" means "crooked water" in Apache.) An interpretive trail leads through the Tuzigoot ruins, explaining different aspects of Sinaguan life; inside the visitor center, a small museum displays many of the artifacts unearthed here. Desert plants, many of which were used by the Sinagua, are identified along the trail.

Just outside Clarkdale off Ariz. 89A. www.nps.gov/tuzi. ✆ **928/634-5564.** $10 adults (combined entry with Montezuma Castle National Monument, above), free for kids 15 and under. Memorial Day weekend to Labor Day weekend daily 8am–6pm; rest of year daily 8am–5pm. Closed Christmas.

A Hike and a Swim

If it's a hot day, you may want to head up to **Sycamore Creek** to cool off in one of the creek's swimming holes. It's only a ¼-mile hike to the first swimming hole, but there are more farther up the creek. To reach the trail head, follow signs to Tuzigoot National Monument; after crossing the bridge over the Verde River, turn left onto Forest Road (F.R.) 131 (signposted for the Sycamore Canyon Wilderness). The road quickly turns to gravel and then dirt and is very rough in places—don't try driving it without a high-clearance vehicle and preferably one with four-wheel-drive. The trail head is 11 miles up this road.

Verde Canyon Railroad ★★ VINTAGE RAILROAD When the town of Jerome was busily mining copper, a railway was built to link the booming town with the territorial capital at nearby Prescott. Because of the rugged mountains between Jerome and Prescott, the railroad was forced to take a longer but less difficult route north along the Verde River before turning south toward Prescott. Today, you can ride these same tracks aboard the Verde Canyon Railroad. The 4-hour route through the canyon traverses the remains of a copper smelter and a stretch of unspoiled desert, inaccessible by car and part of Prescott National Forest. The views of the rocky canyon walls and green waters of the Verde River are quite dramatic, and if you look closely along the way, you'll see ancient Sinagua cliff dwellings. In late winter and early spring, nesting bald eagles can also be spotted. Although the Grand Canyon Railway (p. 240) travels to a more impressive destination, this is a more scenic excursion.

300 N. Broadway, Clarkdale. www.verdecanyonrr.com. ✆ **800/582-7245.** $65 adults, $60 seniors, $45 ages 2–12; 1st-class tickets $80. Call or visit website for schedule.

Where to Stay in Jerome

Connor Hotel of Jerome ★ Housed in a renovated historic hotel, this lodging has spacious rooms with large windows; views of the valley, however, are limited. A few rooms are located directly above the hotel's popular bar, which can be quite noisy on weekends, but most rooms are quiet enough to provide a good night's rest.

164 Main St. www.connorhotel.com. ✆ **800/523-3554** or 928/634-5006 12 units. $90–$165 double. Pets accepted. **Amenities:** Bar; free Wi-Fi.

Ghost City Inn ★ With its long verandas on both floors, this restored old house is hard to miss as you drive into town from Clarkdale. It manages to capture the spirit of Jerome with a mix of Victorian and southwestern decor. Most bedrooms have great views across the Verde Valley (and these are definitely worth requesting). Two units feature antique brass beds. The rooms are on the small side, so if space is a priority, opt for the suite.

541 Main St. www.ghostcityinn.com. ✆ **888/634-4678.** 6 units. $95–$145 double; $145 suite. Rates include full breakfast. 2-night minimum some weekends and holidays. Pets accepted ($25 fee). No children 13 or under. **Amenities:** Free Wi-Fi.

Jerome Grand Hotel ★ Built as a hospital when Jerome was at its height, the Jerome Grand Hotel remains the most imposing structure in town. It's a great place to look at from outside, and it's a great place to look out from, with views impressive even by Jerome standards. (Note that you'll pay a premium for rooms boasting those views.) The rooms are old hospital rooms, but other than that, this is the closest thing Jerome has to a big hotel, with a full restaurant and bar and modern amenities.

200 Hill St. www.jeromegrandhotel.net. ✆ **888/817-6788.** 6 units. $185–$295 double; $395–$525 suite. No pets. **Amenities:** Free Wi-Fi.

Mile High Inn ★ You can't get any quainter than this, right down to the fact that three of the seven units share a bathroom. All the rooms are attractively decorated, some with antiques and some with more modern furnishings. Although the rooms are not very large, a couple do have king-size beds.

309 Main St. www.milehighgrillandinn.com. ✆ **414/634-5094.** 7 units, 4 w/private bath. $85–$105 double w/shared bath; $120–$130 double w/private bath. Rates include full breakfast (except Mon–Wed in winter). 2-night minimum on holidays. **Amenities:** Restaurant; lounge; free Wi-Fi.

Where to Eat in Jerome & the Verde Valley

JEROME

The Asylum ★ SOUTHWESTERN As the name would imply, this restaurant (inside a former hospital building high above downtown Jerome) is a bit out of the ordinary. The menu buys into this as well ("Lunch for the Committed"). But despite the goofy name, it's a serious restaurant, and as befits its place in the Jerome Grand Hotel (see above), the food transcends all of this with Southwestern flair, as in the prickly-pear barbecued pork tenderloin with tomatillo salsa or the mesquite BLT for lunch. Cocktails all get wacky loony-bin names, and there's also a crazy-big wine list.

200 Hill St. www.asylumrestaurant.com. ✆ **928/639-3197.** Reservations recommended. Main courses $10–$16 lunch, $20–$32 dinner. Daily 11am–3:30pm and 5–9pm.

The Bordello of Jerome ★ LIGHT FARE This is a great place for casual and healthful fare in funky, artsy surroundings. You can get burgers made of beef, bison, wild boar, or veggies; and there are a lot of healthy salads with quinoa and the like. The menu has some mildly risqué humor to go with the building's history, which is said to be another town brothel. A Ukulele Orchestra plays in the cafe on alternating Thursday nights.

412 Main St. (at Hull Ave.). https://the-bordello-of-jerome.business.site. ✆ **928/649-5855.** No reservations. Most items $8.50–$13. Mon–Sat 11am–8pm, Sun 11am–4pm. Mon–Wed closes 3–5pm.

Haunted Hamburger ★ AMERICAN Perched precariously high above Jerome's main shopping street, this restaurant seems poised to come crashing down into the Verde Valley far below. Although you can get steaks, fajitas, barbecued ribs, and other dishes here, it would be a mistake not to order the namesake haunted hamburger, which is topped with mushrooms, bacon, cheese, green chilies, grilled onion, and guacamole.

410 Clark St. https://thehauntedhamburger.com. ✆ **928/634-0554.** No reservations. Main courses $11–$17. Daily 11am–9pm.

VERDE VALLEY

In Camp Verde, I always stop at the **Thanks a Latte** coffee shop, 348 S. Main St. (www.greenvalleyroastingcompany.com; ✆ **928/567-6450**) on the road out of town. It's the home of the terrific local coffee roasters, Green Valley. If you need some espresso to get you through the rest of the day, the best place to get it is at Cottonwood's **Crema Coffee & Creamery,** 917 N. Main St. (www.cremacottonwood.com; ✆ **928/649-5785**). Crema also sells sandwiches, soup, pastries, and gelato; it's open Monday through Friday 7am to 4pm, Saturday and Sunday 8am to 4pm.

Bing's Burger Station ★ AMERICAN In what was once a gas station on the edge of old town Cottonwood, you can get some of the best burgers in the region. This burger joint, with its wall of license plates from around the country, is a throwback to the burger stands of the 1950s. The short and simple menu is printed on a pad of paper; mark down what you want on your burger and what sides and drink you want, and hand it to the waiter. Be sure to try one of the fountain sodas (peach, lime, root beer, or mulberry), made with syrups produced exclusively for Bing's.

794 N. Main St., Cottonwood. www.bingsburgers.com. ✆ **928/649-1718**. No reservations. Burgers $6 and up. Tues–Sat 11am–7pm, Sun 11:30am–4pm.

Blazin' M Ranch Wild West Adventure ★ AMERICAN Adjacent to Dead Horse Ranch State Park, the Blazin' M Ranch is classic Arizona-style family entertainment—barbecue and beans accompanied by cowboy music and comedy. Although this place is geared primarily toward the young 'uns, if you're young at heart, you may enjoy the Blazin' M, too. It's definitely more fun if you bring the whole family. Highlights include a reproduction of a Yavapai Apache camp, a mining camp, mechanical horse roping, and a gallery of animated woodcarvings, which features humorous Western scenes. Note that dinner—chicken and ribs, all the fixin's, and dessert—is a prix-fixe $39.95 for adults, though you would not, of course, heard it put quite that way at the Blazin' M!

1875 Mabery Ranch Rd. (off 10th St.), Cottonwood. www.blazinm.com. ✆ **928/634-0334.** Reservations recommended. $40 adults, $35 seniors, $20 ages 5–12. Wed–Sat gates open 4pm, dinner 6:30pm, show 7:30pm. Closed Thurs–Fri in Dec.

Old Town Café ★ LIGHT FARE Good pastries, salads, and sandwiches, such as a grilled panini of smoked turkey, spinach, tomatoes, and mozzarella, make Old Town my favorite lunch spot in the Verde Valley. It's a bright, cheery little cafe with a handful of tables.

1025-A N. Main St., Cottonwood. www.oldtownroaster.com. ✆ **928/634-5980.** No reservations. Salads and sandwiches $7–$10. Tues–Sat 7:30am–3pm.

SEDONA & OAK CREEK CANYON ★★★

66 miles NE of Prescott; 116 miles N of Phoenix; 106 miles S of the Grand Canyon

Just to state the obvious, in few places in the U.S. will you find a town or city in a more beautiful setting. On the outskirts of Sedona, red-rock buttes, eroded canyon walls, and mesas rise into cerulean skies. Those buttes are masterpieces in their own right, each with its own personality and majesty. Off in the distance, the Mogollon Rim looms, its forests of juniper and ponderosa pine dark against the rocks. With a wide band of rosy sandstone predominating in this area, Sedona has come to be known as red-rock country, and each evening at sunset, the rocks put on an unforgettable light show that is reason enough for a visit.

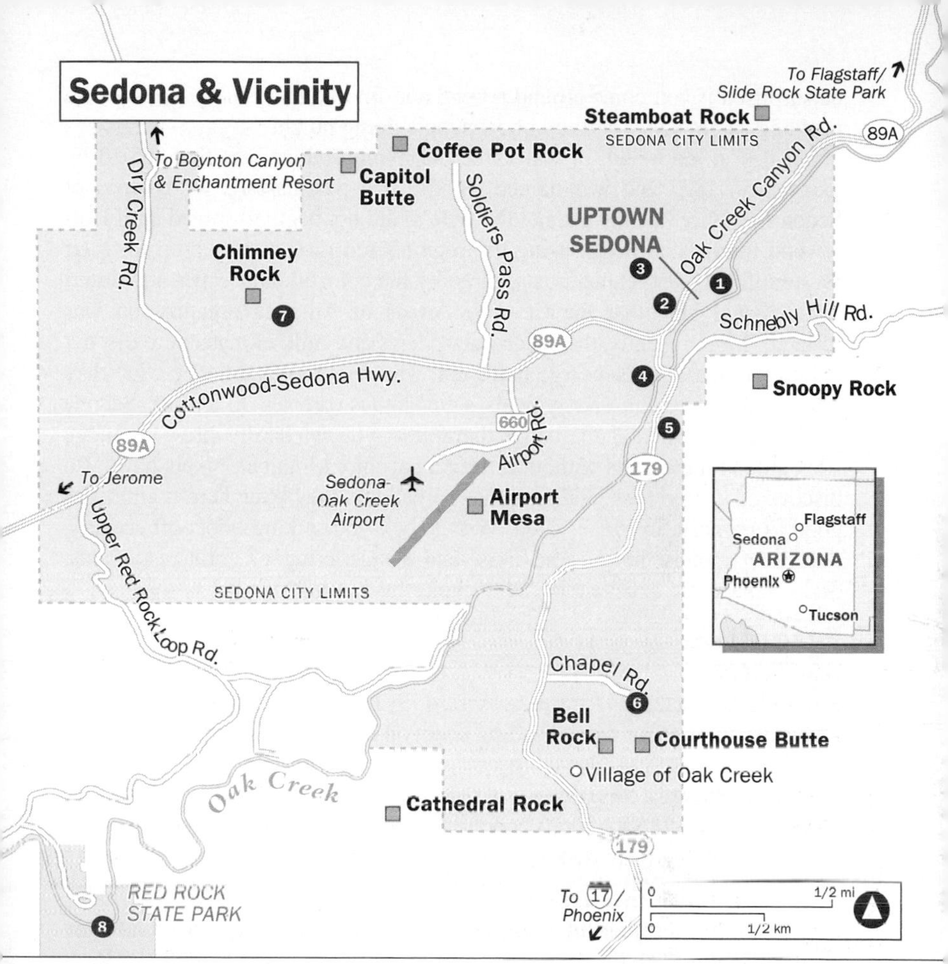

Amitabha Stupa Peace Park **7**
Chapel of the Holy Cross **6**
Hillside Sedona Shopping Center **5**
Red Rock State Park **8**
Sedona Arts Center **1**
Sedona Chamber of Commerce Visitor Center **2**
Sedona Heritage Museum **3**
Tlaquepaque **4**

All this may sound perfectly idyllic, but if you lower your eyes from the red rocks, you'll see the flip side of Sedona—a sprawl of housing developments, highways lined with unattractive strip malls, and bumper-to-bumper traffic. And downtown, which most visitors end up wandering through at least once, alternates serious art stores with trashier places. Yet not even this can mar the beauty of the backdrop.

With national forest surrounding the city (fingers of forest even extend into what would otherwise be the city limits), Sedona has some of the best outdoor access of any city in the Southwest. All around town, alongside highways and down suburban side streets, there are trail heads. Trek down any of these trails and you leave the city behind, entering the world of the red rocks. Just don't be surprised if you come around a bend and find yourself in the middle of a wedding ceremony or a group of 30 people doing tai chi.

Located at the mouth of Oak Creek Canyon, Sedona was first settled by pioneers in 1877 and was named for the first postmaster's wife. Word of Sedona's beauty (the town's, not the wife's) did not begin to spread until Hollywood filmmakers began using the region's red rock as backdrop for their Western films. Next came artists, lured by the colorful landscapes and desert light (it was here that the Cowboy Artists of America organization was formed). More recently, the spectacular views and mild climate were discovered by retirees and New Age believers, who come to experience what they says are unseen cosmic energy fields—the famous vortexes. As a result, Sedona has become a hotbed of alternative therapies—you can hardly throw a smudge stick around these parts without hitting a psychic. Mountain bikers have also discovered the red rock, and word has spread that the biking here is almost as good as up north in Moab, Utah. With knock-your-hiking-boots-off scenery, dozens of motels, hotels, and inns, and a smattering of good restaurants, Sedona makes an excellent base for exploring central Arizona.

Essentials

ARRIVING

From Phoenix, take I-17 north to Ariz. 179; it's about a 2-hour drive. From Flagstaff, it's a 1-hour drive, heading south on I-17 to the turnoff for Ariz. 89A and Sedona. Ariz. 89A also connects Sedona with Prescott.

Sedona Phoenix Shuttle (www.sedona-phoenix-shuttle.com; ✆ **800/448-7988** in AZ, or 928/282-2066) operates several trips daily between Phoenix's Sky Harbor Airport and Sedona. The one-way fare is $55.

VISITOR INFORMATION

The **Sedona Chamber of Commerce Visitor Center/Uptown Gateway Visitor Center,** 331 Forest Rd. (www.visitsedona.com; ✆ **800/288-7336** or 928/282-7722) is at the corner of Ariz. 89A and Forest Road in Uptown Sedona. The visitor center is open Monday through Saturday 8:30am to 5pm, and Sunday and holidays 9am to 3pm.

For information on hiking in the area, contact the Coconino National Forest's **Red Rock District Visitors Center,** 8375 Ariz. 179 (www.fs.fed.us/r3/coconino; ✆ **928/203-2900**), just south of the Village of Oak Creek on the south end of Sedona. It's open daily from 8am to 5pm. About 4 miles north of town, the Forest Service's **Oak Creek Visitor Center** on Ariz. 89A (✆ **928/203-0624**) is another source for maps, park passes, and hunting and fishing licenses; it's open April through November 9am to 4pm.

Another useful website for the area is **www.redrockcountry.org**.

GETTING AROUND

It's only 12 miles from I-17 to Sedona proper, but this is a major tourist destination, and traffic can really bog down on two-lane Ariz. 179 on a Friday afternoon. Whether traveling by car or on foot, you'll need to be patient when navigating traffic in Sedona. Just like you, other drivers are apt to gape at the rocks, so be prepared for slow traffic on roads with good views. You may hear or see references to the **"Y"**; that's the intersection of Ariz. 179 and Ariz. 89A between the Tlaquepaque shopping plaza and Uptown Sedona.

SPECIAL EVENTS

The **Sedona International Film Festival** (www.sedonafilmfestival.com; ✆ **928/282-1177**), held late February to early March, always books plenty of interesting films. In early December at the Tlaquepaque shopping plaza, Sedona celebrates the **Festival of Lights** (www.tlaq.com; ✆ **928/282-4838**) by lighting thousands of luminarias (paper bags partially filled with sand and containing a single candle).

Exploring Sedona Town

Sedona's most notable architectural landmark is the **Chapel of the Holy Cross** ★, 780 Chapel Rd. (www.chapeloftheholycross.com; ✆ **928/282-4069**), a small church built right into the red rock on the south side of town. If you're driving up from Phoenix, you can't miss it—the chapel sits high above the road just off Ariz. 179. With its contemporary styling, it is one of the most architecturally important modern churches in the country. Marguerite Brunswig Staude, a devout Catholic painter, sculptor, and designer, had

vortex **POWER**

For many years now, Sedona has been one of the world's centers for the New Age movement, and large numbers of people make the pilgrimage here to experience the "power vortexes" of the surrounding red-rock country. Around town you'll see bulletin boards and publications advertising such diverse services as past-life regressions, crystal healing, tarot readings, reiki, axiatonal therapy, electromagnetic field balancing, soul recovery, channeling, aromatherapy, myofascial release, and aura photos and videos.

According to believers, a vortex is a site where the earth's unseen lines of power intersect to form a particularly powerful energy field. Aficionados claim there are four vortexes around Sedona. Scientists may scoff, but Sedona's vortexes have become so well known that the visitor centers have several handouts to explain them and a map to guide you to them. (Many of the most spectacular geological features of the Sedona landscape also happen to be vortexes.)

The four main vortexes are Bell Rock, Cathedral Rock, Airport Mesa, and Boynton Canyon. **Bell Rock** and **Airport Mesa** are both said to contain masculine or electric energy that boosts emotional, spiritual, and physical energy. **Cathedral Rock** is said to contain feminine or magnetic energy, good for facilitating relaxation. The **Boynton Canyon** vortex is considered an electromagnetic energy site, which means it has a balance of both masculine and feminine energy.

If you're not familiar with vortexes and want to learn more about the ones in Sedona, consider a vortex tour. As you walk through Uptown you'll see many signs advertising vortex-related services; any of them can help you figure out what you need. Try **Sedona Vortex Adventures** (www.sedonavortexsites.com; ✆ **877/204-3664**) or **Sedona Soul Adventures** (www.sedonasouladventures.com; ✆ **866/508-0094** or 928/282-4562).

Sunset at the Amitabha Stupa

There's just something about Sedona that brings out people's spirituality, and one of the latest spiritual attractions to find a home among the red rocks is the **Amitabha Stupa Park** (www.stupas.org; ✆ **928/282-5195**), a Tibetan Buddhist shrine erected in a residential neighborhood in west Sedona, up a short path that winds through juniper trees. Festooned with prayer flags, the 36-foot-tall stupa is often visited by devout Buddhists, who leave offerings at the base of the stupa; the public is welcome anytime from dawn to dusk. To find the stupa, drive north from Ariz. 89A on Andante Dr. and turn left on Pueblo Dr. Park outside the gate on the right.

the inspiration for the chapel in 1932, but it wasn't until 1957 that her dream was finally realized. The chapel's design is dominated by a simple cross forming the wall that faces the street. The cross and the starkly beautiful chapel seem to grow directly from the rock, allowing the natural beauty of the red rock to speak for itself. It's open Monday through Saturday from 9am to 5pm and Sunday from 10am to 5pm; admission is free. The chapel is on a two-lane road with no outlet; be aware that the parking lots get crowded.

To learn a bit about local history, stop by the **Sedona Heritage Museum,** 735 Jordan Rd. (www.sedonamuseum.org; ✆ **928/282-7038;** daily 11am to 3pm; $7, $10 with audio), in Jordan Historical Park. Housed in a historic home, the museum is furnished with antiques and contains exhibits on the many movies that have been filmed in the area. The farm was once an apple orchard; there's still apple-processing equipment in the barn.

The **Sedona Arts Center,** 15 Art Barn Rd. (www.sedonaartscenter.com; ✆ **888/954-4442** or 928/282-3809), near the north end of Uptown Sedona on Ariz. 89A, has a gallery that specializes in works by local and regional artists.

Exploring Red-Rock Country

If you aren't an active type, you can spend a perfectly contented weekend just sitting and gazing in awe at the rugged cliffs, needle-like pinnacles, and isolated buttes that rise from the green forest floor at the mouth of Oak Creek Canyon. Want to see more without breaking a sweat? Head out into the red rocks on a jeep tour or soar over them in a biplane. Want to go *mano a mano* with this wild landscape? Go for a hike, rent a mountain bike, or go horseback riding.

ALONG ARIZ. 179 SOUTH OF TOWN

Although **Schnebly Hill Road,** which climbs into the red rocks east of Sedona, is a rough dirt road, it's a must for superb views. This road is best driven in a high-clearance vehicle (you can book a jeep tour if you prefer not to drive yourself). Head south of Sedona on Ariz. 179; just past the bridge over Oak Creek (at the Tlaquepaque shopping plaza), look for the turnoff on

Hiking up magnificent Bell Rock, just south of Sedona, is a great introduction to the scenic wonders of red-rock country.

your left. The road starts out paved but soon turns to dirt. As it climbs to the top of the Mogollon Rim, each switchback and cliff-edged curve yields a new and more astonishing view. At the top, the panorama at Schnebly Hill overlook just begs to be savored over a long picnic.

A number of striking rock formations lie south of town. From the Chapel of the Holy Cross (p. 193) on Chapel Road, you can see **Eagle Head Rock** (from the front door of the chapel, look three-quarters of the way up the mountain to see the eagle's head); the **Twin Nuns** (two pinnacles standing side by side); and **Mother and Child Rock** (to the left of the Twin Nuns). A little farther south on Ariz. 179, the aptly named **Bell Rock** rises up; there's a roadside parking area at its foot, and trails lead up to the top. Adjacent to Bell Rock is **Courthouse Butte,** and to the west stands **Cathedral Rock.**

Near the junction of I-17 and Ariz. 179, you can visit one of the premier petroglyph sites in Arizona. The rock art at the **V Bar V Heritage Site** (www.redrockcountry.org; © **928/282-3854**) covers a small cliff face and includes images of herons and turtles. To get here, take the dirt road that leads east for 2⅔ miles from the junction of I-17 and Ariz. 179 to the Beaver Creek Campground. The entrance to the petroglyph site is just past the campground. From the parking area, it's about a half-mile walk to the petroglyphs. The site is open Friday through Monday 9:30am to 3pm. To visit, you'll need a **Red Rock Pass** or another valid pass (below).

WEST OF SEDONA

Heading west out of Sedona on Ariz. 89A, turn left on Airport Road to drive up onto **Airport Mesa,** which commands an unobstructed panorama of Sedona and the red rocks. About halfway up the mesa is a small parking area from which easy trails radiate; at the top of the mesa is a huge parking area and viewpoint park that attracts crowds of sunset gazers. The views from here are among the best in the region.

Located 8 miles west of the "Y," **Boynton Canyon,** a narrow red-rock box canyon, is one of the most beautiful spots in the Sedona area. Today it's the site of the deluxe Enchantment Resort (p. 207), but hundreds of years before there were luxury suites here, there were Sinagua cliff dwellings. Several of these cliff dwellings can still be spotted high on the canyon walls. The Boynton Canyon Trail leads 3 miles into this canyon from a trail head parking area just outside the gates of Enchantment. Drive west of Sedona on Ariz. 89A, turn south on Dry Creek Rd., and follow the signs to Enchantment for about 7 miles, taking a left at the first T intersection (onto Boynton Pass Rd.) and a right at the second T (Boynton Canyon Rd.). On the way to Boynton Canyon, look north from Ariz. 89A to see **Coffee Pot Rock,** also known as Rooster

THE high cost OF RED-ROCK VIEWS

A quick perusal of any Sedona real-estate magazine will convince you that property values around these parts are as high as the Mogollon Rim. However, red-rock real estate is also expensive for those who want only a glimpse of the rocks. With the land around Sedona split up into several types of National Forest Service day-use sites, state parks, and national monuments, visitors find themselves pulling out their wallets just about every time they turn around to look at another rock. Here's the lowdown on what it's going to cost you to do the red rocks right.

A **Red Rock Pass** will allow you to visit Palatki Ruins (p. 197) and the V Bar V petroglyph site (p. 195) and park at any national forest trail-head parking areas. The cost is $5 for a 1-day pass, $15 for a 7-day pass, and $20 for a 12-month pass. Passes are good for everyone in your vehicle.

Be aware that these passes are not valid at Grasshopper Point (p. 198), Call of the Canyon (p. 198), Crescent Moon Picnic Area (p. 197), Red Rock State Park (p. 197), or Slide Rock State Park (p. 198), which charge from $8 to $20 admission per vehicle.

If two or more of you are traveling together and you plan on visiting the Grand Canyon and three or four other national parks or monuments, consider getting an **America the Beautiful Pass** ($80). Good for a year, it will get you into any national park or national monument in the country. If you're 62 or older, get an **America the Beautiful Senior Pass** ($80), which is good for the rest of your life. Persons with disabilities can get a free lifetime **America the Beautiful Access Pass.** Any of these three passes can be used in lieu of a Red Rock Pass.

For more information on the Red Rock passes, visit **www.redrockcountry.org**.

Rock, rising 1,800 feet. Three pinnacles, known as the **Three Golden Chiefs** by the Yavapai tribe, stand beside Coffee Pot Rock. As you drive up Dry Creek Rd., on your right you'll see **Capitol Butte,** which resembles the U.S. Capitol.

West of Boynton Canyon, you can visit a well-preserved set of Sinagua cliff dwellings at **Palatki Heritage Site** (www.fs.usda.gov; ✆ **928/282-3854**). These small ruins, tucked under the red cliffs, are the best place in the area to get a feel for the ancient Native American cultures that once lived in this region. Among the ruins, you'll see numerous pictographs (paintings) created by these long-ago residents. To visit Palatki, you'll need a **Red Rock Pass** (see "The High Cost of Red-Rock Views" box). The ruins are open daily 9:30am to 3pm; call in advance to make a reservation, as there are limited parking spaces. You can get here by driving west from Sedona on Ariz. 89A to F.R. 525, a gravel road leading north to F.R. 795, which dead-ends at the ruins. You can also reach the site from Boynton Canyon; continue west on scenic Boynton Pass Rd. (F.R. 152C), which eventually becomes a sometimes rough dirt road, and at the T intersection, go right onto F.R. 525, then veer right onto F.R. 795. ***Note:*** These dirt roads become impassable to regular cars when they're wet, so don't try coming out here if the roads are at all muddy.

A bit west of the turnoff for Boynton Canyon on Ariz. 89A, Upper Red Rock Loop Rd. leads to **Crescent Moon Picnic Area ★★**, a national forest recreation area that has become a must-see for Sedona visitors. Its popularity stems from a beautiful photograph of Oak Creek with **Cathedral Rock** in the background—an image reproduced countless times on postcards and in Sedona promotional literature. Hiking trails lead up to Cathedral Rock. Admission is $9 per vehicle. Continue on Red Rock Loop Rd. another couple of miles to reach **Red Rock State Park,** 4050 Red Rock Loop Rd. (www.azstateparks.com; ✆ **928/282-6907**), which flanks Oak Creek. The views here take in many of the rocks listed above, and you have the bonus of being right on the creek (though swimming and wading are prohibited). Park admission is $10 per car. The park offers guided walks and interpretive programs.

Exploring Oak Creek Canyon

The **Mogollon Rim** (pronounced *Mug-ee-un*) is a 2,000-foot escarpment cutting diagonally across central Arizona and on into New Mexico. At the top of the Mogollon Rim are the ponderosa pine forests of the high mountains, while at the bottom the lowland deserts begin. Of the many canyons cutting down from the rim, Oak Creek Canyon is the most beautiful—and one of the few with a paved road through it. From just outside Flagstaff to Sedona, Ariz. 89A runs through the canyon, winding its way down from the rim and paralleling Oak Creek. Along the way are overlooks, parks, picnic areas, campgrounds, and a variety of lodges and inns. Between the pine forests of the rim top and the desert below, Oak Creek Canyon is forested with sycamores and other deciduous trees; there is no better time to drive scenic Ariz. 89A than between late September and mid-October, when the canyon is ablaze with red and yellow leaves.

From the north, your first stop south of Flagstaff will be the **Oak Creek Canyon Vista,** which provides a view far down the valley to Sedona and beyond. The overlook is at the edge of the Mogollon Rim, and the road suddenly drops in tight switchbacks just south of here. From this vantage point you can see how one rim of the canyon is lower than the other—Oak Creek Canyon sits on a geologic fault line, and one side of the canyon is moving in a different direction from the other.

Within Oak Creek Canyon you'll find several hikes of different lengths. By far the most spectacular is the 6-mile round-trip **West Fork of Oak Creek Trail ★**, a classic canyon-country hike. At some points, the canyon is no more than 20 feet wide, its steep walls rising more than 200 feet from the creek. You can extend the hike many more miles up the canyon if you want an overnight backpacking trip. The trail head is at the **Call of the Canyon Recreation Area,** on Ariz. 89A 10 miles north of Sedona; there's a $9 day-use fee per vehicle.

In the desert, swimming holes are powerful magnets in the hot summer months, and consequently, **Slide Rock State Park,** 6871 N. Ariz. 89A (www.azstateparks.com; ✆ **928/282-3034**), 7 miles north of Sedona on the site of an old homestead, is the most popular spot in Oak Creek Canyon in summer, with crowds of families and teenagers drawn by its natural water slide and great little swimming hole. On hot days, it's jammed with people splashing in the water and sliding over the algae-covered sandstone bottom of Oak Creek. It's open daily, year-round; entry is $10 per vehicle ($20 in summer). Another popular swimming area is at **Grasshopper Point,** 2 miles north of Sedona on Ariz. 89A. Admission is $8 per vehicle.

If you get thirsty while driving through the canyon, hold out for **Indian Gardens Market,** 3951 N. Ariz. 89A (www.indiangardens.com; ✆ **928/282-7702**), about 4 miles north of Sedona, next to the Oak Creek Visitor Center (p. 192). Here, in the fall, you can usually buy delicious organic apple juice made from apples grown in the canyon. Another 2 miles down Ariz. 89A, just past Grasshopper Point, stop at the overlook at the north end of **Midgely Bridge** for one last view down the canyon.

Organized Tours

For an overview of Sedona town, take a tour on the **Sedona Trolley,** 276 N. Ariz. 89A (www.sedonatrolley.com; ✆ **928/282-4211**), which leaves hourly on two separate tours. One visits the Tlaquepaque shopping plaza, the Chapel of the Holy Cross, and several art galleries, while the other goes out through west Sedona to Boynton Canyon and the Enchantment Resort. Tours are $15 adults ($25 for both tours), $10 ages 12 and under ($20 for both tours).

Sedona Wine Tours (www.theoriginalsedonawinetours.com; ✆ **928/963-1890**) offers a variety of wine tours in the area, starting at $79. They will even pick you up at your hotel. There's also **Wine Tours of Sedona** (www.winetoursofsedona.com; ✆ **928/204-1473**), which offers a variety of wine, brewery, and even chocolate tours in the Verde Valley, starting at $150.

Pink Jeep Tours roar around the Sedona area's rugged canyon terrain.

The red-rock country surrounding Sedona is the city's greatest natural attraction, and there's no better way to explore it than by four-wheel-drive vehicle. Although you may end up feeling like every other tourist in town, you quite simply should not leave Sedona without going on a jeep tour, getting out onto rugged roads and 4×4 trails with spectacular views. The unchallenged leader, **Pink Jeep Tours** (www.pinkjeep.com; ✆ **800/873-3662** or 928/282-5000), has been driving its ubiquitous pink jeeps deep into the Coconino National Forest since 1958. It offers all sorts of tours, starting at 90 minutes ($59 adults, $54 kids), everything from showing you some basics to roaring around rough terrain for hours. Pink Jeep Tours also offers 8- and 10-hour jaunts to the Grand Canyon, 2 hours away from Sedona.

Want to take it up a notch? Head out into the red rocks in a Hummer with **Sedona Offroad Adventures** (www.sedonaoffroadadventures.com; ✆ **928/282-6656**) on tours they say range from "mild to wild." Basic 1-hour treks on the town streets or on easy trails start at $39 adults, $29 kids; a 2-hour "Cliff-Hanger Trail" costs $70 and $69.

For customized tours at your own pace, I recommend contacting Steven "Benny" Benedict at **Earth Tours** (www.earthtours.com; ✆ **928/203-9132**). Benny's operation offers "hikes and spiritual journeys" to spots that even many locals don't know about. Half-day excursions start at $495 per person, and full-day outings are $895 per person.

Just because it's too dark to see the red rocks doesn't mean there's nothing to do in Sedona at night. How about a tour of the heavens? **Evening Sky Tours** (www.eveningskytours.com; ✆ **928/203-0006**) takes advantage of the area's dark night skies to lead people on astronomy tours ($70 adults, $40 kids); I recommend making reservations for these.

As spectacular as Sedona is from the ground, it is even more so from the air. **Guidance Air,** 1200 Airport Rd., Sedona (guidanceair.com; ✆ **928/351-1000**) offers flights from Airport Mesa starting at $99. **Red Rock Helicopter Tours** (www.grandcanyontourcompany.com; ✆ **800/222-6966**) offers short flights to different parts of this colorful region; 75 minutes in the air starts at $115. There's also **Sedona Air Tours** (www.sedonaairtours.com; ✆ **888/866-7433** or 928/204-5939), where a 15-minute basic flight starts at $99. Or, for something slower, how about drifting over the sculpted red buttes in a hot-air balloon? Try **Northern Light Balloon Expeditions** (www.northernlightballoon.com; ✆ **800/230-6222** or 928/282-2274) or **Red Rock Balloon Adventures** (www.redrockballoons.com; ✆ **800/258-3754**); both charge $225 per person.

Outdoor Activities

HIKING

Hiking is the most popular outdoor activity in the Sedona area, with dozens of trails leading off into the red rocks. Not surprisingly, the most convenient trail heads also have the most crowded trails. If you want to ditch the crowds, pick a trail head that is not on Ariz. 179 or Ariz. 89A. Among my personal favorites described below are the Cathedral Rock Trail and the trails off Boynton Pass Rd. ***Note:*** Don't forget to get your Red Rock Pass before heading out for a hike (see the box on p. 196 for details).

This said, the most convenient place to get some red dust on your boots is on the **Bell Rock Pathway ★**, which begins alongside Ariz. 179 just north of the Village of Oak Creek. This trail winds around the base of Bell Rock and accesses many other trails that lead onto the sloping sides of Bell Rock. It's a popular trail and can get crowded, but it is the single best introduction to hiking in Sedona's beautiful red-rock country. It's about 4 miles to go all the way around Bell Rock and adjacent Courthouse Butte.

You'll see fewer tourists if you head to the .75-mile **Cathedral Rock Trail,** which is also located between the Village of Oak Creek and Uptown Sedona. The trail follows cairns (piles of rocks) up the slick-rock slopes on the north side of Cathedral Rock. Turn off Ariz. 179 just south of Sedona at Back o' Beyond Rd. and watch for the trail head at the end of the paved road. Be aware that calling this route a trail is being very generous—in places it is almost a hand-over-hand crawl across the rocks. However, even if you stop when the going gets steep, you'll get great views. For solitude, you can't beat the **Mystic Trail,** which begins at an unmarked roadside pull-off on Chapel Rd. halfway between Ariz. 179 and the Chapel of the Holy Cross. This easy 1-mile out-and-back trail runs between a couple of housing developments, but once you're on the trail, you'll feel all alone.

Another popular set of trails lead into **Boynton Canyon** (site of the Enchantment Resort, p. 207), where you'll glimpse ancient Native American ruins built into the red-rock cliffs. Although the scenery is stupendous, there are usually a lot of other hikers on the trail, and the parking lot tends to fill up early in the day. (For directions to the Boynton Canyon trail head, see p. 196.) Nearby, I'd also recommend the 1.5-mile **Vultee Arch Trail,** which leads to an impressive sandstone arch, or the 1.8-mile round-trip **Devil's Bridge Trail,** which leads to the largest natural sandstone arch in the area. To reach them, drive north on Dry Creek Rd. from Ariz. 89A, bearing right at the "Y" to stay on Forest Rd. 152. The Devil's Bridge turnoff is 1½ miles up that road; the Vultee Arch trail head is 3 miles farther on a rough dirt road.

For the hands-down best views in Sedona, hike all or part of the **Airport Mesa Trail,** a 3.5-mile loop that circles Airport Mesa. With virtually no elevation gain, this is an easy hike. You'll find the trail head about halfway to the top of Airport Mesa on Airport Rd. Try this one as early in the day as possible; by midday, the parking lot is usually full and it stays that way right through sunset.

Hiking in Oak Creek Canyon is also wonderful; for details on the famous **West Fork Oak Creek Trail,** see p. 198.

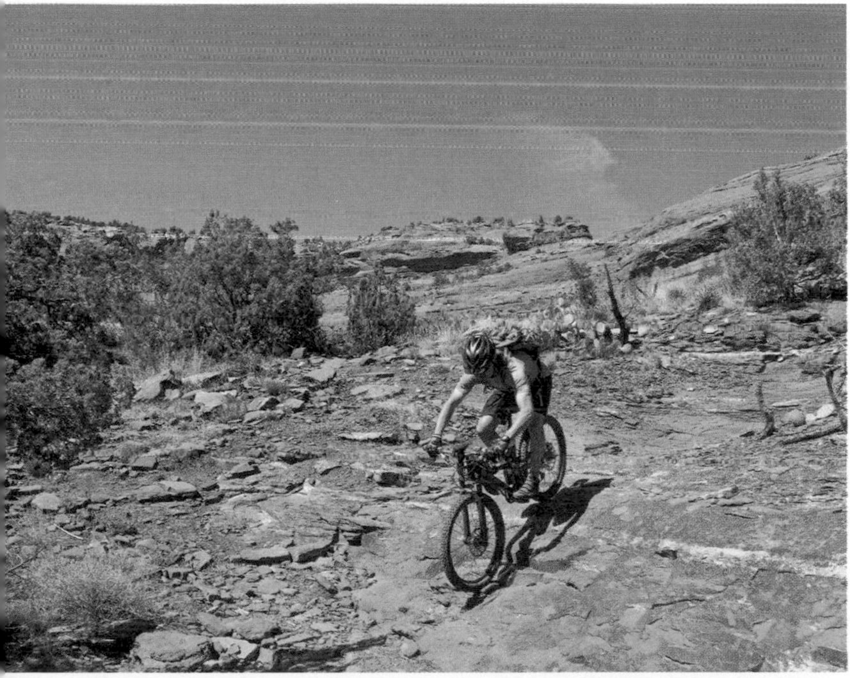

Challenging trails with awesome views lure thrill-seeking mountain bikers to red-rock country.

MOUNTAIN BIKING

Sedona is rapidly becoming one of the Southwest's meccas for mountain biking. The red rock here is every bit as challenging and scenic as the famed slick-rock country of Moab, Utah, and much less crowded. Using Sedona as a base, mountain bikers can ride year-round by heading up to Flagstaff in the heat of summer. One of my favorite rides is around the base of **Bell Rock.** Starting at the parking area on Ariz. 179 just north of the Village of Oak Creek, you'll find not only the easy Bell Rock Path, but also numerous, more challenging trails.

Another great ride starts above Uptown Sedona, where you can take the **Jim Thompson Trail** to Midgely Bridge or a network of trails heading toward Soldier Pass. The riding here is only moderately difficult and the views are superb. To reach these trails, take Jordan Rd. to a left onto Park Ridge Rd., and follow that to its end at a trail head parking area.

Across the street from the Bell Rock Pathway, **Sedona Bike & Bean,** 30 Bell Rock Plaza, on Ariz. 179 in the Village of Oak Creek (www.bike-bean.com; ✆ **928/284-0210**) also rents bikes (and serves coffee). Bikes go for $19 the first hour, $10 for each additional hour. You can also rent bikes from **Mountain Bike Heaven,** 1695 W. Ariz. 89A (www.mountainbikeheaven.com; ✆ **928/282-1312**). Bikes rent for $45 to $65 per day. Either of these stores can sell you a good local trail map or guidebook to the best rides in Arizona.

HORSEBACK RIDING

If you'd rather saddle up a palomino than pedal a bicycle, book a horseback ride through **A Day in the West,** 252 N. Ariz. 89A (www.adayinthewest.com; ✆ **800/973-3662** or 928/282-4320), which charges $95 for a 1½-hour ride along the Verde River. The company does a huge variety of other tours, too, and will come get you at your hotel in Sedona.

GOLF

Surprisingly, Sedona has not yet been ringed with golf courses. However, what few courses there are offer superb views to distract you from your game. South of town off Ariz. 179, the **Oakcreek Country Club,** 690 Bell Rock Blvd. (www.oakcreekcountryclub.com; ✆ **888/284-1660** or 928/284-1660) has an 18-hole course with stunning views. The greens fees range from $67 to $100-plus. Just south of that, the 18-hole course at the **Sedona Golf Resort ★★,** 35 Ridge Trail Dr. (www.sedonagolfresort.com; ✆ **877/733-6630**) offers equally breathtaking views of the red rocks. The greens fee there is $105 ($80 after 1pm).

Shopping in Sedona

Ever since the Cowboy Artists of America organization was founded in Sedona back in 1965 (at what is now the Cowboy Club restaurant, p. 216), this town has had a reputation as an artists' community. There are dozens if not scores of galleries in the area. As in many tourist towns, however, a significant

Designed to resemble a Mexican village, the Tlaquepaque Arts & Crafts Village offers a delightful shopping experience.

percentage of the so-called art leans toward the kitschy. In Sedona you see that phenomenon on steroids; you can find searchingly beautiful Navajo art on display right next to ninja stars "ON SALE SPECIAL TODAY." And that's not to mention all the shops purveying vortex paraphernalia, from crystals and exotic stones to aura pictures, chakra balancing, and, um, "sound vibration energy healing."

The main shopping area, called **Uptown,** is along Ariz. 89A, just east of the roundabout you hit coming into town from the south on Ariz. 179. there's another cluster just south of the Ariz. 179 roundabout, at **Tlaquepaque Arts & Crafts Village,** 336 Ariz. 179 (www.tlaq.com; ✆ **928/282-4838**). With 40-some stores and restaurants, Tlaquepaque is a calming antidote to the ruckus of Uptown. (It's actually easy to pronounce—"ta-lacka-packy"—named after a famous arts-and-crafts neighborhood in the suburbs of Guadalajara.) It's designed to resemble a Mexican village, a maze of narrow alleys and courtyards with fountains, a chapel, and a bell tower—it's worth a visit even if you aren't in a buying mood. Most of its shops sell high-end art, jewelry, women's fashions, and unique gifts. All the restaurants and cafes are terrific, too. I'd also recommend a mall called **Hozho,** on Ariz. 179 just before you cross the Oak Creek bridge; it has a couple of Sedona's better galleries.

Hillside Sedona ★, just south of Tlaquepaque, is dedicated to art galleries and upscale retail shops, and also has a couple of good restaurants.

Clear Creek Trading ★ If you're in the market for a bear-skin rug, a cow skull, or some buffalo horns, do not miss this shop in an old house at the north end of the Uptown shopping district, with rooms full of oddities as well as kitschy tourist souvenirs. 435 N. Ariz. 89A. www.clearcreektrading.com. ✆ **928/204-5805.**

Cowboy Corral ★ Want to dress like Wyatt Earp or Annie Oakley? This shop can outfit you. Definitely not your standard urban cowboy shop, Cowboy Corral goes for the vintage look. They sell guns, too. 219 N. Ariz. 89A. www.cowboycorral.com. ✆ **800/457-2279** or 928/282-2040.

Exposures International Gallery ★ Here's where to go if you've got a big house and need some big art. Exposures is the largest gallery in the state and usually has lots of monument-size sculptures out front. My favorite artist here is Texas sculptor Bill Worrell. 561 Ariz. 179. www.exposuresfineart.com. ✆ **928/282-1125.**

Garland's Indian Jewelry ★★★ With a great location north of town, in the shade of scenic Oak Creek Canyon, and a phenomenal collection of concho belts, squash-blossom necklaces, and bracelets, this is one of the best places in Arizona to shop for Indian jewelry. There are also lots of *katsina* (kachina) dolls for sale. At Indian Gardens, 3953 N. Ariz. 89A (4 mi N of Sedona). www.garlandsjewelry.com. ✆ **928/282-6632.**

Garland's Navajo Rugs ★★★ Garland's isn't just the premier Navajo rug shop in Sedona, it has one of the largest selections of contemporary and antique Navajo rugs in the *country*. It also carries Native American baskets and pottery, Hopi *katsina* dolls, and Navajo sand paintings. 411 Ariz. 179. www.garlandsrugs.com. ✆ **928/282-4070.**

George Kelly Fine Jewelers ★ This store's beautiful, creatively designed jewelry incorporates a wide range of stones, even the occasional meteorite. It's in a stylish shopping mall atop a promontory, overlooking the "Y" from the north. At Hyatt Shops at Piñon Pointe, 101 N. Ariz. 89A., Ste. 23. www.sedonafinejewelry.com. ✆ **928/282-8884.**

The Hike House ★ If you've come to Sedona to hike, be sure to stop by the Hike House. Across Oak Creek from the Tlaquepaque shopping plaza, this shop not only sells hiking gear and clothes, but also has a cafe. An interactive computer trail finder can help you plan your day's hike. 431 Ariz. 179. www.thehikehouse.com. ✆ **928/282-5820.**

Hoel's Indian Shop ★★ Ten miles north of Sedona, in a private residence hidden by trees in Oak Creek Canyon, this Native American arts-and-crafts gallery is one of the finest in the region, selling pieces of the highest quality. It's a good idea to call before coming out to make sure the store will be open. 9589 N. Ariz. 89A. www.hoelsindianshop.com. ✆ **928/282-3925.**

Humiovi ★ On the north side of 89A, this "officially licensed" Hopi art shop has been overseen by the same family for decades and is curated with exquisite taste. They specialize in jewelry, but there's also lots of pottery. "Humiovi" is said to mean "the little seed that sprouts." 247 N. Ariz. 89A. www.humiovisedona.com. ✆ **928/823-9502.**

Hummingbird House ★ Looking for an unusual gift to take home to someone? Tired of the crowds of tourists at Tlaquepaque and in Uptown? Check out this hidden gift shop in an attractively restored historic general store set behind a picket fence. It's on a back street behind the Burger King at the junction of Ariz. 89A and Ariz. 179. 100 Brewer Rd. www.hummingbirdhouse-sedona.com. ✆ **928/282-0705.**

Isadora Handweaving Gallery ★★ One of the top fiber-arts galleries in the country, this tiny shop in the Tlaquepaque shopping plaza has been around for more than 20 years. Gorgeous handmade women's fashions fill the racks, and there are also plenty of beautiful accessories to go with the hand-woven silk jackets, felted scarves, and colorful shawls. At Tlaquepaque, 336 Ariz. 179, Ste. A120. www.isadoragallery.com. ✆ **928/282-6232.**

Lanning Gallery ★ In business for more than 20 years, this gallery in the Hozho Center carries both classic and contemporary art. At Hozho Center, 431 Ariz. 179. www.lanninggallery.com. ✆ **928/282-6865.**

Sedona Arts Center Members Gallery ★ At the north end of Uptown Sedona, this shop is the best place in town to see the work of area artists—everything from jewelry and fiber arts to photography and ceramics. Because it's a nonprofit shop, you won't pay any tax here. 15 Art Barn Rd. www.sedonaartscenter.org/gallery. ✆ **928/282-3865.**

Son Silver West/Robson Design ★ As you come into town from the south, this place is unmissable—a colorful, almost junk-yard-like melange on the west side of Ariz. 179. For those who love everything southwestern, this shop is a treasure-trove of interesting stuff, including Native American and Hispanic art and crafts, antique *santo* (saint) carvings, antique rifles, imported pots, dried-chili *ristras* (garlands), and garden art. 1476 Ariz. 179. www.sonsilverwest.com. ✆ **928/282-3580.**

SEDONA AREA WINERIES

It may be a bit premature to start calling Sedona the next Napa Valley, but there are a few wineries in the area. Three of them, in the community of Page Springs about 20 minutes west of Sedona, are open to the public for tastings. Drive west from Sedona on Ariz. 89A and turn south on Page Springs Rd.; you'll first come to **Javelina Leap Vineyard & Winery,** 1565 N. Page

Springs Rd. (www.javelinaleapwinery.com; ✆ **928/649-2681**), where winemaker and owner Rod Snapp focuses on premium red wines. Javelina Leap produces wines from both estate-grown grapes and grapes from other Arizona vineyards. The tasting room ($8 fee) is open daily 11am to 5pm. Right next door, at **Oak Creek Vineyards and Winery,** 1555 N. Page Springs Rd. (www.oakcreekvineyards.net; ✆ **928/649-0290**); the tasting room ($5 fee) is open daily 10am to 6pm. The most impressive of the three is **Page Springs Cellars ★**, 1500 N. Page Springs Rd. (www.pagespringscellars.com; ✆ **928/639-3004**); Rhone varietals are the specialty of owner Eric Glomski, one of the state's top winemakers. The tasting room ($10 fee) is open Sunday through Thursday 11am to 6pm, Friday and Saturday 11am to 9pm.

Where to Stay Around Sedona

Sedona is one of the most popular destinations in the Southwest, with dozens of hotels and motels around town. Rooms rates are high, particularly in spring and fall, and particularly for rooms with a view of those rocks and canyons. ***Note:*** Terms like "resort" and "bed & breakfast" are used a bit creatively here. Some top-tier places require a 2-night stay on weekends. In this environment, **Airbnb** has come to play a big role in tourist accommodations; there are many deals to be had there and on other overnight rental apps.

SEDONA & OAK CREEK CANYON

Expensive

Amara Hotel, Restaurant & Spa ★★ It's hip, it's convenient, and it's set beside lovely Oak Creek, hidden below the shops of Uptown Sedona above. There's even a swimming hole. How cool is that? This stylish hotel definitely offers the best of both worlds here in Sedona. The resort is hip and sophisticated, yet close to nature, and the minimalist decor and Zen-inspired style make Amara one of Sedona's most tranquil accommodations. From the outside, the hotel fits right in with the red-rock surroundings, while inside, bold splashes of color contrast with black-and-white photos. Guest rooms all have balconies or patios, wonderful pillowtop beds, and furnishings in black and red. The resort also has a small full-service spa.

100 Amara Lane. www.amararesort.com. ✆ **928/282-4828.** 100 units. $179–$550 double; from $279–$550 suite. $29 daily resort fee includes valet parking. Pets accepted ($75 fee). **Amenities:** Restaurant; lounge; concierge; exercise room; Jacuzzi; pool; room service; sauna; full-service spa; Wi-Fi (included in resort fee).

Briar Patch Inn ★★ If you're searching for a tranquil and romantic bed & breakfast amid the cool shade of Oak Creek Canyon, this is the place. Tranquility is guaranteed by the fact that there are no TVs or Wi-Fi in the rooms (there is Wi-Fi in the lobby). Located 3 miles north of Sedona on the banks of Oak Creek, this inn has been run by the same family for some 35 years. Its attractively updated cottages, which date from the 1940s, are surrounded by beautiful grounds (with a swimming hole!) where birdsong and a babbling creek set the mood. A Western/rustic-Mexican style predominates, and most units have fireplaces and kitchenettes. In summer, breakfast is served on a creekside terrace, and spa services like massages and facials take place in a creekside gazebo. While there are no red-rock views, the Briar Patch makes up for that with a delightful combination of solitude and sophistication.

3190 N. Ariz. 89A. www.briarpatchinn.com. ✆ **888/809-3030.** 19 cabins. $285–$495 double. Rates include full breakfast and afternoon snacks. **Amenities:** Concierge; spa services; Wi-Fi in lobby only.

El Portal Sedona ★★★ Owners Steve and Connie Segner have created a distinctive reimagining of a luxury hotel. Built of hand-formed adobe blocks, El Portal is designed to resemble a 200-year-old hacienda; it's a monument to fine craftsmanship. The vine-covered courtyard is a lulling place to read, commune with the plants, or enjoy a fire in the evening; the dining room is high-end rustic, with enormous wood beams (salvaged from a railroad bridge) and all sorts of interesting art cluttering the walls. The whole feeling is an interesting blend of casualness and luxury. You won't have a chatty bellboy nattering on as you tramp a hundred yards to your door, but you will have a gracious hostess give you a quick tour of the facilities and show you to your room—just steps from the lodge—with a minimum of fuss and bother. It's perfect for folks who are happy to spend money on an elegant hotel but hate corporate pretension and officiousness. Each of the enormous guest rooms has its own distinctive character, from Arts and Crafts to cowboy chic. Bathrooms are huge, most rooms have whirlpool tubs, and many have private balconies with red-rock views. There are delightful snacks in the afternoon and exquisite breakfasts. The location is very handy, too, right next to the genteel Tlaquepaque shopping plaza and a 5-minute walk to Uptown.

95 Portal Lane. www.elportalsedona.com. ✆ **800/313-0017** or 928/203-9405. 12 units. $229–$399 double. Rates include afternoon hors d'oeuvres. 2-night minimum weekends and holidays. Pets accepted. **Amenities:** Concierge; access to nearby health club and adjacent resort pools; room service, free Wi-Fi.

Enchantment Resort ★★★ Located at the mouth of Boynton Canyon, this resort more than lives up to its name. The setting is breathtaking (as are the prices), and the pueblo-style architecture blends in with the landscape, as the resort wends its way over nearly a half-mile up the canyon. (There are some wonderful trails in the vicinity, but it's something of a shlep to get back into town for meals or other activities.) Individual casitas can be booked as two-bedroom suites, one-bedroom suites, or single rooms, but it's worth reserving a suite so you can enjoy the casita living rooms, which feature high-beamed ceilings and beehive fireplaces. All rooms have patios with dramatic views. Both the **Che Ah Chi** restaurant (p. 214) and a less formal bar and grill offer tables outdoors; lunch on the terrace should not be missed. Guests have access to the facilities at **Mii amo spa** (see below). With its great red-rocks setting, suites, and myriad outdoor activities (croquet court, pools, and children's programs), Enchantment is a great choice for families looking to get away and stay away.

525 Boynton Canyon Rd. www.enchantmentresort.com. ✆ **800/826-4180** or 928/282-2900. 218 units. $355–$455 double; $565–$665 junior suite; $1,070–$1,980 2-bedroom suite. $34 daily resort fee includes valet parking. **Amenities:** 3 restaurants; 2 lounges; babysitting; bikes; children's programs; concierge; putting green and 6-hole par-3 golf course; health club; 6 Jacuzzis; 5 pools; room service; full-service spa; 6 tennis courts; Wi-Fi (included in resort fee).

L'Auberge de Sedona ★★ You're just beneath the busy center of Sedona, but you'd never know it at this luxurious boutique, styled as a French country retreat. ("Auberge" means "country inn.") The setting is unbeatable: L'Auberge sits on the banks of Oak Creek, shaded by towering sycamore trees; the air is suffused with the rustling sound of flowing water. Along the creek many of the rooms are free-standing rustic cottages, with big porches and outdoor showers. (There are traditional showers inside, too.) There's also a row of units on the cliff above the creek. Everything was redone in the last few years; the interiors are as comfortable and top-tier as you can imagine, right down to the giant TV and those expensive hard-to-figure-out European coffee machines that end up giving you only half a cup of coffee. Rooms are either right on the water or perched above Oak Creek Canyon, the latter with killer views of the iconic red buttes. A daily service fee means no tips to the staff; the hotel has a fleet of shuttles to take you to local restaurants or just up the hill. There are two restaurants, one upscale casual and one swanky; the latter is ingeniously designed to place every table creekside.

301 L'Auberge Lane. www.lauberge.com. ✆ **800/272-6777** or 928/282-1661. 88 units. $209–$999 double; $539–$1,499 cottage. 10% resort fee includes staff tips. Valet parking $27. Pets accepted ($35–$50 per night in basic rooms only). **Amenities:** 2 restaurants; lounge; concierge; fitness room; room service; full-service spa; free Wi-Fi.

The Lodge at Sedona ★ Set amid pine trees a block off Ariz. 89A in west Sedona, this large bed-and-breakfast is one of the more distinctive inns in Sedona, decorated in an Arts and Crafts/Mission style. The best rooms are those on the ground floor. These tend to be large, and several are suites. Suites are only slightly more expensive than deluxe rooms, and some have lovely brick arches separating the living areas. Second-floor rooms are more economical and tend to be fairly small. There's a wellness retreat center on-site as well; all meals (including breakfast) are vegetarian or vegan.

125 Kallof Place. www.lodgeatsedona.com. ✆ **800/619-4467** or 928/204-1942. 14 units. $229–$289 double; $309–$349 suite. Rates include breakfast. Pets accepted ($39 per night, 2-night minimum). No kids 10 and under. **Amenities:** Concierge; access to nearby health club, free Wi-Fi.

Mii amo ★★★ This full-service destination spa inside the gates of the Enchantment Resort (see above) easily claims the state's best spa location. On offer are 3-, 4-, and 7-night stays with all-inclusive prices for meals, various

Getting Pampered in Sedona

While Sedona isn't yet a resort spa destination on par with Phoenix or Tucson, it does have an ever-growing number of spas that can add just the right bit of pampering to your vacation. Longtime local favorite **Therapy on the Rocks,** 676 N. Ariz. 89A (www.myofascialrelease.com; ✆ **928/282-3002**), with its creekside setting, offers massage, myofascial release, and great views of the red rocks. A half-day of therapy here will run you $350. In west Sedona, try **Sedona's New Day Spa,** 1449 W. Ariz. 89A (www.sedonanewdayspa.com; ✆ **928/282-7502**), a beautiful day spa with a resort-like feeling. Massages start at $125; fuller treatments begin at $185. In the Village of Oak Creek, the large **Hilton Eforea Spa,** at the Hilton Sedona Resort, 90 Ridge Trail Dr. (www.hiltonsedonaspa.com; ✆ **928/284-6900**), offers a variety of treatments starting at $132 for massages and $215 for more elaborate treatments. There are also exercise and yoga classes, a pool, and tennis courts.

daily spa treatments, taxes, and fees. You also get all the amenities at the adjoining Enchantment Resort. Designed to resemble a modern Native American–style pueblo, the spa, like Enchantment, is spectacularly located next to the red-rock cliffs of Boynton Canyon, about 7 miles north of west Sedona. Shaded by cottonwood trees, Mii amo is well designed, with indoor and outdoor pools and outdoor massage cabanas at the foot of the cliffs. Guest rooms, which open onto a courtyard, have a bold, contemporary styling (mixed with Native American art and artifacts) that makes them some of the finest accommodations in the state. All units have private patios and gas fireplaces. No other spa in Arizona has a more southwestern feel. Check the website for complete reservation details, which require different arrival times for different packages.

525 Boynton Canyon Rd. www.miiamo.com. ✆ **844/993-9518** or 928/203-8500. 16 units. 3-night packages $3,000–$5,500, about 25% less for double occupancy: 7 nights $6,600–$10,600. Rates include 3 meals per day, 2 daily spa treatments, and a variety of activities. **Amenities:** Restaurant; lounge; bikes; concierge; exercise room; 3 Jacuzzis; 2 pools (indoor & outdoor); room service; full-service spa; access to Enchantment Resort; free Wi-Fi.

Orchard Canyon on Oak Creek ★ This may be the hardest place in the area to book a room—people have been coming here for so many years and like it so much that they reserve a year in advance (however, cancellations do occur). What makes the lodge so special? Maybe it's that you have to drive through the heart of Oak Creek Canyon to get to your log cabin; maybe it's the beautiful gardens or the relaxing atmosphere of an old-time summer getaway. There are 17 well-maintained cabins over 10 breathtakingly verdant acres, complete with tennis court, gardens, an apple orchard, and more. They are rustic—literally made of logs—but comfortable; the larger ones have fireplaces. Meals include organic fruits and vegetables grown on the property, and there's a yoga pavilion overlooking the creek. ***Note:*** Rates include full breakfast and dinner, and an afternoon tea, too.

8067 N. Ariz. 89A. www.enjoyorchardcanyon.com. ✆ **928/282-3343.** 17 units. $335 double. 15% service charge includes breakfast, afternoon tea, and dinner. Closed mid-Nov–early Mar. **Amenities:** Dining room; tennis; free Wi-Fi.

Moderate

Cedars Resort on Oak Creek ★ Located right at the "Y" and set atop a 100-foot cliff, this motel has fabulous views across Oak Creek to the towering red rocks. (Note that I say "motel," rather than the word "resort" in the operation's name.) Guest rooms are large and comfortable, and creekside rooms (for which you pay a premium) have private balconies. For the best views, ask for a "canyon" room—or save money by opting for a room without, and then hang out at the pool and hot tub, both of which have great views of the red rocks. A long stairway leads down to the creek, and the shops of Uptown Sedona are right outside the front door.

20 W. Ariz. 89A. www.sedonacedarsresort.com. ✆ **800/874-2072** or 928/282-7010. 38 units. $139–$179 double. Rates include continental breakfast. **Amenities:** Concierge; exercise room; Jacuzzi; outdoor pool; free Wi-Fi.

Orchards Inn of Sedona ★ For picture-perfect, in-your-face views of the red rocks, few Sedona hotels can compete with the Orchards, which sits on the south side of Ariz. 89A overlooking L'Auberge resort and Oak Creek Canyon and the cliffs beyond. Decorated in soothing neutral tones (why compete with those views?), every room here has glass patio doors to let you see plenty of the scenery. There's a colorful dining room, too.

254 N. Ariz. 89A. www.orchardsinn.com. ✆ **855/474-7719.** 69 units. $129–$249 double. Rates include full breakfast. Free parking. Pets accepted ($10 per night). **Amenities:** Restaurant; lounge; Jacuzzi; outdoor pool, free Wi-Fi.

Sedona Rouge Hotel & Spa ★ This stylish boutique hotel is one of the most distinctive luxury hotels in Sedona, and although it is located right on busy Ariz. 89A in west Sedona, I highly recommend it. Merging contemporary styling with North African details, the hotel manages to create an international ambience. Antique wrought-iron window grates from Tunisia decorate hallways, and guest rooms have Moroccan-inspired tables. Bathrooms, with dual-head rain-type showers, are a real highlight. If you can, try to get a room on the third floor; these have vaulted ceilings that make the rooms seem larger. The tiny lobby is just off an enclosed courtyard with a splashing fountain. A rooftop patio has the best view at the hotel. It's an especially good pick for couples in a romantic mood.

2250 W. Ariz. 89A. www.sedonarouge.com. ✆ **928/203-4111.** 77 units. $189–$340 double; $490–$1,100 suite. Dogs accepted ($50 fee). **Amenities:** Restaurant; lounge; concierge; exercise room; 2 Jacuzzis; outdoor pool; room service; full-service spa; free Wi-Fi.

Sky Ranch Lodge ★ One of Sedona's distinctive features is Airport Mesa, a large hill just south of downtown, which does indeed have a small airport on it. Also up there is this motel, which has a stupendous vista and lush grounds. From here you can see the entire red-rock country, with Sedona filling the valley below. Some rooms are basic; others have exposed wood beams on the ceilings; and some even have fireplaces, balconies, and kitchenettes. Even if you don't have a view from your room, those great views are just steps away. With a pool and plenty of space for running around, this place will keep the kids happy. You can even walk up the road to watch planes and helicopters at the airport.

1105 Airport Rd. www.skyranchlodge.com. ✆ **888/708-6400** or 928/282-6400. 94 units. $140–$240 double. Pets accepted ($10 per night). **Amenities:** Jacuzzi; outdoor pool, free Wi-Fi.

Inexpensive

Forest Houses ★ Set at the upper end of Oak Creek Canyon and built right on the banks of the creek, these rustic houses and apartments date to the 1940s. Built by a stone sculptor, they feature artistic touches that set them apart from other cabins in the canyon. About half of the houses are built right on the creek; some seem to grow straight from the rocks in the streambed. Terraces let you fully enjoy the setting. One of my favorite units is the two-bedroom Cloud House, with stone floors, peeled-log woodwork, and a loft. There are units for 2, 4, 6, and 10 people. This property is certainly not for everyone (no phones, no TVs; you have to drive through the creek to get here; weekend stays require a 2-night minimum, 4 nights in summer), but many who discover the Forest Houses come back year after year.

9275 N. Ariz. 89A. www.foresthousesresort.com. ✆ **928/282-2999.** 16 units. $120–$125 double. 2- to 4-night minimum stay. Children 8 and under stay free in parent's room. Pets accepted ($20 deposit). Closed Jan–mid-Mar. **Amenities:** No Wi-Fi.

Matterhorn Inn ★ In the heart of the Uptown shopping district, this incongruously named hotel is plopped among restaurants and shops on the north side of busy Ariz. 89A, yet all of the attractively furnished guest rooms have excellent views of the red-rock canyon walls. If you lie in bed and keep your eyes on the rocks, you'd never know there was so much going on below you. This place is a great value for Sedona.

230 Apple Ave. www.matterhorninn.com. ✆ **800/372-8207** or 928/282-7176. 23 units. $100–$200 double. Pets accepted ($10 per night). **Amenities:** Jacuzzi; outdoor pool; free Wi-Fi.

Star Motel ★ This is as bare-bones as you will get in Sedona, but you can't beat the location—steps from Uptown's main drag—or the decades of experience the owners of this place bring to the table. The rooms are very small; they're just a little bit bigger than the bed, and the bathroom is closet-sized. But there are small refrigerators in the rooms, everything's clean, the staff is friendly, and for some this will be just what you need.

295 Jordan Rd. www.starmotelsedona.com. ✆ **928/282-3641.** 11 units. $99–$199 double. No pets. **Amenities:** None.

VILLAGE OF OAK CREEK

Expensive

Adobe Village Inn ★ A garden full of bronze statues of children greets you when you pull up to this luxurious inn in the Village of Oak Creek, 6 miles south of Uptown Sedona. The inn lies almost at the foot of Bell Rock and features a variety of themed accommodations. The villas, the Sundance room, and the Sedona suite are the most impressive rooms here. My favorite is the Purple Lizard villa, which opts for a colorful Taos-style interior and an amazing rustic canopy bed. The Wilderness villa resembles a luxurious log cabin. The Lonesome Dove villa is a sort of upscale cowboy cabin with a fireplace, potbellied stove, and round hot tub in a "barrel." Can you say romantic? This inn also operates the Adobe Grand Villas in west Sedona.

150 Canyon Circle Dr. www.adobevillageinn.com. ✆ **928/284-1425.** 15 units. $199–$299 double; $199–$399 suite or villa. Rates include full breakfast. 2-night minimum weekends and holidays. **Amenities:** Concierge; Jacuzzi; outdoor pool, free Wi-Fi.

Canyon Villa ★★ Right at the tippy-top north end of the Village of Oak Creek, with unimpeded views north to the red rocks, this bed-and-breakfast offers comfortable if somewhat throwbacky accommodations; it's all quite nice, but there's a '70s feel to the furnishings and decor. All rooms but one have views, as do the pool area, living room, and dining room. Everything's nice here, but don't expect contemporary or hip. All rooms have balconies or patios, and several have fireplaces. Breakfast is a lavish affair meant to be lingered over, and in the afternoon there's an elaborate spread of appetizers.

40 Canyon Circle Dr. www.canyonvilla.com. ✆ **800/453-1166** or 928/284-1226. 11 units. $239–$359 double. Rates include full breakfast. No children 10 or under. **Amenities:** Concierge; access to nearby health club; outdoor pool; free Wi-Fi.

Hilton Sedona Resort & Spa ★★ If you want a pretty golf course, you can't do better than playing here against those towering views. Same goes for the huge pool area. While golf is the driving force behind most stays here, anyone looking for an active vacation will find plenty to keep them busy. Guest rooms are suites of varying sizes, with fireplaces and balconies or patios. The resort's restaurant plays up its views of the golf course and red rocks. The only drawback here is that, because it's south of the Village of Oak Creek, the resort is a bit of a drive (about 8 miles) to Sedona's shops and restaurants.

90 Ridge Trail Dr. www.hiltonsedonaresort.com. ✆ **877/273-3762** or 928/284-4040. 219 units. $179–$459 double. $20 resort fee includes parking. Pets accepted ($50 fee). **Amenities:** 2 restaurants; 2 lounges; concierge; 18-hole golf course; fitness room; 5 Jacuzzis; 2 pools; room service; sauna; full-service spa; 3 tennis courts; Wi-Fi (included in resort fee).

Las Posadas of Sedona ★ Across the highway from the Hilton resort (above), Las Posadas, done up in a striking rose-red to match the cliffs beyond, is a cross between an all-suites boutique hotel and a bed-and-breakfast inn. All of the rooms are suites, with a separate entrance, a king bed, a kitchenette, a gas fireplace, and a balcony or patio; some have outdoor whirlpool spas. And then there's the gourmet breakfast each morning. Be sure to ask for a room with a view.

26 Ave. de Piedras. www.lasposadasofsedona.com. ✆ **928/284-5288.** 23 units. $185–$270 double. Rates include full breakfast. Pets accepted ($35 per night). No children 11 or under. **Amenities:** Concierge; Jacuzzi; outdoor pool; free Wi-Fi.

Moderate

Red Agave ★ With a gorgeous view of Bell Rock and hiking trails that start at the edge of the property, this is Sedona's premier budget getaway for an active vacation. Affiliated with the nearby Bike & Bean bike shop, Red Agave offers discounts on bike rentals and easy access to miles of great mountain-biking trails. Accommodations are in attractive studios with tile floors, kitchens, and comfortable beds. For families, there are also A-frame cabins with loft sleeping areas. The small pool, two hot tubs, fire pit, and big yard provide lots of options for relaxing.

120 Canyon Circle Dr. www.redagaveresort.net. ✆ **928/284-9327.** 14 units. $179 double; $279 suite. Pets accepted ($60 per pet). **Amenities:** 2 Jacuzzis; small outdoor pool; free Wi-Fi.

Wildflower Inn ★ With the best Bell Rock views of any mid-priced hotels in the Village of Oak Creek, this casual place is a good bet for an affordable Sedona vacation. Not only do many of the rooms have views, but some have fireplaces and others have double whirlpool tubs. There's even a rooftop deck where you can have your breakfast, or a picnic dinner, if you're so inclined. Rustic log furniture in the guest rooms gives this place a bit more character than you'd expect from a motel. The Bell Rock trail head is just across the street.

6086 Ariz. 179. www.sedonawildflowerinn.com. ✆ **928/284-3937.** 28 units. $138–$299 double. Rates include continental breakfast. **Amenities:** Concierge; exercise room; sauna; free Wi-Fi.

Inexpensive

Sedona Village Lodge ★ Set at the back of a big parking lot shared with a shopping plaza, this little hotel in the Village of Oak Creek has great rates. If all you're looking for is an economical place to spend the night and don't need a pool or hot tub, it's a good value. First-floor rooms are smallish with no views; second-floor units are all suites and have great views. (There's no elevator, though.) All rooms have refrigerators and microwaves.

105 Bell Rock Plaza. www.sedonalodge.com. ✆ **800/890-0521** or 928/284-3626. 30 units. $49–$59 double; $79–$89 suite. 2-night minimum holiday weekends and all weekends Mar–May and Sept–Oct. Pets accepted. **Amenities:** Free Wi-Fi.

CAMPGROUNDS

Within Oak Creek Canyon along Ariz. 89A, there are several national forest campgrounds. **Manzanita,** 6 miles north of town, is both the largest and the most pleasant (and the only one open in winter; $20 per night). Other Oak Creek Canyon campgrounds include **Cave Springs,** 13 miles north of town

($22 per night) and **Pine Flat,** 12 miles north of town ($22 per night). The **Beaver Creek Campground,** 3 miles east of I-17 on F.R. 618, which is an extension of Ariz. 179 (take exit 298 off I-17), is a pleasant spot near the V Bar V Heritage Site ($22 per night). Reservations up to 6 months in advance can be made for Manzanita, Cave Springs, and Pine Flat campgrounds by contacting the National Recreation Reservation Service (www.recreation.gov; ✆ **877/444-6777** or 518/885-3639). On the website, search for the campground name and include the Arizona state abbreviation, AZ. There's also a good guide to commercial campgrounds at **www.sedona.net/campgrounds**.

Where to Eat Around Sedona

SEDONA

Expensive

Che Ah Chi ★ AMERICAN The Che Ah Chi, at the exclusive Enchantment Resort (p. 207), has the most memorable setting of any restaurant in Sedona. It is also one of the town's most formal restaurants, which doesn't quite fit with the rugged setting but is in keeping with Enchantment's exclusive character. You're not going to find adventuresome food here, just pristinely prepared basics worthy of the high prices, like a crispy-skin salmon or a confit chicken leg with Brussels sprouts. Because the scenery is every bit as important as the food, make sure you make dinner reservations to take in the sunset on the red rocks (and remember to add in the 15 minutes it takes to get to the resort from downtown Sedona). You can also soak up the views at breakfast and lunch and save quite a bit of money.

At Enchantment Resort, 525 Boynton Canyon Rd. www.enchantmentresort.com. ✆ **928/204-6000.** Reservations required. Main courses $26–$44 dinner; Sun brunch $49 adults ($25 kids 11 and under). Mon–Sat 6:30am–11:30pm, dinner 5:30–9:15pm (last seating).

Cress ★★ NEW AMERICAN This is a serious restaurant with three prix-fixe menus on offer, set in the lovely confines of L'Auberge resort (p. 208), tucked away along Oak Creek beneath the bustle of Uptown Sedona. The chorizo-wrapped shrimp is a great starter, or the roasted beet salad if you want something lighter. Entrees range from delectable seafood, like the pan-seared scallops, or more substantive meats, like the lamb chops. Everything's exquisitely presented, right down to the rococo desserts, like the heart-stopping chocolate construction I had on my last visit. The top-line food and romantic setting—with white tablecloths and softly glowing lanterns alongside Oak Creek—makes this a strong contender for Sedona's don't-miss meal.

301 L'Auberge Ln. www.lauberge.com. ✆ **928/282-3331.** Reservations recommended. Prix-fixe meals $95, $110, and $145, not including wine. Daily 5–9pm.

The Heartline Café ★★ SOUTHWESTERN/INTERNATIONAL The heart line, from Zuni mythology, is a symbol of health and longevity; it is also a symbol for the healthful, creative food served at this family-owned affair that's been in business for decades. The menu is simple but not plain: There's mesquite-crusted rack of lamb, local trout, and free-range chicken. Those searching out variety in vegetarian choices will find it here, too. The beautiful courtyard and traditionally elegant interior are both good places to savor a meal.

1610 Ariz. 89A. www.heartlinecafe.com. ✆ **928/282-3365.** Main courses $25–$32. Daily 5–9pm; closed Tues.

Mariposa ★ NEW LATINO Lisa Dahl is Sedona's best-known chef (see Dahl & Di Luca, below). Her newest outfit has an enviable location, a hilltop beside Ariz. 89A just west of the "Y." In this one she explores a lot of comfort foods with a Latin twist, like a wood-roasted chicken with roasted corn on the side, or a big grilled portobello mushroom with quinoa pilaf—and also some other things just because, like "Lemon Mashed Potatoes with Luscious Lobster Scampi." It's also a great place to stop by late afternoon for a delicious tapas menu, including empanadas and some crunchy fried avocados.

3000 W. Ariz. 89A. www.mariposasedona.com. ✆ **928/282-3331.** Reservations highly recommended. Main courses $22–$29. No credit cards. Lunch 11:30am–2:30pm, tapas menu 4–5pm, dinner 5pm–closing.

Open Range Grill & Tavern ★ SOUTHWESTERN Restaurants with great views here may or may not provide food to match the scenery. Open Range does. The menu offerings are fairly simple, but well prepared and with the occasional unusual ingredient or two. At lunch, there's a tasty grilled-chicken Caesar club sandwich made with sun-dried tomatoes, arugula, and bacon; at lunch or dinner you can get this same dish as a salad. Steaks, pork chops, crab cakes, and salmon dishes all get a Southwestern spin, as does green-chili macaroni and cheese.

In Sedona Center, 320 Ariz. 89A. www.openrangesedona.com. ✆ **928/282-0002.** Reservations accepted for 6 or more. Main courses $22–$33. Daily 11am–8pm.

René at Tlaquepaque ★ CONTINENTAL/AMERICAN For a formal dining experience and traditional French fare, try this perennial favorite, located in Tlaquepaque, the city's upscale south-of-the-border-themed shopping plaza. It's restaurant is one of the best places in Sedona for a special meal secluded from the tourist bustle. The house specialty is the $55 rack of lamb. More adventurous diners may want to try the excellent tenderloin of antelope with whiskey–juniper berry sauce. Finish with a flambéed dessert.

At Tlaquepaque, 336 Ariz. 179, Ste. 118. www.renerestaurantsedona.com. ✆ **928/282-9225.** Reservations recommended. Main courses $11–$27 lunch, $27–$55 dinner. Daily 11:30am–2:30pm and 5:30–8:30pm (Fri–Sat until 9pm). "Lite lunch" menu 2:30–5pm.

Moderate

Café Elote ★ MEXICAN *Elote* is a Mexican preparation of corn on the cob, made with freshly roasted corn slathered with spicy mayonnaise and sprinkled with white *cotija* cheese. Squirt on a little lime, and you have the ultimate south-of-the-border street food. Here at this treat's namesake restaurant, the *elote* is sliced from the cob and served as a sort of dip. This dish alone, maybe with a side of guacamole and a margarita, is reason enough to eat at this highly creative Mexican restaurant. For an entree, try the braised lamb in sweet-and-spicy ancho-chili sauce. This casual and colorful spot feels a bit like a Mexican beach bar. Some great views off the back patio, too.

At the Arabella Hotel, 771 Ariz. 179. www.elotecafe.com. ✆ **928/203-0105.** No reservations. Main courses $17–$22. Tues–Sat 5–9pm.

Cowboy Club Grille & Spirits ★ SOUTHWESTERN The Cowboy Club has history on its side; it lives on at the site of the Oak Creek Tavern, a watering hole for 50 years and the place where the Cowboy Artists of America was formed. With its big booths, huge steer horns over the bar, and cowboy gear adorning the walls, this is Sedona's quintessential New West steakhouse. Start out with fried cactus strips with a prickly-pear sauce. The buffalo tenderloin, served with brandied peppercorn cream sauce, may be the most expensive item on the menu, but it's worth the splurge. Frugal travelers can opt for the buffalo cheeseburger. Service is friendly but can be slow during peak tourist season. The adjacent Silver Saddle Room is a more upscale spin on the same concept, with similar menu prices. The kids should get a kick out of the cowboy decor and, who knows, you may even get them to taste your snake or cactus appetizer.

241 N. Ariz. 89A. cowboyclub.com. ✆ **928/282-4200.** Reservations not accepted for Cowboy Club; recommended for Silver Saddle Room. Main courses $15–$36. Daily 11am–9pm.

Dahl & Di Luca ★ ITALIAN A faux-Tuscan villa interior, complete with a bar in a grotto, makes this the most romantic restaurant in Sedona, and the excellent Italian food makes it that much more unforgettable. Be sure to start with calamari, which is some of the best I've ever had. Pasta dominates here, and portions are big. I like the gnocchi with mushrooms and truffle cream sauce; veal dishes are also excellent, and there are plenty of good seafood, chicken, and vegetarian dishes. The eggplant Parmesan and portobello *alla griglia* are real standouts. Keep in mind that in high season (spring), this place gets packed with tourists and service can, at times, be brusque.

2321 W. Ariz. 89A. www.dahlanddiluca.com. ✆ **928/282-5219.** Reservations recommended. Main courses $13–$36. Daily 5–10pm.

The Hudson ★ NEW AMERICAN This used to be called Shugrues, after the owner, who has now re-imagined it as a "neighborhood place" with an emphasis on comfort food. It's on the top floor of the Hillside Sedona shopping plaza, a short walk from Tlaquepaque. If you come before the sun sets, you'll be treated to unforgettable views through the walls of glass. There are assorted bruschetta to start, and appetizers like sliders, corn chowder, and pretzel bread. Entrees range from Thai scallops to steaks to various pastas.

671 Ariz. 179. www.thehudsonsedona.com. ✆ **928/862-4899.** Main courses $17–$40. Daily 11:30am–9pm.

Secret Garden ★ AMERICAN This is a casual place, with great, made-from-scratch healthy food, served in a unprepossessing, secluded patio and restaurant in Tlaquepaque. Breakfast is the best time to be here, but the comfort food at lunch and dinner—burgers, turkey burgers, a Portobello sandwich, etc.—will take care of you as well. Lots of beers and wines to choose from as well.

In Tlaquepaque, 336 Ariz. 179. www.sedonasecretgardencafe.com. ✆ **928/503-9564.** No reservations. Main courses $16–$28. Daily 11:30am–8:30 or 9pm.

Inexpensive

Dining in Sedona tends to be expensive, so your best bets for economical meals are sandwich shops or ethnic restaurants. For breakfast, locals swear by the **Coffee Pot Restaurant,** 2050 W. Ariz. 89A (www.coffeepotsedona.com; ✆ **928/282-6626**), which has been around for 30 years-plus. In west Sedona, stop by the **West Side Deli,** 2655 W. Ariz. 89A (www.westsidedelisedona.com; ✆ **928/282-8453**) for some of the best deli food in town, for breakfast or lunch. (They close at 3:30pm.) Look at the movie posters on the wall and you'll realize the name of the place is a movie reference as well.

When you need good espresso, perhaps for that long drive to the Grand Canyon, you've got a few good options around town. At the foot of Uptown, the **Pink Java Café,** 206 N. Ariz. 89A (✆ **928/282-0249**), part of the Pink Jeep tours, serves organic coffee; you can't beat the red-rock views from the patio as you sip your latte. In the Village of Oak Creek, try **Firecreek Coffee,** 6586 Ariz. 179 (✆ **928/485-4100**), one of the better coffee roasters in northern Arizona.

The Hideaway House ★ ITALIAN Hidden at the back of a shopping plaza just south of the "Y" with views facing east, this casual family restaurant is as popular with locals as it is with visitors. Basic pizzas, subs, sandwiches, salads, and pastas are the choices here. However, most people come for the knockout views. From the shady porch, you can see the creek below and the red rocks rising across the canyon. There's a particularly good perspective on so-called "Snoopy Rock," which looks for all the world like Snoopy on his dog house. You can also spend time looking for the much smaller "Lucy Rock." Lunch or an early sunset dinner is your best bet.

231 Ariz. 179. www.sedonahideawayhouse.com. ✆ **928/202-4082.** Reservations accepted only for 10 or more. Main courses $13–$32. Daily 11am–9pm (10pm Fri–Sat).

Javelina Cantina ★ MEXICAN Though it's touristy, what this restaurant has going for it is good Mexican food, a lively atmosphere, decent views, and a convenient location in the Hillside shops. The grilled fish tacos are tasty, as is the pork adobo sandwich. The salmon tostadas are also worth trying. Plenty of different margaritas and tequilas are available to accompany your meal. Make a reservation to avoid a wait.

At Hillside Sedona shopping plaza, 671 Ariz. 179. www.javelinacantinasedona.com. ✆ **928/282-1313.** Main courses $9–$18. Daily 11:30am–8:30 or 9pm.

Picazzo's Organic Italian Kitchen ★ PIZZA For down-home pizza in an upscale setting, nothing in Sedona can compare with this artistic pizza place. Throw in an attractive walled patio dining area and a view of Coffee Pot Rock, and you have one of the best values in town. You get a great setting, a great view, and great pizza, and best of all, by eating here you can avoid the crowds in Uptown Sedona. Check out the good by-the-slice lunch specials and half-price appetizers during happy hour. Try the pesto and goat cheese pizza, or a spinach and wild mushroom pizza with Alfredo sauce. Gluten-free pizzas are available, and a lot of vegetarian options as well.

1855 W. Ariz. 89A. www.picazzos.com. ✆ **928/282-4140.** No reservations. Pizzas $15–$31. Sun–Thurs 11am–9pm; Fri–Sat 11am–10pm.

VILLAGE OF OAK CREEK

Moderate

Cucina Rústica ★ MEDITERRANEAN/SOUTHWESTERN With its various distinct dining rooms and numerous antique doors, this sister restaurant to west Sedona's wonderful Dahl & Di Luca (above) feels like a luxurious villa. My favorite room here is one with a central dome lit by what appear to be thousands of stars; for a genuine starlit dinner, ask for a seat on the patio. You can get some of the same delicious dishes served at Dahl & Di Luca, but Cucina Rústica also serves some of the best prawns I've ever had, wrapped in radicchio and prosciutto and then grilled.

7000 Ariz. 179. www.cucinarustica.com. ✆ **928/284-3010.** Reservations recommended. Main courses $13–$34. Daily 5–9pm or 10pm.

Inexpensive

Tara Thai Cuisine ★ THAI Friends who have a house in Sedona love this restaurant, and if you like Thai food, I'm sure you will, too. Not only is the food packed with all those great, exotic Thai flavors, its reasonable prices are a welcome relief in this overpriced tourist town. I like the pad Thai, and, if it's on the menu, be sure to try the mango and sticky rice for dessert. You'll find Tara Thai tucked into a shopping center near the north end of the Village of Oak Creek.

34 Bell Rock Plaza. www.tarathaicuisine.com. ✆ **928/284-9167.** Main courses $12–$16. Weekdays 11am–3pm and 5–9pm; Sat 11am–9pm; Sun noon–9pm.

Sedona Entertainment & Nightlife

To catch some live classical music while you're in town, check the schedule of **Chamber Music Sedona** (www.chambermusicsedona.org; ✆ **877/768-2415** or 928/204-2415). The most popular music venue is the **Sound Bites Grill,** 101 Ariz. 89A (www.soundbitesgrill.com; ✆ **928/282-2713**), which features local players and occasional notable acts like Esteban or Ottmar Leibert.

Otherwise, Sedona doesn't have much in the way of a live music scene, or even a dominant bar scene. Most hotels, of course, have swanky lounges, any of which are worth checking out. **Olde Sedona Bar & Grille,** 1405 W. Ariz. 89A (www.oldesedona.com; ✆ **928/282-5670**) has karaoke, weekly jam sessions, and other entertainment. Down in the Village of Oak Creek, you can do a little dancing at the **Full Moon Saloon,** 7000 N. Ariz. 179 (www.thefullmoonsaloon.com; ✆ **928/284-1872**), in the Tequa Plaza shopping center; it has live music and karaoke several nights a week.

If you're searching for good microbrewed beer, head to the **Oak Creek Brewing Co.,** 2050 Yavapai Dr. (www.oakcreekbrew.com; ✆ **928/204-1300**), north of Ariz. 89A off Coffee Pot Dr., or the affiliated **Oak Creek Brewery and Grill,** 336 Ariz. 179 (www.oakcreekpub.com; ✆ **928/282-3300**) in the Tlaquepaque shopping plaza.

6

THE GRAND CANYON & NORTHERN ARIZONA

The Grand Canyon—the name is at once both apt and inadequate. How can words sum up the grandeur of 2 billion years of the earth's history sliced open by the power of a single river? Once an impassable barrier to explorers and settlers, the Grand Canyon today is a magnet attracting millions of visitors from all over the world. The pastel layers of rock weaving through the canyon's rugged ramparts, the interplay of shadows and light, the wind in the pines, California condors soaring overhead—these sights and sounds never fail to transfix hordes of visitors gazing awestruck into the canyon's seemingly infinite depths.

While the Grand Canyon is undeniably the most awe-inspiring natural attraction in the state, northern Arizona contains other worthwhile (and less crowded) attractions. Only 60 miles south of the great chasm stand the San Francisco Peaks, ancient volcanoes sacred to the Hopi and Navajo as the home of spirits that bring rain to the parched desert below. Amid expansive ponderosa pine forests stands the city of Flagstaff, one of the highest cities in the U.S., with its well-preserved downtown historic district.

THE GRAND CANYON SOUTH RIM ★★★

60 miles N of Williams; 80 miles NE of Flagstaff; 230 miles N of Phoenix; 340 miles N of Tucson

A trip to the Grand Canyon is an unforgettable experience, whether you spend days hiking deep in the canyon, ride the roller-coaster rapids of the Colorado River, or merely stand on the rim peering down in amazement. A mile deep, 277 miles long, and up to 18 miles wide, the canyon is absolutely overwhelming in its grandeur, truly one of the great natural wonders of the world. Clarence Dutton, a 19th-century geologist who published one of the earliest

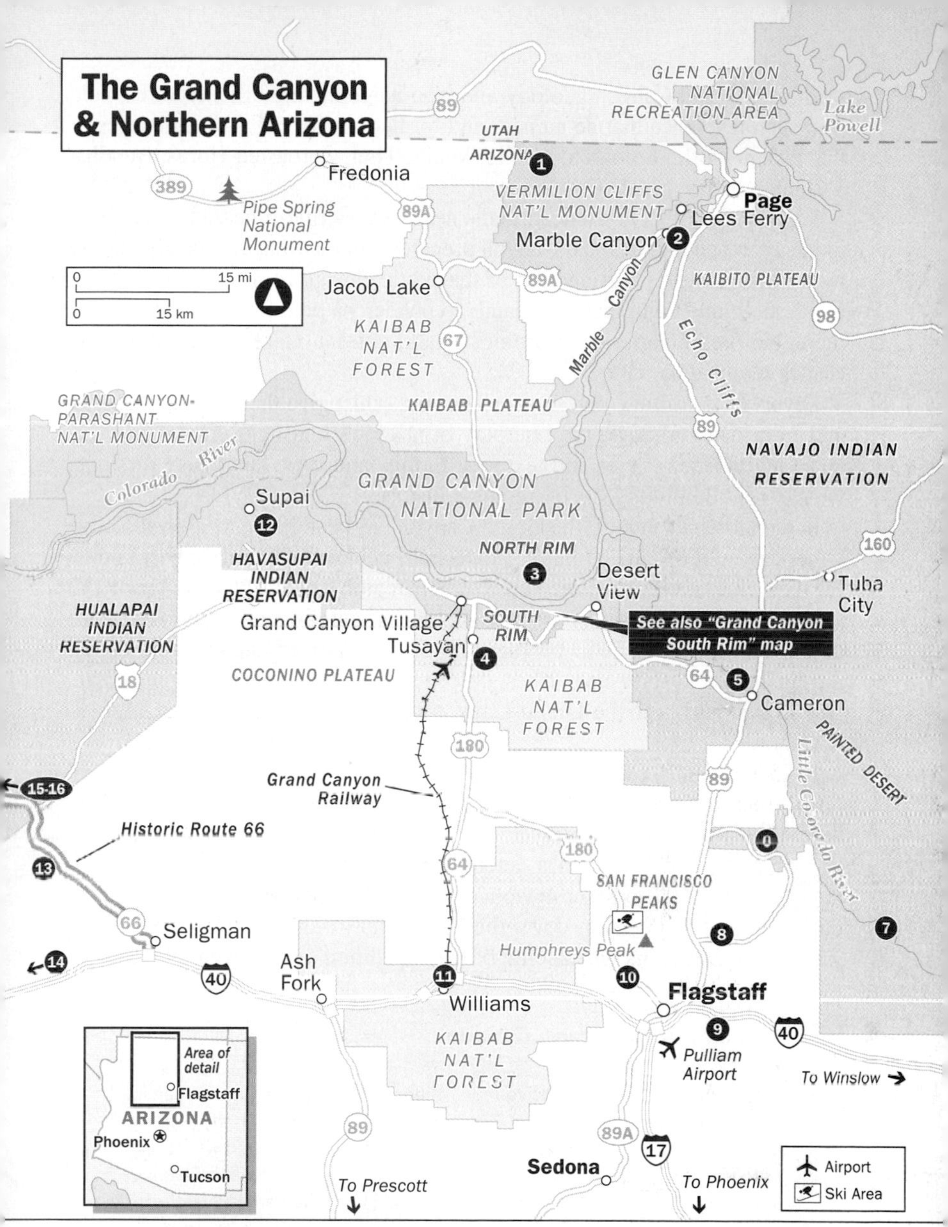

Arizona Snowbowl **10**
Cameron Trading Post **4**
Coyote Buttes **1**
Grand Canyon Caverns **13**
Grand Canyon North Rim **3**
Grand Canyon West Rim **14**
Grand Falls **7**
Havasu Canyon **12**
Kingman **15**
National Geographic Visitor Center **4**
Navajo Bridge **2**
Oatman **16**
Sunset Crater Volcano National Monument **8**
Walnut Canyon National Monument **9**
Williams **11**
Wupatki National Monument **6**

studies of Grand Canyon geology and who named many of its features, held it in such reverence that he named land formations for the gods and sages of the ancient world: Solomon, Apollo, Venus, Thor, Zoroaster, Horus, Buddha, Vishnu, Krishna, Shiva, Confucius.

Something of this reverence infects nearly every first-time visitor. Nothing in the approach to the Grand Canyon prepares you for what awaits. You hardly notice the gradual elevation gain or the subtle change from windswept sagebrush scrubland to juniper woodlands to ponderosa pine forest. Suddenly, it's there. No preliminaries, no warnings. Stark, quiet, a maze of cathedrals and castles sculpted by nature.

Layers of sandstone, limestone, shale, and schist give the canyon its colors, and from dawn to dusk, the interplay of shadows and light creates an ever-changing palette of hues and textures. In this landscape layer cake of stone, we can read 2 billion years of geologic history.

In the more recent past, the Grand Canyon has been home to several Native American cultures, including the Ancestral Puebloans (Anasazi), best known for their cliff dwellings in the Four Corners region (see chapter 7). About 150 years after 13th-century Ancestral Puebloans and Coconino peoples abandoned the canyon, nomadic people from the west moved into the area. Today, the Hualapai and Havasupai tribes, descendants of the ancient Patayan people, still live in and near the Grand Canyon on the south side of the Colorado River.

In 1540, Spanish explorer Garcia Lopez de Cárdenas became the first European to set eyes on the Grand Canyon, but it would be another 329 years before the first expedition traveled through the entire canyon. John Wesley Powell, a one-armed Civil War veteran, was deemed crazy when he set off to navigate the Colorado River in wooden boats. His small band of men spent 98 days traveling 1,000 miles down the Green and Colorado rivers. So difficult was the endeavor that when some of the expedition's boats were wrecked by

Creating the Grand Canyon

Some geologists believe the erosive action of the Colorado River carved the Grand Canyon in a 17-million-year span; others think it took much less time. Either way, it's clear that the canyon has a complex geologic history—it's written all over the landscape.

The story of the Grand Canyon begins eons ago, when vast seas covered this region. Sediments carried by seawater were deposited and, over millions of years, those sediments were turned into limestone and sandstone. According to the most widely accepted theory, the Colorado River began its work of cutting through the plateau when the ancient seabed was thrust upward to form the Kaibab Plateau. Today, 21 sedimentary layers, the oldest of which is more than a billion years old, can be seen in the canyon. Beneath all these layers, at the very bottom, is a stratum of rock so old that it has metamorphosed, under great pressure and heat, from soft shale to a much harder stone. Called Vishnu Schist, this layer is the oldest rock in the Grand Canyon, dating from 2 billion years ago.

powerful rapids, part of the group abandoned the journey and set out on foot, never to be seen again.

Miners, ranchers, loggers, and farmers followed, but they soon found that the Grand Canyon was worth more as a landmark than as land to be worked. The Grand Canyon has become one of the most-visited natural wonders on the planet. By raft, by mule, on foot, and in helicopters and small planes—approximately four million people each year come to gaze into this great chasm.

In the recent past, however, there were those who regarded the canyon as mere wasted space, suitable only for filling with water. Upstream of the Grand Canyon on the Colorado River stands Glen Canyon Dam, which forms Lake Powell (p. 323); downstream lies Lake Mead (p. 478), created by Hoover Dam. The Grand Canyon might have suffered the same fate, but luckily the forces for preservation prevailed. Today, the Grand Canyon is the last major undammed stretch of the Colorado River.

The Colorado—named by early Spanish explorers for the reddish-brown color of its muddy waters—once carried immense loads of silt, much of which now gets deposited on the bottom of Lake Powell. As a result, the water in the Grand Canyon is much clearer (and colder) than it once was. Today, only when rainstorms and snowmelt feed the side canyons of the Grand Canyon does the river still flow murky and red from heavy loads of eroding sandstone.

While the waters of the Colorado are usually clearer than before, the same cannot be said for the air in the canyon. Yes, you'll find smog here, smog that has been blamed on both Las Vegas and Los Angeles to the west and a coal-fired power plant to the east, near Page. Scrubbers have been installed on the power plant's smokestacks, but there isn't much to be done about smog drifting from the west.

Far more visible and frustrating is the traffic congestion at the South Rim during the spring-to-fall busy season. Some five million people visit the park each year, and South Rim traffic in summer has become almost as bad as it is during rush hour in any major city. Finding a parking space can be the biggest challenge of a visit to Grand Canyon National Park. But don't let these inconveniences dissuade you. Despite the crowds, the Grand Canyon more than lives up to its name. It's simply one of the most memorable sights on planet Earth.

Essentials

ARRIVING

In summer you can expect at least a 20- to 30-minute wait at the South Rim entrance gate just to get into the park. If at all possible, travel to the park by some means other than car. Alternatives include taking the Grand Canyon Railway from Williams, flying into Grand Canyon Airport and then taking a taxi, taking the Arizona Shuttle from Flagstaff, or joining a guided tour to the park. You can walk to plenty of scenic overlooks, hiking trails, restaurants,

Over eons, the Colorado River carved through layers of richly colored stone to create the ever-changing spectacle called the Grand Canyon.

and lodges in the Grand Canyon Village area, and free shuttle buses operate along both Hermit Road and Desert View Drive.

BY CAR The South Rim of the Grand Canyon is 60 miles north of Williams (and I-40) via Ariz. 64 and U.S. 180. Flagstaff, the nearest city of any size, is 80 miles southeast. From Flagstaff, you can take either U.S. 180 directly to the South Rim or U.S. 89 to Ariz. 64 and the park's east entrance (the second route has much less traffic). Be sure you have plenty of gasoline in your car before setting out for the canyon; there are few service stations in this remote part of the state, and what gas stations there are charge exorbitant prices. There are no gas stations in the national park itself. You'll find service stations outside the park's south entrance in Tusayan, at **Desert View** near the east entrance (no cash sales in winter), and east of the park at **Cameron.**

Extended waits at the entrance gates, parking problems, and traffic congestion have long been the norm at the canyon during the popular summer months, and even in spring and fall there can be backups at the gates and limited parking space. However, extra ticketing lanes and additional parking lots built in recent years have somewhat alleviated the congestion at the south entrance.

BY PLANE The closest airport with commercial service is in **Flagstaff** (p. 257). From there, you'll need to arrange other transportation the rest of the way to the national park. At the **Grand Canyon Airport** in Tusayan, 6 miles south of Grand Canyon Village, the only regularly scheduled flights are day-tours from Las Vegas on **Scenic Airlines** (www.scenic.com; ✆ **800/634-6801**), **Grand Canyon Airlines** (www.grandcanyonairlines.com; ✆ **866/235-9422** or 702/835-8484), and **Maverick Airlines** (www.maverickairlines.com; ✆ **800/962-3869** or 702/405-4300). Tours of an hour or two cost $140–$160, while longer ones can last from 6½ to 8 hours and cost up to $400.

BY TRAIN The **Grand Canyon Railway** (p. 240) operates excursion trains between Williams and the South Rim of the Grand Canyon.

For long-distance connections, **Amtrak** (www.amtrak.com; ✆ **800/872-7245**) provides service to Flagstaff and Williams. From Flagstaff, bus service goes directly to Grand Canyon Village. From Williams, you can transfer to the Grand Canyon Railway excursion train. ***Note:*** The Amtrak stop in Williams is on the outskirts of town—from there, you'll need to catch a shuttle to the Grand Canyon Railway.

BY BUS **Arizona Shuttle** (www.arizonashuttle.com; ✆ **877/226-8060** or 928/226-8060) buses connect Phoenix, Sedona, and Williams with Flagstaff, where passengers can board shuttles to Grand Canyon Village. One-way adult fares to Flagstaff are $49 from Phoenix, $45 from Sedona, $24 from Williams; the fare from Flagstaff on to the Grand Canyon is $34.

VISITOR INFORMATION

You can get advance information on the Grand Canyon by contacting **Grand Canyon National Park** (www.nps.gov/grca).

When you arrive at the park, stop by the **Grand Canyon Visitor Center,** 4½ miles from the south entrance. Here you'll find an information desk, exhibits, a theater, and a shop selling maps, books, and videos. The center is open daily 8am to 6pm (9am–5pm in winter). Within Grand Canyon Village, **Verkamp's Visitor Center,** near the El Tovar Hotel, is an even more convenient place to get park information; it's open daily 8am to 8pm in summer (until 6pm other months). Displays here focus on the history of development in Grand Canyon Village. Both South Rim entrances hand out a South Rim pocket map and services guides as you enter the park.

Tip: Parks Passes Save Time

You can cut your waiting time at the park entrances by acquiring an **America the Beautiful National Parks Pass** before arriving. The standard pass costs $80 and is good for 1 year. Given the price, this pass is a good value only if you plan to visit several other major national parks or lots of smaller parks and monuments. The **America the Beautiful Senior Pass** ($20, or $80 for a lifetime pass) and **Access Pass** (free of charge) are, on the other hand, exceptional bargains. With any of the three America the Beautiful passes in hand, you can use the express lane. See p. 517 for info.

FEES

The entry fee for Grand Canyon National Park is $35 per car (or $20 per person if coming in on foot or by bicycle). Your admission ticket is good for 7 days. Don't lose it, or you'll have to pay again to reenter the park.

ORIENTATION: GRAND CANYON VILLAGE

The South Rim's Grand Canyon Village is divided roughly into two sections. At the east end are the Grand Canyon Visitor Center, Yavapai Lodge, Trailer Village, and Mather Campground. At the west end are El Tovar Hotel and Bright Angel, Kachina, Thunderbird, and Maswik lodges; as well as several restaurants, the train depot, and the trail head for the Bright Angel Trail.

PARKING

Three large parking lots adjacent to the information plaza are the best places to leave your car; you can easily access the park's free shuttle buses from here. There's also a lot at Market Plaza (the general store), up a side road near Yavapai Lodge. From these parking areas, a paved walking trail leads to the historic section of the village in less than 1.5 miles; most of the route runs right along the rim. You can also park at the Maswik Transportation Center lot. Wherever you park in Grand Canyon Village, you can catch the Village Route bus to the visitor center and other parts of the village. If you park at Yaki Point, you can take the Kaibab Trail Route bus.

GETTING AROUND

If possible, use one of these transportation options to avoid South Rim traffic jams and parking problems.

BY BUS Free shuttle buses operate on three routes within the park. The **Village (Blue) Route** bus circles through Grand Canyon Village throughout the day, with frequent stops at the Grand Canyon Visitor Center, hotels, campgrounds, restaurants, Market Plaza (site of a general store, bank, laundry, and showers), and other facilities. The **Hermit Road (Red) Route** bus takes visitors to eight canyon overlooks west of Bright Angel Lodge (this bus does not operate December–February). The **Kaibab Rim (Orange) Route** bus stops at the Grand Canyon Visitor Center, Mather Point, Yavapai Geology Museum, Pipe Creek Vista, the South Kaibab trail head, and Yaki Point. An early-morning **Hikers' Express bus** to the South Kaibab trail head runs from Bright Angel Lodge, with stops at the Back Country Information Office and the Grand Canyon Visitor Center, to the trail head; it operates 4am to 6am in summer, but as late as 7am to 9am in winter (for the full schedule, see park website). From March through September, the **Tusayan (Purple) Route** operates between the town of Tusayan, outside the park, and Grand Canyon Village, inside the park. To use this shuttle, you must have a valid park entrance pass.

Between mid-May and mid-October, **Trans Canyon** (www.trans-canyonshuttle.com; ✆ **928/638-2820**) offers shuttle-bus service between the South Rim and the North Rim. The vans leave the South Rim at 8am and 1:30pm and arrive at the North Rim at 1:30pm and 6pm. The return trip leaves the

North Rim at 7am and 2pm, arriving at the South Rim at 11:30am and 6:30pm. The fare is $90 each way; reservations are required.

BY TAXI Taxi service is available to and from Grand Canyon Airport, trail heads, and other destinations (✆ **928/638-2631,** ext. 6563). The fare from the airport to Grand Canyon Village is $10 for up to two adults, $5 for each additional person.

FESTIVALS & SPECIAL EVENTS

The **Grand Canyon Music Festival** (www.grandcanyonmusicfest.org; ✆ **800/997-8285** or 928/638-9215), which primarily features chamber music and musicals, takes place in late August and early September. Performances ($15 adults, $10 children) are held indoors at the Shrine of the Ages in Grand Canyon Village. Season tickets for all six performances ($90) are available online.

[FastFACTS] THE GRAND CANYON

Accessibility Check *The Guide* for park programs, services, and facilities that are partially or fully accessible. You can also get the Grand Canyon National Park *Accessibility Guide* at park visitor centers or on the park website. You can pick up an accessibility parking permit at park entrances, visitor centers, and transportation desks. The national park has wheelchairs available at no charge for temporary use inside the park; inquire at the Grand Canyon Visitor Center. All park shuttle buses are wheelchair-accessible. Accessible tours can be arranged at any lodge transportation desk or by calling **Grand Canyon National Park Lodges** (✆ **928/638-2631**).

ATMs There's an ATM at the **Chase** bank (✆ **928/638-2437**) at Market Plaza, near Yavapai Lodge.

Hospitals & Clinics The **North Country Grand Canyon Clinic** (✆ **928/638-2551**) is on Clinic Dr., off Center Rd. (the road that runs past the National Park Service ranger office). The clinic is open daily 8am–6pm (shorter hours Oct–May). It provides 24-hour emergency service as well.

Laundry A coin-operated laundry is located near Mather Campground in the Camper Services building.

Lost & Found Report lost items or turn in found items at the Grand Canyon Visitor Center; ✆ **928/638-7798.** For items lost or found at a hotel, restaurant, or lounge, call ✆ **928/638-2631.**

Police In an emergency, dial ✆ **911.** Ticketing speeders is one of the main occupations of the park's police force, so obey posted speed limits.

Post Office The post office (✆ **928/638-2512**) is at Market Plaza near Yavapai Lodge. It's open Monday through Friday 9am–3:30pm.

Road Conditions For information on road conditions in the Grand Canyon area, call ✆ **888/411-7623** or 511.

Safety The most important safety tip to remember is to be careful near the edge of the canyon. Footing can be unstable and may give way. Keep your distance from wild animals, no matter how friendly they may appear. Avoid hiking alone if at all possible, and keep in mind that the canyon rim is more than a mile above sea level (it's harder to breathe up here). Do not leave valuables in your car or tent.

Wi-Fi & Internet Access Wi-Fi access is limited in the park. Free Wi-Fi is available at the Visitor Center 8am–5pm, with some computers available for public use; at the Canyon Village Market Deli 8am–6pm; and at the Community Library 11:30am–5pm Monday through Saturday.

What to Expect Weather-Wise

The climate at the Grand Canyon is dramatically different from that of Phoenix; there's even a pronounced difference between the rim and the canyon floor. The South Rim's altitude is 7,000 feet, and it gets very cold in winter—you can expect snow anytime between November and May, and winter temperatures can be below 0°F (–18°C) at night, with daytime highs in the 20s or 30s (minus single digits to single digits Celsius). Summer temperatures at the rim range from highs in the 80s (20s Celsius) to lows in the 50s (teens Celsius). The North Rim of the canyon is 1,200 to 1,400 feet higher than the South Rim, and it's much cooler throughout the year; in fact, it's not open to visitors November through April, because the access road is not kept cleared of snow in winter.

On the canyon floor, temperatures are considerably higher. In summer, the mercury can reach 120°F (49°C) with lows in the 70s (20s Celsius), while in winter, temperatures are quite pleasant with highs in the 50s (teens Celsius) and lows in the 30s (single digits Celsius). July, August, and September are the wettest months because of frequent afternoon thunderstorms. April, May, and June are the driest months, but it still might rain or even snow. Down on the canyon floor, there is much less rain year-round.

Exploring the South Rim

GRAND CANYON VILLAGE & VICINITY

Grand Canyon Village is the first stop for the vast majority of the more than five million people who visit the Grand Canyon every year. It's by far the most crowded area in the park, but it also has the most visitor services, overlooks, and historic buildings. As you enter the park through the south entrance, your first unforgettable gasp-inducing glimpse of the canyon is usually at **Mather Point,** down a short paved path from the **Grand Canyon Visitor Center.**

Continuing west toward the village proper, you next come to **Yavapai Point,** which has the best view in the Grand Canyon Village vicinity. (If you can bring yourself to drive past Mather Point and delay your initial glimpse for a few minutes, Yavapai Point actually makes a better first view of the canyon, although parking spaces here are limited.) From Yavapai you can see the Bright Angel Trail, Indian Gardens, Phantom Ranch, the Colorado River, and even the suspension bridge that hikers and mule riders use to cross the river to Phantom Ranch. This is the only bridge across the Colorado for 340 miles, between Hoover Dam downstream and the Navajo Bridge upstream near Lees Ferry. At Yavapai you'll also find the historic **Yavapai Museum of Geology** (open daily 8am–8pm in summer, shorter hours other months), which has big glass walls to take in the extraordinary vistas. Don't miss the geology displays here; they're the park's best introduction to the forces that created the Grand Canyon. Yavapai Point is a particularly good spot for sunrise and sunset photos. From here, the paved **Grand Canyon Greenway** extends 3.5 miles east to the South Kaibab trail head and 3 miles west through Grand Canyon Village.

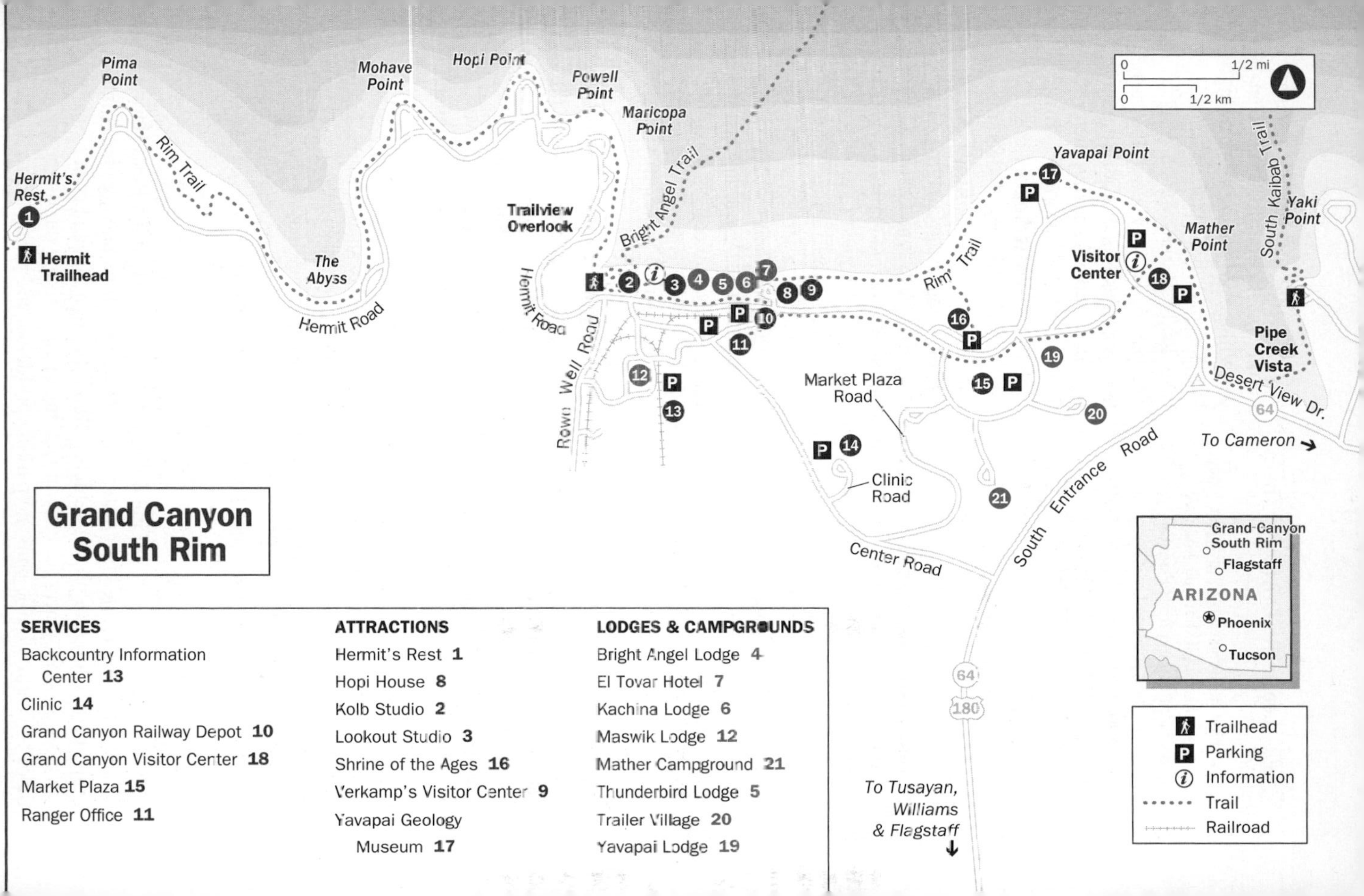
Grand Canyon South Rim
Pima Point
Hermit's Rest
Hermit Trailhead
Rim Trail
Mohave Point
Hopi Point
The Abyss
Hermit Road
Powell Point
Maricopa Point
Trailview Overlook
Bright Angel Trail
Hermit Road
Rowe Well Road
Yavapai Point
Rim Trail
Market Plaza Road
Clinic Road
Center Road
Visitor Center
Mather Point
South Kaibab Trail
Yaki Point
Pipe Creek Vista
Desert View Dr.
64
To Cameron
South Entrance Road
64
180
To Tusayan, Williams & Flagstaff
0 1/2 mi
0 1/2 km
Grand Canyon South Rim
Flagstaff
ARIZONA
Phoenix
Tucson
Trailhead
Parking
Information
Trail
Railroad
SERVICES
Backcountry Information Center 13
Clinic 14
Grand Canyon Railway Depot 10
Grand Canyon Visitor Center 18
Market Plaza 15
Ranger Office 11
ATTRACTIONS
Hermit's Rest 1
Hopi House 8
Kolb Studio 2
Lookout Studio 3
Shrine of the Ages 16
Verkamp's Visitor Center 9
Yavapai Geology Museum 17
LODGES & CAMPGROUNDS
Bright Angel Lodge 4
El Tovar Hotel 7
Kachina Lodge 6
Maswik Lodge 12
Mather Campground 21
Thunderbird Lodge 5
Trailer Village 20
Yavapai Lodge 19

Leave the Driving to Them

We think it's a mistake to give just 1 day to the park. But if that's all you have, and you're coming from Flagstaff, you might be better served by taking a tour. That way, someone else will drive, so that you can enjoy the views. **Canyon Dave** offers knowledgeable geology-focused tours of the South Rim and East Rim (www.grand-canyon-tours-1.com; ✆ **877/845-3283**). Tours begin at $149.

Continuing west from Yavapai Point, you'll come to Grand Canyon Village proper, with its parking lots and park headquarters (a side road leads to the Market Plaza). The paved pathway along the rim here provides lots of good (though crowded) spots for taking pictures. Step inside the historic **El Tovar Hotel** and **Bright Angel Lodge** to take in the wilderness-lodge ambience of their lobbies. Inside Bright Angel Lodge, the **Bright Angel History Room** has displays on architect Mary Elizabeth Jane Colter, who is responsible for much of the park's historic architecture, and the Harvey Girls (see box, p. 291). Notice this room's fireplace—it's designed to replicate all the geologic layers that appear in the canyon. Adjacent to El Tovar, the **Hopi House,** an historic souvenir-and-curio shop resembling a Hopi pueblo, was built in 1905 as a place for Hopi artisans to work and sell their crafts; this was the first shop inside the park. Today, it's full of Native American arts and crafts, including expensive kachina dolls, rugs, jewelry, and pottery. This shop is open daily; hours vary seasonally.

To the west of Bright Angel Lodge, two buildings cling precariously to the rim of the canyon. These are the Kolb and Lookout studios, both of which are listed on the National Register of Historic Places. **Kolb Studio** is named for Ellsworth and Emory Kolb, two brothers who set up a photographic studio here on the rim in 1904. The construction of this studio generated one of the Grand Canyon's first controversies—over whether buildings should be allowed on the canyon rim. The Kolbs had friends in high places, however, and their sprawling studio and movie theater remained. Emory Kolb lived here until his death in 1976. It now serves as a bookstore, while the auditorium houses special exhibits. **Lookout Studio,** built in 1914 from a design by Mary Elizabeth Jane Colter, was the Fred Harvey Company's answer to the Kolb brothers' studio. Note how it incorporates architectural styles of the Hopi and the Ancestral Puebloans, using native limestone and an uneven roofline to blend in with the canyon walls. It now houses a souvenir store and two lookout points. Both the Kolb and Lookout studios are open daily; hours vary seasonally.

HERMIT ROAD

Leading 8 miles west from Grand Canyon Village to Hermit's Rest, Hermit Road has, mile for mile, the greatest concentration of breathtaking viewpoints in the park. Closed to private vehicles March through November, it's one of the most pleasant places for canyon viewing or easy hiking during the busiest times of year: no traffic jams, no parking problems, and plenty of free shuttle buses along the route. Westbound Red buses stop at eight overlooks (Trailview, Maricopa Point, Powell Point, Hopi Point, Mohave Point, the Abyss, Pima Point, and Hermit's Rest); eastbound buses stop at only Pima, Mohave, and Powell points. December through February, you can drive your own vehicle here, but keep in mind that winters usually mean ice and snow; the road is sometimes closed due to hazardous driving conditions.

You probably won't want to stop at every viewpoint, so here are some tips to maximize your excursion. First: The earlier you catch a shuttle bus, the more likely you'll avoid crowds (buses start 1 hour before sunrise, so photographers can get good shots of the canyon in dawn light). Second: The closer you are to Grand Canyon Village, the larger the crowds will be. It's best to head out early and get a couple of miles between you and the village before getting off the shuttle bus.

The first two stops are **Trailview Overlook** and **Maricopa Point,** both on the paved section of the Rim Trail, within 1½ miles of the village. If you just want a short, easy walk on pavement, get out at Maricopa Point and walk back to the village. From either overlook, you can see Bright Angel Trail winding

Return of the Condor

With wingspans approaching 10 feet and weighing as much as 25 pounds, California condors are the largest flying land birds in North America (both mute and trumpeter swans are heavier). In the 1980s, there were only 22 California condors left in the wild; the last few condors were captured and a captive-breeding program was launched in hopes of bringing the species back from the brink of extinction.

Between 1924 and 1996, if you had seen a California condor in Arizona, you would most likely have been in a zoo; none of these giant birds still lived free in a state where once they had been plentiful. In 1996, however, six captive-raised condors were released atop the Vermilion Cliffs (north of Grand Canyon National Park). Since then, between 6 and 10 birds have been released annually, and there are now more than 50 condors flying free over northern Arizona. In 2003, for the first time in more than a century, a pair of condors hatched and raised a chick, and since then, several more condor pairs have successfully raised offspring.

Condors are curious birds, and they are often attracted to human activity. Consequently, they are often seen in or near Grand Canyon Village on the South Rim. Look closely at their wings: if there's a large number on the wing, it's a captive-raised condor, but if there isn't, it's one of the handful of birds hatched in the wild in recent years.

One of the best places to spot condors is en route to the North Rim on House Rock Valley Rd., north of U.S. 98A between Lees Ferry and Jacob Lake. A few miles up this road, you'll find interpretive plaques and a viewpoint from which you can see the condor release site, high atop the cliffs to the east. There's also a small population in the West Canyon that sometimes fly out onto the grasslands near Grand Canyon Caverns (p. 281). For more information on the condor-release program, visit the **Peregrine Fund** website (www.peregrinefund.org), which is the organization that administers the program.

down into the canyon from Grand Canyon Village. As the trail heads for the bottom of the canyon, it crosses the Tonto Plateau, about 3,000 feet below the rim. This is the site of Indian Garden, where there's a campground in a grove of cottonwood trees. The views from these two overlooks are not significantly different from those in the village, so if you've already had a look from that vantage point, you can safely skip them.

Powell Point, the third stop, is the site of a memorial to John Wesley Powell, who, in 1869 with a party of nine men, became the first person to navigate the Colorado River through the Grand Canyon. There's a spectacular view here of Point Imperial and other North Rim landmarks. Also visible at Powell Point are the fenced-off remains of the **Orphan Mine,** a copper mine that began operation in 1893. For a while it went out of business (it was too expensive to transport the copper to a city to sell it), though it re-opened after uranium was discovered in 1951. The mine was shut down in 1969; the area is still closed for ongoing testing for residual contamination.

The next stop, **Hopi Point,** is one of the three best stops along this route. From here you can see a long section of the Colorado River far, far below, looking like a tiny, quiet stream; in reality the section you see is more than 100 yards wide and races through Granite Rapids. Hopi Point juts into the canyon, making it one of the best spots in the park for sunrise and sunset photos (shuttle buses run from 1 hour before sunrise to 1 hour after sunset).

The view is even more spectacular at the next stop, **Mohave Point.** Here you can see the river in two directions. Three rapids are visible; on a quiet day, you can sometimes even hear Hermit Rapids. Like almost all rapids in the Canyon, Hermit Rapids are at the mouth of a side canyon where boulders, loosened by storms and tumbled along flooded streams, get piled up. Don't miss this stop; it's got the best view on Hermit Road.

Next you come to the **Abyss,** the aptly named 3,000-foot drop created by the **Great Mojave Wall.** This vertiginous view is one of the park's most dramatic. The Abyss' walls are red sandstone, which resists erosion more than the soft shale does in the layer below. You can also see some free-standing sandstone pillars (the largest of them is called the **Monument**). For a good road hike, get out here and walk westward to either Pima Point (3 miles) or Hermit's Rest (4 miles).

The **Pima Point** overlook, set back from the road, is another good place to get off the bus. From here, the **Greenway Trail** leads through the forest near the canyon rim, providing good views undisturbed by Hermit Road traffic. From Pima Point, you can see the remains of **Hermit Camp,** which the Santa Fe Railroad built down on the Tonto Plateau. Open from 1911 to 1930, this was developed as a luxury destination, where guests slept in canvas-sided cabins, an early version of today's "glamping."

The final stop on Hermit Road is **Hermit's Rest,** named for Louis Boucher, a prospector who came to the canyon in the 1890s and was known as the Hermit. Built in 1914 as a stagecoach stop, the log-and-stone **Hermit's Rest building,** designed by Mary Elizabeth Jane Colter, is on the National Register

Pack a Lunch

Lunch options are limited inside Grand Canyon National Park, so if you are driving up from Flagstaff, either pack a picnic lunch or stop at someplace in Flagstaff like the **Aspen Deli** (20 N. Beaver St.; ✆ **928/556-8629**) or **Wildflower Bread Company** (530 Piccadilly Dr #10; ✆ **928/233-5010**) for sandwiches to bring along. The newish **Whole Foods** outlet (320 S. Cambridge Lane; ✆ **928/774-5747**) is a good place to snag picnic supplies. Your time is better spent studying the innards of the Earth at some magnificent rimtop vista than waiting in line for a burger and tater tots.

of Historic Places; it's one of the most fascinating structures in the park. There's a snack bar here, making it a great place to linger while you soak up a bit of park history. The steep Hermit Trail, which leads down into the canyon, begins just past Hermit's Rest.

DESERT VIEW DRIVE

While the vast majority of visitors to the Grand Canyon enter through the south entrance and head straight for crowded, congested Grand Canyon Village, you can have a much more enjoyable experience if you take the east entrance instead. From Flagstaff, take U.S. 89 north to Ariz. 64 in Cameron (be sure to stop at the Cameron Trading Post, p. 243) and then head west. Following this route, you'll get great canyon views sooner—even before you enter the park, you can stop at viewpoints on the Navajo Reservation for vistas of the canyon of the Little Colorado River. At every stop you can also shop for Native American crafts and souvenirs at numerous vendors' stalls.

Desert View Drive, the park's only scenic road open to cars year-round, extends for 25 miles between Desert View, just inside the park's east entrance, and Grand Canyon Village. Along Desert View Drive, you'll find not only good viewpoints, but also several picnic areas. Much of this drive is through forests, and canyon views are limited; but where there are viewpoints, they are among the best and least crowded in the park.

Desert View is the first stop on this scenic drive, and with its historic watchtower, general store, snack bar, service station, information center, bookstore, and big parking lot, it is better designed for handling large numbers of tourists than Grand Canyon Village. There's never a wait here, unlike at the south entrance to the park. From anywhere at Desert View, the scenery is breathtaking, but the very best perspective here is from atop the **Desert View Watchtower.** Although the watchtower looks as though it was built centuries ago, it actually dates from 1932, designed by Mary Elizabeth Jane Colter to resemble the prehistoric towers that dot the southwestern landscape. Built as an observation tower and tourist rest stop, the watchtower incorporates Native American designs. The curio shop on the ground floor is a replica of a kiva (sacred ceremonial chamber); the second floor features work by Hopi artist Fred Kabotie and carvings by another Hopi artist, Chester Dennis, with pictographs on the walls that incorporate traditional designs; and the upper two floors' walls and ceiling feature images by artist Fred Geary, reproductions of petroglyphs from throughout the Southwest. From the roof—at 7,522 feet above sea level, it's the highest point on the South Rim—you can see the Colorado River, the Painted Desert to the northeast, the San Francisco Peaks to the south, and Marble Canyon to the north. Several black-mirror "reflectoscopes" provide interesting darkened views of some of the most spectacular sections of the canyon.

Native American art decorates the interior of the Desert View Watchtower, designed by Mary Elizabeth Jane Colter.

A few minutes' drive west, at **Navajo Point,** the Colorado River and Escalante Butte are both visible; there's also a good view of the Desert View Watchtower. **Lipan Point ★★**, the next stop, offers the South Rim's best views of the Colorado River. You can see several stretches of the river from here, including a couple of major rapids. You can also view the **Grand Canyon supergroup:** several strata of rock tilted at an angle to the other layers of rock in the canyon, indicating an earlier period of mountain building. Its red, white, and black rocks, composed of sedimentary rock and layers of lava, pre-date the canyon's main layers of sandstone, limestone, and shale. One of the park's best-kept secrets, a little-known though very rugged trail, begins here at Lipan Point (p. 237).

The next stop along Desert View Drive is the small **Tusayan Museum** (daily 9am–5pm), dedicated to the Hopi tribe and the Ancestral Puebloan people who inhabited the region 800 years ago. Outside the museum, there are ruins of an Ancestral Puebloan village, and inside the museum, artfully displayed exhibits explain various aspects of life in the village. A short self-guided trail leads through the ruins. Free guided tours are available.

Next along the drive is **Moran Point,** where you can see a layer of red shale in the canyon walls and the ancient Vishnu Schist formation at the bottom. This point is named for 19th-century landscape painter Thomas Moran, known for his Grand Canyon works.

The next stop, **Grandview Point,** affords a view of **Horseshoe Mesa,** another interesting feature of the canyon landscape. In the early 1890s, the mesa was the site of the Last Chance Copper Mine; later that same decade, the Grandview Hotel was built here and served canyon visitors until it closed in 1908. The steep, unmaintained **Grandview Trail,** which leads down to Horseshoe

Mesa, makes a good less-traveled alternative to the South Kaibab Trail, although it is considerably more challenging.

The last stop along Desert View Drive is **Yaki Point.** It's not open to private vehicles—the park service would prefer you park your car in Grand Canyon Village and take the Kaibab Trail Route (Orange) shuttle bus from the Grand Canyon Visitor Center to Yaki Point. The reality is that people passing by in cars want to see what this viewpoint is all about, and now park their cars along the main road and walk up the Yaki Point access road. The spectacular view from here encompasses a wide section of the central canyon. The large, flat-topped butte to the northeast is **Wotan's Throne,** one of the canyon's most recognizable features. You'll see a lot of hikers at Yaki Point, since it's also the trail head for the **South Kaibab Trail,** the preferred downhill hiking route to Phantom Ranch. It's a more scenic route than the Bright Angel Trail—if you're planning a day hike into the canyon, this should be your number-one choice. Be sure to bring plenty of water.

Hiking the Grand Canyon

No visit to the canyon is complete without journeying below the rim on one of the park's hiking trails. While the views don't necessarily get any better than they are from the top, they do change considerably. Gazing up at all those thousands of feet of vertical rock walls provides a very different perspective from that atop the rim. Below the rim, you may also see fossils, old mines, petroglyphs, wildflowers, and wildlife. The one thing you won't find on the park's main hiking trails is solitude.

That said, there is no better way to see the canyon than on foot (my apologies to the mules). If you're in good physical condition and have strong legs and knees, you can simply head down the Bright Angel or South Kaibab trail. Keep in mind, though, that these are the two busiest trails, with hundreds of hikers per day. If you want to see fewer other hikers and are in good shape, consider the Grandview Trail or the Hermit Trail instead. If you just want an easy, relatively level walk, take the Rim Trail/Greenway Trail.

Hiking Precautions

The Grand Canyon offers some of the most rugged and strenuous hiking in the United States; anyone attempting even a short walk should be well prepared. Each year, injuries and fatalities are suffered by day hikers who set out without sturdy footgear, or without food and adequate amounts of water. Even a 30-minute hike in summer can dehydrate you, and a long hike in the heat can require drinking more than a gallon of water.

If you go for a day hike in the summer, **carry and drink** at least 2 quarts of water and a couple quarts of Gatorade or other electrolyte-supplement drink. And **do not even think about** hiking from the rim to the Colorado River and back in the same day. Although a few very fit individuals have managed this grueling feat, there are also plenty who have tried and died. Finally, remember that **mules have the right of way.**

DAY HIKES

Hikers tend to gravitate to loop trails, but here on the South Rim, there are no such trails—all hikes are out-and-back. The good news is that the vastly different scenery in every direction makes the route back look entirely different from the route out. The bad news is that most of these out-and-back trails are the reverse of what you usually find: Instead of starting out by toiling up a steep mountain, gravity assists you in hiking down into the canyon. There are few natural turnarounds, and it's easy to hike farther than you realize, only to face an arduous slog coming back, when you're already tired. Here's a rule of thumb: Expect to take 2 hours climbing back for every hour spent going down. Know your limits and turn around before you become tired.

For an easy, flat hike, your main option is the **Rim Trail ★**, which stretches for 13 miles from the South Kaibab trail head east of Grand Canyon Village to Hermit's Rest, 8 miles west of the village. Most of this trail is paved; the portion that passes through Grand Canyon Village is always the most crowded stretch of trail in the park. From Powell Point west, it becomes a dirt path for about 3 miles; most of this stretch follows Hermit Road, which means you'll have traffic noise (although only from shuttle buses for most of the year). The last 2.8 miles is part of the paved Greenway Trail. To avoid crowds and get the most enjoyment out of a Rim Trail hike, head out as early in the morning as you can, taking the shuttle to the Abyss. From here it's a 4-mile hike to Hermit's Rest; for more than half of this distance, the trail isn't as close to the road as it is around Grand Canyon Village. Hermit's Rest makes a great place to rest, and from here you can catch a shuttle back to the village. Alternatively, take the shuttle all the way to Hermit's Rest and then hike east, catching a shuttle back whenever you start to feel tired.

The **Bright Angel Trail ★★**, which starts just west of Bright Angel Lodge in Grand Canyon Village, is the most popular trail into the canyon, mostly because it starts right where the greatest number of park visitors tend to congregate (near the ice-cream parlor and the hotels). It's also the route traditionally used for mule rides into the canyon. Bear in mind that this trail follows a narrow side canyon for several miles, and thus has somewhat limited views. On the other hand, it's the only maintained South Rim trail into the canyon that has potable water, and it has some good turnaround points. **1½ Mile Resthouse** (1,131 ft. below the rim) and **3 Mile Resthouse** (2,112 ft. below the rim) have water except in winter, when the water is turned off. These rest houses are named for their distance from the rim; if you hike to **3 Mile Resthouse,** you will have a 3-mile hike back up. Destinations for longer day hikes include **Indian Garden** (9 miles round-trip) and **Plateau Point** (12 miles round-trip), which are both slightly more than 3,000 feet below the rim. There is year-round water at Indian Garden.

Beginning near Yaki Point, east of Grand Canyon Village, the **South Kaibab Trail ★★★** is the preferred route down to **Phantom Ranch.** This trail offers the best views of any of the trails into the canyon; if you have time for only one day hike, make it the South Kaibab Trail. From the trail head, it's 3 miles round-trip to **Cedar Ridge** and 6 miles round-trip to **Skeleton Point.** The hike is strenuous, and there's no water available along the trail.

If you're an experienced mountain or desert hiker with good, sturdy boots, consider the unmaintained **Hermit Trail ★**, which begins at Hermit's Rest, 8 miles west of Grand Canyon Village at the end of Hermit Road. It's a 5-mile round-trip hike to **Santa Maria Spring** (the trail plunges 1,600–1,700 ft. in the first 1.5 miles) and a 7-mile round-trip hike to **Dripping Springs.** Water from these two springs must be treated with a water filter, iodine, or purification tablets, or by boiled for at least 10 minutes, so you're better off just carrying sufficient water for your hike. Beyond Santa Maria Spring, the Hermit Trail descends to the Colorado River, a 17-mile hike from the trail head. Note that Hermit Road is closed to private vehicles March through November; during these months, you'll need to take the shuttle bus to the trail head. If you take the first bus of the day, you'll likely have the trail almost all to yourself.

The **Grandview Trail ★**, which begins at Grandview Point 12 miles east of Grand Canyon Village, is another steep, unmaintained trail that's only for the most physically fit hikers. A strenuous 6-mile round-trip hike leads to **Horseshoe Mesa,** 2,600 feet below the trail head. No water is available, so carry at least a gallon. Just to give you an idea of how steep this trail is, you'll lose more than 2,000 feet of elevation in the first .8 mile down to **Coconino Saddle.**

Even more challenging is the **Tanner Trail ★**, which starts just downhill from the parking lot at Lipan Point, near the east end of Desert View Drive. It's so rarely used that the National Park Service doesn't even mark it on the maps it hands out to park visitors (probably for good reason—the park service doesn't want to have to rescue folks who might collapse from dehydration hiking back up). Once a trail used by horse thieves to move stolen horses between Utah and Arizona, it's one of the shortest, steepest, and most challenging trails into the canyon. Passing through the hottest part of the canyon, it's exposed to the sun most of the day; the trail is badly eroded, with a loose, slippery gravel section along the Redwall Limestone formation, raising the imminent risk of a serious, potentially deadly fall. You must be in excellent shape, with good knees and strong quadriceps, and don't even think of setting foot on this trail unless you're wearing very sturdy boots with excellent ankle support. Take lots of water and drink it. How far can you hike on this trail? Well, that's up to you. It's 3 miles and a 1,700-foot elevation drop to **Escalante Butte,** where there's a good view of Marble Canyon, Hance Rapids, and the bottom of the canyon.

BACKPACKING

Backpacking the Grand Canyon is an unforgettable experience. Although most people simply hike down to Phantom Ranch and back, there are many miles of trails deep in the canyon. Keep in mind, however, that to backpack the canyon, you'll need to do a lot of planning. A **Backcountry Use Permit** is required of all hikers planning to overnight in the canyon, unless you'll be staying at Phantom Ranch in a cabin or dormitory. Only a limited number of overnight hikers are allowed into the canyon on any given day, so it's important to make permit requests as soon as possible. You can submit permit requests in person, by mail, or by fax. Contact the **Backcountry Information Center,** Grand Canyon National Park, P.O. Box 129, Grand Canyon, AZ 86023 (www.nps.gov/grca; ✆ **928/638-7875** for information Monday–Friday 1–5pm MST; fax 928/638-2125). The office accepts written permit requests 5 months ahead, starting the first of every month. In person, verbal permit requests can be made only 4 months in advance. Holiday periods are the most popular—if you want to hike over the Labor Day weekend, be sure to make your reservation on May 1. If you show up without a hiking permit, go to the **Backcountry Information Center** adjacent to Maswik Lodge (daily 8am–noon and 1–5pm) and put your name on the waiting list. When applying for a permit, you must specify your exact itinerary, and once in the canyon you must stick to that itinerary. Backpacking fees include a nonrefundable $10 backcountry permit fee and a $8 per-person per-night backcountry camping fee, on top of the park entry fee you'll pay when you arrive at the Grand Canyon.

There are **campgrounds** at Indian Garden, Bright Angel Campground (near Phantom Ranch), and Cottonwood; hikers are limited to 2 nights per trip at each of these campgrounds (except November 15–February 28, when 4 nights are allowed at each campground). Other nights can be spent camping at undesignated sites in certain regions of the park.

Maps are available through the **Grand Canyon Association** (www.grandcanyon.org; ✆ **800/858-2808** or 928/638-2481) and at bookstores and gift shops within the national park.

The best times of year to backpack are spring and fall. In summer, temperatures at the bottom of the canyon are frequently above 100°F (38°C), while in winter, ice and snow at higher elevations make footing on trails precarious (crampons are recommended). Plan to carry at least 2 quarts, preferably 1 gallon, of water whenever backpacking in the canyon.

The Grand Canyon is a rugged, unforgiving landscape, and many people might prefer to backpack with a professional guide. To arrange a guided backpacking trip into the canyon, contact **Discovery Treks** (www.discoverytreks.com; ✆ **480/247-9266**), which offers 3- to 5-day all-inclusive hikes with rates starting at $975 per person.

Organized Tours & Excursions

BUS TOURS

Rather leave the driving to someone else so you can enjoy the scenery? Opt for a bus or van tour of the Grand Canyon with **Xanterra South Rim** (www.grandcanyonlodges.com; ✆ **888/297-2757,** 303/297-2757 outside the U.S., 928/638-2631 for same-day reservations). To book these, call the numbers listed, or stop by the transportation desks at Bright Angel, Maswik, or Yavapai lodges in Grand Canyon Village. You'll pay $27.50 for a 1½-hour sunrise or sunset tour, $36 for a Hermit's Rest tour, $65 for a Desert View tour, or $80 for a combination of any two tours.

TRAIL RIDES BY MULE & HORSE ★

Mule rides into the canyon have been popular since the beginning of the 20th century, when the Bright Angel Trail was a toll road. After looking at the steep drop-offs and narrow path of the Bright Angel Trail, you might decide this isn't exactly the place to trust your life to a mule. Never fear: Wranglers will quickly reassure that you they haven't lost a rider yet. Three-hour mule rides meander along the Rim through the forest to eventually arrive at the Abyss, a spectacular viewpoint along Hermit Road. Overnight mule trips go all the way down to the canyon floor at Phantom Ranch, where cabins and dormitories are available. From November to March, a 2-night Phantom Ranch trip is offered; other times of year, you'll ride down one day and back up the next. Mule trips range from $143 for the 3-hour ride, to $600 for an overnight ride, to $863 for the 2-night ride. Couples get discounts on overnight rides. Riders must be at least 9 years old; weigh less than 200 pounds fully dressed; be at least 4 feet, 7 inches tall; and speak and understand English fluently. Pregnant women are not allowed. Especially in summer, these rides often book up 6 months or more in advance (you can make reservations up to 13 months ahead). For more information or to make a reservation, contact **Xanterra Parks &**

Excursions into the canyon's depths on muleback are very popular—make reservations months in advance.

Resorts (www.grandcanyonlodges.com; ✆ **888/297-2757** or 303/297-2757). For last-minute bookings (up to 5 days ahead of your desired date), contact **Xanterra South Rim** at its Arizona phone number (✆ **928/638-2631**) on the remote chance that there's space available. If you arrive at the canyon without a reservation, stop by the Bright Angel Transportation Desk and put your name on the next day's waiting list. Hey, you never know.

For more casual horseback riding outside of the Canyon, head to **Apache Stables** (www.apachestables.com; ✆ **928/638-2891**), located outside the park a mile north of Tusayan on Moqui Drive. A 1-hour ride costs $52.50, a 2-hour ride is $92.50. There are also wagon rides and campfire rides (be sure to bring something to cook over the fire). The stables are closed in winter.

THE GRAND CANYON RAILWAY ★★

In the early 20th century, most visitors to the Grand Canyon arrived by train, and it's still possible to travel to the canyon along the steel rails. The **Grand Canyon Railway** (www.thetrain.com; ✆ **800/843-8724** or 303/843-8724) runs from Williams to Grand Canyon Village, using either diesel engines or, occasionally, early-20th-century steam engines (they now run on waste vegetable oil). Trains depart from the Williams Depot, housed in the historic 1908 Fray Marcos Hotel, which also has a railroad museum, gift shop, and cafe. (Grand Canyon Railway also operates the adjacent Grand Canyon Railway Hotel.) At Grand Canyon Village, trains stop at the 1910 log railway terminal in front of El Tovar Hotel.

There are four classes of service to choose from: coach, first class, observation dome (upstairs in the dome car), and luxury parlor class. Actors posing as cowboys provide entertainment aboard the train. It's 8-hours round-trip, including a 3¼- to 3¾-hour layover at the canyon. Round-trip fares (not including tax or the national park entrance fee) range from $67 to $219 for adults, $25.50 to $120 for children 2 to 12.

Not only is this a fun, scenic trip, it also avoids the traffic congestion and parking problems in Grand Canyon Village. When booking your train trip, you can also book a bus tour in the park, which will help you make the most of your limited time on the Rim. Or, if you want, book a room/train package so you can stay overnight in the park.

Tip for families: In November, December, and January, the railway runs a Polar Express service to "the North Pole," complete with a visit from Santa.

INTERPRETIVE PROGRAMS

Any number of interpretive programs are scheduled throughout the year at various South Rim locations. Ranger-led walks explore different aspects of the canyon, from nature hikes to fossil trips to guided tours of the Tusayan Ruin; rangers also give geology talks, lecture on the cultural and natural resources of the canyon, and hold stargazing gatherings. Many programs are held at Mather Point Amphitheater and the Shrine of the Ages. Consult your copy of *The Guide* for information on times and meeting points.

A Bird's-Eye View

Despite controversies over noise and safety (there have been a few crashes over the years), airplane and helicopter flights over the Grand Canyon remain one of the most popular ways to see this natural wonder. If you want to join the crowds buzzing above the canyon, you'll find several companies operating out of Grand Canyon Airport in Tusayan. Air tours last anywhere from 30 minutes to about 2 hours. Companies offering tours by small plane include **Air Grand Canyon** (www.airgrandcanyon.com; ✆ **800/247-4726** or 928/638-2686) and **Grand Canyon Airlines** (www.grandcanyonairlines.com; ✆ **866/235-9422** or 928/638-2359), which has been offering air tours since 1927. Fifty-minute plane flights cost $108 to $159. Helicopter tours are available from **Maverick Helicopters** (www.maverickhelicopter.com; ✆ **888/261-4414** or 702/261-0007), **Grand Canyon Helicopters** (www.grandcanyonhelicoptersaz.com; ✆ **855/326-9617** or 702/835-8477), and **Papillon Grand Canyon Helicopters** (www.papillon.com; ✆ **888/635-7272** or 702/736-7243). Helicopter rates range from $149 to $209 for a 25- to 40-minute flight and $299 for a 45- to 55-minute flight. Children sometimes receive a discount (usually around $20).

THE GRAND CANYON FIELD INSTITUTE

If you're the active type or want more of an educational experience, consider a trip with the **Grand Canyon Field Institute** (www.grandcanyon.org/classes-tours; ✆ **866/471-4435** or 928/638-2485). Co-sponsored by Grand Canyon National Park and the Grand Canyon Association, the Field Institute schedules a wide variety of guided educational trips, such as challenging backpacking trips through the canyon (some for women only) and programs lasting anywhere from a day to more than a week. Subjects covered include wilderness studies, geology, natural history, human history, photography, and art.

JEEP TOURS

To explore parts of Grand Canyon National Park that most visitors never see, contact **Grand Canyon Jeep Tours & Safaris** (www.grandcanyonjeeptours.com; ✆ **800/320-5337** or 928/638-5337), which offers three different tours visiting the park and the adjacent Kaibab National Forest. Prices range from $79 to $95 for adults and $69 to $80 for children.

RAFTING THE COLORADO RIVER ★★★

Ever since John Wesley Powell proved it was possible to travel by boat down the tumultuous Colorado, running the big river has beckoned adventurers. Today, anyone from grade-schoolers to grandmothers can join the ranks of those who've made the run. However, be prepared for some of the most furious white water in the world.

Numerous companies offer trips through various sections of the canyon. You can spend as little as half a day on the Colorado (downstream from Glen Canyon Dam; p. 325) or more than 2 weeks. You can go down the river in a huge motorized rubber raft (the quickest and noisiest way to see the entire canyon), a paddle- or oar-powered raft (more thrills and, if you have to help paddle, more of a workout), or a wooden dory (the biggest thrill of all). In a motorized raft, you can travel from Lees Ferry to Lake Mead in 8 days; if you opt for a dory or an oar- or paddle-powered raft, expect to spend 5 to 6 days getting from Lees Ferry to Phantom Ranch, or 7 to 9 days from Phantom Ranch to Diamond Creek, just above Lake Mead. You can also hike in or out of Phantom Ranch for a combination rafting-and-hiking adventure. Aside from the half-day trips near Glen Canyon Dam, any Grand Canyon rafting trip will involve lots of monster rapids.

Most trips start from **Lees Ferry** near Page and Lake Powell. The main rafting season is April through October, but some companies operate year-round. Rafting trips tend to book up more than a year in advance; some companies begin taking reservations as early as January for the following year's trips. A few rafting trips charge as little as $250 per day, but most fall in the $300 to $350 per day range; rates depend on the length of the trip and the type of boat used.

The following companies are well established in guiding visitors down the Colorado River to the Grand Canyon:

- **Arizona Raft Adventures,** 4050 E. Huntington Rd., Flagstaff (www.azraft.com; ✆ **800/786-7238** or 928/526-8200); 6- to 16-day motor, oar, and paddle trips. Although this is not one of the larger companies operating on the river, it offers lots of different trips, including some focusing on natural history and others that double as yoga workshops. They also do trips in paddle rafts that allow you to help navigate and provide the power while shooting the canyon's rapids.
- **Canyoneers,** P.O. Box 2997, Flagstaff (www.canyoneers.com; ✆ **800/525-0924** or 928/526-0924); 3- to 10-day motorized-raft trips and 6- to 14-day oar-powered trips. Way back in 1938, this was the first company to take paying customers down the Colorado, and Canyoneers is still one of the top companies on the river.
- **Grand Canyon Expeditions Company,** P.O. Box O, Kanab, Utah (www.gcex.com; ✆ **800/544-2691** or 435/644-2691); 8- and 9-day motorized trips and 14- and 16-day dory trips. If you've got the time, these dory trips are a fine homage to John Wesley Powell's expedition 150 years ago; they're among the most thrilling adventures in the world.
- **Grand Canyon Whitewater,** 1000 N. Humphreys St. Suite 202, Flagstaff (www.grandcanyonwhitewater.com; ✆ **800/343-3121** or 928/779-2979); 4- to 8-day motorized-raft trips and 5- to 13-day oar trips.
- **Hatch River Expeditions,** 5348 E. Burris Lane, Flagstaff (www.hatchriverexpeditions.com; ✆ **800/856-8966** or 928/526-4700); 4- to 8-day motorized trips and 6-, 7-, and 12-day oar trips. All of this company's trips, except their upper-canyon expedition, end with a helicopter flight out of the canyon. In business since 1929, Hatch River claims to be the oldest commercial rafting company in the U.S. With so much experience, you can count on Hatch to provide a great trip.

- **Outdoors Unlimited,** 6900 Townsend Winona Rd., Flagstaff (www.outdoors unlimited.com; ✆ **800/637-7238**); 5- to 15-day oar and paddle trips. This company has been taking people through the canyon for more than 40 years and usually sends them home very happy.
- **Wilderness River Adventures,** P.O. Box 717, Page (www.riveradventures.com; ✆ **800/992-8022**); 3- to 8-day motorized-raft trips and 5- to 14-day oar trips. The 4-day trips (actually 3½ days) involve hiking out from Phantom Ranch. This is one of the bigger companies operating on the canyon, offering a wide variety of trips—it's a good place to start if you're not sure what type of trip you want to do.

For information on 1-day rafting trips at the west end of the Grand Canyon, see p. 280. For information on half-day trips near Page, see p. 330.

Attractions Outside the Canyon

In Tusayan, outside the south entrance to the park, the **National Geographic Visitor Center,** 450 Ariz. 64 (www.explorethecanyon.com; ✆ **928/638-2468**) shows a 34-minute IMAX film covering the history and geology of the canyon throughout the day on a six-story screen. Admission is $13.59, $12.50 seniors and military, and $10.33 for children. March to October, there are shows daily 8:30am to 8:30pm; November to February, shows are daily between 10:30am and 6:30pm. The visitor center also has interactive exhibits and a cafe.

Outside the east entrance to the park, the **Cameron Trading Post** (www.camerontradingpost.com; ✆ **800/338-7385** or 928/679-2231), at the crossroads where Ariz. 64 branches off U.S. 89, is one of the best trading posts in the state. The original stone trading post, a historic building, now houses a gallery of Indian artifacts, clothing, and jewelry. This gallery sells museum-quality pieces, but even if you don't have $10,000 to drop on a rug or basket, you can still look around. The more modern main trading post is the largest trading post in northern Arizona. Don't miss the beautiful terraced gardens in back of the original trading post.

If you aren't completely beat at the end of the day, check the entertainment schedule at Tusayan's **Grand Hotel** (✆ **928/638-3333**). Cowboy singers, country bands, and Native American dancers all perform here regularly.

Where to Stay on the South Rim

The Grand Canyon is one of the most popular national parks in the country, and hotel rooms both within and just outside the park are in high demand. Make reservations as far in advance as possible. Don't expect to find a room if you show up in summer without a reservation—you'll probably have to drive back to Williams or Flagstaff to find a vacancy. However, occasionally it's possible, due to cancellations and no-shows, to get a same-day reservation at a national park property; it's a long shot, but it happens. Same-day reservations can be made by calling ✆ **928/638-2631.**

Even if you aren't staying here, stop in the lobby of the vintage El Tovar Hotel to admire its mix of luxury and rustic lodge charm.

INSIDE THE PARK

All hotels inside the park are operated by **Xanterra South Rim/Xanterra Parks & Resorts;** to make reservations at any of the in-park hotels listed below, contact Xanterra at www.grandcanyonlodges.com; ✆ **888/297-2757** or 303/297-2757. Reservations are taken up to 13 months in advance, beginning on the first of the month. If you want to stay in one of the historic rim cabins at Bright Angel Lodge, reserve at least a year in advance. The one exception are the small, very basic rooms with shared bathrooms at Bright Angel Lodge; they're often the last in the park to book up. If you're trying to get a last-minute reservation, they may be your best bet.

Expensive

El Tovar Hotel ★★ El Tovar Hotel, which first opened its doors in 1905, is the park's premier lodge. Built of local rock and Oregon pine by Hopi craftsmen, it's a rustic yet luxurious mountain lodge perching on the edge of the canyon (only a few rooms have views, however). The lobby, entered from a veranda set with rustic furniture, has a small fireplace, cathedral ceiling, and log walls with moose, deer, and antelope heads on display. Guest rooms are comfortable and attractively decorated, but the standard units are rather small, as are the bathrooms. For more legroom, book a deluxe unit. Suites, with private terraces and stunning views, are extremely spacious. **El Tovar Dining Room** (p. 249) serves a mix of continental and Southwestern cuisine; it's the best restaurant in the village. Just off the lobby is a cocktail lounge with a view.

Grand Canyon Village. ✆ **928/638-2631.** 78 units. $217–$263 double; $352–$538 suite. **Amenities:** Restaurant; lounge; concierge; room service; free Wi-Fi.

Moderate

Thunderbird & Kachina Lodges ★ If you want great views, these hotels are your best bets—but only if you get a room with a view. These two side-by-side hotels, dating from the 1960s, are a far cry from what you might imagine a national park hotel would look like. They do, however, have the most modern rooms on the canyon rim, and the biggest windows of any of the hotels. If you get a second-story room on the canyon side of either hotel, you'll get some of the best views in the park (these rooms at the Kachina Lodge get the nod for *the* best views). Book early—these are some of the park's most popular accommodations. Just remember, if it's not a view room, you'll be staring at the parking lot, and the lodge will not guarantee canyon-view rooms.

Grand Canyon Village. ✆ **928/638-2631.** 104 units. $225–$243 double. **Amenities:** Free Wi-Fi.

Yavapai Lodge ★ Located at the east end of Grand Canyon Village (a 1-mile hike from the main part of the village, but convenient to the Grand Canyon Visitor Center), the Yavapai is the largest lodge in the park, comprised of several buildings; this is where you'll likely wind up if you wait too long to make a reservation. Unfortunately, it's the least-appealing hotel in the park, with no canyon views (it's also less expensive than the Thunderbird and Kachina lodges). If you stay here, try for a room in the nicer Yavapai East wing, which is set under shady pines.

Grand Canyon Village. ✆ **928/638-2631.** 358 units. $161 double (winter discounts available). **Amenities:** Restaurant; free Wi-Fi.

Inexpensive

Bright Angel Lodge & Cabins ★★ Bright Angel Lodge, which began operation in 1896 as a collection of tents and cabins on the edge of the canyon, is the most affordable lodge in the park. With its flagstone-floor lobby and huge fireplace, it has a genuine, if crowded, mountain-lodge atmosphere. It also happens to offer the greatest variety of accommodations in the park. The best and most popular units are the rim cabins, which should be booked a year in advance. In fact, any rooms here should be booked as far in advance as possible. Most of the rooms and cabins feature rustic furnishings. The Buckey Suite, the oldest structure on the canyon rim, is arguably the best room in the park, with a canyon view, gas fireplace, and king-size bed.

Grand Canyon Village. ✆ **928/638-2631.** 90 units (20 w/shared bath). $85 double w/ shared bath; $110 double w/private bath; $140–$217 cabin; $171–$469 suite. **Amenities:** 2 restaurants; snack bar; lounge; free Wi-Fi.

Maswik Lodge ★ Set back ¼ mile or so from the rim, the Maswik Lodge offers spacious rooms and cabins that have been comfortably modernized without losing their appealing rustic character. If you don't mind roughing it a bit, the 28 old cabins, available only in summer, have lots of character, with high ceilings and ceiling fans—they're my top choice away from the rim. If you prefer modern appointments, lots of space, and air-conditioning, opt for one of the large Maswik North rooms, which also have refrigerators and coffeemakers. Second-floor rooms have high ceilings and balconies. ***Note:*** As of 2019, the Maswik South buildings are being demolished and replaced with a new lodge, so confusion is likely to reign for the next couple of years.

Grand Canyon Village. ✆ **928/638-2631.** 250 units. $112–$215 double (winter discounts available). **Amenities:** Restaurant; lounge; free Wi-Fi.

Phantom Ranch ★ Built in 1922, Phantom Ranch, the only lodge at the bottom of the Grand Canyon, has a classic ranch atmosphere. Accommodations are in rustic stone-walled cabins or 10-bed gender-segregated dormitories. Evaporative coolers keep both the cabins and the dorms cool in summer. Make reservations as early as possible, and don't forget to reconfirm. An online lottery offers the hope that you can skip ahead of the line, but as with all lotteries the odds are—well, certainly not with us. Family-style meals must be reserved in advance. The dinner menu consists of beef-and-vegetable stew ($29) and steak ($48); breakfasts ($24) are hearty, and sack lunches ($21) are available as well. Between meals, the dining hall becomes a canteen selling snacks, drinks, gifts, and necessities. After dinner, it serves as a beer hall. There's a public phone here, and mule-back duffel transfer ($64) between Grand Canyon Village and Phantom Ranch can be arranged.

Grand Canyon floor. No phone. 11 cabins, 40 dorm beds. $149 double in cabin; $51 dormitory bed. Mule-trip overnights (all meals included) $477 for 1 person, $843 for 2 people. 2-night trips available Nov–Mar. **Amenities:** Restaurant; lounge.

IN TUSAYAN (OUTSIDE THE SOUTH ENTRANCE)

If you can't get a reservation for a room in the park, this is the next closest place to stay, in a line of hotels along U.S. 180/Ariz. 64. During the day, the area can be very noisy, with helicopters and airplanes constantly taking off from the airport, but at night things calm down. Hotels outside the park are popular with tour groups, which keep them full throughout the summer.

Best Western Grand Canyon Squire Inn ★ With a pool in the summer and a video-game room and bowling alley year-round, this hotel offers plenty to distract the kids. Parents will likely appreciate the large guest rooms with comfortable easy chairs and big windows. In the lobby, which is more Las Vegas glitz than mountain rustic, cases are filled with old cowboy paraphernalia. Down in the basement you'll find an impressive Western sculpture and a waterfall wall. The **Coronado Room** restaurant (p. 250) is a plus.

74 Ariz. 64. www.grandcanyonsquire.com. ✆ **800/622-6966** or 928/638-2681. 318 units. $100–$430 double. Children 12 and under stay free in parent's room. **Amenities:** 3 restaurants; 2 lounges; exercise room; Jacuzzi; outdoor pool; sauna; free Wi-Fi.

Canyon Plaza Resort ★ Despite the word "resort" in the name, the Canyon Plaza's setting is none too pretty, behind the IMAX theater and surrounded by parking lots. Guest rooms are large and comfortable, however, with balconies or patios. The hotel is built around two enclosed skylit courtyards, one of which houses a restaurant and the other a bar and whirlpool. Families should opt for a suite, with its separate small living room. Unfortunately, the hotel is very popular with tour groups and can often feel crowded.

406 Canyon Plaza Lane. www.grandcanyonplaza.com. ✆ **800/995-2521** or 928/638-2673. 232 units. Early Mar–late Oct double $251; late Oct–early Mar double $100–$188. Rates include continental breakfast. Children 16 and under stay free in parent's room. Pets under 40 lbs. accepted ($50 per night). **Amenities:** Restaurant; lounge; hot tub; outdoor pool; free Wi-Fi.

Grand Hotel ★★ With its mountain lodge–style lobby—a flagstone fireplace, log-beam ceiling, and fake ponderosa-pine tree trunks holding up the roof—this modern hotel is your best bet outside the park. Just off the lobby are a dining room (with evening entertainment ranging from Native American dancers to country-music bands; see p. 250), a small bar that even has a few saddles for bar stools, and an espresso stand. Guest rooms are spacious, with a few Western touches, and some have small balconies.

149 Ariz. 64. www.grandcanyongrandhotel.com. ✆ **888/634-7263** or 928/638-3333. 121 units. Doubles $370–$400; mid-Oct–mid-Mar $100–$130. Children 12 and under stay free in parent's room. **Amenities:** Restaurant; lounge; exercise room; Jacuzzi; indoor pool; free Wi-Fi.

Holiday Inn Express Hotel & Suites—Grand Canyon ★ With modern, well-designed, and predictably clean and comfortable guest rooms, this hotel also has a separate building with 32 large suites that are ideal for families. These suites are among the nicest accommodations inside or outside the park. ***Parents take note:*** The main building offers "Kids' Suites" that have bunk beds, three TVs, and a video-game machine.

226 N. Ariz. 64. www.gcanyon.com. ✆ **888/473-2269** or 928/638-3000. 194 units. $120–$270 double; $200–$360 suite. Rates include full breakfast. Children 19 and under stay free in parent's room. **Amenities:** 2 Jacuzzis; indoor pool; free Wi-Fi.

Red Feather Lodge ★ With more than 200 units, this combination motel/hotel is often slow to fill up, so it's a good choice for last-minute bookings. Try to get one of the newer rooms, which are a bit more comfortable; the older ones date to the lodge's opening in 1963. In summer, the pool makes this place a good bet for families, and there's a reasonably priced Mexican restaurant on-site.

300 Ariz. 64. www.redfeatherlodge.com. ✆ **800/538-2345** or 928/638-2414. 225 units. Mar–Oct $132–$275; Nov–Apr $79–$275. Children 17 and under stay free in parent's room. Pets accepted ($25 per night plus $5 for each additional pet up to 3). **Amenities:** Restaurant; Jacuzzi; outdoor pool; laundry facilities; fitness center; free Wi-Fi.

FARTHER AFIELD

Cameron Trading Post Motel ★ Located 54 miles north of Flagstaff on U.S. 89, at the junction with the road to the national park's east entrance, this motel offers some of the most attractive rooms in the vicinity of the Grand

Canyon. Adjacent to the historic Cameron Trading Post (p. 243), the motel is built around the shady oasis of the old trading post's terraced gardens. Guest rooms feature southwestern-style furniture. Most have balconies, and some have views of the Little Colorado River (which, however, rarely has much water in it). Don't miss the Navajo tacos in the dining room; the small ones are plenty big enough for a meal.

466 U.S. 89, Cameron. www.camerontradingpost.com. ✆ **800/338-7385** or 928/679-2231. 62 units. Doubles Nov–Feb $89, Mar–Oct $129; suites Nov–Feb $139–$169, Mar–Oct $169–$199. Pets accepted ($25 fee). **Amenities:** Restaurant; free Wi-Fi.

CAMPGROUNDS

Inside the Park

On the South Rim, there are two campgrounds and an RV park. **Mather Campground,** in Grand Canyon Village, has 327 campsites ($18 per night). Reservations can be made up to 6 months in advance and are required for stays between March and late November. Contact the National Recreation Reservation Service (www.recreation.gov; ✆ **877/444-6777** or 518/885-3639). In winter, campsites are available on a first-come, first-served basis, at $15 per night; reservations not accepted. **Desert View Campground,** with 50 sites ($12 per night), is 25 miles east of Grand Canyon Village and open from mid-April to mid-October. No reservations are accepted; on arrival, campers must self-register at the automated fee machine. The **Trailer Village RV park,** in Grand Canyon Village, has 75 RV sites and charges $41 per night (for two adults) for full hookup. Reservations can be made up to 13 months in advance online via **DNC Parks & Resorts** (www.visitgrandcanyon.com). For same-day reservations at all these campgrounds, call ✆ **928/638-2631.**

Outside the Park

Two miles south of Tusayan, the U.S. Forest Service's **Ten-X Campground** has 70 campsites ($10 per night), open May through early October. There are no shower or laundry facilities and no utility hookups. It's usually your best bet for finding a site late in the day.

You can also camp just about anywhere within the **Kaibab National Forest,** which borders Grand Canyon National Park. Several dirt roads lead into the forest from the highway, and although you won't find designated campsites or toilets along these roads, you will find spots where others have obviously camped before. This so-called dispersed camping is usually used by campers who haven't found sites in campgrounds. One of the most popular roads for this sort of camping is on the west side of the highway between Tusayan and the park's south entrance. For more information, contact the **Tusayan Ranger District,** Kaibab National Forest, 176 Lincoln Log Loop (P.O. Box 3088), Grand Canyon (www.fs.usda.gov/kaibab; ✆ **928/638-2443**).

Where to Eat Around the South Rim

INSIDE THE PARK

If you're looking for a quick, inexpensive meal, there are plenty of options. In Grand Canyon Village, choices include a restaurant at the **Yavapai Lodge,** a food court at the **Maswik Lodge,** and a delicatessen at **Canyon Village Marketplace** on Market Plaza. The **Bright Angel Fountain,** at the back of the Bright Angel Lodge, serves hot dogs, sandwiches, and ice cream—as you might expect, it's always crowded on hot days. One out-of-the-ordinary place for a quick bite is the **Hermit's Rest Snack Bar** at the west end of Hermit Road, set in a stone building designed by Mary Elizabeth Jane Colter. At Desert View (near the east entrance to the park), there's the **Desert View Trading Post Cafeteria.** All of these places are open daily, and all serve meals for $15 and under.

The Arizona Room ★★ SOUTHWESTERN Boasting the best view of the three dining establishments right on the South Rim, the Arizona Room is immensely popular and a favorite restaurant in the park. Its Southwestern menu is almost as creative as that of El Tovar Dining Room (below), featuring lots of regionally sourced artisanal foods. There is often a long wait for a table here (they don't take reservations) so arrive early, which should assure you of getting a good table without too much of a wait. Once you finally sit down to eat, I recommend both the pan-seared salmon fillet with tomato salsa and the baby back ribs with chipotle glaze. ***Tip:*** It's also open for lunch part of the year, giving you another great option for dining with a billion-dollar view.

At the Bright Angel Lodge. ✆ **928/638-2631.** No reservations. Main courses $7.50–$13 lunch, $18–$34 dinner. Daily 5–9:30pm (Mar–Oct also lunch daily 11:30am–3pm). Closed Jan–Feb.

El Tovar Dining Room ★★ CONTINENTAL/SOUTHWESTERN If you're staying at the Grand Canyon, you'll want to have dinner in the hotel's rustic yet elegant dining room. But before making reservations at the most expensive restaurant in the park, be aware that few tables have views of the canyon. Limited views aside, the meals served here are the best on the South Rim. The menu includes a bit of Southwestern flavor, but for the most part, it sticks to familiar continental dishes. The New York steak is a good bet, as is the wild salmon tostada. Start your meal with the interesting little roulades (flavorful bite-size tortilla roll-ups). Service is generally quite good. Have a drink in the bar before dinner (you might even be able to snag a table with a view), or save it for wine with dinner—the El Tovar boasts an award-winning list of more than 100 wines.

At El Tovar Hotel. ✆ **928/638-2631,** ext. 6432. Reservations highly recommended for dinner; reservations accepted 30 days in advance. Main courses $13–$25 lunch, $29–$40 dinner. Daily 7am–9pm.

Harvey House Café ★ AMERICAN Perched on the rim of the canyon, this casual Southwestern-themed restaurant in the historic Bright Angel Lodge stays packed with families throughout the day. The food is good and relatively simple, with plenty of choices for all tastes. The dinner menu includes everything from burgers to fajitas to spaghetti (foods calculated to comfort tired and hungry hikers). House favorites for lunch are the sourdough bread bowls full of chili or stew. Beer and wine are available, and service is generally friendly and efficient.

At the Bright Angel Lodge. ✆ **928/638-2631.** No reservations. Main courses $8–$14 breakfast, $7–$12 lunch, $10–$19 dinner. Daily 7am–9pm.

IN TUSAYAN (OUTSIDE THE SOUTH ENTRANCE)

In addition to the restaurants listed below, you'll find a steakhouse and a pizza place, as well as familiar chains such as McDonald's, Pizza Hut, and Wendy's.

Canyon Star Restaurant and Saloon ★ AMERICAN/MEXICAN This place aims to compete with El Tovar Dining Room (above) and the Arizona Room (above), serving adequate but expensive Southwestern cuisine a la carte—meaning the pricey main dishes don't come with sides. The fare includes salmon, barbecue chicken, and well-cooked steaks. The meal is accompanied by live entertainment—evening shows include cowboy music and performances of Native American songs and dances. This place is big, so there usually isn't too long a wait for a table; even if there is, you can relax in the saloon, perhaps on a bar stool with a saddle. ***One note:*** Diners frequently complain that the food here takes a long time to appear from the kitchen.

At the Grand Hotel, 149 Ariz. 64. ✆ **928/638-3333.** Reservations recommended in summer. Main courses $10–$20 lunch, $11–$30 dinner. Daily 2pm–11pm.

Coronado Room ★ SOUTHWESTERN The Coronado Room's classic fare might seem dated to some tastes, but it certainly sticks to the ribs. Appetizers like calamari and Maryland crab cakes seem a little unlikely a mile and a half above sea level; the entrees are more successful, including a twin pork chop, lamb lollipop, buffalo short ribs, steaks, and seafood, and, as a nod to vegetarians, a roast eggplant entree. If you want to be adventurous, they also serve a very good elk tenderloin.

At the Best Western Grand Canyon Squire Inn, 100 Ariz. 64. ✆ **928/638-2681.** Reservations recommended. Main courses $19–$39. Daily 5–10pm.

THE GRAND CANYON NORTH RIM ★★★

216 miles N of Grand Canyon Village (South Rim); 354 miles N of Phoenix; 125 miles W of Page/Lake Powell

Although the North Rim of the Grand Canyon is only 10 miles from the South Rim as the raven flies, it's more than 200 miles by road, and because it is such a long drive from population centers such as Phoenix and Las Vegas, the North Rim gets much less crowded than the South Rim. What's more, it's not even open from early November through mid-May, due to occasional heavy snowfall. There are far fewer activities or establishments here than on the South Rim (no helicopter or plane rides, no IMAX theater, no McDonald's). Most of the millions of people who annually visit the Grand Canyon never make it to this side—and that is exactly why the North Rim is the preferred place to visit if your schedule allows. Crowds, traffic congestion, and parking problems are not unheard of here, but they're a fraction of the headaches you'll encounter on the South Rim.

The North Rim is on the Kaibab Plateau—named from the Paiute word for "mountain lying down"—which is more than 8,000 feet high on average. At this higher elevation, instead of the South Rim's mix of junipers and ponderosa pines, you'll see dense forests of ponderosa pines, Douglas firs, and aspens interspersed with large meadows, giving the North Rim a much more alpine feel than the South Rim. The additional 1,000 feet of elevation also means that the North Rim gets considerably more snow in winter than the South Rim. The highway south from Jacob Lake is not plowed in winter, when Grand Canyon Lodge closes down.

Essentials

ARRIVING The North Rim is at the end of Ariz. 67 (the North Rim Pkwy.), about an hour's drive south of Jacob's Lake and U.S. 89A. It's nearly a 4-hour drive from Flagstaff.

Between mid-May and mid-October, **Trans Canyon** (www.trans-canyonshuttle.com; ✆ **928/638-2820**) offers shuttle-bus service between the South Rim and the North Rim. Vans leave the South Rim at 8am and 1:30pm and arrive at the North Rim at 1:30pm and 6pm; other vans leave the North Rim at 7am and 2pm to arrive at the South Rim at 11:30am and 6:30pm. The fare is $90 each way. Reservations are required.

FEES The park entry fee is $35 per car and is good for 1 week. Your receipt serves as your admission pass. (See box on p. 225 for details on America the Beautiful park passes.)

VISITOR INFORMATION For information before leaving home, contact **Grand Canyon National Park** (www.nps.gov/grca; ✆ **928/638-7888**). At the entrance gate, you'll be given a North Rim pocket map and services guide. Within the park, the **North Rim Visitor Center,** adjacent to the Grand Canyon Lodge, is open mid-May to mid-October daily 8am to 6pm.

Exploring the North Rim

While it's hard to beat the view from a chair on the terrace of the Grand Canyon Lodge, the best North Rim spots for seeing the canyon are Bright Angel Point, Point Imperial, and Cape Royal. A half-mile trail near the Grand Canyon Lodge leads to **Bright Angel Point ★**, where you can see and hear Roaring Springs, 3,600 feet below the rim, the North Rim's only water source. From here you can even see Grand Canyon Village on the South Rim.

An Important Note

Visitor facilities at the North Rim are open only from mid-May to mid-October. From mid-October to November (or until snow closes the North Rim Parkway), the park is open for day use only. The campground may be open after mid-October, weather permitting.

The North Rim offers entirely different Grand Canyon views. From the Cape Royal overlook, Wotan's Throne can be seen in its full majesty.

At 8,803 feet, **Point Imperial ★** is the highest point on the North Rim, affording a sweeping view of the eastern Grand Canyon, the great staircase of stone called the Vermilion Cliffs, the northern reaches of the Painted Desert, and the confluence of the Little Colorado and Colorado rivers. The promontory, which lies about 5 road miles northeast of the park entrance, is easily accessible by car. The **Point Imperial/Nankoweap Trail** leads north from Point Imperial along the rim of the canyon.

You can continue on the same road another 17 miles to **Cape Royal ★★**, the most spectacular setting on the North Rim. Note that the route becomes more and more sinuous here; it's best left to rugged vehicles and drivers not bothered by precipitous heights. Along the way you'll pass several other scenic overlooks. Across the road from the **Walhalla Overlook** are the ruins of an Ancestral Puebloan structure, and, just before Cape Royal, the **Angel's Window Overlook** gives you a breathtaking view of the natural bridge that forms Angel's Window. Once at Cape Royal, you can follow a trail across this natural bridge to a towering promontory overlooking the canyon.

Once you've had your fill of simply taking in the views, you may want to stretch your legs on a trail or two. The shortest is the .5-mile paved trail to Bright Angel Point, along which you'll have plenty of company but also plenty of breathtaking vistas. For a relatively easy hike away from the crowds, try part of the 9.6-mile **Widforss Point Trail** (a quarter-mile south of the road to Cape Royal, turn west onto a dirt road that leads 1 mile to the trail head).

If you have time for only one hike here, however, make it the **North Kaibab Trail.** Only extremely fit hikers with a camping permit should tackle the full trail, which leads 14 miles down to Phantom Ranch and the Colorado River, an almost 6,000-ft. drop in elevation. For a day hike, try **Roaring Springs,** a 9.5-mile round-trip hike descending 3,000 feet, which takes 7 to 8 hours. To shorten this hike, turn around after 2 miles at the **Supai Tunnel,** which is only 1,500 feet or so below the rim.

To see the canyon from a saddle, contact **Grand Canyon Trail Rides** (www.canyonrides.com; ✆ **435/679-8665**), which offers mule rides varying in length from 1 hour ($45) to a half-day ($90). One half-day ride goes down into the canyon to the Supai Tunnel.

En Route to the North Rim: The Arizona Strip

FROM THE SOUTH & EAST: LEES FERRY

About 15 miles north of its intersection with U.S. 89, U.S. 89A crosses the Colorado River at **Lees Ferry** in Marble Canyon. The original **Navajo Bridge** over the river here was replaced in 1995, and the old bridge is now open to pedestrians. From the bridge, 470 feet above the Colorado River, there's a beautiful view of Marble Canyon. At the west end of the bridge, the Navajo Bridge Interpretive Center, operated by the National Park Service, is partly housed in a stone building built during the Depression by the Civilian Conservation Corps (CCC). At the east end of the bridge, which is on the Navajo Reservation, interpretive signs tell the story of Lees Ferry from the Native American perspective.

Lees Ferry, which is the southern tip of the Glen Canyon National Recreation Area (p. 325), is the starting point for raft trips through the Grand Canyon; for many years it was the only place to cross the Colorado River for hundreds of miles in either direction. This stretch of the river is legendary among anglers for its trophy trout fishing. **Lees Ferry Anglers** (www.leesferry.com; ✆ **800/962-9755** or 928/355-2261), 11 miles west of the bridge on U.S. 89A, is fishing headquarters for the region. It sells all manner of fly-fishing tackle, rents waders and boats, and offers advice about good spots to try your luck; it also operates a guide service. A guide and boat cost $425 per day for one person, $525 per day for two people.

Continuing west, 89A passes under the **Vermilion Cliffs,** so named for their deep-red coloring and now the namesake of the **Vermilion Cliffs National Monument** (www.blm.gov/visit/vermilion-cliffs; ✆ **435/688-3200**). At the base of these cliffs, huge boulders balance on narrow columns of eroded soil, an otherworldly sight. Access to the national monument is very limited, and for the most part, a four-wheel-drive vehicle is required. Along this unpopulated stretch of road are three rustic lodges (p. 256).

Along this same stretch of road, a gravel road leads north to the **Coyote Buttes ★★★**, some of the most unusual rock formations in Arizona. Basically, these striated conical sandstone hills are petrified sand dunes, which should give you a good idea of why one area of the Coyote Buttes is called the Wave. The buttes are a favorite of photographers. You must have a permit ($7 per person) to visit this area, and only 20 people a day are allowed in (with a maximum group size of six people). Half of the available permits are issued by lottery (applications must be submitted 4 months in advance); the other half are distributed to people try their luck by just showing up in person. For more information, contact the Bureau of Land Management's **Arizona Strip Field Office** (www.blm.gov/programs/recreation/permits-and-passes/lotteries-and-permit-systems/arizona/coyote-buttes; ✆ **435/688-3200**). There's no actual trail to the buttes—you have to navigate by way of the photos and map that you'll be sent when you receive your permit.

One last detour to consider: An area known as the **East Rim,** not to be confused with the East Rim across the river, lies just outside the park in Kaibab National Forest; it's a great place to go to escape the crowds. A few miles north of the park entrance, about ¾ mile south of DeMotte Campground, turn east on gravel Forest Road (F.R.) 611. Follow F.R. 611 for about 1½ miles; from here you can either continue 3 miles to the **East Rim Viewpoint,** or turn onto F.R. 610, go 6 miles, and turn onto F.R. 219 for another 4 miles to the **Marble Viewpoint.** For more information, contact the **North Kaibab Ranger Station** (www.fs.usda.gov/kaibab; ✆ **928/643-7395**), or in summer, the **Kaibab Plateau Visitors Center** (✆ **928/643-7298**), in Jacob Lake at the junction of Ariz. 67 and U.S. 89A.

FROM THE NORTH: FREDONIA & JACOB LAKE

North of the North Rim lies a remote and sparsely populated region of the state known as the Arizona Strip. To learn more about the pioneer history of this area, take Ariz. 389 west from Fredonia for 14 miles to **Pipe Spring National Monument,** 406 N. Pipe Spring Rd., Fredonia (www.nps.gov/pisp; ✆ **928/643-7105**). Here you'll see an early Mormon ranch house, known as Winsor Castle, built in the style of a fort for protection from Indians (occasionally the wives of polygamists hiding out from the law also stayed here). A small museum contains exhibits on both Mormon settlers and the Paiute Indians who have long inhabited this region. There are tours throughout the day, and in summer there are living-history demonstrations. The monument is open daily 8am to 5pm March through August, 8:30am to 4:30pm September through April (closed New Year's Day, Thanksgiving, and Christmas). Admission is $10 per adult.

If you have an interest in Native American rock art, make time to hike in remote **Snake Gulch,** which has some of the most impressive and extensive pictographs in the state. The red-and-yellow pictographs in this remote canyon date from the Basketmaker period (300 B.C.–A.D. 800). The first ones are in a shallow cave about 2 miles from the trail head; continue down the canyon for 2 or 3 miles to find many more shallow caves with pictographs. The easiest way to reach the Snake Gulch trail head is from Fredonia, driving 21 miles south on paved F.R. 22, which turns into F.R. 422 for another 1½ miles. Turn right (west) on F.R. 423 for 1.3 miles to F.R. 642, which heads north 2.6 miles to the trail head. You can also get there from Jacob Lake, turning west off Ariz. 67 just south of the Jacob Lake Visitor Center onto F.R. 461, which leads 9 miles to F.R. 422. Much of this route is on gravel roads, but they should be passable to regular passenger vehicles unless it has rained or snowed recently. Carry plenty of water, especially in summer, when it can be extremely hot here. Spring and fall are the best times to visit. For more information, contact the **North Kaibab Ranger District,** 430 S. Main St. (P.O. Box 248), Fredonia (www.fs.usda.gov/kaibab; ✆ **928/643-7395.**

Where to Stay on the North Rim

INSIDE THE PARK

Grand Canyon Lodge ★★ Perched right on the canyon rim, this classic mountain lodge is as impressive a lodge as any you'll find in a national park; it's listed on the National Register of Historic Places. The stone-and-log main building has a soaring ceiling and a viewing room set up with chairs facing a wall of glass; on either side of this room are flagstone terraces furnished with rustic chairs. Accommodations vary from standard motel units to rustic mountain cabins to comfortable modern cabins. The frontier cabins, although cramped and paneled with dark wood, were renovated in 2009 and capture the feeling of a mountain retreat better than the other options. The two-bedroom pioneer cabins, good for families, were also remodeled in 2009. Only a few units have canyon views, but the dining hall has two walls of glass so you can gaze onto the canyon at every meal.

North Rim. (Contact Forever Resorts, 7501 E. McCormick Pkwy., Scottsdale.) www.grandcanyonlodgenorth.com. ✆ **877/386-4383** or 480/337-1320. 218 units. $141 double; $155–$228 cabin. Children 15 and under stay free in parent's room. Closed mid-Oct–mid-May. **Amenities:** 3 restaurants; lounge; bikes; free Wi-Fi.

OUTSIDE THE PARK

Five miles north of the park on Ariz. 67, the **Kaibab Lodge** (kaibablodge.com; ✆ **928/638-2389**) offers rustic cabins and a dining room and gift shop, at rates from $100 to $200. You'll also find lots of budget accommodations in Kanab, Utah, 37 miles northwest of Jacob Lake via U.S. 89A.

Jacob Lake Inn ★ About 30 miles north of the North Rim park entrance, this lodge at the crossroads of Jacob Lake is always a busy spot in summer. While most of the units here are old cabins that tend to be cramped and old-fashioned, there are also two dozen modern motel-style rooms in a contemporary mountain-rustic lodge. I recommend these latter rooms, which are the inn's only rooms with TVs, telephones, and high-speed Internet access. They're more expensive than the cabins, but they are the nicest rooms in the area. Stock up on cookies at the inn's bakery.

Ariz. 67/U.S. 89A, Jacob Lake. www.jacoblake.com. ✆ **928/643-7232.** 62 units. $96–$128 cabin double; $159 motel/lodge double (lower rates in winter). Pets accepted in most rooms ($10 per night). **Amenities:** Restaurant; free Wi-Fi.

EN ROUTE TO THE PARK

If you don't have a reservation at the North Rim's Grand Canyon Lodge, call the places recommended below to see if you can get a reservation. If so, you can continue on to the North Rim the next morning. Lodges anywhere near the canyon fill up early in the day if they aren't already fully booked with reservations made months in advance.

Cliff Dwellers Lodge ★ Affiliated with Lees Ferry Anglers, this motel is the area's de facto fly anglers' headquarters and tends to stay filled up with people who are here to fish for the Colorado's huge rainbow trout. Its newer, more expensive rooms are standard motel units with combination tub/showers; they're the best and most predictable rooms in the Vermilion Cliffs area. Older rooms, in an interesting stone-walled building, have knotty pine walls and showers only. The lodge is close to some spectacular balanced rocks, and it's about 11 miles east to Lees Ferry. The views are unforgettable; the restaurant is good if perhaps a touch pricey.

U.S. 89A milepost 547, Marble Canyon. www.cliffdwellerslodge.com. ✆ **800/962-9755** or 928/355-2261. 20 units. $80–$100 double (lower rates in winter). **Amenities:** Restaurant; no Wi-Fi.

Lees Ferry Lodge at Vermilion Cliffs ★ Located at the foot of the Vermilion Cliffs, 4 miles west of the Colorado River, Lees Ferry Lodge, built in 1929 of native stone and rough-hewn timber beams, is a small place with simple, rustic accommodations. However, the lodge's restaurant serves as a sort of de facto community center for area residents, and owner Maggie Sacher, an Illinois transplant, is usually on hand to answer questions and share stories. The patio seating area in front of the lodge has fabulous views, and the restaurant has a great old-fashioned atmosphere. With its rustic character and friendly feel, this is a fine place to stay in the area.

U.S. 89A, Marble Canyon. www.vermilioncliffs.com. ✆ **928/355-2231.** 10 units. $70–$90 double. Children 4 and under stay free in parent's room. Pets accepted. **Amenities:** Restaurant; no Wi-Fi.

Marble Canyon Lodge ★ The Marble Canyon Lodge, built in the 1920s just west of the Navajo Bridge, is the closest lodge to the put-in spot for people rafting the Grand Canyon, and consequently this lodge is popular primarily with rafters. Accommodations are mostly in aging motel-style rooms that lack the modernity of the rooms at Cliff Dwellers Lodge or the character of the rooms at the Lees Ferry Lodge at Vermilion Cliffs. In addition to the restaurant, a general store specializes in rafting supplies.

U.S. 89A, Marble Canyon. www.marblecanyoncompany.com. ✆ **800/726-1789** or 928/355-2225. 56 units. $79–$89 double. Children 11 and under stay free in parent's room. Pets accepted. **Amenities:** Restaurant; lounge; no Wi-Fi.

CAMPGROUNDS

Just north of Grand Canyon Lodge, the **North Rim Campground** (✆ **928/638-7888** or 928/638-7814), with 90 sites and no hookups for RVs, is the only campground at the North Rim. It's open mid-May to mid-October.

Reservations are recommended and can be made up to 6 months in advance by calling the National Recreation Reservation Service (www.recreation.gov; ✆ **877/444-6777** or 518/885-3639). Campsites cost $18 to $25 per night.

Two nearby campgrounds are just outside the park in the Kaibab National Forest. The closest to the park entrance, the **DeMotte Campground** (May 15–Oct 15), has 38 sites and charges $20. **Jacob Lake Campground** (May 15–Oct 15), 30 miles north of the park entrance, has 51 sites and also charges $20 per night. Neither campground takes reservations. You can also camp anywhere in the Kaibab National Forest as long as you're more than 200 feet from a main roadway or a quarter-mile from a water source. So if you can't find a site in a campground, simply pull off the highway in the national forest and park your RV or pitch your tent. Contact the North Kaibab Ranger District, 430 S. Main St., Fredonia (www.fs.usda.gov/kaibab; ✆ **928/643-7395**) for information.

The **Kaibab Camper Village** (www.kaibabcampervillage.com; ✆ **800/525-0924**, 928/643-7804 May 14–Oct 15, or 928/635-5251 other months) is a privately owned campground in the crossroads of Jacob Lake, 30 miles north of the park entrance. It's open from mid-May to mid-October and has around 100 sites. Rates are $20 for tent sites, $40–$45 for RV sites with full hookups. Make reservations well in advance.

Where to Eat on the North Rim

INSIDE THE PARK

Grand Canyon Lodge (p. 255) has a dining room with a splendid view. More casual choices at the lodge include a cafeteria and a saloon that serves light meals.

OUTSIDE THE PARK

Your only choices for a meal outside the park are the **Kaibab Lodge** (www.kaibablodge.com; ✆ **928/638-2389**), just north of the entrance, and the **Jacob Lake Inn** (www.jacoblake.com; ✆ **928/643-7232**), 45 miles north at the junction with U.S. 89A.

FLAGSTAFF ★★

150 miles N of Phoenix; 32 miles E of Williams; 80 miles S of Grand Canyon Village

Born of the railroads and named for a flagpole, Flagstaff is the main jumping-off point for trips to the Grand Canyon, but it's also home to Northern Arizona University, whose students ensure that this is a lively, liberal town. With its wide variety of restaurants, three national monuments nearby, and one of the state's finest museums, Flagstaff makes an ideal base for exploring northern Arizona.

The San Francisco Peaks, just north of the city, are the site of the Arizona Snowbowl ski area, one of the state's main winter playgrounds. In summer, miles of trails through these same mountains attract hikers and mountain bikers; ride the chairlift and you'll get a panoramic vista that stretches 70 miles north to the Grand Canyon. Volcanic eruptions 900 to 1,000 years ago turned the land east of the San Francisco Peaks into fertile farmland, which the Sinagua people cultivated. Today the ruins of their ancient villages, scattered across lonely, windswept plains, are all that remain of their culture, but their living descendants remain on the land today on the Hopi mesas.

It was as a railroad town that Flagstaff made its fortunes, and the historic downtown offers a glimpse of the days when the city's fortunes rode the rails. The railroad still runs right through the middle of Flagstaff, and though the train horns don't sound within the city limits, the ground still rumbles when the train passes. It makes a picturesque frame for an Arizona city that is emerging as a destination worthy of visiting on its own, quite apart from the neighboring attractions.

Essentials

ARRIVING Flagstaff is on I-40, one of the main U.S. east-west interstates. I-17 starts here and heads south to Phoenix, a 2¼-hour drive. Ariz. 89A connects Flagstaff to Sedona by way of Oak Creek Canyon (45 minutes), and U.S. 180 leads to the South Rim of the Grand Canyon (1½ hours).

Flagstaff Pulliam **Airport** is 3 miles south of Flagstaff off I-17. **Amtrak** (www.amtrak.com; ✆ **800/872-7245**) offers service to Flagstaff from Chicago and Los Angeles. The train station is at 1 E. Rte. 66. The **Greyhound** bus station (www.greyhound.com) is at 880 E. Butler Ave. (✆ **928/774-4573**).

GETTING AROUND Call **A Friendly Cab** (www.afriendlycab.com; ✆ **800/853-4445** or 928/774-4444) if you need a taxi. The standard rate is $3 plus $1.70 a mile. **Mountain Line Transit** (www.mountainline.az.gov; ✆ **928/779-6624**) provides public bus transit around the city; the fare is $1.25, or $2.50 for a day pass.

VISITOR INFORMATION The **Flagstaff Visitor Center,** 1 E. Rte. 66 (www.flagstaffarizona.org; ✆ **800/379-0065** or 928/774-9541), located in the Amtrak station, is open Monday to Saturday 8am to 5pm and Sunday 9am to 4pm; it's closed Thanksgiving, Christmas, and New Year's Day. Be sure to see the marvelous model train that glides around the center's gift shop.

Exploring Flagstaff

Heading into Flagstaff from the south, I-17 becomes Milton Rd., which leads past Northern Arizona University. Eventually it merges with Historic Route 66, hangs a right, and then runs parallel to the railroad tracks through downtown, where it intersects with San Francisco St., downtown's main street. Humphreys St. leads north out of town toward the San Francisco Peaks and the Grand Canyon's South Rim.

Downtown Flag, as the residents abbreviate the town's name, is the city's **historic district,** an eclectic mix of bistros, breweries, bookstores, bars, and boutiques, to say nothing of outdoor sports shops and New Age stores, all speaking to the various constituencies that make the town their home. Its old brick buildings now hold shops selling Native American crafts, works by local

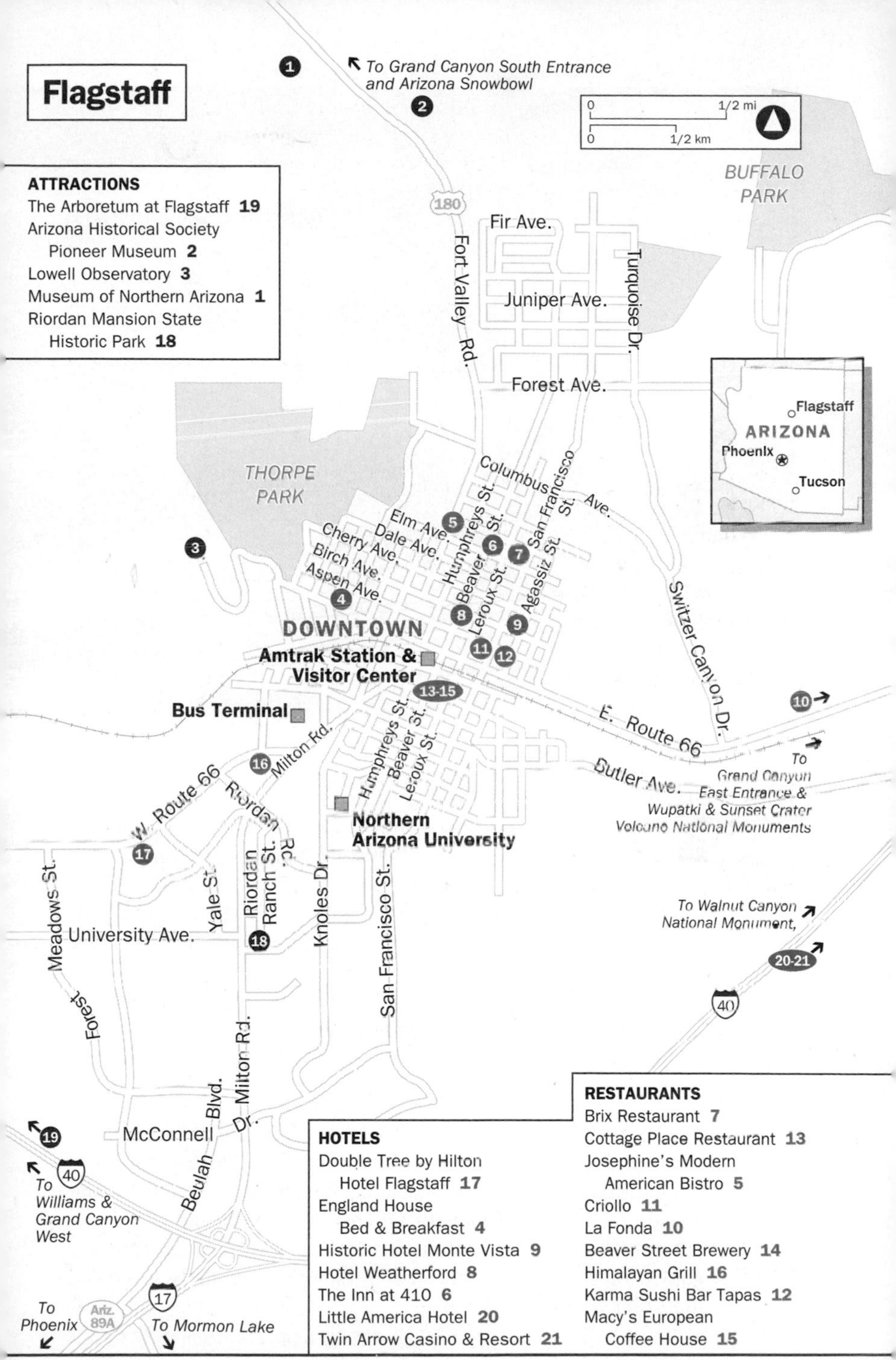
Flagstaff
ATTRACTIONS
The Arboretum at Flagstaff 19
Arizona Historical Society Pioneer Museum 2
Lowell Observatory 3
Museum of Northern Arizona 1
Riordan Mansion State Historic Park 18
To Grand Canyon South Entrance and Arizona Snowbowl
0 1/2 mi
0 1/2 km
BUFFALO PARK
180
Fir Ave.
Fort Valley Rd.
Juniper Ave.
Turquoise Dr.
Forest Ave.
Flagstaff
ARIZONA
Phoenix
Tucson
THORPE PARK
Columbus Ave.
San Francisco St.
Humphreys St.
Elm Ave.
Dale Ave.
Cherry Ave.
Birch Ave.
Aspen Ave.
Beaver St.
Leroux St.
Agassiz St.
Switzer Canyon Dr.
DOWNTOWN
Amtrak Station & Visitor Center
13-15
Bus Terminal
E. Route 66
Butler Ave.
Milton Rd.
W. Route 66
Riordan Rd.
Humphreys St.
Beaver St.
Leroux St.
Northern Arizona University
To Grand Canyon East Entrance & Wupatki & Sunset Crater Volcano National Monuments
Meadows St.
Yale St.
Riordan Ranch St.
Knoles Dr.
San Francisco St.
University Ave.
To Walnut Canyon National Monument,
20-21
40
Forest
Milton Rd.
Beulah Blvd.
McConnell Dr.
To Williams & Grand Canyon West
40
17
To Phoenix
Ariz. 89A
To Mormon Lake
HOTELS
Double Tree by Hilton Hotel Flagstaff 17
England House Bed & Breakfast 4
Historic Hotel Monte Vista 9
Hotel Weatherford 8
The Inn at 410 6
Little America Hotel 20
Twin Arrow Casino & Resort 21
RESTAURANTS
Brix Restaurant 7
Cottage Place Restaurant 13
Josephine's Modern American Bistro 5
Criollo 11
La Fonda 10
Beaver Street Brewery 14
Himalayan Grill 16
Karma Sushi Bar Tapas 12
Macy's European Coffee House 15

Flagstaff's historic train station sits in the heart of downtown, right on old Route 66.

artists, Route 66 souvenirs, and various other Arizona mementos such as rocks, minerals, and crystals. **Puchteca Indian Goods,** 20 N. San Francisco St. (✆ **928/774-2414**) has some really interesting Native American jewelry and pottery; across the street, the **Artists Gallery,** 17 N. San Francisco St. (www.flagstaffartistsgallery.com; ✆ **928/773-0958**) is full of art by local artists. Bibliophiles should check out **Starrlight Books,** 15 N. Leroux St. (✆ **928/774-6813**), which sells first editions and other hard-bound books as well as contemporary work, including plenty of books about the region. If you need any outdoor gear, **Babbitt's Backcountry Outfitters,** 12 E. Aspen Ave. (www.babbittsbackcountry.com; ✆ **928/774-4775**) has an extensive inventory of equipment for just about any outdoor pursuit.

The Arboretum at Flagstaff ★ GARDENS Covering 200 acres, this arboretum, the highest-elevation research garden in the U.S., focuses on plants of the high desert, coniferous forests, and alpine tundra, all of which environments are found in the Flagstaff vicinity. On the grounds you can visit a butterfly garden, an herb garden, a shade garden, and a passive solar greenhouse. There are guided tours daily at 11am and 1pm, as well as regularly scheduled bird and wildflower walks.

4001 S. Woody Mountain Rd. www.thearb.org. ✆ **928/774-1442.** $10 adults, $7 seniors and students, $5 ages 3–17, free for kids 2 and under. Wed–Mon 9am–4pm (until 5pm Memorial Day–Labor Day). Closed Nov–Mar.

Arizona Historical Society Pioneer Museum ★ MUSEUM Housed in a stone building constructed in 1908 as a hospital for the indigent (in other words, a poor farm), this small historical museum contains a historical collection from northern Arizona's pioneer days. Barbed wire, livestock brands, saddles, and trapping and timber displays round out the collection.

2340 N. Fort Valley Rd. www.arizonahistoricalsociety.org. ✆ **928/774-6272.** $6 adults, $5 seniors and adult students, $3 students 7–17, free for kids 6 and under. Mon-Sat 9am–5pm (10am–4pm Nov–Apr); Sun 10am–4pm Memorial Day–Labor Day. Closed New Year's Day, Thanksgiving, and Christmas.

Lowell Observatory ★ OBSERVATORY Located atop aptly named Mars Hill, this is one of the oldest astronomical observatories in the Southwest, founded in 1894 by Percival Lowell. Over the years the observatory has played important roles in contemporary astronomy—among the work carried out here were Lowell's study of the planet Mars and the calculations that led him to predict the existence of Pluto. (Thirteen years after Lowell's death, Pluto was finally discovered, almost exactly where he had predicted it would be.) The facility consists of outdoor displays, several observatories, and a visitor center with lots of fun and educational exhibits. During the day, there are guided tours every hour between 11am and 3pm; at 10am, 1pm, and 4pm, you can look at the sun through a small telescope that was designed for safe viewing. However, the main attraction is the chance to observe the stars and planets through the observatory's 24-inch telescope. Keep in mind that the telescope domes are not heated, so if you come up to stargaze, be sure to dress appropriately. There are no programs on cloudy nights.

1400 W. Mars Hill Rd. www.lowell.edu. ✆ **928/774-3358.** $15 adults, $14 seniors and students, $8 kids 5–17. Mon–Sat 10am–10pm, Sun 10am–5pm. Closed New Year's Day, Easter, Thanksgiving, and Dec 24–25.

Museum of Northern Arizona ★★ MUSEUM Small but surprisingly thorough, this museum is an ideal first stop on an exploration of northern Arizona. The recently renovated ethnography exhibit is a model of interpretation, with tribal stories told in the voices of the people themselves. You'll learn, through state-of-the-art exhibits, about the archaeology, ethnology, geology, biology, and fine arts of the region. The cornerstone of the museum is an exhibit exploring life on the Colorado Plateau from 15,000 B.C. to the present. Among the other displays are a life-size kiva (ceremonial room) and

Desert Sunset Panorama

For an unforgettable sunset view, head south of town to what people hereabouts call the **Edge of the World:** an overlook at the head of Ariz. 89A as it climbs out of the Verde Valley over the towering Mogollon Rim. There you'll see the red rocks of Sedona spread out far below, colored even more vividly by the setting sun.

a small but interesting collection of kachinas. The large gift shop is full of contemporary Native American arts and crafts, and during the summer special exhibits and sales focus on Hopi and Navajo arts and crafts.

The museum itself is built of native stone, with a courtyard where vegetation from all six life zones of northern Arizona grows. Outside, a short self-guided nature trail leads through a narrow canyon.

3101 N. Fort Valley Rd. (2 mi N of downtown on U.S. 180). www.musnaz.org. ✆ **928/774-5213.** $12 adults, $10 seniors and military, $8 students, free for kids under 10. Daily 10am–5pm. Closed New Year's Day, Thanksgiving, and Christmas.

Riordan Mansion State Historic Park ★ MANSION Built in 1904 for local timber barons Michael and Timothy Riordan, this 13,000-square-foot, 40-room mansion—Arizona's finest example of an Arts and Crafts–era building—is actually two houses connected by a large central hall. Each brother and his family occupied half of the house (the rooflines were constructed differently so visitors could tell the two sides apart). Its exterior is faced with log slabs to look like a giant log cabin; inside, mission-style furnishings and touches of Art Nouveau styling make it clear that this family kept up with the fashions of their time. The west wing holds displays on, among other things, Stickley furniture. Guided tours provide a glimpse into the lives of two of Flagstaff's most influential pioneers. Incidentally, the Riordan Mansion was designed by Charles Whittlesey, the creator of Grand Canyon's El Tovar Hotel (p. 244).

409 W. Riordan Rd. (off S. Milton Rd., just N of I-17/I-40 jct.). www.azstateparks.com. ✆ **928/779-4395.** $10 adults, $5 ages 7–13. May–Oct daily 9:30am–5pm; Nov–Apr Thurs–Mon 9:30am–5pm. Guided tours hourly 10am–4pm. Closed Christmas.

OUTLYING ATTRACTIONS

Sunset Crater Volcano National Monument ★ NATURAL ATTRACTION Dotting the landscape northeast of Flagstaff are more than 400 volcanic craters, of which Sunset Crater Volcano is the youngest. Taking its name from the colors of the cinders near its summit, Sunset Crater Volcano stands 1,000 feet tall and began forming around 1040. Over a period of more than 150 years, the volcano erupted repeatedly (creating the red-and-yellow cinder cone seen today), eventually covering an 800-sq.-mile area with ash, lava, and cinders. A 1-mile interpretive trail passes through a desolate landscape of lava flows, cinders, and ash as it skirts the volcano's base. If you want to climb to the top of a cinder cone, take the 1-mile Lenox Crater Trail. In the visitor center (at the west entrance to the national monument), you can learn more about the formation of Sunset Crater and about volcanoes in general. Near the visitor center, the 44-site **Bonito Campground,** open early May to mid-October, charges $24 for a campsite.

14 mi N of Flagstaff off U.S. 89. www.nps.gov/sucr. ✆ **928/526-0502.** Entry $25 per vehicle (combined admission w/Wupatki National Monument, below). Daily sunrise–sunset; visitor center daily 9am–5pm. Visitor center closed Christmas.

Walnut Canyon National Monument ★ ANCIENT SITE In this 400-foot-deep wooded canyon east of Flagstaff, the remains of 300 small

Visitors can even walk inside the small but remarkably intact Sinagua ruins in Walnut Canyon.

13th century Sinagua cliff dwellings can be seen in the undercut layers of limestone. These cliff dwellings, though not as impressive as the ruins at Montezuma Castle National Monument (p. 185) or nearby Wupatki National Monument (below), are worth visiting for the chance to explore the well-preserved rooms, which the canyon setting protected from the elements (and from enemies). The same Sinagua people who built and then abandoned the stone pueblos in Wupatki National Monument migrated southward to settle for 150 years in Walnut Canyon. A self-guided trail leads from the visitor center on the canyon rim down 185 feet to a section of the canyon wall where 25 cliff dwellings can be viewed up close (some can even be entered). Bring binoculars so that you can scan the canyon walls for other cliff dwellings. Twice a month from Memorial Day to Labor Day (on the first and last Saturday), guided hikes are led into the monument's backcountry (reservations required). There's a picnic area near the visitor center.

7½ mi E of Flagstaff on Walnut Canyon Rd. (exit 204 off I-40). www.nps.gov/waca. ✆ **928/526-3367.** $15 adults, free for kids 15 and under. May–Oct daily 8am–5pm; Nov–Apr daily 9am–5pm. Visitor center closed Christmas.

Wupatki National Monument ★★ ANCIENT SITE The landscape northeast of Flagstaff is a desolate, sparsely populated region carpeted with volcanic ash deposited in the 11th century. The area also contains hundreds of archaeological sites, the most impressive being the pueblo ruins left by the

Sinagua ("wupatki" means "without water" in Spanish), who inhabited this area from around 1100 until around 1250. Contemporary Hopis and Zunis claim them as their ancestors, and it is easy to see the similarity between the stone-walled pueblos here and traditional homes on the nearby Hopi Reservation. Today the ruins of several ancient villages are preserved in this national monument, the largest being **Wupatki Ruin,** in the southeastern part of the monument. Here the Sinagua built a sprawling three-story pueblo containing nearly 100 rooms. They also constructed what is believed to be a ball court, which, although quite different in design from courts built by the Aztec and Maya peoples farther south, suggests a similar game was played in this region. Another circular stone structure just below the main ruins may have been an amphitheater or a dance plaza. The most unusual feature of Wupatki, however, is a natural phenomenon: a blowhole, which may have been the reason this pueblo was constructed here. A network of small underground tunnels and chambers acts as a giant barometer, blowing air through the blowhole when the underground air is under greater pressure than the outside air. On hot days, cool air rushes out of the blowhole with amazing force. Several other ruins within the national monument are easily accessible by car: **Nalakihu, Citadel,** and **Lomaki** are the closest to U.S. 89; **Wukoki,** built atop a huge sandstone boulder near Wupatki, is particularly picturesque. The visitor center adjacent to the Wupatki ruins has some interesting exhibits on the Sinagua and Ancestral Puebloan people. November through March, there are reservation-only guided hikes on Saturdays. All hikes begin at noon and last from 2 to 3 hours.

The huge pueblo ruins of Wupatki rise out of a desolate, windswept landscape.

33 mi N of Flagstaff off U.S. 89. www.nps.gov/wupa. ✆ **928/679-2365.** Entry $25 per vehicle (combined admission w/Sunset Crater Volcano National Monument, above). Daily sunrise–sunset; visitor center daily 9am–5pm (closed Christmas).

Outdoor Activities

Flagstaff is northern Arizona's center for outdoor activities. Chief among them is skiing at **Arizona Snowbowl** (www.snowbowl.ski; ✆ **928/779-1951**), on the slopes of Mount Agassiz, from which you can see all the way to the North Rim of the Grand Canyon. Snowbowl has 4 chairlifts, 32 runs, and 2,300 vertical feet of slopes (an excellent mix of beginner, intermediate, and

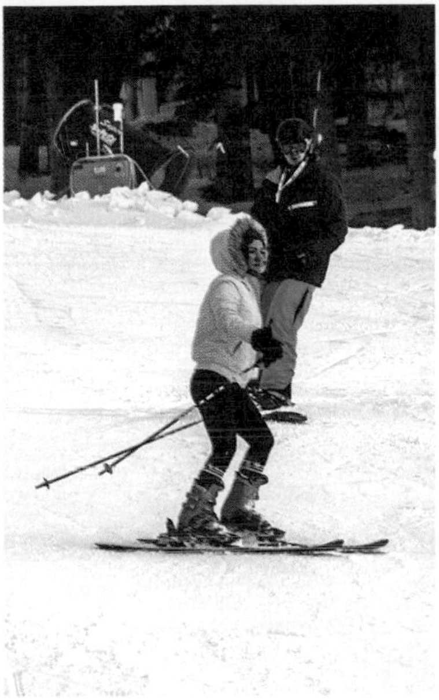

From the slopes of Flagstaff's Arizona Snowbowl, skiers can glimpse the Grand Canyon North Rim in the distance.

advanced slopes), as well as ski rentals and a children's ski program. It's the ski area most easily accessed from Phoenix, so Snowbowl sees a lot of weekend traffic from the snow-starved denizens of the desert. Conditions are, however, very unreliable; it can be shut down for weeks on end when there's not enough snow. All-day lift tickets are $79 adults, $66 teens 13 to 17, $47 seniors, $44 ages 8 to 12, and free for kids 7 and under and seniors 70 and over. In summer, you can ride a chairlift almost to the summit of Mount Agassiz and enjoy sweeping views across seemingly all of northern Arizona. In summer the round-trip lift-ticket costs $19 adults, $15 seniors and kids 8 to 12. To get here, take U.S. 180 N from Flagstaff for 7 miles and turn right onto Snow Bowl Rd.

When no snow is on the ground, there are plenty of trails for hiking amid the San Francisco Peaks, and many national forest trails are open to mountain bikes. Late September, when the aspens have turned a brilliant golden yellow, is one of the best times of year for a hike in Flagstaff's mountains. If you've got the stamina, do the **Humphreys Trail,** which climbs more than 3,300 feet in 4.5 miles. Needless to say, the views from the 12,633-foot summit, the highest point in Arizona, are stupendous. The trail head is 7 miles north of Flagstaff on U.S. 180 N (turn right on Snow Bowl Rd. and go to the parking area by the ski lodge).

For a short hike with a big payoff, the 2.5-mile round-trip hike to **Red Mountain** leads to a fascinating red-walled cinder cone that long ago collapsed to reveal its strange interior walls. Its trail head is north of Flagstaff on U.S. 180, at milepost 247 (a forest road leads west for about a quarter-mile to the trail head parking area).

Another fine local hike explores the **Picture Canyon Preserve,** a 478-acre rocky patch of forest 4 miles east of Flagstaff on Route 66 (take El Paso Flagstaff Rd. 1 mile to the parking area). A 2.8-mile loop trail takes you up and down a steep but low canyon to a waterfall, a petroglyph site, ponds, and an ancient pithouse; part of the 800-mile-long Arizona Trail passes through Picture Canyon as well.

For information on other hikes in the Coconino National Forest, contact the **Flagstaff Ranger Districts,** 5075 N. U.S. 89, Flagstaff 86004 (www.fs.usda.gov/coconino; ✆ **928/526-0866**).

Grand Falls: The Muddy Niagara

At 185 feet tall, Grand Falls, 33 miles east of Flagstaff on the Little Colorado River, are higher than Niagara Falls. Granted, they don't carry nearly the volume of water Niagara does—in fact, most of the year there's no water at all in Grand Falls. They run only during the spring snowmelt season (in years when there has been any snow) and after summer monsoons. Consequently, to see these falls, you need to have good timing. You also need a high-clearance vehicle, because the last 10 miles of the route are on a washboard gravel road that can be impassable if it has rained.

To find Grand Falls, drive north from Flagstaff on U.S. 89A a couple miles to Townsend-Winona Rd., where you turn east and go 8 miles to Leupp Rd. Turn left on Leupp and follow it 14 miles into the Navajo Reservation to Indian Route 70 (you may see a sign for GRAND FALLS BIBLE CHURCH). Turn left (north) onto this gravel road and drive 10 miles to the Little Colorado River. Now turn around and go back ¼ mile to the unmarked rough dirt track on your right. The falls are a few hundred yards down this dirt road.

Where to Stay in Flagstaff

Double Tree by Hilton Hotel Flagstaff ★ With its elegant marble-floored lobby, this is easily the most upscale lodging in Flagstaff. A ballroom, crystal chandelier, luxurious furnishings, and contemporary sculpture lend grandeur to the public spaces. Guest rooms are quite comfortable and have Serta Perfect Sleeper beds. The on-site Japanese teppanyaki and sushi restaurant is one of the best in Arizona.

1175 W. Rte. 66. www.doubletree3.hilton.com. ✆ **928/773-8888.** 183 units. $185–$195 double; $205–$235 suite. Pets allowed ($50 per pet). **Amenities:** 2 restaurants; lounge; exercise room; pool; room service; sauna; free Wi-Fi.

England House Bed & Breakfast ★★ Just 3 blocks from Flagstaff's historic downtown, this B&B is in a beautiful two-story Victorian red-sandstone house built in 1902. This old house was lovingly restored by owners Richard and Laurel Dunn, whose devotion to details has given the England House a delightful period authenticity. The three large guest rooms, all on the second floor, are furnished with 1870s French antiques. There's also a small guest room, called the Pantry (though it isn't really *that* small), on the ground floor. Two rooms are outfitted with Tempur-Pedic mattresses. Breakfasts are served in a bright sunroom just off the kitchen.

614 W. Santa Fe Ave. www.englandhousebandb.com. ✆ **928/214-7350.** 4 units. $139–$209 double. Rates include full breakfast. No children 11 or under. **Amenities:** Concierge; free Wi-Fi.

Historic Hotel Monte Vista ★ This hotel is definitely not for everyone. Although it is historic, it is also a bit run-down and appeals primarily to young travelers who appreciate the low rates and the nightclub just off the lobby. So why stay here? In its day, the Monte Vista hosted the likes of Clark Gable, John Wayne, Carole Lombard, and Gary Cooper, and today, the hotel is supposedly haunted (ask at the front desk for the list of resident ghosts). Opened in 1927, the Monte Vista now has creatively decorated rooms that vary in size and decor. Although the hotel has plenty of old-fashioned flair, don't expect perfection. Check out a room first to see if this is your kind of place.

100 N. San Francisco St. www.hotelmontevista.com. ✆ **928/779-6971.** 50 units, 5 w/shared bath. $65–$85 double w/shared bath, $90–$125 double w/private bath, $120–$175 suite. Children 17 and under stay free in parent's room. **Amenities:** Restaurant; lounge; free Wi-Fi.

Hotel Weatherford ★ This historic hotel in downtown Flagstaff is a relaxed sort of place popular with young travelers; it has loads of character. The distinctive stone-walled 1897 building has a wraparound veranda on its third floor, where you'll also find the beautifully restored Zane Grey Bar and Ballroom. Downstairs are a casual restaurant and the ever-popular Charly's Pub & Grill (p. 271), which has been booking live rock, blues, and jazz acts for more than 3 decades. Charly's serves one of the best Navajo tacos in Flagstaff—it's a favorite hangout of locals in the know. The hotel is the site of Flagstaff's annual New Year's Eve giant pine-cone drop.

23 N. Leroux St. www.weatherfordhotel.com. ✆ **928/779-1919.** 17 units, 3 w/shared bath. $70–$115 double w/shared bath; $115–$175 double w/private bath; $195–$205 suite. Children 12 and under stay free in parent's room. **Amenities:** Restaurant; 3 lounges; free Wi-Fi.

The Inn at 410 ★★ Situated only 2 blocks from historic downtown Flagstaff, this restored 1894 Craftsman home is one of the best B&Bs in Arizona, providing convenience, pleasant surroundings, comfortable rooms, and delicious breakfasts. Guests can lounge and enjoy afternoon tea on the front porch, in the comfortable dining room, or in the garden. Each guest room features a distinctive theme that conjures up the inn's Western heritage. All rooms have fireplaces, and three have two-person whirlpool tubs. Some of the guest rooms are in an adjacent building that overlooks the gardens. **Brix** (below), one of Flagstaff's best restaurants, is right next door.

410 N. Leroux St. www.inn410.com. ✆ **800/774-2008** or 928/774-0088. 10 units. $185–$325 double. 2-night minimum weekends Apr–Oct. Rates include full breakfast and afternoon refreshments. No children 8 or under. **Amenities:** Concierge; exercise room and access to nearby health club; free Wi-Fi.

Little America Hotel ★ Set on 500 acres of ponderosa pine forest, with a trail that winds for 2 miles through the property, this hotel on the east side of Flagstaff might seem at first to be little more than a giant truck stop. However, on closer inspection, you'll find that behind the truck stop stands a surprisingly luxurious and economical hotel set beneath shady pines. The decor tends toward a blend of midcentury modern and contemporary, with plenty of space to stretch out and relax. Rooms vary in size, but all have small private balconies.

2515 E. Butler Ave. (exit 198 off I-40). www.flagstaff.littleamerica.com. ✆ **800/865-1401** or 928/779-2741. 247 units. $199–$299 double; $499–$759 suite. Children 17 and under stay free in parent's room. **Amenities:** Restaurant; lounge; free airport transfers; concierge; exercise room; Jacuzzi; pool; room service; free Wi-Fi.

Twin Arrows Casino and Resort ★ Owned by the Navajo Nation, this recently built five-story casino complex sits on the broad plain that opens a few miles east of hilly, forested Flagstaff and affords superb views of the San Francisco Peaks. Gamblers will appreciate the variety of table games and slots, while foodies have a choice of six restaurants that range from a pricey steakhouse (with, for instance, a $42 porterhouse) to an inexpensive ($9.99) all-day buffet that features Native American dishes. Rooms are spacious and well appointed, and the King Mountain View rooms have that grand vista of the (usually) snowclad peaks a few miles to the west. Stay in the Presidential Suite, if you win downstairs, and the executive chef will cook you a meal in your very own private dining room. The sole downside is the entertainment, which tends to be generic country bands.

22181 Resort Blvd. www.twinarrows.com. ✆ **855/946-8946** or 928/856-7200. 200 rooms. $85–$209 double. **Amenities:** 6 restaurants; fitness center; indoor heated pool; whirlpool; free Wi-Fi.

Where to Eat in Flagstaff

If you're headed north to the Grand Canyon and need a good espresso to get you there, stop at **Late for the Train Espresso,** 1800 N. Fort Valley Rd. (www.lateforthetrain.com; ✆ **928/773-0308**), on U.S. 180 as you drive north out of town. Just look for the old gas station. There's another location downtown at 22 E. Birch Ave. (✆ **928/779-5975**), as well as a kiosk inside the Flagstaff Medical Center at 1200 N. Beaver St. (✆ **928/214-3943**). On cold mornings, though, only one Flagstaff coffee drink will do, and that's the "Hot Monte" at the Hotel Monte Vista's **Rendezvous Coffee House/Martini Bar,** 100 N. San Francisco St. (www.hotelmontevista.com; ✆ **928/779-6971**). It's made with espresso supplied by the local Fire Creek roasters, along with chocolate, milk, cinnamon, and cayenne. If you need to stock up on picnic supplies, try **Whole Foods,** 320 S. Cambridge Lane at Butler Ave. (✆ **928/774-5747**). For good old-fashioned pies, head east of downtown Flagstaff to **Miz Zip's,** 2924 E. Rte. 66 (✆ **928/526-0104**)—just don't try using one of those newfangled credit cards at the cash-only establishment.

EXPENSIVE

Brix Restaurant and Wine Bar ★★ NEW AMERICAN Although it's a bit hard to find (tucked into a corner of an old brick carriage house), Brix, Flagstaff's most contemporary restaurant, is well worth searching out. The menu relies on fresh, seasonal, locally sourced ingredients, so it changes regularly. However, any time of year you'll find a great selection of artisanal cheeses, which make a good starter to a meal here. The chef's creativity shines through in such dishes as scallops with red lentils and rack of elk with red cabbage spätzle and grilled broccolini. There's an excellent wine list to accompany the food.

413 N. San Francisco St. www.brixflagstaff.com. ✆ **928/213-1021.** Reservations recommended. Main courses $29–$41. Tues–Sun 5–9pm.

Cottage Place Restaurant ★ CONTINENTAL/NEW AMERICAN On the south side of the railroad tracks in a neighborhood mostly frequented by college students, Cottage Place is just what its name implies—an unpretentious little cottage. It reopened in 2017 after years of service as a fine dining establishment with a slightly more casual air—but despite the casual appearance, dining here is a formal affair, at least by Flagstaff standards. The menu, which tends toward the rich side, is farmhouse French, with an emphasis on fresh produce and seasonal ingredients. House specialties include steak frites, pork tenderloin, and other carnivorean treats, though there are a couple of choices for vegetarians as well.

126 W. Cottage Ave. www.cottageplace.com. ✆ **928/774-8431.** Reservations recommended. Main courses $20–$32. Tues–Sat 5–9pm; Sun 10am–3pm.

Josephine's Modern American Bistro ★ REGIONAL AMERICAN Housed in a restored Craftsman bungalow with a beautiful stone fireplace and a wide front porch for summer dining, this restaurant combines a historical setting with excellent food that draws on a wide range of influences. The pork osso buco with green-chili polenta is a real winner. At lunch, try the crab-cake po' boy sandwich, a rarity on regional menus. There's a good selection of reasonably priced wines, too.

503 N. Humphreys St. www.josephinesrestaurant.com. ✆ **928/779-3400.** Reservations recommended. Main courses $10–$14 lunch, $20–$33 dinner. Lunch Mon–Fri 11:30am–2pm, dinner Mon–Thurs 5pm–9pm, Fri–Sat 5pm–9:30 pm, brunch Sat–Sun 9am–2pm.

MODERATE

Criollo ★ LATIN AMERICAN Utilizing locally grown and sustainably produced ingredients as much as possible, this casually hip restaurant in downtown Flagstaff, part of the same family as Brix Restaurant and Wine Bar (above), serves flavorful food from a range of Latin American countries. The chicken mole burrito and the fish tacos are excellent, as is the *hallaca*, a tamale made with a banana-leaf wrapper instead of a corn husk. There are lots of small plates in case you just want a light meal, and the bar whips up some very interesting cocktails, such as a charred grapefruit margarita.

16 N. San Francisco St. www.criollolatinkitchen.com. ✆ **928/774-0541.** Reservations recommended. Main courses $11–$22 lunch, $12–$29 dinner. Daily 11am–9 pm.

La Fonda ★ MEXICAN Although it's definitively in Arizona and the Southwest, Flagstaff has never boasted much in the way of regional—and especially Mexican—cuisine. A noteworthy exception is La Fonda, opened in 1958 in the city's nondescript Sunnyside neighborhood; it's easily the equal of just about anything Tucson or Phoenix has to offer. The García family's offerings are *muy aútentico*, right down to the *menudo*, or cow tripe stew, on the breakfast menu. If you're not fond of innards, you'll find plenty of other choices, including chicken enchiladas made with blue-corn tamales and mouth- (and eye-) watering green chile.

1900 N. 2nd St. www.lafondaflg.com. ✆ **928/779-0296.** Main courses $12–$22. Mon–Sat 10am–9pm, Sun 10am–8pm.

INEXPENSIVE

Beaver Street Brewery ★ AMERICAN/PIZZA This big microbrewery, cafe, and billiards parlor on the south side of the railroad tracks serves up several good brews, and it also does great pizzas and salads. The Beaver Street pizza, made with roasted-garlic pesto, sun-dried tomatoes, fresh basil, and goat cheese, is particularly tasty. Among the large, filling salads, the Mongolian beef is a standout, served on a bed of greens with sesame-ginger dressing. This place stays packed with college students, but a good pint of ale helps any wait pass quickly, especially if you can grab a seat by the woodstove. The brewery also operates the adjacent **Beaver Street Brews & Cues,** 3 S. Beaver St., which has pool tables and a vintage bar.

11 S. Beaver St. www.beaverstreetbrewery.com. ✆ **928/779-0079.** No reservations. Main courses $13–$18. Sun–Wed 11am–10pm; Thurs 11am–11pm; Fri–Sat 11am–midnight.

Himalayan Grill ★ INDIAN/TIBETAN Set in a little strip mall south of downtown Flagstaff, Himalayan Grill specializes in Indian cuisine. The less familiar Nepalese and Tibetan dishes like *momos* (similar to Japanese *gyoza* or Chinese potstickers), though, are the more memorable entries on the menu. Here you can get them stuffed with either meat or vegetables. Follow your *momos* with a bowl of *thupka* (a hearty noodle soup) or *chau chau* (pan-fried noodles). Both of these latter dishes can be ordered with chicken or lamb. At lunch, there's a $9 buffet, and on Sundays, brunch is served.

801 S. Milton Ave. www.himalayangrill.com. ✆ **928/213-5444.** Main courses $10–$21. Daily 11am–2:30pm and 5–10pm.

Karma Sushi Bar Tapas ★ JAPANESE Located on historic Route 66 directly across from the Flagstaff Visitor Center, this stylish sushi place is a favorite of local college students. The food is all sushi and small plates, so it's light—a good antidote to one too many cowboy-size steaks. Especially recommended: the caterpillar roll (eel, cucumber, artificial crab, and avocado slices) and the black cat roll (tempura asparagus, spicy lobster, mango, and avocado with black sesame seeds).

6 E. Rte. 66. www.karmaflagstaff.com. ✆ **928/774-6100.** Sushi $4.50–$17; main courses $9–$21. Sun–Wed 11am–10pm; Thurs–Sat 11am–11pm.

Macy's European Coffee House & Bakery ★ COFFEEHOUSE/ BAKERY Good espresso and baked goodies—including some monster cinnamon rolls—draw people in here the first time, but there are also decent vegetarian pasta dishes, soups, salads, and other college-town standbys. This is Flagstaff's counterculture hangout, attracting both students and professors.

If you're feeling virtuous, you can have a dandy bowl of oatmeal instead of a delicious pastry—but the pastries are awfully tempting.

14 S. Beaver St. www.macyscoffee.net. © **928/774-2243.** Meals $4–$8. Daily 6am–6pm.

Flagstaff Entertainment & Nightlife

For events taking place during your visit, check *Flagstaff Live* (www.flaglive.com), a free weekly newspaper available at shops and restaurants downtown. The university has many musical and theatrical groups that perform throughout most of the year, and several clubs around town book a variety of live acts.

Downtown's **Orpheum Theater,** 15 W. Aspen St. (www.orpheumflagstaff.com; © **928/556-1580**) gets the best of touring rock, folk, and country acts, so be sure to check the schedule while you're in town. On the first Friday of the month in summer, also check out **Downtown Friday Nights** (www.heritagesquaretrust.org; © **928/853-4292**), when the whole city, it seems, turns out on Heritage Square to enjoy each other's company and listen to live music. During the warmer months, regular outdoor concerts are performed at the **Pepsi Amphitheater,** Fort Tuthill County Park (www.pepsiamphitheater.com; © **928/774-0899**), located at exit 337 off I-17 south of Flagstaff.

Flagstaff has no end of good brewpubs—well, a dozen, anyway. Among them are the **Beaver Street Brewery** (above), which also operates the **Lumberyard Brewing Company Taproom and Grille,** 5 S. San Francisco St. (www.lumberyardbrewingcompany.com; © **928/779-2739**). Also try **Mother Road,** 7 S. Mikes Pike (www.motherroadbeer.com; © **928/774-0492**), which whips up some remarkable brews and is a fun place to hang out. Climb the stairs to the **FLG Terroir ★,** 17 N. San Francisco St. (www.flgterroir.com; © **928/773-9463**), a wine bar located above the Artists Gallery in downtown Flagstaff with an extensive wine (more than 500 labels) and beer list and an inventive menu of light dishes. Also check out **Cuveé 928,** 6 E. Aspen Ave. (www.cuvee928winebar.com; © **928/214-9463**), a watering hole right on Heritage Square in downtown Flagstaff with an extensive list of wines from all over the world, as well as a number of bespoke cocktails.

For a lively scene, check out the **Museum Club,** 3404 E. Rte. 66 (© **928/526-9434**), a Flagstaff institution and one of America's classic roadhouses. Built in the early 1900s and often called the Zoo, this cavernous log saloon is filled with deer antlers, stuffed animals, and trophy heads. There's live music (mostly country) on weekends. The Club reopened under new management in 2018 after briefly closing for the first time in more than 80 years, and it's back to its rambunctious self.

Other places around town with live music include **Charly's Pub,** 23 N. Leroux St. (www.weatherfordhotel.com; © **928/779-1919**), inside the historic Weatherford Hotel (p. 267). This place has long been a popular student hangout featuring live blues and rock, and it serves some of the best Navajo tacos in town. For a mellower scene, see what's on the schedule at the **Campus Coffee Bean,** 1800 S. Milton Rd. (www.campuscoffeebean.com; © **928/556-0660**).

WILLIAMS

32 miles W of Flagstaff; 58 miles S of the Grand Canyon; 220 miles E of Las Vegas, NV

Although it's almost 60 miles south of the Grand Canyon, Williams is still the closest real town to the national park. Consequently, it has dozens of motels, hotels, and B&Bs catering to those unable to get a room in or just outside the park, as well as a handful of the obligatory on-your-way-to-the-Grand-Canyon tourist traps nearby. Williams is also where you'll find the depot for the Grand Canyon Railway excursion train, a fun alternative to dealing with traffic congestion in Grand Canyon National Park.

Founded in 1880 as a railroading and logging town, Williams also has a bit of Western history to boast about, which makes it an interesting place to explore for a morning or afternoon. Old brick commercial buildings dating from the late 19th century line the main street, while modest Victorian homes sit on tree-shaded streets spreading south from the railroad tracks. In recent years, however, mid-20th-century history has taken center stage: Williams was the last town on historic Route 66 to be bypassed by I-40, and the town now plays up its Route 66 heritage.

Named for famed mountain man Bill Williams, the town sits at the edge of a ponderosa pine forest atop the Mogollon Rim. Surrounding Williams is the Kaibab National Forest; within the forest not far from town are good fishing lakes, hiking and mountain-biking trails, and a small downhill ski area.

Essentials

ARRIVING Williams is on I-40 just west of the junction with Ariz. 64, which leads north to the South Rim of the Grand Canyon. **Amtrak** (✆ **800/872-7245**) has service to Williams on its Southwest Chief line. There's no station, though—the train stops on the outskirts of town, where a shuttle van from the Grand Canyon Railway Hotel will pick you up and drive you into town. Since most people coming to Williams by train are continuing on to the Grand Canyon on the Grand Canyon Railway, this arrangement works well. For info on the **Grand Canyon Railway** excursion trains to Grand Canyon Village, see below.

VISITOR INFORMATION The **Williams Visitors Center,** 200 W. Railroad Ave. (http://experiencewilliams.com; ✆ **928/635-4061**) is open daily from 8am to 5pm. The center has some interesting historical displays, and the shop carries books on the Grand Canyon and trail maps for the adjacent national forest. Ask here for advice on area hiking, mountain biking, and fishing.

Exploring Williams

These days, most people coming to Williams are here to board the **Grand Canyon Railway ★★**, Williams Depot, 233 N. Grand Canyon Blvd. (www.thetrain.com; ✆ **800/843-8724** or 303/843-8724), which operates vintage steam and diesel locomotives between Williams and Grand Canyon Village.

Tourist shops in Williams play up the town's Route 66 connection.

Round-trip fares (not including tax or the national park entrance fee) range from $67 to $219 for adults, $25.50 to $120 for children 2 to 12. Although this is primarily a day-excursion train, it's possible to ride up one day and return on a different day—just let the reservations clerk know that's what you want to do. Be sure you have overnight reservations at a hotel in the park before you do this, however. The same company that operates the train also manages the **Maswik Lodge** in Grand Canyon Village.

Route 66 fans will want to drive Williams's main street, which, not surprisingly, is named Route 66. Along this stretch of the old highway, you can check out the town's vintage buildings, many of which house shops selling Route 66 souvenirs. A few antiques stores sell collectibles from the heyday of the famous highway. Both east and west of town you can drive more sections of the "Mother Road" on either side of the interstate, but these are fairly dull stretches of road, interesting only to Route 66 die-hards. The best section is 24 miles west of Williams at exit 139: The longest uninterrupted stretch of Route 66 extends from here all the way from Seligman to Kingman to Oatman (see box, p. 284).

Grand Canyon Deer Farm ★ ZOO If you have kids with you, be sure to stop at this private petting zoo east of town, where you'll find both axis deer and reindeer, as well as miniature horses, donkeys, and cattle. Best of all, you get to pet and feed the deer and some of the other animals. You'll also see bison, llamas, a camel, coatimundis, and even wallabies and marmosets. Between April and August, you're likely to see newborns.

6769 E. Deer Farm Rd. (I-40 exit 171). www.deerfarm.com. ✆ **928/635-4073.** $14 adults, $12.50 seniors, $8 ages 3–13, free for kids 2 and under. Mid-Mar–mid-Oct daily 9am–6pm; mid-Oct–mid-Mar daily 10am–5pm. Closed Thanksgiving and Christmas.

Planes of Fame Air Museum ★ MUSEUM Fans of old fighter planes may want to spend a little time wandering around the hangar at this museum in Valle, 30 miles north of Williams on Ariz. 64. Among the aircraft on display are American, Japanese, and Russian fighters. You can also see an old Ford Trimotor, the sort of plane that once flew tourists over the Grand Canyon.

Valle Airport, 755 Mustang Way, Valle. ✆ **928/635-1000.** www.planesoffame.org. $10 adults, $8 military and veterans, $5 ages 5–11, free for kids 4 and under. Daily 9am–5pm. Closed Thanksgiving and Christmas.

Where to Stay in Williams

In addition to the following choices, a slew of budget motels, both chains and independents, line Route 66 as it rolls through Williams.

The Canyon Motel & RV Park ★ You'll find this updated 1940s Route 66 motor lodge on the eastern outskirts of Williams, tucked against the trees. While the setting and the rooms in 1940s flagstone cottages are nice enough, the real attractions are the railroad cars parked in the front yard, where you can spend the night in a caboose or a Pullman car, a fun experience. An indoor pool, horseshoe pit, swing set, and nature trails provide plenty of entertainment for the whole family. There's also a deluxe RV park here.

1900 E. Rodeo Rd. www.thecanyonmotel.com. ✆ **800/482-3955** or 928/635-9371. 23 units. $40–$99 double; $206 caboose; $140 Pullman double. **Amenities:** Indoor pool; coin-op laundry; free Wi-Fi.

Grand Canyon Railway Hotel ★ Operated by the Grand Canyon Railway, this hotel combines modern comforts with the style of a classic Western railroad hotel. The high-ceilinged lobby features a large flagstone fireplace and paintings of the Grand Canyon. The very comfortable guest rooms are decorated with southwestern styling; ask for a unit in the wing with the fitness room, pool, and hot tub. The hotel's elegant lounge, which boasts a 100-year-old English bar, serves simple meals, and there's an adjacent buffet-style restaurant. Although this hotel does not accept pets, they do have a pet "resort."

233 N. Grand Canyon Blvd. www.thetrain.com. ✆ **800/843-8724** or 928/635-4010. 298 units. $170–$279 double, $229–$370 suite. Railroad/hotel packages available (mid-Mar–mid-Oct and holidays $235 per person; mid-Oct–mid-Mar $160 per person). Children 15 and under stay free in parent's room. **Amenities:** Restaurant; lounge; exercise room; indoor pool; free Wi-Fi.

The Red Garter Inn ★ The Wild West lives again at this restored 1897 bordello, but these days the only tarts that come with the rooms are in the bakery downstairs. Located across the street from the Grand Canyon Railway terminal at the top of a steep flight of stairs, this B&B sports high ceilings, attractive wood trim, and reproduction period furnishings. Walls in a couple of rooms have graffiti written by bordello visitors in the early 20th century. Historical atmosphere makes this a top choice for a stay in Williams.

137 W. Railroad Ave. www.redgarter.com. ✆ **800/328-1484** or 928/635-1484. 4 units. $164–$199 double. Rates include full breakfast. No children 7 or under. **Amenities:** Restaurant; free Wi-Fi.

CAMPGROUNDS

Near Williams in the Kaibab National Forest, there are several campgrounds, including **Kaibab Lake** (4 miles NE of Williams off Ariz. 64, with 63 sites at $24–$40 per night); **Dogtown Lake** (6½ miles SE of Williams off 4th St./Perkinsville Rd./F.R. 173, with 52 sites at $24 per night); and **White Horse Lake** (19 miles SE of Williams off 4th St./Perkinsville Rd./F.R. 173, with 94 sites ($24 per night).

Where to Eat in Williams

Grabbing a quick bite to eat isn't hard in Williams—any number of cafes, diners, and family restaurants cluster along historic Route 66.

Red Raven Restaurant ★ NEW AMERICAN A cheeseburger and a milkshake may be the meal of choice for most visitors to this Route 66 town, but here at the Red Raven, culinary horizons are a bit broader. Start your meal with Southwestern egg rolls served with a smoky chipotle dipping sauce. Then try the pork loin with cilantro pesto or the basil-butter salmon with cranberry–pine nut couscous. There are also plenty of steaks. Although it's fairly casual, this is by far the most sophisticated restaurant in town.

135 W. Rte. 66. www.redravenrestaurant.com. ✆ **928/635-4980.** Reservations recommended. Main courses $9–$16 lunch, $17–$40 dinner. Daily 11am–2pm and 5–9pm.

Rod's Steak House ★ AMERICAN For a good dinner in Williams, just look for the red neon steer at the east end of town. The menu here may be short, but the food is reliable, and Rod's has been a Williams go-to since 1946. Prime rib au jus, the house specialty, comes in three different weights to fit your hunger. If you're not in the mood for steak, opt for barbecued ribs, trout, fried chicken, or, if you're old-school, beef liver.

301 E. Rte. 66. ✆ **928/635-2671.** www.rods-steakhouse.com. Reservations recommended. Main courses $8–$13 lunch, $16–$42 dinner. Mon–Sat 11am–9:30pm.

HAVASU CANYON ★★ & GRAND CANYON WEST

Havasu Canyon: 200 miles W of Grand Canyon Village; 70 miles N of Ariz. 66; 155 miles NW of Flagstaff; 115 miles NE of Kingman

Grand Canyon West: 240 miles W of Grand Canyon Village; 70 miles N of Kingman; 115 miles E of Las Vegas, NV

With five million people each year visiting the South Rim of the Grand Canyon (p. 220), creating inevitable traffic congestion and parking hassles, you may want to consider an alternative to the South Rim. The North Rim (p. 250) is one option, but it's closed from November to mid-May, and in summer it too has its share of clogged traffic. So where else can you go?

A visit to Havasu Canyon, on the Havasupai Indian Reservation, is one alternative, where a 20-mile round-trip hike or horseback ride—similar to that from Grand Canyon Village to Phantom Ranch—takes you to a decidedly different canyon floor setting, with stunning blue-green waterfalls. You'll need a permit, however—day hiking is not permitted at Havasu Canyon—which requires advance planning; otherwise, you'll have to content yourself with a long look from the rim.

West of there, there's also Grand Canyon West, on the Hualapai Indian Reservation. Best known for its much-hyped Skywalk, it's primarily a tour-bus destination from Las Vegas, well supplied with cafeteria-style restaurants, contrived attractions, and as much buzzing helicopter and small-plane traffic as any busy airport (this is the only place where you can fly down into the canyon). Still, if you have very little time to spare but desperately want to see something that looks like the Grand Canyon, it may be just the answer for you.

Essentials

ARRIVING You can't reach **Havasu Canyon**'s Supai village by car: Indian Rte. 18, which runs north from Ariz. 66, ends 8 miles from Supai, at Hualapai Hilltop. The trail head for the trail into the canyon is here. The turnoff from Ariz. 66 is 7 miles east of Peach Springs and 31 miles west of Seligman. The easiest and fastest way to reach Havasu Canyon is by helicopter from Hualapai Hilltop. Flights are operated by **Airwest Helicopters** (www.airwesthelicopters.com; ✆ **623/516-2790**). The one-way fare is $85.

The best route to **Grand Canyon West** is to head northwest out of Kingman on U.S. 93. After 27 miles, turn right onto Pearce Ferry Rd. (signed for Dolan Springs and Meadview) for 28 miles, then turn right onto Diamond Bar Rd., which is signed for Grand Canyon West. After 14 miles on this road, you'll enter the Hualapai Indian Reservation. About 6 miles farther, you'll reach the **Grand Canyon West Terminal** (there's actually an airstrip here), where visitor permits and bus-tour tickets are sold. You can also drive to Grand Canyon West from Peach Springs via Buck and Doe Rd., but that route includes almost 50 miles of gravel road, which isn't passable if it has rained any time recently. Many visitors also come on day tours from Las Vegas; **TakeTours** (www.taketours.com; ✆ **617/500-7002**) offers a Hoover Dam and Grand Canyon West trip for $95.

VISITOR INFORMATION For information on Havasu Canyon, contact **Havasupai Tourism,** P.O. Box 160, Supai, AZ 86435 (http://theofficialhavasupaitribe.com; ✆ **928/448-2121**), which handles all campground reservations. The phone line is not often answered; the website is your best bet. For Grand Canyon West details, contact **Hualapai Tourism** (www.grandcanyonwest.com; ✆ **888/868-9378** or 928/769-2636).

Exploring Havasu Canyon ★★★

Imagine hiking for hours through a dusty brown landscape of rocks and cacti. The sun overhead is blistering and bright. The air is hot and dry. Rock walls rise higher and higher as you continue your descent through a mazelike canyon. Eventually, the narrow canyon opens into a wide plain shaded by cottonwood trees, a sure sign of water, and within a few minutes you hear the sound of a babbling stream. The water, when you finally reach it, is cool and crystal clear. Following the stream, you pass through a dusty Indian village of small homes. Not surprisingly, in a village 8 miles beyond the last road, every yard seems to be a corral for horses.

As the trail descends again, following the stream, you spot the first waterfall. At the foot of the falls, the creek's waters are now a brilliant turquoise blue. The sandstone walls rising above look redder than before. No, you aren't

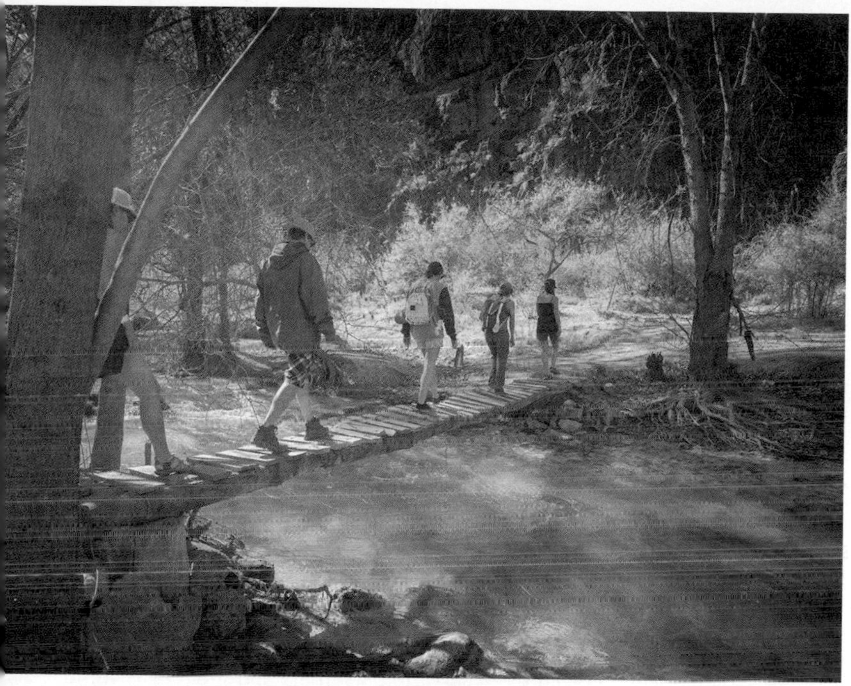

A hike into Havasu Canyon reveals astonishing turquoise pools and waterfalls.

having a heat-induced hallucination—the water really is turquoise, filling travertine terraces that form deep pools of cool water. Welcome to Havasu Canyon, home of the Havasupai tribe, whose name means "people of the blue-green waters." For centuries, the Havasupai have called this idyllic desert oasis home.

You must have a reservation to enter Havasu Canyon. There is no entrance fee as such; instead, fees are structured around camping and lodging. Staying at the Canyon's one **motel,** such as it is (p. 281), costs a staggering $175 per night—and a $90 tribal fee on top of that. Reservations for **campsites** for 2018 opened in February and were quickly booked for the entire year. Plan to jump on it as soon as the season begins (p. 281). A 1-night stay at a campground costs $140.56 per person; 2 nights are $171.11, and 3 nights (the maximum stay) are $207.67. If you're staying on Friday, Saturday, or Sunday, add $18.33 per night per person. This weekend fee, instituted in 2018, is a response to supply and demand: There are thousands of people clamoring to come in, and room for only a few, who must then pay premium—underscore premium—prices for the privilege. Reservations are prepaid and nonrefundable, and altering them in any way costs an added $100.

If you plan to hike down into the canyon, start early to avoid the heat of the day. The hike is beautiful, but it's 10 miles to the campground. The steepest part of the trail is the first mile or so from Hualapai Hilltop; after that it's relatively flat.

Havasu Flood Alert

In August 2008, a massive flood roared through Havasu Canyon, gouging a new creek channel that created two new waterfalls but bypassed one of the former falls. Then, in 2010, two flash floods stranded campers in the canyon, prompting a temporary closure. There is speculation that the flood of 2008 has made the campground more prone to flooding. Floods have occurred here regularly over the years, though the canyon has always been quick to heal any damage. Be sure to check current conditions when planning a trip to Havasupai; if possible, plan your visit for spring, when flash flooding is less likely.

Through **Havasupai Tourism** (http://theofficialhavasupaitribe.com; ✆ **928/448-2121**), you can hire a horse to carry you or your gear down into the canyon from Hualapai Hilltop. Horses cost $264 round-trip for four bags weighing a total of 130 pounds. Many people who hike in decide it's worth the money to ride out, or at least have their backpacks carried out. Be sure to confirm your horse reservation at least a week before driving to Hualapai Hilltop. Sometimes no horses are available, and it's a long drive back to the nearest town. There are also pack mules that will carry your gear into and out of the canyon. If you're staying at Havasupai Lodge, you can also make these equine arrangements through the lodge (p. 281).

Here's a great way to avoid the reservation scramble and 3-day-stay limit: Go into Havasu Canyon with a guide. **Arizona Outback Adventures** (www.aoa-adventures.com; ✆ **866/455-1601** or 480/945-2881) leads 3- to 5-day hikes into Havasu Canyon, charging $995 to $1,645 per person (plus $400–$475 tribal fees). **Discovery Treks** (www.discoverytreks.com; ✆ **888/256-8731** or 480/247-9266), offers a 3-day trip for $847 per person, plus $400 tribal fee, and **Wildland Trekking** (www.wildlandtrekking.com; ✆ **800/715-4453**), which operates out of Flagstaff, offers a 3-day trip for $1,015 per person, plus $420 tribal fee.

Exploring Grand Canyon West

Located on the Hualapai Indian Reservation on the south side of the Colorado River, **Grand Canyon West** (www.grandcanyonwest.com; ✆ **888/868-9378**) commands a view of the little-visited west end of Grand Canyon National Park. The view is not as spectacular as at either the South Rim or the North Rim, but Grand Canyon West has one thing they don't: Because it's on Hualapai reservation land, it is one of the only places where helicopters are legally allowed to take passengers down into the canyon. (At this point, only the north side of the Colorado is within Grand Canyon National Park.) **Papillon Helicopters** (www.papillon.com; ✆ **888/635-7272** or 702/736-7243) charges $254 per person for a quick trip to the bottom of the canyon and a boat ride on the Colorado River. Tours booked through the **Hualapai Tribe** (www.grandcanyonwest.com) are somewhat less expensive, running between $99 and $147.

The Skywalk at Grand Canyon West.

Because this is the closest spot to Las Vegas with access to the Grand Canyon, busloads of visitors come and go throughout the day, and the air is always filled with the noise of helicopters.

Grand Canyon West has ambitions to become a major destination, with plans in the works for a full-fledged resort and airport. The first phase of this development is the **Skywalk,** a horseshoe-shaped glass observation platform jutting over a side canyon of the Grand Canyon. From its deck you can glimpse the Colorado River, a short horizontal distance away—and 4,000 feet below. However, you'll have to cough up a minimum of $82.38 for the privilege of walking out on the Skywalk, for a view that's only marginally better than the view from solid ground. You'll also have to pay to ride the **shuttle bus** that takes visitors from the airstrip to the actual rim of the canyon. The shuttle stops at Eagle Point, site of the Skywalk and a collection of traditional Native American dwellings; at Guano Point, where bat guano was once mined commercially; and at Hualapai Ranch, a faux cowtown offering wagon and horseback rides, cowboy cookouts, and gunfight shows. Tours operate daily throughout the year; prices start at $49.92 per person without the Skywalk ($82.38–$94.90 with Skywalk). A horseback ride can be added for $10.85–$81.38. A helicopter ride down into the canyon and a brief boat trip on the Colorado River can be added for $202. Reservations are recommended (go to www.grandcanyonwest.com).

To be frank, Grand Canyon West and the Skywalk are pretty much the biggest tourist rip-off in the state and can be recommended only as a side trip from Las Vegas for travelers who absolutely must fly into the canyon. However, the 2-hour drive out here from Kingman (see "Arriving," p. 283) is one of the most scenic routes in Arizona. Along **Diamond Bar Road,** you'll be driving below the Grand Wash Cliffs, and for much of the way, the route traverses a dense forest of Joshua trees.

> **Take Me to the River**
>
> Want to visit the Grand Canyon floor by car, but you don't have a vehicle with you? You can do the Diamond Creek Road drive in comfort in a van with **Grand Canyon Custom Tours** (http://grandcanyoncustomtours.com; ✆ **928/779-3163**). These full-day tours start in Flagstaff or Williams and include a visit to Grand Canyon Caverns (see box below). The cost is $269 per person.

For adventurous types, there's another excellent alternative to the Grand Canyon West tourist hub: Drive **Diamond Creek Road** from Peach Springs to the Colorado River and the Grand Canyon floor. The dirt road—which, though graded, can be rough and slick—is best traveled in a high-clearance, four-wheel-drive vehicle; it winds through a series of wide side canyons on the way to the river. The route is idyllic, and to be sure, it's the only car route other than the one Thelma and Louise took that goes all the way to that brown, chugging river in the Grand Canyon. There's a $25 tribal fee to drive the 20 miles from Peach Springs to the riverside **Diamond Creek Campground;** purchase permits at the Hualapai Lodge (below). The trip takes about an hour each way.

Here at the west end of the canyon, it's also possible to do a 1-day rafting trip. Operated by **Hualapai River Runners,** a tribal rafting company (www.grandcanyonwest.com; ✆ **928/769-2636**), these trips are offered between March and October. Expect a mix of white water and flat water. Although it's not as exciting as longer trips in the main section of the canyon, you'll still plow through some pretty big waves. Be ready to get wet. Trips also visit a couple of side canyons where you can get out and do some exploring. Raft trips depart from the Hualapai Lodge in Peach Springs (below) and cost $451 per person, including a helicopter ride to the river.

Where to Stay & Eat Near Havasu Canyon & Grand Canyon West

IN PEACH SPRINGS

Peach Springs, on the Hualapai Indian Reservation, is the nearest base for visiting Grand Canyon West, and it's only a couple of hours from the trail head for Havasu Canyon.

The Caverns Inn ★ Ever dreamed of spending the night 220 feet underground? The underground cavern suite at this old Route 66 motel is surprisingly popular for an accommodation that costs $900 a night. Most of the inn's rooms are far more traditional (and far more economical). Built on the site of the Grand Canyon Caverns (see box below), the Caverns Inn is not as modern

The Grand Canyon Underground

Just outside Peach Springs on the Hualapai Reservation, **Grand Canyon Caverns** (www.gccaverns.com; ✆ **928/422-3223** or 928/422-4565) are an unusual phenomenon: dry caverns formed by lava flows as they encounter limestone. A 210-foot elevator ride takes visitors down to the caverns, which were once a designated fallout shelter (you'll still see supplies stored in one large chamber). They're open daily Memorial Day to October 15, 9am to 5pm, and other months daily 10am to 4pm. Admission is $21 adults, $16 seniors, and $14 kids 4 to 12. Explorers' Tours ($80 adults and kids) head into parts of the caverns that aren't seen on the regular tour. Recently discovered side caverns have been added to the menu with the 2½-hour Wild Tour ($100 per person, ages 8 and older only).

as the nearby Hualapai Lodge, but rooms are comfortable and service is good. Horseback rides and guided jeep tours to the bottom of the Grand Canyon can be arranged, and there's a general store with camping supplies and food.

Mile Marker 115, Rte. 66, Peach Springs. www.gccaverns.com. ✆ **928/422-3223.** 49 units. $100–$130 double; $900 cavern suite. Children 12 and under stay free in parent's room. Pets accepted ($25 deposit plus $5 per night). **Amenities:** Restaurant; lounge; outdoor pool; free Wi-Fi.

Hualapai Lodge ★ Although fairly basic, this lodge offers the most luxurious accommodations anywhere in the region. Guest rooms are spacious and modern, with a few bits of regional decor for character. Most guests are here to visit Grand Canyon West, go rafting with Hualapai River Runners, or hike into Havasu Canyon. The dining room is just about the only place in town to get a meal; it serves some Native American dishes. Light sleepers should be aware that there is a railroad track behind the hotel.

900 Rte. 66, Peach Springs. www.grandcanyonwest.com. ✆ **928/769-2230.** 54 units. $169 double. Children 16 and under stay free in parent's room. Pets accepted ($25 per day). **Amenities:** Restaurant; gym; Jacuzzi; outdoor pool; room service; free Wi-Fi.

IN HAVASU CANYON

Havasu Campground, 2 miles beyond Supai village between Havasu Falls and Mooney Falls, is the canyon's only campground. Campsites are mostly in the shade of cottonwood trees on either side of Havasu Creek, and picnic tables are provided. No firewood is available, so be sure to bring a camp stove. Spring water is available, but it needs to be purified before you drink it. To reserve a campsite, contact **Havasupai Tourism,** P.O. Box 160, Supai, AZ 86435 (http://theofficialhavasupaitribe.com; ✆ **928/448-2141**).

Havasupai Lodge ★ Located in Supai village, this lodge offers, aside from the campground, the only accommodations in the canyon. The two-story building features standard motel-style rooms that lack only TVs and telephones, neither of which is much in demand at this isolated retreat. The only real drawback of this comfortable though basic lodge is that it's 2 miles from Havasu Falls and 3 miles from Mooney Falls. A cafe, across from the general store, serves breakfast, lunch, and dinner. It's a very casual place, and while prices are high for what you get, remember that all ingredients have had to be packed in by horse. ***Note:*** Reservations must be prepaid, and refunds are offered only if you cancel more than 2 weeks before your stay date.

P.O. Box 159, Supai. http://theofficialhavasupaitribe.com. ✆ **928/448-2111** or 928/448-2201. 24 units. $175 double plus $90 entrance fee. **Amenities:** Cafe; store; no Wi-Fi.

KINGMAN

180 miles SW of Grand Canyon Village; 150 miles W of Flagstaff; 30 miles E of Laughlin, NV; 90 miles SE of Las Vegas, NV

The only town of any size between the Grand Canyon and Las Vegas, Kingman is primarily a place to gas up before heading out across the desert. However, the city does have interesting little museums and downtown historic buildings, and it has one other claim to fame: It's right on the longest surviving stretch of historic Route 66.

If Kingman today is more way station than destination, it's not surprising, considering its history. In 1857, Lieutenant Edward Fitzgerald Beale passed through this region, leading a special corps of camel-mounted soldiers on a road-surveying expedition (the road he surveyed would, some 60 years later, become the National Old Trails Highway, the precursor to Route 66). Soon after, in the 1870s, gold and silver were discovered in the nearby hills, and in the early 1880s the railroad laid its tracks through what would become Kingman. As a railroad town, it flourished briefly around the start of the 20th century; buildings constructed in that heyday give today's downtown a whiff of historical character. Mining towns in the nearby hills, such as Oatman and Chloride, boomed until the 1920s, but after the mines played out and were abandoned, the region suffered.

Then, in the 1930s, tens of thousands of the impoverished and unemployed passed through, following Route 66 from the Dust Bowl to the promised land of California, and Kingman thrived as an important wayside stop. Though Route 66 has long since been replaced by I-40, over the years the historic highway has taken on legendary status. Today, people come from all over the world searching for pieces of the past.

Kingman's Native Son

What, you've never heard of Andy Devine? In Kingman, you'll see his name everywhere. Devine was born in Flagstaff in 1905, but his family moved here the next year, and it became his home town. Known for his distinctive squeaky voice, the actor starred in hundreds of films beginning in the silent-screen era; he was perhaps best known as cowboy sidekick Jingles on the 1950s TV Western *Wild Bill Hickok*, as well as the driver in the 1939 John Ford/John Wayne classic *Stagecoach*. Devine died in 1977, but here in Kingman his memory lives on—in a room in the local museum, in the name of the town's main thoroughfare, and every September when the town celebrates Andy Devine Days.

Essentials

ARRIVING Kingman is located at the junction of I-40 and U.S. 93, which heads northwest to Las Vegas; Route 66 runs through the middle of town. **Amtrak** (✆ **800/872-7245**) offers rail service to Kingman from Chicago and Los Angeles. The station is at 4th St. and Andy Devine Ave./Rte. 66.

VISITOR INFORMATION The **Powerhouse Tourist Information & Visitor Center,** 120 W. Rte. 66 (www.gokingman.com; ✆ **928/753-6106**), is open daily 8am to 5pm. It is set in a restored 1907 powerhouse that also houses the Historic Route 66 Museum, a Route 66 gift shop, and a model railroad.

Exploring the Kingman Area

There isn't much to do right in Kingman; the town's three paying attractions can be visited on one combination ticket, costing $4 for adults, $3 for seniors, and free for ages 12 and under. Right by the visitor center, the **Historic Route 66 Museum,** 120 W. Rte. 66 (www.kingmantourism.org; ✆ **928/753-9889**) has exhibits on the history of not just Route 66, but also the roads, railroads, and trails that preceded it. A great collection of old photos taken during the Depression, and even an "Okie" truck, are on display. You'll also see a Studebaker Champion and mock-ups of a gas station, diner, hotel lobby, and barbershop. Hours are daily from 9am to 5pm. You can get a taste of local history (including plenty of Andy Devine memorabilia) at the **Mohave Museum of History and Arts,** 400 W. Beale St. (www.mohavemuseum.org; ✆ **928/753-3195**), open Monday through Friday 9am to 5pm, Saturday 1 to 5pm. At the museum, you can pick up a walking tour map of the town's many vintage buildings, some of which are on the National Register of Historic Places, including the **Bonelli House,** 430 E. Spring St. (✆ **928/753-1413**). This two-story stone home, built in 1915, is furnished much as it may have been at that time. It's open Monday through Friday 11am to 3pm (last tour starts at 2:30pm).

When you're tired of the heat and want to cool off, head southeast of Kingman to **Hualapai Mountain Park,** 6250 Hualapai Mountain Rd. (www.mcparks.com; ✆ **928/681-5700**), which covers 2,300 acres at elevations between 4,984 and 8,417 feet. The park offers picnicking, hiking, mountain biking, camping, and rustic rental cabins built in the 1930s by the Civilian Conservation Corps. Daily admission is $7 per vehicle.

OATMAN

Located 30 miles southwest of Kingman on old Route 66, the busy little mining camp of **Oatman** is a classic Wild West ghost town full of tourist shops selling tacky souvenirs. Founded in 1906 when gold was discovered here, Oatman quickly grew into a lively town of 12,000 people and was an important stop on Route 66. In 1942, when the U.S. government closed down many of Arizona's gold-mining operations, Oatman's population plummeted. Today the once-abandoned old buildings have been preserved and the historic look of Oatman has attracted numerous filmmakers over the years; *How the West Was Won* is just one of several movies shot here. Famously, Clark Gable and Carole Lombard honeymooned in Oatman in 1939, and the **Oatman Hotel**

GET YOUR KICKS ON route 66

It was the Mother Road, the Main Street of America, and for thousands of Midwesterners devastated by the Dust Bowl days of the 1930s, the road to a better life. On the last leg of its journey from Chicago to California, Route 66 meandered across the vast empty landscape of northern Arizona, and today, much of this road is still visible.

Officially dedicated in 1926, Route 66 was the first highway in America to be uniformly signed from one state to the next. Less than half of the highway's 2,200-mile route was paved, and in those days, the stretch between Winslow and Ash Fork was so muddy in winter that drivers had their cars shipped by railroad between the two points. By the 1930s, however, the entire length of Route 66 had been paved, and the westward migration was underway.

In the years following World War II, unprecedented numbers of Americans took to Route 66 for a different reason: Postwar prosperity and affordable cars made leisure travel accessible to the middle classes, who set out en masse to discover the West. Motor courts, cafes, and tourist traps sprang up along the highway's length, increasingly using eye-catching signs and billboards to lure passing motorists. Neon lit up the once-lonely stretches of highway.

By the 1950s, Route 66 just couldn't handle the traffic. After President Eisenhower initiated the National Interstate Highway System, Route 66 was slowly replaced by a four-lane divided highway. Many of the towns along the old highway were bypassed, and motorists stopped frequenting such roadside establishments as Pope's General Store and the Oatman Hotel. Many closed, while others were replaced by their more modern equivalents. Some, however, managed to survive, and they appear along the road like strange time capsules from another era, vestiges of Route 66's legendary past.

The **Wigwam Motel** (p. 305) in Holbrook is one of the most distinctive Route 66 landmarks. Built around 1940, these concrete wigwams (actually tepees) still contain many of their original furnishings. Also in Holbrook are several rock shops with giant signs—and life-size concrete dinosaurs.

Flagstaff, the largest town along the Arizona stretch of Route 66, became a major layover spot. Motor courts flourished on the road leading into town from the east. Today, this road has been officially renamed Route 66 by the city of Flagstaff, and a few of the old motor courts remain. Downtown Flagstaff has quite a few shops where you can pick up Route 66 memorabilia.

About 65 miles west of Flagstaff and 24 miles west of Williams, you can find the longest remaining stretch of old Route 66. Extending for 160 miles from Ash Fork to Topock, this lonely blacktop passes through some of the most remote country in Arizona (and goes right through the town of Kingman). In **Seligman,** at the east end of this stretch of the highway, you'll find **Delgadillo's Snow Cap,** 301 E. Rte. 66 (✆ **928/422-3291**), which serves up fast food amid outrageous decor (closed in winter).

(181 Main St.; ✆ **928/768-4408**) claims that the couple's ghosts still haunt the place. You can't stay in the hotel these days, but you can grab a bite in its restaurant, which is pretty good if touristy.

One of Oatman's biggest attractions is its population of feral burros—descendants of pack animals used by gold miners—that roam the streets begging for handouts. Be careful—they bite!

Next door at **Angel & Vilma Delgadillo's Route 66 Gift Shop & Visitor's Center,** 217 E. Rte. 66 (www.route66giftshop.com; ✆ **928/422-3352**) you'll be entertained by the descendants of the late founding owner Angel Delgadillo, one of Route 66's most famous residents. The walls of Angel's old one-chair barbershop are covered with photos and business cards of happy customers.

After leaving Seligman, the highway passes through such waysides as Peach Springs, Truxton, Valentine, and Hackberry—and some stunningly beautiful country. Keep your eyes open for condors, part of the population introduced into the Grand Canyon a couple of decades ago. Before reaching Peach Springs, you'll come to **Grand Canyon Caverns** (p. 281), once a near-mandatory stop for families traveling Route 66. In Hackberry, be sure to stop at the **Hackberry General Store & Visitor's Center,** 11255 E. Ariz. 66 (www.hackberrygeneralstore.com; ✆ **928/769-2605**), which is filled with Route 66 memorabilia and other old stuff from the 1950s and 1960s. At Valle Vista, near Kingman, the highway goes into a 7-mile-long curve that some claim is the longest continuous curve on a U.S. highway.

After the drive through the wilderness west of Seligman, Kingman feels like a veritable metropolis; its bold neon signs once brought a sigh of relief to the tired and the hungry. Today, it boasts dozens of modern motels and is still primarily a resting spot for the road-weary. **Mr. D'z Route 66 Diner** (below), a modern rendition of a 1950s diner (housed in an old gas station/cafe), serves burgers and blue-plate specials. Across the street at 120 W. Rte. 66, a restored 1907 powerhouse is home to the **Historic Route 66 Association of Arizona** (www.azrt66.com; ✆ **928/753-5001**), the **Historic Route 66 Museum** (p. 283), and the **Powerhouse Visitor Center.** Each year over the first weekend in May, Kingman hosts the **Historic Route 66 Fun Run,** a drive along 150 miles of old Route 66 between Topock and Seligman.

The last stretch of Route 66 in Arizona heads southwest out of Kingman through the rugged Sacramento Mountains. At the base of the mountains, before the road climbs up into switchbacks that stymied many an Okie's jalopy back in the day, stop in at the **Cool Springs Station** (www.route66coolspringsaz.com; ✆ **928/768-8366**) for a soda and a browse through the quirky gift shop.

Route 66 then passes through **Oatman,** which almost became a ghost town after the local gold mining industry shut down and the new interstate highway pulled money out of town. Today, mock gunfights and nosy wild burros entice motorists to stop, and shops playing up Route 66's heritage line the wooden sidewalks.

After dropping down out of the mountains, the road once crossed the Colorado River on a narrow metal bridge. Although the bridge is still there, it now carries a pipeline instead of traffic. The Oatman-Topock Highway now runs south, intersecting with I-40 at the California border.

Annual events staged here are among the strangest in the state, including January bed races, a Fourth of July high-noon sidewalk egg fry, and a Christmas season bush-decorating competition. Saloons and restaurants provide options for a meal and a chance to soak up the Oatman atmosphere for a while. For more info, contact the **Oatman Chamber of Commerce** (www.oatmangoldroad.org; ✆ **928/768-6222**).

Feral burros roam the streets of Oatman, a mining ghost town that now promotes its Route 66 heritage.

Where to Stay & Eat Around Kingman

Most budget motel chains have branches in Kingman, along with a few locally owned places, and rates are among the lowest in the state. Newer and more expensive hotels, including a La Quinta Inn (✆ **928/529-5070**) and a Hampton Inn (✆ **928/692-0200**), can be found on Stockton Hill Rd. (I-40 exit 51).

DamBar & Steak House ★ STEAK This steakhouse has long been Kingman's favorite place for dinner out. It's hard to miss—just look for the steer on the roof of a rustic wooden building. Inside, the atmosphere is casual, with wooden booths and sawdust on the floor. Mesquite-broiled steaks are the name of the game here, but there are plenty of other hearty dishes as well. On Friday and Saturday nights, there's live country music.

1960 E. Andy Devine Ave. www.dambarsteakhouse.com. ✆ **928/753-3523.** Reservations recommended on weekends and in summer. Main courses $13–$36. Daily 11am–10pm.

Mr. D'z Route 66 Diner ★ AMERICAN Painted an eye-catching turquoise and pink, this modern version of a vintage roadside diner is a big hit with car buffs and people doing Route 66. The retro color scheme continues inside, where you can snuggle into a booth or grab a stool at the counter. Punch in a few 1950s tunes on the jukebox, and order up a Route 66 bacon cheeseburger and a root beer float. It's kitschy as all get-out, but a lot of fun.

105 E. Andy Devine Ave. www.mrdzrt66diner.com. ✆ **928/718-0066.** Main courses $5.50–$17. Daily 7am–9pm.

THE FOUR CORNERS REGION: LAND OF THE HOPI & NAVAJO

7

Where in the U.S. can you stand in four states at the same time? The answer is way up in the northeastern corner of Arizona, where this state meets New Mexico, Colorado, and Utah. This novelty of the United State's westward expansion has long captured the imagination of travelers, for such a junction isn't something you see every day—and neither, for most of us, are the towering mesas, tall mountains, and multicolored desert that surround the site.

However, Four Corners is much more than a surveyor's gimmick. The term also refers to this entire region, most of which is Navajo and Hopi reservation land. These tribes have lived on these lands for hundreds of years. The Navajo, with their traditional octagonal or hexagonal log homes (called hogans) scattered across the countryside, were herders of sheep, goats, and cattle. The Hopi, on the other hand, congregated in villages atop mesas and built houses of stone.

And these two tribes are only the most recent Native Americans to inhabit this land. The Ancestral Puebloans (formerly called Anasazis) left their mark on countless canyons throughout the Four Corners region, the most spectacular being the ruins in Canyon de Chelly and Navajo national monuments. (For more on the Ancestral Puebloans, see p. 13.)

The Four Corners region happens to have some of the most spectacular landscapes in the state. Among the most dramatic landscape features are the 1,000-foot buttes of Monument Valley, which for years have symbolized the Wild West of John Wayne movies and car commercials. Here you'll also find Arizona's most scenic reservoir, Lake Powell, a flooded version of the Grand Canyon. With its miles of blue water mirroring red-rock canyon walls hundreds of

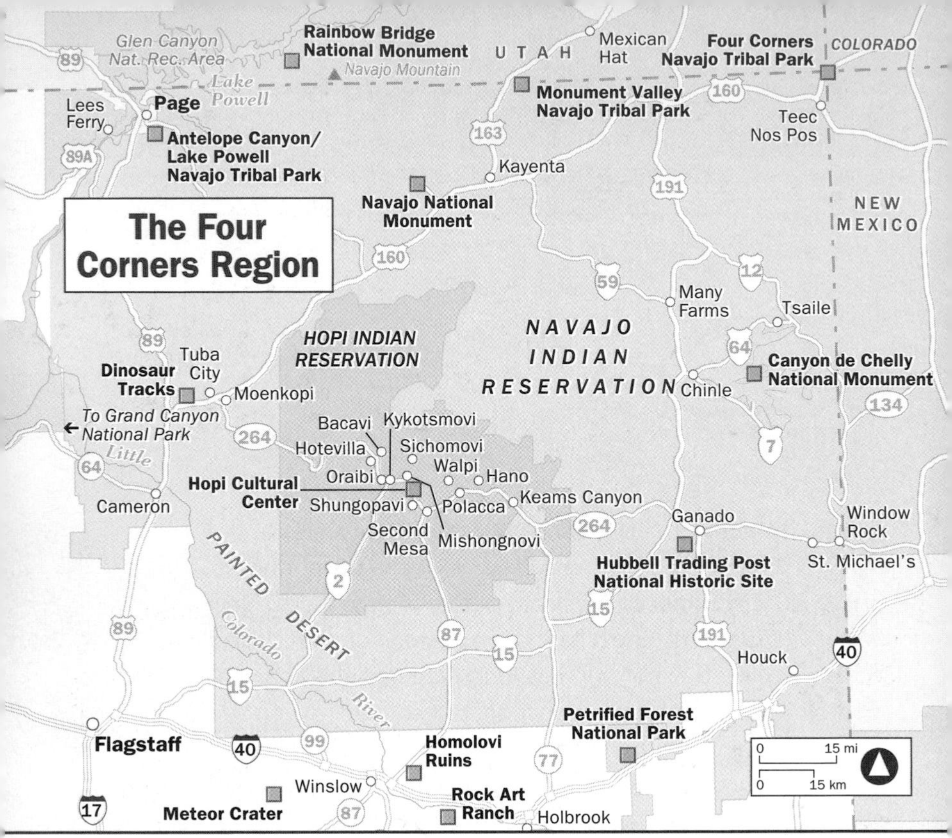

feet high, Lake Powell is one of northern Arizona's curious contrasts—a vast artificial reservoir in the middle of barren desert canyons.

Be forewarned, however: The Four Corners region also claims some of the most desolate, wind-swept, and monotonous landscapes in the state. Be sure to fill up on both gas and coffee before heading out on the highway for another 100-mile drive to the next destination. And one more thing to keep in mind: While the rest of Arizona does not observe daylight saving time, the Navajo Nation does—meaning that for much of the year you'll be an hour later when on Navajo land.

WINSLOW

55 miles E of Flagstaff; 70 miles S of Second Mesa; 33 miles W of Holbrook

It's hard to imagine that a town could build its tourist fortunes on a mention in a pop song, but that is exactly what Winslow has done, decades after the Eagles sang about "standin' on a corner in Winslow, Arizona," in the hit song "Take It Easy," written by Glenn Frey and Jackson Browne (the latter of whom still turns up in town from time to time). On the corner of Second St. and Kinsley Ave., the town even has an official Standin' on the Corner Park (complete with a mural of a girl in a flatbed Ford, to match the song's road-weary lyrics).

Nearby is the beautifully restored La Posada, one of the Southwest's historic railroad hotels. Twenty miles west of town is mile-wide Meteor Crater. And northeast of town, Homolovi Ruins State Park preserves significant archaeological sites from the Ancestral Puebloan culture. If you happen to be a rock climber, you'll find great climbing routes in the Moenkopi section of Jacks Canyon south of town.

Essentials

ARRIVING Winslow is on I-40 at the junction with Ariz. 87, which leads north to the Hopi mesas and south to Payson. **Amtrak** (✆ **800/872-7245**) trains stop in Winslow at La Posada hotel, 501 E. Second St.

VISITOR INFORMATION The **Winslow Chamber of Commerce,** 523 W. Second St. (✆ **928/289-2434;** www.winslowarizona.org) is housed in the town's restored Hubbell Trading Post. Besides the visitor center it has exhibits on Winslow's history.

Exploring the Winslow Area

In downtown Winslow, near that famous corner, you'll find the little **Old Trails Museum,** 212 Kinsley Ave. at Second St. (www.oldtrailsmuseum.org; ✆ **928/289-5861**), a focal point of community memory. Set in a former bank, complete with its original vault, the museum has exhibits on Route 66 and the Harvey Girls (who once worked in the nearby La Posada hotel; see p. 291). It's open Tuesday through Saturday from 10am to 4pm. Admission is free.

For a nice change of pace, stop by the **SNOWDRIFT Art Space,** 120 W. Second St. (www.snowdriftart.com; ✆ **928/289-8201**), an art gallery/studio owned by artist Daniel Lutzick, who was one of the people who helped get the historic La Posada hotel up and running again. Call for a guided tour.

On the windswept plains northeast of Winslow, 1¼ miles north of I-40 at exit 257, **Homolovi Ruins State Park** (www.azstateparks.com; ✆ **928/289-4106**) preserves more than 300 Ancestral Puebloan archaeological sites, several of which have been partially excavated, including a 1,400-room pueblo. The ruins represent a pueblo that was once among the most impressive in the Southwest, a peer of Wupatki and Walnut Canyon. There is a $7 entry fee per vehicle, payable at the visitor center. Be sure to arrive before 4pm to allow plenty of time to see the largest ruin, Homolovi II. If you're there on the first Saturday of

You, too, can stand on a corner in Winslow, Arizona, just as in the Eagles' hit song "Take It Easy."

the month (except in August and December), come over after dark for a stargazing party using the park's big telescope.

Continuing north from the state park, you'll find the little-known and little-visited **Little Painted Desert County Park ★**. It offers a sweeping, astonishing view of 660 acres of weathered Painted Desert sand hills below a steep rim, an unsuspected treasure that can only be seen from that tall cliff. To reach the park, continue north on Ariz. 87 from Homolovi Ruins State Park for another 12 miles. Look out for two ramadas on the left (there is a park entrance sign, but it's too weathered to read). And once you leave the highway, watch out for potholes deep enough to swallow an RV.

Meteor Crater ★ GEOLOGICAL SITE At 550 feet deep and 2.4 miles in circumference, the Barringer Meteorite Crater is the best-preserved meteorite impact crater on Earth. The meteorite, which is estimated to be roughly 150 feet in diameter, was traveling at 26,000 mph when it slammed into the earth 50,000 years ago. Within seconds, more than 175 million tons of rock had been displaced, leaving a gaping crater. Today, you can stand on the rim of the crater (there are observation decks and a short trail) and marvel at the power, equivalent to 20 million tons of TNT, that created this otherworldly setting. So closely does this crater resemble craters on the surface of the moon that in the 1960s, NASA came here to train Apollo astronauts.

On the rim of the crater, a museum has exhibits on astrogeology and space exploration, as well as a film on meteorites. On display are a 1,400-pound meteorite and an Apollo space capsule. Throughout the day, there are 1-hour hiking tours along the rim. If you can make time for one of these informative, not too strenuous sessions, you should.

20 mi W of Winslow, at exit 233 off I-40. www.meteorcrater.com. ✆ **800/289-5898** or 928/289-5898. $18 adults, $16 seniors, $9 children 5 and under. Memorial Day–Labor Day daily 7am–7pm; rest of year daily 8am–5pm. Closed Christmas.

Where to Stay in Winslow

In addition to the following historic hotel, you'll find lots of budget chain motels in Winslow.

Communing with the Spirits of the Past

Located on part of the old Hashknife Outfit, the largest ranch in the country during the late 19th century, **Rock Art Ranch ★★** (✆ **928/386-5047** or 928/288-3260) is one of the finest ancient rock art sites in the state. The setting is absolutely enchanting, in narrow little Chevelon Canyon, which is almost invisible until you are right beside it. Pecked into the canyon's walls are hundreds of Ancestral Puebloan petroglyphs, or rock art carvings, that span more than 8,000 years. Tours (reservations required) are available Monday through Saturday (call to get rate information and directions to the ranch). Also on the ranch are a museum of Ancestral Puebloan artifacts and a bunkhouse that dates from the Hashknife days. If you're interested in petroglyphs, Rock Art Ranch should not be missed.

La Posada ★★★ La Posada hotel is a southwestern treasure, a cousin of many other fine historically significant buildings (including Union Station in downtown Los Angeles) that are still in use decades after first being built. Designed by Mary Elizabeth Jane Colter, architect of many of the buildings on the South Rim of the Grand Canyon, this railroad hotel first opened in 1930. Colter gave La Posada the feel of an old Spanish hacienda and even created a fictitious history for the building. In the lobby you'll see numerous pieces of original furniture, as well as reproductions of pieces once found in the hotel. After falling into disuse after World War II, the hotel was restored to its former glory in the late 1990s and has been an extraordinarily popular destination ever since. The nicest rooms, with period Art Deco and modernist furnishings but modern amenities, are the large units named for famous guests—Albert Einstein, Howard Hughes, and Harry Truman. Even the less expensive, smaller rooms are fine, decorated in the same retro fashion; just be aware that such rooms tend to be closer to the train tracks at the back of the hotel, and passing trains can be surprisingly loud. The hotel's **Turquoise Room** (below) is by far the best restaurant in the entire Four Corners region. La Posada is reason enough to overnight in Winslow. Even if you can't stay, stop by to look at this beautiful place and its oasis-like gardens.

303 E. 2nd St. (Rte. 66), Winslow. www.laposada.org. ✆ **928/289-4366.** 45 units. $129–$169 double. Pets accepted ($10 fee). **Amenities:** Restaurant; lounge; access to nearby health club; room service; free Wi-Fi.

Where to Eat in Winslow

E&O Kitchen ★ MEXICAN A little less than a mile due west of La Posada lies Winslow's small regional airport, the design for which just happens to have been personally approved by noted aviator Charles Lindbergh, who often checked in at the famed railroad hotel. The E&O Kitchen, tucked into the airport, isn't easy to find, but it's well worth a visit for the delicious Mexican dishes that come fresh out of the kitchen. It's fun to watch small planes come and go as you eat, too. Apart from the Turquoise Room, it's the best food in Winslow.

703 Airport Rd. ✆ **928/289-5352.** Mon–Thurs 11am–5:30pm, Fri 11am–7pm, Sat 11am–5pm.

The Turquoise Room ★★ NEW AMERICAN/SOUTHWESTERN When Fred Harvey began his railroad hospitality career, his objective was to provide decent meals to the traveling public. (See the "Fred Harvey & His Girls" box, below.) Here, in La Posada's reincarnated dining room, chef/owner John Sharpe prepares not just decent meals, but superb meals, the likes of which you won't find anywhere else in northern Arizona. In summer, herbs and vegetables often come from the hotel's own gardens, and wild game is a specialty. The wait staff, many of them local Native American men and women, will have plenty of specials to suggest, making use of fresh, authentic ingredients. On top of all this, you can watch the trains rolling by just outside the window while you dine.

At La Posada, 303 E. 2nd St. www.theturquoiseroom.net. ✆ **928/289-2888.** Reservations recommended. Main courses $9–$16 lunch, $17–$36 dinner. Daily 7am–4:15pm and 5–9pm.

FRED HARVEY & HIS girls

Unless you grew up in the Southwest and can remember back to pre–World War II days, you may have never heard of Fred Harvey and the Harvey Girls. But if you spend much time in northern Arizona, you're likely to run into quite a few references to the Harvey Girls and their boss.

Fred Harvey was the Southwest's most famous mogul of railroad hospitality and was an early promoter of tourism in the Grand Canyon State. Harvey, an English immigrant who was working for a railroad in the years shortly after the Civil War, developed a distaste for the food served at railroad stations. He decided he could do a better job, and in 1876 he opened his first Harvey House railway-station restaurant for the Santa Fe Railroad. By the time of his death in 1901, Harvey operated 47 restaurants, 30 diners, and 15 hotels across the West.

The women who worked as waitresses in the Harvey House restaurants came to be called Harvey Girls. Known for their distinctive black dresses, white aprons, and black bow ties (which women servers at Winslow's Turquoise Room in the La Posada hotel [above] still wear for period effect), Harvey Girls had to adhere to very strict behavior codes. In fact, in the late 19th century, they were considered the only real "ladies" in the West, aside from schoolteachers. So celebrated were they in their day that in the 1940s, Judy Garland starred in a Technicolor MGM musical called *The Harvey Girls*. Garland played a Harvey Girl who battles the evil town dance-hall queen (played by Angela Lansbury) for the soul of the local saloonkeeper.

THE HOPI RESERVATION

67 miles N of Winslow; 250 miles NE of Phoenix; 100 miles SW of Canyon de Chelly; 140 miles SE of Page/Lake Powell

The Hopi Reservation, often referred to as Hopiland or just Hopi, has at its center a grouping of three mesas upon which the Hopi have been living for centuries. (Their ancestors moved away from other pueblos in the region after the decline of ancient Ancestral Puebloan centers such as Chaco Canyon and Mesa Verde.) Completely encircled by the Navajo Nation, this remote region, with its flat-topped mesas and barren landscape, is the center of the universe for the Hopi people.

Here tradition-minded Hopi, whose name means "peaceful people," follow their ancient customs. They still grow corn and other crops at the foot of their mesas in much the same way as indigenous peoples of the Southwest have for centuries. Many aspects of pueblo culture remain intact, although much of the culture is hidden from visitors' view. The Hopi perform elaborate religious and social dances throughout the year, but most of these dances aren't open to outsiders. Some, however, are replicated at festivals outside the mesas, such as the **Suvoyuki Hopi Festival,** held the first Saturday in August at Homolovi State Park; the **Hopi Festival of Arts & Culture,** held the weekend before July 4 in Flagstaff; and the **Hopi Festival at Heritage Square,** held the last weekend of September, also in Flagstaff. See p. 30 for details.

Lying within view of the San Francisco Peaks to the west, where the rain spirits called the *katsina* are said to dwell, the mesas are home to two of the oldest continuously inhabited villages in North America—Walpi and Old

Oraibi. Although these two communities reflect their historic role, serving as a direct tie to the pueblos of the Ancestral Puebloan culture, most villages on the reservation are scattered collections of modern homes. They're not destinations unto themselves, although you can also take a guided tour of Walpi village. The main reason for a visit to this area is the chance to buy crafts directly from the Hopi, at numerous crafts shops and studios along Ariz. 264, which sell kachinas, baskets, pottery, and silver jewelry.

Important note: When visiting the Hopi pueblos, remember that you are a guest and your privileges can be revoked at any time. Respect all posted signs at village entrances, and remember that *photographing, sketching, and recording are prohibited in the villages and at ceremonies.* Also, kivas (ceremonial rooms) and ruins are off-limits. Be aware, too, that alcohol is prohibited on Hopi and Navajo tribal lands.

Essentials

ARRIVING This is one of the state's most remote regions. Distances are great, but highways are generally in good condition. Ariz. 87 leads from Winslow to Second Mesa, and Ariz. 264 runs from Tuba City in the west to the New Mexico state line in the east.

VISITOR INFORMATION For advance information, contact the **Hopi Office of Cultural Preservation** (www8.nau.edu/hcpo-p; ✆ **928/734-3612**). The Moenkopi Legacy Inn's website (**www.experiencehopi.com**) is another good place for information on visiting the Hopi reservation.

Exploring the Hopi Villages

With the exception of Upper and Lower Moenkopi, which are near the Navajo town of Tuba City, and the recently settled Yuh Weh Loo Pah Ki community east of Keams Canyon, the Hopi villages are scattered along roughly 20 miles of Ariz. 264. **Old Oraibi** is the oldest, but there are no official tours of this village, and visitors are not likely to feel very welcome here unless they've been invited to visit by a resident. **Walpi,** one of only two villages with organized tours, is the best place for visitors to learn more about life in the Hopi villages. Most of the Hopi villages listed below aren't especially picturesque, but they do have quite a few crafts galleries and stores selling silver jewelry.

FIRST MESA At the top of First Mesa, parts of the village of **Walpi** still look much like the ruins of Ancestral Puebloan villages in Canyon de Chelly, Navajo National Monument, and Wupatki National Monument. Small stone houses seem to grow directly from the rock of the mesa top, and ladders jut from the roofs of kivas. The view from the village stretches for hundreds of miles—it's easy to see why the Hopi settled on this spot. Walpi was originally located lower on the slopes of First Mesa, but after the Pueblo Revolt of 1680 brought on fear of reprisal from the Spanish, villagers moved to the top of the mesa so that they could better defend themselves in the event of a Spanish attack.

Immediately adjacent to Walpi are the two villages of **Sichomovi,** founded in 1750 as a colony of Walpi, and **Hano,** founded by Tewa peoples who were most likely seeking refuge from the Spanish after the Pueblo Revolt of 1680.

Neither of these villages has the ancient character of Walpi. At the foot of First Mesa, the settlement of **Polacca** was founded in the late 1800s by Walpi villagers who wanted to be closer to the trading post and school.

SECOND MESA Second Mesa is today the center of tourism in Hopiland, with the **Hopi Cultural Center** (below) located here. Villages on Second Mesa include **Shungopavi,** which was moved to its present site after Old Shungopavi was abandoned in 1680 following the Pueblo Revolt. Old Shungopavi is said to have been the first Hopi village; it was founded by the Bear Clan. Shungopavi is notable for its silver jewelry and its coiled plaques (flat baskets).

Mishongnovi, which means "place of the black man," is named for the leader of a clan that came here from the San Francisco Peaks around 1200. The original Mishongnovi village, located at the base of the mesa, was abandoned in the 1690s, and the village was reestablished at the current site atop the mesa. The Snake Dance is held here during odd-numbered years.

Sipaulovi, located on the eastern edge of the mesa, was founded after the Pueblo Revolt of 1680.

THIRD MESA **Oraibi,** which lays claim to being the oldest continuously occupied town in the United States, is located on Third Mesa. The village dates from 1150 and, according to legend, was founded by people from Old Shungopavi. A Spanish mission was established in Oraibi in 1629; the ruins are still visible north of the village. Today, Oraibi is a mix of old stone houses and modern ones, mostly constructed of cinder blocks. Blue-corn *piki* bread, dolls, and other traditional goods are available for sale, and you may even be invited into someone's home to see the crafts they have to offer. For this reason, Old Oraibi is the most interesting village in which to shop for local crafts, especially weavings, baskets, and jewelry.

For centuries, Oraibi was the largest of the Hopi villages, but in 1906, a schism arose as a result of divisive Bureau of Indian Affairs policies, causing many villagers to leave and form **Hotevilla.** This is considered the most conservative of the Hopi villages, and it has had frequent confrontations with the federal government. **Kykotsmovi,** also known as Lower Oraibi or New Oraibi, was founded in 1890 by villagers from Oraibi who wanted to be closer to the school and trading post. This village is the seat of the Hopi Tribal Government. **Bacavi** was founded in 1907 by villagers who had left Oraibi to help found Hotevilla, but later decided they wanted to return to Oraibi. The people of Oraibi would not let them return, however. Rather than go back to Hotevilla, they founded a new village.

MOENKOPI Forty miles west of the Hopi mesas, this village was founded in 1870 by people from Oraibi. Moenkopi sits in the center of a wide green valley where plentiful water makes farming more reliable. Divided into the villages of Upper Moenkopi and Lower Moenkopi, Moenkopi is only a few miles from Tuba City off U.S. 160.

VISITING THE THREE MESAS

Start your visit to the Hopi pueblos at the **Hopi Cultural Center,** on Ariz. 264 in Second Mesa (✆ **(928) 734-2401**). This combination museum, motel, and restaurant is the tourism headquarters for the area. Check at the Center for hours, which can be irregular, and entrance fees to the museum.

The most rewarding Hopi village to visit is **Walpi ★**, on First Mesa. Guided 1-hour walking tours of this tiny village are usually offered daily between 9am and 3pm (8am to 4pm in summer). Your tour leaders will be local Hopis, who will share with you the history of the village and explain a bit about the local culture. Tours are arranged by the First Mesa Consolidated Villages' Tourism Program and cost $20. To sign up for a tour, call in advance (✆ **928/737-2670**).

Another interesting village to visit is the historic community of **Keams Canyon,** at the far eastern end of First Mesa on Highway 264. The village is named after a pretty little canyon about 1½ miles to the north, where you'll find, carved into the stone walls, an inscription left by Colonel Christopher "Kit" Carson. It was Carson who led the war on the Navajo during the summer of 1863 and who, to defeat the tribe, burned their crops, leaving the Navajo with no winter supplies. The inscription reads simply 1ST REGT. N.M. VOLS. AUG 13TH 1863 COL. C. CARSON COM. To find the inscription, turn off Ariz. 264 in Keams Canyon and drive north on the main road through the community. You'll also find some picnic tables along this road.

Please be aware that travel off 264 into any Hopi-owned areas other than the villages is allowed only in the company of a certified Hopi guide.

CULTURAL TOURS

To get the most out of a visit to the Hopi mesas, it is best to take a guided tour. With a guide, you will learn much more about this rather insular culture than you ever could on your own. Tour companies frequently use local guides and stop at the homes of working artisans. This all adds up to a more in-depth and educational visit to one of the oldest cultures on the continent. For information on authorized guides, see www.experiencehopi.com/authorized-hopi-guides.

Bertram Tsavadawa at **Ancient Pathways Tours** (✆ **928/797-8145**) specializes in tours to Hopi petroglyph sites, including Dawa Park, with its significant trove of more than 15,000 pieces of rock art. Three-hour tours cost $75 for adults and $35 for children under 18; 6-hour tours cost $165 for adults and $85 for kids. One-hour tours of Old Oraibi ($15) are also available.

Micah Loma'omvaya, an anthropologist, heads **Hopi Tours** (www.hopitours.vistaprintdigital.com; ✆ **928/349-3063**, text only), which offers 2-hour petroglyph tours for $45 per person, among other packages; half-day and full-day weekend tours are also available.

Half-day and full-day tours are also offered by Gary Tso of the **Left-Handed Hunter Tour Company** (lhhunter68@hopitelecom.net; ✆ **928/734-2567**). Half-day tours cost $160 for two people, and full-day tours cost $265 for two people.

Personalized tours by Hopi artist Evelyn Fredericks (www.evelynfredericks.com/tours.html; ✆ **928/255-2112**) take in petroglyph sites, Old Oraibi, Walpi, and the studios of local artists; the cost is $150 for one person and $50 per person thereafter, with no charge for children under age 18. (Add $15 per person for Walpi.)

Hopi Dances & Ceremonies

The Hopi have developed the most complex religious ceremonies of any of the Southwest tribes. The masked kachina dances for which they are most famous are held from January to July. However, most kachina dances are closed to the non-Hopi public. Social dances (usually open to the public) are held August through February. If you're on the reservation during these months, ask if any dances are taking place.

The kachina season lasts from the winter solstice until shortly after the summer solstice. The actual dates for dances are usually announced only shortly before the ceremonies are to be held. Preparations for the dances take place inside kivas (traditional ceremonial rooms) that are entered from the roof by means of a ladder; the dances themselves are usually held in a village square or street.

With ludicrous and sometimes lewd mimicry, clowns known as *koyemsi*, *koshares*, and *tsukus* entertain spectators between the dances, bringing a lighthearted counterpoint to the very serious nature of the kachina dances. Non-Hopis attending dances are often playfully targeted for attention by these clowns.

Despite the importance of the kachina dances, it is the **Snake Dance** that has captured the attention of many non-Hopis. The Snake Dance involves the handling of both poisonous and nonpoisonous snakes. The ceremony takes place over 16 days, with the first 4 days dedicated to collecting snakes from the four cardinal directions. Later, footraces are held from the bottom of the mesa to the top. On the last day of the ceremony, the actual Snake Dance is performed. Men of the Snake Society form pairs of dancers—one to carry the snake in his mouth and the other to distract the snake with an eagle feather. When all the snakes have been danced around the plaza, they are rushed down to their homes at the bottom of the mesa to carry the Hopi prayers for rain to the spirits of the underworld.

Masked dancers known as kachinas (or, in Hopi, *katsinas*) play an important role in tribal ceremonies.

The Spirit of the Hopi *Katsinas*

Whether in the form of dolls or as masked dancers, kachinas—or, as artists more often refer to them, *katsinas*—represent the spirits of everything from plants and animals to ancestors and sacred places. More than 300 kachinas appear on a regular basis in Hopi ceremonies, and another 200 appear occasionally. The kachina spirits are said to live in the San Francisco Peaks to the southwest and at Spring of the Shadows in the east. According to legend, the kachinas lived with the Hopi long ago, but the Hopi people made the kachinas angry, causing them to leave. Before departing, though, the kachinas taught the Hopi how to perform their ceremonies.

Today, the kachina ceremonies, performed by men wearing elaborate costumes and masks, serve several purposes. Most important, they bring clouds and rain to water the all-important corn crop, but they also ensure health, happiness, long life, and harmony in the universe. As part of the kachina ceremonies, dancers often bring carved wooden kachina dolls to village children to introduce them to the various spirits.

Check with the **Hopi Office of Cultural Preservation** (p. 293) to check which ceremonies and dances are open to non-Hopi visitors.

Shopping for Hopi Crafts

Across the reservation, dozens of small shops sell crafts and jewelry of different quality, and some homes, especially at the foot of First Mesa, have signs indicating that they sell crafts. Shops often sell the work of only a few individuals, so you should stop at several to get an idea of the variety of work available. Also, if you visit Walpi or Oraibi, you can find villagers selling various crafts, including kachina dolls. The quality will usually not be as high as that in shops, but then, the prices won't be as high, either. For information on arts and artists you might wish to seek out, visit the **Hopi Arts Trail** website (http://hopiartstrail.com).

If you're in the market for Hopi silver jewelry, stop in at **Hopi Fine Arts** (© **928/737-2222**), at the foot of Second Mesa at the junction of Ariz. 264 and Ariz. 87. Owned by the renowned trader and collector Alph Secakuku, this shop also has a good selection of kachina dolls and some beautiful coil and wicker plaque baskets. Hours are limited in the winter.

One of the best places to get a quick education in Hopi art and crafts is **Tsakurshovi** ★ (© **928/734-2478**), a tiny shop 1½ miles east of the Hopi Cultural Center on Second Mesa. (The name means "pointed hill.") Tsakurshovi has a huge selection of traditional kachina dolls and Hopi overlay jewelry. Owners Janice and Joseph Day are happy to share their expertise with visitors. Here you can also buy a "Don't Worry Be Hopi" T-shirt, made famous by an NPR story a dozen years back.

In Oraibi, visit **Hamana So-oh's Arts & Crafts** (© **928/206-6392**), a great place to buy Hopi artwork of all kinds. The shop is open year-round except during the Bean Dances, which take place in February.

At Keams Canyon, 30 miles east of Second Mesa on Ariz. 264, **McGee's Indian Art Gallery** (www.hopiart.com; © **928/738-2295**) is the best place on

Eat Local, Shop Local, in Hopiland

The Hopi and Navajo reservations both offer some interesting opportunities to eat locally and shop locally, and in so doing patronize small businesses and individuals, which is one of the key aspects of eco-travel.

On the Hopi reservation, residents of the village of **Walpi** lead tours of this ancient cliff-top village (p. 293). On these walking tours, village residents sell handicrafts and sometimes traditional *piki* bread, a paper-thin bread made from blue corn, which has long been a staple food of the Hopi.

If you walk through the village of **Old Oraibi,** village residents also sell handicrafts, particularly small wooden dolls. Throughout the Hopi Reservation, you'll see signs in front of people's homes advertising traditional crafts for sale.

the reservation to shop for high-quality contemporary kachina dolls. The first trading post to open on this site was built in 1879, and the McGee family has owned the business since 1937. The gallery is adjacent to a grocery store that is the current incarnation of the old trading post.

Where to Stay & Eat in Hopiland

Options are limited on the Hopi reservation itself; visitors generally stay at hotels in either Winslow (p. 290) to the south, or Tuba City to the west. If you've brought your food along, you'll find picnic tables just east of Oraibi on top of the mesa. These tables have an amazing view!

Hopi Cultural Center Restaurant & Inn ★ Although it isn't much, this simple motel is one of only two accommodations on the Hopi reservation. While the Moenkopi Legacy Inn in Moenkopi/Tuba City is newer and more comfortable, the Hopi Cultural Center is more centrally located if you are planning to spend a couple of days in the area. Guest rooms are comfortable enough, though the grounds are quite desolate. The restaurant menu includes some traditional dishes, including *noqkwivi*, or Hopi stew, made with hominy, lamb, and green chili, and a Hopi taco, with ground beef, cheese, and fixings heaped on a blue-corn tortilla. (Remember that alcohol is prohibited at Hopi—forget about a cold beer with which to wash down these tasty dishes.) There's also a small museum on the grounds. Because it is the only lodging for miles around, be sure you have a reservation before heading up for an overnight visit.

Second Mesa. www.hopiculturalcenter.com. ✆ **928/734-2401.** 33 units. $136 double. Children 12 and under stay free in parent's room. Pets accepted ($50 deposit). **Amenities:** Restaurant; free Wi-Fi.

En Route to or from the Hopi Mesas

On the west side of the reservation, in Tuba City, the **Tuba City Trading Post,** Main St. and Moenave Ave. (✆ **928/283-5441**), was built in 1906 of local stone. Its octagonal design is meant to resemble a Navajo hogan or traditional home (there's also a real hogan on the grounds). The trading post sells Native American crafts, with an emphasis on books, music, and jewelry. Across the parking lot from the trading post and next to the Quality Inn (below), you'll find **Hogan Espresso,** 10 N. Main St. (✆ **928/283-4545**), one of the few places on the reservation where you can get espresso. It's open Monday to Friday from 7am to 7pm, Saturday from 9am to 7pm, and Sunday 9am to 4pm. Another rarity, but less rare as time rolls on: Hogan Espresso offers free Wi-Fi to go along with its delicious coffee.

Behind the trading post, you'll find the **Explore Navajo Interactive Museum** (✆ **928/640-0684**), housed in a tentlike structure used for the 2002 Salt Lake City Olympics. A good introduction to Navajo culture, the museum includes a traditional Navajo hogan. (There is also a Navajo code talkers museum in the trading post, open 8am to 5pm daily.) In summer, the museum is open Monday through Friday from 9am to 5pm and Saturday from 9 am to 4 pm; call for hours in other months. Admission is $9 for adults, $7 for seniors, and $6 for children ages 7 to 12.

West of Tuba City and just off U.S. 160, you can see **dinosaur footprints** ★ preserved in the stone surface of the desert. There are usually a few people waiting at the site to guide visitors to the best footprints (these guides will expect a tip of a few dollars). The scenery out your car window is some of the strangest in the region—you'll see lots of red-rock sandstone formations that resemble petrified sand dunes.

WHERE TO STAY IN TUBA CITY

Moenkopi Legacy Inn & Suites ★★ With a facade designed to resemble a Hopi village, the Moenkopi Legacy Inn, which opened in 2010, is by far the best hotel in the area. The lobby, with its peeled-log columns, stone chimney, and soaring ceiling, is reminiscent of the interiors of traditional Hopi homes, and incorporates numerous traditional Hopi symbols. Guest rooms are large, comfortable, and modern, and feature old photos of Hopi villages. In the courtyard, there's a small artificial stream beside the swimming pool. There's a small gift shop off the lobby, and display cases feature works by local artists and artisans. The Inn also offers all-day tours of the Hopi Mesas for $145 a person ($89 for 12 and under with a paid adult), with lunch at the Hopi Cultural Center and water included.

Jct. Ariz. 160 and Ariz. 264. www.experiencehopi.com. ✆ **928/283-4500.** 100 units. $115–$155 double; $155–$175 suite. Rates include continental breakfast. Children 17 and under stay free in parents' room. **Amenities:** Lounge (no alcohol served); exercise room; Jacuzzi; outdoor saltwater pool; free Wi-Fi.

Quality Inn Navajo Nation ★ Located in the bustling Navajo community of Tuba City (where you'll find gas stations, fast-food restaurants, and grocery stores), this modern hotel is adjacent to the historic Tuba City Trading Post. The hotel offers comfortable rooms of average size, but the green lawns, shade trees, and old trading post (complete with hogan) are what really set this place apart. This hotel is also adjacent to the Explore Navajo Interactive Museum (above). The nearby Moenkopi Legacy Inn may be newer, but the trading post and museum here make this a more interesting choice in the area.

10 N. Main St. www.explorenavajo.com. ✆ **928/283-4545.** 80 units. $144–$159 double. Rates include full breakfast. Children 17 and under stay free in parent's room. Pets accepted ($10 per night). **Amenities:** Restaurant; exercise room; free Wi-Fi.

A NATIVE AMERICAN crafts PRIMER

The Four Corners region is taken up almost entirely by the Navajo and Hopi reservations, so Native American crafts are ubiquitous. You'll see jewelry for sale by the side of desolate roads, Navajo rugs in tiny trading posts, and Hopi kachinas being sold out of village homes. The information below will help you make an informed purchase.

Hopi Kachina Dolls These elaborately decorated wooden dolls are representations of the spirits of plants, animals, ancestors, and sacred places. Traditionally, they were given to children to initiate them into the pantheon of kachina spirits, which play important roles in ensuring rain and harmony in the universe. Kachinas have long been popular with collectors, and Hopi carvers have changed their style over the years to cater to the collectors' market. Older kachinas were carved from a single piece of cottonwood, sometimes with arms simply painted on. This older style is much simpler and stiffer than the contemporary style that emphasizes action poses and realistic proportions.

A great deal of carving and painting goes into each kachina, and prices today are in the hundreds of dollars for even the simplest. The *tsuku*, or clown kachinas, which are usually painted with bold horizontal black-and-white stripes and often depicted in humorous situations or carrying slices of watermelon, are popular with tourists and collectors. In the past few years, young carvers have been returning to the traditional style of kachina, so it's now easier to find these simpler images for sale.

Hopi Overlay Silver Work Most Hopi silver work is done in the overlay style, which was introduced to tribal artisans after World War II, when the GI Bill provided funds for former soldiers to study silversmithing at a school founded by Hopi artist Fred Kabotie. (Fred's grandson, Ed Kabotie, is an artist and musician who wrote the parody song "Don't Worry Be Hopi.") The overlay process basically uses two sheets of silver, one with a design cut from it. Heat fuses the two sheets, forming a raised image. Designs often borrow from other Hopi crafts such as basketry and pottery, and from ancient Ancestral Puebloan pottery. Belt buckles, earrings, bolo ties, and bracelets are all popular.

Hopi Baskets On Third Mesa, wicker plaques and baskets are made from rabbit brush and sumac, and colored with bright aniline dyes. On Second Mesa, coiled plaques and baskets are created from dyed yucca fibers. Throughout the reservation, yucca-fiber sifters are made by plaiting over a willow ring.

THE PETRIFIED FOREST & PAINTED DESERT ★

25 miles E of Holbrook; 90 miles E of Flagstaff; 118 miles S of Canyon de Chelly; 180 miles N of Phoenix

Petrified wood has long fascinated people, and although it can be found in almost every state and every continent, the "forest" of downed logs in northeastern Arizona is by far the most extensive. This petrified forest—a landscape of fallen trees whose cells, millions of years ago, were filled with sand that turned to stone—has been a center of attention since antiquity.

When, in the 1850s, Mormon pioneers discovered this vast treasure-trove of petrified wood, scattered like stone kindling across the landscape, they

Hopi Pottery Contemporary Hopi pottery tends toward geometric designs in variety of styles, including a yellow-orange ware decorated with black-and-white designs and white pottery with red-and-black designs. The most famous Hopi potter, Nampeyo, who died in 1942, is credited with bringing Hopi pottery to the attention of collectors. Today, members of the Nampeyo family are still active as potters. Most pottery is produced on First Mesa.

Navajo Silver Work Whereas the Hopi create overlay silver work from sheets of silver and the Zuni use silver work simply as a base for their skilled lapidary or stone-cutting work, Navajo silversmiths typically highlight the silver itself. Silversmithing caught on with Navajo men in the 1880s, when Lorenzo Hubbell, who had established a trading post in the area, hired Mexican silversmiths as teachers. The earliest pieces of Navajo jewelry were replicas of Spanish ornaments, but as the Navajo silversmiths became more proficient, they began to develop their own designs. The squash-blossom necklace, with its horseshoe-shape pendant, is one of the most distinctive Navajo designs.

Navajo Rugs After the Navajo acquired sheep and goats from the Spanish, they learned weaving from the pueblo tribes; by the early 1800s, their weavings were widely recognized as the finest in the Southwest. Women were the weavers among the Navajo, and they primarily wove blankets. By the end of the 19th century, the craft was beginning to die out, as ready-made blankets became more economical. When Lorenzo Hubbell set up his trading post, he recognized a potential market in the East for the woven blankets—if they could be made heavy enough to be used as rugs. Today the cost of Navajo rugs, which take hundreds of hours to make, has become almost prohibitively expensive, but there are still enough women practicing the craft to keep it alive.

The best rugs are those made with homespun yarn and natural vegetal dyes, although commercially manufactured yarns and dyes are increasingly used to keep costs down. Some weavers are now using wool from Churro sheep, which are descended from sheep that may have been brought to this region by Spanish settlers more than 300 years ago. There are more than 15 regional styles of rugs and there is quite a bit of overlapping and borrowing. Bigger and bolder patterns are likely to cost quite a bit less than very complex and highly detailed patterns.

began exporting it wholesale to the East. Within 50 years, so much had been removed that the pioneering environmentalist John Muir, who lived for a time in the nearby hamlet of Adamana, agitated with his friend Theodore Roosevelt to preserve the place. In 1906 several areas were set aside as the Petrified Forest National Monument, which, in 1962, became a national park. A 27-mile scenic drive winds through the petrified forest (and a small corner of the Painted Desert), providing a fascinating high-desert experience.

Essentials

ARRIVING The north entrance to Petrified Forest National Park is 25 miles east of Holbrook on I-40. The south entrance is 20 miles east of Holbrook on U.S. 180.

Turning Wood to Stone

It may be hard to believe as you drive across the arid landscape of the Petrified Forest, but at one time this area was a vast steamy swamp. That was 225 million years ago, when dinosaurs and huge amphibians ruled the earth, and now-extinct species of giant trees grew on the high ground around the swamp. Fallen trees were washed downstream, gathered in piles in quiet backwaters, and eventually were covered over with silt, mud, and volcanic ash. As water seeped through this soil, it dissolved the silica in the volcanic ash and redeposited it inside the cells of the logs. Eventually, the silica recrystallized into stone to form petrified wood, with minerals such as iron, manganese, and carbon contributing its distinctive colors.

This region was later inundated with water, and thick deposits of sediment buried the logs ever deeper. Eventually, the land was transformed yet again as a geologic upheaval thrust the lake bottom up above sea level. This upthrust of the land cracked the logs into the segments we see today. Wind and water gradually eroded the landscape to create the Painted Desert, and the petrified logs were once again exposed on the surface of the land.

FEES & HOURS The entry fee is $20 per car. The park is open daily 7am to 6pm.

VISITOR INFORMATION For details on the Petrified Forest or the Painted Desert, contact **Petrified Forest National Park** (www.nps.gov/pefo; ✆ **928/524-6228**). For info on Holbrook and the surrounding region, contact the **Holbrook Chamber of Commerce Visitor Center & Museum** (www.holbrookchamberofcommerce.com; ✆ **928/524-6558**).

Exploring the Petrified Forest

Petrified Forest National Park has both a north and a south entrance. If you are coming from the west, it's better to start at the southern entrance and work your way north along the park's 27-mile scenic road, which has more than 20 overlooks. This way, you'll see the most impressive displays of petrified logs early in your visit and save the Painted Desert vistas for last. (The description below follows this route.) If you're coming from the east, start at the northern entrance and work your way south.

The **Rainbow Forest Museum** (✆ **928/524-6822**), just inside the south entrance to the park, is the best place to begin your tour. Here you can learn all about petrified wood, watch an introductory film, and otherwise get oriented. Exhibits chronicle the area's geologic and human history. There are also displays on the reptiles and dinosaurs that once inhabited this region. The museum sells maps and books and also issues free backpacking permits. The Rainbow Forest Museum is open daily 8am to 5pm. Adjacent to the museum is a snack bar.

Behind the museum, the **Giant Logs self-guided trail** winds across a hillside strewn with logs that are 4 to 5 feet in diameter. Almost directly across the parking lot from the museum is the entrance to the **Long Logs** and **Agate**

The Giant Logs trail is strewn with ancient tree trunks transformed by colorful crystallized minerals.

House areas. On the 1.6-mile Long Logs trail, you can see more big trees, while at Agate House, a 2-mile round-trip hike will lead you to the ruins of a pueblo built from colorful petrified wood. These two trails can be combined into a 2.5-mile hike.

Heading north, you'll pass by the unusual formations known as the **Flattops.** These structures were caused by the erosion of softer mineral deposits from beneath a harder layer of sandstone. This is one of the park's wilderness areas. The **Crystal Forest** is the next stop to the north, named for the beautiful amethyst and quartz crystals once found in the cracks of petrified logs. (Concern over the removal of these crystals was what led to the protection of the petrified forest.) A .75-mile loop trail winds past the logs that once held the crystals.

At the **Jasper Forest Overlook,** you can see logs that include petrified roots, and a little bit farther north, at the **Agate Bridge** stop, you can see a petrified log that forms a natural agate bridge. Continuing north, you'll reach **Blue Mesa,** where pieces of petrified wood form capstones over easily eroded clay soils. As wind and water wear away at the clay beneath a piece of stone, the balance of the stone becomes more and more precarious until it eventually comes toppling down. A 1-mile loop trail here leads into the park's badlands.

Erosion has played a major role in the formation of the Painted Desert, and to the north of Blue Mesa you'll see some of the most

No Souvenirs, Please!

At both the southern and northern entrances to the park are places where repentant visitors can leave pieces of petrified wood they've picked up during their visit. Local lore has it that bad luck befalls anyone who removes such artifacts from the Park. Whether you believe it or not, it behooves us short-timers on this planet to leave things where they are, taking away only memories—and also avoiding prosecution for breaking federal laws.

interesting erosional features of the area. It's quite evident why these hills of sandstone and clay are known as the **Teepees.** The layers of different color are due to manganese, iron, and other minerals in the soil.

At **Newspaper Rock,** you can see a dense concentration of petroglyphs left by generations of Native Americans. A steel overlook with several sets of tower-viewer binoculars hangs over a low cliff opposite the petroglyphs, allowing visitors to get a good look at them. At nearby **Puerco Pueblo,** the park's largest archaeological site, you can view the remains of homes built by the people who created the park's petroglyphs. This pueblo was probably occupied around A.D. 1400. Don't miss the petroglyphs on its back side.

Exploring the Painted Desert

North of Puerco Pueblo, the road crosses I-40. From here to the Painted Desert Visitor Center, there are eight overlooks onto the southernmost edge of the **Painted Desert.** Named for the vivid colors of the soil and stone that cover the land here, the Painted Desert is a dreamscape of pastels washed across a barren expanse of eroded hills. The colors are created by minerals dissolved in sandstone and clay soils that were deposited during different geologic periods. There's a picnic area at Chinde Point overlook.

At Kachina Point, you'll find the **Painted Desert Inn,** a renovated historic building that's now operated as a bookstore and museum. Built in 1924 and expanded by the Civilian Conservation Corps, the inn is noteworthy for both its architecture and the Fred Kabotie murals on the interior walls. Hours are 9am to 4:30pm daily. From here, there's access to the park's other wilderness area. Between Kachina Point and Tawa Point, you can do an easy 1-mile

Vividly colored bands of soil stripe the hills of the Painted Desert.

round-trip hike along the rim of the Painted Desert. An even more interesting route leads down into the Painted Desert from behind the Painted Desert Inn.

Just inside the northern entrance to the park, the **Painted Desert Visitor Center** (✆ **928/524-6228**) is open daily from 8am to 5pm. Here you can watch a short film that explains the process by which wood becomes fossilized (it's the same film that's shown at the Rainbow Forest Museum). Adjacent to the visitor center are a cafeteria, bookshop, and gas station.

Exploring Holbrook

Although the Petrified Forest National Park is the main reason for visiting this area, you might want to stop by downtown Holbrook's **Old West Museum,** 100 E. Arizona St. (✆ **928/524-6558**), which also houses the Holbrook Chamber of Commerce visitor center. This old and dusty museum, housed in the 1898 Historic Navajo County Courthouse, has exhibits on local history but is most interesting for its old jail cells. It's open daily from 8am to 5pm; admission is free. On weekday evenings in June and July, there are Native American dance performances in front of the visitor center.

Although it is against the law to collect petrified wood inside Petrified Forest National Park, there are several rock shops in Holbrook where you can buy legally collected pieces of petrified wood in all shapes and sizes. You'll find them lined up along the main street through town and out on U.S. 180, the highway leading to the park's south entrance. The biggest and best of these rock shops is **Jim Gray's Petrified Wood Co.,** 147 U.S. 180 (www.petrifiedwoodco.com; ✆ **928/524-1842**), which has everything from raw rocks to petrified wood coffee tables that sell for thousands of dollars. This store also has a fascinating display of minerals and fossils. It's open daily from 7am to 7 or 8pm in the summer (8am–6pm in other months; closed Thanksgiving and Christmas).

Where to Stay in Holbrook

Holbrook, the town nearest to Petrified Forest National Park, offers lots of budget chain motels charging very reasonable rates.

Wigwam Motel ★ If you're looking to capture a bit of Route 66 history, don't miss this collection of concrete wigwams. This unique motel was built in the 1940s, when unusual architecture was springing up all along famous Route 66. The motel has been owned by the same family since it was built and still has the original rustic furniture. Old cars are kept in the parking lot for an added dose of Route 66 character.

811 W. Hopi Dr. www.galerie-kokopelli.com/wigwam. ✆ **928/524-3048.** 15 units. $69–$76 double. Pets accepted ($5 per night). **Amenities:** No Wi-Fi.

Where to Eat in Holbrook

While there are plenty of inexpensive restaurants in Holbrook, none is particularly memorable or recommendable. Your best bet is to drive over to Winslow to the Turquoise Room at La Posada hotel (p. 291).

THE WINDOW ROCK & GANADO AREAS

74 miles NE of Petrified Forest National Park; 91 miles E of Second Mesa; 190 miles E of Flagstaff; 68 miles SE of Canyon de Chelly National Monument

> **What Time Is It?**
>
> Contrary to the rest of the state, the Navajo Nation observes daylight saving time in summer. If you're coming from elsewhere in Arizona, the time here will be 1 hour later in months when daylight saving is in effect. The Hopi Reservation, however, does not observe daylight saving time, even though it is completely surrounded by the Navajo Nation.

Window Rock, the capital of the Navajo Nation, is less than a mile from the New Mexico state line. It's named for a huge natural opening in a sandstone cliff just outside town, a landmark preserved as the **Window Rock Tribal Park,** located 2 miles north of Ariz. 264 (go north on Indian Rte. 12 and then turn east onto Window Rock Blvd.).

As the Navajo Nation's capital, Window Rock is the site of government offices, a museum and cultural center, and a zoo. A few miles to the west is the **St. Michaels Historical Museum**, in the community of St. Michaels. About a half-hour's drive west of St. Michaels is the **Hubbell Trading Post,** in the community of Ganado.

Essentials

ARRIVING To reach Window Rock from Flagstaff or Holbrook, take I-40 east to Lupton and go north on Indian Rte. 12.

SPECIAL EVENTS Unlike the village ceremonies of the Hopi, Navajo religious ceremonies tend to be held in the privacy of family hogans. However, the public is welcome to attend numerous fairs, powwows, and rodeos throughout the year. The biggest of these is the **Navajo Nation Fair** (www.navajonationfair.org; (✆ **928/871-6478**), held in Window Rock in early September. It features traditional dances, a rodeo, a powwow, a Miss Navajo Pageant, and arts-and-crafts exhibits and sales. The Fourth of July Celebration Rodeo, also held in Window Rock, is a not-to-be-missed experience if you're in the area.

VISITOR INFORMATION For advance information, contact **Navajo Tourism** (www.discovernavajo.com; ✆ **928/810-8501**).

Exploring the Window Rock & Ganado Area

Hubbell Trading Post National Historic Site ★ STORE/HISTORIC SITE Located just outside the town of Ganado, 26 miles west of Window Rock, the Hubbell Trading Post is the oldest continuously operating trading post on the Navajo Nation, established in 1876 by Lorenzo Hubbell, who did more to popularize the arts and crafts of the Navajo people than any other person. Hubbell was in large part responsible for the revival of Navajo weaving in the late 19th century.

navajo **HISTORY 101**

The **Navajo Nation,** the largest reservation in the U.S., is home to nearly 200,000 Navajos and covers an area of 26,000 square miles in northeastern Arizona and parts of New Mexico and Utah. Although the reservation today has modern towns with supermarkets, shopping centers, and hotels, many Navajos still follow a pastoral lifestyle. Their flocks of goats and sheep, and herds of cattle and horses, have free range of the reservation and often graze beside the highway.

Compared to the Hopi and Zuni peoples, the Navajo are relative newcomers to the Southwest. Their Athabaskan language is closely related to the languages spoken by Native Americans in the Pacific Northwest, and it is a close cousin of the languages spoken by the neighboring Apaches. It's believed that the Navajo migrated southward from northern Canada beginning around 1000, arriving in the Southwest sometime after 1400, though possibly earlier. At this time, they were still hunters and gatherers, but contact with the pueblo tribes, which had long before adopted an agricultural lifestyle, began to change the Navajo into farmers.

When the Spanish arrived in the Southwest in the early 17th century and began to encroach upon Navajo land, the Navajo began raiding Spanish settlements for horses, sheep, and goats. In 1805, the Spanish sent a military expedition into the Navajo's chief stronghold, Canyon de Chelly, and killed 115 people, who, by some accounts, may have been all women, children, and old men. This massacre, however, did not put an end to the conflicts between the Navajo and Spanish settlers. In 1846, when this region became part of the United States, American settlers encountered the same problems that the Spanish had, and eventually the Navajo were defeated and moved onto this reservation. (See p. 170 for the story of the Navajo Long Walk.)

Today, the Navajo are chiefly herders but have had to turn to other livelihoods as well. Weaving and silver work have become lucrative businesses for some craftspeople, although the amount of money these trades garner for the tribe as a whole is not significant. Many Navajos now take jobs as migrant workers. Gas and oil leases and coal mining on the reservation provide additional income. Fortunately, the Navajo have recognized the tourism potential of their spectacular land. **Monument Valley** (p. 318) is operated as a tribal park, as is the **Four Corners** monument (p. 323). Numerous Navajo-owned tour companies also operate on the reservation.

As you travel the reservation, you may notice small hexagonal or octagonal buildings with rounded roofs. These are hogans, the traditional homes of the Navajo, and are usually made of wood and earth with the doorway facing east to greet the new day. Although most Navajos now live in Western-style houses, a family usually has a hogan for religious ceremonies.

On the reservations, trading posts are much more than just a place to trade crafts for imported goods—for many years they were the main gathering spot for meeting people from other parts of the reservation, serving as a sort of gossip fence and newsroom. In Hubbell Trading Post's general store, you'll still see basic foodstuffs for sale (not much variety here) and bolts of the cloth Navajo women use for sewing their traditional skirts and blouses. However, today this trading post is more of a living museum. Visitors can explore the

The capital of the Navajo Nation, Window Rock, is named for this striking natural sandstone rock formation.

grounds on their own or take a guided tour ($5), and can often watch Navajo weavers in the slow process of creating a rug.

The rug room is filled with a variety of traditional and contemporary Navajo pieces. And although it's possible to buy a small 12×18-inch rug for around $100, most cost thousands of dollars, especially anything done in the famed Ganado Red style that is a hallmark of the area. In another room are baskets, kachinas, and jewelry by Navajo, Hopi, and Zuni artisans.

Twice a year, usually in May and September or October, there are auctions of Native American crafts, sometimes at the trading post but now more often in Gallup, New Mexico, an hour's drive away. For more information, visit https://friendsofhubbell.org or call ✆ **602/571-1122.**

Ariz. 264, Ganado. www.nps.gov/hutr. ✆ **928/755-3475.** Free admission. Apr 30–Sept 8 daily 8am–6pm; Sept 9–Apr 29 daily 8am–5pm. Visitor center winter hours are sometimes shorter; call ahead to check. Closed New Year's Day, Thanksgiving, and Christmas.

Navajo Museum, Library & Visitor's Center ★ CULTURAL CENTER This museum and cultural center is housed in a large building patterned after a traditional hogan. Inside you'll see rotating exhibits of contemporary crafts and art, as well as exhibits on modern Navajo culture. There's also a gift shop.

Ariz. 264 at Loop Rd., adjacent to Navajo Zoo, Window Rock. www.navajonationmuseum.org. ✆ **928/871-7941.** Free admission. Mon–Sat 8am–5pm.

Navajo Nation Zoo & Botanical Park ★ ZOO Located in back of the Navajo Nation Inn, this zoo and botanical park features animals and plants that are significant in Navajo history and culture, such as bears, cougars, and wolves. The setting is very dramatic, with several sandstone "haystack" rocks, and some of the animal enclosures are quite large, incorporating natural rock outcroppings.

Ariz. 264, Window Rock. www.navajozoo.org. ✆ **928/871-6574.** Free admission. Mon–Sat 10am–4:30pm. Closed New Year's Day, Thanksgiving, and Christmas.

St. Michaels Historical Museum ★ MUSEUM In the community of St. Michaels, 4 miles west of Window Rock, this museum chronicles the lives and influence of Franciscan friars who started a mission in this area in the 1670s. The museum is in a small building adjacent to the impressive stone mission church. Back in the early years of the 20th century, a friar here photographed the Navajos of the area, and the chance to see some of these historical photos is one of the best reasons to visit this museum. The Navajo Nation Tourism Department just across the street is a good source of information.

St. Michaels, just south of Ariz. 264. ✆ **928/871-4171.** Free admission. Memorial Day–Labor Day daily 9am–5pm; other months, call for hours.

Shopping for Navajo Crafts

The **Hubbell Trading Post** (above), although a National Historic Site, is still an active trading post and has an outstanding selection of rugs, as well as lots of jewelry. In Window Rock, be sure to visit the **Navajo Arts and Crafts Enterprise** (www.gonavajo.com; (✆ **800/871-1829** or 928/871-4090), next to the Quality Inn Navajo Nation Capital. Operating since 1941, this store sells silver-and-turquoise jewelry, Navajo rugs, baskets, pottery, and Native American clothing. The store is open Monday through Saturday from 9am to 8pm and Sunday from noon to 6pm.

For more on Navajo traditional crafts, see "A Native American Crafts Primer," p. 300.

Where to Stay Around Window Rock

Navajoland Inn & Suites ★ Two miles west of Window Rock near the historic St. Michaels Mission, this hotel is centrally located for exploring west to the Hopi mesas, north to Canyon de Chelly, and south to Petrified Forest National Park. With its indoor pool and exercise room, this is your best bet in the area, especially if you're traveling with the family.

392 W. Ariz. 264, St. Michaels. www.navajolandsuites.com. ✆ **928/871-5690.** 73 units. $80–$100 double; $110 suite. Children 12 and under stay free in parent's room. Pets accepted ($20 per day). **Amenities:** Exercise room; Jacuzzi; indoor pool; sauna; restaurant and snack bar; free Wi-Fi.

Quality Inn Navajo Nation Capital ★ Located in Window Rock, the administrative center of the Navajo Nation, this hotel features southwestern-style furnishings in a calming desert-sand color scheme. The restaurant serves American and traditional Navajo dishes, including mutton stew and fry bread.

48 W. Ariz. 264, Window Rock. www.explorenavajo.com. ✆ **800/662-6189** or 928/871-4108. 56 units. $92–$130 double. Rates include continental breakfast. Children 17 and under stay free in parent's room. Pets accepted ($50 refundable deposit). **Amenities:** Restaurant; exercise room; gift shop; free Wi-Fi.

Where to Eat Around Window Rock

In Window Rock, your best bet is the **Quality Inn Navajo Nation Capital** (above), which serves moderately priced American, Mexican, and Navajo food. Try the Navajo tacos or mutton stew. The restaurant is open daily from 6am to 9pm.

At the **Ch'ihootso Indian Marketplace** (✆ **928/871-5443**), at the junction of Ariz. 264 and Indian Rte. 12, you'll find several tiny restaurants that

> **Eat Local, Shop Local, in the Navajo Nation**
>
> The Hopi and Navajo reservations both offer some interesting opportunities to eat locally and shop locally, and in so doing patronize small businesses and individuals, which is one of the key aspects of eco-travel.
>
> On the Navajo Nation, you can sample traditional foods at the **Ch'ihootso Indian Marketplace** in Window Rock (above). The steam corn soup served at several of the little food vendors' stalls here is a particular favorite of local families.
>
> Anywhere on the Navajo Nation where there is a scenic view, you'll find jewelry vendors set up by the side of the road. Their wares tend to be inexpensive, certainly as compared to the finer work sold at the trading posts.

specialize in traditional Navajo dishes such as mutton stew and fry bread. On weekends, a crafts/flea market is in the parking lot here. Hours vary.

CANYON DE CHELLY NATIONAL MONUMENT ★★★

68 miles NW of Window Rock; 222 miles NE of Flagstaff; 110 miles SE of Navajo National Monument; 110 miles SE of Monument Valley Navajo Tribal Park

It's hard to imagine narrow canyons less than 1,000 feet deep being as impressive as the Grand Canyon, but in some ways Canyon de Chelly National Monument is just that. Gaze down from the rim at an ancient cliff dwelling as the whinnying of horses and clanging of goats' bells drifts up from far below, and you'll be struck by the continuity of human existence. For more than 2,000 years, people have called these canyons home, and today the canyon is the site of not only prehistoric dwelling sites, but also the summer homes of Navajo farmers and shepherds.

Canyon de Chelly National Monument consists primarily of two major canyons—Canyon de Chelly (pronounced "Canyon duh Shay," a name derived from the Navajo word *tsegi,* meaning "rock canyon") and Canyon del Muerto (Spanish for "Canyon of the Dead"). The canyons extend for more than 100 miles through the rugged slickrock landscape of northeastern Arizona, draining the seasonal snowmelt runoff from the Chuska Mountains.

In summer, Canyon de Chelly's smooth sandstone walls of red and yellow contrast sharply with the greens of corn, pastures, and cottonwoods on the canyon floor. Vast stone amphitheaters form the caves in which the Ancestral Puebloans built their homes, and as you watch shadows and light paint an ever-changing canyon panorama, it's easy to see why the Navajo consider this sacred ground. The many mysteriously abandoned cliff dwellings and the breathtaking natural beauty make Canyon de Chelly as worthy of a visit as the Grand Canyon.

Essentials

ARRIVING From Flagstaff, the easiest route to Canyon de Chelly is I-40 to U.S. 191 to Ganado. At Ganado, drive west on Ariz. 264 and pick up U.S. 191

N. to Chinle. If you're coming down from Monument Valley or Navajo National Monument, Navajo Rte. 59, which connects U.S. 160 and U.S. 191, is an excellent road with plenty of beautiful scenery.

FEES Admission to the monument is free.

SPECIAL EVENTS The annual **Central Navajo Fair,** held in Chinle in August, includes, among other activities, a rodeo, a powwow (Native American drumming and dancing), and Navajo food stalls.

VISITOR INFORMATION Before leaving home, you can contact **Canyon de Chelly National Monument,** P.O. Box 588, Chinle, AZ 86503 (www.nps.gov/cach; (✆ **928/674-5500**) for information. The monument itself is open daily from sunrise to sunset. The visitor center is open daily 8am to 5pm (closed Christmas). Remember that the Navajo Nation observes daylight saving time.

Exploring the Canyon

Your first stop should be the **visitor center** (above), in front of which is an example of a traditional crib-style hogan, a hexagonal structure of logs and earth that Navajos use as both a home and a ceremonial center. Inside the visitor center, a small museum explores the history of Canyon de Chelly, and there's often a silversmith demonstrating Navajo jewelry-making techniques. Interpretive programs are offered at the monument from Memorial Day to Labor Day. Check at the visitor center for daily activities, such as campfire programs and natural-history programs.

From the visitor center, most people tour the canyon by car. Very different views of the monument's system of canyons are provided by the 15-mile North Rim and 16-mile South Rim drives. The North Rim Drive overlooks Canyon del Muerto, while the South Rim Drive overlooks Canyon de Chelly. With stops, the drive along either rim road can easily take 2 to 3 hours. If you have time for only one, make it the South Rim Drive, which provides both a dramatic view of Spider Rock and the chance to hike down into the canyon on the only trail you can explore without hiring a guide. If, on the other hand, you're more interested in the history and prehistory of this area, opt for the North Rim Drive, which overlooks several historically significant sites within the canyon.

THE NORTH RIM DRIVE

The first stop on the North Rim is the **Ledge Ruin Overlook.** On the opposite wall, about 100 feet up from the canyon floor, you can see the Ledge Ruin. This site was occupied by the Ancestral Puebloans between 1050 and 1275. Nearby, at the unmarked Dekaa Kiva Viewpoint, you can see a lone kiva (circular ceremonial building). This structure was reached by means of toeholds cut into the soft sandstone cliff wall.

The second stop is the **Antelope House Overlook,** which is the all-around most interesting overlook in the monument. Not only do you get to hike a quarter-mile over the rugged rimrock landscape, but you also get to view ruins, rock art, and impressive cliff walls. The Antelope House ruin takes its name from the antelope paintings, believed to date back to the 1830s, on a nearby cliff wall. Beneath the ruins of Antelope House, archaeologists have

Taking Photos on the Reservations

Before taking a photograph of a Navajo, always ask permission. If it's granted, a tip of $1 or more is expected. Photography is not allowed at all in Hopi villages.

found the remains of an earlier pit house dating from A.D. 693. Although most of the Ancestral Puebloan cliff dwellings were abandoned sometime after a drought began in 1276, Antelope House had already been abandoned by 1260, possibly because of damage caused by flooding. Across the wash from Antelope House, an ancient tomb, known as the **Tomb of the Weaver,** was discovered by archaeologists in the 1920s. The tomb contained the well-preserved body of an old man wrapped in a blanket of golden eagle feathers and accompanied by cornmeal, shelled and husked corn, pine nuts, beans, salt, and thick skeins of cotton. Also visible from this overlook is **Navajo Fortress,** a red-sandstone butte that the Navajo once used as a refuge from attackers. A steep trail and system of log ladders led to the top of the butte, and by hauling the ladders up behind them, the Navajo could escape from any pursuers.

The third stop is **Mummy Cave Overlook,** named for two mummies found in burial urns below the ruins. Archaeological evidence indicates that this giant amphitheater consisting of two caves was occupied for 1,000 years, from A.D. 300 to 1300. In the two caves and on the shelf between are 80 rooms, including three kivas. The central structure between the two caves includes an interesting three-story building characteristic of the architecture in Mesa Verde National Park in Colorado. Archaeologists speculate that a group of Ancestral Puebloans migrated here from New Mexico. Much of the original plasterwork is still intact and indicates that the buildings were colorfully decorated.

The fourth and last stop on the North Rim is the **Massacre Cave Overlook,** which got its name after an 1805 Spanish military expedition killed more than 115 Navajos at this site. The Navajo at the time had been raiding Spanish settlements that were encroaching on their territory. Accounts of the battle at Massacre Cave differ. One version claims there were only women, children, and old men taking shelter in the cave, but the official Spanish records claim 90 warriors and 25 women and children were killed. Also visible from this overlook is **Yucca Cave,** which was occupied about 1,000 years ago.

THE SOUTH RIM DRIVE

The South Rim Drive climbs slowly but steadily, and at each stop you're a little bit higher above the canyon floor. Near the mouth of the canyon is the **Tunnel Overlook,** where a short narrow canyon feeds into Chinle Wash, a wash formed by the streams that cut through the canyons of the national monument. *Tsegi* is a Navajo word meaning "rock canyon," and at the nearby **Tsegi Overlook,** that's just what you'll see when you gaze down from the viewpoint.

The next stop is the **Junction Overlook,** so named because it overlooks the junction of Canyon del Muerto and Canyon de Chelly. Here you can see the **Junction Ruin,** which has 10 rooms and a kiva. Ancestral Puebloans occupied this ruin during the Great Pueblo Period, which lasted from around 1100

To view the White House Ruin, one of Canyon de Chelly's largest sites, take the 2½-mile round-trip White House Ruins Trail.

until shortly before 1300. **First Ruin,** which is perched precariously on a long narrow ledge, is also visible. There are 22 rooms and two kivas in this ruin. Good luck picking out the two canyons in this maze of curving cliff walls.

The third stop is **White House Overlook,** from which you can see the 80-room **White House Ruin,** which is among the largest ruin sites in the canyon. These buildings were inhabited between 1040 and 1275. From this overlook, you have your only opportunity to descend into Canyon de Chelly without a guide or ranger. The **White House Ruins Trail ★★** descends 600 feet to the canyon floor and crosses Chinle Wash before reaching the White House Ruin. The buildings of this ruin were constructed both on the canyon floor and 50 feet up the cliff wall in a small cave. Although you cannot enter the ruins, you can get close enough to get a good look. You may enter the canyon without a Navajo guide on this trail only. Do not wander off this trail, and please respect the privacy of the Navajo living here. The 2½-mile round-trip hike takes about 2 hours. Be sure to carry water.

Notice the black streaks on the sandstone walls above the White House Ruins. These streaks, known as desert varnish, are formed by seeping water, which reacts with iron in the sandstone (iron is what gives the walls their reddish hue). To create the canyon's many petroglyphs, Ancestral Puebloan artists would chip away at the desert varnish. Later, the Navajo used paints to create pictographs of animals and historical events, such as the Spanish military expedition that killed 115 Navajos at Massacre Cave. Many of these petroglyphs and pictographs can be seen if you take a guided tour into the canyon.

The fifth stop is **Sliding House Overlook.** These ruins were built on a narrow shelf and appear to be sliding down into the canyon. Inhabited from about 900 until 1200, Sliding House contained between 30 and 50 rooms. This overlook is already more than 700 feet above the canyon floor, with sheer walls giving the narrow canyon a very foreboding appearance.

On the last access road to the canyon rim, you'll come to the **Face Rock Overlook,** which provides yet another dizzying glimpse of the ever-deepening canyon. Here you gaze 1,000 feet down to the bottom. However, it is the next stop—**Spider Rock Overlook ★★**—that offers the monument's most spectacular view. This viewpoint overlooks the junction of Canyon de Chelly and Monument Canyon. The monolithic pinnacle known as Spider Rock rises 800 feet from the canyon floor, its two free-standing towers forming a natural monument. Across the canyon from Spider Rock is the similarly striking **Speaking Rock,** which is connected to the far canyon wall.

OTHER WAYS TO SEE THE CANYON

Access to the floor of Canyon de Chelly is restricted. Unless you're on the White House Trail (above), you must be on an organized tour or accompanied by an authorized guide in order to enter the canyon. If you want to see a lot of the canyon and don't happen to be driving your own four-wheel-drive vehicle, the best way to see Canyon de Chelly and Canyon del Muerto is on a jeep tour or what locals call **shake-and-bake tours ★**. These latter tours are in rugged military-type trucks that have seats installed in the truck beds. In summer, these excursions really live up to the name. (In winter, the trucks are enclosed to keep out the elements.) Tours make frequent stops for photographs and to visit ruins, Navajo farms, and rock art. **Thunderbird Lodge** (www.thunderbirdlodge.com; (✆ **800/679-2473**), which uses unusual six-wheel-drive trucks for its tours, operates half-day tours costing $70 and full-day trips costing $150 per person. The half-day tours operate year-round with departures from the hotel (below) at 9am and 2pm. A sunset tour is offered from April through October. Full-day tours operate spring through fall, departing at 9am and returning at 5pm. Similar tours are offered by **Canyon de Chelly Tours** (www.canyondechellytours.com; ✆ **928/349-1600**), which departs from the Holiday Inn (below) and will take you into the canyon in a Unimog truck (a powerful four-wheel-drive off-road vehicle). These 3-hour tours, which operate from March to October, cost $75. Reservations are recommended.

For a more personalized experience, go out in a jeep in a small group. My favorite guide is Daniel Staley, who operates **Beauty Way Jeep Tours** (http://canyondechellybeautywayjeeptours.com; ✆ **928/674-3772,** text 928/797-0836). Descendants of Chauncey Neboiya, the first Navajo archaeologist, Daniel and his sons continue a guiding tradition that goes back more than 60 years. A 3-hour tour costs $175 for one to three people; a 4-hour tour costs $240; and a 5-hour tour costs $305. Longer tours and overnight camping trips can also be arranged.

You can find other guides, approved by the National Park Service, at www.nps.gov/cach.

For a more traditional means of transportation, you can go on a guided horseback ride. Drive east along South Rim Drive to **Totsonii Ranch ★** (www.webreserv.com/totsoniiranchaz; ✆ **928/221-4205**), which is 1¼ miles past the end of the paved stretch of this road. Rides from here visit a remote part of the canyon (including the Spider Rock area); call for rates and available rides.

If you're physically fit and enjoy hiking, consider hiring a **Navajo guide** to lead you into the canyon. Hikes can start at the White House Ruin trail, near the Spider Rock overlook, or from near the Antelope House overlook. These latter two starting points are trails that are not open to the public without a guide and should be your top choices. The hike from Antelope House gets my vote for best option for a hike. The monument visitor center maintains a list of guides, and guides can often be hired at the visitor center. The guide fee is usually $15 per hour with a 3-hour minimum.

Shopping

The **Thunderbird Lodge Gift Shop** in Chinle (✆ **800/679-2473**) is well worth a stop while you're in the area (see below for more on the lodge). It has a large collection of rugs, as well as a good selection of pottery and plenty of souvenirs. Anywhere visitors gather in the canyon (such as at ruins and petroglyph sites), you're likely to encounter craftspeople selling jewelry and other types of handwork. These craftspeople accept cash, personal checks, traveler's checks, and sometimes credit cards.

Forget About Wine with Dinner

Alcohol is prohibited on both the Navajo and Hopi reservations. Unfortunately, however, despite this prohibition, drunk drivers are a problem on the reservation, so stay alert.

Where to Stay Near Canyon de Chelly

Holiday Inn–Canyon de Chelly ★ Between the town of Chinle and the national monument entrance, this modern hotel is on the site of the old Garcia Trading Post, which has been incorporated into the restaurant and gift shop building (although the building no longer has any historical character). All guest rooms have patios or balconies, and most face the cottonwood-shaded pool courtyard. Because Canyon de Chelly truck tours leave from the parking lot here and because the restaurant serves the best food in town, this should be your top choice for a room in Chinle.

Indian Rte. 7, Garcia Trading Post, Chinle. www.ihg.com/holidayinn/hotels/us/en/reservation. ✆ **888/465-4329** or 928/674-5000. 108 units. $103–$120 double. Children 19 and under stay free in parent's room; children 12 and under eat free. **Amenities:** Restaurant; concierge; exercise room; outdoor pool; room service; free Wi-Fi.

Thunderbird Lodge ★ Built on the site of an early trading post at the mouth of Canyon de Chelly, Thunderbird Lodge is the closest hotel to the national monument. The red-adobe construction of the lodge itself is reminiscent of ancient pueblos, and the presence on the property of an old stone-walled trading post gives this place lots of character. However, the rooms here are not quite as modern or as comfortable as those at the nearby Holiday Inn. The old trading post now is a cafeteria that serves a few Navajo dishes. There's also a shop that sells Navajo rugs.

Indian Rte. 7, Chinle. www.thunderbirdlodge.com. ✆ **800/679-2473** or 928/674-5841. 73 units. Mar–Oct $100–$120 double, $130 suite; Nov–Feb $70–$90 double, $100 suite. Children 12 and under stay free in parent's room. Pets accepted ($10 fee). **Amenities:** Restaurant; free Wi-Fi.

CAMPGROUNDS

Adjacent to the Thunderbird Lodge is the free **Cottonwood Campground,** which has around 100 sites but does not take reservations. On South Rim Drive 10 miles east of the Canyon de Chelly visitor center, you'll find the private **Spider Rock Campground** (www.spiderrockcampground.com; © **928/781-2016**), which has more than 30 spaces and charges $11 per night. This campground also has RV spaces for $16 a night and a couple of hogans for rent; call for rates.

Where to Eat Near Canyon de Chelly

Other than a handful of fast-food restaurants in Chinle, the only places to eat in town are hotel dining rooms. While the cafeteria at the Thunderbird Lodge has a memorable setting in a historic trading post, the food is forgettable. The food at the Holiday Inn's dining room is a bit better, though the service isn't. If you need an espresso, stop by **Changing Woman Cafe** (© **928/674-5260**), which is in a hogan under the trees across from the national monument's Cottonwood Campground. The coffee is organic, and the cafe owner, Victoria Begay, also offers a variety of four-wheel-drive, hiking, and camping tours.

NAVAJO NATIONAL MONUMENT ★

110 miles NW of Canyon de Chelly; 140 miles NE of Flagstaff; 60 miles SW of Monument Valley; 90 miles E of Page

Navajo National Monument, 30 miles west of Kayenta and 60 miles northeast of Tuba City, encompasses three of the largest and best-preserved Ancestral Puebloan cliff dwellings in the region—Betatakin, Keet Seel, and Inscription House. It's possible to visit both Betatakin and Keet Seel, but, due to its fragility, Inscription House is closed to the public. The name Navajo National Monument is a bit misleading. Although the Navajo do inhabit the area now, the cliff dwellings were built by Kayenta Ancestral Puebloans, the ancestors of today's Hopi and Pueblo peoples. The Navajo did not arrive in this area until after the cliff dwellings had been abandoned.

For reasons unknown, the well-constructed cliff dwellings here were abandoned around the middle of the 13th century. Tree rings suggest that a drought in the latter part of the 13th century prevented the Ancestral Puebloans from growing sufficient crops. In Tsegi Canyon, however, there's another theory for the abandonment. The canyon was usually flooded each year by spring and summer snowmelt, which made farming quite productive, but in the mid-1200s, weather patterns changed and streams began cutting deep into the soil, forming narrow little canyons called arroyos, which lowered the water table and made farming much more difficult.

Essentials

ARRIVING Navajo National Monument can be reached by taking U.S. 89 N. to U.S. 160 to Ariz. 564 N.

VISITOR INFORMATION For information, contact **Navajo National Monument** (www.nps.gov/nava; ✆ **928/672-2700**). Late May through early September, the visitor center is open daily from 8am to 5:30pm; in winter the visitor center is open daily from 9am to 5pm. The monument is open daily from sunrise to sunset and admission is free.

Exploring the Monument

A visit to Navajo National Monument is definitely not a point-and-shoot experience. You're going to have to expend some energy if you want to see what this monument is all about. The shortest distance you'll have to walk is 1 mile, which is the round-trip from the visitor center to the Betatakin overlook. However, if you want to actually get close to these ruins, you're looking at strenuous day or overnight hikes.

Your first stop should be the **visitor center,** which has informative displays on the Ancestral Puebloan and Navajo cultures, including numerous artifacts from Tsegi Canyon. You can also watch a couple of short films or a slide show.

The only one of the monument's three ruins that can be seen easily is **Betatakin** ★, which means "ledge house" in Navajo. Built in a huge amphitheater-like alcove in the canyon wall, Betatakin was occupied only from 1250 to 1300 and may have housed 125 people. A 1-mile round-trip paved trail from the visitor center leads to overlooks of Betatakin. The strenuous 5-mile round-trip hike to Betatakin itself is led by a ranger, takes 3 to 5 hours, and involves descending more than 700 feet to the floor of Tsegi Canyon and later returning to the rim. Between late May and early September, these guided hikes are offered daily at 8:15 and 10am. (Remember, daylight saving time *is* observed here on the Navajo Nation.) Other months, tours leave only on weekends at 10am, but call to make sure the tour will be going out. These hikes are offered on a first-come, first-served basis. All participants should carry 1 to 2 quarts of water. While this is a fascinating hike, you will be hiking with a large group.

Keet Seel ★, which means "broken pieces of pottery" in Navajo, has a much longer history than Betatakin, with occupation beginning as early as A.D. 950 and continuing until 1300. At one point, Keet Seel may have housed 150 people. The 17-mile round-trip hike is quite strenuous and involves going a thousand feet up and down switchbacks, negotiating loose rock, sliding down a sandy hill, and otherwise exerting a lot of energy. During the summer, hikers usually stay overnight at a primitive campground near the ruins, but in the winter, if the hike is offered at all, it is done as a day hike. You must carry enough water for your trip—up to 2 gallons in summer—because none is available along the trail. These hikes are offered between late May and mid-September, and reservations can be made up to 5 months in advance. Hikes are sometimes offered in other months. Note that all hikers must attend a mandatory orientation, preferably the day before their hike. Hiking to Keet Seel also requires a free special permit from the Navajo Nation, available by calling the Visitor Center for a reservation; only 20 slots are open per day.

Where to Stay Near the Navajo National Monument

There is no lodge at the national monument, but there are two campgrounds. **Sunset View Campground** (31 sites), near the visitor center, is open all year, while **Canyon View Campground** (14 sites), a mile north off Tsegi Canyon Rd., is open only between April and September. Both campgrounds are free, and neither takes reservations. Sunset View has water and restrooms. The nearest reliable motels are 30 miles away in Kayenta (p. 321). See www.nps.gov/nava/planyourvisit/placestogo.htm for more information.

MONUMENT VALLEY NAVAJO TRIBAL PARK ★★★

60 miles NE of Navajo National Monument; 110 miles NW of Canyon de Chelly; 200 miles NE of Flagstaff; 150 miles E of Page

In its role as sculptor, nature has, in the north central part of the Navajo Nation, created a garden of monoliths and spires unequaled anywhere on earth. Whether you've been here or not, you've almost certainly seen images of Monument Valley before. This otherworldly landscape has been an object of fascination for years, and since Hollywood director John Ford first came here in the 1930s, it has served as backdrop for countless movies, TV shows, and commercials.

Located 30 miles north of Kayenta and straddling the Arizona-Utah state line (you actually go into Utah to get to the park entrance), Monument Valley is a vast flat plain punctuated by natural sandstone cathedrals. These huge monoliths rise up from the sagebrush with sheer walls that capture the light of the rising and setting sun and transform it into fiery hues. Evocative names including the Mittens, Three Sisters, Camel Butte, Elephant Butte, the Thumb, and Totem Pole reflect the shapes the sandstone has taken under the erosive forces of nature.

While it may at first seem as if this strange landscape is a barren wasteland, it is actually still home to a few hardy Navajo families. The Navajo have been living in the valley for generations, herding their sheep through the sagebrush scrublands, and some families continue to reside here today. In fact, human habitation in Monument Valley dates back hundreds of years. Within the park are more than 100 Ancestral Puebloan archaeological sites, ruins, and petroglyphs dating from before 1300.

Essentials

ARRIVING Monument Valley Navajo Tribal Park is 200 miles northeast of Flagstaff. Take U.S. 89 north to U.S. 160 to Kayenta, then drive north 24 miles on U.S. 163.

FEES Admission to the park is $20 per vehicle up to four people (free for children 9 and under). ***Note:*** Because this is a tribal park and not a federal park, America the Beautiful passes are not valid here.

Stay overnight near Monument Valley to view its majestic buttes at their most spectacular time of day: sunset.

VISITOR INFORMATION For information, contact **Monument Valley Navajo Tribal Park** (www.navajonationparks.org; ✆ **435/727-5874** or 435/727-5879). May through September, the park is open daily from 6am to 8pm; between October and April, it's open daily from 8am to 4:30pm. The park is closed on Christmas.

Exploring Monument Valley

This is big country and, like the Grand Canyon, primarily a point-and-shoot experience for most visitors. Because this is reservation land and people still live in Monument Valley, most backcountry and off-road travel is prohibited unless you're with a licensed guide. So basically, with one exception, your options for seeing the park on your own are limited. You can take a few pictures from the overlook beside the visitor center and the View Hotel, drive the park's Valley Drive (a scenic but very rough 17-mile dirt road), take a jeep or van tour, or go on a guided hike or horseback ride. At the visitor center, you'll find a small museum and a large gift shop, and at the View Hotel you'll find a restaurant with a knockout view. A quarter-mile away from the visitor center there's a picnic area.

Although **Valley Drive** is best driven in a high-clearance vehicle, plenty of people drive the loop in rental cars and other standard passenger vehicles. Take it slow, and you should do fine. However, if the first stretch of rocky, rutted road convinces you to change your mind about the drive, just return to the visitor center and book a jeep or van tour and let someone else pay the repair bills. Along the loop drive, you'll pass 11 very scenic viewpoints that provide ample opportunities for photographing the valley's many natural monuments. At many of these viewpoints, you'll also encounter Navajos selling jewelry and other crafts. At John Ford's Point, so named because it was a favorite shooting location for film director John Ford, you can see scenes straight out of Ford's movies with John Wayne. To the southwest, for instance, are Mitchell and Gray Whiskers buttes, so prominent in *The Searchers*. To the northeast stands West Mitten Butte, which figures in *She Wore a Yellow Ribbon*. Farther along the 17-mile loop drive that leads to and around Rain God Mesa, take the spur road about a mile beyond Lookout Point to catch a view of East Mitten Butte and Merrick Butte; you'll be on the same spot that the storied vehicle bearing John Wayne and company traveled in *Stagecoach*.

There are two exceptions to the no-traveling-off-road rule. The 3.3-mile **Wildcat Trail ★★** is a loop hiking trail off Highway 163 that circles West Mitten Butte and provides the only opportunity to get close to this picturesque butte. As you circle the butte, you'll get all kinds of different perspectives, even one that completely eliminates the "thumb." Be sure to carry plenty of water. Be aware that the loose sand can make for a difficult slog, so wear good hiking boots, not casual shoes. The other trail open without a guide is the **Mesa Rim Trail,** a .5-mile trail along the mesa above the View Hotel.

Please be aware that rock climbing is not allowed on Navajo tribal land.

TAKING A TOUR

If you're trying to decide whether to take a tour, here's some little-publicized information that might help. Most tours don't just drive the 17-mile loop; they go off into a part of the valley that's closed to anyone who is not on a tour. There you'll get close-up looks at several natural arches and stop at some beautiful petroglyphs. Before booking a tour, make sure that the tour will go to this "closed" section of the valley.

There are always plenty of jeep tour companies waiting for business in the park's main parking lot. If you're staying at Goulding's Lodge (below), then your best bet is to go out with **Goulding's Tours** (www.gouldings.com; ✆ **435/727-3231**), which has its office right at the lodge, just a few miles from the park entrance. Goulding's offers tours ranging from a few hours to a full day, costing from $60 to $135 (call for more information). **Monument Valley Simpson's Trailhandler Tours** (www.trailhandlertours.com; ✆ **877/686-2848** or 435/727-3362), another reliable company, charges $69 to $200 for a 2½-hour tour ($35 for children 6–12); a 1½-hour tour is also available, but the extra hour, at only $12 more for adults, takes in a lot more territory. **Sacred Monument Tours** (www.monumentvalley.net; ✆ **435/727-3218** or 928/380-4527) charges $75 for a 2½-hour jeep tour; a variety of other tours are also available. Sacred Monument Tours also offers horseback tours, with a 1-hour tour beginning at $80, a 2-hour tour beginning at $110, and a 3-hour tour beginning at $150 per adult rider.

Because jeep and van tours are such a big business here, there's a steady stream of the vehicles on Valley Drive throughout the day. One way to get away from the rumble of engines is to go out on a guided hike. **Kéyah Hózhóní Tours** (www.monumentvalley.com; ✆ **928/309-7440**) offers hiking tours ($100 per person), all-day photo tours ($250 per person), and overnight camping trips ($550 for one or two people). Keep in mind that conditions are likely to be very hot in summer. The guides, Carlos and Carl Phillips, are flexible in their hours and glad to plan tours around individual needs.

Monumental Sunsets

Monument Valley is photogenic at any time of day, but especially at sunset, when the lengthening shadows make for a nice play of light with the spires and buttes. Drive along U.S. 163 about 5 miles north of Kayenta, where the 7,096-foot rise called Agathla Peak, the root of an ancient volcano, looms to the east. It has a nice haunted quality that's especially well served by a full moon, and it's one of the most memorable vistas in the already spectacular region.

Attractions Outside the Park

Before leaving the area, you might want to visit **Goulding's Museum & Trading Post,** at Goulding's Lodge (below). This old trading post was the home of the Gouldings for many years, and it's set up as they had it back in the 1920s and 1930s. There are also displays about the many movies that have been shot here. The trading post hours vary with the seasons; admission is by donation.

Inside Kayenta's **Burger King,** which is next door to the Hampton Inn, there's an interesting exhibit on the Navajo code talkers of World War II. The code talkers were Native American soldiers, including many young Navajos, who used their own languages to transmit coded messages, primarily in the South Pacific.

Where to Stay & Eat Near Monument Valley

In addition to the lodgings listed here, the prices of which have risen dramatically in recent years, you'll find several budget motels north of Monument Valley in the Utah towns of Mexican Hat and Bluff. There are restaurants at both the View Hotel and Goulding's Lodge, but, aside from the great views, both are serviceable at best and will make you wish you'd packed a meal.

Goulding's Lodge ★ For decades this was the only lodge actually located in Monument Valley, and although you can now stay inside the park at the Navajo-owned View Hotel, Goulding's is still a good bet. It's one of the most popular hotels in the area, so be sure to make your reservation well in advance. Goulding's offers great views (especially at sunrise) from the private balconies of its large guest rooms, which include one-bedroom suites and two-bedroom apartments. The restaurant serves Navajo and American dishes, and also boasts views that are enough to make any meal an event. Unfortunately, although the setting is memorable, the service in the restaurant can be somewhat lacking. The lodge also has a museum.

Monument Valley, UT. www.gouldings.com. ✆ **435/727-3231.** 63 units. Rates begin at $223 for a standard room with two beds. Children 9 and under stay free in parent's room. Pets accepted ($20 fee). **Amenities:** Restaurant; exercise room; indoor pool; free Wi-Fi.

Hampton Inn–Navajo Nation ★ This is the most modern lodging right in the town of Kayenta and, as such, should be your first choice if you can't get a room in Monument Valley itself. The Hampton Inn is built in a contemporary Santa Fe style and has spacious, comfortable guest rooms. In the hotel's dining room, you can get a few Navajo dishes. Adjacent to the hotel, you'll find the Navajo Cultural Center and a Burger King that has an interesting display on the Navajo code talkers of World War II.

U.S. 160, Kayenta. www.hamptoninn.com. ✆ **800/426-7866** or 928/697-3170. 73 units. $185–$225 double. Rates include full breakfast. Children 18 and under stay free in parent's room. Pets accepted ($20 fee plus $20 per night). **Amenities:** Restaurant; outdoor pool; room service; free Wi-Fi.

Kayenta Monument Valley Inn ★ This hotel, right in the center of Kayenta, is very popular with tour groups and is almost always crowded. Although the grounds are dusty and a bit run-down, rooms are spacious and clean and have all been extensively renovated in the past few years. Part of the hotel's dining room is designed to look like an Ancestral Puebloan ruin, and the menu offers both American and Navajo cuisine.

U.S. 160 and U.S. 163, Kayenta. www.kayentamonumentvalleyinn.com. ✆ **866/306-5458** or 928/697-3221. 164 units. Early Sept–June $163–$239 double; July–early Sept $179–$259 double. Children 18 and under stay free in parent's room. **Amenities:** Restaurant; exercise room; outdoor pool; room service; free Wi-Fi.

The View Hotel ★★ This Navajo-owned hotel inside Monument Valley Navajo Tribal Park is the only hotel inside the park. As such, it should be your first choice for accommodations in the area. With the park's most famous and picturesque buttes right outside the windows, you need do nothing more than sit back and watch the play of light on red-rock pinnacles. The rooms themselves are comfortable enough, though little better than standard freeway off-ramp motel rooms. What you're paying for here is the view, not the room itself. The same is true of the restaurant, which constantly disappoints.

Monument Valley, UT. www.monumentvalleyview.com. ✆ **435/727-5555.** 96 units. Mid-Mar–mid-Nov $149–$229 double, $185–$319 suite; mid-Nov–mid-Mar $99–$129 double, $175–$199 suite. **Amenities:** Restaurant; exercise room; free Wi-Fi.

Wetherill Inn ★ Located in Kayenta a mile north of the junction of U.S. 160 and U.S. 163, and 20 miles south of Monument Valley, the Wetherill Inn doesn't look like much from the outside, but guest rooms are the most modern rooms in Kayenta. While the hotel offers neither the convenience of the View Hotel or Goulding's Lodge nor the amenities of the nearby Holiday Inn or Hampton Inn, if you just want a nice room for the night, this is a good bet. A cafe next door serves Navajo and American food.

1000 Main St., Kayenta. www.wetherill-inn.com. ✆ **928/697-3231.** 54 units. May 1–Oct 15 $152 double; Oct 16–Nov 15 and Apr $107 double; Nov 16–Mar 31 $92 double. Children 12 and under stay free in parent's room. Rates include continental breakfast. **Amenities:** Indoor pool; free Wi-Fi.

CAMPGROUNDS

If you're headed to Monument Valley Navajo Tribal Park, you can camp at **Goulding's Campground** (www.gouldings.com; ✆ **435/727-3231**), which charges $30 per night per tent site. There are also small cabins that go for $139 per night and RV sites with full hookups from $52 to $62 a night. This campground is open year-round (limited services November to mid-March) and has

More Big Rocks

Monument Valley isn't the only place in this region with impressive rocks. **Square Butte,** midway between Lake Powell and Kayenta on Highway 98, is a spectacular red-rock mirror of the far more imposing Navajo Mountain due north. East of Kayenta on U.S. 160, watch for the red sandstone cliffs known as **Baby Rocks.** East of Tuba City, also on U.S. 160, watch for the two sandstone towers known as **Elephant Feet.** Everywhere you look here, it's a wonderland of stone.

an indoor pool, hot showers, a playground, a coin-op laundry, a convenience store, and Wi-Fi.

Driving on to Colorado or New Mexico: The Four Corners Meet

It's an offbeat treat to visit the **Four Corners Monument** (https://navajonationparks.org; ✆ **928/871-6647**), where you can stand in four states—Arizona, Colorado, Utah, and New Mexico—at once. Located north of Teec Nos Pos in the very northeast corner of the state, this park is the only place in the United States where the corners of four states come together. The scenery is a little nondescript, considering the majesty of the surrounding countryside, and the exact point is just a cement pad surrounded by flags and vendor stalls. The park also has a few picnic tables and a snack bar serving, among other things, Navajo fry bread. The park is open daily from 8am to 7pm, and admission is $3. The Teec Nos Pos Trading Post, by the way, sells ice, groceries, and well-priced art and craft goods. It's definitely worth a visit.

A trick of the map, maybe, but it's a unique travel experience: standing at the meeting place of four states.

LAKE POWELL ★★ & PAGE

98 miles NW of Kayenta; 272 miles N of Phoenix; 130 miles E of Grand Canyon North Rim; 130 miles NE of Grand Canyon South Rim

Had the early Spanish explorers of Arizona suddenly come upon Lake Powell after slogging for months across desolate desert, they would have either taken it for a mirage or fallen to their knees and rejoiced. Surrounded by hundreds of miles of parched desert, this reservoir, created by the damming of the

Dammed If You Do...

When the Glen Canyon Dam was first proposed, an angry outcry arose. Many people felt that Glen Canyon was even more beautiful than the Grand Canyon and should be preserved in its natural state. Preservationists lost the battle, however, and construction of the dam began in 1960, with completion in 1963. It took another 17 years for Lake Powell to fill to capacity, during which time the rising lake saw service as a movie set for such films as *The Greatest Story Ever Told* and *Planet of the Apes*. Today, the lake is a watery powerboat playground, and houseboats and water-skiers cruise where once only birdsong and the splashing of waterfalls filled the canyon air. These days most people seem to agree, though, that Lake Powell is as amazing a sight as the Grand Canyon, and it draws almost as many visitors each year as its downriver neighbor.

Colorado River at Glen Canyon, seems unreal when first glimpsed. Yet real it is, and it draws people from around the region with its promise of relief from the heat—even though the place, in truth, can be infernally hot for much of the year.

While Lake Powell is something of a man-made wonder, one of the natural wonders of the world—**Rainbow Bridge**—can also be found on its shores. Called *nonnozhoshi* by the Navajo, or "the rainbow turned to stone," this is the largest natural bridge on earth and stretches 275 feet across a side canyon off Lake Powell.

The town of Page, originally a camp constructed to house the workers who built the dam, has many motels and inexpensive restaurants, and is the main base for most visitors to the area.

Essentials

ARRIVING Page is connected to Flagstaff by U.S. 89. Ariz. 98 leads southeast onto the Navajo Indian Reservation and connects with U.S. 160 to Kayenta and Four Corners.

FEES Admission to Glen Canyon National Recreation Area is $25 per car (good for 1 week). There is also a $30-per-week boat fee if you bring your own boat.

VISITOR INFORMATION For further information on the Lake Powell area, contact the **Glen Canyon National Recreation Area** (www.nps.gov/glca; ✆ **928/608-6404**); the **Page–Lake Powell Chamber of Commerce,** 34 S. Lake Powell Blvd., Page (www.pagechamber.com; ✆ **928/645-2741**); or the **John Wesley Powell Memorial Museum,** 6 N. Lake Powell Blvd., Page (www.powellmuseum.org; ✆ **928/645-9496**), which houses the Page Lake Powell Visitor Center.

Exploring the Lake Powell Area

Until the flooding of Glen Canyon formed Lake Powell, this area was one of the most remote regions in the contiguous 48 states. However, since the construction of Glen Canyon Dam in the 1960s, this remote and rugged landscape

Wake-boarding on Lake Powell, one of the state's most popular recreation areas.

has become one of the country's most popular national recreation areas. Today, the lake and much of the surrounding land, designated the **Glen Canyon National Recreation Area,** attracts around two million visitors each year. The otherworldly setting amid the slickrock canyons of northern Arizona and southern Utah is a tapestry of colors, the blues and greens of the lake contrasting with the reds and oranges of the surrounding sandstone cliffs. This interplay of colors and vast desert landscapes easily makes Lake Powell the most beautiful of Arizona's many reservoirs.

Built to provide water for the desert communities of the Southwest and West, **Glen Canyon Dam** stands 710 feet above the bedrock and contains almost 5 million cubic yards of concrete. The dam also provides hydroelectric power, and deep within its massive wall of concrete are huge power turbines. At the **Carl Hayden Visitor Center** (**✆ 928/608-6200**), located beside the dam on U.S. 89 just north of Page, you can tour the dam and learn about its construction. (Tours are $5 and last about an hour.) Between mid-May and mid-September, the visitor center is open daily 8am to 6pm; November to February, it's open daily 8am to 4pm; other months, it's open daily 8am to 5pm (it's closed New Year's Day, Thanksgiving, and Christmas).

More than 500 feet deep in some places, and bounded by nearly 2,000 miles of shoreline, **Lake Powell** is a maze of convoluted canyons where rock walls often rise hundreds of feet straight out of the water. In places, the long, winding canyons are so narrow there isn't even room to turn a motorboat around. The only way to truly appreciate this lake is from a boat, whether a houseboat, a runabout, or a sea kayak. Water-skiing, jet-skiing, and fishing have long been the most popular on-water activities, and the lake is a hive of activity, especially in the summer months. Head up-lake from Wahweap Marina, and you'll soon get away from the crowds and into some of the narrower reaches of the lake.

So, What's with the Bathtub Ring?

You'll notice that the red-rock cliff walls above the waters of Lake Powell are no longer red but are instead coated with what looks like a layer of white soap scum. Those are calcium carbonate deposits left on the rock after more than a decade of drought that, at its worst, left the lake level more than 130 feet below what is called "full pool" (when the reservoir is full). Currently, the lake level is down around 100 feet, low enough that some launch ramps are now unusable.

If you don't have your own boat, you can at least see a small part of the lake on a boat tour. A variety of tours depart from **Wahweap Marina** (www.lakepowell.com; ✆ **888/896-3829** or 928/645-2433), which is 5 miles north of the Glen Canyon Dam on Lake Shore Drive. Your best bet is either the 1½-hour **Antelope Canyon Cruise** ($47 for adults, $32 for children) or the 2½-hour **Canyon Adventure Cruise** ($75 for adults, $49 for children). To see more of the lake, opt for the full-day tour to Rainbow Bridge. Dinner cruises are also offered.

If you'd like to see more of the area than is visible from car or boat, consider taking an air tour with **Westwind Scenic Air Tours** (www.westwindairservice.com; ✆ **928/645-2494**), which offers several tours of northern Arizona and southern Utah, including flights over Rainbow Bridge and Monument Valley. Flights board at the **Page Airport** (238 10th Ave.; ✆ **928/645-4240**). Sample rates are $135 for a 30-minute flight over Rainbow Bridge (minimum two passengers) and $273 for a 90-minute flight over Monument Valley (minimum three passengers). Children 12 and under get a 10% discount.

RAINBOW BRIDGE NATIONAL MONUMENT

Rainbow Bridge ★★★, the world's largest natural bridge and one of the most spectacular sights in the Southwest, rises from the bedrock of a narrow canyon roughly 40 miles up the lake from Wahweap Marina and Glen Canyon Dam. Carved by wind and water over the ages, Rainbow Bridge is an awesome reminder of the powers of erosion that have sculpted this entire region. This massive natural arch of sandstone, 290 feet high with a span of 275 feet, sits within **Rainbow Bridge National Monument** (www.nps.gov/rabr; ✆ **928/608-6200**), which is administered by Glen Canyon National Recreation Area. Entrance is free.

Rainbow Bridge is accessible only by boat or by way of a 14-mile-long hiking trail; most visitors opt for boating. **Lake Powell Resorts and Marinas** (www.lakepowell.com; ✆ **888/896-3829** or 928/645-2433) offers 6-hour tours ($122 for adults, $77 for children), departing from the Wahweap Marina in Page (100 Wahweap Blvd.; ✆ **928/645-1027**), which cruise through some of the most spectacular scenery on earth. Tours include a box lunch and a bit more exploring after visiting Rainbow Bridge. ***Note:*** Because the lake's water level is so low from years of drought, the boat stops more than a half-mile from Rainbow Bridge; passengers have to hike from there to see the sandstone arch.

The hike to Rainbow Bridge is about 25 miles round-trip and should be done as an overnight backpacking trip. It requires a Navajo Nation camping and hiking permit ($12 per day), available through the **Navajo Parks and Recreation Department** in Window Rock (www.navajonationparks.org; ✆ **928/871-6647**), at the **Antelope Canyon Tribal Park Office** (✆ **928/698-2808**), 3 miles south of Page on Navajo Rte. 20 (beside the LeChee Chapter House), or at the **Cameron Visitor Center** (✆ **928/679-2303**) in the community of Cameron near the turnoff for the Grand Canyon.

ANTELOPE CANYON

If you've spent any time in Arizona, chances are you've noticed photos of a narrow sandstone canyon only a few feet wide. The pinkish-orange walls of the canyon seem to glow with an inner light, and beams of sunlight slice the darkness of the deep slot canyon. Sound familiar? If you've seen this, you were probably looking at a photo of Antelope Canyon (sometimes called Corkscrew Canyon). Located 2½ miles southeast of Page off Ariz. 98 (at milepost 299), this photogenic canyon comprises the **Antelope Canyon/Lake Powell Navajo Tribal Park ★★★** (✆ **928/698-2808**), which is on the Navajo Nation. To visit, you will need to join a tour licensed by the Navajo Nation. Most tours last 1½ hours and leave from Page. **Antelope Canyon Tours,** 22 S. Lake Powell Blvd. (www.antelopecanyon.com; ✆ **866/645-9102** or 928/645-9102) operates tours to Upper Antelope Canyon and charges $45.50 for adults, $35.50 for ages 8 to 12, and $27.50 for kids 6 to 7. (Rates are discounted in January and February.) Photographic tours cost $108 (no kids allowed on these). For more on visiting Antelope Canyon with authorized tour operators, see the Navajo Nation Parks & Recreation website, **www.navajonationparks.org.** Just remember that if there's even the slightest chance of rain in the region, you should not venture into this canyon, which is subject to flash floods. In the past, people who have ignored bad weather predictions have been killed by such floods.

Antelope Canyon's stunning stonescapes can only be seen with a licensed Navajo Nation tour guide.

Overland Canyon Tours, 48 S. Lake Powell Blvd. (www.overlandcanyontours.com; ✆ **928/608-4072**) offers tours to nearby Canyon X, which is much less visited than Antelope Canyon and is a good choice for serious photographers who want to avoid the crowds. A 3-hour tour costs $80, with children under 8 admitted free.

ATTRACTIONS IN PAGE

In the town of Page, the **John Wesley Powell Memorial Museum** (6 N. Lake Powell Blvd.; www.powellmuseum.org; ✆ **928/645-9496**) tells the story of the intrepid adventurer for whom the lake is named. In 1869, Powell, a one-armed Civil War veteran, led a small band of men on the first boat expedition to travel the length of the Grand Canyon, spending more than 3 months fighting the rapids of the Green and Colorado rivers. Besides documenting the Powell expedition with photographs, etchings, and dioramas, the museum displays Native American artifacts ranging from Ancestral Puebloan pottery to contemporary Navajo and Hopi crafts. The museum is also an information center for Page, Lake Powell, and the surrounding region. Admission is free, but donations are welcome. It's open daily from 9am to 5pm.

Between April and October, you can learn about Navajo culture at **Navajo Village Heritage Center** (www.navajovillage.com; ✆ **928/660-0304**), a living-history center on the northeast corner of Ariz. 98 and Coppermine Rd. (on the south side of Page). Evening performances here center on programs of Native American dancing, but there are also demonstrations by weavers, silversmiths, and other artisans. Tours last 2½ hours, cost $50 ($30 for children), and include dinner. Reservations are required. This is definitely touristy, but you will come away with a better sense of Navajo culture.

Outdoor Activities Around Lake Powell

While simply exploring the lake's maze of canyons on a narrated tour is satisfying enough for many visitors, the most popular activities are still houseboating, water-skiing, riding personal watercraft, and fishing. At the **Wahweap Marina** (www.lakepowell.com; ✆ **888/896-3829** or 928/645-2433), about 5 miles north of the Glen Canyon Dam, you can rent various types of boats, along with personal watercraft and water skis. Rates range from $450 to $800 per day, depending on the type of boat. Personal watercraft go for $450 per day, and sea kayaks rent for $50 per day. For information on renting houseboats, see p. 330. A variety of boats, including ski boats and kayaks, can also be rented at **Antelope Point Marina,** 537 Marina Pkwy., Navajo Rte. 22B (www.antelopepointlakepowell.com; ✆ **928/645-5900**). Expect to pay $375 to $425 per day for a ski boat and $30 to $45 per day for a kayak.

FISHING

Smallmouth, largemouth, and striped bass, as well as walleye, catfish, crappie, and carp, are all plentiful year-round in Lake Powell. Because the lake lies within both Arizona and Utah, you'll need to know which state's waters you're fishing in whenever you cast your line out, and you'll need the appropriate license. (Be sure to pick up a copy of the Arizona and Utah state fishing regulations, or ask about applicable regulations at any of the marinas.) In Wahweap, you can arrange licenses to fish the entire lake at **Lake Powell Resorts and Marinas** (✆ **928/645-2433**), which also sells bait and tackle and a provide you with advice on fishing this massive reservoir. Other marinas he lake also sell licenses, bait, and tackle. The best season is March through November, but walleye are most often caught during the cooler months.

If you'd rather try your hand at catching enormous rainbow trout, try downstream of the Glen Canyon Dam, where cold waters provide ideal conditions for trophy trout. Unfortunately, there isn't much access to this stretch of river. You'll need a trout stamp to fish for the rainbows. If you want a guide to take you where the fish are biting, contact Bill McBurney at **Ambassador Guide Service** (www.ambassadorguides.com; ✆ **928/606-5829**); his rates are $400 for a half-day and $700 for a full day.

GOLF

The 18-hole **Lake Powell National Golf Course** ★, 400 Clubhouse Dr. (www.lakepowellgolfing.com; ✆ **928/645-2023**) is one of the most spectacular in the state. The fairways wrap around the base of the red-sandstone bluff atop which sits the town of Page. The views stretch on forever, and in places, eroded sandstone walls come right down to the greens and fairways. Greens fees run $39 to $52 for 18 holes.

HIKING

If you're looking for a quick, easy hike with great views, head north on North Navajo Drive from downtown Page. At the end of this street is the main trail head for Page's **Rimview Trail.** This trail runs along the edge of Manson Mesa, upon which Page is built, and has views of Lake Powell and miles of red-rock country. The entire loop trail is 8 miles long, but if you want to do a shorter hike, then just head east (clockwise) from the trail head and walk for as long as you care to. If you happen to have your mountain bike with you, the trail is a great ride.

At Lees Ferry, a 39-mile drive from Page at the southern tip of the national recreation area (see p. 253), you'll find three short trails (Cathedral Wash, River, and Spencer). The most interesting is the 2-mile **Cathedral Wash Trail,** which follows a dry wash through a narrow canyon with unusual rock formations (beware of flash floods). The trail head is at the second turnout after turning off U.S. 89A. The **River Trail,** a 2-mile round-trip hike along the river, starts at the Lees Ferry boat ramp about 5 miles north of U.S. 89A at Marble Canyon. The 4-mile round-trip **Spencer Trail,** which branches off the River Trail, leads to the top of a 1,700-foot cliff for spectacular views of Marble Canyon.

Canyoneering backpackers may want to try the famed **Paria Canyon Trail** ★, which runs from Utah (trail head on U.S. 89) to Lees Ferry. Between 38 and 47 miles long (depending on where you start), it follows the meandering route of a narrow slot canyon. Hiking Paria is a challenge—but a life-changer, too. Paria Canyon hikers must apply online in advance for a permit (https://www.blm.gov/az/paria/index.cfm?usearea=PC); the cost is $5 per day per person and another $5 a day if you bring your dog.

KAYAKING

If roaring engines aren't your speed, you might want to consider exploring Lake Powell by sea kayak. While afternoon winds can sometimes make paddling difficult, the air is often quite still in the morning. With a sea kayak, you can even explore canyons too narrow for powerboats. Kayak tours of Lake Powell are organized by **Twin Finn Diving,** 816 Copper Mine Rd. (www.twinfinn.com; ✆ **928/660-0778**), ranging in length from a couple of hours to 5 days and in price from $90 to $1,200. Twin Finn rents kayaks, too; call for prices and to reserve a craft. Guided kayak trips are also offered by **Kayak Powell** (www.kayaklakepowell.com; ✆ **888/854-7862**), which charges $95 for a half-day tour; $495 for a 2-day tour. Kayak Powell also rents kayaks and canoes, ranging from $35 to $60 per day. In Page, **Lake Powell Paddleboards and Kayaks** (www.lakepowellpaddleboard.com; ✆ **928/645-4017**) rents both those watercraft: a kayak goes for $30 a day and a paddleboard for $40 a day.

RAFTING & FLOATING TRIPS

While most of Glen Canyon National Recreation Area consists of the impounded waters of Lake Powell, the recreation area also contains a short stretch of the Colorado River that still flows swift and free. To see this stretch of river, try a float trip from Glen Canyon Dam to Lees Ferry (see p. 253 in chapter 6 for more on Lees Ferry). Operated by **Wilderness River Adventures** (www.riveradventures.com; ✆ **888/922-0822**) from March through early December, these half-day trips in motorized rafts cost $94 for adults and $83 for children ages 4 to 15. Try to reserve at least 2 weeks in advance. **Kayak Powell** (see above) offers all-day self-guided kayak and canoe trips on this stretch of the Colorado River at regular boat rental rates.

SWIMMING

If you're just looking for a good place for a swim near Lake Powell Resort, take the Coves Loop just west of the marina. Of the three coves, the third one, which has a sandy beach, is the best. The Chains area, another good place to jump off the rocks and otherwise lounge by the lake, is outside Page down a rough dirt road just before you reach Glen Canyon Dam.

Where to Stay In Page & Lake Powell

HOUSEBOATS

Although there are plenty of hotels and motels in and near Page, the most popular accommodations here are not waterfront hotel rooms, but houseboats, which function as floating vacation homes. With a houseboat, which is as easy to operate as a car, you can explore Lake Powell's beautiful red-rock country, far from any roads. No special license or prior experience is necessary, and plenty of hands-on instruction is given before you leave the marina. Because Lake Powell houseboating is extremely popular with visitors from all over the world, it's important to make reservations as far in advance as possible, especially if you plan to visit in summer.

Antelope Point Resort & Marina ★★ At this marina, built atop the world's largest floating platform of its kind, you can rent some of the newest and most luxurious houseboats on the lake (the larger ones even have outdoor hot tubs). There are 59-foot, 70-foot, and 75-foot boats available, ranging in quality from deluxe to luxury. You can also rent speedboats ($375–$425 per day), personal watercraft ($375 per day), and sea kayaks ($30–$45 per day),

Oh Say Can You See

The entire Colorado Plateau is a region of one spectacular view after another, but two scenic vistas in the Glen Canyon area merit special mention.

As you drive down the hill from Page on Lake Powell Boulevard (the road toward Glen Canyon Dam from Page), go straight through the intersection instead of turning right toward the dam. Here you'll find a parking area and a short path to the **Glen Canyon Dam Overlook,** a viewing platform perched on the edge of sheer cliff walls. Far below lie the clear green waters of the Colorado River, while upstream looms Glen Canyon Dam.

If you're up for a short hike, grab the camera and head to the **Horseshoe Bend ★** viewpoint. Horseshoe Bend is a huge loop of the Colorado River, and the viewpoint is hundreds of feet above the water on the edge of a cliff. It's about a half-mile to the viewpoint from the trail head, which is 5 miles south of the Carl Hayden Visitor Center on U.S. 89, just south of milepost 545.

which will allow you to explore smaller waterways that your houseboat can't navigate. To reach the marina, which has a floating restaurant, a market, and a cafe for ice cream and coffee, head east out of Page on Ariz. 98 and drive 5 miles to the signed Antelope Point Marina turnoff.

537 Marina Pkwy., Page. www.lakepowellhouseboating.com. ✆ **800/255-5561.** $5,111–$14,562 per week. Pets accepted ($100 fee). **Amenities:** Watersports equipment/rentals.

Lake Powell Resorts & Marinas ★ This is the original houseboat-rental operation on Lake Powell, and houseboats here range in size from 46 to 75 feet, sleep anywhere from 8 to 12 people, and come complete with showers and a fully equipped kitchen. For deluxe on-the-water accommodations, opt for one of the 62-foot "Journey" houseboats. If you're coming in the summer, splurge on a boat with some sort of cooling system.

100 Lakeshore Dr., Page. www.lakepowell.com. ✆ **888/896-3829** or 928/645-2433. Mid-June–mid-Aug $2,370–$15,000 per week; lower rates other months. 3-, 4-, 5-, and 6-night rates also available on most houseboats. Pets accepted ($10 per day).

HOTELS & MOTELS IN PAGE

Best Western Arizonainn ★ Perched right at the edge of the mesa on which Page is built, this modern motel has a fine view across miles of desert. While the guest rooms are unremarkable and are basically just standard motel rooms, about half have lake views. Be sure to ask for one of these. If you can't get a room with a view, you can at least hang out by the pool; it's got that same 100-mile view.

716 Rimview Dr. www.bestwestern.com. ✆ **928/645-8868.** 102 units. May–Sept $120–$160 double; Oct–Apr $94–$160 double. Rates include continental breakfast. Children 17 and under stay free in parent's room. No pets. **Amenities:** Free airport transfers; exercise room; Jacuzzi; outdoor pool; free Wi-Fi.

Courtyard by Marriott ★ Set at the foot of the mesa on which Page is built and adjacent to the Lake Powell National Golf Course (p. 329), this is the top in-town choice. It's also the closest you'll come to a golf resort in this part of the state. Although you'll pay a premium for views of the golf course or lake, it's a worthwhile investment. Guest rooms are larger than those at most area lodgings. Moderately priced meals are served in a casual restaurant that has a terrace overlooking the distant lake. The 18-hole golf course has great views of the surrounding landscape.

600 Clubhouse Dr. www.marriott.com/pgacy. ✆ **928/645-5000.** 153 units. $195–$209 double. Children 17 and under stay free in parent's room. Pets accepted. **Amenities:** Restaurant; lounge; 18-hole golf course; exercise room; Jacuzzi; seasonal outdoor pool; free Wi-Fi.

Lake Powell Resort ★ This hotel at the sprawling Wahweap Marina 5 miles north of Page should be your first lodging choice in the area. The Lake Powell Resort features lots of resort amenities and activities, but it is often overwhelmed by busloads of tour groups, and service is often overtaxed by the volume. Guest rooms are arranged in several long two-story wings, and every unit has either a balcony or a patio. Half of the rooms have lake views; those in the west wing have the better vantage point, since the east wing overlooks a coal-fired power plant. The **Rainbow Room** (below) offers fine dining.

100 Lakeshore Dr. www.lakepowell.com. ✆ **888/896-3829** or 928/645-2433. 348 units. $108–$138 double, $249–$284 suite. Children 17 and under stay free in parent's room. Pets accepted ($20 fee). **Amenities:** 2 restaurants; snack bar; lounge; free airport transfers; concierge; exercise room; Jacuzzi; 2 outdoor pools; room service; sauna; watersports equipment/rentals; free Wi-Fi.

CAMPGROUNDS

There are campgrounds at Wahweap and Lees Ferry in Arizona, and at Bullfrog, Hite, and Halls Crossing in Utah. Because of the lake's popularity, these campgrounds stay packed for much of the year. **Wahweap** (✆ **888/896-3829**) charges $30 per night (reservations available online at www.lakepowell.com). Some scrubby trees provide a bit of shade at the Wahweap site, but the wind and sun make this a rather bleak spot in summer. Down in the Glen Canyon recreation area's southern tip, the **Lees Ferry Campground** (www.nps.gov/glca/planyourvisit/camping.htm; ✆ **928/608-6200**), about 5 miles north of the Navajo Bridge on Lees Ferry Rd., has a 55-site campground charging $20 per night. Reservations are not accepted.

Where to Eat in Page

Blue Buddha Sushi Lounge ★ JAPANESE Maybe it's the sight of all that Lake Powell water and maybe it's the hip, urban vibe, but whatever the reason, this sushi restaurant is a big hit in Page. This stylish lounge/restaurant attracts a young crowd who come for creative sushi rolls. Blue lights and Buddha statues everywhere set the mood.

644 N. Navajo Dr. www.bluebuddhasushilounge.com. ✆ **928/645-0007.** Reservations recommended. Main courses $14–$25; sushi $8–$12. Tues–Sat 5–9pm.

The Dam Bar & Grille ★ AMERICAN This theme restaurant is a warehouse-size space designed to conjure images of the interior of Glen

Canyon Dam. Inside, cement walls, hard hats, and a big transformer that sends out bolts of neon "electricity" will put you in a "dam" good mood. Sandwiches, pastas, and steaks dominate the menu, but the slow-roasted chicken is my favorite dish. The lounge area is a popular local hangout, and next door is the affiliated Gunsmoke Saloon nightclub. Kids will love the cool dam decor and old boats around the inside of the restaurant.

644 N. Navajo Dr. www.damplaza.com. © **928/645-2161.** Reservations recommended in summer. Main courses $10–$25. Daily 11am–11pm.

Jádí Tooh ★ AMERICAN It's not every day you eat in a floating restaurant, much less the only floating restaurant on the vast inland sea that is Lake Powell. With big walls of glass (some of which roll up like garage doors) and a large patio off the bar, this place is the perfect spot for lingering over a meal and drinks, especially on a hot summer day. The water lapping at the floats and the sandstone rising all around make this the quintessential Lake Powell dining experience. The menu doesn't stretch the bounds of creativity (a few pizzas, sandwiches, and salads at lunch and primarily steaks at dinner), but the setting can't be beat.

Antelope Point Marina, 537 Marina Pkwy., Navajo Rte. 22B. www.antelopepointlakepowell.com. © **928/645-5900.** Main courses $8.75–$26. Daily 11am–9pm (closed Mon–Wed in winter).

Rainbow Room ★ AMERICAN/SOUTHWESTERN With sweeping vistas of Lake Powell through the walls of glass, the Rainbow Room is both Page's top restaurant and its most touristy. The menu is short and includes a few dishes with Southwestern flavor, and many of the ingredients are organic. The steaks are good—and the beef is Arizona-grown. Be prepared for a wait; this place, open for breakfast and dinner, regularly feeds busloads of tourists. The adjacent bar has a knockout view through a long wall of glass.

Lake Powell Resort, 100 Lakeshore Dr. © **888/896-3829.** Reservations recommended. Main courses $8–$14 breakfast, $19–$35 dinner. Daily 6am–10am and 5–9pm. Closed Nov–Feb.

EASTERN ARIZONA'S HIGH COUNTRY

8

The saguaro cactus may be Arizona's preeminent symbol, but it could just as appropriately be the ponderosa pine—Arizona happens to have the world's largest forest of that coniferous giant. The tall mountains and dense pine forests of eastern Arizona's highlands, long home to the Apache people, are an outdoor enthusiast's paradise and a cool, welcome getaway from the desert far below.

Folks from Phoenix and its surrounding cities discovered long ago how cool the nearby White Mountains' forests are; for many decades they've built cabins and weekend homes in this area, making their way up the twisting, turning Beeline Highway to the high country. In only a few hours, you can drive up from the cacti and creosote bushes to meadows, mountain lakes, and pine forests. In this sparsely populated region, which features some of the most rugged topography in the world, towns with such apt names as Alpine, Lakeside, and Pinetop are now second homes for thousands of residents of the desert metropolises.

Dividing the arid lowlands from the cool highland forests is the Mogollon Rim (pronounced *Mug*-ee-own by the locals), a high escarpment that stretches for 200 miles from central Arizona into New Mexico. Along this impressive wall of rock, the climatic and vegetative change is dramatic, with sunshine at the base and snow squalls at the top. This scenic area was made famous by Western author Zane Grey, who lived in a cabin near Payson and set many of his novels and stories here.

Trout fishing, hiking, horseback riding, and hunting are the main warm-weather pastimes of eastern Arizona, and when winter weather reports from up north have Phoenicians dreaming about snow, many head to the White Mountains for a bit of skiing. Sunrise Park Resort, operated by the White Mountain Apache Tribe, is the state's biggest and busiest downhill ski area. There are also plenty of cross-country ski trails in the area.

Much of eastern Arizona is the reservation of the White Mountain Apache Tribe. Recreational activities abound here, but remember that the Apache Tribe requires visitors to have reservation fishing permits and outdoor recreation permits. Fishing is particularly popular on the reservation, which isn't surprising, considering there are 400 miles of trout streams and 25 lakes stocked with rainbow and brown trout.

PAYSON & THE MOGOLLON RIM COUNTRY

94 miles NE of Phoenix; 90 miles SE of Flagstaff; 90 miles SW of Winslow; 100 miles W of Pinetop-Lakeside

Payson, 94 miles from Phoenix and 5,000 feet above sea level, is one of the closest places for Phoenicians to find relief from the summer heat, and though it is not quite high enough to be considered the mountains, it certainly isn't the desert (summer temperatures are 20° cooler than in the Valley of the Sun). The 200-mile-long Mogollon Rim, an escarpment whose cliffs tower nearly half a mile above the forest below, is only 22 miles north of town, and the surrounding Tonto National Forest provides opportunities for hiking, swimming, fishing, and hunting. The nearly perfect climate of Payson has also made the town a popular retirement spot. Summer highs are usually in the 80s or 90s (30s Celsius), while winter highs are usually in the 50s and 60s (teens Celsius).

Essentials

ARRIVING Ariz. 87, the Beeline Highway, connects Payson to Phoenix and Winslow. Ariz. 260 runs east from Payson, climbing the Mogollon Rim and continuing into the White Mountains.

The cliffs of the Mogollan Rim tower over the desert below.

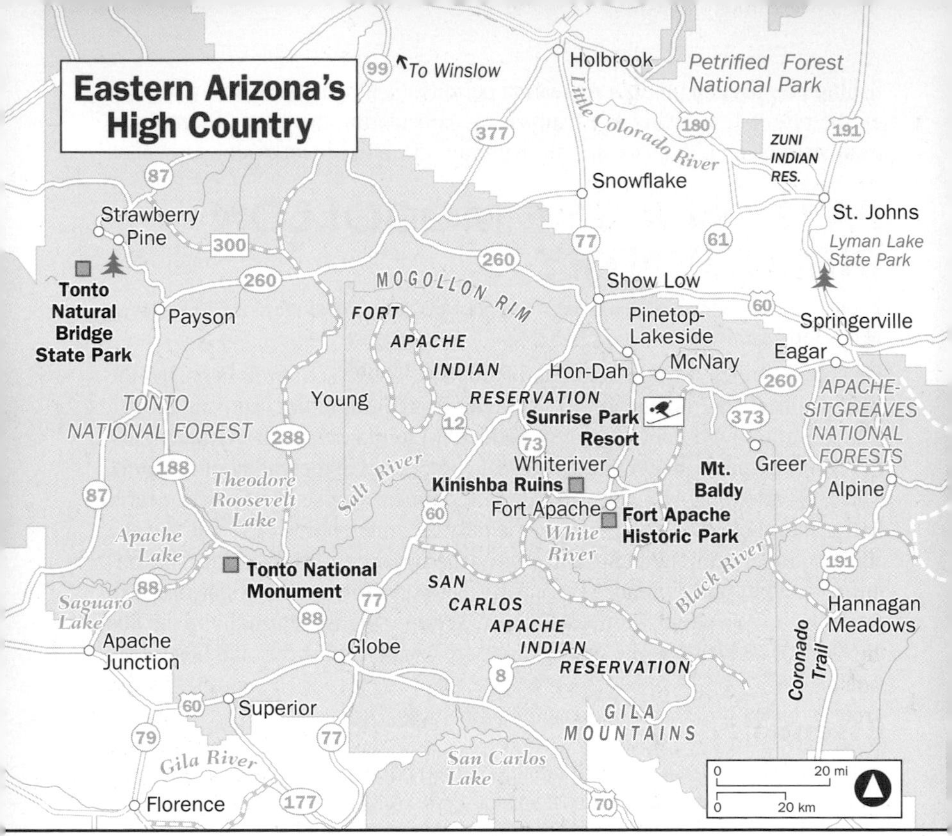

SPECIAL EVENTS Held every year since 1884 (when it started as a friendly gathering of local ranchers and cowboys), the **August Doins Rodeo** claims to be the world's oldest continuous rodeo. The rodeo is held the third weekend in August.

VISITOR INFORMATION Contact the Rim Country Regional Chamber of Commerce (www.rimcountrychamber.com; ✆ **928/474-4515**).

Exploring Payson & the Mogollon Rim

To get a background on the area's history, go to Green Valley Park, where the **Rim Country Museum,** 700 Green Valley Pkwy. (http://rimcountrymuseum.org; ✆ **928/474-3483**) is housed in the oldest forest ranger station and residence still standing in the Southwest. Inside you'll find displays on the region as well as a special Zane Grey exhibit and a reconstruction of the cabin Grey lived in on and off from 1921 to 1929, before an argument with Arizona Game & Fish rangers led to his promise to leave Arizona and never return. Grey made good on it, even though 28 of his 57 novels have Arizona settings. The museum is open Wednesday through Monday from 10am to 4pm. Admission is $5 for adults, $4 for seniors, and $3 for children 12 to 18.

About 5 miles north of town, off Ariz. 87 on Houston Mesa Road, you can visit the ruins of **Shoofly Village** in the Tonto National Forest. This village

Western writer Zane Grey's cabin in Payson, now part of the Rim Country Museum.

was first occupied nearly a thousand years ago by peoples related to the Hohokam and Salado. It once contained 79 rooms, though today only rock foundations remain. An interpretive trail helps bring the site to life.

If you're feeling lucky, spend some time and money at the **Mazatzal Casino** (www.mazatzalcasino.com; ✆ **800/777-7529** or 928/474-6044), a half-mile south of Payson on Ariz. 87. The casino is run by the Tonto Apaches.

The area's most popular attraction is **Tonto Natural Bridge State Park,** 10 miles northwest of Payson on Ariz. 87 (www.azstateparks.com; ✆ **928/476-4202**), which preserves the largest natural travertine bridge in the world. In 1877, gold prospector David Gowan, while being chased by Apaches, became the first white man to see this natural bridge, which stands 183 feet high and 150 feet across at its widest point. Admission to the park is $7 for adults and $4 for children 7 to 13. The park is open Thursday through Monday from 9am to 5pm.

About 15 miles north of Payson on Ariz. 87 is the village of **Pine,** and another 3 miles beyond this, the village of **Strawberry.** Here, in a quiet setting in the forest, you'll find a few shops selling antiques and crafts and, on Ariz. 87 in Pine, the **Pine-Strawberry Museum** (www.pinestrawhs.org; ✆ **928/476-3547**), a small museum that chronicles the history of this area. From May 15 to October 15, the museum is open Monday through Thursday from 10am to 2pm and Friday through Sunday from 10am to 4pm; other months the museum is open Monday through Saturday 10am to 2pm. Admission is $1 (kids 10 and under get in for free). From Strawberry, drive west 1¾ miles on Fossil Creek Road to visit the old **Strawberry Schoolhouse** (www.pinestrawhs.org/schoolhouse.html), a restored log building dating from 1885 and billed as the oldest standing schoolhouse in Arizona. It's open mid-May to mid-October Saturday from 10am to 4pm and Sunday from noon to

Tonto Natural Bridge, a soaring arch of travertine limestone.

4pm; mid-June through early August, the schoolhouse is als
Monday from 10am to 4pm.

If you continue west past the schoolhouse, the gravel **Fossil**
leads 10 miles down into a deep and spectacular canyon. It's
but if you like views, it's well worth the white knuckles an
tom, **Fossil Creek** offers some of the most idyllic little swi
could ever hope to find. If you make it down here on a w
might have a swimming hole all to yourself. A permit is requ
April 1 to October 1 and can be obtained at www.recreation

One of the most popular scenic drives in the area is alo
Mogollon Rim on 45-mile-long **Forest Road (F.R.) 300.** As
the edge of the rim, you'll get stunning views of the forest
are plenty of places to stop, including lakes, picnic areas,
campgrounds. This is a good gravel road and can be negotia
a standard passenger car. In winter, however, the road is no
access the rim road from Payson, head east on Ariz. 260 or
for 30 miles and watch for signs.

Outdoor Activities

The **Highline Trail** is a beautiful 51-mile hike along the lo
Mogollon Rim, with fine mountain vistas, intriguing rock
towering stands of Ponderosa pines. Following years of negl
rebuilt in 2017 and, though still challenging, has been gre
you'd like to go horseback riding on the Highline, try **Kohl's**
on Hwy. 260, 17 miles north of Payson (✆ **928/478-0030**). A
$65.

You can find out more about this and other area trails at the
Station, 1009 E. Ariz. 260 (www.fs.usda.gov/tonto; ✆ **928/4**
east end of town. Several area trails are open for mountain b
bikes can be rented at **Rim Country Recreation** (✆ **928/978**

A Pleasant Valley Detour

For a bit of back-road adventure, head south from the Mogollon Rim to the remote community of **Young,** which sits in the middle of the aptly named Pleasant Valley. The town can be reached only via well-graded gravel roads—24 miles of gravel if you come from the north, 32 miles from the south—which is why a trip to Young is an adventure.

Why visit Young? Most people come just to see the land that spawned the worst range war and family feud in the West. Known as the Pleasant Valley War or Graham-Tewksbury Fe
over conflicts about she
the valley, and eventually
of lives. Zane Grey mem
1880s range war in his n
Man.

To get there, head eas
miles from Payson on Ari
south for another 26 mil
(Young Highway), which
becomes Ariz. 288. If you
288 south to Ariz. 188, it
drive to Globe (p. 161).

Where to Stay in Payson

Majestic Mountain Inn ★ Although located in town, this hotel was built in an attractive, modern mountain-lodge style that makes it the most appealing place to stay right in Payson. There's a large stone chimney and fireplace in the lobby, and all of the deluxe and luxury rooms have fireplaces. The luxury units also have tile floors and a double whirlpool tub facing the fireplace. The standard rooms aren't as spacious or luxurious, but are still quite comfortable.

602 E. Ariz. 260. www.majesticmountaininn.com. ✆ **928/474-0185.** 50 units. $69–$149 double. Rates include continental breakfast. Children 17 and under stay free in parent's room. Pets accepted ($25 fee). **Amenities:** Access to nearby health club; outdoor pool; free Wi-Fi.

CAMPGROUNDS

East of Payson on Ariz. 260 are several national forest campgrounds, including **Upper Tonto Creek** and **Christopher Creek** campgrounds, which are the best developed and most scenic in the Payson area. Neither of these campgrounds takes reservations. Information is available from the **Payson Ranger Station,** 1009 E. Ariz. 260 (www.fs.usda.gov/tonto; ✆ **928/474-7900**), at the east end of town.

Where to Eat in Payson

Fargo's Steakhouse ★ STEAK This modern steakhouse next door to the Majestic Mountain Inn is the classiest restaurant in town and has a contemporary mountain-lodge atmosphere. The menu doesn't break any new ground, but you can get reliable steaks. Start with tenderloin skewers with Cajun dipping sauce or the bacon-wrapped scallops. Steak eaters on a diet will want to consider the black and blue Caesar salad.

620 E. Ariz. 260. www.fargossteakhouse.com. ✆ **928/474-7455.** Reservations recommended for parties of 6 or more. Main courses $9.50–$14 lunch, $14–$34 dinner. Sun–Thurs 11am–9pm; Fri–Sat 11am–10pm.

Gerardo's Firewood Café ★ ITALIAN Although it's nothing fancy, this casual southern Italian restaurant on the north side of Payson is a local favorite. The classics, including lasagna, spaghetti and meatballs, and shrimp scampi, are all on the menu, along with plenty of pizzas, a good selection of vegetarian pasta dishes, and a gluten-free pasta primavera.

512 N. Beeline Hwy. www.gerardosbistro.com. ✆ **928/468-6500.** Reservations recommended. Main courses $14–$19. Mon–Thurs 11am–8:30pm; Fri–Sat 11am–9pm; Sunday 12pm–8pm.

PINETOP-LAKESIDE

90 miles NE of Payson; 185 miles NE of Phoenix; 50 miles S of Holbrook; 140 miles SE of Flagstaff

Dozens of motels and cabin resorts string along Arizona Highway 260 in the busy community of Pinetop-Lakeside, two towns that grew together over the years, together with neighboring Show Low, named after a legendary card game. At first glance, it's easy to dismiss the place as one long commercial strip, what with all the shopping centers and budget motels, but Pinetop-Lakeside has spent many years entertaining families during the summer months, and it has plenty of diversions to keep visitors busy. If you're looking for a romantic weekend or solitude, continue farther into the White Mountains to Greer (p. 344).

Pinetop-Lakeside is well situated for anyone who enjoys the outdoors, with Apache and Sitgreaves national forests on one side and the unspoiled lands of the White Mountain Apaches' Fort Apache Indian Reservation on the other. Nearby are several lakes with good fishing; nearly 200 miles of hiking, mountain-biking, and cross-country ski trails; horseback riding; and downhill skiing. Although summer is the busy season, Pinetop-Lakeside becomes something of a ski resort in winter. Sunrise Park Resort ski area (p. 346) is only 30 miles away, and on weekends the town is packed with skiers.

Essentials

GETTING THERE Pinetop-Lakeside is located on Ariz. 260 and is 90 miles east of Payson.

VISITOR INFORMATION For information on this area, contact the **Pinetop-Lakeside Chamber of Commerce** (www.pinetoplakesidechamber.com; ✆ **800/573-4031** or 928/367-4290).

Exploring the Pinetop-Lakeside Area

Within the town itself, attractions are mostly of the commercial kind (movie theater, mini-golf, go-karts), with the exception of **Woodland Lake Park** at the east end of Pinetop (below). But you don't have to go far outside town to find sites of interest.

In 1870, the U.S. government established Fort Apache in the Arizona highlands just south of modern-day Pinetop. Today, the town is called Whiteriver, and it lies within the Fort Apache Reservation, just south of Pinetop-Lakeside. In Whiteriver, approximately 22 miles south of Pinetop on Ariz. 73, the **Apache Cultural Center & Museum** (www.wmat.us/wmaculture.html; ✆ **928/338-4625**) stands on the grounds of the **Fort Apache Historic Park,** a collection of more than 20 historic buildings that have been carefully restored. Inside a log building known as General Crook's Cabin, there's a museum with small but informative exhibits on Apache culture. Down a short trail you'll find a re-creation of a traditional Apache village. The center is open Monday through Friday (plus Saturdays in summer) from 8am to 5pm. Admission is $5 for adults, $3 for students, and free for children 7 and under.

Also in the reservation nearby, the **Kinishba Ruins** is a 500-room pueblo ruin nearly 800 years old. The Spanish explorer Coronado visited here when he passed through in search of the Seven Cities of Cíbola. Look for the ruins off a marked dirt road 7 miles west of Whiteriver on Ariz. 73.

For more information on visiting the Fort Apache Indian Reservation, contact the **White Mountain Apache Tribe** (http://wmat.us; ✆ **(928) 338-4346**).

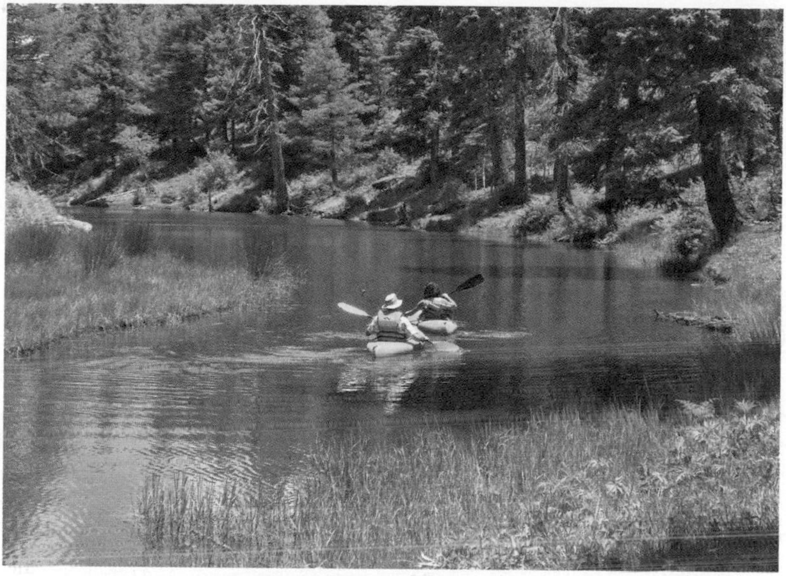

The Apache-Sitgreaves National Forest is studded with woodland lakes perfect for fishing, canoeing, and kayaking.

Owned and operated by the White Mountain Apache Tribe, the **Hon-Dah Casino,** 777 Ariz. 260 (www.hon-dah.com; © **800/929-8744** or 928/369-0299) has 800 slot machines and poker and blackjack tables. It's open daily round-the-clock, at the junction of Ariz. 73 and Ariz. 260, about 4 miles east of Pinetop-Lakeside.

Outdoor Activities

Old forts and casinos aside, it's the outdoors (and the cool weather) that really draws people here. Fishing, hiking, mountain biking, and horseback riding are among the most popular activities.

FISHING

If you're up here to catch the big one, you can try for native Apache trout, as well as stocked rainbows, browns, and brookies. This is also the southernmost spot in the United States where you can fish for arctic graylings, at **Lee Valley Lake** (Arizona's highest lake, at 9,420 feet) and a few other spots. Right in the Pinetop-Lakeside area, try **Woodland Lake,** in Woodland Lake Park, toward the east end of Pinetop and just south of Ariz. 260, or **Show Low Lake,** east of Lakeside and north of Ariz. 260. On the nearby Fort Apache Indian Reservation, there's good fishing in **Hawley Lake,** which is east of Pinetop-Lakeside and south of Ariz. 260. If you plan to fish here or at any other lake on Apache land, be sure to get a reservation fishing license ($9 per day). Licenses are available at **Hon-Dah Ski & Outdoor Sport,** at Ariz. 260 and Ariz. 73 (© **928/369-7669**) or online via the **White Mountain Apache Tribe** (http://wmatoutdoors.org).

GOLF

Several area golf courses are open to the public, including **Pinetop Lakes Golf & Country Club,** 4643 Buck Springs Rd., Pinetop (www.pinetoplakes golf.com; ✆ **928/369-4531**), considered one of the best executive courses in the state and only $25 for 18 holes; **Silver Creek Golf Club,** 2051 Silver Lake Blvd., Show Low (www.silvercreekgolfclub.com; ✆ **928/537-2744**), with fees of $37 to $56 for 18 holes; and the **Bison Golf & Country Club,** 1 N. Bison Preserve Dr., Show Low (www.bisongolf.net; ✆ **928/537-4564**), which costs $47 to $60 for 18 holes.

HIKING & MOUNTAIN BIKING

Meandering through the forests surrounding Pinetop-Lakeside are the 180 miles of trails of the **White Mountains Trail System.** Many of these trails are easily accessible (in fact, some are right in town) and are open to both hikers and mountain bikers. The trails at Pinetop's **Woodland Lake Park,** just off Ariz. 260 near the east end of Pinetop, run 6 miles, including a paved path around the lake. For a panoramic vista of the Mogollon Rim, hike the short, flat **Mogollon Rim Interpretive Trail** off Ariz. 260 on the west side of Lakeside. For another short but pleasant stroll, check out the **Big Springs Environmental Study Area,** on Woodland Road in Lakeside. This quiet little preserve encompasses a small meadow through which flows a spring-fed stream. There is often good bird-watching here. You can spot more birds at Woodland Lake Park, mentioned above, and at **Jacques Marsh,** 2 miles north of Ariz. 260 on Porter Mountain Road in Lakeside. For more information on area trails, contact the **Lakeside Ranger District,** 2022 W. White Mountain Blvd., Lakeside (www.fs.usda.gov/asnf; ✆ **928/368-2100**), on Ariz. 260 in Lakeside, or the **Pinetop-Lakeside Chamber of Commerce** (p. 340).

HORSEBACK RIDING

Between mid-May and the end of October, you can saddle up at **Porter Mountain Stables,** 1497 Flag Hollow Rd. (www.portermtnstables.com; ✆ **928/368-5306**), which charges $35 for adults ($33 for children) for a 1-hour ride, $54 for adults ($51 for children) for a 2-hour ride. Half-day, all-day, and sunset rides are also offered.

RAFTING

About 50 miles south of Show Low, U.S. 60 crosses a bridge over the narrow and scenic canyon of the Salt River. This stretch of the river is a favorite of whitewater rafters, and several companies offer rafting trips of varying lengths if water levels permit. (In 2018, the rafting season was cancelled because of insufficient flow.) Try **Arizona Rafting** (https://saltriverraftingarizona.com; ✆ **800/231-7238**), **Canyon Rio Rafting** (www.canyonrio.com; ✆ **800/272-3353**), or **Mild to Wild Rafting** (www.mild2wildrafting.com; ✆ **800/567-6745**).

Where to Stay in Pinetop-Lakeside

Hon-Dah Resort Casino & Conference Center ★ This hotel, adjacent to the Hon-Dah Casino a few miles east of Pinetop-Lakeside, is the largest and most luxurious lodging in the White Mountains. As with most casino hotels, it was designed to impress. The portico is big enough to hold a basketball court, and inside the front door is an artificial rock wall upon which are mounted stuffed animals, including a cougar, a bobcat, a bear, ducks, and even a bugling elk. Most of the guest rooms are spacious as well.

777 Ariz. 260 (at junction with Ariz. 73), Pinetop. www.hon-dah.com. ✆ **800/929-8744** or 928/369-0299. 128 units. $109–$119 double; $170–$199 suite. **Amenities:** Restaurant; 2 lounges; Jacuzzi; year-round outdoor pool; room service; sauna; free Wi-Fi.

Lake of the Woods ★ Set on its own private lake right on Ariz. 260, Lake of the Woods is a 25-acre rustic mountain resort that caters primarily to families. Cabins and houses range from tiny to huge, with rustic and modern side by side. The smallest sleep two or three, while the largest can take up to 20; all have kitchens and fireplaces. Some are on the edge of the lake, while others are tucked away under the pines; be sure to request a location away from the busy highway and ask for a newer cabin, as the accommodations vary considerably in quality. Kids, in particular, love this place: They can fish in the lake, row a boat, or play in the snow. The owners of Lake of the Woods also operate **Lazy Oaks,** a 15-unit resort on nearby Rainbow Lake.

2244 W. White Mountain Blvd., Lakeside. www.lakeofthewoodsaz.com. ✆ **928/368-5353.** 33 units. $79–$269 cabin for 2 people. 3- to 4 night minimum stay in summer and on some holidays. Children 1 and under stay free in parent's cabin. Pets accepted. **Amenities:** 2 Jacuzzis; sauna; recreation room; watersports equipment/rentals; free Wi-Fi.

CAMPGROUNDS

There are numerous campgrounds in the Pinetop-Lakeside area, including Fool Hollow, Lewis Canyon, and Lakeside. Of these, **Fool Hollow Lake Recreation Area,** 1500 N. Fool Hollow Lake Rd., Show Low (www.azstateparks.com; ✆ **928/537-3680**) is the nicest. There are numerous campgrounds nearby on the Fort Apache Indian Reservation. For information about these campgrounds, contact the **White Mountain Apache Tribe Game and Fish,** 100 W. Fatco Rd., Whiteriver (www.wmatoutdoors.org; ✆ **928/338-4385**).

Where to Eat in Pinetop-Lakeside

Charlie Clark's Steak House ★ AMERICAN Charlie Clark's, the oldest steakhouse in the White Mountains, has been serving up thick, juicy steaks since 1938 (before that, during Prohibition, the building was used as a sort of backwoods speakeasy). Mesquite-broiled steaks and chicken, as well as seafood and prime rib, fill the menu.

1701 E. White Mountain Blvd., Pinetop. www.charlieclarks.com. ✆ **888/333-0259** or 928/367-4900. Reservations available. Main courses $10–$17 lunch, $16–$33 dinner. Sun–Thurs 11am–9pm; Fri–Sat 11am–10pm.

Darbi's Café ★ AMERICAN A popular place for any of the day's three squares, Darbi's serves unpretentious but expertly made food of a classic Arizona diner sort: huevos rancheros and chicken-fried steak in the morning, burgers and salads in the afternoon, meatloaf and catfish in the evening.

There's something for everyone on the menu, plus a full bar and a delightful patio for al fresco wining and dining.

235 E. White Mountain Blvd., Pinetop. www.darbiscafe.com. © **928/367-6556.** Reservations available for parties of 6 or more. Main courses $7–$12 breakfast, $9–$15 lunch, $15–$22 dinner. Sun–Tues 6am–2pm; Wed–Sat 6am–8pm.

GREER & SUNRISE PARK ★

51 miles SE of Show Low; 98 miles SE of Holbrook; 222 miles NE of Phoenix

The tiny community of Greer, set in lush meadows on either side of the Little Colorado River and surrounded by forests, is by far the most picturesque mountain community in Arizona. The elevation of 8,525 feet usually ensures snow in winter and pleasantly cool temperatures in summer, a combination that has turned Greer into an upscale mountain getaway, popular with lowlanders. Modern log homes are springing up all over the valley, but Greer is still free of the sort of strip-mall developments that have forever changed the character of Payson and Pinetop-Lakeside.

Greer is also the closest community to the popular **Sunrise Park Resort** ski area (p. 346), which gives the village more of a ski-resort atmosphere.

Essentials

ARRIVING From Phoenix, take U.S. 87 N. to Payson and then go east on Ariz. 260, or take U.S. 60 east from Phoenix through Globe and Show Low to Ariz. 260. Greer is just a few miles south of Ariz. 260 on Ariz. 373.

VISITOR INFORMATION Online, contact the **Business Council of Greer** (www.greerarizona.com).

Exploring Greer

Lying 5 miles south of Ariz. 260 on unspoiled Ariz. 273, the pine-shaded center of Greer is low-key and pleasantly un-townlike. The Little Colorado River, which flows through Greer on its way to the Grand Canyon, is little more than a babbling brook here. Still, it's known for its trout fishing, one of the main draws in these parts. North of town, the river has been dammed into three reservoirs, known as the **Greer Lakes,** that are top fishing spots (below). Also at the north end of town, **Butler Canyon** is worth exploring; turn east off Main St. onto East Fork Rd./CR 1121 to access an easy 1-mile nature trail that loops through the cool, verdant canyon. Follow Main St. another quarter-mile toward town and turn west onto Osborne Rd. to access the **West Fork Trail,** which climbs 7 miles through forests and meadows to the top of 11,590-foot **Mount Baldy ★**, the second-highest peak in Arizona, a mountain sacred to the White Mountain Apaches. At the south end of town at 8 Main St. is the trailhead for the **East Fork Trail,** which also leads 7 miles to the top of Mount Baldy; this trail starts with a steep 600-foot climb but then becomes a much easier ascent.

A 3-minute drive on Main St./Ariz. 373 north from Greer's town center, the **Butterfly Lodge Museum** (www.butterflylodgemuseum.org; © **928/735-7514**)

is set in a restored cabin built in 1914 by James Willard Schultz (a writer) and his son, Hart Merriam Schultz (a painter). It's now a memorial to these two unusual creative individuals, with period furnishings, artifacts, and examples of both men's work. It's open Memorial Day to Labor Day Thursday through Sunday (and holidays) from 10am to 5pm. Admission is $2 for adults and $1 for ages 12 to 17.

Winter is one of the busiest seasons in Greer because the town is so close to the **Sunrise Park Resort** ski area, about a 20-mile drive west from the center of Greer if you go via Ariz. 260. There's a shorter route through the mountains (Ariz. 273), but it usually takes longer and is closed in winter.

Outdoor Activities

FISHING

The Greer Lakes—Bunch, River, and Tunnel reservoirs—are popular spots, and all three hold brown and rainbow trout. On **River Reservoir,** try the shallows at the south end. On **Tunnel Reservoir,** you can often do well from shore, especially if you're fly-fishing, though there is a boat launch. However, **Big Lake,** south of Greer, has the best fishing reputation here. Fishing is also good on **Sunrise Lake;** be sure to get a Fort Apache Indian Reservation fishing license ($7 per day for adults, available at the Sunrise General Store) in addition to the state fishing license the other lakes require.

HIKING & MOUNTAIN BIKING

Come summer, the ski slopes and cross-country ski trails at **Sunrise Park Resort** (below) become **mountain-biking trails** and, when combined with the nearby **Pole Knoll trail system** (14 miles west of Springerville/Eagar on Ariz. 260), provide mountain bikers with 35 miles of trails of varying degrees of difficulty. In the summer, mountain bikers can get an all-day Sunrise lift pass for $37. A single lift ride to the top of the mountain is $19 for adults and $13 for seniors, active military, and children 12 and under. Sunrise Park also boasts a zip line, climbing wall, 300-foot slide, and other fun things to do.

This area offers some of the finest mountain hiking in Arizona, including **Mount Baldy ★**. Lying on the edge of the Fort Apache Indian Reservation, the peak is sacred to the Apaches; non-Apaches are not allowed to go to the summit. The **West Baldy Trail,** the most popular and scenic route, begins 6 miles south of Sunrise Park Resort ski area (off the gravel extension of Ariz. 273) and follows the West Fork of the Little Colorado River. This 16.7-mile (out and back) trail climbs roughly 2,000 feet and is moderately strenuous, although the high elevation often leaves lowland hikers gasping for breath. From Greer, the **East Fork Trail** and **West Fork Trail** (above) also ascend Mount Baldy.

HORSEBACK RIDING

The **Sprucedale Ranch** (www.sprucedaleranch.com; ✆ **928/333-4984**), a working spread located in the mountains above Greer, offers short (2-hour) and day-long rides with a seasoned wrangler. If you're ambitious to lead a cowboy life, you can even join the vaqueros in May and October for authentic horse drives to and from winter and summer pastures and, in October, a cattle roundup.

SKIING

Located just off Ariz. 260 on Ariz. 273, the **Sunrise Park Resort** ski area (www.sunriseskipark.com; ✆ **800/772-7669** or 928/735-7669) is the largest and most popular ski and snowboarding area in Arizona. Operated by the White Mountain Apache Tribe, it usually opens in November, although thaws and long stretches without snow can make winters a bit unreliable. There are some good advanced runs, but beginner and intermediate skiers will really be in heaven. The ski area encompasses three mountains, including 11,000-foot-tall Apache Peak. A ski school offers a variety of lessons. Lift tickets cost $68 for adults, $56 for teens, and $39 for kids 12 and under. Ski rentals are available here and at numerous shops in Pinetop-Lakeside. The ski area's **Sunrise Park Hotel** offers motor-lodge-style rooms from $59 to $269; call ✆ **800/772-7669** for reservations.

Ski lifts at Sunrise Park Resort, Arizona's largest ski area.

More than 13 miles of groomed cross-country ski trails wind their way through forests of ponderosa pines and across high snow-covered meadows at Sunrise. These trails begin at the **Sunrise General Store** (✆ **928/735-7669, ext. 2180**), located at the turnoff for the downhill area. All-day trail passes are $12 ($20 on weekends), and rental equipment is available. When there is enough snow, there are also good opportunities for cross-country skiing within Greer itself—at 8,500 feet, the alpine scenery in this area is quiet and serene.

Where to Stay in Greer

Greer Lodge ★ Set alongside the Little Colorado River and a small trout pond, the Greer Lodge is a longtime favorite that just underwent a substantial upgrade, with a dozen new cabins and thoroughly remodeled existing log motel units. The cabins sleep anywhere between four and twelve guests; all are on the water in a splendidly picturesque setting.

80 Main St., Greer. www.greerlodgeaz.com. ✆ **928/225-7620.** 20 units. $199–$499. Pets accepted in some cabins ($20). **Amenities:** Lake; horseshoes; Wi-Fi $10 per visit.

Greer Peaks Lodge ★ Set on a hillside at the upper end of the valley, this luxurious lodge is just a few steps away from the waters of the Little Colorado River, which at this point is little more than a creek. The lodge, with its two-story stone fireplace, log beams above the lobby, and wide expanse of decks, is a great place to soak up Greer's mountain-getaway atmosphere.

There's a wide range of accommodations, from rooms (most of which are huge) and suites in the main lodge to spacious cabins. Throughout the lodge, the emphasis is on comfort and tranquility. The restaurant is one of your best bets in Greer for a reliable meal. Many of the cabins rented by the lodge are not right on this property but elsewhere around the village of Greer.

1 Main St. (P.O. Box 1), Greer. http://greerpeakslodge.com. ✆ **928/735-7617.** 14 units. $135 double; $275–$295 suite; $95–$1,560 cabin. Children 5 and under stay free in parent's room. 2-night minimum winter weekends, 3-night minimum summer holidays. Pets accepted in some cabins ($20 fee). **Amenities:** Restaurant; exercise room; 2 Jacuzzis; room service; sauna; free Wi-Fi.

CAMPGROUNDS

In the immediate vicinity of Greer are a couple of nice campgrounds in Apache and Sitgreaves National Forests. Contact the **National Recreation Reservation Service** (www.recreation.gov; ✆ **877/444-6777**) to make reservations for both the **Rolfe C. Hoyer Campground** ($24 per night), 1 mile north of Greer on Ariz. 373, and the **Winn Campground** ($14 per night), 12 miles southwest of Greer on Ariz. 273 (the road past Sunrise Park Resort). Because of its proximity to Greer and the Greer Lakes, Rolfe C. Hoyer is your best choice in the area. There are also several campgrounds nearby on the Fort Apache Indian Reservation (no reservations accepted). Contact the **White Mountain Apache Tribe Game and Fish,** 100 W. Fatco Rd., Whiteriver (www.wmatoutdoors.org; ✆ **928/338-4385**).

Where to Eat in Greer

For filling breakfasts and delicious sweet rolls and cobbler, rendezvous at the **Rendezvous Diner,** 117 Main St. (✆ **928/735-7483**), which is housed in a log cabin that dates back to 1909. The diner is open Wednesday through Monday from 7am to 4pm (7am to 3pm in winter). The restaurant at the **Greer Peaks Lodge** (above) is another top choice in town.

Molly Butler Lodge ★ AMERICAN Although it may not look it, this restaurant has been in business since 1910 and is one of the oldest restaurants in the state. Much updated over the years, the Molly Butler now sports a mountain-rustic look. While the menu sticks to simple fare, it's the most reliable menu in town. The steaks are your best choices, but the chili's good, too. The bar here is a favorite après-fishing hangout and has live music on Friday and Saturday nights.

109 Main St. www.mollybutlerlodge.com. ✆ **928/735-7226.** Main courses $10–$24. Lunch Tues–Sat 11am–2:30pm; Dinner daily 5pm–9pm.

SPRINGERVILLE & EAGAR

Springerville: 17 miles NE of Greer; 56 miles E of Show Low; 82 miles SE of Holbrook; 227 miles NE of Phoenix

Together the adjacent towns of Springerville and Eagar constitute the northeastern gateway to the White Mountains. Although the towns themselves are at the foot of the mountains, the vistas from around Springerville and Eagar take in all the area's peaks. Both towns also like to play up their Wild West backgrounds—in fact, the famed actor John Wayne liked the area so much that he had a ranch along the Little Colorado River just west of Eagar. The ranch, now owned by the Hopi Tribe, produces prize Hereford cattle descended from Wayne's herd.

Volcanic activity between 300,000 and 700,000 years ago left the land north of the twin towns dotted with cinder cones, giving the landscape its distinctive character. With 405 extinct volcanic vents, the Springerville Volcanic Field covers an area bigger than the state of Rhode Island; it's the third-largest volcanic field of its kind in the continental United States (after the San Francisco Field near Flagstaff and the Medicine Lake Field in California). For a brochure outlining a tour of the volcanic field, contact the Springerville-Eagar Regional Chamber of Commerce (below).

Essentials

ARRIVING Springerville and Eagar lie at the junction of U.S. 60, U.S. 180/191, and Ariz. 260. From Phoenix, there are two routes: Ariz. 87 N. to Payson and then east on Ariz. 260, or U.S. 60 east to Globe and then north to Show Low and on to Springerville (or you can take Ariz. 260 from Show Low to Springerville). From Holbrook, take U.S. 180 southeast to St. Johns and U.S. 180/191 south to Springerville. From southern Arizona, U.S. 191 is very slow but very scenic.

VISITOR INFORMATION For information on the area, contact the **Springerville-Eagar Regional Chamber of Commerce** (www.springervilleeagarchamber.com; ✆ **928/333-2123**).

Exploring the Springerville-Eagar Area

A couple of small local museums are worth visiting; for both, you'll need to plan ahead. The **Reneé Cushman Art Museum,** housed in the LDS (Mormon) Church in Springerville, consists of one woman's personal collection of European art and antiques, among them an etching attributed to Rembrandt and three pen-and-ink drawings by Tiepolo. The antique furniture dates back to the Renaissance. The museum is open by appointment only; admission is free. Contact the **Springerville-Eagar Regional Chamber of Commerce** (www.springervilleeagarchamber.com; ✆ **928/333-2123**) to arrange a visit.

Local history and old automated musical instruments are the focus of the **Little House Museum** at X Diamond Ranch (www.xdiamondranch.net; ✆ **928/333-2286**), 7 miles west of Eagar on South Fork Rd., off Ariz. 260. This working cattle ranch was founded in the 1880s by John and Molly Butler (of Molly Butler Lodge in Greer, see p. 347) and is still run by the family. Tales of colorful Wild West characters as told by the guide are as much a part of the museum as the displays. Museum visits are by reservation only and cost $10 for adults and $4 for kids 11 and under. The X Diamond Ranch also has a Native American archaeological site that is open to the public. Combination museum and archaeological site tours are $14 adults, $7 children.

Casa Malpais Archaeological Park and Museum ★★ ANCIENT SITE Declared a National Landmark in 1964, the Casa Malpais ruins are unique in Arizona in that the pueblo, which was constructed around 1250 and occupied until about 1400, was built to take advantage of existing caves. Many of these caves form a system of catacomb-like rooms under the pueblo. To visit the ruin you must take a guided tour, leaving from the Casa Malpais museum in downtown Springerville. At the museum (admission free), you'll find exhibits on both the Mogollon people and dinosaurs that once roamed this region.

418 E. Main St., Springerville. www.casamalpais.org. ✆ **928/333-5375.** Guided tours $10 adults, $8 seniors, $5 children. Museum Tues–Sat 8am–4pm; closed holidays. Tours Mar–Nov daily 9 and 11am and 2pm (weather permitting).

Lyman Lake State Park ★ ANCIENT SITE Although this state park is most popular with anglers and water-skiers, it also contains petroglyphs that date back thousands of years and the ruins of an early Ancestral Puebloan village, Rattlesnake Point Pueblo. Ancient rock art can be viewed along the Peninsula Petroglyph Trail and the Ultimate Petroglyph Trail.

On U.S. 180/191, 18 mi N of Springerville. www.azstateparks.com. ✆ **928/337-4441.** Entrance fee $7 per vehicle, $3 individual/bicycle.

Outdoor Activities

For a chance to see pronghorn antelope, elk, and mule deer, head south of Eagar to the **Sipe White Mountain Wildlife Area.** This 1,362-acre grassy valley at the foot of the White Mountains was once a cattle ranch, and today the old ranch house serves as a visitor center (open daily 8am to 5pm from mid-May to mid-October). Several miles of hiking trails wind through forest and pasture and past lakes and ponds. There's good bird-watching here, too, especially for hummingbirds. Be aware that hunting is allowed on the property in season. Sipe is 5 miles down a gravel road that begins 2 miles south of Eagar off U.S. 180/191. For more information, contact the **Arizona Game & Fish Department,** Pinetop Regional Office, 2878 E. White Mountain Blvd., in Pinetop (www.azgfd.com; ✆ **928/367-4281**).

Off Ariz. 260 between Eagar and Greer (take CR 4124), the **X Diamond Ranch** (www.xdiamondranch.net; ✆ **928/333-2286;** see below) maintains a section of the Little Colorado River as a fly-fishing stream. The half-day fishing rate is $40, while a full day costs $50.

Where to Stay Around Springerville

X Diamond Ranch ★★ Well known in the area for its Little House Museum (p. 348) and trout fishing on the Little Colorado River (p. 344), this historic ranch off Ariz. 260 between Eagar and Greer also rents a variety of smartly outfitted pine-paneled cabins, ranging in size from two to four bedrooms. There's no restaurant on the premises, but cabins have full kitchens. Smoking is prohibited indoors in cabins and the ranch house. A conference room is available for meetings, seating up to 140 people.

P.O. Box 113, Greer. www.xdiamondranch.net. ✆ **928/333-2286.** 7 units. Apr–Oct $115–$185 double. Children 1 and under stay free in parent's room. Pets permitted ($25 per visit). **Amenities:** Fishing; free Wi-Fi.

Where to Eat Around Springerville

In the predominantly Mormon high country of eastern Arizona, caffeine isn't easy to come by. Still, a good espresso can be found at the **Wildfire Espresso & Smoothie Bar,** 89 N. Main St., Eagar (© **928/333-3851**). It's open Monday through Friday from 7:30am to 5pm and Saturday from 10am to 4pm. Most restaurants serve coffee as well.

Avery's ★ AMERICAN If you're in the mood for BBQ and all the fixings, then Avery's is your White Mountains destination of choice. The walk-up counter, part of a sprawling gas station/convenience store, always has a line—and not just because it's about the only game in town.

262 W. Main St., Springerville. © **928/333-1111.** www.averysaz.com. Main courses $6–$13. Mon–Sat 11am–8:30 pm.

Los Dos Molinos ★ NEW MEXICAN With restaurants in Phoenix and Mesa, Los Dos Molinos is legendary for its spicy New Mexican food, such as *adovada* ribs (pork marinated in chili sauce) and blue corn tamales. The green chile is hotter than the red chile, but you can ask for some of each and decide for yourself.

900 E. Main St., Springerville. www.losdosmolinosphoenix.com. © **928/333-4846.** Reservations recommended for large parties. Main courses $5–$10. Tues–Sat 11am–9pm.

THE CORONADO TRAIL ★

Alpine: 28 miles S of Springerville; 75 miles E of Pinetop-Lakeside; 95 miles N of Clifton

Winding southward from the Springerville-Eagar area to Clifton and Morenci for 100 miles, the Coronado Trail (U.S. 191) is one of the most remote, little-traveled—and, truth be told, dangerous—paved roads in the state. Because this road is so narrow and winding, with dozens of 15 mph curves, it's slow going—meant for people who aren't in a hurry to get anywhere anytime soon, and who don't mind sharing a clifftop highway with one logging truck after another.

The road runs through a beautiful area, however, often called the Alps of Arizona. Even if you don't drive the length of the route, it's worth exploring some of its outdoor pleasures.

Olden Days, Golden Days

The Coronado Trail, which until recently bore the ominous highway number 666, is named for the Spanish explorer Francisco Vásquez de Coronado, who came to Arizona in search of gold in the early 1540s. Although he never found it, his party did make it as far north as the Hopi pueblos and traveled through this region on their march northward from Mexico. Centuries later, the discovery of huge copper reserves would make the fortunes of the towns of Clifton and Morenci, at the southern end of the Coronado Trail.

Essentials

ARRIVING Alpine is 28 miles south of Springerville and Eagar at the junction of U.S. 191, which continues south to Clifton and Morenci, and U.S. 180, which leads east into New Mexico.

VISITOR INFORMATION For more information on the region, contact the **Alpine Area Chamber of Commerce** (www.alpinearizona.com; ✆ **928/339-4656**). For outdoor info, contact the Apache and Sitgreaves National Forests' **Alpine Ranger District** (https://www.fs.usda.gov/asnf; ✆ **928/339-5000**).

Exploring Alpine & the Coronado Trail

Coronado may not have found the gold he was looking for in this part of Arizona, but in the fall, when the aspens turn color, the mountainsides around here are dazzlingly gold. There are only a few places in Arizona where the fall color is worth a drive, and this is one of them. It's one of the most popular times of year in this area.

Alpine, at the northern end of the Coronado Trail, is the main base for today's explorers, who tend to be outdoor types in search of uncrowded trails and streams where the trout are biting. Located near the New Mexico state line, Alpine offers a few basic lodges and restaurants, plus easy access to the region's many trails.

Golden aspens in autumn in the White Mountains.

Picturesquely set in a wide grassy valley at 8,030 feet, Alpine certainly lives up to its name. Alpine is surrounded by the **Apache** and **Sitgreaves National Forests,** which together have miles of trails and numerous campgrounds. In spring, wildflowers abound and the trout fishing is excellent. In summer, there's hiking and mountain biking on forest trails. In autumn, the aspens in the Golden Bowl on the mountainside above Alpine turn a brilliant yellow, and in winter, visitors come for cross-country skiing, snowmobiling, and ice-fishing.

South of Alpine 23 miles along U.S. 191, **Hannagan Meadows** is another good stop along the trail, summer or winter. Here you'll find excellent hiking, mountain biking, and cross-country ski trails. Hannagan Meadows also provides access to the **Blue Range Primitive Area,** which is popular with hikers and offers fine trout fishing.

OUTDOOR ACTIVITIES AROUND ALPINE

Eight miles west of Alpine (take U.S. 191 to CR 8854), there's cross-country skiing at the **Williams Valley Winter Recreation Area** (www.fs.usda.gov/recarea/asnf/recreation/wintersports), which doubles as a mountain-biking trail system in summer. Be warned that this fire-prone area is sometimes closed in summer as a safeguard.

For fishing, try **Luna Lake,** 4 miles east of Alpine off U.S. 180. Around the lake you'll also find some easy-to-moderate mountain-bike trails that usually offer good wildlife-viewing opportunities.

The best hike in the area is the trail up **Escudilla Mountain,** 10 miles north of Alpine (take U.S. 191 to Ariz. 56), where you'll see some of the best autumn displays of aspens. The Escudilla National Recreation Trail leads 3 miles to the summit of the mountain (6 miles round-trip), involving more than 1,300 feet of elevation gain.

Where to Stay & Eat Along the Coronado Trail

Between Springerville-Eagar and Clifton-Morenci, there are nearly a dozen National Forest Service campgrounds. If fishing and boating interest you, head to **Luna Lake Campground,** just east of Alpine on U.S. 180, where the daily campsite fee is $16. Reserve a Luna Lake campsite through the **National Recreation Reservation Service** (www.recreation.gov; ✆ **877/444-6777**). For a more tranquil forest setting, try the free **Hannagan Campground** (reservations not accepted), which makes a good base for exploring the Coronado

Wolf Sightings

A Mexican gray wolf recovery project has been underway here in the remote wilderness for 2 decades. The reintroduction has so far met with mixed success, as wolves have been killed by cars, people, disease, and even mountain lions. Some wolves have had to be recaptured because they strayed out of the area set aside for them or because they had encounters with humans. Keep your eyes open, and you may be lucky enough to see a wolf in the wild.

Trail. For information on these campgrounds, contact the **Alpine Ranger District** (✆ **928/339-5000**).

If you're looking for someplace to eat, Alpine has a couple of basic restaurants. Both lodges below have restaurants.

Hannagan Meadow Lodge ★ Located 23 miles south of Alpine at an elevation of 9,100 feet, this rustic lodge, dating back to 1926, is set amid cool forests on the winding route of the Coronado Trail. It's a good spot for a quiet getaway or a family vacation. The comfortable, if dated, accommodations range from rustic pine-paneled cabins to lodge rooms done up primarily with pastel-colored quilts and wrought-iron beds. In summer, the lodge is a base for exploring hundreds of miles of hiking trails, and offers horseback riding. In winter, the lodge rents cross-country skis and snowshoes to its guests and offers snowmobile tours for $65 an hour.

HC 61, Alpine. www.hannaganmeadow.com. ✆ **928/339-4370.** 17 units. $85–$120 double; $150–$200 cabin. Children stay free in parent's room. Pets accepted in cabins ($20 fee). **Amenities:** Restaurant; free Wi-Fi.

Tal-Wi-Wi Lodge ★ Four miles north of Alpine on U.S. 191, Tal-Wi-Wi Lodge is nothing fancy—just a rustic lodge popular with anglers and hunters—but it's a good choice in an area with few options. Five deluxe rooms, located in a new building, have gas fireplaces; two have hot tubs. In both buildings, furnishings are rustic yet comfortable, with wood-paneled walls and large front porches. The lodge's new fitness center is the best gym in the area. The dining room serves country breakfasts and dinners. The lodge is closed mid-October to mid-April.

U.S. 191 (P.O. Box 169), Alpine. www.talwiwilodge.com. ✆ **928/339-4319.** 20 units. $85–$140 double. 2-night minimum stay summer holiday weekends. Pets accepted ($10 per day). **Amenities:** Restaurant, lounge; fitness room; free Wi-Fi.

9

TUCSON

Encircled by mountain ranges and bookended by the two units of Saguaro National Park, Arizona's second-largest city has everything for the vacationer that Phoenix has to offer, plus a bit more. There are world-class golf resorts, excellent restaurants, art museums and galleries, an active cultural life, and, of course, plenty of great weather. Tucson also has a long history that melds Native American, Hispanic, and Anglo roots. With a national park, a national forest, and other natural areas and historic sites just beyond the city limits, Tucson richly celebrates its Sonoran Desert setting.

Founded by the Spanish in 1775, Tucson was built on the site of a much older Native American village. The city's name comes from *chuk shon*, which, in the language of the indigenous Tohono O'odham, or Desert People, means "spring at the base of black mountain," a reference to Sentinel Peak (now known simply as "A Mountain," because of the large letter A planted on its slopes by the University of Arizona). From 1867 to 1877, Tucson was the territorial capital of Arizona, but that honor eventually went to Phoenix—punishment, historians say, for the fact that Tucson briefly sided with the Confederacy during the Civil War. Once the capital moved, Tucson did not develop as quickly as Phoenix, and as a result still preserves bits of its Hispanic and Western heritage. Back in the days of urban renewal, Tucson activists turned back the bulldozers and managed to preserve at least some of the city's old Mexican character. Though much of the old city was destroyed, preservationists are bringing back its ghosts every year. Today, advocates for controlled growth are fighting hard to preserve both Tucson's desert environment and the city's unique character. The inevitable sprawl has ringed much of Tucson with vast suburbs, but the city is still far from becoming another Phoenix.

There's an ongoing struggle here to retain an identity distinct from other southwestern cities. One great engine for renewal came in 2014, when a modern version of downtown's old streetcar went into service. With it, block by block, downtown has been remade, and downtown Tucson has become a vibrant urban center featuring dozens of good restaurants and bars, museums and art galleries, and music venues surrounded by historic neighborhoods.

At some point in the last few years, Tucson went to bed an overgrown cowtown and woke up a full-fledged modern city. The town had spread as far as it could, from mountain range to mountain range in a valley 30 miles wide by 30 miles long—the only way left to grow was up. Downtown now bristles with tall buildings, and cranes putting more of them up. Even so, with the Santa Catalina Mountains for a dramatic backdrop, Tucson remains Arizona's most beautiful and most livable city. Whether you're taking in the mountain vistas from the tee box of the 12th hole, the saddle of a palomino, or a table for two, Tucson makes a memorable vacation destination.

ESSENTIALS

Not nearly as large and spread out as Phoenix and the Valley of the Sun, Tucson is small enough to be convenient, yet large enough to be sophisticated. The mountains ringing Tucson are bigger and closer to town than those in Phoenix, and the desert here is more easily accessed. You can always know which direction you're heading by looking at those mountain ranges: the Santa Catalina Mountains, the tallest, lie to the north; the jagged, comparatively low Tucson Mountains are west; the imposing, rocky Rincon Mountains are east; and the Santa Rita Mountains, their tallest peak an ancient volcano, lie to the south.

Arriving

BY PLANE Located 6 miles south of downtown, **Tucson International Airport,** 7250 S. Tucson Blvd. (www.tucsonairport.org; ✆ **520/573-8100**) is served by a number of major airlines.

Visitor centers in both baggage-claim areas can give you brochures and reserve a hotel room if you haven't done so already.

GETTING FROM THE AIRPORT TO YOUR LODGINGS

Many resorts and hotels in Tucson provide a free or competitively priced airport shuttle service. **Arizona Stagecoach** (www.azstagecoach.com; ✆ **877/782-4355** or 520/889-1000) operates 24-hour van service to downtown Tucson and the foothills resorts. Fares to foothills resorts are around $38 one-way and $66 round-trip. It takes between 45 minutes and 1 hour to reach the foothills resorts. To return to the airport, it's best to call at least a day before your scheduled departure.

You'll find taxis waiting outside baggage claim, or you can call **Yellow Cab** (www.yellowcabtucson.com; ✆ **520/624-6611**) or **VIP Taxi** (www.viptaxi.com; ✆ **520/300-3000**). The rate at the airport is $5 for the first mile and $2.60 for every mile thereafter, with a minimum fare of $16. A taxi to downtown costs around $25, to the foothills resorts $32 to $55.

Sun Tran (www.suntran.com; ✆ **520/792-9222**), the local public transit system, operates bus service to and from the airport. The fare is $1.75. Route 25 runs north/south along Park Avenue between the airport and the Laos Transit Center, 205 W. Irvington Rd., and the downtown Ronstadt Transit Center,

215 E. Congress St., where transfers can be made to other routes. Route 11 travels north/south through midtown along Palo Verde Road and Alvernon Way between the airport and the Tucson Jewish Community Center near Dodge Blvd. and River Road. Both routes generally run every 30 minutes from 5:30am to 10:30pm weekdays, and every 60 minutes from 6am to 7pm on weekends and holidays.

BY CAR **I-10,** the main east-west interstate across the southern United States, passes through Tucson and connects to Phoenix. **I-19** connects Tucson with the Mexican border at Nogales. **Ariz. 86** links Tucson with the Organ Pipe Cactus National Monument and the Tohono O'odham Indian Reservation to the southwest, while **Ariz. 77** links with Globe, Holbrook, and the Hopi and Navajo reservations to the north.

If you're headed downtown, take the Congress Street exit off I-10. If you're going to one of the foothills resorts north of downtown, you'll probably want to take the Orange Grove or Ina Road exit off I-10.

BY TRAIN Tucson is served by **Amtrak** (www.amtrak.com; © **800/872-7245**) passenger rail service. The *Sunset Limited*, which runs between New Orleans and Los Angeles, stops in Tucson, as does the *Texas Eagle*, which runs between Los Angeles and Chicago. The **train station** is at 400 N. Toole Ave., in the heart of downtown. You'll see taxis waiting to meet the train.

BY BUS **Greyhound** (www.greyhound.com; © **800/231-2222** or 520/792-3475) connects Tucson to the rest of the United States through its extensive system. The bus station is at 801 E. 12th St.

Visitor Information

The **Metropolitan Tucson Convention & Visitors Bureau (MTCVB),** 100 S. Church Ave. (at Broadway; www.visittucson.org; © **800/638-8350** or 520/624-1817), is an excellent source of information on Tucson and its environs. The visitor center (at 811 N. Euclid Ave.) is open Monday through Friday from 9am to 5pm, Saturday and Sunday from 9am to 4pm.

City Layout

MAIN ARTERIES & STREETS Tucson is laid out on a grid that's fairly regular everywhere except the oldest parts of downtown; some of the midcentury developments in midtown also have odd diagonal streets called "stravenues." In the flatlands, major thoroughfares are spaced at 1-mile intervals, with smaller streets filling in the squares created by the major roads. In the foothills, where Tucson's most recent growth has occurred, the grid system breaks down completely because of the hilly terrain.

The main **east-west roads** are (from south to north) 22nd Street, Broadway Boulevard, Speedway Boulevard, Grant Road (with Tanque Verde Road as an extension), and Ina Road/Skyline Drive/Sunrise Road. The main **north-south roads** are (from west to east) Miracle Mile/Oracle Road, Stone/Sixth Avenue, Campbell Avenue, Country Club Road, Alvernon Road, Swan Road, Wilmot

Overlooking the Tucson skyline from the west, Sentinel Peak bears a big letter "A" for the University of Arizona.

Road, and Kolb Road. **I-10** cuts diagonally across the Tucson metropolitan area from northwest to southeast.

In **downtown Tucson,** Congress Street and Broadway Boulevard are the main east-west streets; Broadway splits into the one-way, westbound Congress Street when it enters the western end of downtown, with Broadway one-way eastbound until leaving downtown. Stone Avenue, Sixth Avenue, and Fourth Avenue are the main north-south streets.

FINDING AN ADDRESS Because Tucson is laid out on a grid, finding an address is relatively easy. The zero (or starting) point for all Tucson addresses is the corner of Stone Avenue, which runs north and south, and Congress Street, which runs east and west. From this point, streets are designated either north, south, east, or west. Addresses usually, but not always, increase by 100 with each block, so an address of 4321 E. Broadway Blvd. should be 43 blocks—or 4.3 miles, at 10 blocks per mile—east of Stone Avenue. In the downtown area, many of the streets and avenues are numbered, with numbered streets running east and west, and numbered avenues running north and south.

STREET MAPS The best way to find your way around Tucson is to pick up a free map at the airport visitor center or the MTCVB (above). Maps handed out by car-rental agencies are not very detailed but will do for some purposes. Local gas stations and convenience stores also sell detailed maps.

Neighborhoods in Brief

DOWNTOWN

Tucson's main business district has also recently become a vibrant area, full of restaurants, bars, galleries, and shops, that buzzes until 2am. It is served by a streetcar that runs from the university to the west side.

EL PRESIDIO HISTORIC DISTRICT

Named for the Spanish military garrison that once stood here, this neighborhood is bounded by Alameda Street, Main Avenue, Franklin Street, and Church Avenue. In the 1880s, this was the city's most affluent neighborhood, and many large homes from that era have been restored. The Tucson Museum of Art is a major draw here.

BARRIO HISTÓRICO DISTRICT

Another 19th-century neighborhood, the Barrio Histórico is bounded on the north by Cushing Street, on the west by railroad tracks, on the south by 18th Street, and on the east by Stone Avenue. The Barrio Histórico is characterized by Sonoran-style adobe row houses. A few restaurants dot the neighborhood, most at the southern end, but most restored buildings serve as offices and private residences. This remains a borderline neighborhood; try to avoid it late at night.

UNIVERSITY DISTRICT/MIDTOWN

Northeast of downtown Tucson lie several different neighborhoods surrounding the University of Arizona. Just to the west, Fourth Avenue is a favorite shopping and nightlife district for college students. Neighborhoods to the east are largely residential but have a few good hotels. Stretching north from the university, Campbell Avenue has the city's greatest concentration of interesting budget restaurants.

EAST TUCSON

East of the University District all the way to the eastern unit of Saguaro National Park, sprawling East Tucson has lots of hotels, including several all-suites properties, plenty of good restaurants, and both the national park and Sabino Canyon Recreation Area.

WEST TUCSON

Along the flank of the Tucson Mountains, the west side is home to several top attractions, including the Arizona-Sonora Desert Museum, Old Tucson Studios, and the west unit of Saguaro National Park, but it doesn't have many recommendable restaurants or places to stay.

ORO VALLEY & MARANA

These two suburbs northwest of Tucson are where all the city's recent development has taken place. Here you'll find the posh Ritz-Carlton Dove Mountain resort and several good restaurants. The area has stupendous views of the west slopes of the Santa Catalina Mountains, with access to the mountains at Catalina State Park.

THE FOOTHILLS

This huge affluent area in northern Tucson boasts elegant shopping plazas, modern malls, world-class resorts, golf courses, and expensive residential neighborhoods, surrounded by hilly desert at the foot of the Santa Catalina Mountains.

GETTING AROUND

By Car

Unless you plan to stay by the pool or on the golf course, you'll want to rent a car while visiting Tucson. Luckily, rates are a little lower than rates in Phoenix. At press time, Alamo was charging around $250 per week ($325 with taxes and surcharges included) during high season for a compact car with unlimited mileage in Tucson. See p. 506 for info on car rental savings.

Parking is at a premium in downtown Tucson, and parking tickets at expired meters are a major source of revenue for the city. There are two huge parking lots on the south side of the Tucson Convention Center, a couple of small lots on either side of the Tucson Museum of Art (one at Main Ave. and Paseo Redondo, and one at the corner of Council St. and Court Ave.), and parking garages beneath the main library (101 N. Stone Ave.) and El Presidio Park (on Alameda St.). Other garages and parking lots are scattered throughout downtown. Outside the crowded downtown area, with the exception of the University, parking is abundant and free. Almost all Tucson hotels and resorts provide free parking.

By Public Transportation

BY BUS Covering much of the Tucson metropolitan area, **Sun Tran** (www.suntran.com; ✆ **520/792-9222**) public buses charge $1.75 per ride for adults and students, 75¢ for seniors, and free for children 5 and under. Day passes are available on buses for $4.

Downtown Tucson's **Ronstadt Transit Center,** 215 E. Congress St., is served by about 30 regular and express bus routes to all parts of Tucson. The bus system, however, does *not* extend to such major attractions as the Arizona-Sonora Desert Museum, Old Tucson, or Saguaro National Park.

BY STREETCAR Launched in 2014, Tucson's modern streetcar proved an instant hit, transporting travelers from the Banner University of Arizona Medical Center to the Mercado San Agustín west of downtown, a distance of about 4 miles; it'll get you close to everywhere you'll want to travel downtown and in the University area. The streetcar runs every 10–15 minutes on weekdays and every 15–30 minutes on weekends. A day pass costs $4.50, which you can buy online (www.sunlinkstreetcar.com) or at vending machines at streetcar stops. Note that you cannot purchase individual ride tickets on board the streetcar. Your pass will be charged $1.75 for each ride you take.

By Taxi

If you need a taxi, you'll have to phone for one. **Yellow Cab** (www.yellowcabtucson.com; ✆ **520/624-6611**), **Discount Cab** (www.discountcab.com; ✆ **520/388-9000**), and **VIP Taxi** (www.viptaxi.com; ✆ **520/300-3000**) provide service throughout the city. The general rate is $5 for the first mile and $2.60 for every mile thereafter; some companies impose minimum fares. Although distances in Tucson are not as great as those in Phoenix, it's still a good 10 or more miles from the foothills resorts to downtown Tucson, so expect to pay $25 or thereabouts for a taxi. Most resorts have shuttle vans or can arrange taxi service to major attractions.

On Foot

Downtown Tucson is compact and best explored on foot. (Narrow streets in the historic districts make driving a challenge.) Several major attractions—including the Arizona-Sonora Desert Museum, Old Tucson Studios, Saguaro National Park, and Sabino Canyon—can be reached only by car, but be aware that they require quite a bit of walking once you arrive. Be sure to bring a good pair of walking shoes.

[Fast FACTS] TUCSON

Dentist Call the **Arizona Dental Association** (✆ **800/866-2732;** www.azda.org) for a referral.

Doctor For a doctor referral, ask at your hotel, or call the **Northwest Medical Center** (✆ **520/742-9000;** www.northwestmedicalcenter.com).

Emergencies For fire, police, or medical emergencies, phone ✆ **911.**

Hospitals The **Tucson Medical Center** is at 5301 E. Grant Rd. (✆ **520/327-5461;** www.tmcaz.com). The **Banner-University Medical Center Tucson** is at 1501 N. Campbell Ave. (✆ **520/694-0111;** www.bannerhealth.com/locations/tucson/banner-university-medical-center-tucson).

Lost Property If you lose something at the airport, call ✆ **520/573-8156.** If you lose something on a Sun Tran bus, call ✆ **520/792-9222.**

Newspapers & Magazines The ***Arizona Daily Star*** is Tucson's morning daily. ***Tucson Weekly*** is the city's news-and-lifestyle journal, published on Thursday. ***Zócalo*** is a lively arts and local history/culture monthly.

Pharmacies Contact Walgreens (✆ **800/925-4733;** www.walgreens.com) for the Walgreens pharmacy nearest you; some are open 24 hours a day.

Police In case of an emergency, phone ✆ **911.**

Post Office There's a post office in downtown Tucson at 141 S. Sixth Ave. (✆ **800/275-8777** or 520/903-1958; www.usps.com); it's open Monday through Friday from 9am to 5pm.

Safety Tucson is surprisingly safe for a city of its size. However, downtown attracts a lot of street people and panhandlers. Be particularly alert if you're down here for a performance of some sort. Just to the south of downtown lies a poorer section of the city that's best avoided after dark unless you are certain of where you're going. Take the same precautions you would in any other city.

When driving, be aware that many streets in the Tucson area are subject to flooding when it rains. Heed warnings about possible flooded areas and don't try to cross a low area that has become flooded. Find an alternate route instead.

Taxes In addition to the 5.6% **sales tax** levied by the state, Tucson levies a 2.6% city sales tax, for a total of 8.6%. **Car-rental** taxes, surcharges, and fees add up to around 30% on weekly rentals at the Tucson International Airport. The **hotel tax** in the Tucson area is 12.1%.

Weather For the local weather forecast, call the **National Weather Service** (✆ **520/881-3333**).

EXPLORING TUCSON

Tucson blends the old and the new, with roots extending thousands of years into the Native American past and tendrils projecting far into the future, in forward-looking places such as Biosphere II and a cluster of astronomical observatories. You can taste the city's rich history in its many museums—and taste its flavors in restaurants and food trucks around town (Tucson is one of only two international Cities of Gastronomy in the United States). Look in any direction, and you'll find something fun, inspiring, and delicious.

The **Tucson Attractions Passport** is a great way to save money on admissions to many of the city's top attractions. The passport, available at the Tucson Visitors Center, 811 N. Euclid Ave. (www.visittucson.org; ✆ **800/638-8350**), costs $24 and gets you discounted admissions to the Arizona-Sonora Desert Museum, Kitt Peak National Observatory, Old Tucson Studios, Biosphere 2, the Pima Air & Space Museum, Tohono Chul Park, the Tucson

The full spectrum of desert life, from hummingbirds to this handsome mountain lion, is on display at the Arizona-Sonora Desert Museum.

Museum of Art, and many other attractions in Tucson and across southern Arizona. You can also download the Tucson Attractions Passport as a free app and make purchases through it.

The Tucson Area's Top Attractions

Arizona-Sonora Desert Museum ★★★ NATURE CENTER/ZOO More zoo than museum proper, ASDM is one of the best of its kind in the country. The Sonoran Desert, which spans central southern Arizona and parts of northern Mexico, contains within its boundaries not only arid lands, but also forested mountains, springs, rivers, wetlands, grasslands, and streams. Exhibits here encompass the full spectrum of Sonoran Desert life—from plants and insects to fish, reptiles, and mammals—and all are on display in very natural settings. Coyotes and javelinas (peccaries) seem very much at home in their compounds, which are surrounded by nearly invisible fences, making it seem as if there's nothing between you and the animals. You'll also see black bears and mountain lions, tarantulas and scorpions, prairie dogs and desert bighorn sheep. The walk-in hummingbird aviary is a special treat, with hummers of many species whizzing by your head and sometimes pausing to take stock of you. So, too, is the raptor free flight display, staged in all but summer, when birds of prey such as hawks, owls, and ravens are set loose to demonstrate their remarkable skills. Don't be surprised if you end up staying here hours longer than you had intended. ***Tip:*** The grounds are quite extensive, so wear good walking shoes; a brimmed hat and sunscreen lotion are also advisable. If you get hungry, there are two excellent dining options—the cafeteria-style Ironwood Terraces and the more upscale Ocotillo Café.

Arizona History Museum **23**
Arizona State Museum **24**
Arizona-Sonora Desert Museum **1**
ASARCO Mineral Discovery Center **30**
Biosphere 2 **11**
Center for Creative Photography **21**
Children's Museum Tucson **8**
Colossal Cave Mountain Park **33**
De Grazia Gallery in the Sun **13**
Downtown History Museum **6**
El Tiradito **10**
Flandrau: The UA Science Center **20**
Fort Lowell Museum **17**
Golf n' Stuff **19**
Jewish Community Center Sculpture Park **15**
The Mini-Time Machine Museum of Miniatures **16**
Mission San Xavier del Bac **29**
Museum of Contemporary Art **9**
Old Tucson Studios **2**
Pima Air & Space Museum **32**
Presidio San Agustin del Tucson **5**
Reid Park Zoo **27**
Sabino Canyon Recreation Area **14**
Saguaro National Park **3**
Southern Arizona Transportation Museum **7**
Steward Observatory Mirror Lab **25**
Titan Missile Museum **31**
Tohono Chul Park **12**
Trail Dust Town **18**
Tucson Botanical Gardens **26**
Tucson Museum of Art & Historic Block **4**
Tucson Rodeo Parade Museum **28**
The University of Arizona Museum of Art **22**

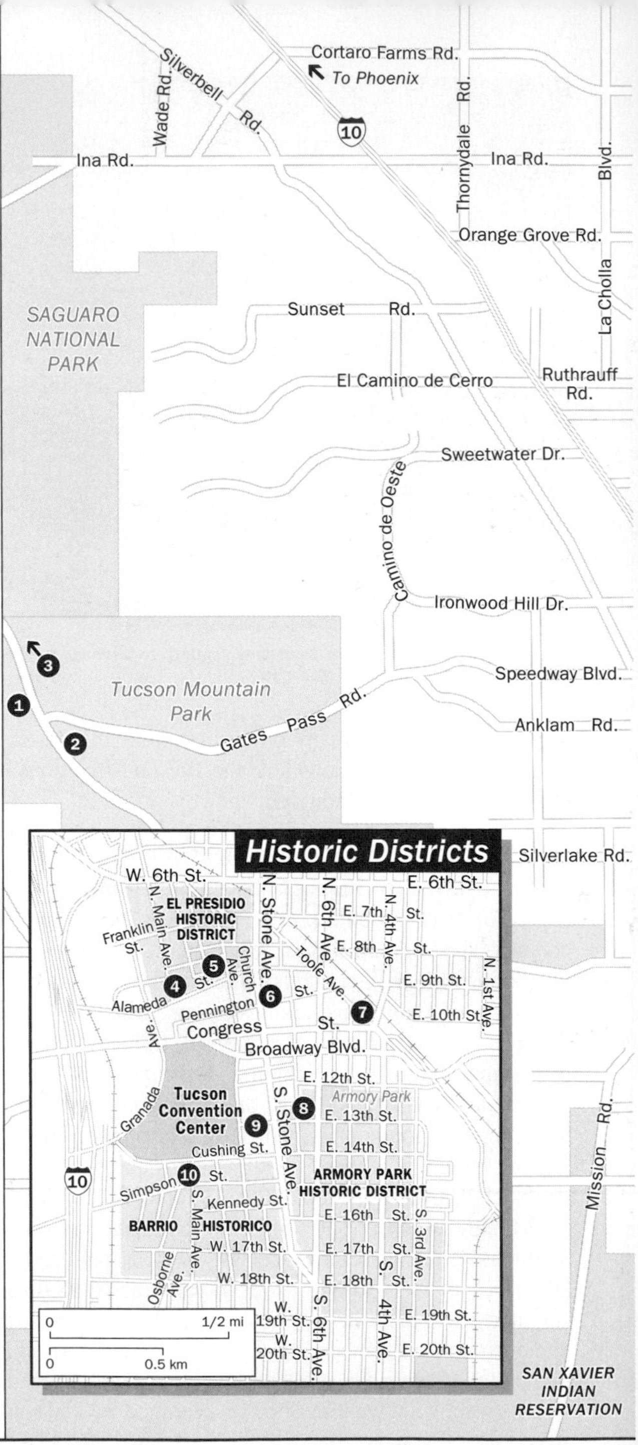

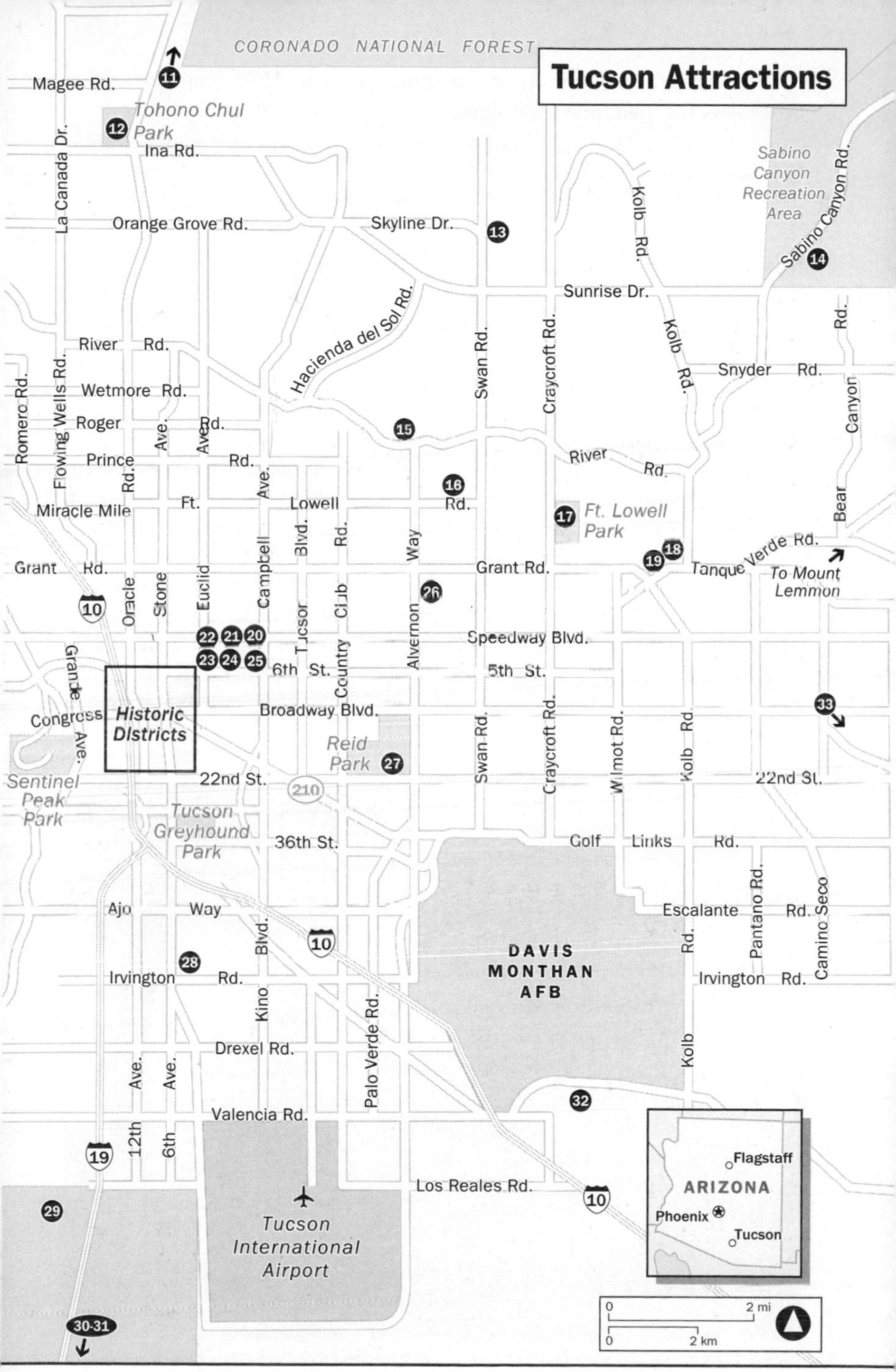

Tucson Attractions
CORONADO NATIONAL FOREST
Magee Rd.
Tohono Chul Park
Ina Rd.
La Canada Dr.
Orange Grove Rd.
Skyline Dr.
Sabino Canyon Recreation Area
Sabino Canyon Rd.
Kolb Rd.
Sunrise Dr.
Hacienda del Sol Rd.
Swan Rd.
Craycroft Rd.
Snyder Rd.
Canyon
Bear
River Rd.
Wetmore Rd.
Roger Rd.
Prince Rd.
Romero Rd.
Flowing Wells Rd.
Miracle Mile
Ft. Lowell Rd.
Ft. Lowell Park
Tanque Verde Rd.
To Mount Lemmon
Grant Rd.
Oracle Rd.
Stone Ave.
Euclid Ave.
Campbell Ave.
Tucson Blvd.
Country Club Rd.
Alvernon Way
Speedway Blvd.
6th St.
5th St.
Broadway Blvd.
Grande Ave.
Congress
Historic Districts
Reid Park
Sentinel Peak Park
22nd St.
Wilmot Rd.
Tucson Greyhound Park
36th St.
Golf Links Rd.
Escalante Rd.
Pantano Rd.
Camino Seco
Ajo Way
Kino Blvd.
DAVIS MONTHAN AFB
Irvington Rd.
Drexel Rd.
Palo Verde Rd.
12th Ave.
6th Ave.
Valencia Rd.
Los Reales Rd.
Tucson International Airport
ARIZONA
Flagstaff
Phoenix
Tucson
0 2 mi
0 2 km

To get here from downtown, go west on Speedway Blvd., which becomes Gates Pass Rd., and follow the signs.

2021 N. Kinney Rd., 14 mi W of downtown. www.desertmuseum.org. ✆ **520/883-2702.** $22 adults, $20 seniors, $9 ages 3–12, $18 military, $17 AZ and Sonora residents. Oct–Feb daily 8:30am–5pm; Mar–May and Sept daily 7:30am–5pm; June–Aug Sun–Fri 7am–5pm, Sat 7am–10pm.

Mission San Xavier del Bac ★★★ CHURCH/HISTORIC SITE Called the White Dove of the Desert, Mission San Xavier del Bac is a blindingly white adobe building that rises from a sere, brown landscape. Considered the finest example of mission architecture in the Southwest, the beautiful church was built between 1783 and 1797, incorporating Moorish, Byzantine, and Mexican Renaissance architectural styles. The church, however, was never actually completed, which becomes apparent only when the two bell towers are compared—one is topped with a dome, while the other has none.

Colorful murals cover the interior walls, and behind the altar are elaborate decorations. To the left of the main altar, in a glass sarcophagus, stands a statue of St. Francis Xavier, the mission's patron saint. A visit to San Xavier's little museum, alongside the chapel, provides a bit of historical perspective; you can also explore more of the mission, such as the farm fields and station of the cross beyond the walls. To the east of the church, atop a small hill, you'll find not only an interesting view of the church, but also a replica of the famous grotto in Lourdes, France. There are often food stalls selling fry bread in the parking lot in front of the church.

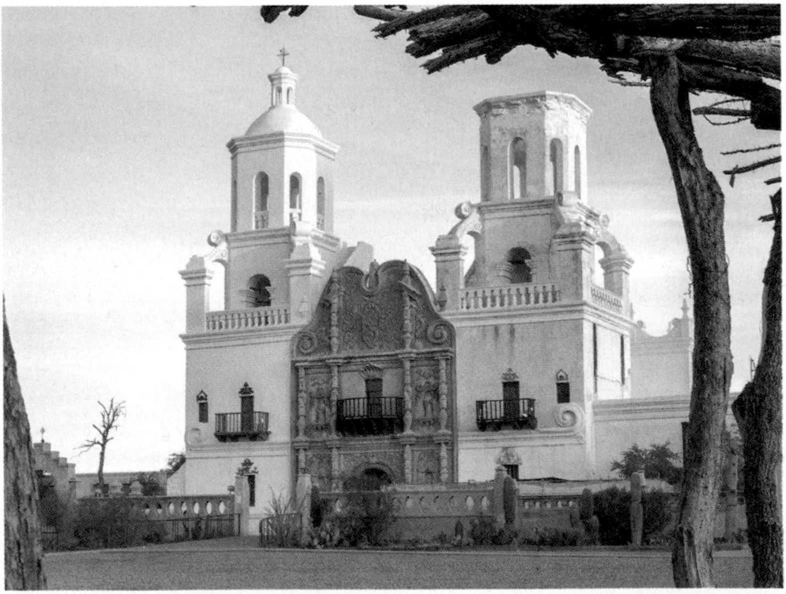

On the San Xavier reservation south of Tucson, San Xavier del Bac is considered the finest mission church in the Southwest.

Be aware that San Xavier is still an active Roman Catholic church, serving the San Xavier Indian Reservation, with frequent services; behave accordingly. Sunday masses are held at 7am, 10am, and 11:30am. Docents are always on hand to answer questions. To get here, take I-19 south 9 miles to exit 92 and turn right.

1950 W. San Xavier Rd. www.sanxaviermission.org. ✆ **520/294-2624.** Free admission; donations accepted. Daily 7am–5pm.

Old Tucson Studios ★ ATTRACTION Despite the name, this is not the historical location of the old city of Tucson—it's a Western town originally built as the set for the 1939 movie *Arizona.* In the years since, Old Tucson has been used in the filming of John Wayne's *Rio Lobo, Rio Bravo*, and *El Dorado;* Clint Eastwood's *The Outlaw Josey Wales;* Kirk Douglas's *Gunfight at the O.K. Corral;* Paul Newman's *The Life and Times of Judge Roy Bean;* and, more recently, *Tombstone* and *Geronimo.*

Today, in addition to serving as a site for film, TV, and advertising productions (call ahead to find out if any filming is scheduled), Old Tucson has become a Wild West theme park with family-oriented activities and entertainment. Throughout the day, there are staged shootouts in the streets, stunt demonstrations, a cancan musical revue, and other performances. Train and kiddie rides, restaurants, and gift shops round out the experience.

To get here, take Speedway Blvd. west, continuing in the same direction when it becomes Gates Pass Blvd., and turn left on S. Kinney Rd.

201 S. Kinney Rd. www.oldtucson.com. ✆ **520/883-0100.** $20 adults, $18 seniors and military, $11 ages 4–11; discounts for Pima County residents. Daily 10am–5pm, closed Sept 4–27, Thanksgiving Day, Dec 24–25, and for occasional special events.

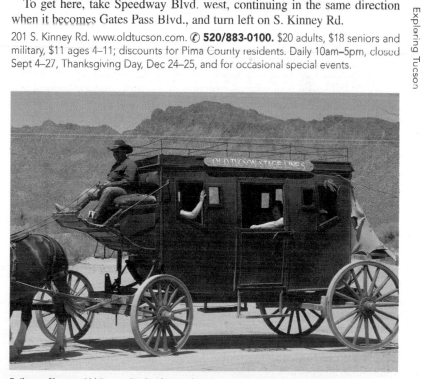

Built as a film set, Old Tucson Studios has evolved into a Wild West theme attraction.

Saguaro National Park ★★★ NATURE PRESERVE The quintessential symbol of the American desert, saguaro cacti occur naturally only here in the Sonoran Desert. Sensitive to fire and frost, and exceedingly slow to mature, these massive, treelike cacti grow naturally in great profusion around Tucson, but have long been threatened by development and by plant collectors. In 1933, to protect these desert giants, the federal government set aside two large tracts of land as a saguaro preserve. This preserve eventually became Saguaro National Park. The two units of the park, one on the east side of the city (Rincon Mountain District) and one on the west (Tucson Mountain District), preserve not only dense stands of saguaros, but also the many other wild inhabitants of this part of the Sonoran Desert. Both units have loop roads, nature trails, hiking trails, and picnic grounds.

The **west unit** of the park is more popular with visitors because of its proximity to both the Arizona-Sonora Desert Museum (p. 361) and Old Tucson Studios (above); it's your best choice if you're trying to see a lot of Tucson in a short amount of time. This section also happens to have the most impressive stands of saguaros. Be sure to take the scenic **Bajada Loop Drive,** where you'll find dramatic views and several hiking trails (the Hugh Morris Trail involves a long, steep climb, but great views are the reward). To reach the west unit of the park, follow Speedway Boulevard west from downtown Tucson (it becomes Gates Pass Blvd.). Stop in at the visitor center for an overview of the park's natural history.

Sunset on Signal Hill

A hike to Signal Hill, located off the Bajada Loop Drive in Saguaro National Park's west unit and only a quarter-mile walk from the parking area, will reward you with not only a grand sunset vista away from the crowds at Gates Pass, but also the sight of dozens of petroglyphs.

The **east unit** of the park contains an older area of saguaro "forest" at the foot of the Rincon Mountains. This section is popular with hikers because most of it has no roads. It also has a visitor center, a loop scenic drive, a picnic area, and a trail open to mountain bikes (the paved loop drive is a great road-bike ride). To reach the east unit of the park, take Speedway Boulevard east, then head south on Freeman Road to Old Spanish Trail.

www.nps.gov/sagu. Tucson Mt. District visitor center: 2700 N. Kinney Rd. ✆ **520/733-5158.** Rincon Mt. District visitor center: 3693 S. Old Spanish Trail. ✆ **520/733-5153.** Entry fee $15 per car, $5 per hiker or biker. Tucson Mt. District open to vehicles daily sunrise–sunset; Rincon Mt. District open to vehicles daily 7am–sunset; both open to hikers 24 hr. a day. Visitor centers daily 9am–5pm; closed Christmas.

The Historic Districts

If you're interested in the history of Tucson, join a walking tour of the Old Pueblo. Begin with a $3 guided tour of the **Downtown History Museum** (below), arm yourself with a street map, and go explore. Tours of downtown Tucson are also offered several times each week by local historian Ken Scoville of **Old Pueblo Walking tours** (www.oldpueblotours.com; ✆ **520/230-9345**), who charges $79 per adult ($69 children) for half-day tours.

Seeing It All from "A Mountain"

The best way to get a feel for the geography of the Tucson area is to drive to the top of a mountain—but not just any mountain. **"A Mountain"** (officially called Sentinel Peak) rises just west of downtown Tucson on the far side of I-10. The peak gets its common name from the giant whitewashed letter *A* (for University of Arizona) near the summit. To get here, drive west to the end of Congress Street and turn left on Sentinel Peak Road. The park is open daily from dawn to dusk.

Tip: Don't visit this neighborhood on Mondays, when all of the attractions listed below are closed.

Downtown History Museum ★ MUSEUM If you want to learn more about the history of Tucson, this is the museum to visit. Exhibits cover Spanish presidio days, American army days, merchants, and schools. Through the use of artifacts and old photos, these exhibits help bring the city's past to life. One of the most curious exhibits focuses on the gangster John Dillinger, who was arrested here in Tucson in 1934.

140 N. Stone Ave., in the Wells Fargo Bank bldg. www.arizonahistoricalsociety.org. ✆ **520/770-1473.** Free admission, donations accepted. Wed–Fri 11am–3pm. Closed major holidays. Bus: All downtown-bound buses. Streetcar: Park Ave. & 2nd St.

Museum of Contemporary Art ★ MUSEUM Among the newest museums in Tucson, the Museum of Contemporary Art is housed in the city's old downtown fire station, conveniently close to dozens of restaurants and art galleries. While it holds nowhere near the inventory of its big sisters in places like Chicago and New York, Tucson's MOCA contains contemporary artworks from around the globe, as well as works by numerous local artists. There's always something going on in the big studio space, from talks to children's workshops; check the calendar for what's happening while you're here. The last Sunday of the month is always free.

265 S. Church Ave. www.mocatucson.org. ✆ **520/624-5019.** $5 adults, $3 students and seniors. Wed–Sun noon–5pm. Bus: All downtown-bound buses. Streetcar: Stone Ave. & Congress St.

Presidio San Agustin del Tucson ★ HISTORIC SITE At this reconstruction of part of the Spanish fort that was Tucson's birthplace, you'll really get a sense of the early history of this city. Within its adobe-block walls and in an adjacent adobe building, displays illuminate various aspects of Tuscon's founding years. Most months between fall and spring, there is a Saturday living-history event here.

196 N. Court Ave. www.tucsonpresidio.com. ✆ **520/791-4873.** $5 adults, $1 children 6–14. Wed–Sun 10am–4pm. Bus: All downtown-bound buses. Streetcar: Church Ave. & Congress St.

Southern Arizona Transportation Museum ★ MUSEUM Housed in a building adjacent to the former Southern Pacific Railroad Depot, built in

THE shrine THAT STOPPED A FREEWAY

The southern Arizona landscape is dotted with roadside shrines, symbols of the region's Hispanic and Roman Catholic heritage. Most are simple crosses decorated with plastic flowers and dedicated to people who have been killed in auto accidents. One shrine, however, stands out from all the rest: Tucson's **El Tiradito.** Not only does this crumbling shrine attract the devout, but it once also stopped a freeway.

El Tiradito, on South Granada Avenue at West Cushing Street, is the only shrine in the United States dedicated to a sinner buried in unconsecrated soil. Several stories tell of how this shrine came to be, but the best of them concerns a young Mexican American man who was having an affair with a railroad conductor's wife. Caught in the act, he was chopped to bits, his body scattered along the railroad tracks—thus "El Tiradito," Spanish for "the Little Castaway." Because he had been caught in the act of adultery and died without confessing his sins, his body could not be interred in the church cemetery, so he was buried where he fell.

The people of the neighborhood soon began burning candles on the spot to try to save the soul of the young man, and eventually people began burning candles in hopes that their own wishes would come true. They believed that if the candle burned through the night, their prayers would be answered. The shrine eventually grew into a substantial little structure, and in 1927 was dedicated by its owner to the city of Tucson. In 1940, the shrine became an official Tucson monument.

Such status was not enough to protect the shrine from urban renewal, however. When the federal government announced that it would level the shrine to build a new freeway through the center of Tucson, the city's citizens were outraged. Their protests eventually resulted in the shrine being named to the National Register of Historic Places, and the freeway was moved a few hundred yards to the west.

To this day, devout Catholics from the surrounding neighborhood still burn candles at the shrine that stopped a freeway. A visit after dark, perhaps in conjunction with dinner next door at **El Minuto** (p. 401), a popular Mexican restaurant, is a somber experience that will easily convince you of how important this shrine is to the neighborhood.

1941, this little museum is worth a visit if only to wander around the depot grounds. The museum's exhibits focus on the history of the railroad in southern Arizona; on the grounds are an old steam engine and a statue of Doc Holliday and Wyatt Earp, who shot a man to death nearby, just a few months after the famed gunfight at the O.K. Corral in Tombstone (p. 454). The museum is right next door to the current Amtrak station.

414 N. Toole Ave. www.tucsonhistoricdepot.org. ✆ **520/623-2223.** Free admission. Tues–Thurs 11am–3pm; Fri–Sat 10am–4pm; Sun 11am–3pm. Bus: All downtown-bound buses. Streetcar: 6th Ave. & Congress St.

Tucson Museum of Art & Historic Block ★★ MUSEUM COMPLEX
This complex includes galleries housed in historic adobe homes, a courtyard frequently used to display sculptures, and a large modern building that often mounts the most interesting exhibits in town. One highlight is the **Palice Pavilion–Art of the Americas** exhibit, which consists of a large collection of

pre-Columbian art that represents 3,000 years of life in Mexico and Central and South America. This collection is housed in the historic Stevens/Duffield House, which also contains Spanish colonial artifacts and Latin American folk art. The noteworthy **Goodman Pavilion of Western Art** comprises an extensive collection that depicts cowboys, horses, and the wide-open spaces of the American West.

On the block surrounding the museum, you'll see a number of restored homes, dating from 1850 to 1907, all built on the former site of the Tucson presidio, and all open to the public. A map and brochures are available at the museum's front desk; October through April, guided tours of the historic block and nearby **Corbett House** are available (free with museum admission).

140 N. Main Ave. www.tucsonmuseumofart.org. ✆ **520/624-2333.** $12 adults, $10 seniors, $7 students, free for veterans and kids 12 and under; free 1st Thurs of month 5pm–8pm; free AZ and Sonora residents on 2nd Sun of month. Tues–Sun 10am–5pm. Closed Thanksgiving, Christmas. Bus: All downtown-bound buses. Streetcar: Church Ave. & Congress St.

University District Attractions

Arizona History Museum ★ MUSEUM As the state's oldest historical museum, this repository of all things Arizonan is a treasure-trove for the history buff. If you've never explored a real mine, you can do the next best thing by exploring the museum's full-scale reproduction of an underground mine tunnel. You'll see an assayer's office, miner's tent, stamp mill, and blacksmith's shop in the mining exhibit. A transportation exhibit displays stagecoaches and the horseless carriages that revolutionized life in the Southwest, while a range of temporary exhibits give a pretty good idea of what it was like back then.

949 E. 2nd St. www.arizonahistoricalsociety.org. ✆ **520/628-5774.** $10 adults, $8 seniors, $4 students ages 7–17, free for kids 6 and under. Mon–Thurs 9am–4pm, Fri 9am–8pm, Sat 11am–4pm. Closed major holidays. Bus: 1, 4, 5. Streetcar: University Blvd.

Arizona State Museum ★ MUSEUM The oldest anthropological museum in the Southwest offers one of the state's most interesting exhibits on prehistoric and contemporary Native American cultures. Paths of Life: American Indians of the Southwest focuses on 10 different tribes from around the

Rattlesnake Crossing

Generally speaking, rattlesnakes should not be crossed, but there is one Tucson rattler that should not be avoided. I am referring here to the city's unusual **Diamondback Bridge,** a snake-shaped pedestrian bridge designed by Tucson artist Simon Donovan that spans E. Broadway Boulevard just east of downtown Tucson. From the north end, you enter through the giant vipers open mouth (watch out for the fangs). At the south end of the bridge, a giant rattle is raised in the air, and if you're lucky you just might hear it buzzing as you pass. The bridge is best accessed from the south end of the Fourth Avenue shopping district. Just walk east on E. Ninth Street, turn right on N. Third Avenue, and then follow the bike path through Iron Horse Park.

Southwest and northern Mexico, not only displaying a wide range of artifacts, but also exploring the lifestyles and cultural traditions of Indians living in the region today. In addition, the museum showcases a collection of some 20,000 ceramic pieces, spanning 2,000 years of life in the desert Southwest.

University of Arizona campus, 1013 E. University Blvd. at Park Ave. www.statemuseum.arizona.edu. ✆ **520/621-6302.** $5 adults, free for kids 17 and under. Mon–Sat 10am–5pm. Closed major holidays. Bus: 1, 4, 5. Streetcar: University Blvd.

Center for Creative Photography ★★ GALLERY Have you ever wished you could see an original Ansel Adams print up close, or perhaps an Edward Weston or a Richard Avedon? You can at the Center for Creative Photography. Originally conceived by Ansel Adams, the center now holds more than 90,000 works by more than 2,200 of the world's best photographers, making it one of the best and largest collections in the world. The center mounts fascinating exhibits year-round and is also a research facility that preserves the photographic archives of more than 240 photographers, including Adams. While the main gallery is open on a regular basis, you must make an appointment to view images from the archives.

University of Arizona campus, 1030 N. Olive Rd. (east of Park Ave. and Speedway Blvd.). www.creativephotography.org. ✆ **520/621-7968.** Free admission, donations encouraged. Tues–Fri 9am–4pm; Sat 1–4pm. Closed major holidays. Bus: 1, 4, 5. Streetcar: Olive and Second St.

Flandrau: The UA Science Center ★★ SCIENCE CENTER Located on the University of Arizona campus, Flandrau is the most convenient place in Arizona to do a little stargazing through a professional telescope. On clear nights, astronomers train Flandrau's 16-inch telescope on whatever objects in the night sky are most interesting. You might get a close-up look at the craters of the moon or the rings of Saturn. The science center also has a large mineral collection, exhibits related to University science research, a fine gift shop, and regularly scheduled laser-light shows and 3D movies in the state-of-the-art planetarium.

University of Arizona campus, 1601 E. University Blvd., at Cherry Ave. www.flandrau.org. ✆ **520/621-7827.** $16 adults; $12 seniors, military, college students, and children 4–15; free for kids 4 and under. Telescope viewing free. Mon–Thurs 9am–5pm, Fri 9am–10pm,

Mirror, Mirror in the Hall

The mountaintops of southern Arizona are dotted with astronomical observatories, and one thing many of them have in common is that they use massive glass mirrors to reflect the light of distant stars. At the University of Arizona's **Steward Observatory Mirror Lab** (http://mirrorlab.as.arizona.edu; ✆ **520/626-8792**), you can tour a facility that has made mirrors for telescopes all over the world. Keep in mind that some of these mirrors are more than 25 feet in diameter. The mirrors are cast and polished inside a facility *under* the east wing of the UA football stadium (not actually a hall). Monday through Friday at 1 and 3pm, there are 90-minute tours of the mirror lab ($20 adults; $18 seniors and military; $10 children and students 10–20). Reservations are required.

Art in the Open Air

Although it isn't very big, the **Jewish Community Center Sculpture Park,** 3800 E. River Rd. (www.tucsonjcc.org/programs/arts/sculpture-garden; ✆ **520/299-3000**) exhibits some excellent sculptures and is well worth wandering through. It's just off the Rillito River Park path, so you can combine a visit to the sculpture park with a walk or bike ride along the (usually) dry riverbed. You'll find the community center at the north end of North Dodge Boulevard.

Sat 10am–10pm, Sun 12pm–5pm. Telescope viewing (weather permitting) Wed–Sat 7–10pm. Closed major holidays. Bus: 1, 3, 4, 5, 6, 9, 15. Streetcar: 2nd Street/Cherry Ave.

The University of Arizona Museum of Art ★★ MUSEUM With European and American works dating from the Renaissance up to the 20th century, the art collections at this museum are even more extensive and diverse than those of the Tucson Museum of Art. Tintoretto, Rembrandt, Picasso, O'Keeffe, Warhol, and Rothko are all represented. Another highlight, the *Retablo of Ciudad Rodrigo*, consists of 26 paintings from 15th-century Spain that were originally placed above a cathedral altar. The museum also has an extensive collection of 20th-century sculpture that includes more than 60 clay and plaster models and sketches by Jacques Lipchitz.

University of Arizona campus, 1031 N. Olive Rd. (at Park Ave. and Speedway Blvd.). www.artmuseum.arizona.edu. ✆ **520/621-7567.** $8 adults, $6.50 seniors, free for Museum members, students, and children. Tues–Fri 9am–4pm, Sat 9am–5pm, Sun noon–5pm. Closed major holidays. Bus: 1, 4, 5. Streetcar: Olive and Second St.

Other Attractions Around Town

De Grazia Gallery in the Sun ★★ HISTORIC HOME/MUSEUM Prolific southwestern artist Ettore "Ted" De Grazia (1909–1982) was a Tucson favorite son, and his home, a sprawling, funky adobe building on 10 acres of land in the foothills, is a city landmark. De Grazia is said to be the most reproduced artist in the world, since so many of his images of big-eyed children were used as greeting cards during the 1950s and 1960s. Today De Grazia's images seem trite and maudlin, but in his day he was a very successful artist. This gallery is packed with original paintings, even though, near the end of his life, De Grazia burned several hundred thousand dollars' worth of his paintings in a protest of IRS inheritance taxes. The gift shop has lots of reproductions and other objects with De Grazia images—you might even find an original De Grazia for sale.

6300 N. Swan Rd. www.degrazia.org. ✆ **800/545-2185** or 520/299-9191. Free admission. Daily 10am–4pm. Closed New Year's Day, Easter, Thanksgiving, and Christmas.

Fort Lowell Museum ★ MUSEUM Located in Fort Lowell Park, this museum occupies the site of a cavalry outpost that was active between 1873 and 1891. The museum chronicles the history of life at the fort, with some of the ruins of the original fort preserved for viewing. Before it was a fort, this site was a Hohokam village; artifacts uncovered from archaeological digs are also on display. Another display focuses on medical facilities at the fort (renowned medical researcher Walter Reed, who discovered how yellow fever is transmitted, was the base surgeon here in 1876). Here you'll learn that, despite Hollywood's version of history, illness, not injury from Indian attacks, was the biggest medical problem during the wars with the Apaches.

2900 N. Craycroft Rd. www.arizonahistoricalsociety.org. ✆ **520/885-3832.** Free admission, donations accepted. Thurs–Sat 10am–4pm. Closed major holidays. Bus: 34.

Tucson Rodeo Parade Museum ★ MUSEUM A parade must be pretty special to warrant its own museum, and Tucson's Fiesta de los Vaqueros Rodeo Parade is indeed special. It's the longest nonmotorized parade in the country, including all manner of horse-drawn carriages, buggies, and wagons. If you aren't in town for the rodeo, which is in late February, you can still see lots of those old horse-drawn vehicles at this museum. Included in the collection is the original surrey with the fringe on top that was used in the filming of *Oklahoma!* (which was shot not in Oklahoma but in southern Arizona, south of the town of Patagonia). There's also a beautiful carriage used by Ava Gardner during the filming of *The Life and Times of Judge Roy Bean.* There are more than 150 vehicles on display, as well as a wide variety of other exhibits on early Tucson history. The only drawback of this fascinating museum is that it's open only a few months of the year (early January to early April).

4823 S. 6th Ave. www.tucsonrodeoparade.com. ✆ **520/294-3636.** $12 adults, $9 seniors, $2 kids 15 and under. Mon–Sat 9:30am–3:30pm (11am–1pm during rodeo week). Closed mid-Apr–early Jan, and certain days during rodeo week (late Feb). Bus: 8.

Outlying Attractions

ASARCO Mineral Discovery Center ★ MUSEUM To learn more about Tucson's copper-mining past and present, head 15 miles south of Tucson to tour this huge open-pit copper mine, still an active working mine. One-hour mine tours are offered four times a day (call for summer days and hours). The center also has exhibits and a video about the copper mining process, and large items of vintage mining equipment are set around the desert landscape outside. You might want to combine this with a visit to the nearby **Titan Missile Museum** (p. 374).

1421 W. Pima Mine Rd., Sahuarita (take exit 80 from I-19). www.mineraldiscovery.com. ✆ **520/625-7513.** Free admission; tours $10 adults, $8 seniors, $7 ages 5–12. Tues–Fri 9am–3pm; Sat 10am–5pm.

Biosphere 2 ★★ ATTRACTION For 2 years, beginning in September 1991, four men and four women were locked inside this airtight 3-acre greenhouse in the desert, 35 miles north of Tucson near the town of Oracle. During their tenure in Biosphere 2 (Earth is considered Biosphere 1), they conducted experiments on how the Earth, basically a giant greenhouse, manages to support all the planet's life forms. Today there are no longer any people living in Biosphere 2, and the former research facility is operated as equal parts science center and tourist attraction. Tours take visitors inside the giant greenhouse and into the mechanisms that helped keep this sealed environment going for

The giant greenhouse of the Biosphere 2 science center is a futuristic sight in the desert hills north of Tucson.

2 years. The futuristic building rising out of the desert hill country is an impressive sight.

32540 S. Biosphere Rd., Oracle (off Ariz. 77 at mile marker 96.5). www.b2science.org. ✆ **520/621-4800.** $20 adults, $18 seniors and military, $15 students, $13 ages 6–12. Daily 9am–4pm. Closed Thanksgiving and Christmas.

Colossal Cave Mountain Park ★ CAVERN It seems nearly every cave in the Southwest has its legends of bandits and buried loot, and Colossal Cave—which isn't exactly colossal but is certainly impressive—is no exception. A 45-minute tour through this cavern combines a bit of Western lore with a bit of geology, for an experience that both kids and adults will enjoy. Although there was much damage to the formations here before the cave was protected, the narrow passageways and dramatic lighting keep the tours interesting. For more adventurous types, some tours venture into little-visited parts of the cave. This private 2,400-acre park, southeast of Tucson, also offers horseback riding ($47 for a 1-hr. ride) and has a small museum, picnic areas, snack bars, and a gift shop.

16721 E. Old Spanish Trail Rd., Vail (take Vail exit from I-10). www.colossalcave.com. ✆ **520/647-7275.** $5 per car for park entry; tours $18 adults, $9 ages 5–12, $14 military and first responders, $8 military dependent 5–12. Daily 8am–5pm, closed Thanksgiving Day and Christmas Day.

Pima Air & Space Museum ★★ MUSEUM Located just south of Davis-Monthan Air Force Base, the Pima Air & Space Museum houses one of the largest collections of historic aircraft in the world. On display are more than 275 aircraft, including a mock-up of an X-15A-2 (the world's fastest aircraft), an SR-71 Blackbird, several Russian MIGs, a "Superguppy," and a B-17G "Flying Fortress." Tours are available. The museum also offers 90-minute guided tours of Davis-Monthan's **AMARG** (Arizona Maintenance and

Military aircraft on display at the Pima Air & Space Museum south of Tucson.

Regeneration Group) facility, nicknamed the Boneyard: Here, thousands of mothballed military planes are lined up in neat rows under the Arizona sun. You must reserve 10 business days in advance for these tours, which are offered Monday through Friday and cost $10.

6000 E. Valencia Rd. (take Valencia Rd. exit from I-10). www.pimaair.org. ✆ **520/574-0462.** $16.50 adults, $13.25 Pima County residents, $13.75 seniors and military, $10 kids 7–12, free for kids 6 and under. Daily 9am–5pm. Closed Thanksgiving and Christmas.

Titan Missile Museum ★ If you've ever wondered what it would be like to have your finger on the button of a nuclear missile, here's your opportunity to find out. This deactivated intercontinental ballistic missile (ICBM) silo, called the Copper Penny, is now a museum—and is the only museum in the country that allows visitors to descend into a former missile silo. There's a huge Titan missile on display, and, even without its nuclear warhead, it is a terrifying sight. The guided tours do a great job of explaining not only the ICBM system, but also what life was like for the people who worked here. Operated by the Pima Air & Space Museum, this museum is located 25 miles south of Tucson near the community of Green Valley. On the first and third Saturday of each month, there are Beyond the Blast Door tours, which take visitors into areas not on the normal tour. You can even spend the night in the silo; inquire at the Museum for details.

1580 W. Duval Mine Rd., Sahuarita (exit 69 off I-19). www.titanmissilemuseum.org. ✆ **520/625-7736.** Admission $10.50 adults, $9.50 seniors, $7 children 7–12; Beyond the Blast Door Tour $20. Daily 8:45am–5:00pm; in summer 9:45am–4pm except Sat, 8:45am–5pm. Closed Thanksgiving and Christmas. Take I-19 south to Green Valley; take exit 69 west a half-mile to main entrance.

Parks, Gardens & Zoos

Reid Park Zoo ★ ZOO Although relatively small and overshadowed by the Arizona-Sonora Desert Museum, the Reid Park Zoo makes a fun in-town destination for families. Africa, Asia, and South America enclosures display African and Asian elephants, white rhinoceroses, giraffes, anteaters, capybaras (the world's largest rodents), and rheas (sort of like ostriches). Get here early, when the animals are more active and before the crowds hit. There's a good playground in the adjacent park.

1100 S. Randolph Way (at 22nd St. btw. Country Club Rd. and Alvernon Way). www.reidparkzoo.org. ✆ **520/791-4022.** $10.50 adults, $8.50 seniors, $6.50 children 2–14. Oct–May daily 9am–4pm; Jun–Sept 8am–3pm. Closed Thanksgiving and Christmas. Bus: 7.

Sabino Canyon Recreation Area ★★ PARK At the base of the Santa Catalina Mountains on the northeastern edge of the city, Sabino Canyon is a fabulous place to commune with the desert for a morning or an afternoon. This desert oasis has impressive scenery, hiking trails, and a stream; you can splash in the canyon's waterfalls and swim in natural pools (water conditions permitting), but it is just as enjoyable simply to gaze at the beauty of crystal-clear water flowing through a rocky canyon guarded by saguaro cacti. There are numerous picnic tables in the canyon, and many miles of hiking trails wind their way into the mountains, making it one of the best places in the city for a day hike. A **narrated tram** shuttles visitors up and down the lower canyon throughout the day, and between April and November (but not July or August), there are moonlight tram rides three times a month (usually the nights before the full moon). The **Bear Canyon tram** is used by hikers heading up the 2.5-mile trail to the picturesque **Seven Falls,** a favorite destination within this recreation area.

Another good way to experience the park is by bicycling up the paved road during the limited hours when bikes are allowed: Sunday through Tuesday,

Driving the Catalina Highway

Within a span of only 25 miles, the **Catalina Highway,** which begins off Tanque Verde Rd. on Tucson's northeast side, climbs roughly 1 mile in elevation from the lowland desert landscape of cacti and ocotillo bushes to forests of ponderosa pines. As it passes through several different life zones, this route is the climate-zone equivalent of driving from Mexico to Canada. When you look at it this way, the $5 fee for driving this twisty-turny road seems like nothing compared to the cost of a flight to Canada (and that fee will also get you into Sabino Canyon, above). Along the way, there are numerous overlooks, some of which are head-spinningly vertiginous. Other spots are particularly popular with rock climbers. Be sure to stop at Windy Point, with its sweeping view of the entire Tucson Valley. There are numerous hiking trails, picnic areas, and campgrounds along the route. For more information, contact the **Coronado National Forest Santa Catalina Ranger District,** 5700 N. Sabino Canyon Rd. (www.fs.usda.gov/coronado; ✆ **520/749-8700**).

Thursday, and Friday before 9am and after 5pm. This is a strenuous uphill ride for most of the way, but the scenery is beautiful.

5900 N. Sabino Canyon Rd. www.fs.usda.gov/coronado or www.sabinocanyon.com. ✆ **520/749-8700,** 520/749-2861 for shuttle info, 520/749-2327 for moonlight shuttle reservations. Parking $5 (also good for driving the Catalina Hwy.). Park open daily dawn–dusk. Sabino Canyon tram rides $10 adults, $5 kids 3–12; Bear Canyon tram $4 adults, $2 kids 3–12. Trams run daily 9am–4pm or 4:30pm.

Tohono Chul Park ★★ GARDENS In fewer than 50 acres, Tohono Chul—the name means "desert corner" in the language of the Tohono O'odham, or Desert People—provides an excellent introduction to the plant and animal life of the desert. You'll see a forest of cholla cacti as well as a garden of small pincushion cacti. From mid-February to April, the wildflower displays here are gorgeous (if enough rain has fallen in the previous months). The park also includes an ethnobotanical garden; a garden for children that encourages them to touch, listen, and smell; a demonstration garden; natural areas; an exhibit house for art displays; a bistro (open 8am–5pm); and two very good gift shops. Park docents lead guided tours throughout the day. Special events take place throughout the cooler months of the year. If you're in town at Christmastime, the holiday display of lights is a must-see.

7366 N. Paseo del Norte (off Ina Rd. W Oracle Rd.). www.tohonochulpark.org. ✆ **520/742-6455.** $13 adults; $10 seniors, military, and students; $3 ages 5–12. Grounds daily 8am–5pm. Exhibit house daily 9am–5pm. Buildings closed New Year's Day, July 4th, Thanksgiving, and Christmas (free admission to grounds these days). Bus: 16.

Tucson Botanical Gardens ★ GARDENS Set amid residential neighborhoods in midtown Tucson, these gardens are an oasis of greenery and, though small, are well worth a visit if you're interested in desert plant life, landscaping, or gardening. On the 5½-acre grounds, there are a dozen different gardens that not only have visual appeal, but also are educational. You can learn about creating a garden for birds or for butterflies, and then see what sort of crops the Native Americans of this region have traditionally grown. A sensory garden stimulates all five senses. A toy train layout and a tropical butterfly house (open fall through spring) make this a surprisingly good place to bring the kids.

2150 N. Alvernon Way. www.tucsonbotanical.org. ✆ **520/326-9686.** $15 adults; $13 seniors, military, and students; $8 ages 4–12. Sat–Wed 7:30am–4:30pm, Thurs–Fri 7:30am–8pm. Closed New Year's Day, July 4th, Thanksgiving, and Dec 24–25. Bus: 9 or 11.

Especially for Kids

In addition to the museums listed below, two of the greatest places to take kids in the Tucson area are the **Arizona-Sonora Desert Museum** (p. 361) and **Old Tucson Studios** (p. 365). Kids will also get a kick out of the **Sabino Canyon** tram ride (p. 375), the **Reid Park Zoo** (p. 375), **Flandrau Science Center** (p. 370), and the **Pima Air & Space Museum** (p. 373).

They'll also enjoy **Trail Dust Town,** 6541 E. Tanque Verde Rd. (www.traildusttown.com; ✆ **520/296-4551**), a Wild West–themed shopping and dining center. It has a full-size carousel, a miniature train to ride, the Museum of the Horse Soldier (open daily 1–7pm; $2.50 admission), shootout shows, and a family steakhouse. A day pass with unlimited rides and admissions costs $12. Basically, it's a sort of scaled-down Old Tucson. Right next door you'll also find **Golf n' Stuff,** 6503 E. Tanque Verde Rd. (www.golfnstuff.com; (✆ **520/296-2366**), which has two miniature-golf courses, bumper boats, go-karts, batting cages, laser tag, a climbing wall, and a videogame arcade. An all-park pass is $22 per person.

The city of Tucson operates 17 public pools that are available to visitors for a daily rate of $2 adults, $1 children; weekly and annual passes are also available. See **www.tucsonaz.gov/parks/pools-and-splash-pads** for information. Pima County operates additional pools outside the city limits, with daily admission $3 adults, $1.50 seniors, and $1 children. See **www.webcms.pima.gov** for information. Of the county parks, **Brandi Fenton Park** (3482 E. River Rd.) is perhaps the most scenic, and though it has only a splash pad and no pool, it's always full of kids.

Children's Museum Tucson ★ ACTIVITY CENTER This museum, in the historic Carnegie Library in downtown Tucson, is filled with fun and educational hands-on activities. Exhibits include a music room, a room where kids can paint with light, an enchanted rainforest, an ocean discovery center, and an electricity gallery. Expect to find such perennial kid favorites as a fire truck, a toy train, and dinosaur sculptures. Activities are featured daily.

200 S. 6th Ave. www.childrensmuseumtucson.org. ✆ **520/792-9985.** $9 per person (babies under 12 months free); $3 on Mon in summer and 3rd Mon of each month. Mon 9am–7pm, Tues–Fri 9am–5pm; Sat–Sun 10am–5pm. Closed Easter, Thanksgiving, and Christmas. Bus: All downtown-bound buses.

The Mini-Time Machine Museum of Miniatures ★ MUSEUM More than 400 miniature houses fill this private museum, everything from a rococo palace to an old English pub to a Craftsman bungalow patterned after Pasadena's famous Gamble house (designed by architects Charles and Henry Greene). There are miniature houses from all over the world, including a Mexican cantina and Thai spirit houses. One wing of the museum, the Enchanted Realm Gallery, is devoted to haunted and enchanted houses that are full of witches and fairies. Keep an eye out for the miniature violin-maker's studio inside an actual violin.

4455 E. Camp Lowell Dr. www.theminitimemachine.org. ✆ **520/881-0606.** $9 adults, $8 seniors, $6 ages 4–17; $6 for all on Thurs. Tues–Sat 9am–4pm, Sun noon–4pm. Closed major holidays. Bus: 34.

OUTDOOR ACTIVITIES

BICYCLING Tucson is one of the best bicycling cities in the country, so rated by national publications and organizations, and the dirt roads and trails of the surrounding national forest and desert are perfect for mountain biking. At **Fair Wheel Bikes,** 1110 E. Sixth St. (www.fairwheelbikes.com; ✆ **520/884-9018**), carbon-fiber bikes are available for rent; call for rates and reservations.

The foothills around Tucson offer mountain bikers a good workout.

The number-one choice in town for cyclists in halfway decent shape is the road up **Sabino Canyon** (p. 375). Keep in mind, however, that bicycles are allowed on this road only 5 days a week and then only before 9am and after 5pm (the road is closed to bikes all day Wednesday and Saturday). For a much easier ride, try **The Loop,** a 131-mile-long, car-free paved bike path that encircles the city. It's a fantastic way to get around town without dodging traffic. The oldest section of the loop, the **Rillito River Park path,** runs for 12 miles between Craycroft Road and I-10, paralleling River Road and the usually dry bed of the Rillito River.

There are lots of great mountain-bike rides in the Tucson area, too. For an easy and very scenic dirt-road loop through forests of saguaros, head to the west unit of Saguaro National Park (p. 366) and ride the 6-mile **Bajada Loop Drive.** You can turn this into a 12-mile ride (half on paved road) by starting at the Red Hills Visitor Center.

Within the city of Tucson, there are 36 stations where, for $8 a day, you can rent a **TugoBike** (http://tugobikeshare.com) and travel wherever you like, as long as you return it to one of those stations. If you're going to be here for more than a few days, save money with a $18 monthly pass.

BIRD-WATCHING Southern Arizona has some of the best bird-watching in the country, and although the best spots are east and south of Tucson (see chapters 8 and 10), there are a few places around the city that birders will enjoy seeking out. Check the **Tucson Audubon Society's Rare Bird Alert** (www.tucsonaudubon.org; ✆ **520/629-0510**) to find out which birds have been spotted in the area lately.

The city's premier birding spot is the **Sweetwater Wetland,** a man-made wetland just west of I-10 and north of Prince Road. Created as part of a wastewater treatment facility, these wetlands now have an extensive network of trails that wind past numerous ponds and canals, with several viewing platforms. The area has enough different types of wildlife habitat to attract a wide variety of bird species. To find the wetlands, take I-10 south to the Prince Road exit, and at the end of the exit ramp, turn right onto Sweetwater Drive.

In the northeast corner of the city, **Roy P. Drachman Agua Caliente Regional Park,** 12325 E. Roger Rd. (off N. Soldier Trail), is another great birding place, with year-round warm springs that are a magnet for dozens of species, including waterfowl, great blue herons, black phoebes, soras, and vermilion flycatchers. (To get here, follow Tanque Verde Rd. east 6 miles from the Sabino Canyon Rd. intersection and turn left onto Soldier Trail.) Other good places include **Sabino Canyon Recreation Area** (p. 375), the path to the waterfall at **Loews Ventana Canyon Resort** (p. 391), and the **Rillito River path** between Craycroft and Swan roads.

If you have more time, there's prime bird watching about 40 miles south of the city in **Madera Canyon ★**, within the **Coronado National Forest** (www.fs.usda.gov/coronado; ✆ **520/281-2296**). With year-round water, Madera Canyon attracts a surprising variety of bird life—more than a dozen species of hummingbirds and an equal number of flycatchers, warblers, tanagers, buntings, grosbeaks, and many rare birds not found in any other state. Before birding became a hot activity, this canyon was popular with families looking to escape the Tucson heat, and its shady picnic areas and trails still get a lot of use by non-birders. If you're heading out for the day, arrive early—parking is very limited. To reach Madera Canyon, take the Continental Road/Madera Canyon exit off I-19 and drive 12 miles southeast. The canyon is open daily from dawn to dusk; there's a $5 day-use fee. There's also a campground (**Bog Springs Campground;** $10 per night; no reservations). For information on the canyon's **Santa Rita Lodge** and **Chuparosa Inn,** see p. 395.

GOLF Although there aren't quite as many golf courses in Tucson as in Phoenix, this is still a golfer's town, with more than 40 courses to choose from. For last-minute tee-time reservations, contact **Standby Golf** (www.discountteetimes.com; ✆ **800/655-5345** or 480/874-3133). No fee is charged for this service.

Numerous resort courses allow non-guests to play. Perhaps the most famous of these are the two 18-hole courses at **Ventana Canyon Golf and Racquet Club ★★**, 6200 N. Clubhouse Lane (www.ventanacanyonclub.com; ✆ **520/577-4015**). These Tom Fazio–designed courses offer challenging desert-style target play that is nearly legendary. The 3rd hole on the Mountain Course is one of the most photographed holes in the West. In winter, the greens fee is $149 ($99 for twilight play). You'll spend a bit less if you're staying at Loews Ventana Canyon Resort or the Lodge at Ventana Canyon, and summer rates are a bargain, ranging from $55 to $59.

As famous as the Ventana Canyon courses is the 27-hole **Omni Tucson National Resort ★**, 2727 W. Club Dr. (www.tucsonnational.com; ✆ **520/297-2271**), a traditional course familiar to golfers as the site for many years of the annual Tucson Open. One of the 9-hole courses here is a desert-style target course, which makes this a good place for an introduction to desert golfing. The greens fee for 18 holes is $200 in winter ($120 after 2pm)—a rate that drops to $150 and $100, respectively, for resort guests.

El Conquistador Country Club, 10555 N. La Cañada Dr., Oro Valley (www.elconquistadorcc.com; ✆ **520/544-1801**), with two 18-hole courses and a 9-hole course, offers stunning (and very distracting) views of the Santa Catalina Mountains. Greens fees are $79 to $99 in winter. At the 27-hole Arnold Palmer–designed course at **Starr Pass Tucson Golf Club,** 3645 W. Starr Pass Blvd. (www.jwmarriottstarrpass.com/Arizona-Golf-Resort/Starr-Pass-4.html; ✆ **520/670-0400**), the fairways play up to the narrow Starr Pass, which was once a stagecoach route. The greens fee is $250 in winter (discounts for twilight play and students).

There are many public courses around town. The **Arizona National,** 9777 E. Sabino Greens Dr. (www.arizonanationalgolfclub.com; ✆ **520/749-3636**) incorporates stands of cacti and rocky outcroppings into the course layout. Greens fees are $60 to $90 in winter. **Heritage Highlands at Dove Mountain,** 4949B W. Heritage Club Blvd., Marana (www.heritagehighlands.com; ✆ **520/579-7000**) is a championship desert course at the foot of the Tortolita Mountains; the greens fee is $79 in winter and $109 in spring.

Tucson Parks and Recreation operates five municipal golf courses, of which the **Randolph North** and **Randolph Dell Urich,** 600 S. Alvernon Way (✆ **520/791-4161**) are the premier courses. The former has been the site of Tucson's LPGA tournament. Greens fees for 18 holes at these two courses are $44, with discounts for seniors and Pima County residents. Other municipal courses include **El Rio,** 1400 W. Speedway Blvd. (✆ **520/791-4229**); **Silverbell,** 3600 N. Silverbell Rd. (✆ **520/791-5235**); and **Fred Enke,** 8251 E. Irvington Rd. (✆ **520/791-2539**). El Rio, the original site of the Tucson Open, and Enke were recently refurbished, though the city government has also made noises recently about selling them to developers. Enke is the city's only desert-style golf course. Greens fees for 18 holes at these three courses are $43 in winter. For information and reservations for any of the municipal courses, visit **www.tucsoncitygolf.com**.

Hummer in the Desert

With desert mountain ranges encircling the city, Tucson is a great place for a rugged off-road adventure. To explore some rugged sections of the Sonoran Desert, contact **Hummer Tours of Tucson** (www.hummertoursoftucson.com; ✆ **520/977-6615**). The company uses these tough off-road vehicles to explore some hard-to-get-to places, including the old fire road that runs up the north side of Mount Lemmon to the top of the Santa Catalina Mountains.

HIKING Tucson is one of the country's premier hiking destinations. The city is nearly surrounded by mountains, most of which are

Desert hiking in Saguaro National Park.

protected as city and state parks, national forest, or national park, and within these public areas are hundreds of miles of hiking trails.

Saguaro National Park (www.nps.gov/sagu; © **520/733-5153** for the east unit or © **520/733-5158** for the west unit) flanks Tucson on both the east and the west, with units accessible off Old Spanish Trail east of Tucson and past the end of Speedway Boulevard west of the city. Here you can observe Sonoran Desert vegetation and wildlife, and hike among the huge saguaro cacti for which the park is named. For saguaro-spotting, the west unit is the better choice. See p. 366 for details. Adjacent to Saguaro National Park, **Tucson Mountain Park,** at the west end of Speedway Boulevard, preserves a similar landscape. The parking area at Gates Pass, on Speedway, is a favorite sunset spot.

Popular **Sabino Canyon** (p. 375), off Sabino Canyon Road, is one of Tucson's best hiking areas. A cold mountain stream here cascades over waterfalls and forms pools that make great swimming holes. The 5-mile round-trip **Seven Falls Trail ★**, which follows Bear Canyon deep into the mountains, is a favorite spot for many hikers. You can take a tram to the trail head or add extra miles by hiking from the main parking lot.

Several convenient hiking options are in Tucson's northern foothills, where the city limits push right to the boundary of the Coronado National Forest. The **Ventana Canyon Trail** begins at a parking area adjacent to the Loews Ventana Canyon Resort (off Sunrise Dr. west of Sabino Canyon Rd.) and leads into the Ventana Canyon Wilderness. A few miles west, the **Finger Rock Trail** starts at the top of a section of Alvernon Road accessed from Skyline Drive, while over near the Westward Look Wyndham Grand Resort (p. 392), the **Pima Canyon Trail ★** leads into the Ventana Canyon Wilderness (reach it off Ina Rd. just east of Oracle Rd). Both of these trails provide classic desert canyon hikes of whatever length you feel like (a dam at 3 miles on the Pima Canyon trail makes a good turnaround point). South of the El Conquistador Golf & Tennis Resort (p. 393), the **Linda Vista Trail** begins just off Oracle Road on Linda Vista Boulevard, and winds up Pusch Ridge through dense stands of prickly pear cactus. Higher up on the trail, there are some large saguaros. Because this trail is shaded by Pusch Ridge in the morning, it's a good choice for a morning hike on a day that's going to be hot.

On the rugged northwest face of the Santa Catalina Mountains, between 2,500 and 3,000 feet in elevation, **Catalina State Park,** 11570 N. Oracle Rd.

(www.azstateparks.com/Catalina; ✆ **520/628-5798**) offers various trails that lead into the Pusch Ridge Wilderness. The park's best day hike is the 5.5-mile round-trip to **Romero Pools,** where small natural pools of water set amid the rocks are a refreshing destination on a hot day (expect plenty of other people on a weekend). This hike involves about 1,000 feet of elevation gain. Admission to the park is $7 per vehicle. Within the park is a Hohokam ruin. On winter weekends there are free guided hikes here.

One of the reasons Tucson is such a livable city is the presence of the cool (and, in winter, sometimes snow-covered) pine forests of 8,250-foot Mount Lemmon. Within the **Mount Lemmon Recreation Area,** at the end of the Catalina Highway, you'll find many miles of trails. A hearty hiker can set out from the lowland desert and hike up into alpine forests (although it's easier to hike from the top down). For a more leisurely excursion, drive up onto the mountain to start your hike. There is a $5-per-vehicle charge to use most of the sites within this recreation area; stop at the roadside ticket kiosk at the base of the mountain to pay your fee. For more information, contact the **Coronado National Forest Santa Catalina Ranger District,** 5700 N. Sabino Canyon Rd. (www.fs.usda.gov/coronado; ✆ **520/749-8700**).

HORSEBACK RIDING If you want to play cowboy or cowgirl, there are plenty of stables around Tucson where you can saddle up. In addition to providing guided trail rides, some of the stables below offer sunset rides with cookouts. Although reservations are not always required, they're a good idea. You can also opt to stay at a guest ranch (p. 396) and do as much riding as your muscles can stand.

All Around Trail Horses is a consortium of two Tucson-area ranches located near the eastern unit of Saguaro National Park, as well as another ranch in southwestern Colorado. Saguaro Stables and La Posta Quemada Ranch offer trail rides into Coronado National Forest, Colossal Cave Park, and other locations in the Rincon Mountains. Check the website (**www.allaroundtrailhorses.com**) for rates and schedules. Also affiliated with this group, **Spanish Trail Outfitters** (✆ **520/631-3787**) offers rides at the Westward Look Wyndham Grand Resort. Rates are $43 for a 1-hour ride, $54 for a 1½-hour ride, and $64 for a sunset ride.

HOT-AIR BALLOONING The ballooning season in Tucson runs October to April or May. **Balloon America** (www.balloonridesusa.com; ✆ **520/299-7744**) offers flights over the foothills of the Santa Catalina Mountains ($249 per person; private flight for two, $749), complete with a drone video showing you in flight. Check the website for discounts. **Fleur de Tucson Balloon Tours** (www.fleurdetucson.net; ✆ **520/403-8547**) offers rides over the Tucson Mountains and Saguaro National Park. Rates are $250 per person, including brunch and a champagne toast.

SKIING Located 35 miles from Tucson, **Mount Lemmon Ski Valley,** 10300 Ski Run Rd. (www.skithelemmon.com; ✆ **520/576-1321**) is the southernmost ski area in the United States, with 22 runs for experienced downhill skiers as well as beginners. The season here isn't very reliable—Ski Valley didn't even open in 2017 and 2018—so be sure to call first to make sure it's open. Locals recommend not using your own skis or snowboard (too many exposed rocks). The ski area often opens only after a new dump of snow, so be sure to call the road-condition information line (✆ **520/547-7510**) before driving up. Check the website for current lift-ticket prices.

TENNIS Convenient to downtown, the **Reffkin Tennis Center,** 50 S. Alvernon Way (www.reffkintenniscenter.com; ✆ **520/791-4896**) is the Southwest's largest public tennis facility, with 25 lighted courts. During the day, court time is $3 per person for 1½ hours; at night, it's $12 per court. Most Tucson hotels and resorts also provide courts for guest use.

WILDFLOWER VIEWING Bloom time varies from year to year, but March and April are good times to view native wildflowers in the Tucson area. While the crowns of white blossoms worn by saguaro cacti are among the most visible blooms in the area, other cacti are far more colorful. **Saguaro National Park** (p. 366) and **Sabino Canyon** (p. 375) are among the best local spots to see saguaros, other cactus species, and various wildflowers in bloom.

SPAS

Health spas are big business in Tucson, and full-service spas can cost $400 to $500 or more per day. However, for under $100 you can avail yourself of a spa treatment or two (massages, facials, seaweed wraps, salt scrubs, and the like) and maybe even get to spend the day lounging by the pool at some exclusive resort.

The **Elizabeth Arden Red Door Spa ★**, at the Westin La Paloma Resort & Spa, 3666 E. Sunrise Dr. (www.reddoorspas.com; ✆ **866/733-3667** or 520/742-7866), focuses on skin-care services, but plenty of body wraps and massages are available as well. With a 50-minute treatment ($140), you can use the spa's facilities for the day, although unlike other spas in town, you won't find aerobics classes here—the Red Door is more about relaxation than fitness. Spa packages range in price from $65 to $220.

For a variety of services and a gorgeous location, you just can't beat the **Lakeside Spa at Loews Ventana Canyon Resort,** 7000 N. Resort Dr. (www.loewshotels.com/ventana-canyon/discover/lakeside-spa; ✆ **520/529-7830**), wedged between the rugged Santa Catalinas and the manicured fairways of the resort's fabled golf course. Soothed by the scent of aromatherapy, you can treat yourself to herbal wraps, mud treatments, massages, facials, complete salon services, and much more. Fifty-minute treatments run $110 to $145. With any 50-minute body treatment, you get use of the spa's facilities, pool, and fitness classes for the day.

With five locations around the Tucson area, **Gadabout Salon Spas** (www.gadabout.com) offers drop-in mud baths, facials, and massages as well as hair and nail services; body treatments and massages start at $90 for a 50-minute massage. Locations include St. Philip's Plaza, 1990 E. River Rd.

(✆ **520/577-2000**); 6393 E. Grant Rd. (✆ **520/885-0000**); 3207 E. Speedway Blvd. (✆ **520/325-0000**); 6960 E. Sunrise Dr. (✆ **520/615-9700**); and 8303 N. Oracle Rd. (✆ **520/742-0000**).

Finally, if money is no object, you can book into Tucson's storied **Canyon Ranch,** 8700 E. Rockcliffe Rd. (www.canyonranch.com; ✆ **800/742-9000** or 520/749-9655), a wellness resort of international renown (p. 396).

WHERE TO STAY IN TUCSON

Phoenix still holds the title of Resort Capital of Arizona, but Tucson isn't far behind—and Tucson resorts boast much more spectacular settings than their rivals in Phoenix and Scottsdale. As far as non-resort accommodations go, Tucson has a wider variety than Phoenix, with a better stock of bed-and-breakfast inns both in historic neighborhoods and in the desert outskirts, and two guest ranches within a 20-minute drive. Business and budget travelers are well served with all-suite and conference hotels, as well as plenty of budget chain motels.

SEASONS Tucson hotels and resorts experience wide fluctuations in rates from season to season. At the more expensive hotels and resorts, summer rates (usually in effect from May to September), are often less than half what they are in winter. Considering that temperatures usually aren't unbearable May and September, those are good months to visit if you're looking to save money. When making late-spring or early-fall reservations, always be sure to ask when rates are scheduled to go up or down. You'll save quite a bit if you avoid the last week in January and most of February, when the winter gem and mineral shows are in town and hotels generally charge premium rates.

BED & BREAKFASTS If you're looking to stay in a B&B, try **Airbnb.com** or **Wimdu.com** (for rentals and less formal B&Bs) or contact the **Arizona Association of Bed & Breakfast Inns** (www.arizona-bed-breakfast.com) and **Arizona Trails Travel Services** (www.arizonatrails.com; ✆ **888/799-4284** or 480/837-4284).

Downtown & the University Area

EXPENSIVE

Arizona Inn ★★★ With its pink-stucco buildings and immaculately tended flower gardens, the Arizona Inn is an oasis of tranquility, and an unforgettable place to spend a vacation. Opened in 1930 by Isabella Greenway, Arizona's first congresswoman, the inn is still family-owned and -operated, and imbued with Old Arizona charm. Playing a game of croquet, taking high tea in the library, or lounging by the pool, you might feel as if you were in a different and decidedly more gracious time. Guest rooms vary in size and decor, but most have a mix of reproduction antiques and original pieces made for the inn years ago by disabled World War I veterans. Some units have gas fireplaces, and most suites have private patios or enclosed sun porches. The inn's **Main Dining Room** (p. 402) is a casually elegant space. Fragrant flowering trees and vines surround the small pool.

2200 E. Elm St. www.arizonainn.com. ✆ **800/933-1093** or 520/325-1541. 95 units. $149–$359 double; $349–$609 suite. Children 12 and under stay free in parent's room. **Amenities:** 3 restaurants; 2 lounges; babysitting; bikes; concierge; exercise room; outdoor pool; room service; saunas; 2 tennis courts; free Wi-Fi.

Doubletree by Hilton Hotel Tucson at Reid Park ★★ With its pleasant orange tree–shaded pool area and 14 acres of landscaping, this in-town high-rise hotel, midway between the airport and downtown Tucson, is something of an in-town budget resort (the Randolph Park municipal golf course is right across the street, and the University of Arizona baseball stadium is within easy walking distance). Guest rooms boast bright colors and bold contemporary designs, and there's a big exercise room by the pool. The hotel does a lot of convention business and sometimes feels crowded, but the gardens, with their citrus trees (feel free to pick the fruit) and lawns, are always tranquil. Guest rooms are divided between a nine-story tower that offers views of the valley (even-numbered rooms face the heated outdoor pool, odd-numbered rooms face the mountains) and a two-story building with patio rooms overlooking the garden and pool area.

445 S. Alvernon Way. www.doubletree1.hilton.com. ✆ **520/881-4200.** 295 units. Dec–May $159–$195 double, $209–$259 suite; June–Sept $99 double, $149–$199 suite; Oct–Nov $139 double, $139 suite. Children 17 and under stay free in parent's room. Pets accepted ($50 deposit). **Amenities:** 2 restaurants; 2 lounges; concierge; exercise room; Jacuzzi; outdoor pool; room service; 3 tennis courts; Wi-Fi ($10 per day).

MODERATE

Catalina Park Inn ★★ Close to downtown west of the University of Arizona and overlooking a shady park, this 1927 home has been lovingly restored by owners Mark Hall and Paul Richard. From the outside, the B&B has the look of a Mediterranean villa; many interesting and playful touches enliven the classic interior. The huge Catalina Room in the basement is a guest favorite, conjuring up the inside of an adobe, but a whirlpool tub in a former cedar closet. Two upstairs rooms have balconies; two units in a separate casita (cottage) across the garden offer more contemporary styling. The B&B closes in summer but is open mid-September to mid-May.

309 E. 1st St. www.catalinaparkinn.com. ✆ **520/792-4541.** 6 units. $125–$195 double. Children 10 and under stay free in parent's room. Rates include full breakfast. Small dogs accepted in casitas ($20 fee). **Amenities:** Concierge; free Wi-Fi.

Lodge on the Desert ★ Dating from 1936 and set amid neatly manicured lawns and gardens, this classic old Arizona resort was completely remodeled and expanded in 2009. The relaxing retreat looks a bit like a Mexican village, with narrow pathways winding between buildings. Guest rooms are in both hacienda-style adobe buildings, tucked amid cacti and orange trees, and newly constructed adobe-style two-story buildings. Rooms feature a mix of contemporary and southwestern furnishings; many units have

Arizona Inn 22
Canyon Ranch Health Resort 17
Casa Tierra Adobe Bed & Breakfast Inn 4
Catalina Park Inn 18
Comfort Suites at Sabino Canyon 29
Courtyard Tucson Williams Center 25
Doubletree by Hilton Tucson-Reid Park 26
Downtown Clifton 21
Embassy Suites Tucson-Paloma Village 10
DoubleTree Suites by Hilton Tucson-Williams Center 24
Extended StayAmerica Tucson 27
Hacienda del Sol Guest Ranch Resort 12
Hilton Tucson El Conquistador Golf & Tennis Resort 8
Homewood Suites at St. Philip's Plaza 13
Hotel Congress 19
JW Marriott Starr Pass Resort & Spa 2
La Posada Lodge and Casitas 14
The Lodge at Ventana Canyon 16
Lodge on the Desert 23
Loews Ventana Canyon Resort 15
Miraval Arizona Resort 7
Paca de Paja Bed & Breakfast 5
Omni Tucson National Resort 6
Radisson Suites Tucson 28
The Royal Elizabeth 20
Starr Pass Golf Suites 3
Tanque Verde Ranch 30
The Westin La Paloma Resort & Spa 11
Westward Look Wyndham Grand Resort 9
White Stallion Ranch 1

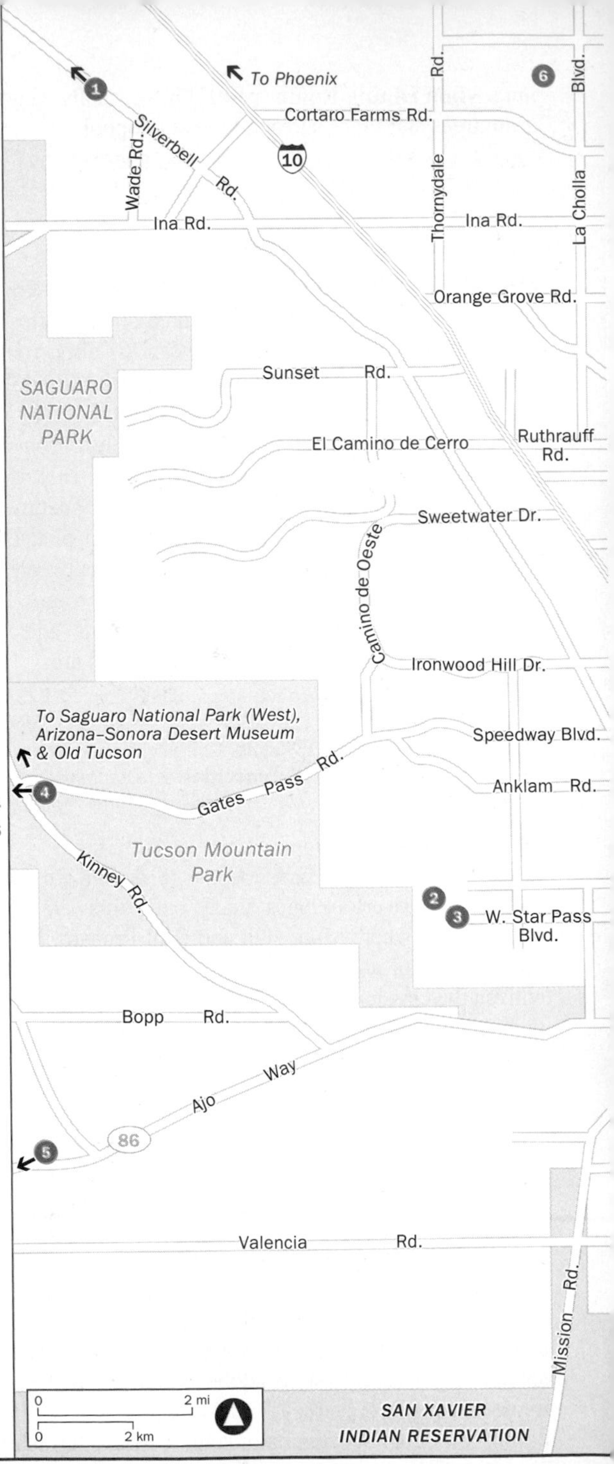

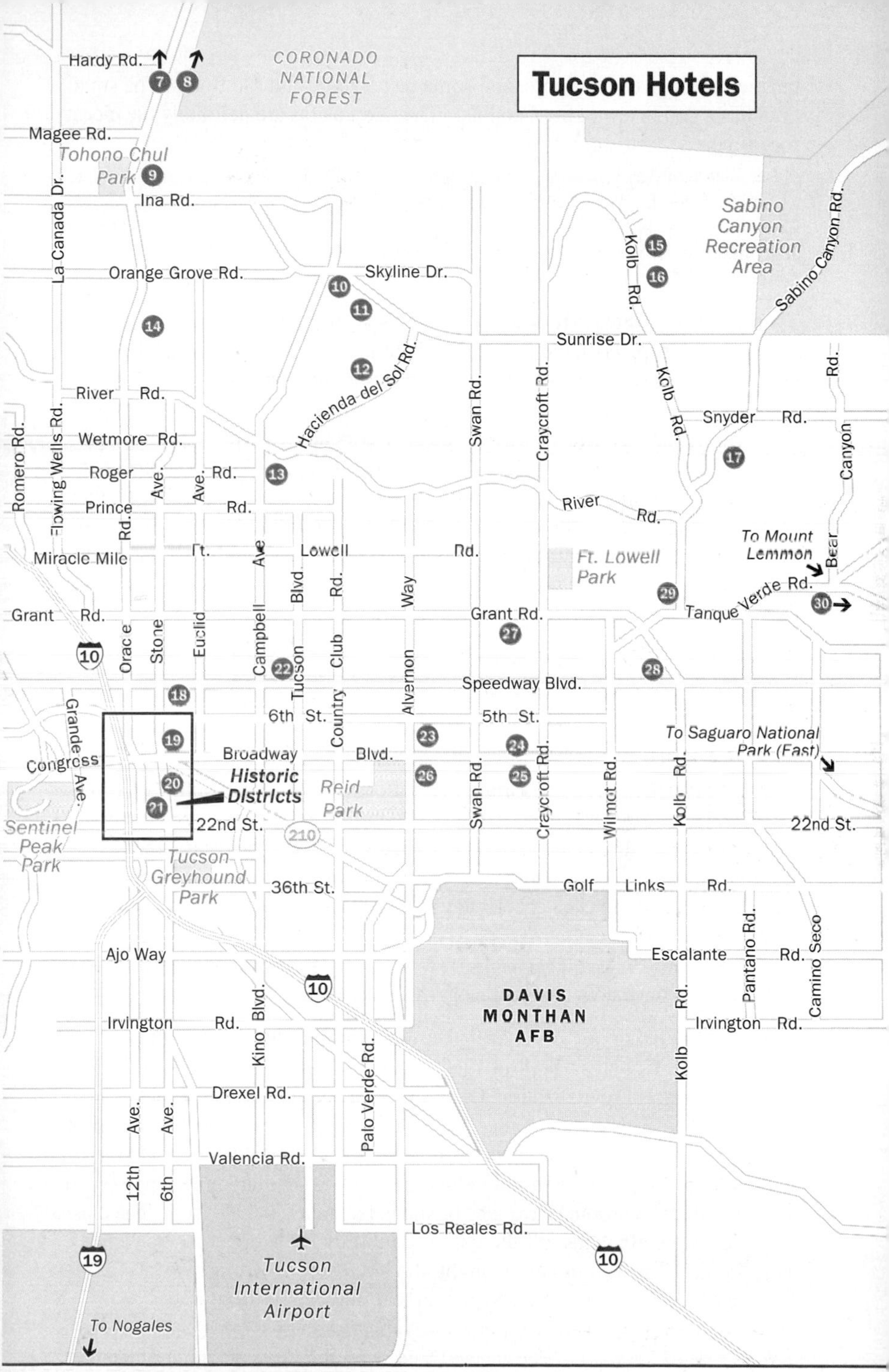

Tucson Hotels
CORONADO NATIONAL FOREST
Hardy Rd.
Magee Rd.
Tohono Chul Park
Ina Rd.
La Canada Dr.
Orange Grove Rd.
Skyline Dr.
Sabino Canyon Recreation Area
Sabino Canyon Rd.
Kolb Rd.
Sunrise Dr.
Hacienda del Sol Rd.
Swan Rd.
Craycroft Rd.
River Rd.
Snyder Rd.
Wetmore Rd.
Flowing Wells Rd.
Romero Rd.
Roger Rd.
Prince Rd.
Oracle Rd.
Stone Ave.
Euclid Ave.
River Rd.
Bear Canyon Rd.
Miracle Mile
Ft. Lowell Rd.
Ft. Lowell Park
To Mount Lemmon
Tanque Verde Rd.
Campbell Ave
Tucson Blvd
Country Club Rd.
Alvernon Way
Grant Rd.
10
Speedway Blvd.
6th St.
5th St.
Grande Ave.
Congress
Broadway Blvd.
Historic Districts
Reid Park
To Saguaro National Park (East)
Wilmot Rd.
Sentinel Peak Park
22nd St.
210
Tucson Greyhound Park
36th St.
Golf Links Rd.
Ajo Way
Escalante Rd.
Pantano Rd.
Camino Seco
DAVIS MONTHAN AFB
Irvington Rd.
Kino Blvd.
Drexel Rd.
12th Ave.
6th Ave.
Palo Verde Rd.
Valencia Rd.
Los Reales Rd.
19
Tucson International Airport
To Nogales

beamed ceilings or fireplaces, and some have patios and tile floors. The small pool has a good view of the Catalinas. The new casitas are definitely the nicest rooms here.

306 N. Alvernon Way. www.lodgeonthedesert.com. ✆ **520/320-2000.** 103 units. Jan–late May $269–$299 double, $329–$349 suite; late May–mid-Sept $139–$169 double, $199–$215 suite; mid-Sept–Dec $159–$179 double, $209–$229 suite. Children 17 and under stay free in parent's room. Dogs accepted ($25 per night, may not be left unattended). **Amenities:** Restaurant; lounge; Jacuzzi; outdoor pool; room service; free Wi-Fi.

The Royal Elizabeth ★★ Just a block from downtown's Temple of Music and Art (p. 419), the Royal Elizabeth is an 1878 Victorian adobe mansion that features an unusual combination of architectural styles, making for a uniquely southwestern-style inn. The old home looks thoroughly unpretentious from the outside, but inside you'll find beautiful woodwork and gorgeous Victorian-era antique furnishings. Guest rooms are as gorgeous as the public areas, with high ceilings, beautiful antiques, and hardwood floors; they all open off a large, high-ceilinged central hall. The immediate neighborhood has some charming territorial architecture mixed in with a few newish buildings; art galleries, the Tucson Museum of Art, hipster bars, and several good restaurants are within walking distance.

204 S. Scott Ave. www.royalelizabeth.com. ✆ **877/670-9022** or 520/670-9022. 6 units. $169–$325 double. Rates include breakfast at nearby restaurant. Children 9 and under stay free in parent's room. **Amenities:** Concierge; access to nearby health club; Jacuzzi; outdoor pool; free Wi-Fi.

INEXPENSIVE

Downtown Clifton ★ Originally built in 1947, the Downtown Clifton, near the Temple of Music and Art (p. 419), has been restored with an emphasis on modernist funkiness. Every room features a queen bed and large-screen TV that streams Netflix, Hulu, and the like, and the art on the walls is available for sale. You can even check out a record player and discs from the hotel's large vinyl library.

485 S. Stone Ave. www.downtowntucsonhotel.com. ✆ **520/623-3163.** $109 double. Dogs allowed. **Amenities:** Concierge; gift shop; free Wi-Fi.

Hotel Congress ★ Anchoring the western entrance to downtown Tucson, the Hotel Congress, built in 1919 to serve railroad passengers, is the hub of the city's recent revitalization. Operating as a budget hotel, it attracts young globe-trotters. Although the place is utterly basic, the lobby has loads of southwestern elegance. Guest rooms remain true to their historical character, with antique telephones and old radios, so don't expect anything fancy (such as TVs). Most bathrooms have tubs or showers, but a few have both. The classic little **Cup Cafe** is just off the lobby (think Edward Hopper meets Gen X), as is the tiny **Tap Room** bar. At night, the hotel's **Club Congress** (p. 422) is a popular (and loud) dance club (pick up earplugs at the front desk).

311 E. Congress St. www.hotelcongress.com. ✆ **800/722-8848** or 520/622-8848. 40 units. $79–$109 double (lower rates in summer). Pets accepted ($10 per night). **Amenities:** Restaurant; bar; nightclub; free Wi-Fi.

East Tucson

EXPENSIVE

Courtyard Tucson Williams Center ★ Set a block off busy E. Broadway Boulevard amid tall palm trees, this modern business hotel is in such a pretty setting that it makes a good choice for vacationers as well as business travelers. Rooms are large and modern, but it's the courtyard with its pond, small waterfall, and pleasant pool area that really makes this an enjoyable place to stay. Because this is a business hotel, rates are lower on weekends.

201 S. Williams Blvd. www.marriott.com/tusce. ✆ **800/321-2211** or 520/745-6000. 153 units. $134–$242 double; $329 suite. Children 17 and under stay free in parent's room. **Amenities:** Restaurant; lounge; exercise room; Jacuzzi; outdoor pool; free Wi-Fi.

MODERATE

DoubleTree Suites by Hilton Tuscon-Williams Center ★ Sporting an old-Mexico, elegant feel, this newish hotel is one of Tucson's favorite lodgings. You'll surely feel like you're on vacation when you're here, even if you are in the middle of a business district. Guest rooms are two-room suites, which makes this place great for families, and the courtyard pool area, although not very large, provides plenty of opportunities for soaking up the sun on warm days.

5335 E. Broadway Blvd. www.tucsonwilliamscenter.embassysuites.com. ✆ **800/362-2779** or 520/745-2700. 142 units. Sept–May $143–$210 double; June–Aug $112–$128 double. Rates include full breakfast and evening social hour. Children 17 and under stay free in parent's room. **Amenities:** Exercise room; Jacuzzi; outdoor pool; room service; free Wi-Fi.

Radisson Suites Tucson ★★ With large and very attractive rooms, this all-suite chain hotel is a good choice for those who need plenty of space and those who want to be in the east-side business corridor. The five-story brick building is arranged around two long garden courtyards, one of which has a large pool and whirlpool. The pool and gardens are among the nicest at any non-resort hotel in Tucson and are the best reasons to stay here. Some rooms have Sleep Number® beds, and rooms on the fourth and fifth floors on the east side have nice mountain views.

6555 E. Speedway Blvd. www.radissontucson.com. ✆ **800/333-3333** or 520/721-7100. 299 suites. Oct–May $130–$245 double; June–Sept $92–$245 double. Children 17 and under stay free in parent's room. Pets accepted ($75 fee). **Amenities:** Restaurant; lounge; concierge; exercise room; Jacuzzi; pool; room service; free Wi-Fi.

INEXPENSIVE

Comfort Suites at Sabino Canyon ★ Although it looks rather stark from the outside and shares a parking lot with a shopping center, this Comfort Suites is surprisingly pleasant inside, built around four tranquil and lushly planted garden courtyards. Most of the rooms are quite large, and some have kitchenettes. This is a good economical choice close to Sabino Canyon, the Mount Lemmon Highway, and Saguaro National Park's east unit.

7007 E. Tanque Verde Rd. www.choicehotels.com. ✆ **800/424-6423** or 520/298-2300. 90 units. $111–$144 double. Rates include full breakfast and evening social hour.

Children 17 and under stay free in parent's room. Pets accepted ($25 per night). **Amenities:** Access to nearby gym; Jacuzzi; outdoor pool; free Wi-Fi.

Extended StayAmerica Tucson ★ This east-side hotel, located across the street from the Tucson Medical Center, is pretty basic, but the rooms are clean and the rates are low. Guest rooms also have full kitchens, so you can save even more money on your Tucson stay by cooking in your room.

5050 E. Grant Rd. www.extendedstayamerica.com. ✆ **800/804-3724** or 520/795-9510. 120 units. $69–$110 double (lower weekly rates). Children 17 and under stay free in parent's room. Pets accepted ($25 per night, $150 maximum). **Amenities:** Pool; exercise room; free Wi-Fi.

The Foothills

EXPENSIVE

Embassy Suites Tucson–Paloma Village ★ Situated at the intersection of Skyline Drive and Campbell Road, this hotel is surrounded by upscale shopping centers and is close to some of Tucson's best restaurants. Although the suites here are small by Embassy Suites standards, you will still get two rooms, which makes this a good choice for families. Some suites have mountain views, while others overlook the dense desert vegetation of a dry wash. The pool area has limited mountain views. The full breakfast and afternoon snacks can help you save on meal costs.

3110 E. Skyline Dr. www.tucsonpalomavillage.embassysuites.com. ✆ **800/362-2779** or 520/352-4000. 120 units. Jan–Apr $289–$309 double; May and Sept–Nov $179–$199 double; June–Aug $214–$229 double; Dec $259–$279 double. Rates include full breakfast and evening social hour. Children 17 and under stay free in parent's room. **Amenities:** Exercise room; Jacuzzi; outdoor pool; room service; free Wi-Fi.

Hacienda del Sol Guest Ranch Resort ★★ With its colorful Southwest styling, historical character, mature cactus gardens, and ridge-top setting, Hacienda del Sol is one of Tucson's most distinctive getaways. The lodge's basic rooms, set around flower-filled courtyards, are evocative of old Mexican inns, with a rustic, colorful character and decidedly artistic flair. If you prefer more modern, spacious accommodations, ask for a suite; if you want loads of space and the chance to stay where Katharine Hepburn and Spencer Tracy may have stayed, ask for the casita grande. With large terraces for alfresco dining, **The Grill** (p. 407) is one of Tucson's best restaurants. During the day, you can lounge by the small pool, get a spa treatment, or go for a horseback ride.

5501 N. Hacienda del Sol Rd. www.haciendadelsol.com. ✆ **800/728-6514** or 520/299-1501. 30 units. $302–$432 double, $352–$536 suite. Children 12 and under stay free in parent's room. Pets accepted ($50 fee). **Amenities:** 2 restaurants; lounge; concierge; access to nearby health club; Jacuzzi; outdoor pool; room service; spa; free Wi-Fi.

The Lodge at Ventana Canyon ★★ This boutique golf resort at the base of the Santa Catalina Mountains shares the same two Tom Fazio–designed golf courses as Loews Ventana Canyon Resort (below). Stay here, though, and you'll get more personal service, since the Lodge at Ventana Canyon is part of a gated country club community; when you stay here you feel more like a resident than a hotel guest, and it has a more relaxed feel than the Hilton Tucson El Conquistador Resort or the Omni Tucson National Resort. Accommodations are in spacious suites, most of which have mission-style furnishings, small kitchens, large bathrooms with oversize tubs, and walls of windows facing the mountains. A few units have balconies, cathedral ceilings, and spiral stairs that lead to sleeping lofts. The third hole of the resort's Mountain Course is one of Tucson's most photographed holes.

6200 N. Clubhouse Lane. www.thelodgeatventanacanyon.com. ✆ **800/828-5701** or 520/577-1400. 50 units. $84–$311 1-bedroom suite, $159–$401 2-bedroom suite. $25 nightly service fee charged. Children 11 and under stay free in parent's room. Pets accepted ($100 fee). **Amenities:** Restaurant; snack bar; lounge; children's programs; concierge; 2 18-hole golf courses; gym; 2 Jacuzzis; outdoor pool; room service; full-service spa; 11 tennis courts; Wi-Fi (included in service fee).

Loews Ventana Canyon Resort ★★★ With two fabled desert-style golf courses out the front door and a national forest trail out the back, this luxurious resort is a great choice for both golfers and hikers. The craggy peaks of the Santa Catalina Mountains rise behind the property, and the distinctive architecture and flagstone floors in the lobby lend a rugged but luxurious character. Guest rooms have balconies that overlook city lights or mountains. Bathrooms include tubs for two, and some rooms have fireplaces. The lobby lounge serves afternoon tea before becoming an evening piano bar. In addition to numerous other amenities, the resort has a nature trail with a waterfall and plenty to keep the kids busy, including a playground. A hiking trail leads from the hotel into its namesake canyon.

7000 N. Resort Dr. https://www.loewshotels.com/ventana-canyon. ✆ **800/234-5117** or 520/299-2020. 398 units. $149–$329 double, $339–$569 suite. Children 17 and under stay free in parent's room. $29 per night resort fee. Valet parking $9. Pets accepted ($25 fee). **Amenities:** 4 restaurants; 3 lounges; babysitting; bikes; children's programs; concierge; 2 18-hole golf courses; exercise room and access to nearby health club; 2 Jacuzzis; 2 outdoor pools; room service; full-service spa; 3 tennis courts; Wi-Fi (free).

The Westin La Paloma Resort & Spa ★★★ If grand scale is what you're looking for, this is the place. Everything about the Westin La Paloma is big—big portico, big lobby, big pool area—and from the resort's sunset-pink mission-revival buildings, there are big views. While adults will appreciate the resort's tennis courts, exercise facilities, and poolside lounge chairs, kids will love the 177-foot water slide. Guest rooms are in 27 low-rise buildings surrounded by desert landscaping. Couples should opt for the king rooms (ask for a mountain or golf-course view if you don't mind spending a bit more). Southwestern cuisine is the specialty at the on-site restaurant. The resort's spa is a Red Door Spa by Elizabeth Arden.

3800 E. Sunrise Dr. www.westinlapalomaresort.com. ✆ **800/937-8461** or 520/742-6000. 487 units. $79–$314 double, $179–$414 suite. $29 per night resort fee. Children 17 and under stay free in parent's room. Valet parking $15. Pets accepted. **Amenities:** 5 restaurants; 2 lounges; babysitting; children's programs; concierge; 27-hole golf course; health club and full-service spa; 4 Jacuzzis; 5 pools (1 for adults only); room service; 10 tennis courts; Wi-Fi ($13 per night).

Westward Look Wyndham Grand Resort ★★ With the desert at its doorstep, this resort, which underwent a $14-million renovation in 2009, is a favorite of mine. Built in 1912 as a private estate, Westward Look is the oldest resort in Tucson, and although it doesn't have a golf course, it has horseback-riding stables, a nature trail, an excellent spa, and plenty of tennis courts. The large guest rooms have a southwestern flavor and private patios or balconies with city views. For the ultimate in Southwest luxury, opt for one of the stargazer spa suites, which have outdoor hot tubs. GOLD, the resort's main restaurant, utilizes herbs and vegetables grown on-site, and the Lookout Grille is a favorite local hangout for watching sports on big-screen TVs. If you aren't a golfer but do enjoy resort amenities, this is one of your best bets in Tucson.

245 E. Ina Rd. www.westwardlook.com. ✆ **800/722-2500** or 520/297-1151. 244 units. Jan–Apr $229–$499 double; May $109–$359 double; June–Sept $99–$259 double; Oct–Dec $169–$399 double. $15 per day resort fee. Children 17 and under stay free in parent's room. Pets accepted. **Amenities:** 2 restaurants; 2 lounges; bikes; children's programs; concierge; gym; 3 Jacuzzis; 3 pools; room service; full-service spa; 8 tennis courts; Wi-Fi (included in resort fee).

MODERATE

Homewood Suites at St. Philip's Plaza ★ Located on the edge of the foothills in the St. Philip's Plaza shopping center, within walking distance of several good restaurants, this hotel offers a great location and a good value. Bikes are available to guests, and out the hotel's back door is a paved pathway along the (usually bone-dry) Rillito River. Spacious guest rooms have double vanities, wet bars, and two TVs—basically, everything you need for a long, comfortable stay.

4250 N. Campbell Ave. http://homewoodsuites3.hilton.com. ✆ **520/577-0007.** 122 units. Oct–May $139–$289 double; June–Sept $159–$169 double. Rates include continental breakfast. Children 17 and under stay free in parent's room. Pets under 35 lbs. accepted ($75 deposit). **Amenities:** Bikes; exercise room, access to nearby health club; Jacuzzi; outdoor pool; free Wi-Fi.

La Posada Lodge and Casitas ★ Although this hotel fronts busy Oracle Road, once you check in and park yourself on your patio overlooking the pool or the grassy courtyard, you'll forget all about the traffic out front. There are several different types of rooms here, but my favorites are the "Western"-style rooms, which have a sort of retro south-of-the-border decor that includes headboards painted with classic Mexican scenes. Casitas, which are the largest and most expensive rooms here, have a similar decor. There are also some fun rooms with a 1950s retro feel. The attractive rooms, pleasant pool area, and on-site Mexican restaurant together make this an excellent and economical choice.

5900 N. Oracle Rd. www.laposadalodge.com. ✆ **520/887-4800.** 72 units. $111–$169 double. Rates include full breakfast. Children 17 and under stay free in parent's room. Pets under 70 lbs. accepted ($25 fee). **Amenities:** Restaurant; lounge; exercise room; Jacuzzi; outdoor pool; free Wi-Fi.

West Tucson, Oro Valley & Marana

EXPENSIVE

Hilton Tucson El Conquistador Golf & Tennis Resort ★★ Although El Conquistador is a bit out of the way, the view of the Santa Catalina Mountains rising behind the property makes this northern foothills resort one of my favorites in Tucson. Sunsets are truly spectacular. Most guest rooms are built around a central courtyard with manicured lawns and a large oasis of swimming pools, one of which has a long water slide. The pool area and the nearby horseback-riding stables make the Hilton an excellent choice for families. All rooms feature southwestern-influenced contemporary furniture, spacious marble bathrooms, and balconies or patios. Be sure to ask for a mountain-view room. Golf on the resort's three courses is the favorite pastime, but this is not so exclusively a golf resort as the Lodge at Ventana Canyon or the Omni Tucson National Resort.

10000 N. Oracle Rd. www.hiltonelconquistador.com. ✆ **800/325-7832** or 520/544-5000. 428 units. Jan–late May $339–$379 double, from $389 suite; late May early Sept $119–$149 double, from $153 suite; early Sept–Dec $246–$277 double, from $289 suite. Children 18 and under stay free in parent's room. Valet parking $15 (self-parking available). Pets under 75 lbs. accepted ($75 fee). **Amenities:** 4 restaurants; 2 lounges; children's programs; concierge; 1 9-hole and 2 18-hole golf courses; health club and spa; 3 Jacuzzis; 4 pools; room service; saunas; 31 tennis courts; Wi-Fi ($10 per day).

JW Marriott Starr Pass Resort & Spa ★ Set on the edge of Tucson Mountain Park, this sprawling resort on the far west side of Tucson is a golfers favorite but also makes a good choice for families and outdoorsy types. Kids will love the family-friendly pool area, while hikers and mountain bikers have access to miles of trails through the adjacent park. With its many restaurants, this resort is designed to be a destination—you could very easily spend several days just hanging out and never venturing out to see Tucson's sights. Unfortunately, low-flying fighter jets from nearby Davis-Monthan Air Force Base often disturb the tranquility of the resort. Then again, you can always retreat to the plush bed in your room.

3800 W. Starr Pass Blvd. www.jwmarriottstarrpass.com. ✆ **888/527-8989** or 520/792-3500. 575 units. Mid-Oct–May $259–$299 double, from $409 suite; June–mid-Oct $169 double, from $269 suite. $29 per night resort fee. Children 17 and under stay free in parent's room. Valet parking $20; self-parking $10. **Amenities:** 5 restaurants; 4 lounges; espresso bar; children's programs; concierge; exercise room; 2 Jacuzzis; 3 outdoor pools; room service; full-service spa; Wi-Fi ($16.95 per day).

Omni Tucson National Resort ★★ Golf is the name of the game at this boutique resort, which, though a bit out of the resort mainstream, is looking good after a major makeover a few years back. The spacious rooms, with warm contemporary styling and balconies or patios, are some of the most luxurious in town, and most cling to the edges of the golf course. The golf course here is far more forgiving than those shared by the Lodge at Ventana

Canyon and Loews Ventana Canyon, which makes this a good choice for golfers not up to the challenge of desert-style golf courses.

2727 W. Club Dr. (off Magee Rd.). www.omnihotels.com. ✆ **800/843-6664** or 520/297-2271. 128 units. Jan–Apr $199–$299 double; May $119–$329 double; June–Aug $89–$120 double; Sept–Dec $150–$209 double. $20 per night resort fee. Children 17 and under stay free in parent's room. Pets accepted ($50 fee). **Amenities:** 3 restaurants; lounge; concierge; 2 18-hole golf courses; health club and full-service spa; 2 Jacuzzis; 2 pools; room service; sauna; 4 tennis courts; Wi-Fi (free).

MODERATE

Casa Tierra Adobe Bed & Breakfast Inn ★ If you've come to Tucson to be in the desert, then this secluded B&B west of Saguaro National Park is a good choice. Built to look as if it has been here since Spanish colonial days, the modern adobe home is surrounded by cactus and paloverde trees, with great views across a landscape full of saguaros to the mountains; sunsets are enough to take your breath away. Guest rooms, which have wrought-iron sleigh beds, open onto a central courtyard surrounded by a covered seating area. Two outdoor hot tubs make perfect stargazing spots, and there's a telescope on the property.

11155 W. Calle Pima. www.casatierratucson.com. ✆ **866/254-0006** or 520/578-3058. 4 units. May–Sept $150–$175 double, $195–$265 suite; Oct–Apr $165–$195 double, $215–$285 suite. Rates include full vegetarian breakfast. 2-night min. stay. Closed June 15–Aug 16. **Amenities:** Concierge; exercise room; Jacuzzi; free Wi-Fi.

Paca de Paja Bed & Breakfast ★ Although this inn has only one suite and is 30 minutes west of Tucson, it's a great choice for anyone coming to Arizona to experience the desert. It's a very energy-efficient straw-bale house, its walls constructed of straw that is then covered with stucco. Owner/innkeeper Caroline Wilson also harvests rainwater to irrigate her garden, which is designed to minimize water usage. A nature trail on the property meanders through a dense cactus forest, and lots of other opportunities to explore the desert are within a 30-minute drive. The guest suite has a sitting room full of natural-history books and an outdoor living area, which gives guests loads of room to enjoy.

16242 Pinacate Ave. www.pacadepaja.com. ✆ **888/326-4588** or 520/822-2065. 1 unit. Dec–Apr $160 double ($130 per night for 2 or more nights); May–Nov $150 double ($120 per night for 2 or more nights). Rates include full breakfast. No credit cards. **Amenities:** Bikes; free Wi-Fi.

INEXPENSIVE

Starr Pass Golf Suites ★ The most economically priced golf resort in the city, Starr Pass is located 3 miles west of I-10. It's a condominium resort, however, which means you shouldn't expect the sort of service you get at other resorts. Accommodations are in privately owned Santa Fe–style casitas rented as two-bedroom units, master suites, or standard hotel-style rooms. The small hotel-style rooms are a bit cramped and not nearly as lavishly appointed as the comfortable master suites, which have fireplaces, full kitchens, balconies, and a southwestern style. The desert-style 27-hole golf course is one of the best courses in the city. There are also hiking/biking trails on the property. A free shuttle runs to the main Marriott Starr Pass resort (above).

3645 W. Starr Pass Blvd. www.shellhospitality.com. ✆ **800/503-2898** or 520/670-0500. 80 units. $69–$109 double, $119–$169 suite, $159–$259 casita. Children 17 and under stay free in parent's room. **Amenities:** Restaurant; lounge; bikes; 27-hole golf course; exercise room; Jacuzzi; outdoor pool; 2 tennis courts; free Wi-Fi.

Outlying Areas

NORTH OF TUCSON

Aravaipa Farms Orchard and Inn ★★ A romantic getaway near one of the state's most spectacular desert-wilderness areas, this B&B is located 60 miles north of Tucson on Aravaipa Creek. The inn is 7 miles from the highway, 3 of those miles up a well-maintained dirt road and then across a stream (high-clearance vehicles recommended), so it's a long way to a restaurant. Consequently, the inn provides all meals for $55 per person Wednesday through Saturday (and can make arrangements for meals the other days). Guests entertain themselves hiking in the Aravaipa Canyon Wilderness, bird-watching, and cooling off in the creek. The casitas are eclectically decorated in a mix of folk art and rustic Mexican furnishings, with tile floors, stone-walled showers, and shady verandas. For a romantic weekend or a vigorous vacation, this inn makes an ideal base. The innkeepers also rent out a three-bedroom house that sleeps up to six people.

89395 E. Aravaipa Rd., Winkelman. www.aravaipafarms.com. ✆ **520/357-6901.** 5 units. $219–$239 double, $449–$599 house. Children by prior arrangement. **Amenities:** Dining room; outdoor pool; free Wi-Fi.

SOUTH OF TUCSON

Chuparosa Inn ★ Tucked amid the shady trees of Madera Canyon, this rustic inn is built of stone and wood, and, with its tower at the front entrance, looks a bit like a miniature castle. It's beautiful, and a delightful place to stay for couples wanting to get away from the city roar, or for those who've come up the canyon to do some bird-watching (the objective of many guests here). The inn's name is a Spanish term for "hummingbird," and if you visit in the warmer months, you're likely to see plenty of the colorful little birds (14 species have been spotted here, and there are regularly scheduled hummingbird banding programs). Three rooms have kitchenettes, and one a full kitchen.

1300 W. Madera Canyon Rd., Madera Canyon. www.chuparosainn.com. ✆ **520/393-7370.** 4 units. $200–$275. Rates include continental breakfast and tax. 2-night min. Children 12 and over only. **Amenities:** Free Wi-Fi.

Santa Rita Lodge Nature Resort ★ In the shady depths of Madera Canyon, this lodge primarily hosts bird-watchers and hikers. The rooms are not as nice as those at the Chuparosa Inn (above), but the birding is as good as it gets. The simply furnished rooms and cabins are large and comfortable, and all have kitchenettes where you can do a bit of cooking. The nearest restaurants are 13 miles away, so bring food for your stay.

1218 S. Madera Canyon Rd., Madera Canyon. www.santaritalodge.com. ✆ **520/625-8746.** 12 units. $115–$175 double. Pets accepted ($25 per night). **Amenities:** Free Wi-Fi.

Spa Resorts

Canyon Ranch Health Resort ★★★ Canyon Ranch offers the sort of complete spa experience that's available at only a handful of places around the country (and then only if you have both money and fat to burn). On staff are doctors, nurses, life-management therapists, exercise physiologists, counselors, massage therapists, and tennis and golf pros. Services offered include health and fitness assessments; health, nutrition, exercise, and stress-management evaluations; fitness classes; massage therapy; therapeutic body treatments; facials, manicures, pedicures, and haircuts; makeup consultations; cooking demonstrations; and art classes. Guests stay in a variety of spacious, comfortable accommodations. Three gourmet, low-calorie meals are served daily. If you're serious about getting healthy or leading a more fulfilled life, this is your place in the sun.

8600 E. Rockcliff Rd. www.canyonranch.com. ✆ **800/742-9000** or 520/749-9000. 185 units. $1,000–$1,500 double. Rates include all meals, classes, and allowances for spa and wellness services. Pets under 30 lbs. accepted ($250 per stay). No children 13 or under (except for infants in care of personal nannies). **Amenities:** 2 dining rooms; free airport transfers; bikes; concierge; 7 exercise rooms; 8 Jacuzzis; 3 outdoor pools; aquatic center; room service; saunas; spa complex; 7 tennis courts; free Wi-Fi.

Miraval Arizona ★★★ Tucson's other world-class destination spa emphasizes stress management, self-discovery, and relaxation. To this end, activities at the all-inclusive resort, now a Hyatt property, include meditation, yoga, art classes, and a variety of confidence-building activities; more active types can go hiking, mountain biking, and rock climbing. Of course, there are also plenty of more traditional spa offerings such as massages, wraps, scrubs, facials, manicures, and pedicures. The spa offers a variety of lifestyle-management workshops, fitness/nutrition consultations, exercise classes, and an "equine experience" program. The main pool is a gorgeous three-tiered leisure pool surrounded by waterfalls and desert landscaping. Guest rooms, many of which have views of the Santa Catalina Mountains, are done up in a southwestern style. Miraval has LEED-certified sustainable rooms, and its dining room uses local and organic ingredients as much as possible.

5000 E. Via Estancia. www.miravalresorts.com. ✆ **855/234-1672.** 116 units. $349–$939 double, plus 23% resort fee and taxes. Rates include all meals, classes, and allowances for spa services and golf. No children. **Amenities:** Restaurant; snack bar; lounge; free airport transfers; bikes; concierge; exercise room; 5 Jacuzzis; 5 pools; room service; saunas; spa complex; 2 tennis courts; free Wi-Fi.

Guest Ranches

Tanque Verde Ranch ★★ Want to spend long days in the saddle but don't want to give up resort luxuries? Then Tanque Verde Ranch, which was founded in 1868 and still has some of its original buildings, is for you. This is far and away the most luxurious guest ranch in Tucson. With Saguaro National Park and the Coronado National Forest bordering the ranch, there's plenty of room for horseback riding. There are also nature trails and a nature center, and at the end of the day, a spa provides ample opportunity to recover from too many hours in the saddle. Guest rooms are spacious and comfortable, with fireplaces and patios in many units. Some of the large casitas are among the most luxurious accommodations in the state. The dining room, which overlooks the Rincon Mountains, sets impressive buffets.

14301 E. Speedway Blvd. www.tanqueverderanch.com. ✆ **800/234-3833** or 520/296-6275. 76 units. $150–$499 double. All-inclusive rates include all meals and ranch activities. Children 3 and under stay free in parent's room. **Amenities:** Dining room; lounge; free airport transfers w/4-night stay; bikes; children's programs; exercise room; access to nearby health club; 2 Jacuzzis; 2 pools (indoor and outdoor); spa; 5 tennis courts; free Wi-Fi.

White Stallion Ranch ★ Set on 3,000 acres of desert, the White Stallion Ranch is perfect for those who crave wide-open spaces. Operated since 1965 by the True family, this spread has a more authentic feel than any other guest ranch in the area. A variety of horseback rides are offered, and a petting zoo keeps kids entertained. There are also nature trails, guided nature walks and hikes, hayrides, weekly rodeos, and team cattle penning. Guest rooms vary considerably in size and comfort, from tiny, spartan single units to deluxe two-bedroom suites, as well as the home-sized Hacienda, suitable for larger families and groups. Renovated rooms are worth requesting.

9251 W. Twin Peaks Rd. www.whitestallion.com. ✆ **888/977-2624** or 520/297-0252. 43 units. Rates per person: Mid-June–late Sept $216–$291 double, $208–$265 suite; Oct–mid-Jun $230–$359 double, $263–$325 suite. 15% service charge per night. Rates include all meals. 4- to 6-night min. stay in winter. Children 2 and under stay free in parent's room. **Amenities:** Dining room; lounge; free airport transfers with 4-night stay; concierge; exercise room; Jacuzzi; small outdoor pool, sauna; tennis court; free Wi-Fi.

WHERE TO EAT IN TUCSON

Variety, they say, is the spice of life, and Tucson certainly dishes up plenty of variety (and spice) when it comes to eating out. For its wealth of eating opportunities and the quality of the food served here, in 2015 Tucson was named a UNESCO World City of Gastronomy, the first in the United States. (San Antonio, Texas, earned the second title a couple of years later.) Tucson is a city that lives for spice, and in the realm of fiery foods, Sonoran-style Mexican reigns supreme.

If you're one of those rare people who aren't fans of Mexican food, don't despair—there are plenty of other restaurants serving everything from the finest French cuisine to innovative American, Italian, Asian, and African food. Southwestern food, Mexican-inspired but a creation of the region, is prevalent, too, and you should be sure to dine at a Southwestern restaurant early in your visit. This cuisine can be brilliantly creative, and after trying it, you may want *all* your meals to be Southwestern.

On the other hand, if you're on a tight dining budget, look for early-bird dinners, which are quite popular with retirees.

Arizona Inn – Main Dining Room 31
Azul 15
Beyond Bread 22
Blanco Tacos + Tequila 14
Blue Willow 29
Brooklyn Pizza Company 10
Brushfire BBQ Co. 24
Café à la C'Art 4
Café Poca Cosa 7
Downtown Kitchen + Cocktails 5
Eclectic Café 39
Eegee's 35
El Charro Café 9
El Corral Restaurant 18
El Guero Canelo 25
El Minuto Cafe 28
Feast 34
Flying V Bar & Grill 43
Frank's/Francisco's 33
Ghini's French Café 21
The Grill 17
Harvest Restaurant 11
Hub Restaurant & Creamery 6
Kingfisher Bar & Grill 32
L'il Abner's Steakhouse 1
Little Anthony's Diner 41
Lovin' Spoonfuls 23
Mariscos Chihuahua 26
Maynard's Market & Kitchen 8
Mi Nidito 43
Parish Gastropub 13
Pat's Drive-In 27
Pinnacle Peak Steakhouse 38
Saguaro Corners 42
Scordato's 20
Seis Kitchen 3
Teresa's Mosaic Café 2
Tucson Tamale Company 36
Vero Amore 37
Wildflower 12
Yoshimatsu Healthy Japanese Eatery 20
Zinburger Wine & Burger Bar 19
Zona '78 40

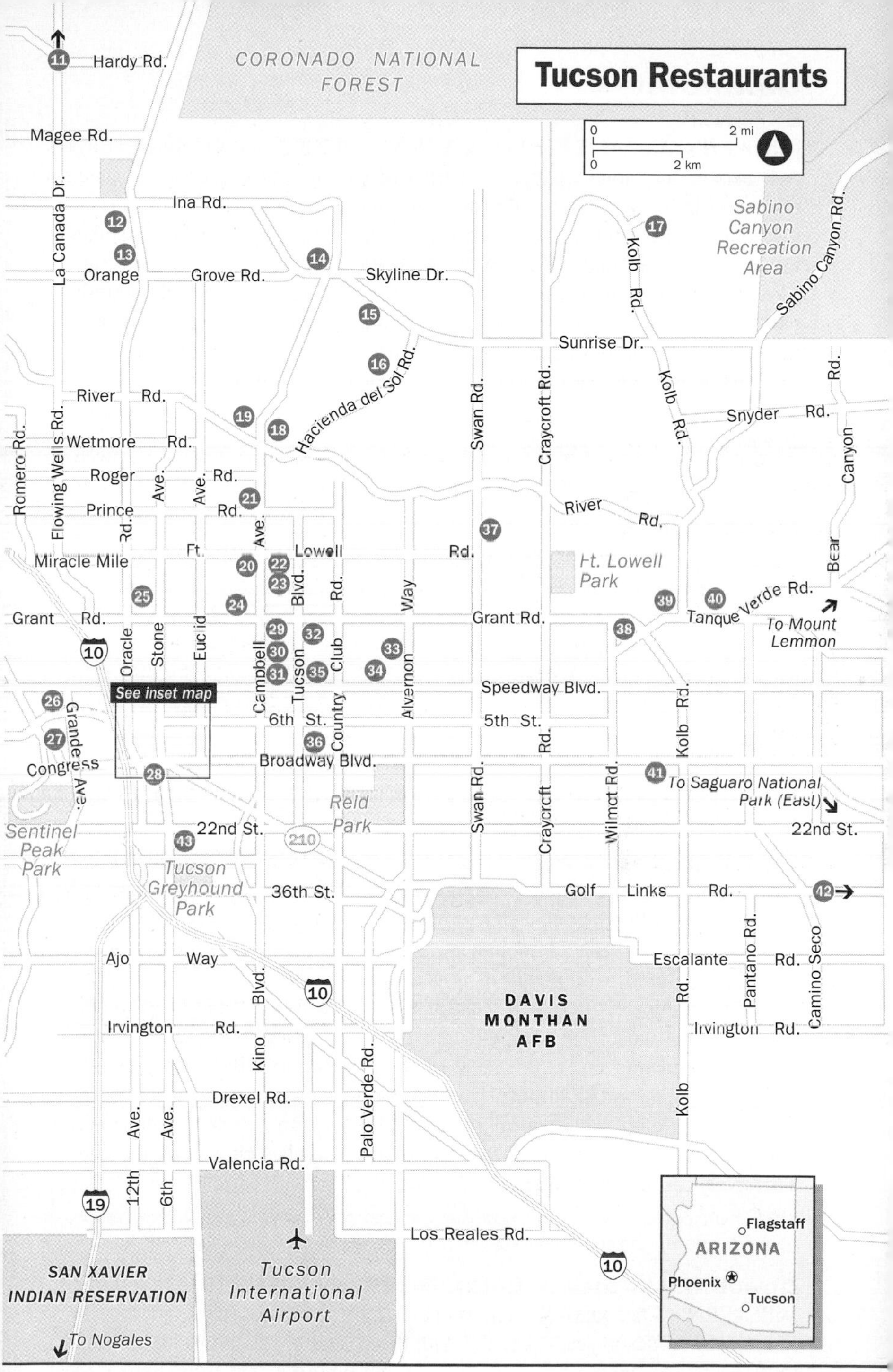

Tucson Restaurants
CORONADO NATIONAL FOREST
Sabino Canyon Recreation Area
Ft. Lowell Park
Reid Park
Sentinel Peak Park
Tucson Greyhound Park
DAVIS MONTHAN AFB
SAN XAVIER INDIAN RESERVATION
Tucson International Airport
To Nogales
To Mount Lemmon
To Saguaro National Park (East)
See inset map
Hardy Rd.
Magee Rd.
Ina Rd.
Orange Grove Rd.
Skyline Dr.
Sunrise Dr.
River Rd.
Wetmore Rd.
Roger Rd.
Prince Rd.
Miracle Mile
Ft. Lowell Rd.
Grant Rd.
Speedway Blvd.
6th St.
5th St.
Broadway Blvd.
Congress
22nd St.
36th St.
Golf Links Rd.
Ajo Way
Escalante Rd.
Irvington Rd.
Drexel Rd.
Valencia Rd.
Los Reales Rd.
Snyder Rd.
Tanque Verde Rd.
La Canada Dr.
Romero Rd.
Flowing Wells Rd.
Oracle Rd.
Stone Ave.
Euclid Ave.
Campbell Ave.
Tucson Blvd.
Country Club Rd.
Alvernon Way
Swan Rd.
Craycroft Rd.
Wilmot Rd.
Kolb Rd.
Hacienda del Sol Rd.
Sabino Canyon Rd.
Bear Canyon Rd.
Pantano Rd.
Camino Seco
Grande Ave.
Kino Blvd.
Palo Verde Rd.
12th Ave.
6th Ave.
10
19
210
0 2 mi
0 2 km
ARIZONA
Flagstaff
Phoenix
Tucson
11
12
13
14
15
16
17
18
19
20
21
22
23
24
25
26
27
28
29
30
31
32
33
34
35
36
37
38
39
40
41
42
43

Downtown

EXPENSIVE

Maynard's Market & Kitchen ★★ NEW AMERICAN/SOUTHWESTERN A cousin of the Hotel Congress's **Cup Cafe** across the street (p. 388), this restaurant in Tucson's restored downtown train station carries out a railroad theme, with old trolley track used for a foot rail at the bar and railroad spikes turned into table lamps. Serving steak, seafood, and a variety of specials, Maynard's is a great downtown dining option. As much as possible ingredients are organic, local, or sustainably produced. Sunday brunch is a local favorite. There's also a little market here where you can grab gourmet-to-go food; the market also serves sandwiches, salads, and drinks.

400 N. Toole Ave. www.maynardsmarkettucson.com. ✆ **520/545-0577.** Reservations recommended. Main courses $19–$38. Tues–Thurs 5pm–9pm; Fri–Sat 5pm–midnight; Sun 9am–2pm. Market: Main courses $7–$10; Mon–Thurs 7am–8pm; Fri–Sat 7am–9pm; Sun 9am–8pm.

MODERATE

Café à la C'Art ★ LIGHT FARE In the courtyard on the grounds of the Tucson Museum of Art, this cafe serves up tasty sandwiches and sophisticated main courses; it's a good spot for a meal break if you're downtown wandering the Presidio neighborhood or touring the museum. Try the Parmesan-crusted turkey croissant or the Cuban sandwich, made with roasted pork and ham. Wash it all down with some fresh lemonade, and be sure to save room for dessert.

150 N. Main Ave. www.cafealacarttucson.com. ✆ **520/628-8533.** No reservations. Sandwiches and salads $12–$13; entrees $11–$20. Sun–Tues 8am–3pm; Wed–Sat 8am–9pm.

Café Poca Cosa ★★ CONTEMPORARY MEXICAN At this stylish downtown restaurant, the cooking of owner/chef Suzana Davila has earned a devoted local following, as well as write-ups in just about every major international food magazine. Although nominally Mexican, this food is not just *any* Mexican food; with plenty of Southwestern cross-currents, it's imaginative and different. Expect such creations as grilled beef with a jalapeño chili and tomatillo sauce; chicken with a dark mole sauce made with Kahlúa, chocolate, almonds, and chilies; and plenty of fresh, locally grown greens as accompaniments and highlights. The menu is posted on portable blackboards, so you never know what you might find on any given day. However, you're always good with the *plato* Poca Cosa, a trio of dishes chosen by the chef. This lively restaurant is an excellent value.

110 E. Pennington St. www.cafepocacosatucson.com. ✆ **520/622-6400.** Reservations recommended. Main courses $13–$15 lunch, $24–$25 dinner. Tues–Sat 11am–9pm.

Downtown Kitchen + Cocktails ★★ NEW AMERICAN/SOUTHWESTERN Chef Janos Wilder, Tucson's most celebrated chef, got his start in downtown Tucson years ago, and with this casual restaurant he has returned to his roots. Downtown's eclectic menu draws on influences from all over the world, and its bar is a favorite hangout for local cultural influencers and movers and shakers. Consider making a meal of several small plates such as the flavor-packed "fat noodles," pork belly donuts, and calamari with mango and gingered carrots. Imaginative cocktails are a highlight.

135 S. Sixth Ave. www.downtownkitchen.com. ✆ **520/623-7700.** Reservations recommended. Main courses $19–$28. Daily 4–9pm.

INEXPENSIVE

El Minuto Café ★ MEXICAN Downtown at the edge of the Barrio Histórico next to El Tiradito shrine, El Minuto is a meeting ground for Anglos and Latinos, who come for the lively atmosphere and Mexican home-cooking. In business since 1936, this establishment is a neighborhood landmark and a prototype that other Mexican restaurants often try to emulate. Cheese crisps (that is, Mexican pizzas) are a specialty, and the enchiladas, especially *carne seca* (dried meat), are tasty. The chile con carne is another local favorite. This is a fun place for people-watching—you'll find all types, from kids to businessmen in suits.

354 S. Main Ave. www.elminutotucson.com. ✆ **520/882-4145.** No reservations. Main courses $8–$17.50. Sun–Thurs 11am–9pm; Fri–Sat 11am–10pm.

Hub Restaurant and Ice Creamery ★ AMERICAN Hub has proved to be a—well, a hub of the new downtown, shaped by the arrival of the urban streetcar and the rebirth of Congress Street as a dining destination. Hub's food ranges from burgers and meatloaf to elegant variations on comfort classics such as lobster mac and cheese. The most expensive thing on the menu, a take on steak frites, is still less expensive than at other venues downtown—and it's delicious. Save room for the house-made ice cream.

266 Congress St. www.hubdowntown.com. ✆ **520/207-8201.** Reservations for private dining room only. Main courses $10–$25. Daily 11am–midnight.

The Secret of *Carne Seca*

Housed in an old stone building in El Presidio Historic District, **El Charro Cafe** ★ is Tucson's oldest family-operated Mexican restaurant, and it's legendary around these parts for its *carne seca,* a traditional air-dried beef that is a bit like shredded beef jerky. To see how they make *carne seca,* just glance up at the restaurant's roof as you approach: The large metal cage is filled with beef drying in the desert sun. You'll rarely find *carne seca* on a Mexican menu outside of Tucson, so indulge while you're here. El Charro also claims to be ground zero for the deep-fried burrito called the chimichanga, and though historical fact points elsewhere, it's an enjoyable local legend. The adjacent **¡Toma!** (p. 424), a colorful bar/cantina, is under the same ownership. There are other El Charro locations at 6910 E. Sunrise Dr. (✆ **520/514-1922**), and 7725 N. Oracle Rd., Oro Valley (✆ **520/229-1922**), as well as in Concourse B of Tucson International Airport.

311 N. Court Ave. www.elcharrocafe.com. ✆ **520/622-1922.** Reservations recommended for dinner. Main courses $8–$25. Mon–Thurs and Sun 10am–9pm; Fri–Sat 10am–10pm.

Mi Nidito ★★ MEXICAN When he was president, Bill Clinton stopped by Mi Nidito, a beloved culinary venue on Tucson's south side, and demolished half the menu. Ever since, Mi Nidito has boasted the "President's combination" plate, and it's a delicious doozy. It takes a Secret Service detail to bust through the crowd, though; diners must usually wait outside for at least half an hour before getting a table. It's worth the wait.

1813 S. Fourth Ave. www.minidito.net. ✆ **520/622-5081.** Main dishes $8–$17. Fri–Sat 11am–2am; Sun, Wed, and Thurs 11am–10:30pm.

Seís Kitchen ★ MEXICAN Tucson's finest street taco, Mexico City–style, used to be found in a food truck called Seís, Spanish for "six," after the six Mexican food regions from which the menu drew. Then the owners found a location in Tucson's ultrahip Mercado San Agustín, the anchor of a booming west-of-the-freeway downtown scene. From opening to closing, you'll find a long line at the order window, but plenty of seats in the spacious, leafy plaza. Try the fiery chicken *tinga* or the pork *al pastor,* to name just a couple of possibilities. Top it off with an order of *calabacitas*, or stewed squash. A second location in the Joesler Village shopping center across from St. Philip's Plaza (1765 E. River Rd. #131; ✆ **520/612-7630**) is just as good as the mothership. The food truck is still in service for catering, too.

130 S. Avenida Del Convento #130. www.seiskitchen.com. ✆ **520/622-2002.** Main dishes $8–$12. Sun–Thurs 8am–8pm; Fri–Sat 8am–9pm.

Central Tucson & the University Area

EXPENSIVE

Arizona Inn—Main Dining Room ★★ FRENCH/AMERICAN The dining room at the Arizona Inn, one of the state's first resorts, is consistently excellent. Pink-stucco pueblo-style buildings surround the courtyard and the bar patio, romantic dining spots that overlooking colorful manicured gardens. The menu changes regularly, but includes plenty of classic dishes such as vichyssoise, bouillabaisse, and boeuf bourguignon, plus a handful of Southwestern-inspired offerings. Presentation is artistic, and fresh ingredients are emphasized. The homemade ice creams are fabulous. Lighter fare is served at the next-door bar, which is one of Tucson's best-loved watering holes.

2200 E. Elm St. www.arizonainn.com. ✆ **520/325-1541.** Reservations recommended. Main courses $14–$19 lunch, $29–$42 dinner; tasting menu $55 ($75 w/wine). Breakfast daily 6:30–11am, lunch Mon–Fri 11:30am–2pm, brunch Sat–Sun 11:30–2pm, dinner daily 5:30–9:30pm.

MODERATE

Kingfisher Bar & Grill ★★ SEAFOOD If you're serious about seafood, Kingfisher is definitely one of your best bets for a memorable meal in Tucson. The freshest seafood, artfully blended with bright flavors and imaginative ingredients, is deftly prepared as appetizers, sandwiches, and main dishes. You may have difficulty deciding whether to begin with oysters, house-smoked trout, or ceviche—so why not tackle them all and call it a meal? By the way, the warm cabbage salad is a must—delicious! The atmosphere is upscale and lively, and the bar and late-night menu are a hit with night owls. Be sure to save room for one of the prizewinning desserts, too—and if you're in town in summertime, check in for the delightful "road trip" menus that visit different regions of the country.

2564 E. Grant Rd. www.kingfishertucson.com. ✆ **520/323-7739.** Reservations recommended. Main courses $13–$17 lunch, $16–$32 dinner. Mon–Fri 11am–midnight; Sat–Sun 5pm–midnight. Closed July 1–July 15.

INEXPENSIVE

Beyond Bread ★ AMERICAN/BAKERY Although ostensibly a bakery, this place is really a bustling sandwich shop that also sells great breads and pastries. You can even get hot breakfasts here, but most Tucsonans dash in for coffee and a treat from the pastry case. The sandwich list is long and inventive, with both hot and cold varieties, and they all come on the great bread that's baked on the premises. Most of the sandwiches are so big that you could split them between two people if you weren't too hungry. Soups and salads are on the menu, too. Other locations are on the east side of town at Monterey Village, 6260 E. Speedway Blvd. (✆ **520/747-7477**), and in the foothills at 421 W. Ina Rd. (✆ **520/461-1111**).

3026 N. Campbell Ave. www.beyondbread.com. ✆ **520/322-9965.** Main courses $5–$11. Mon–Fri 6:30am–8pm; Sat 7am–8pm; Sun 7am–6pm.

Blue Willow ★ AMERICAN The crowds of people waiting on the front patio for a table on weekend mornings should be a clue that this place does great breakfasts. Better yet, the breakfasts are massive, and they're available all day long. The Blue Willow Special—made with scrambled eggs, green chilies, tomatoes, chopped corn tortillas, cheddar cheese, salsa, and sour cream—is a much-beloved choice, but the Mexican-inspired chorizo scramble is another dish worth trying. Be sure to browse around the little gift shop at the front of the restaurant; it has a wonderfully eclectic selection.

2616 N. Campbell Ave. www.bluewillowtucson.com. ✆ **520/327-7577.** Main courses $6–$20. Mon–Fri 7am–9pm; Sat–Sun 8am–9pm.

Brooklyn Pizza Company ★ PIZZA Solar-powered pizza? That's what the sign says, and if you look on the roof of the building housing this little pizza joint, you'll see dozens of photovoltaic panels. While the pizzas themselves are baked in a gas-fired oven, everything else in the restaurant runs on the power of the sun. Now that's eco-friendly! There are lunch, late-night, and happy-hour specials, plus house-made gelatos. The **Sky Bar** (p. 423) next door is a fun place to hang out while you're waiting for your pizza to cook.

534 N. 4th Ave. www.brooklynpizzacompany.com. ✆ **520/622-6868.** No reservations. Pizzas $7–$19. Daily 11am–11pm; late-night pizza slices served until 2:30am Thurs–Sat.

Brushfire BBQ Co. ★ BARBECUE At this tiny barbecue joint, you pick the size of your meal (regular or hungry), the type of sauce you want (they've got six flavors), and what sides you'd like (be sure to get the flavored slaw of the day). Those are a lot of choices to make on an empty stomach, but once you've made them, the payoff is some of the best barbecue in Tucson. Be sure to get an order of messy fries, topped with hot sauce, cheese, and pork, brisket, or sausage.

2745 N. Campbell Ave. www.brushfirebbq.com. ✆ **520/624-3223.** Main courses $8.50–$25. Mon–Thurs 11am–9pm, Sat 11am–10pm, Sun 10am–9pm.

Frank's and Francisco's ★ AMERICAN/MEXICAN By day Frank's, not far from the Tucson Botanical Gardens, is an unassuming greasy spoon whose marquee warns, "Elegant dining elsewhere." The dining at Frank's is just fine, though, with the best chicken-fried steak and home fries in town, and breakfast and lunch specials that will fill you up for under a ten-spot. By night, the chefs at Frank's turn the place into Francisco's, with Michoacán-style Mexican cuisine, including cheesy *caramelos*, savory charro beans, and superb street-style tacos. As another slogan has it, "Eat, pay, and get out"—but you'll have a blast while you're doing it.

3843 E. Pima St. www.franksrestaurant.com. ✆ **520/881-2710.** Main dishes $5–$10. Frank's: Mon–Fri 6am–2pm, Sat 7am–2pm, Sun 8am–2pm; Francisco's: Tues–Sat 4pm–10pm.

Ghini's French Caffe ★★ FRENCH A French cafe and breakfast spot in the middle of Tucson? *Mais oui!* This casual little spot is a real gem. The owner is from Marseille and reproduces plenty of favorites from the home country. At breakfast, there are flaky croissants, a Marseille-style omelet made with anchovies, and wonderful Provençal-style fried eggs with tomatoes, garlic, and thyme. Lunchtime brings interesting salads, sandwiches made with baguettes, and a good range of simple pastas. Everything is available to go.

1803 E. Prince Rd. www.ghiniscafe.com. ✆ **520/326-9095.** Sandwiches and pastas $7.50–$15. Tues–Thurs 7am–3pm; Fri–Sat 7am–9pm; Sun 8am–2pm.

Hot Dogs, Sonoran-Style

You might think it a scenario out of a detective show, but the early days of Sonoran-style hot dogs in Tucson were accompanied by industrial espionage, extortion, and considerable bad blood. The dust settled, and one pioneer stood standing: **El Guero Canelo ★** (www.elguerocanelo.com), which in 2018 was awarded a coveted James Beard America's Classics prize for its take on the *salchicha rojo*. The hot dog, wrapped in bacon and slathered with beans and salsa, will thrill the connoisseur, and the restaurant scene itself is a pure joy. For a slice of authentic Tucson culture, this place is not to be missed. The original El Guero Canelo is at 5201 S. 12th Ave. (✆ **520/295-9005**), and there are locations in central Tucson (2480 N. Oracle Rd.; ✆ **520/882-8977**), on the East Side (5802 E 22nd St.; ✆ **520/790-6000**), South Tucson's hip new "meat market," or *carniceria* (4519 S 12th Ave.; ✆ **520/889-3935**), and even, as an act of clemency toward its northern neighbor, on the west side of Phoenix (5131 W. McDowell Rd.; ✆ **602/278-8560**). Main courses run between $2.50 and $8; it's open Monday–Thursday 10am–10pm; Friday–Saturday 8am–midnight; Sunday 8am–10pm.

Lovin' Spoonfuls ★ VEGAN Chili dogs, turkey sandwiches, tuna melts, bacon cheeseburgers. The menu at this casual little place may not sound too interesting until you realize that not one of those dishes actually has meat in it. This is a vegan restaurant, so there are no eggs or dairy products to be seen (or tasted). If you're already a vegetarian or vegan, you may not want to eat anywhere else while you're in Tucson. Oh, and there are organic beers and wines to accompany your meal.

2990 N. Campbell Ave. www.lovinspoonfuls.com. ✆ **520/325-7766.** Main courses $6–$9.50 lunch, $9.50–$13.50 dinner. Mon–Fri 11am–9pm; Sat 9:30am–9pm; Sun 10am–3pm.

Tucson Tamale Company ★ MEXICAN Tamales, stuffed cornmeal dumplings steamed in corn husks, are a staple among the Southwest's Hispanic population, but the owners of this restaurant are taking tamales to a broader audience. To that end, the tamales here are made without lard and sometimes include some very nontraditional ingredients. There are vegan tamales (one with spinach and mushrooms), as well as a Wisconsin grilled cheese tamale. For traditionalists, however, there are tamales made with things like pork loin and green chilies, chicken and tomatillos, and beef sirloin and chipotle peppers. In recent years, branch stores have opened on the north side (7286 N. Oracle Rd.; ✆ **520/403-1888**) and east side (7159 E. Tanque Verde Rd.; ✆ **520/298-8404**).

2545 E. Broadway. www.tucsontamale.com. ✆ **520/305-4760.** Main courses $7, with larger takeout quantities available. Mon–Sat 9am–9pm.

Yoshimatsu Healthy Japanese Eatery ★ JAPANESE Yoshimatsu is an authentic Japanese restaurant in a city with a sizable Japanese population, largely because of Davis-Monthan Air Force Base. Not only is there a long menu of health-conscious Japanese dishes, but the decor in this ultracasual place features little glass cases displaying all manner of Japanese toys and action figures. The okonomiyaki, sort of a Japanese pizza, is a signature dish. A stylish little sushi bar is attached to the restaurant.

2741 N. Campbell Ave. www.yoshimatsuaz.com. ✆ **520/320-1574.** Main courses $7.50–$17. Sun–Thurs 11am–9pm; Fri–Sat 11am–10pm.

East Tucson

MODERATE

Feast ★★ INTERNATIONAL Feast has evolved from a takeaway place to an elegant sit-down restaurant, its menu propelled by a highly innovative chef. The menu changes periodically, but duck meatballs, vegetable dumplings, and beef short ribs turn up regularly.

3719 E. Speedway Blvd. www.eatatfeast.com. ✆ **520/326-9363.** Reservations recommended. Main courses $18–$28. Tues–Sat 11am–9pm; Sun 10am–9pm.

Zona 78 ★ PIZZA Try the Tuscany, which is covered with Italian sausage, mozzarella, kalamata olives, fennel, roasted garlic, onions, mushrooms, and fresh basil. This pie is just bursting with flavors. To really get the most out of a visit to Zona 78, you need to bring enough people so that you can order the big antipasti plate. There's a second Zona 78 on the west side at 78 W. River Rd. (✆ **520/888-7878**).

7301 E. Tanque Verde Rd. www.zona78.com. ✆ **520/296-7878.** Reservations recommended. Main courses $14.50–$25. Daily 11am–10pm.

INEXPENSIVE

Eegee's ★ LIGHT FARE In 1971, two kids, Ed Irving and Bob Greenberg, concocted a particularly delicious slushy lemonade and, driving a beat-up panel truck, took a batch to a construction site on Tucson's east side. The construction workers loved the cold treat, but they clamored for food as well. So it was that Eegee's, formed from the first and last names of the partners, was born. Today there are two dozen Eegee's scattered around Tucson, with a satellite up the road in Casa Grande, serving that slushy lemonade and other drinks along with grinders, subs, fries, and salads. See the website for locations apart from the flagship store on Tucson's east side.

5601 E. Speedway Blvd. www.eegees.com. ✆ **520/296-1013.** Sandwiches $2.89–$3.49; salads $3.29–$4.99; fries $1.99–$2.79. Daily 9:30am–10pm.

Little Anthony's Diner ★ AMERICAN This place is primarily for kids, although lots of big kids enjoy the 1950s music and decor. The menu includes such offerings as a La Bamba burger and Chubby Checker triple-decker club sandwich, along with a healthy salad-driven menu dubbed "Things Elvis Wouldn't Eat." Daily specials and bottomless soft drinks make feeding the family fairly inexpensive, and a video-game room will keep your kids entertained while you finish your milkshake. If you want to make a night of it (and you make a reservation far enough in advance), you can take in an old-fashioned melodrama next door at the Gaslight Theatre (p. 421). Together, these two places make for a fun night out with the family.

7010 E. Broadway Blvd. (in back of Gaslight Plaza). www.littleanthonysdiner.com. ✆ **520/296-0456.** Burgers and sandwiches $7.50–$10, pizza $10–$17. Mon 7:30am–9pm; Tues–Thurs 7:30am–10pm; Fri–Sat 7:30am–11pm; Sun 7:30am–9pm.

Saguaro Corners ★ ECLECTIC This cavernous far-eastside hangout is an ideal place to stop for a nosh on the way home from a day exploring Saguaro National Park. The menu is all over the map, ranging from tacos and pasta to steaks and shrimp and grits, but somehow it all works, and the clientele and staff are the epitome of western friendliness.

3750 S. Old Spanish Trail. www.saguarocorners.net. ✆ **520/886-2020.** Main courses $12–$18. Mon–Thurs 11am–8:30pm, Fri 11am–9:30pm, Sat 9am–9:30pm, Sun 9am–8:30pm.

Vero Amore ★★ ITALIAN Everyone loves pizza, but some people are absolutely fanatical about it. Solidly in the fanatics category are the owners of this cozy midtown pizza place, whose menu has grown from pizzas to include treats like Caprese salad, steak, pasta dishes, and gelato. Vero Amore adheres to the rigid Neapolitan (Italian) pizza-making standards that require pizzas to have thin crusts and be made with Italian flour and Italian tomatoes. The pizzas also have to be baked in a very hot wood-fired oven. Put this all together and you get pizzas that are simple in presentation yet packed with flavor. Comfortable and casual, Vero Amore is a good lunch choice if you find yourself on the near-east side of the city in the middle of the day. There's a second location in Marana at 12130 N. Dove Mountain Blvd., Ste. 104 (✆ **520/579-2292**).

3305 N. Swan Rd., Ste. 105. www.veroamorepizza.com. ✆ **520/325-4122.** Main courses $11–$25. Sun–Thurs 11am–9pm; Fri–Sat 11am–10pm.

The Foothills

EXPENSIVE

Azul ★★ NEW AMERICAN Fine dining restaurants have a tough time in Tucson, a town where locals have countless inexpensive choices and prefer the casual to the formal. Still, Azul is just the kind of place to take a date for dinner or a business prospect for lunch, elegant without being overbearing—and, to boot, located in one of Tucson's most visually impressive resorts. The menu isn't terribly adventurous, but the chef does good things with salmon, steak, Yucatán-style chicken, and even a vegetarian quinoa-stuffed poblano pepper. You won't find better views of the Santa Catalina Mountains, either.

At the Westin La Paloma, 3770 E. Sunrise Dr. ✆ **520/615-6100.** Breakfast and lunch $15–$24, dinner $17–$39, prix-fixe $49+. Breakfast 6:30am–11am daily; lunch/brunch 11am–2pm daily; dinner Sun–Thurs 5pm–9pm, Fri–Sat 5pm–10pm.

Flying V Bar & Grill ★ SOUTHWESTERN Creative Southwestern dishes that emphasize local ingredients, some even sourced from local Tohono O'odham farmers, make this restaurant at the Loews Ventana Canyon Resort a good bet for anyone wanting to sample some regional flavors. Popular dishes include guacamole prepared tableside, pork tacos, shrimp and scallop ceviche, and a bacon-rich brussels sprout salad. The steaks and lamb are some of the best on any Tucson grill. With lots of shareable small plates, this is a great place for grazing.

At Loews Ventana Canyon Resort, 7000 N. Resort Dr. https://www.loewshotels.com/ventana-canyon. ✆ **520/299-2020.** Reservations recommended. Main courses $18–$48. Sun–Thurs 5:30–9pm; Fri–Sat 5:30–10pm.

The Grill ★★ REGIONAL AMERICAN Great food, historical Southwest character, views, live jazz, design by the storied architect Josias Joesler—this place has it all. Located in a 1920s hacienda-style building at the Hacienda del Sol resort (p. 390), the Grill is one of Tucson's best restaurants. The menu changes regularly and always manages to keep up with the latest culinary trends. For a starter, you might try grilled octopus or blue crab and fire roasted corn tartare. Despite the hefty price at $48, the New York strip steak is deservedly the most popular entree on the menu and big enough for two people to share. Sunday brunch here is a real treat. The main patio overlooks the Catalinas and the fairways of the adjacent golf course.

At the Hacienda del Sol Guest Ranch Resort, 5501 N. Hacienda del Sol Rd. www.haciendadelsol.com. ✆ **520/529-3500.** Reservations recommended. Main courses $25–$48. Mon–Sat 5–9:30pm; Sun brunch 9:30am–2pm, dinner 5pm–9pm.

MODERATE

Blanco Tacos + Tequila ★ MEXICAN The retro Swedish-modern decor at this restaurant is about as far as you can get from the usual perpetual-fiesta styling of most Mexican restaurants. However, Blanco, from the same restaurant group responsible for Wildflower (below), is far from an average Mexican restaurant. The food here doesn't break any new ground, but the fish tacos are some of the best in Tucson. Dishes are made with fresh ingredients, and even the rice and vegetables that come with meals are well done. Service is friendly and there are great views from the deck. There's a great tequila list, and the bar makes some fun cocktails.

La Encantada Center, 2905 E. Skyline Dr., Ste. 246. www.foxrc.com/restaurants/blanco-tacos-tequila. ✆ **520/232-1007.** No reservations. Main courses $12–$19. Sun–Thurs 11am–9pm; Fri–Sat 11am–10pm.

The Parish Gastropub ★ AMERICAN Some days you need a beer. Some days you need bacon popcorn. Some days you need hushpuppies—or an eggplant croquette, or a slab of mesquite-broiled salmon. On such days, Tucsonans head to The Parish, an inconspicuous but comfortable bistro in a nondescript strip mall on a corner of busy Oracle Road. Everything on the menu is a treat, but, as its name suggests, The Parish is at its best when serving up Cajun and Creole dishes that would do New Orleans proud.

6453 N. Oracle Rd. www.theparishtucson.com ✆ **520/797-1233.** Main courses $9–$30. Mon 11am–10pm, Tues–Sat 11am–midnight, Sun 10am–3pm (brunch) and 4:30pm–10pm (dinner).

Scordato's ★★ ITALIAN Helmed by Daniel Scordato, scion of Tucson's best-known Italian culinary dynasty, Scordato's has the best pizza in Tucson, along with a range of Italian dishes that are far from ordinary. Try, for instance, the grilled asparagus and arugula salad, or the penne with wafer-thin sliced pork tenderloin. The 12-inch pizzas are in the Neapolitan style, thin and crunchy, and come in a variety of configurations, including a stunning robiola, fontina, and mozzarella cheese with chopped kalamata olives, roasted mushrooms, and fresh arugula. You'll want to explore the extensive wine list, too.

4911 N. Stone Ave. (at River Rd.). www.scordatospizzeria.com. ✆ **520/529-2700.** Reservations for parties of 6 or more only. Main courses $10–$17. Mon–Sat 11am–9pm, Sun 4pm–9 pm.

Market Timing

Saturday and Sunday mornings are great times to stop by St. Philip's Plaza, just across the street from a historic Episcopalian church on the corner of Campbell Avenue and River Road. On weekend mornings, there is a wonderful little farmers' market here. You can pick up organic bread, prickly-pear cactus juice and jelly, homemade tamales, Mexican cheeses, and plenty of produce. Stock up here, and then head to Sabino Canyon Recreation Area for a picnic.

Wildflower ★ NEW AMERICAN Stylish comfort food in large portions is the order of the day at this chic and casually elegant northwest-Tucson bistro. The heaping plate of fried calamari with *mizuna* greens is a good bet for a starter, and entrees run the gamut from a comforting mesquite-broiled cheeseburger with Swiss cheese to bacon-wrapped pork tenderloin. Both pasta and salmon also show up in reliable guises. Bottles of wine are half-price on Tuesdays.

At Casas Adobes Shopping Plaza, 7037 N. Oracle Rd. (at Ina Rd.). https://www.foxrc.com/restaurants/wildflower-american-cuisine. ✆ **520/219-4230.** Reservations recommended. Main courses $11–$24 lunch, $22–$34 dinner. Daily 11am–9pm.

INEXPENSIVE

Eclectic Café ★ AMERICAN/MEXICAN After a day of hiking at Sabino Canyon, the Eclectic, founded in 1980 by the mastermind behind Frank's and Francisco's (p. 404), is a fun and delicious refueling station—and also a good place to stoke up before any such enterprise. A weekend breakfast favorite is the Mexico City–style tortilla-and-salsa dish called *chilaquiles,* while lunch and dinner offer a wide range of salads, quiches, crepes, sandwiches, and a full menu of Mexican dishes. There's almost too much choice here, but Tucsonans, a brave lot, make do.

7053 E. Tanque Verde Rd. (at Sabino Canyon Rd.). www.eclecticcafetucson.com. ✆ **520/885-2842.** Main dishes $8–15. Mon–Fri 11am–9pm, Sat 8am–9pm, Sun 8am–8pm.

Zinburger Wine & Burger Bar ★ AMERICAN Burgers and beer? Yes. Burgers and wine? It doesn't seem like a logical pairing, but it works, and there are five Arizona Zinburgers to prove it, three in the Phoenix area and two in Tucson. Kids aren't barred from the place, and there's a kids' menu, but it's really—well, a hip, noisy booze-and-burger joint for grown-ups, with good food and plenty of good wine to boot.

In Joesler Village, 1865 E. River Rd. www.zinburgeraz.com. ✆ **520/299-7799.** No reservations. Main courses $9–$16. Sun–Thurs 11am–9pm; Fri–Sat 11am–10pm.

West Tucson, Oro Valley & Marana

MODERATE

Harvest Restaurant ★★ NEW AMERICAN/SOUTHWESTERN This Oro Valley restaurant, affiliated with both the Grill at Hacienda del Sol (p. 390) and Tucson's two Zona 78s (p. 405), emphasizes fresh, local, seasonal ingredients. It's an excellent choice if you're staying in the northwest foothills area. The empanadas have a lusciously flaky crust and come with a tangy *chimichurri* sauce. Likewise, if you want a great burger, this is the place. Dinner features numerous healthful dishes making use of fish, whole grains, and veggies. The attention to ingredients also extends to the cocktail menu, which features seasonal drinks made with fresh-squeezed juices.

10355 N. La Cañada Dr., Oro Valley. www.harvestov.com. ✆ **520/731-1100.** www.marketrg.com. Reservations recommended. Main courses $10–$14 lunch, $14–$25 dinner. Daily 11am–9pm.

INEXPENSIVE

Mariscos Chihuahua ★ MEXICAN In the dining room of this funky little westside Mexican joint, a life-size marlin leaps out of a wall that has been painted with a mural of the open ocean. This unusual decor should give you a hint about what they serve here—seafood, Mexican seafood. Fish, shrimp, and octopus, prepared in numerous styles, are the specialty here. You can start with a delicious ceviche tostada and then have spicy shrimp *endiablados* or a Sinaloa-style fish filet (made with a creamy green-pepper sauce). Wash your meal down with an inexpensive margarita or a *michelada*, a popular Mexican drink that mixes beer and tomato juice. You'll find Mariscos Chihuahua just south of Speedway Boulevard west of I-10 and downtown Tucson.

1009 N. Grande Ave. ✆ **520/623-3563.** No reservations. Main courses $8–$18. Daily 9am–9pm.

Pat's Drive-In ★ AMERICAN In business for more than 60 years, Pat's was originally located in the heart of downtown, then expanded to four locations, then shrank to this last one, an old-fashioned drive-in, with its distinctive red-and-white striped paint job, famous in Tucson for its chili dogs. The dogs come in both mild and spicy versions and should be accompanied by some of the great French fries. Be forewarned, these dogs are messy. You'll find Pat's just south of Speedway west of I-10.

1202 W. Niagara St. ✆ **520/624-0891.** Main dishes $1.50–$6. No credit cards. Sun–Thurs 11am–9pm; Fri–Sat 11am–10pm.

Teresa's Mosaic Café ★★ MEXICAN A mile or so west of I-10, this casual Mexican restaurant, with colorful mosaic tile tables, mirror frames, and a kitchen counter, may be hidden behind a McDonald's on the corner of Grant and Silverbell roads, but it's well worth finding for breakfast or lunch. Try the legendary *huevos rancheros*, *chilaquiles* (another popular Mexican breakfast dish), or chorizo and eggs for breakfast, and don't pass up the fresh lemonade or *horchata* (spiced rice milk). This is an especially good spot for a meal if you're on your way to the Arizona-Sonora Desert Museum, Old Tucson, or Saguaro National Park's west unit.

2455 N. Silverbell Rd. ✆ **520/624-4512.** Reservations recommended on weekends. Main courses $8.50–$16. Mon–Sat 7:30am–9pm; Sun 7:30am–2pm.

Cowboy Steakhouses

El Corral Restaurant ★ STEAK Fun, inexpensive, and atmospheric, this is one of Tucson's most iconic steakhouses. Good prime rib and cheap prices make this place hugely popular with retirees and families. The restaurant doesn't accept reservations, so expect long lines or come before or after regular dinner hours. Inside, the hacienda building has a genuine old-timey feeling, with flagstone floors and wood paneling that make it dark and cozy. In keeping with the name, there's a traditional corral fence of mesquite

For Caffeine Cravings & Sugar Buzzes

For some of the best espresso in Tucson, head to **Raging Sage Coffee Roasters,** 2458 N. Campbell Ave. (www.ragingsage.com; ✆ **520/320-5203**), a Tucson treasure for coffee lovers for 20 years. If you need a pick-me-up in the University of Arizona area, try **Caffe Luce,** 943 E. University Blvd., no. 191 (www.maingatesquare.com/caffe-luce; ✆ **520/207-5504**), directly across the street from the campus, or **Seven Cups,** 2516 E. Sixth St. (www.sevencups.com; ✆ **520/881-4072**), a traditional Chinese tearoom in a hip residential neighborhood near the University of Arizona.

To satisfy sugar cravings, stop in at the **Cup Cafe,** at Hotel Congress, 311 E. Congress St. (www.hotelcongress.com; ✆ **520/798-1618**), or at the **Kingfisher** (p. 402), one of the city's best dessert providers. At **La Baguette Bakery,** 1797 E. Prince Rd. (www.ghiniscafe.com/page.cfm/bakery; ✆ **520/322-6297**), affiliated with Ghini's French Caffe (p. 404), you can get all kinds of delicious French pastries. **AJ's Fine Foods,** 2805 E. Skyline Dr. (www.ajsfinefoods.com; ✆ **520/232-6340**), a gourmet supermarket in La Encantada shopping center at the northwest corner of Skyline Drive and Campbell Avenue, is another good place to grab a pastry. Out on the east side, a much-loved source of pastry and caffeine is the aptly named **Le Buzz Café,** 9121 E. Tanque Verde Rd. (www.lebuzzcaffe.com; ✆ **520/749-3903**), just off the Catalina Highway and the road to Mount Lemmon.

On a hot day, head to **Frost, A Gelato Shoppe,** 7131 N. Oracle Rd., Ste. 101 (www.frostgelato.com; ✆ **520/797-0188**), a great little gelateria in the Casas Adobes shopping center. Other Frosts can be found at 7301 E. Tanque Verde Rd. (✆ **520/886-0354**), which is conveniently close to Sabino Canyon, and at 2905 E. Skyline Dr., Ste. 286 (✆ **520/299-0315**), in La Encantada shopping center.

branches around the restaurant parking lot. Prime rib is the house specialty, but you can also get steaks, chicken, pork ribs, and burgers.

2201 E. River Rd. www.elcorraltucson.com. ✆ **520/299-6092.** Main courses $10–$32. Mon–Fri 5–10pm; Sat–Sun 4:30–10pm.

Li'l Abner's Steakhouse ★ STEAK Just around corner from White Stallion Ranch, Lil Abner's is an old Tucson institution, founded in 1947 in what was then the deepest, darkest desert. Specializing in thick-cut steaks, ribs, beans, and Western music, the steakhouse is now surrounded by the ever-growing district where northwest Tucson meets Marana. The best seating for most of the year is out on the huge patio under sheltering mesquite trees, family-style. The meals are family-style, too, with gigantic racks of ribs and 2-pound steaks available, as well as more modest cuts for single diners.

8500 N. Silverbell Rd. http://lilabnerssteakhouse.com. ✆ **520/744-2800.** Main courses $19–$29. Mon–Thurs 5pm–9pm; Fri–Sun 5pm–10pm.

Pinnacle Peak Steakhouse ★ STEAK Located in the Wild-West–themed Trail Dust Town entertainment center (p. 376), the Pinnacle Peak Steakhouse specializes in family dining in a fun cowboy atmosphere. Stroll the wooden sidewalks past the opera house and saloon to the grand old dining rooms of the restaurant. Once through the doors, you'll be surprised at the authenticity of the place, which really does resemble a dining room in old Tombstone. Be prepared for crowds—this place is very popular with tour buses. Oh, and by the way, wear a necktie into this place, and you'll have it cut off! Actually, lots of people wear ties just so they can have them added to the collection tacked to the ceiling.

6541 E. Tanque Verde Rd. www.pinnaclepeaktucson.com. ✆ **520/296-0911.** Main courses $11–$33. Mon–Fri 5–10pm; Sat–Sun 4:30–10pm.

TUCSON SHOPPING

Although the Tucson shopping scene is overshadowed by that of Scottsdale and Phoenix, the city does have a respectable diversity of merchants. Tucsonans have a strong sense of their place in the Southwest, and southwestern clothing, food, crafts, furniture, and art abound (and often at reasonable prices), as do shopping centers built in a southwestern architectural style.

The city's population center continues to move steadily northward, so it is in the northern foothills that you'll find most of the city's large enclosed shopping malls, as well as tasteful small shopping plazas full of boutiques and galleries.

Top Shopping Areas & Malls

Along Fourth Avenue between Congress Street and Speedway Boulevard (just north of downtown Tucson), more than 50 shops, galleries, and restaurants make up the **Fourth Avenue historic shopping and entertainment district.** The buildings here were constructed in the early 1900s, and the proximity to the University of Arizona helps keep this district bustling. Many of the shops cater primarily to student needs and interests.

El Presidio Historic District, around the Tucson Museum of Art, is the city's center for crafts shops. This area is home to Old Town Artisans (p. 415) and the Tucson Museum of Art shop (p. 415). The city's **"Lost Barrio"** district, on the corner of Southwest Park Avenue and 12th Street (a block off Broadway), is a good place to look for Mexican imports and southwestern-style home furnishings at good prices.

Casas Adobes Plaza ★ With clothing stores, several good restaurants, and a Whole Foods, this little hacienda-style historic shopping center in the foothills is a pleasant place for a shopping stop. 7001–7153 N. Oracle Rd. www.casasadobesplaza.com. ✆ **520/299-2610.**

La Encantada ★★ Tucson's toniest and most spectacularly scenic mall is nestled at the upper end of Campbell Avenue, at Skyline Drive, in the shadow of the Santa Catalina Mountains. The mall has a Crate & Barrel, a Williams-Sonoma shop, an Apple Store, and many other high-end shops and restaurants. 2905 E. Skyline Dr., www.laencantadashoppingcenter.com. ✆ **520/299-3566.**

Plaza Palomino ★ Built in the style of a Spanish hacienda with a courtyard and fountains, this little shopping center is home to some of Tucson's most interesting specialty shops, as well as galleries and restaurants. There's a farmers' market here on Saturday mornings. 2900–2990 N. Swan Rd. (at Fort Lowell Rd.). www.plazapalomino.com. ✆ **520/323-1005.**

St. Philip's Plaza ★★ This upscale southwestern-style shopping center contains a couple of good restaurants, a beauty salon/day spa, and numerous shops and galleries. On Saturday and Sunday mornings, there's a farmers' market. Makes a great one-stop Tucson shopping outing. 4280 N. Campbell Ave. (at River Rd.) www.stphilipsplaza.com. ✆ **520/529-2775.**

Tucson Mall ★ You'll find more than 200 retailers in this busy, two-story skylit complex, the largest of the northern foothills malls. Locals like to walk the mall for exercise. www.shoptucsonmall.com. 4500 N. Oracle Rd. ✆ **520/293-7331.**

Antiques & Collectibles

Michael D. Higgins Antique Indian Art ★ This little shop specializes in pre-Columbian artifacts and Native American artwork, but also carries a few examples of African, Asian, and other ethnographic art. It's open Thursday through Saturday only, from 11am to 5pm. 4351 E. Grant Rd. www.mhiggins.com. ✆ **520/577-8330.**

Morning Star Antiques ★ Adjoining Morning Star Traders (p. 418), Morning Star Antiques carries an excellent selection of antique Spanish and Mexican furniture, as well as other unusual and rustic pieces. 2020 E. Speedway Blvd. www.morningstartraders.com. ✆ **520/881-2112.**

Art

Tucson's gallery scene is not concentrated, but scattered across the foothills and other affluent suburbs. One hot spot is the corner of Campbell Avenue and Skyline Drive, where you'll find **Gallery Row,** a stylishly modern southwestern shopping plaza with several contemporary art galleries. Behind this complex, at 6420 N. Campbell Ave., a small courtyard complex is home to **Sanders Galleries** (www.sandersgalleries.com; ✆ **520/299-1763**) and **Settlers West Galleries** (www.settlerswest.com; ✆ **520/299-2607**), both of which specialize in Western art, as well as **Gallery West** (www.indianartwest.com; ✆ **520/529-7002**), specializing in American Indian art.

Davis Dominguez Gallery ★★ Located just a couple of blocks off Fourth Avenue in downtown Tucson, this huge gallery features some of the best and most creative contemporary art in the city. It's open only by appointment in July and August. 154 E. 6th St. www.davisdominguez.com. ✆ **866/629-9759** or 520/629-9759.

Etherton Gallery ★★ For more than 35 years, this gallery has been presenting some of the most distinctive art to be found in Tucson, including contemporary and historical photographs. A favorite of museums and serious collectors, Etherton Gallery isn't afraid to present work with strong themes. A smaller location is at the Temple of Music and Art, 330 S. Scott Ave. (✆ **520/624-7370**). 135 S. 6th Ave. www.ethertongallery.com. ✆ **520/624-7370.**

Jane Hamilton Fine Art ★ This gallery's boldly colored contemporary art really stands out; many artworks reflect a desert aesthetic. At Plaza Colonial Center, 2890 E. Skyline Dr., Ste. 180. www.janehamiltonfineart.com. ✆ **520/529-4886.**

Medicine Man Gallery/Mark Sublette Modern ★★★ This gallery has the finest and most tasteful traditional Western art you'll find anywhere in Arizona. Artists represented include Ed Mell, Maynard Dixon, and Howard Post; most of the gallery's artists have received national attention. There's an excellent selection of Native American crafts as well; see p. 418 for more details. The gallery also houses a small Maynard Dixon Museum. 6872 E. Sunrise Dr., Suite 130. www.medicinemangallery.com ✆ **800/422-9382** or 520/722-7798.

Philabaum Contemporary Art Glass ★★ For more than 30 years, this gallery has been exposing Tucson to the latest trends in contemporary glass art. The gallery is full of lovely and colorful pieces by Tucson's own Tom Philabaum and more than 30 other artists from around the country. 711 S. 6th Ave. www.philabaumglass.com. ✆ **520/884-7404.**

Books

Barnes & Noble has two Tucson locations: 5130 E. Broadway Blvd. (✆ **520/512-1166**) and 7325 N. La Cholla Blvd., Ste. 100, in the Foothills Mall (✆ **520/742-6402**).

Antigone ★★ A longtime fixture on Fourth Avenue, Antigone is Tucson's premier literary bookstore, featuring visiting authors from around the country as well as local writers. Three book-nerdy young employees recently took over ownership, and a decades-long tradition promises to continue for a long while to come. 411 N. Fourth Ave. www.antigonebooks.com. ✆ **520/792-3715.**

Bookmans ★ This big bookstore, housed in a strip mall next to a busy Whole Foods location, is crammed full of used books and recordings, and has long been a favorite of Tucsonans. There are other Bookmans stores at 6230 E. Speedway Blvd. (✆ **520/748-9555**) and 3733 W. Ina Rd. (✆ **520/579-0303**). 3330 E. Speedway. www.bookmans.com. ✆ **520/325-5767.**

The Book Stop ★★ Fifty years on and counting, the Book Stop is Tucson's favorite used book emporium. As befits any good secondhand store, the shelves are packed to the rafters, and there are plenty of first editions and other rarities to ogle. Prices are reasonable, too, making the Book Stop a must-stop destination for bookish travelers. 214 N. Fourth Ave. www.bookstoptucson.com. ✆ **520/326-6661.**

Clues Unlimited ★ If you forgot to pack your vacation reading, drop by this fun little store, which specializes in mysteries. Its owners have deep knowledge of the genre. 3154 E. Fort Lowell Rd. www.cluesunlimited.com. ✆ **520/326-8533.**

Crafts

See also Native American Arts, Crafts & Jewelry, p. 417.

Old Town Artisans ★★ Housed in a restored 1850s adobe building covering an entire city block in El Presidio Historic District, this unique shopping plaza houses several shops brimming with traditional and contemporary southwestern designs. There's also free Wi-Fi in the courtyard, and a nice little cafe, **La Cocina,** that features free performances by local musicians Wednesday through Saturday evenings. 201 N. Court Ave. www.oldtownartisanstucson.com. ✆ **800/782-8072** or 520/623-6024.

Tucson Museum of Art Shop ★★ The Tucson Museum's gift shop offers a colorful and changing selection of southwestern crafts, mostly by local and regional artists, as well as cool tchotchkes. 140 N. Main Ave. www.tucsonmuseumofart.org. ✆ **520/624-2333.**

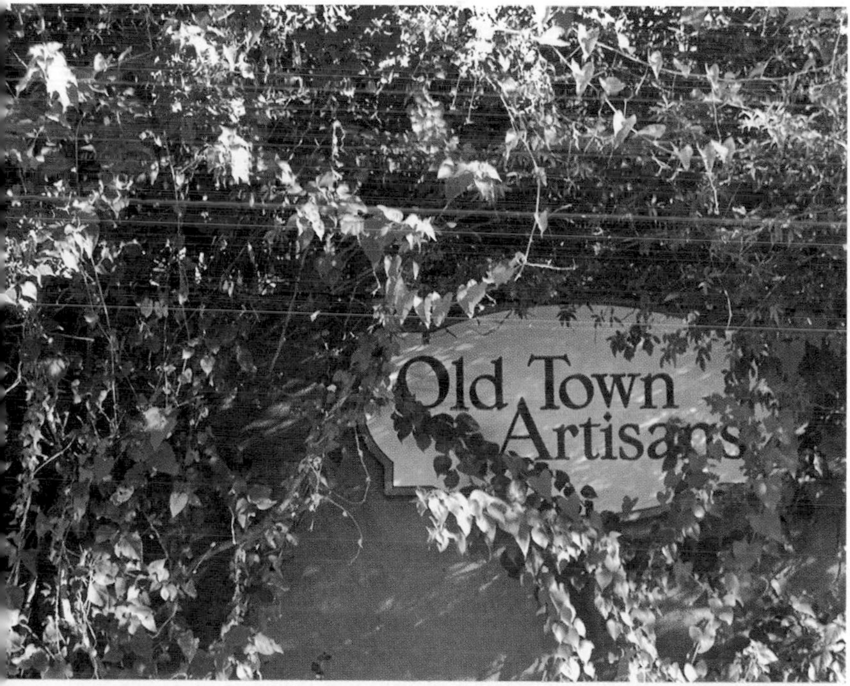

In the historic district, Old Town Artisans houses a range of shops selling traditional and contemporary crafts.

Seeing Stars

Amateur astronomers, take note. Because of all the great star-viewing opportunities in southern Arizona, Tucson has a large number of stargazers, and they all shop at **Stellar Vision Astronomy Shop** (3721 E. 37th St., www.stellarvisiontucson.com; ✆ **520/571-0877**). It's packed with new and used telescopes of all shapes and sizes, as well as books and star charts. **Starizona,** on the northwest side of town (5757 N Oracle Rd Suite 103, http://starizona.com; ✆ **520/292-5010**), is similarly well stocked with goodies for stargazers.

Fashion

See also the listing for the Beth Friedman Collection under "Jewelry," below. For cowboy and cowgirl attire, see p. 418.

Dark Star Leather ★★ In the market for a distinctive leather jacket, belt, or purse? Stop by this locally owned shop in Plaza Palomino, where exotic leathers are used in one-of-a-kind designs. You can sometimes find great deals on sale items. 2940 N. Swan Rd., Ste. 129. www.darkstarleather.com. ✆ **520/881-4700.**

Maya Palace Boutique and Bridal Shop ★★ Ethnic-inspired but sophisticated women's clothing in natural fabrics is sold here by a friendly staff, who help customers of all ages put together a southwestern chic look, from casual to dressy. It's also a premier destination for wedding-bound brides and their parties. In Plaza Palomino, 2930 N. Swan Rd., Suite 120. www.mayapalace.com. ✆ **520/748-0817.**

Gifts & Souvenirs

B&B Cactus Farm ★ Devoted exclusively to cacti and succulents, this plant nursery is worth a visit just to see the amazing variety on display. (It's a good place to stop on the way to or from Saguaro National Park East.) The store can pack your purchase for traveling or ship it anywhere in the United States. 11550 E. Speedway Blvd. www.bandbcactus.com. ✆ **520/721-4687.**

DAH Rock Shop ★ Can't make it to Tucson for the annual gem and mineral shows? Don't despair. At this cluttered shop, you can pick through shelves crammed with all manner of rare minerals and exotic stones. 3401 N. Dodge Blvd. www.dahrockshopaz.com. ✆ **520/323-0781.**

Native Seeds/SEARCH ★★ Gardeners, cooks, and just about anyone in search of an unusual gift will likely be fascinated by this shop, operated by a nonprofit organization dedicated to preserving the biodiversity of native southwest seeds. The shelves are full of heirloom beans, corn, chiles, and other seeds from a wide variety of native desert plants. You'll also find gourds and inexpensive Tarahumara Indian baskets, bottled sauces and salsas made from native plants, and books about native agriculture. 3061 N. Campbell Ave. www.nativeseeds.org. ✆ **520/622-5561.**

Picánte Designs ★ Hispanic-themed icons and accessories here include *milagros*, Day of the Dead skeletons, Mexican crosses, jewelry, greeting cards, and folk art from around the world. This is a great place to shop for distinctive south-of-the-border kitschy gifts. 2932 E. Broadway. www.picantetucson.com. ✆ **520/320-5699.**

Tohono Chul Museum Shops ★★ The two shops here are packed with Mexican folk art, nature-themed toys, household items, T-shirts, and books. They're an absolute must after a visit to surrounding Tohono Chul Park (p. 376), which is landscaped with desert plants. 7366 N. Paseo del Norte (1 block W of corner of Ina and Oracle rds.). www.tohonochulpark.org. ✆ **520/742-6455.**

UN Center/UNICEF ★ If your tastes run to ethnic imports, be sure to check out this great little gift shop. Not only is there a lot of cool stuff from all over the world, but when you buy something here, you'll also be helping underprivileged children. Monterey Village, 6242 E. Speedway Blvd. www.untucson.org. ✆ **520/881-7060.**

Jewelry

Beth Friedman Collection ★ Selling a well-chosen collection of jewelry by Native American craftspeople and international designers, this shop also carries some extravagant cowgirl get-ups in velvet and lace, as well as contemporary women's fashions. Next to Joesler Village at 6266 N. Via Jaspeada. www.shoptiques.com/boutiques/beth-friedman. ✆ **520/577-6858.**

Mexican & Latin American Imports

The **"Lost Barrio,"** on the corner of Southwest Park Avenue and 12th Street (a block south of Broadway), is a good place to look for Mexican imports and southwestern-style home furnishings at good prices.

Antigua de Mexico ★ This warehouse-like shop is absolutely packed with crafts from Mexico—oversize ceramics and painted plates, wooden and wrought-iron furniture, and punched-metal frames and framed mirrors. Smaller items include crucifixes and candlesticks. 3235 W. Orange Grove Rd. www.antiguademexico.us. ✆ **520/742-7114.**

Native American Art, Crafts & Jewelry

Bahti Indian Arts ★★ Family-owned for more than 50 years, this store sells exquisitely made Native American crafts—jewelry, baskets, sculpture, paintings, books, weavings, kachina dolls, Zuni fetishes, and much more. Bahti is the first place to shop if you're looking for southwestern ethnographic arts and crafts. At St. Philip's Plaza, 4330 N. Campbell Ave., Ste. 73. www.bahti.com. ✆ **520/577-0290.**

Gallery West ★ Located right below Anthony's in the Catalinas restaurant, this tiny shop specializes in very expensive Native American artifacts (mostly pre-1940s) such as New Mexico Pueblo pots, Apache and Pima baskets, 19th-century Plains Indian beadwork, Navajo weavings, and kachinas. Also for sale is plenty of both contemporary and vintage jewelry. 6420 N. Campbell Ave. (at Skyline Dr.). www.indianartwest.com. ✆ **520/529-7002.**

Medicine Man Gallery/Mark Sublette Modern ★ This shop has the best and biggest selection of old Navajo rugs in the city. There are also Mexican and other Hispanic textiles, Acoma pottery, basketry, and other Indian crafts, as well as artwork by cowboy artists (p. 414). 6872 E. Sunrise Dr., Suite 130. www.medicinemangallery.com. ✆ **800/422-9382** or 520/722-7798.

Morning Star Traders ★★★ With hardwood floors and a museum-like atmosphere, this store features Native American crafts of the highest quality, including antique Navajo rugs, kachinas, furniture, and a huge selection of old Native American jewelry. This just may be the best store of its type in the entire state. An adjoining shop, Morning Star Antiques (p. 413), carries an impressive selection of antique furniture. 2020 E. Speedway Blvd. www.morningstartraders.com. ✆ **520/881-2112.**

Western Wear

Arizona Hatters ★ Under new ownership but a Tucson fixture since 1935, Arizona Hatters carries the best names in cowboy hats, from Stetson to Bailey to Resistol. The shop specializes in custom-fitting hats to the customer's head and face. 2790 N. Campbell Ave. www.arizonahatters.com. ✆ **520/775-3015.**

Boot Barn ★ Here's the place to put together your Western-wear ensemble under one roof. A national chain, it's the largest such store in Tucson and can outfit you and your kids in the latest cowboy fashions, from hats to boots. Two other Tucson locations are at 6701 E. Broadway (✆ **520/731-3422**) and 3776 South 16th Ave. (✆ **520/622-4500**). In Northwest Plaza, 3719 N. Oracle Rd. (at Prince Rd.). www.bootbarn.com. ✆ **520/888-1161.**

TUCSON ENTERTAINMENT & NIGHTLIFE

Tucson after dark is a fairly easy landscape to negotiate, compared to the vast cultural sprawl of Phoenix. Nightlife is more concentrated here, with the **Downtown Arts District** at the center of the action, featuring the Temple of Music and Art, the Tucson Convention Center Music Hall, and several nightclubs. The **University of Arizona campus,** a mile away, is another entertainment nexus.

The free ***Tucson Weekly*** contains thorough listings of concerts, theater and dance performances, and club offerings. Each Thursday, the entertainment section of the ***Arizona Daily Star*** ("Caliente") is a good source of information for what's going on around town.

The Performing Arts

There's a fair amount of cultural overlap between Tucson and Phoenix—two of Tucson's major companies, the **Arizona Opera** (www.azopera.org) and the **Arizona Theatre Company** (www.arizonatheatre.org), spend half their time in Phoenix, while **Ballet Arizona** (www.balletaz.org), headquartered in Phoenix, presents a full range of classical dance programs in Tucson. Tucson also has its own **Tucson Symphony Orchestra** and **Ballet Tucson** (http://ballet tucson.org), and it sustains a diversified theater scene. Usually, the best way to purchase tickets is directly from the company's box office.

Tickets to **Tucson Convention Center** events (but not the symphony or the opera) and other venues around town may be available by calling **Ticketmaster** (www.ticketmaster.com; ✆ **800/745-3000** or 866/448-7849) or by stopping by the **TCC box office,** 260 S. Church Ave. (http://tucsonconventioncenter.com; ✆ **520/791-4101**).

PERFORMING ARTS CENTERS & CONCERT HALLS

Tucson's largest performance venue, the **Tucson Convention Center,** is the home to the Tucson Symphony Orchestra and the Arizona Opera Company, along with hosting many touring companies. The box office is open Monday through Friday from 10:30am to 5:30pm.

The centerpiece of the Tucson theater scene is the **Temple of Music and Art,** 330 S. Scott Ave. (http://arizonatheatre.org/atc-tucson; ✆ **520/622-2823**), a restored historic theater dating from 1927. The 627-seat Alice Holsclaw Theatre is the Temple's main stage, but there's also the 90-seat Cabaret Theatre. Call for box office hours.

University of Arizona Centennial Hall, 1020 E. University Blvd. at Park Avenue (www.uapresents.org; ✆ **520/621-3341**), on the UA campus, stages Broadway shows and performances by national and international musical acts. A big stage and excellent sound system permit large-scale productions. Subscriptions may be purchased through uapresents.org or by calling ✆ **520/621-3341.** All other tickets sales are through Ticketmaster, ✆ **800/745-3000.**

Originally opened in 1930, downtown Tucson's **Fox Theatre,** 17 W.

The restored Fox Theatre, first opened in 1930, presents everything from films to live music.

Congress St. (www.foxtucson.com; ✆ **520/547-3040**), a restored movie palace, is now the city's most beautiful place to catch live music, a play, or even a classic or independent film. The box office is open Tuesday through Friday 11am to 6pm, and on performance Saturdays and Sundays from 2 hours before show time.

The **Center for the Arts Proscenium Theatre,** Pima Community College (West Campus), 2202 W. Anklam Rd. (www.pima.edu/community/the-arts/center-arts; ✆ **520/206-6986**) is another good place to check for classical music performances. It offers a wide variety of shows.

OUTDOOR VENUES & SERIES

Weather permitting, Tucsonans head to Reid Park's **DeMeester Outdoor Performance Center,** at Country Club Road and East 22nd Street (https://www.tucsonaz.gov/parks/GeneCReidPark; ✆ **520/791-4873**) for performances under the stars. This amphitheater stages live theater performances, as well as frequent concerts (many of which are free).

CLASSICAL MUSIC, OPERA & DANCE

Both the **Tucson Symphony Orchestra** (www.tucsonsymphony.org; ✆ **520/882-8585**), which is the oldest continuously performing symphony in the Southwest, and the **Arizona Opera Company** (www.azopera.org; ✆ **520/293-4336**), the state's premier opera company, perform at the Tucson Convention Center Music Hall and other venues in the city. Single fares are available through Ticketmaster (www.ticketmaster.com), with season subscriptions available through the organizations themselves.

At the **University of Arizona Fred Fox School of Music** (www.music.arizona.edu; ✆ **520/621-1162**) performances include classical music and opera, held in the Music Building's Crowder and Holsclaw halls, near the intersection of Speedway Boulevard and Park Avenue on the UA campus. You can also catch performances by the UA Dance Ensemble in the **Stevie Eller Dance Theatre**—the bold contemporary architecture of this building makes seeing a performance here a double treat. Call the above number for information.

THEATER

Tucson doesn't have a lot of theater companies, but what few it does have stage a surprisingly eclectic sampling of classic and contemporary plays. **Arizona Theatre Company** (http://arizonatheatre.org/atc-tucson; ✆ **520/622-2823**), which performs at the Temple of Music and Art, is the state's top professional theater company, splitting its time between Tucson and Phoenix. Each season sees a mix of comedy, drama, and Broadway-style musical shows. The **Invisible Theatre,** 1400 N. First Ave. (www.invisibletheatre.com; ✆ **520/882-9721**), a tiny theater in a converted laundry building, has been home to Tucson's most experimental theater for nearly 50 years (it does off-Broadway shows). Tickets run $35 for single admission.

The West just wouldn't be the West without good old-fashioned melodramas, and the **Gaslight Theatre,** 7010 E. Broadway Blvd. (www.thegaslighttheatre.com; ✆ **520/886-9428**) is where evil villains, stalwart heroes, and defenseless heroines pound the boards. You can boo and hiss, cheer and sigh as the predictable stories unfold on stage. It's great fun for kids and adults, with plenty of pop-culture references. Tickets are $22 adults, $20 students and seniors, and $12 kids 12 and under. Performances are held nightly, with two shows on Friday and Saturday nights, plus a Sunday matinee. Tickets often sell out a month in advance.

The Club & Music Scene

COMEDY

Laffs Comedy Caffé ★ This stand-up comedy club features local and professional comedians from around the country Thursday through Saturday nights, with the stage open to all comers on Thursdays. A full bar and a limited menu are available. At the Village, 2900 E. Broadway Blvd., Ste. 154. www.laffscomedyclub.com. ✆ **520/323-8669.** Cover free Thurs, $12–$17.50 Fri–Sat.

COUNTRY

The Maverick ★ Since 1962, the Maverick, in different incarnations and different locations around town, has been Tucson's favorite country-music dance club. It's now located at the crossroads of busy Tanque Verde and Kolb roads, with live country music every night from Tuesday through Saturday. Country dance lessons are especially popular with a Tucson crowd. 6622 E. Tanque Verde Rd. www.tucsonmaverick.com. ✆ **520/298-0430.** No cover to $5.

JAZZ

The **Tucson Jazz Society** (www.tucsonjazz.org; ✆ **520/903-1265**) books well-known jazz musicians for performances each year and sponsors different series at various locations around the city. Tickets are usually between $15 and $35. The society also mounts a **jazz festival** from mid- to late January each year. Their website lists various jazz nights at restaurants all over Tucson.

The Grill/Terraza Garden Patio & Lounge ★★ No other jazz venue in Tucson has more flavor of the Southwest than this restaurant/lounge perched high on a ridge top overlooking the city. There are live bands (jazz, blues, flamenco) Friday and Saturday nights, and a pianist on other nights. Hacienda del Sol Guest Ranch Resort, 5501 N. Hacienda del Sol Rd. www.haciendadelsol.com. ✆ **520/529-3500.**

ROCK, BLUES & REGGAE

Chicago Bar ★ Transplanted Chicagoans love to watch their home teams on the TVs at this neighborhood bar, but there's also live music nightly. Sure, blues gets played a lot, but so do reggae and rock and about everything in between. 5954 E. Speedway Blvd. www.chicagobartucson.com. ✆ **520/748-8169.** No cover to $5.

Get Your Mariachi On

Tucson is the mariachi capital of the United States, and no one should visit without spending at least one evening listening to some of these strolling musicians. At the **St. Augustine Cathedral,** 192 S. Stone Ave. (http://cathedral-staugustine.org; ✆ **520/623-6351**) there is even a mariachi Mass every Sunday at 8am. In April, Tucson's International Mariachi Conference (www.tucsonmariachi.org) draws hundreds of participants. **Guadalajara Grill ★,** 1220 E. Prince Rd. (✆ **520/323-1022**), a large Mexican restaurant just west of North Campbell Avenue, is a great place to catch an evening of lively mariachi music; it's convenient to several of the foothills resorts. Musicians perform Sunday through Thursday 6–9pm, Friday and Saturday 6–10pm.

Club Congress ★ Just off the lobby of the restored Hotel Congress (p. 388), Club Congress is Tucson's main alternative-music venue, with several nights of live music each week. Over the years such bands as Nirvana, Dick Dale, and the Goo Goo Dolls have played here, although more recently, the club has tended to book primarily local and regional acts. 311 E. Congress St. www.hotelcongress.com. ✆ **520/622-8848.** No cover to $25.

The Rialto Theatre ★ This renovated 1919 vaudeville theater, although not a nightclub, is now Tucson's main venue for performances by bands that are too big to play across the street at Club Congress. 318 E. Congress St. http://eventbritesites.com/tf/rialtotheatre. ✆ **520/740-1000.** Tickets $10–$70.

The Bar, Lounge & Pub Scene

Audubon Bar ★ If you're looking for a quiet, comfortable scene, the piano music in this classic lounge at the Arizona Inn (p. 384) is sure to soothe your soul. Before or after drinks, you can stroll the resort's beautiful gardens. 2200 E. Elm St. www.arizonainn.com. ✆ **520/325-1541.**

Barrio Brewing Co. ★ Located in a warehouse district southeast of downtown and a few blocks south of Broadway, this big brewpub, which is affiliated with Gentle Ben's Brewing Co. (below), isn't easy to find, but it is definitely worth searching out. Grab a seat on the loading-dock patio and sip a stout as the sun goes down. 800 E. 16th St. (at E. Euclid Ave. and Toole St.). www.barriobrewing.com. ✆ **520/791-2739.**

The Canyon's Crown ★ It's so cool and dark and appropriately atmospheric inside this eastside English pub that you'd never know that sunshine and blue skies lurk just outside the door. This is a great place to stop for a pint after hiking at Sabino Canyon. 6958 E. Tanque Verde Rd. www.canyonscrown.com. ✆ **520/885-8277.**

Cascade at Loews Ventana Canyon ★ With a view of the Catalinas, this plush lounge—Tucson's ultimate piano bar—is perfect for romance or relaxation at the start or end of a night on the town. Sunday through Thursday nights, there's live piano music or a jazz band, and on Fridays and Saturdays, there's a live band and dancing. At Loews Ventana Canyon Resort, 7000 N. Resort Dr. www.loewshotels.com. ✆ **520/299-2020.**

Cushing Street Bar & Restaurant ★★ On the edge of the Barrio Histórico district just south of the Tucson Convention Center, this restaurant/bar in a historic 1860s adobe building has loads of old Tucson character. There's live jazz on Friday and Saturday nights and occasionally other nights in the month. 198 W. Cushing St. www.cushingstreet.com. ✆ **520/622-7984.**

Famous Sam's ★ With seven branches around the city, Famous Sam's mixes the classic bar and grill vibe with off-track betting on horse and dog races. It keeps a lot of Tucson's sports fans happy with its cheap prices and large portions. Locations include 7129 E. Golf Links Rd. (✆ **520/296-1245**) and 2320 N. Silverbell Rd. (✆ **520/884-7267**). www.famoussams.com.

Gentle Ben's Brewing Co. ★ Just off the UA campus, Gentle Ben's is Tucson's favorite microbrewery and, not surprisingly, attracts primarily a college crowd. A big, modern place with plenty of outdoor seating, it's been a magnet for nearly half a century. 865 E. University Blvd. www.gentlebens.com. ✆ **520/624-4177.**

The Kon Tiki ★ With a Polynesian luau theme, this joint is not some modern-day designer's idea of the 1950s; this is the real thing, a dimly lit but joyful place for those who love a retro vibe. But be careful—those sweet tropical cocktails can pack a Hawaiian punch! 4625 E. Broadway Blvd. www.kontikitucson.com. ✆ **520/323-7193.**

Saint Charles Tavern ★ A recent and welcome entry in Tucson's hip bar scene, the Saint Charles Tavern opened on a burgeoning South Fourth Avenue in 2017. It's a touch noisy, especially on nights when live music is on offer, but not so much that you can't have a good conversation, and the service is impeccable. An outside beer garden is the perfect place to sit on cool evenings. 1632 S. Fourth Ave. ✆ **520/888-5925.**

The Shanty ★★ A favorite hangout of politicians, journalists, writers, artists, and other movers and shakers since the 1930s, the Shanty also sports one of the city's best beer selections, with representative brews from around the world. Pull up a barstool, admire the fine art on the wall, and enjoy the parade. 401 E. 9th St. ✆ **520/623-2664.**

The Shelter ★ Housed in an unusual round building that supposedly was once a fallout shelter (thus the name of the bar), this place is totally retro, with lots of JFK memorabilia on the walls. There are even vintage pinball machines. Fun and funky. 4155 E. Grant Rd. www.facebook.com/TheShelterCocktailLounge. ✆ **520/326-1345.**

Sky Bar ★ A perfect match for this stargazing city, this bar sets up telescopes on the patio at night, projects images from space on screens around the room, and has regularly scheduled astronomy lectures and presentations. As if this astronomical orientation isn't cool enough, the Sky Bar is also solar powered, utilizing power from a photovoltaic array on the roof. Brooklyn Pizza (p. 403) is next door. 536 N. Fourth Ave. www.skybartucson.com. ✆ **520/622-4300.**

¡Toma! ★ With a Mexican hat fountain/sculpture in the courtyard, this fun and festive bar in El Presidio Historic District is owned by the family that operates El Charro Cafe next door (p. 401). Drop by for half-price margaritas and appetizers during happy hour (Monday–Friday 3–6pm). 311 N. Court Ave. ✆ **520/622-1922.**

GAY & LESBIAN BARS & CLUBS

Brodies Tavern ★ Billing itself as three bars under one roof, Brodies boasts a sports bar, a beer and shot station, and a patio bar with pool tables. Though advertised as a LGBT hangout, the clientele is decidedly male. 2449 N. Stone Ave. http://brodiestavernbackpocket.net. ✆ **520/622-0447.**

IBT's ★ On funky Fourth Avenue, IBT's has long been the most popular gay men's dance bar in town. The music ranges from 1980s retro to hip-hop, and regular drag shows add to the fun. There's always an interesting crowd. 616 N. 4th Ave. www.ibtstucson.com. ✆ **520/882-3053.**

Spectator Sports

COLLEGE SPORTS The **University of Arizona's Wildcats** teams provide action year-round (www.arizonaathletics.com; ✆ **800/452-2287** or 520/621-2287). The Pac-10 **football team** plays at UA's Arizona Stadium; most tickets cost between $20 and $60—though some seats go for ten times that amount. For a winter visitor, getting a ticket for UA's championship-contending Wildcats **basketball team** is more of a challenge, and more daunting to the wallet. The best bargain, and in a fantastic setting, is UA Wildcat **baseball,** with games played in the old Hi Corbett field (featured prominently in the film *Major League*) in Reid Park. Tickets are a bargain $7–$12, and you can walk up to the box office and get a seat on any just about any game day. UA women's **softball,** also played at a championship level, is another fun option.

GOLF TOURNAMENTS The **World Golf Championships–Accenture Match Play Championship** (www.pgatour.com; ✆ **520/207-0595**), Tucson's main PGA tournament, is held in late February at the Jack Nicklaus Signature Golf Course at Ritz-Carlton Golf Club at Dove Mountain. Daily tickets are $25 to $55. The **Cologuard Classic** is held at the Omni Tucson National Resort at about the same time, with tickets at $20.

HORSE/GREYHOUND RACING For 6 weeks each winter, the **Rillito Park Racetrack,** 4502 N. First Ave. (www.rillitoracetrack; ✆ **520/293-5011**), the birthplace of both the photo finish and organized quarter horse and Arabian racing, hosts quarter horse and thoroughbred racing. The ponies run on weekends in January and February. General admission is $5, and clubhouse admission is $10. Greyhounds race year-round at **Tucson Greyhound Park,**

2601 S. Third Ave. (www.tucsongreyhound.com; ✆ **520/884-7576**). Admission is free. Races are held Monday through Saturday evenings. To reach the track, take exit 261 off I-10.

Casinos

Casino del Sol ★ Operated by the Pascua Yaqui tribe, this is one of the two largest casinos in southern Arizona, with plenty of slot machines, plus keno, bingo, and a card room. It's 15 miles southwest of Tucson off I-19 (take the Valencia Rd. exit and drive west). 5655 W. Valencia Rd. www.casinodelsol.com. ✆ **855/765-7829.**

Desert Diamond Casino ★ Operated by the Tohono O'odham tribe and just off I-19 south of Tucson, this casino offers the same variety of slot and video poker machines found at other casinos in the state. A card room, bingo, and keno round out the options. 1100 W. Pima Mine Rd., Sahuarita (take exit 80 off I-19). www.ddcaz.com. ✆ **866/332-9467** or 520/294-7777.

SOUTHERN ARIZONA

10

Southern Arizona is a place where the cactus forests of the Sonoran Desert meet the agave-spiked grasslands of the Chihuahuan Desert, where old hippies and old cowboys live side by side, where military bases abut conservation areas and national monuments, where small towns and historic ranches shelter under tall mountain ranges. You can find jaguars in the forests and fine wines on the plains—and everywhere you look, you can find a rich history of Native Americans, the Wild West, and the modern age.

Southern Arizona was the first part of the Southwest explored by the Spanish. As early as 1540, a Spanish expedition led by the conquistador Francisco Vásquez de Coronado passed through this region. Nearly 150 years later, Father Eusebio Francisco Kino founded a string of Jesuit missions across the region the Spanish called the Pimeria Alta, an area that would later become northern Mexico and eventually southern Arizona. Converting the Indians and building mission churches, Father Kino left a long-lasting mark on this region. Two of the missions he founded still stand—San Xavier del Bac (p. 364), 9 miles south of present-day Tucson, and San José de Tumacácori (p. 433), south of Tubac.

More than 450 years after Coronado marched through this region, the valley of the San Pedro River is undergoing something of a population explosion, especially in the city of Sierra Vista, where retirement communities sprawl across the landscape. Nearby, in the once nearly abandoned copper-mining town of Bisbee, urban refugees and artists have opened numerous galleries and B&Bs, making this one of the most interesting small towns in the state.

The combination of low deserts, high plains, and towering mountains has given this region a fascinating diversity of landscapes. Giant saguaros cover the slopes of the Sonoran Desert throughout much of southern Arizona, and in the far western parts of this region, organ pipe cacti reach the northern limit of their range. In the cool mountains, which biologists call "sky islands," cacti give way to pines, and passing clouds bring snow and rain. Narrow canyons and broad valleys, fed by the rain and snowmelt, provide habitat for hundreds of species of birds and other wildlife. Southeastern Arizona is a birding destination of worldwide importance—nearly half of North America's bird species wing their way through here at some point each year.

The region's mild climate has also given rise to a small but steadily growing wine industry, and touring these wineries and vineyards is a favorite weekend excursion for Tucson and Phoenix residents. When planning a trip through southern Arizona, it's well worth mapping out a route that will let you stop at a winery or two.

ORGAN PIPE CACTUS NATIONAL MONUMENT ★★

135 miles S of Phoenix; 140 miles W of Tucson; 185 miles SE of Yuma

Located roughly midway between Yuma and Tucson, Organ Pipe Cactus National Monument is a preserve for this rare cactus. The organ pipe cactus resembles the saguaro cactus in many ways, but instead of forming a single main trunk, organ pipes have many trunks, some 20 feet tall, that Anglo miners who came to the region thought resembled organ pipes.

This rugged region has few towns or services. To the west lie the inaccessible Cabeza Prieta National Wildlife Refuge and the Barry M. Goldwater Air Force Range (a bombing range), and to the east is the large Tohono O'odham

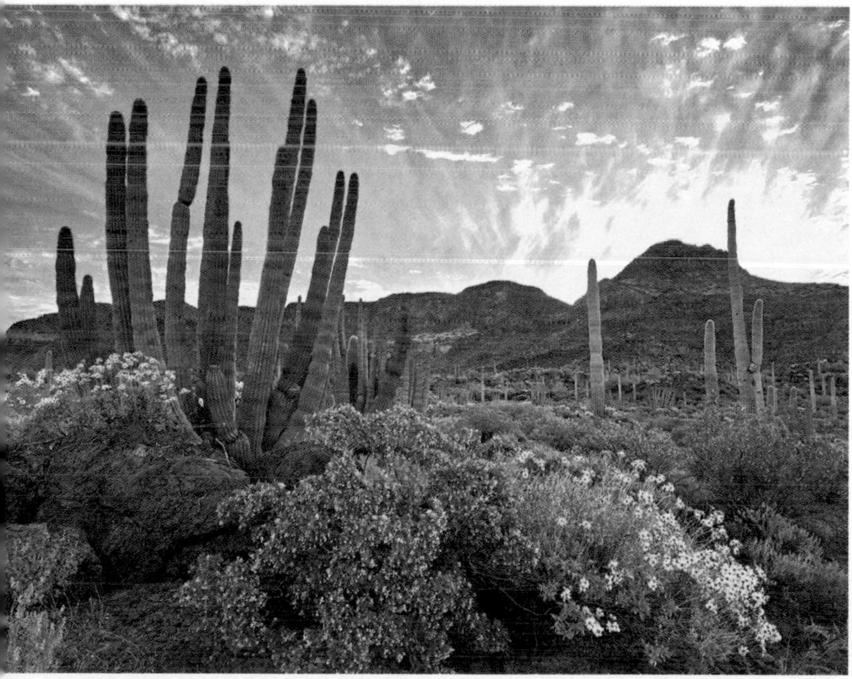

The distinctive organ pipe cactus, with its many branching spiny trunks, grows only in this rugged area of southern Arizona.

Amerind Foundation Museum **16**
Bisbee **15**
Buenos Aires National Wildlife Refuge **2**
Cave Creek Canyon **21**
Chirihuaca National Monument **20**
Cochise Stronghold **17**
Coronado National Memorial **11**
Douglas **22**
Fort Bowie National Historic Site **19**
Fort Huachuca Museum **9**
Kartchner Caverns State Park **13**
Las Cienegas National Conservation Area **8**
Nogales **5**
Organ Pipe Cactus National Monument **1**
Patagonia Lake State Park **6**
Patagonia-Sonoitas Creek Preserve **7**
Ramsey Canyon **10**
San Pedro Riparian National Conservation Area **12**
Slaughter Ranch **23**
Tombstone **14**
Tubac **3**
Tumacácori **4**
Willcox **18**

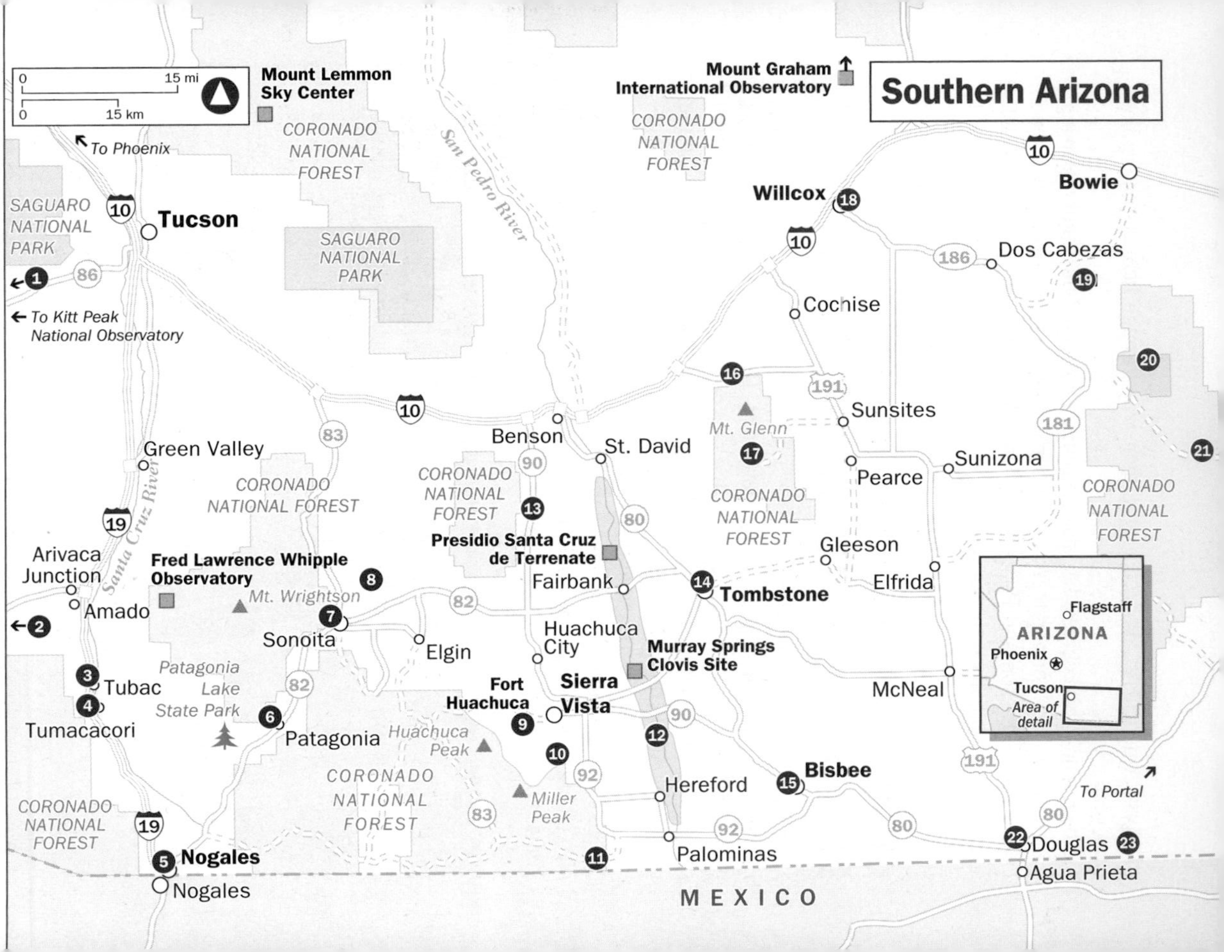

Indian Reservation. The only motels in the area are in the small town of Ajo, a former company town built to house copper-mine workers. Its downtown plaza, with tall palm trees, covered walkways, and arches, has the look and feel of a Mexican town square with a little Arabic and midcentury modernist architecture thrown in for good measure. Be sure to gas up your car before leaving Ajo if you're heading to Organ Pipe.

Essentials

ARRIVING From Tucson, take Ariz. 86 west to Why and turn south on Ariz. 85. From Yuma, take I-8 east to Gila Bend and go south on Ariz. 85.

FEES The park entry fee is $25 per car.

VISITOR INFORMATION Contact **Organ Pipe Cactus National Monument** (www.nps.gov/orpi; ✆ **520/387-6849**). The Kris Eggle Visitor Center is open daily 8am to 5pm, although the park itself is open 24 hours a day. The visitor center is closed Thanksgiving and Christmas.

Exploring the Monument

Two well-graded gravel roads lead through different sections of this large national monument, and many visitors are content to just drive through this unusual landscape. For the best scenery in the park, follow **Ajo Mountain Drive,** a 21-mile one-way loop that meanders through the rugged foothills of the Ajo Mountains. Along this route, you can get out and hike the Arch Canyon, Estes Canyon, or Bull Pasture trails. Alternatively, if you are short on time, take **Puerto Blanco Drive,** a 5-mile route leading to the Pinkley Peak picnic area. Guides available at the park's visitor center explain natural features of the landscape along both drives. In winter, there are guided van tours of Ajo Mountain Drive, as well as guided hikes; call the visitor center a week in advance to reserve a seat on the van tour ($5). Be sure to check with the national monument to ask about road conditions and to leave information about where you'll be before planning any hikes. Carry plenty of water and food, no matter what time of year.

Where to Stay & Eat Near Organ Pipe Cactus NM

There are two campgrounds within the park. Campsites are $12 in primitive **Alamo Campground** and $20 in the more developed **Twin Peaks Campground.** The nearest lodgings are in Ajo, with several old and very basic motels as well as a B&B (see below). There's a good Mexican restaurant, **Marcela's,** on the main drag, along with a coffee shop in the historic plaza. There are also a couple of chain restaurants. There's nowhere to eat between Ajo and Phoenix, apart from a grocery store and hit-or-miss cafe in Sells, so you'll want to find someplace in town. There are also plenty of budget chain motels and restaurants in the town of Gila Bend, 70 miles north of the monument.

Guest House Inn Bed & Breakfast ★ Built in 1925 as a guesthouse for mining executives, this B&B has attractive gardens in the front yard, a mesquite thicket off to one side, and a modern southwestern feel to its interior decor. Guest rooms are simply furnished with reproduction antique and southwestern furnishings. There are sunrooms on both the north and the south sides of the house.

700 Guest House Rd., Ajo. www.guesthouseinn.biz. © **520/387-6133.** 4 units. $89 double. Rates include full breakfast. **Amenities:** Free Wi-Fi.

En Route to Tucson

If you're on your way from Organ Pipe Cactus National Monument to Tucson via Ariz. 86, you will pass through the large Tohono O'odham Indian Reservation. To learn more about this tribe, stop at the **Tohono O'odham Nation Cultural Center & Museum,** Fresnal Canyon Rd., Topawa (www.tonation-nsn.gov/cultural-center-museum; © **520/383-0200**), south of the community of Sells. The museum is in a beautiful modern building with attractive gardens, and, although displays are designed primarily for tribal members, there is also plenty to interest anyone not from the reservation. A gift shop sells baskets, native wild foods, and other interesting gift items. The museum is open Monday through Saturday from 10am to 4pm; admission is free. To find it, drive 9 miles south from Sells on Indian Rte. 19; at the water tower, turn left onto Fresnal Canyon Rd. and drive ¼ mile.

Farther east on Ariz. 86, you can shop for Tohono O'odham baskets and silver jewelry at **Coyote Store,** Ariz. 86, Milepost 140 (© **520/383-5555**). It's east of the turnoff for **Kitt Peak National Observatory** (p. 437), a must-visit spot along this route.

TUBAC ★★ & BUENOS AIRES NATIONAL WILDLIFE REFUGE ★

45 miles S of Tucson; 21 miles N of Nogales; 84 miles W of Sierra Vista

In the fertile valley of the Santa Cruz River 45 miles south of Tucson, Tubac is one of Arizona's largest arts communities and home to a large retirement community. The town's old buildings house more than 80 shops selling fine arts, crafts, unusual gifts, and lots of southwestern souvenirs, making Tubac one of southern Arizona's most popular destinations. ***Note:*** Many of the local artists leave town during the summer, and shops tend to close on summer weekdays. From October to May, however, shops are open daily.

In 1691, Father Eusebio Francisco Kino established Tumacácori as one of the first Spanish missions in what would eventually become Arizona. At that time, Tubac was a Tohono O'odham village, but by the 1730s, the Spanish had begun settling in the region, which they called Pimeria Alta. After a Pima uprising in 1751, Spanish forces were sent into the area to protect the settlers, and in 1752 Tubac became a presidio (fort).

A Notorious Ranch

If you're on the way to Tubac from Tucson on a Tuesday or Saturday morning between 8:30 and 11am, stop in at the **Historic Hacienda de Canoa** (5375 S. I-19 Frontage Rd., just south of the Green Valley Hospital) for a brief visit. Admission is free, and guided tours are offered during those hours. The hacienda, or ranch headquarters, was once the center of operations of a huge cattle ranch—and infamous for its days-long drinking parties, which the Belgian mystery writer Georges Simenon, who spent time here, chronicled in his novel *Bottom of the Bottle*.

While the European history of this area dates back more than 300 years, human habitation of the region dates far back into prehistory. Archaeologists have found evidence that people have lived along the Santa Cruz River for nearly 10,000 years. The Hohokam were here from about A.D. 300 until the decline of their agricultural civilization around 1500; when the Spanish arrived some 200 years later, they found the Hohokam's descendants, the Tohono O'odham (Desert People, once called the Papago) and, farther north, Akimel O'odham (River People, better known as the Pima) inhabiting this region.

Tubac's other claim to fame is that Juan Bautista de Anza III, the second commander of the presidio, set out from here in 1775 to find an overland route to California. De Anza led 240 settlers and more than 1,000 head of cattle on this grueling expedition; when they finally reached the coast of California, they founded the settlement of San Francisco. A year after de Anza's journey to the Pacific, the garrison was moved from Tubac to Tucson, and, with no protection from marauding Apaches, Tubac's settlers soon moved away. Soldiers were stationed here again in 1787, but lack of funds closed down the presidio in 1821 when Mexican independence brought Tubac under a new flag. It was not until this region became U.S. territory that settlers returned. By 1860, Tubac was briefly the largest town in Arizona. To learn about the area's history, visit Tubac Presidio State Historic Park (p. 432) and Tumacácori National Historical Park (p. 433).

Essentials

ARRIVING The Santa Cruz Valley towns of Amado, Tubac, and Tumacácori are all due south of Tucson on I-19.

SPECIAL EVENTS Each year in February, artists from all over the country participate in the **Tubac Festival of the Arts.** On the third weekend in October, the **Anza Day Celebration** commemorates Capt. Juan Bautista de Anza's 1775 westward trek that led to the founding of San Francisco.

VISITOR INFORMATION For information on Tubac and Tumacácori, contact the **Tubac Chamber of Commerce,** 2 Tubac Rd. (www.tubacaz.com; ✆ **520/398-2704**).

Exploring Tubac

Tubac Center of the Arts ★ ARTS CENTER Tubac is an arts community, and this Spanish colonial building serves as its center for cultural activities. Throughout the season, the center features workshops, traveling exhibitions, juried shows, an annual crafts show, and theater and music performances. The quality of the art at these shows is generally better than what's found in most of the surrounding stores. There is also a good little gift shop here.

9 Plaza Rd. www.tubacarts.org. ✆ **520/398-2371.** Admission by donation. Mon–Sat 10am–4:30pm; Sun 1–4:30pm. Closed major holidays and Sun May–Sept.

Tubac Presidio State Historic Park ★ HISTORIC SITE Although little remains of the old presidio (fort) other than buried foundation walls, this small park does a good job of presenting the region's Spanish colonial history. Park exhibits focus on the Spanish soldiers, Native Americans, religion, and contemporary Hispanic culture in southern Arizona. Also on the grounds is the old Tubac School, built in 1885 and the oldest schoolhouse in the state. Living-history presentations are staged October through March on the first and third Fridays of the month between noon and 3:30pm. Among the characters you'll meet are Spanish soldiers, settlers, and friars.

1 Burruel St. www.azstateparks.com/tubac. ✆ **520/398-2252.** $5 adults, $2 children 7–13, free for kids 6 and under. Daily 9am–5pm. Closed Christmas.

The historic Tubac school is Arizona's oldest schoolhouse.

The 200-year-old mission church at Tumacácori, an evocative ruin of one of Arizona's earliest Hispanic settlements.

Tumacácori National Historical Park ★ HISTORIC SITE Founded in 1691 by Jesuit missionary and explorer Father Eusebio Francisco Kino, San José de Tumacácori mission was one of the first Anglo settlements in what is today Arizona. Father Kino's mission was to convert the Pima Indians, and for the first 60 years, the mission was successful. However, in 1751, during the Pima Revolt, the mission was destroyed. For the next 70 years, this mission struggled to survive; in the 1820s an adobe mission church was constructed. Today, the mission ruins are a silent and haunting reminder of the role Spanish missionaries played in settling the Southwest. Much of the old adobe church still stands, and its Spanish architectural influences can readily be seen. A small museum contains exhibits on mission life and the history of the region. On weekends between January and April, Native American and Mexican craftspeople give demonstrations of indigenous crafts. January through March, there are also tours to the nearby mission ruins of Calabazas and Guevavi. These tours are by reservation and cost $25 per person. **La Fiesta de Tumacácori,** a celebration of Indian, Hispanic, and Anglo cultures, is held the first weekend of December.

1891 E. Frontage Rd. (3 mi S of Tubac, at exit 29 off I-19). www.nps.gov/tuma. ✆ **520/398-2341.** $5 adults, free for kids 15 and under. Daily 9am–5pm. Closed Thanksgiving and Christmas.

TUBAC SHOPPING

While tourist brochures tout Tubac as an artists' community, the town is more of a southwestern souvenir mecca. There are a few genuine art galleries here, but you have to look hard amid the tourist shops to find the real gems.

For some of the area's better fine art, visit the **Karin Newby Gallery,** 15 Tubac Rd. (www.karinnewbygallery.com; ✆ **888/398-9662** or 520/398-9662), which also has a large sculpture garden. For traditional Western art, some by members of the prestigious Cowboy Artists of America, visit **Big Horn Galleries,** La Entrada de Tubac, Bldg. K (www.bighorngalleries.com; ✆ **520/398-9209**).

One of the more genuine Tubac-area institutions is the **Santa Cruz Chili & Spice Company** ★, 1868 E. Frontage Rd. (www.santacruzchili.com; ✆ **520/398-2591**) near Tumacácori National Historical Park. At this combination store and packing plant, you'll find all things hot (chiles, hot sauces, salsas) arranged on the shelves, including an amazing assortment of familiar and obscure spices. In back, you can see various herbs being prepared and packaged. The shop is open Monday through Friday from 8am to 5pm and Saturday from 10am to 5pm (until 3pm in summer).

Exploring Buenos Aires National Wildlife Refuge ★

If you're a bird-watcher, you'll definitely want to make the trip to **Buenos Aires National Wildlife Refuge** (www.fws.gov/refuge/Buenos_Aires; ✆ **520/823-4251**), about 28 miles northwest of Tubac. To get here, head north from Tubac on I-19 to Arivaca Junction, then drive west on a winding two-lane road. The refuge begins just outside the small community of Arivaca. Grab a cup of fresh-roasted coffee on the way at the **Gadsden Coffee Company** (16850 W Arivaca Rd.; ✆ **520/398-3251**).

Your first stop should be **Arivaca Cienega,** a quarter of a mile east of Arivaca. *Cienega* is Spanish for "marsh," and that is exactly what you'll find here. A boardwalk leads across this marsh, which is fed by seven springs that provide year-round water and consequently attract a wide variety of bird life. Vermilion flycatchers are quite common here, and this is one of the few places

Going Nuts in Sahuarita

As you drive south from Tucson to Tubac, you pass through the town of Sahuarita, home to one of the largest pecan farms in the country. More than 6,000 acres surrounding Sahuarita are planted with pecan trees. At the **Pecan Store,** 1625 E. Sahuarita Rd., Sahuarita (www.pecanstore.com; ✆ **800/327-3226** or 520/791-2062), you can go "nuts" stocking up on everything from fresh pecans to chocolate toffee pecans to mesquite-spiced pecans. The store is open Monday through Saturday 9am to 5pm, Sunday 10am to 4pm (daily 10am–4pm in summer). Rather drive through those pecan groves than take the interstate? Drive south on South Sixth Ave. in Tucson, which becomes the Old Nogales Highway and joins I-19 in Green Valley.

The Ruby Road

If you enjoy scenic drives and don't mind gravel roads with deep potholes and thrilling cliffs, don't pass up the opportunity to drive the **Ruby Road** from Arivaca through Coronado National Forest to Peña Blanca Lake and Nogales. This road winds its way through the mountains just north of the Mexican border, passing Arivaca Lake before reaching picturesque Peña Blanca Lake, where the pavement resumes. Along the way, you'll pass the privately owned ghost town of **Ruby** (http://rubyaz.com; ✆ **520/744-4471**), which is open to the public Thursday through Sunday from 9am to dusk (admission $12). Call first to make sure the caretaker is available.

in the United States where you can see a gray hawk. Other good birding spots within the refuge include **Arivaca Creek,** 2 miles west of Arivaca, and **Aguirre Lake,** a seasonal lake a half-mile north of the refuge headquarters, which is off Ariz. 286 north of Sasabe. The refuge is also home to pronghorn antelopes, javelinas, coatimundis, white-tailed deer, mule deer, and coyotes.

The headquarters' **visitor center** is a good place to spot one of the refuge's rarest birds, the masked bobwhite quail. These quail disappeared from Arizona in the late 19th century, but have been reintroduced in the refuge. Other birds you might spot outside the visitor center include Bendire's thrashers, Chihuahuan ravens, canyon towhees, and green-tailed towhees. The visitor center is open daily 9am to 4pm (closed New Year's Day, Thanksgiving, Christmas, and summer weekends).

From November through April, guided birding walks are offered Saturday mornings at 8am, and 5-mile guided hikes in Brown Canyon are offered on the second and fourth Saturdays of the month (reservations required). There is primitive **camping** at 83 designated spots along rough gravel roads. Look for the brown campsite signs along the road, and bring your own water.

These roads also offer good mountain biking and horseback riding. If you're looking for a strenuous hike, try the 5-mile round-trip **Mustang Trail,** which climbs from Arivaca Creek into the surrounding dry hills; the trail head is 2 miles west of Arivaca.

Outdoor Activities

Linking Tubac with Tumacácori, the 8-mile **de Anza Trail** passes through forests and grasslands and follows the Santa Cruz River for much of its route. It's part of the **Juan Bautista de Anza National Historic Trail,** which stretches from Nogales to San Francisco, commemorating the overland journey of the Spanish captain who led a small band of colonists overland to California in 1775 and 1776, founding what is now the city of San Francisco. Today, birdwatching is the most popular activity along the trail. History buffs will also get to see an excavation of part of the Spanish colonial settlement of Tubac. The most convenient trailhead is beside Tubac Presidio State Historic Park (p. 432).

If golf is more your speed, you can play a round at the **Tubac Golf Resort & Spa** (www.tubacgolfresort.com; ✆ **520/398-2021**), just north of Tubac off

East Frontage Rd. Greens fees range from $99 to $109 in winter ($79–$89 after noon) but are a bargain $49 in summer ($39 after noon).

Where to Stay

IN AMADO

Amado Territory Inn ★ This modern inn, just off I-19 at the crossroads of Amado, is built in the territorial style and has a bit of the feel of an old Arizona ranch house. Guest rooms are outfitted in a mix of Mexican rustic furnishings and reproduction antiques, much like homes would have been furnished in Arizona more than 100 years ago. Rooms on the second floor feature balconies with views across the farm fields of the Santa Cruz Valley, while those on the ground floor have patios.

3001 E. Frontage Rd. www.amadoterritoryinn.com. ✆ **888/398-8684** or 520/398-8684. 14 units. Nov–June $130–$165 double, $250 suite; July–Oct $105–$130 double, $220 suite. Rates include full breakfast. Children 13 and over welcome. Pets accepted. **Amenities:** Restaurant; spa services; free Wi-Fi.

IN TUBAC

Freedom on the Go B&B ★ If waking up to the neighing of horses and the bleating of alpacas is appealing, you'll love this small ranch a few minutes outside Tubac. If you're a birder, that's one more reason to like the place, which swarms with winged creatures. Breakfasts are delicious, and vegetarian options are available.

35 Camino Cocinero Rd. www.bedandbreakfast.com/az-tubac-freedomonthegoranch.html. ✆ **520/444-6481.** 2 units. $80 single; $105 double. Full breakfast included. **Amenities:** Free Wi-Fi.

Tubac Golf Resort & Spa ★★ This economical golf resort is built on the Otero Ranch, which dates back to 1789 and is the oldest Spanish land-grant ranch in the Southwest. Today, with its green fairways, the resort is a lush oasis amid the dry hills of the Santa Cruz Valley and is luxurious enough to compete with many of Tucson's resorts. It has more a classic southwestern ambience than most of the Tucson golf resorts, however, and because it is fairly small, it has a low-key feel that I like. Red-tile roofs and brick archways throughout the resort conjure its Spanish heritage, while spacious modern guest rooms are set amid expansive lawns. Casitas have patios, beamed ceilings, and beehive fireplaces; newer rooms are worth requesting.

1 Otero Rd. (P.O. Box 1297). www.tubacgolfresort.com. ✆ **520/398-2211.** 98 units. $134–$319 double; $179–$339 suite. Children 12 and under stay free in parent's room. Pets accepted ($25 daily fee; no more than two pets). **Amenities:** 2 restaurants; lounge; babysitting; bikes; concierge; 27-hole golf course; exercise room; 2 Jacuzzis; outdoor pool; room service; full-service spa; tennis court; free Wi-Fi.

Where to Eat in Tubac & Tumacácori

In addition to the restaurants mentioned on p. 438, **Stables,** at the Tubac Golf Resort & Spa (above), serves good steaks. If you need a latte or a muffin while you're in town, stop by the **Tubac Deli & Coffee Co.,** 6 Plaza Rd. (www.tubacdeli.com; ✆ **520/398-3330**).

STARRY, STARRY nights

Southern Arizona's clear skies and the absence of lights in the surrounding desert make the night sky here as brilliant as anywhere on earth. This fact has not gone unnoticed by the world's astronomers, and consequently, southern Arizona has come to be known as the Astronomy Capital of the World.

Many observatories are open to the public, but you'll need to make tour reservations well in advance. In addition to the ones listed below, the **Flandrau: The UA Science Center** (p. 370) in Tucson offers public viewings. In Flagstaff, there are public viewing programs at the **Lowell Observatory** (p. 261).

In the Quinlan Mountains atop 6,875-foot Kitt Peak, **Kitt Peak National Observatory ★** (www.noao.edu/kpno; ✆ **520/318-8726**) is the largest and most famous astronomical observatory in the region, with the world's largest collection of optical telescopes. This is the region's only major observatory to offer public nighttime viewing. Day visitors can stop in at the visitor center (daily 9am–3:45pm), explore a museum, and take a guided tour (10am, 11:30am, and 1:30pm). Admission to the visitor center is free; single tours are $11 adults ($13 for all three tours) and $7 for ages 7 to 12 ($8 for all three tours). The observatory is 56 miles southwest of Tucson off Ariz. 86 (allow 90 min. for the drive). Nighttime stargazing (reservations required, call 2–4 weeks in advance) costs $55 for adults ($50 if reserved online); $52 for students and seniors ($47 if reserved online). The visitor center is closed New Year's Day, Thanksgiving, and Christmas.

Atop 8,550-foot Mount Hopkins, the **Fred Lawrence Whipple Observatory** (www.cfa.harvard.edu/facilities/flwo; ✆ **520/670-5707**) is the largest observatory operated by the Smithsonian Astrophysical Observatory. Six-hour tours are offered mid-March through November on Monday, Wednesday, and Friday ($10 adults, $5 kids 6 to 12; no children 5 or under). Reservations are required and should be made 4 to 6 weeks in advance. No food is available here, so bring a picnic lunch. The observatory's visitor center (Monday–Friday 8:30am–4:30pm; closed federal holidays) is reached by taking I-19 south from Tucson to exit 56; turn right on E. Frontage Rd., drive south 3 miles, turn left on Elephant Head Rd., and then turn right on Mount Hopkins Rd.

The **Mount Graham International Observatory,** near the town of Safford (34 miles north of I-10 on U.S. 191), offers 7-hour tours that include lunch but do not include viewing through the observatory's telescopes. Tours are arranged through **Eastern Arizona College's Discovery Park Campus,** 1651 W. Discovery Park Blvd., Safford (www.eac.edu/discoverypark; ✆ **928/428-6260**). The tours operate from May through October and cost $40 (reservations are required).

Affiliated with the University of Arizona, the **Mount Lemmon Sky Center** (http://skycenter.arizona.edu; ✆ **520/626-8122**), 27 miles northeast of Tucson near the summit of Mount Lemmon, has a 24-inch telescope; celestial objects you'll see during night-sky viewing programs include binary stars, star clusters, nebulae, galaxies, planets, and the moon. These SkyNights programs cost $65 for adults ($40 for children), last 5 hours, and include a light dinner and astronomy lecture. Allow 90 minutes to drive to the center from midtown Tucson. Bring warm clothes—mountain nights can be very cold, even when it's warm in the desert below.

Elvira's Restaurant ★★ MEXICAN This Mexican restaurant, its ceiling decorated with hundreds of unusual glass "teardrop" ornaments, was originally south of the border in Nogales, Mexico, where it was a popular dinner destination for gringos. Because safety concerns and passport requirements have been keeping Americans from crossing the border into Mexico, Elvira's has moved north to Tubac and Tucson, making it much easier to enjoy the restaurant's complex and flavorful *mole* dishes and the unusual flank-steak *molcajete,* served in a stone dish traditionally used for grinding guacamole. Try the Frida Kahlo, a chile stuffed with squash blossoms and corn. The margaritas here are notoriously strong.

2221 E. Frontage Rd., Ste. A101–102. www.elvirasrestaurant.com. ✆ **520/398-9421.** Reservations recommended. Main courses $12–$26. Tues–Thurs 11am–9pm; Fri–Sat 11am–10pm; Sun 11am–3pm.

Tubac Jack's ★ MEXICAN Though not the must-stop that Elvira's is, Tubac Jack's, which got its start in 1956, does decent seafood and makes a good plate of carnitas, or mesquite-smoked pork, that also turns up in the signature green chile stew and pulled-pork sandwich.

7 Plaza Rd. http://tubacjacks.com. ✆ **520/398-3161.** Main dishes $13–$19. Thurs–Fri and Sun 11am–9pm, Sat 11am–10pm.

Wisdom's Café ★ MEXICAN Located between Tubac and Tumacácori (look for the giant chicken statues out front), this roadside diner is a Santa Cruz Valley institution, in business since 1944. With a cement floor and walls hung with old cowboy stuff, it feels a bit like a cross between a cave and an old barn. The menu is short but includes some twists on standard Mexican fare, including tostadas, tacos, and enchiladas made with turkey. Don't eat too much, though, or you won't have room for this restaurant's main draw—huge fruit burritos that are basically Mexican fruit pies. Wisdom's recently opened a second location in Tubac (La Entrada Shopping Plaza, 4 Plaza Rd.; ✆ **520/216-7664**) in case a hunger pang should hit.

1931 E. Frontage Rd., Tumacácori. www.wisdomscafe.com. ✆ **520/398-2397.** Main courses $6–$16. Mon–Sat 11am–3pm and 5–8pm.

NOGALES

63 miles S of Tucson; 175 miles S of Phoenix; 65 miles W of Sierra Vista

Situated on the Mexican border, the twin towns of Nogales, Arizona, and Nogales, Sonora, Mexico (known jointly as Ambos Nogales), form a bustling border community. All day long, U.S. citizens cross into Mexico to shop for bargains on Mexican handicrafts, pharmaceuticals, tequila, and Kahlúa, while Mexican citizens cross into the United States to buy consumer goods and appliances.

Essentials

ARRIVING Nogales is the last town on I-19 before the Mexican border. Ariz. 82 leads northeast from town toward Sonoita and Sierra Vista.

VISITOR INFORMATION Contact the **Nogales Chamber of Commerce,** 123 W. Kino Park Way (www.thenogaleschamber.org; ✆ **520/287-3685**).

Exploring North & South of the Border

Most people who visit Nogales, Arizona, are here to cross the border to Nogales, Mexico. The favorable exchange rate makes shopping in Mexico very popular with Americans, although many of the items for sale in Mexico can sometimes be found at lower prices in Tucson. Many people now cross the border specifically to purchase prescription drugs, and pharmacies line the streets near the border crossing.

Nogales, Mexico, is a typical border town filled with tiny shops selling crafts and souvenirs. Some of the better deals are on wool rugs, which cost a fraction of what a Navajo rug costs but are not nearly as well made. Pottery is another popular buy, as is multicolored glassware. Dozens of restaurants serve simple Mexican food and cheap margaritas. For a real border experience, try **La Roca** (Calle Ochoa 52–105, www.larocarestaurant.com; ✆ **520/313-6313**), a cavernous restaurant carved into a cliff face. The food is exceptional, and it's an easy walk to the border crossing. La Roca is open 7 days a week, often until midnight.

Plenty of other shops and restaurants in Nogales, Mexico, are within walking distance of the border, so unless you plan to continue farther into Mexico, it's not a good idea to take your car. There are numerous pay parking lots and garages on the U.S. side of the border where your vehicle will be secure for the day. If you should take your car into Mexico, be sure to get Mexican auto insurance beforehand—your U.S. auto insurance will not be valid. If you are a member of the American Automobile Association, you can get Mexican auto insurance through the AAA office in Tucson. You can also get insurance through **Sanborn's** (www.sanbornsinsurance.com; ✆ **800/222-0158**).

Most businesses in Nogales, Mexico, accept U.S. dollars. You may bring back $800 worth of merchandise duty-free, including 1 liter of liquor (if you are 21 or older). You now need either a passport, a passport card, a Trusted Traveler Card, or some other U.S. government–accepted identification document to cross the border into Mexico and return to the U.S. Be sure to verify that you have appropriate documentation before entering Mexico; visit www.travel.state.gov for more info.

These Boots Were Made for Ridin'

Cowboys and cowgirls in search of the ultimate pair of boots should be sure to schedule a visit to Nogales's **Paul Bond Boot Company,** 915 W. Paul Bond Dr. (www.paulbondboots.com; ✆ **520/281-0512**), where you can shop for cowboy boots that are both functional and works of art. These boots can sell for $1,200 or more, although you can also get boots for as little as $550. This boot maker has been in business in Nogales since the 1950s. Take exit 4 (Mariposa Rd.) off I-19 and drive west. Look for the company's trademark, a statue of a white horse, atop a low hill.

Note: Nogales has had a high crime rate in recent years, but tourists have not been targeted. Still, it's advisable to check the current situation before crossing the border.

Where to Stay & Eat in Nogales

If you're planning to spend time in Nogales, you can find plenty of places to stay across the border in Mexico for a fraction of the cost of American hotels—and they're just as good. A local favorite is the **Hotel Fray Marcos de Niza** (Calle Campillo 91, www.hotelfraymarcos.com; ✆ **866/947-5969**), an easy walk from the border, with a good restaurant and bar.

Best Western Sonora Inn & Suites ★ A no-frills but perfectly acceptable choice of lodging is the Nogales branch of the Best Western chain, which sits close to the Mariposa Road international crossing and is a favorite of business travelers, truckers, and Border Patrol agents. The road rumbles with truck traffic into the night, but once the crossing closes at 10pm the area is agreeably quiet.

750 W Shell Rd. www.bestwesternnogales.com. ✆ **520/375-6500.** $89–$109 double, $109–$129 suite. Rates include breakfast. Pets not accepted. **Amenities:** Outdoor pool; free Wi-Fi.

Hacienda Corona de Guevavi ★ Few lodging places anywhere in Arizona capture the character of the state better than this historic hilltop ranch house outside of Nogales. Originally the headquarters of the Guevavi Ranch, the sprawling home was once a favorite getaway for John Wayne, but it had been abandoned when Phil and Wendy Stover bought the hacienda and embarked on a major restoration. Today the inn, which is built around courtyards and quiet gardens, has five very tastefully decorated guest rooms, all but one of which reflect the inn's southwestern heritage. The one room that does not have a southwestern flavor has the feel of a room at an African safari lodge. There are also several casitas (guesthouses) available for families. Dinners and horseback riding can be arranged, and guests' horses can be boarded for $20 a day.

348 S. River Rd., Nogales. www.haciendacorona.com. ✆ **520/287-6503.** 8 units. $199–$239 double. Rates include full breakfast and evening hors d'oeuvres. No children 6 or under in main house (young children accepted in casitas). Pets accepted in casitas ($100 refundable deposit, plus $5 per night). **Amenities:** Concierge; outdoor pool; free Wi-Fi in common areas.

Zula's ★ GREEK/MEXICAN Nogales is a resolutely international city (it was originally named Isaacson, after two Jewish storekeepers who settled in the canyon in the 1870s). It should come as no surprise, then, that many of the city's old families are Lebanese, Syrian, German, French—and Greek, which brings us to Zula's, southern Arizona's favorite Greek-Mexican eatery, more formally and tongue-twistingly called Papachoris' Zulas Restaurant. You can get enchiladas, a hamburger and shake, a Greek salad, steak tampiqueña, chicken parmigiana, an omelet—just about anything, really, including refried beans, which one waggish server calls "Mexican caviar." It's a favorite hangout for locals, and for good reason.

982 N Grand Ave. ✆ **520/287-2892.** Main dishes $9–$19. Wed–Mon 7am–8pm.

PATAGONIA ★★ & SONOITA ★

Patagonia: 18 miles NW of Nogales; 60 miles SE of Tucson; 171 miles SE of Phoenix; 50 miles SW of Tombstone

A mild climate, a few good restaurants, bed-and-breakfast inns, and a handful of wineries have turned the small communities of Patagonia and Sonoita into a favorite weekend getaway for Tucsonans. Sonoita Creek, one of the only perennial streams in southern Arizona, attracts an amazing variety of bird life and, consequently, this area also attracts flocks of bird-watchers from all over the country.

Patagonia and Sonoita are only about 12 miles apart, but they have decidedly different characters. Patagonia, a historic mining and ranching town surrounded by the Patagonia Mountains, is a sleepy little hamlet with tree-shaded streets, quite a few old adobe buildings, and a big park in the middle of town. The town's main draw, especially for bird-watchers, is the Nature Conservancy preserve on the western edge of town. Sonoita, on the other hand, sits out on the windswept high plains; it's really a highway crossroads with a few surrounding housing developments, not a town as such. The landscape around Sonoita, however, is filled with expensive new homes on small ranches, and not far away are the vineyards of one of Arizona's main wine regions.

Essentials

ARRIVING Sonoita is at the junction of Ariz. 83 and Ariz. 82. Patagonia is 12 miles southwest of Sonoita on Ariz. 82.

VISITOR INFORMATION The **Patagonia Area Business Association Tourist Information Center,** 317 McKeown Ave. (www.patagoniaaz.com; ✆ **888/794-0060**) is open Monday through Saturday from 10am to 5pm and Sunday from 10am to 4pm.

Exploring the Patagonia-Sonoita Area

If the landscape here gives you a sense of déjà vu, that's probably because you've seen it in numerous movies and television shows. Over the years, this area has been a backdrop for such films as *Oklahoma!, Red River, A Star Is Born,* and *David and Bathsheba,* and such TV programs as *Little House on the Prairie* and *The Young Riders.* Harshaw Road, which begins just south of the main road through downtown, will take you to this beautiful grassland; the graded dirt road is passable in most weathers by ordinary passenger cars.

The **Patagonia–Sonoita Creek Preserve** (www.nature.org; ✆ **520/394-2400**), owned by the Nature Conservancy, protects 2 miles of Sonoita Creek riparian (riverside) habitat, which is important to migratory birds. More than 300 species of birds have been spotted at the preserve, which makes it a

The rarely seen elegant trogon is a frequent visitor to the Sonoita Creek State Natural Area, just one of many prime birding sites around here.

popular destination with birders from all over the country. Among the rare birds that can be seen are 22 species of flycatchers, kingbirds, and phoebes, plus the Montezuma quail. A forest of cottonwood trees, some more than 100 feet tall, lines the creek. At one time, such forests grew along all the rivers in the region; today, this is one of southern Arizona's best remaining examples of a cottonwood-willow riparian forest. The sanctuary is just outside Patagonia on a dirt road that parallels Ariz. 82 (turn west on Fourth Avenue, then south on Pennsylvania Street, drive through the creek, and continue about 1 mile). From April to September, hours are Wednesday through Sunday 6:30am to 4pm; from October to March, it's open Wednesday through Sunday 7:30am to 4pm. Admission is $6 ($3 for Nature Conservancy members); a $10 pass is available admitting you to both this preserve and the Ramsey Canyon Preserve (p. 449). Naturalist-guided walks through the preserve are sometimes offered; reservations are not required.

On your way to or from the Nature Conservancy Preserve trails, be sure to drop by the **Paton Center,** also owned by the Nature Conservancy. Numerous hummingbird feeders and a variety of other feeders attract an amazing range of birds to the yard, making this a favorite stop of avid birders. The center is at 477 Pennsylvania Rd., after you cross the creek.

Another required birders' stop in the area is at the **Patagonia Roadside Rest Area,** 4¼ miles south of Patagonia on Ariz. 82. This pull-off is a good place to look for rose-throated becards, varied buntings, and zone-tailed hawks.

Birdwatchers will also want to visit **Las Cienegas National Conservation Area** (www.blm.gov/national-conservation-lands/arizona/las-cienegas; ✆ **520/258-7200**), a 45,000-acre preserve with grasslands, wetlands, and oak forests. This is a good place to look for the rarely seen gray hawk. Access is off the east side of Ariz. 83, about 7 miles north of Sonoita.

Patagonia Lake State Park (https://azstateparks.com/patagonia-lake; ✆ **520/287-6965**), about 7 miles southwest of Patagonia off Ariz. 82, is a popular boating and fishing lake formed by the damming of Sonoita Creek. The lake is 2½ miles long and stocked in winter with rainbow trout. Other times of the year, people fish for bass, crappie, bluegill, and catfish. Park facilities include a picnic ground, campground, and swimming beach, and you can rent boats ranging from pontoon boats to canoes and kayaks. The entrance fee is $15–$20 per vehicle, which includes the adjacent **Sonoita Creek State Natural Area** (✆ **520/287-6965**), a 5,000-acre preserve along the banks of Sonoita Creek. This natural area is also known as an excellent bird-watching site, and guided birding walks are offered on a regular basis. Elegant trogons, among the most beautiful of southern Arizona's rare birds, are often spotted here. Hike-in campsites are $12; reservations can be made at the Patagonia Lake State Park website above.

Navajo Rugs

In the market for a Navajo rug? Get in touch with Steve Getzwiller at **Nizhoni Ranch Gallery** (www.navajorug.com; ✆ **520/455-5020**), located off Pinto Trail, on the south end of Sonoita. Here you'll find one of Arizona's best selections of contemporary and old Navajo rugs.

Outdoor Activities

If you'd like to have a local birding guide take you out and help you identify the area's many species of flycatchers, contact Matt Brown at the **Patagonia Birding & Butterfly Co.** (www.lifebirds.com; ✆ **520/604-6300**). The base rate is $25 an hour, with another $5 an hour for each additional person.

To book a trail ride through the area's grasslands, contact **Arizona Horseback Experience** (www.horsebackexperience.com; ✆ **520/455-5696**). A 3-hour ride is $105, and a wine-tasting ride to a local winery is $160.

Patagonia Shopping

Mesquite Grove Gallery, 371 McKeown Ave. (✆ **520/394-2356**) has a good selection of works by area artists. At **Global Arts Gallery & Lillian's Closet,** 315 McKeown Ave. (www.globalartsgallery.com; (✆ **520/394-0077**), you'll find a wide range of ethnic arts, fine art, jewelry, and women's clothing. Also be sure to visit **La Galeria Dia de los Muertos,** 266 Naugle Ave. (✆ **520/394-2035**).

HIGH PLAINS wine COUNTRY

Sonoita is little more than a crossroads with a few shops and restaurants, but surrounding the community are miles of rolling grasslands with a mix of luxury-home "ranchettes" and actual cattle ranches, all with spectacular big-sky views. Out on those high plains, more than just deer and antelope play. Oenophiles roam, as well. With a dozen wineries between Sonoita and Elgin, this is Arizona's biggest little wine country (there are also concentrations of wineries to the east near Willcox and in the Sedona area of central Arizona). Most of the wineries are located in or near the village of **Elgin,** 10 miles east of Sonoita.

Right in the middle of Sonoita, you'll find **Dos Cabezas WineWorks,** 3248 Ariz. 82 (www.doscabezaswinery.com; ✆ **520/841-1193**), with a tasting room open Thursday through Sunday from 10:30am to 4:30pm ($10–$13 tasting fee). Dos Cabezas also offers casitas ($130–$200) for overnight stays. Five miles south of Sonoita, **Lightning Ridge Cellars,** 2368 Ariz. 83 (www.lightningridgecellars.com; ✆ **520/455-5383**) makes several surprisingly good red wines, primarily from estate-grown grapes. The tasting room is open Friday through Sunday from 11am to 4pm, and the tasting fee is $11. Just west of Elgin, **Callaghan Vineyards ★**, 336 Elgin Rd. (www.callaghanvineyards.com; ✆ **520/455-5322**) is open for tastings Thursday through Sunday from 11am to 4pm ($10 tasting fee). This winery produces by far the best wines in the region and, arguably, the best wines in the state. Next door to Callaghan is **Flying Leap Vineyard,** 342 Elgin Rd. (www.flyingleapvineyards; ✆ **520/455-5499**), a small winery and distillery with a casual tasting room in the winery itself. Call for hours; Flying Leap also has tasting rooms in Willcox, Tucson, and Bisbee. Next door to this winery, **Kief-Joshua Vineyards,** 370 Elgin Rd. (www.kj-vineyards.com; ✆ **520/455-5582**) boasts the most elegant tasting room in the area. It's open daily from 11am to 5pm ($10 tasting fee).

If you have one too many sips while touring vineyards and aren't staying within walking distance, call Ken's Shuttle Service (✆ **520/604-6939**) for transportation.

This little cottage, associated with Grayce's Gift and Candle Shop, was created by Grayce Arnold, who assembled a collection of hundreds of Mexican skeleton figures used in Mexico's Dia de los Muertos (Day of the Dead) celebration. The gallery is usually open on weekends; call ahead on weekdays.

Where to Stay

IN PATAGONIA

Circle Z Ranch ★ In business since 1926, this is the oldest continuously operating guest ranch in Arizona. Over the years, it has served as a backdrop for numerous movies and TV shows, including *Gunsmoke* and John Wayne's *Red River.* The 6,500-acre ranch on the banks of Sonoita Creek is bordered by the Nature Conservancy's Patagonia–Sonoita Creek Sanctuary, Patagonia State Park, and the Coronado National Forest. More than 165 miles of nearby trails ensure that everyone gets in plenty of riding in a variety of terrain, from desert hills to grasslands to the riparian forest along the creek. The adobe cottages provide an authentic ranch feel that's appreciated by guests hoping to find a genuine bit of the Old West.

Ariz. 82 (btw. Nogales and Patagonia). www.circlez.com. © **888/854-2525** or 520/394-2525. 24 units. $1,992–$2,452 double per week, plus 15% service charge. Lower rates for kids 15 and under. Nightly rates sometimes available, with 3-night minimum. Rates include all meals and horseback riding. Closed early May–late Oct. **Amenities:** Dining room; outdoor pool; tennis court; Wi-Fi in common area.

Duquesne House Inn & Gardens ★ This historic adobe building 1 block off Patagonia's main street was built in 1898 as a boarding house for miners. Today the little building, with its shady front porch, is your best choice for overnight accommodations in Patagonia. Each of the three suites has its own entrance, sitting room, and bedroom, and is decorated in an eclectic southwestern style. The studio apartment has its own kitchenette. My favorite room has an ornate woodstove and claw-foot tub. At the back of the house, an enclosed porch overlooks the large garden.

357 Duquesne Ave. www.theduquesnehouse.com. © **520/394-2732.** 4 units. $140 double ($115 Tues–Wed). Rates include breakfast (no breakfast Tues–Wed). **Amenities:** Free Wi-Fi.

IN SONOITA

Xanadu Ranch GetAway ★ To "B" or not to "B," that is the question at Xanadu Ranch, which calls itself a hybrid B&B. What this means is that you can opt for a breakfast basket or not, your choice. You can also opt to bring your own horse with you if you wish, since this place is also a "horse motel." The ranch owners, Bernie and Karen Kauk, don't offer horseback riding, but they can put you in touch with people who do. Rooms are spacious and comfortable, and the setting, on a hill south of town, provides great views and awesome sunsets. Despite the name, the Bunkhouse is the nicest (and newest) room on the ranch. This makes a good base both for touring the wine country and bird-watching.

92 S. Los Encinos Rd. www.xanaduranchgetaway.com. © **520/455-0050.** 4 units. $105–$189 double (lower rates for longer stays, discounts for cash payment). Pets accepted ($25 per stay). **Amenities:** Free Wi-Fi.

Where to Eat

IN PATAGONIA

For good coffee and pastries, check out **Gathering Grounds,** 319 McKeown Ave. (© **520/394-2009**), which also serves ice cream and has a deli.

Velvet Elvis Pizza Company ★ ITALIAN This casual hangout sums up the unusual character of Patagonia's residents. Faux-finished walls ooze artiness, while paeans to pop culture include shrines to both the Virgin Mary and Elvis. The menu features a variety of pizzas heaped with veggies, cheeses, and meats; if you plan a day in advance, you can call in an order for the Inca pizza (made with a quinoa-flour crust). Add an organic salad and accompany it with some fresh juice, microbrew, espresso, or wine.

292 Naugle Ave. www.facebook.com/velvetelvispizza. ✆ **520/394-2102.** Reservations accepted for parties of 6 or more. Pizzas $12–$45; other dishes $7.50–$10. Wed 11:30am–8pm, Thurs–Sun 11:30am–8:30pm.

IN SONOITA

Canela ★★ SOUTHWESTERN At the crossroads of Sonoita, this little restaurant is the most upscale restaurant between Tucson and Bisbee; it's an absolute must if you are in the area for a wine-country getaway. The menu changes frequently to take advantage of what's fresh and seasonal, but may include sunchoke soup garnished with paprika and sunchoke chips; crispy sweetbreads with local spinach, black olives, cream, and grilled lemon; roasted Churro (heirloom) leg of lamb; or Arizona beef hanger steak with local cress and honey-thyme mashed sweet potatoes, and *chimichurri* sauce. The Sunday brunch is a great way to begin an afternoon of wine tasting at area wineries.

3252 Ariz. 82. www.canelabistro.com. ✆ **520/455-5873.** Reservations recommended. Main courses $17–$24. Thurs–Sat 3–9pm; Sun 10am–3pm. Closed July–Aug.

The Steak Out ★ STEAK This is ranch country, and this big barn of a place is where the ranchers and everyone else for miles around head when they want a good steak. A classic cowboy atmosphere prevails—there's even a mounted steer head just inside the front door. The restaurant's name and the scent of a mesquite fire should be all the hints you need about what to order—a grilled steak, preferably the exceedingly tender filet mignon. Wash it down with a beer, and you've got the perfect cowboy dinner.

3200 S. Sonoita Hwy. (jct. of Ariz. 82 and Ariz. 83). www.azsteakout.com. ✆ **520/455-5205.** Reservations recommended. Main courses $8–$36. Mon–Thurs 5–9pm; Fri 5–10pm; Sat 11am–10pm; Sun 11am–9pm.

The Vineyard Café ★ AMERICAN Owned by a local couple who worked in East Coast restaurants for years before returning home to raise grapes, the Vineyard Café offers a delicious but simple range of omelets, salads, Mexican dishes, and light fare. Dinner is offered on Friday and Saturday nights, with a changing menu and extensive wine list that are worth exploring.

3252 Highway 82. www.vineyardcafesonoita.com. ✆ **520/455-4779.** Reservations recommended for dinner. Main courses $8–$12. Wed 11am–3pm; Thurs 7:30am–3pm; Fri–Sat 7:30am–7:30pm; Sun 9am–2pm.

SIERRA VISTA & THE SAN PEDRO VALLEY ★

70 miles SE of Tucson; 189 miles SE of Phoenix; 33 miles SW of Tombstone; 33 miles W of Bisbee

At an elevation of 4,620 feet above sea level, Sierra Vista is blessed with the perfect climate—never too hot, never too cold. This fact more than anything else has contributed to Sierra Vista becoming one of the fastest-growing cities in Arizona. Although the city itself is a modern, sprawling community outside the gates of the U.S. Army's Fort Huachuca, it is wedged between the Huachuca Mountains and the valley of the San Pedro River. Consequently, Sierra Vista makes a good base for exploring the region's natural attractions—the San Pedro Riparian National Conservation Area, Coronado National Memorial, and the Nature Conservancy's Ramsey Canyon Preserve. No other area of the United States attracts more attention from birders, who come in hopes of spotting some of the 300 bird species that have been sighted in southeastern Arizona.

At the head of the valley, the town of **Benson,** about 35 miles north of Sierra Vista, has several attractions as well, including **Kartchner Caverns State Park,** the region's biggest attraction.

Essentials

ARRIVING Sierra Vista is at the junction of Ariz. 90 and Ariz. 92, about 35 miles south of I-10.

SPECIAL EVENTS In February, cowboy poets, singers, and musicians congregate at the **Cochise Cowboy Poetry & Music Gathering** (www.cowboypoets.com). Though tiny by comparison to its Tucson cousin, the **Huachuca Gem, Mineral, and Jewelry Show** (http://www.huachucamineralandgemclub.info/Gem_Show.html), held in mid-October, highlights the work of gemologists and jewelry makers from around the country.

VISITOR INFORMATION Contact the **Sierra Vista Convention & Visitors Bureau,** 3020 Tacoma St. (www.visitsierravista.com; ✆ **800/288-3861** or 520/417-6960).

Exploring the San Pedro Valley

Near Benson, the remarkable **Singing Wind Bookshop** (Singing Wind Rd.; ✆ **520/586-2425**), on a ranch down a dirt road north of town, has been in business more than 30 years. It started out with just a couple shelves of books; now the inventory is well into the thousands, with an emphasis on the Southwest, natural sciences, and children's literature. Take exit 304 from I-10, drive north 2¼ miles, and take a right (east) onto Singing Wind Rd. Drive to the end, opening and closing the gate. The store is open daily from 9am to 5pm.

Arizona Folklore Preserve ★ MUSIC VENUE Set beneath the shady cottonwoods and sycamores of Ramsey Canyon, the Arizona Folklore Preserve is the brainchild of Dolan Ellis, Arizona's official state balladeer, and his wife, Rose. Ellis was first appointed state balladeer back in 1966 and has been writing songs about Arizona for more than 45 years. He performs most weekends and often welcomes musical guests to the stage of this performance hall. Take Ariz. 92 south from Sierra Vista and turn right onto Ramsey Canyon Rd.

56 E. Folklore Trail, Sierra Vista. www.arizonafolklore.com. ✆ **520/378-6165.** $15 adults, $6 students 17 and under. Showtime Sat–Sun 2pm. Reservations recommended.

Coronado National Memorial ★ NATURE PRESERVE/HISTORIC SITE About 20 miles south of Sierra Vista, this 5,000-acre preserve is dedicated to Francisco Vásquez de Coronado, the first European to explore this region. In 1540, Coronado, leading more than 700 people, left Compostela, Mexico, in search of the fabled Seven Cities of Cíbola, said to be rich in gold and jewels. Sometime between 1540 and 1542, Coronado led his band of weary men and women up the valley of the San Pedro River, which this monument overlooks. At the visitor center, you can learn about Coronado's fruitless quest for riches and check out the wildlife observation area. A quarter-mile from the visitor center, a ¾-mile trail leads to 600-foot-long **Coronado Cave.** (You'll need to bring your own flashlight.) Drive up to 6,575-foot **Montezuma Pass,** in the center of the memorial, which provides far-reaching views of Sonora, Mexico, to the south, the San Pedro River to the east, and several mountain ranges and valleys to the west. Along the .8-mile round-trip **Coronado Peak Trail,** you'll also have good views of the valley and can read quotations from the journals of Coronado's followers. There are also some longer trails where you'll see few other hikers. From Ariz. 92, follow S. Coronado Memorial Dr. 5 miles south to the monument's visitor center.

A Holy Bird Sanctuary

In the community of St. David, 5 miles south of Benson on Ariz. 80, the **Holy Trinity Monastery** (www.holytrinitymonastery.org; ✆ **520/720-4642**), which is near the banks of the San Pedro River, has a 1.3-mile birding trail.

4101 E. Montezuma Canyon Rd., Hereford. www.nps.gov/coro. ✆ **520/366-5515.** Free admission. Visitor center daily 8am–4pm; memorial daily dawn–dusk. Closed Thanksgiving and Christmas.

Fort Huachuca Museum ★ HISTORIC SITE Fort Huachuca, an army base at the mouth of Huachuca Canyon just west of Sierra Vista, was established in 1877. The buildings of the old post have been declared a National Historic Landmark, and one is now a museum dedicated to the many forts that dotted the Southwest in the latter 19th century, as well as to the African American "buffalo soldiers" who served there. Exhibits include quotes by soldiers that give an idea of what it was like to serve back then. The associated **U.S. Army Intelligence Museum,** at Hungerford and Cristi streets, has displays on early code machines, surveillance drones, and other pieces of equipment formerly used for intelligence gathering.

At the Fort Huachuca U.S. Army base, 21201 Grierson Rd., Sierra Vista. ✆ **520/533-5736.** Admission by donation. Mon–Fri 9am–4pm. Closed all federal holidays.

Kartchner Caverns State Park ★★ NATURAL ATTRACTION These caverns are among the largest and most beautiful in the country, and because they are wet caverns, stalactites, stalagmites, soda straws, and other cave formations are still growing. Within the caverns are two huge rooms, each larger than a football field with ceilings more than 100 feet high. These two rooms can be visited on two separate tours. On the shorter Rotunda/Throne Room Tour, you'll see, in the Rotunda Room, thousands of delicate soda straws. The highlight, though, is the Throne Room, at the center of which is a 58-foot-tall column. The second, and longer, tour visits the Big Room and leads past many strange and rare cave formations. Within the park are several miles of aboveground hiking trails. A campground ($25 per night) provides a convenient place to stay in the area.

The caverns are popular and tours are limited; make a reservation in advance, especially if you want to visit on a weekend. However, it is sometimes possible to get same-day tickets.

Off Ariz. 90, 9 mi S of Benson. www.azstateparks.com. ✆ **520/586-2283** for reservations, 520/586-4100 for information. $7 per car (up to 4 adults). Tours $23 adults, $13 children 7–13, kids under 7 not allowed on Big Room Tour. Park open 8am–6pm. Closed Christmas; no Big Room Tours mid-Apr–mid-Oct.

Ramsey Canyon Preserve ★★ NATURE PRESERVE Each year, beginning in late spring, a buzzing fills the air in Ramsey Canyon, but instead of reaching for the bug repellant, visitors reach for their binoculars. It's not the buzzing of bees or mosquitoes that fills the air, but rather the whirring wings of hummingbirds. Over the years, 14 species of these diminutive birds have been sighted here. Because Ramsey Creek, which flows through the canyon, is a year-round stream, it attracts a wide variety of wildlife, including bears, bobcats, and more than 170 bird species. A short nature trail leads through the canyon, and a second trail leads higher up the canyon. Keep an eye out for a rare species of frog, *Rana subaquavocalis,* that lives only here. April and May

Beautiful Ramsey Canyon attracts an amazing number of birds, especially hummingbirds.

are the busiest times; May and August are the best times to see hummingbirds. Between March and October, guided walks are offered Tuesday, Thursday, and Saturday at 9am.

27 Ramsey Canyon Rd., off Ariz. 92, 5 mi S of Sierra Vista. www.nature.org. ✆ **520/378-2785.** $6 adults ($3 for Nature Conservancy members); free 1st Sat of month. Mar–Oct Thurs–Mon 8am–5pm; Nov–Feb Thurs–Mon 9am–4pm. Closed New Year's Day, Thanksgiving, and Christmas.

San Pedro Riparian National Conservation Area ★ NATURE PRESERVE Over the past century, roughly 90% of Arizona's free-flowing year-round rivers and streams have disappeared due to human use of desert waters. These rivers and streams once supported riparian areas that provided water, food, and protection to myriad plants, animals, and even humans. You can get an idea of what such riparian areas were like by visiting this sprawling preserve 8 miles east of Sierra Vista. Fossil findings from this area indicate that people were living along this river as long as 13,000 years ago. At that time, this area was a swamp, not a desert. Today, the San Pedro River is all that remains of this ancient wetland, and, due to an earthquake a century ago, much of the San Pedro's water now flows underground. Don't expect a wide, rushing river when you visit the San Pedro; it would be called a creek anywhere but Arizona. Still, the water attracts wildlife, especially birds, and the conservation area is very popular with birders, who have a chance of spotting more than 350 species here.

Within the riparian area is the **Murray Springs Clovis Site** (just north of Ariz. 90 about 5 miles east of Sierra Vista), where 16 spear points and the remains of a 13,000-year-old mammoth kill were found in the 1960s. A short trail through the site has numerous interpretive signs about the finds.

For a glimpse of the region's Spanish history, visit the ruins of the **Presidio Santa Cruz de Terrenate** (about 20 miles northeast of Sierra Vista off Ariz. 82 near the ghost town of Fairbank), a military outpost established in 1775 or 1776 but never completed due to constant Apache attacks. Today only decaying

Ghost of the Past

Within the San Pedro conservation area, the former railroad town of **Fairbank** was founded in the 1880s to serve nearby silver-mining towns. It once had a population of nearly 15,000 people; today it's a ghost town. Drive Ariz. 82 to the bridge over the San Pedro River to find the remains of several buildings from Fairbank's heyday. Only one has been restored and opened to the public: the old Fairbank School, now the **Fairbank Schoolhouse Museum and Store** (✆ **520/457-3062**), open Friday through Sunday from 9:30am to 4:30pm; admission is free. From Fairbank, several miles of hiking trails lead along the San Pedro River. You can walk to two other ghost towns, **Millville** and **Charleston,** but there is very little to see at either of these old town sites. It is also possible to walk from Fairbank to the ruins of the Presidio Santa Cruz de Terrenate (see above).

adobe walls remain. Take Ariz. 82 east from U.S. 90; at milepost 60, drive north 1¾ miles on Ironhorse Ranch Road. It's a 1.3-mile hike to the site.

Where Ariz. 90 crosses the San Pedro, the **San Pedro House,** a 1930s ranch house, now serves as a visitor center and bookstore, open daily 9:30am to 4:30pm. Here you can pick up information on guided walks and hikes, bird walks, bird-banding sessions, and other events throughout the year. Outside the old ranch house, there's a huge old cottonwood tree.

Ariz. 90. www.blm.gov/visit/san-pedro. ✆ **520/258-7200.** Free admission. Parking areas sunrise–sunset.

Outdoor Activities

BIRDING

Bird-watching is big business in these parts, with birders' B&Bs, bird refuges, and even birding festivals. The **Southwest Wings Birding and Nature Festival** (www.swwings.org), one of southern Arizona's biggest annual birding events, is held each year in early August in Sierra Vista.

Serious birders may want to visit this area on a guided tour. Your best bet is **Mark Pretti Nature Tours** (www.markprettinaturetours.com; ✆ **520/803-6889**), run by the former resident naturalist at Ramsey Canyon Preserve. A half-day birding tour costs $120 and a full-day tour costs $200 to $220. Three-day ($625) and 7- to 8-day ($1,300–$1,400) trips are also offered. Melody Kehl of **Melody's Birding Adventures** (www.cbiz.nctopia.com/outdoor; ✆ **520/245-4085**) is another reliable local guide, her rates start at $250 for a 10-hour day. **High Lonesome Birdtours** (www.hilonesometours.com; ✆ **443/838-6589**), another local tour company, charges $2,450 per person for a 7-day birding trip.

To join a guided bird walk along the San Pedro River, a birding hike up Miller Canyon in the Huachuca Mountains, an owl-watching night hike, or a hummingbird banding session, contact the **Southeastern Arizona Bird Observatory** (www.sabo.org; ✆ **520/432-1388**). Most activities cost $10 to $20, although there are also half-day trips for $45, day trips for $70, and multiday trips for as much as $1,450. Workshops and tours are also offered.

South of Ramsey Canyon off Ariz. 92, a road through **Carr Canyon** climbs up to some of the higher elevations in the Huachuca Mountains. Keep your eyes open for buff-breasted flycatchers, red crossbills, and red-faced warblers. The one-lane road is narrow and winding (usually navigable by passenger car), and not for the acrophobic. It climbs 5 miles up into the mountains to the old mining camp of Reef Townsite.

The **Environmental Operations Park,** 3 miles east of Ariz. 92 at 7201 Ariz. 90, a grasslands and wetlands restoration site at Sierra Vista's sewage treatment facility, is a good place to see yellow-headed blackbirds, ducks, peregrines, and harriers from fall to spring. For more information, contact the City of Sierra Vista (✆ **520/458-3315**) or the Southeastern Arizona Bird Observatory (✆ **520/432-1388**).

Hummingbird Heaven

If it's summer and you're looking to add as many hummingbirds as possible to your life list, take a drive up Miller Canyon (south of Ramsey Canyon) to **Beatty's Guest Ranch and Orchard,** 2173 E. Miller Canyon Rd., Hereford (www.beattysguestranch.com; ✆ **520/378-2728**), where a public hummingbird-viewing area is set up. A total of 15 species of hummers have been sighted here, and several times, 14 species have been seen in 1 day. Cabins are available for rent for serious birders and backcountry enthusiasts.

HIKING

Hikers will find numerous trails in the Huachuca Mountains west of Sierra Vista. There are trails at **Garden Canyon** on Fort Huachuca, at **Ramsey Canyon Preserve,** at **Carr Canyon** in Coronado National Forest, and within **Coronado National Memorial.** For information on hiking in the Coronado National Forest, contact the **Sierra Vista Ranger District,** 5990 S. Hwy. 92 (www.fs.usda.gov/coronado; ✆ **520/378-0311**), 8 miles south of Sierra Vista.

HORSEBACK RIDING

The **Double R Guest Ranch** (http://doublerguestranch.com; ✆ **520/212-6943**), located north of Benson on the way to the tiny town of Pomerene, is an equestrian's dream. The guest ranch rents horses to ride on guided expeditions along the San Pedro River and into the Rincon Mountains, and there's enough bird life here to keep any 10 ornithologists busy. An hour's ride costs $45, while a full-day trip is a bargain $180.

Where to Stay

IN BENSON

Comfort Inn ★ There's very little lodging near Kartchner Caverns; this off-ramp budget hotel in Benson is a decent option, with a lobby done up in Santa Fe style with flagstone floors and rustic southwestern furniture. Guest rooms are strictly hotel modern, but they are roomy and reliable.

630 S. Village Loop. www.choicehotels.com. ✆ **520/586-8800.** 62 units. $89–$95 double. Rates include continental breakfast. Children 19 and under stay free in parent's room. **Amenities:** Exercise room; outdoor pool; free Wi-Fi.

IN SIERRA VISTA

Lazy Dog Ranch ★ This small B&B is an excellent choice for birdwatchers, located as it is within the San Pedro Riparian National Conservation Area, with the river flowing past the edge of the property. Both accommodations are quite large and decorated with southwestern style. One unit is a cottage off the courtyard; the other unit has a kitchenette. In that courtyard you'll find both a fire pit (for cool nights) and a swimming pool (for warm days). There are hiking trails nearby. Around the inn, you'll find lots of art and artifacts from owners Michael and Catherine McCormack's world travels, and, yes, there are lazy dogs in residence.

3123 N. Thistle Rd. www.lazydogranch.net. ✆ **520/458-5583.** 2 units. $135 double. 2-night minimum on weekends. Rates include continental breakfast. Children 10 and under stay free in parent's room. Pets accepted ($10 per night). **Amenities:** Seasonal outdoor pool; free Wi-Fi.

IN HEREFORD

Casa de San Pedro ★ Built with bird-watching tour groups in mind, this modern inn is set on the west side of the San Pedro River on 10 acres of land. The inn is built in the territorial style around a courtyard garden and has large, comfortable hotel-style guest rooms and a large common room where birders gather to swap tales of the day's sightings. The inn also offers birding, cultural, and history tours. This is by far the most upscale inn in the region.

8933 S. Yell Lane. www.bedandbirds.com. ✆ **520/366-1300.** 10 units. $175–$250 double. Rates include full breakfast. No children 11 or under. **Amenities:** Concierge; Jacuzzi; outdoor pool; free Wi-Fi.

Ramsey Canyon Inn Bed & Breakfast ★ Adjacent to the Nature Conservancy's Ramsey Canyon Preserve, this inn is the most convenient choice in the area for birders who are here to see the canyon's famous hummingbirds. The property straddles Ramsey Creek, with guest rooms in the main house and housekeeping suites reached by a footbridge over the creek. In addition to a large gourmet breakfast, guests get pie in the afternoon. Book early during the birding season. It's also an eco-friendly choice, with on-demand water heaters, gray-water irrigation of the inn's orchard, and use of organic ingredients as often as possible.

29 Ramsey Canyon Dr. www.ramseycanyoninn.com. ✆ **520/378-3010.** 9 units. $135–$160 double; $160–$175 suite. Rates include full breakfast (except in housekeeping suites). No children 15 or under in inn; children accepted in suites. **Amenities:** Free Wi-Fi.

CAMPGROUNDS

There are two Coronado National Forest campgrounds—14-site **Reef Townsite** and 8-site **Ramsey Vista**—up winding Carr Canyon Road south of Sierra Vista off Ariz. 92. Both charge $10 per night. For information, contact the Coronado National Forest Sierra Vista Ranger District (www.fs.usda.gov/coronado; ✆ **520/378-0311**).

Where to Eat in Sierra Vista

In addition to the restaurants below, Sierra Vista supports quite a number of Asian restaurants, with an emphasis on Chinese, Japanese, and Korean cuisine. Remember, too, that you're only a half-hour drive from Bisbee, which has a number of restaurants (p. 464).

The German Café ★ GERMAN German food in Arizona. *Jawohl*, thanks to all the service personnel who've been stationed in Germany over the years. The German Café is *echt Deutsch*, serving the usual suspects: bratwurst, knockwurst, wiener schnitzel, and, of course, heaps of sauerkraut. They do a great job of it, too.

1232 E. Fry Blvd. ✆ **520/456-1705.** Main dishes $12–$20. Mon–Sat 11am–9pm.

Tanuki Sushi ★ JAPANESE There are times when only sushi and udon will do, and when those times come, Tanaka, in downtown Sierra Vista, does a fine job. The menu includes a few Korean dishes, but the Japanese concoctions are highlights, with a full menu of tempura and other hot dishes as well.

1221 E. Fry Blvd. ✆ **520/459-6583.** Main dishes $10–$15. Mon–Sat 4:30pm–9pm.

TOMBSTONE ★

70 miles SE of Tucson; 181 miles SE of Phoenix; 24 miles N of Bisbee

All it took was a brief blaze of gunfire more than 125 years ago to seal the fate of this former silver-mining boomtown. On these very streets, outside a livery stable known as the O.K. Corral, Wyatt Earp, his brothers Virgil and Morgan, and their friend Doc Holliday took on the outlaws Ike Clanton and Frank and Tom McLaury on October 26, 1881. Today, Tombstone, "the town too tough to die," is one of Arizona's most popular attractions. I'll leave it up to you to decide whether it is more of a tacky tourist trap or a genuine historical attraction.

Tombstone was named by Ed Schieffelin, a silver prospector who ventured into this area at a time when the region's Apaches were fighting to preserve their way of life. Schieffelin was warned that all he would find here was his own tombstone, so when he discovered silver, he named the strike Tombstone. Within a few years, the town of Tombstone was larger than San Francisco, and between 1880 and 1887, an estimated $37 million worth of silver was mined here. Such wealth created a sturdy little town, and as the Cochise County seat of the time, Tombstone boasted several imposing buildings, including the

A Tombstone in Tombstone

When you're finished with downtown Tombstone, head south down the main drag to pay your respects to town founder Ed Schieffelin, who had the eccentric wish to be buried in Tombstone under something like a cairn or a pyramid, the kind of stone pile a miner would use to mark a claim. His friends built that monument, with a touching plaque commemorating him as "a dutiful son, faithful husband, kind brother, and true friend." It's easy to drive into and out of Tombstone without noticing the thing, but look closely just past the Border Patrol inspection station, and you'll see it down in a draw. Allen Street, the tourist hub in town, turns into a dirt road that will take you to the monument itself, a very bumpy 4 miles among low hills and century plants.

county courthouse, which is now a state park. After a fire in 1882 destroyed much of the town, new and grander buildings were erected. In 1887, however, underground water flooded the silver mines, and despite attempts to pump the water out, the mines were never reopened. With the demise of the mines, the boom came to an end and the population rapidly dwindled.

Today, Tombstone's historic district consists of some original late-19th-century buildings and newer structures built in the same style. Most house souvenir shops and restaurants.

Essentials

ARRIVING From Tucson, take I-10 east to Benson and then Ariz. 80 south to Tombstone. From Sierra Vista, take Ariz. 90 north to Ariz. 82, heading east.

SPECIAL EVENTS Tombstone's biggest annual celebration is **Wyatt Earp Days** (www.wyattearpdays.com), held in late May, which includes an 1880s fashion show and plenty of gunfights. On the third weekend in October, **Helldorado Days** (http://tombstonehelldoradodays.com) commemorates the gunfight at the O.K. Corral with countless shootouts in the streets, mock hangings, and a parade.

VISITOR INFORMATION Stop by the **Tombstone Chamber of Commerce Visitor Center,** 395 E. Allen St. (www.tombstonechamber.com; ✆ **888/457-3929** or 520/457-3929).

Exploring Tombstone

As portrayed in novels, movies, and TV shows, the shootout has come to epitomize the Wild West, and nowhere is this great American phenomenon more glorified than in Tombstone, where the star attraction is the famous **O.K. Corral,** 308 E. Allen St. (www.ok-corral.com; ✆ **520/457-3456**), site of a 30-second gun battle that has taken on mythic proportions over the years. Inside the corral, you'll find not only displays on the shootout, but also an exhibit focusing on local photographer C. S. Fly, who ran the boardinghouse where Doc Holliday was staying at the time of the shootout.

Next door is **Tombstone's Historama,** a kitschy multimedia affair that rehashes the well-known history of Tombstone's "bad old days" and has a recorded narration by Vincent Price. The O.K. Corral and Tombstone's Historama are open daily from 9am to 5pm; a $6 admission fee covers both sites (free for kids 5 and under); $10 covers both plus a shootout reenactment almost on the very site of the original gunfight.

If you aren't able to catch one of the staged shootouts at the O.K. Corral (daily at 2pm), don't despair—there are plenty of other shootouts staged regularly in Tombstone (usually between noon and 4pm). Expect to pay $6 for adults, $4 for seniors, and $3 for children at any of these shows. For a little fun and games, try to catch the Tombstone Cowboys shootout at **Helldorado Town,** Fourth and Toughnut streets (no phone). These shootouts, which are staged two to three times a day, are more hysterical than historical.

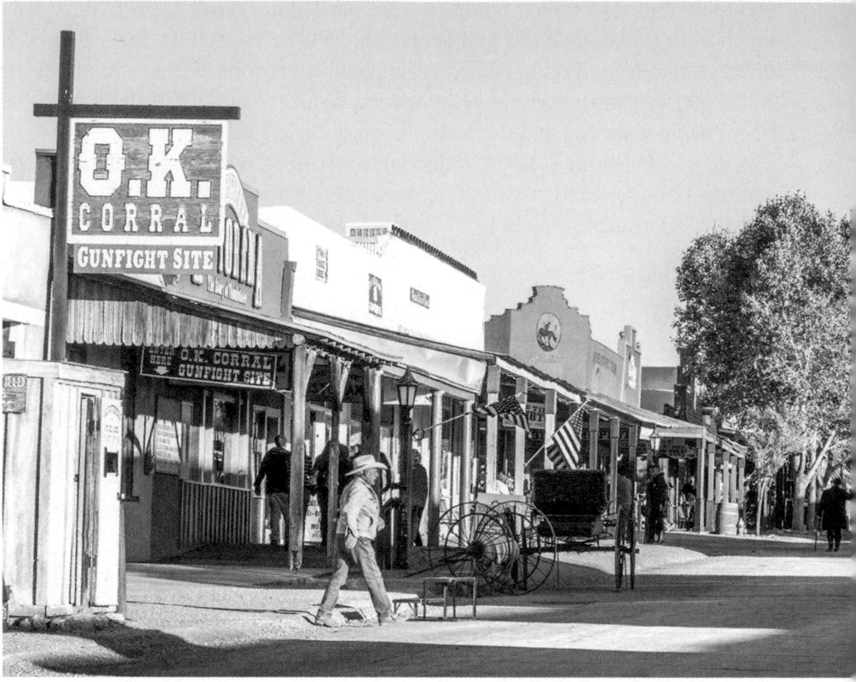

Thanks to its Wild West mystique, the frontier town of Tombstone today draws tourists with a mix of history and kitschy attractions.

When the smoke cleared in 1881, three men lay dead. They were later carted off to the **Boot Hill Graveyard,** 408 N. Ariz. 80 (✆ **520/457-3300**), on the north edge of town. The graves of Clanton and the McLaury brothers, as well as those of others who died in gunfights or by hanging, are well marked. Entertaining epitaphs grace the grave markers; Among the most famous is that of Lester Moore: HERE LIES LESTER MOORE, FOUR SLUGS FROM A 44, NO LES, NO MORE. The cemetery is open to the public daily 8am to dusk. Enter through a gift shop on Ariz. 80.

When the residents of Tombstone weren't shooting each other in the streets, they were likely to be found in the saloons and bawdy houses that lined Allen Street. Most famous was the **Bird Cage Theatre,** Allen and Sixth streets (www.tombstonebirdcage.com; ✆ **520/457-3421**), so named for the cagelike cribs (sort of like box seats) suspended from the ceiling. These velvet-draped cages were used by prostitutes to ply their trade. For old Tombstone atmosphere, this place is hard to beat. Admission is $12 for adults, $11 for seniors, $10 for children 8 to 18; the theater is open daily from 9am to 6pm. There are also nightly ghost tours for $20; call for hours.

When it's time for a cold beer, Tombstone has a couple of very lively old saloons. The restored **Crystal Palace Saloon,** 436 E. Allen St. (www.crystal

palacesaloon.com; ✆ **520/457-3611**), built in 1879, is a favorite hangout of the town's costumed actors and other would-be cowboys and cowgirls. **Big Nose Kate's,** 417 E. Allen St. (www.bignosekates.info; ✆ **520/457-3107**), is an equally entertaining spot full of Wild West character and characters, or would-be characters.

Tombstone has long been a tourist town, and its streets are lined with souvenir shops selling wind chimes, dream catchers, and loads of cowboy souvenirs; of course, there are several places where you can dress up in old-fashioned clothes and get your picture taken. However, there are also some interesting little museums around town. At the **Rose Tree Inn Museum,** at Fourth and Toughnut streets (http://tombstonerosetree.com; ✆ **520/457-3326**), you can see the world's largest rose tree. Inside are antique furnishings from Tombstone's heyday in the 1880s. The museum is open daily from 9am to 5pm (closed Thanksgiving and Christmas). Admission is $5 (free for children 13 and under).

The most imposing building in town, **Tombstone Courthouse State Park,** 223 Toughnut St. (www.azstateparks.com; (✆ **520/457-3311**) provides a much less sensationalized version of local history. Built in 1882, the courthouse is now a museum containing artifacts, photos, and newspaper clippings that chronicle Tombstone's lively past. In the courtyard, you can still see the gallows that once ended the lives of outlaws. The park is open daily from 9am to 5pm (closed on Christmas); the entrance fee is $7 for adults and $2 for children 7 to 13.

At the **Tombstone Epitaph Museum,** Fifth Street between Allen and Fremont streets (www.tombstone-epitaph.com; ✆ **520/457-2211**), you can inspect the office of the town's old newspaper, *The Tombstone Epitaph,* and learn about John Clum, who founded the paper after a colorful career as an Apache Indian agent. The museum is open daily from 9:30am to 6pm; admission is free.

Perhaps the best place in town to sort out the truth of Tombstone's history is the privately owned **Tombstone Western Heritage Museum ★**, Fremont and Sixth streets (www.thetombstonemuseum.com; ✆ **520/457-3800**), which holds the town's most fascinating collection of Tombstone artifacts and ephemera. Included in this impressive collection are items that once belonged to Wyatt and Virgil Earp, rare photos of the Earps and the outlaws of Tombstone, and all kinds of original documents dating to the days of the shootout at the O.K. Corral. The museum is open Monday through Saturday 10am to 5pm, Sunday 1 to 5pm; admission is $7.50 for adults and $3 for children 12 to 18 ($13 for families).

For more Tombstone history, stop by the **Wyatt Earp House & Gallery,** 102 E. Fremont St. (✆ **520/457-3111**), a tiny adobe house that may or may not once have been the home of Wyatt Earp. Lovingly restored a few years ago with representative furnishings of the time, the old house also operates as a small art gallery selling Western and Southwestern art.

ORGANIZED TOURS

To further immerse yourself in Tombstone's Wild West history, take a walk around town with a guide from **Tombstone Walking Tour** (www.tombstonewalkingtours.com; ✆ **520/457-9876**). A 90-minute tour costs $20 for adults, $10 for children. Alternatively, take one of **Old Tombstone Tours'** (http://oldtombstonetours.net; ✆ **520/457-3018**) 20-minute stagecoach rides around the town's historic district ($10 adults; $5 children). Stagecoaches leave from in front of the O.K. Corral.

To see some of the landscapes once roamed by the Earps and the Clantons, get out of town on a jeep tour. Tours are offered by **Into the West Jeep Tours** (wwwintothewestjeeptours.com; ✆ **520/559-2151** or 520/559-2228). Expect to pay $95 to $125 for a tour (two-person minimum).

Where to Stay in Tombstone

Tombstone Monument Ranch ★ Located in the hills a couple of miles from Tombstone, this guest ranch is something of a Western theme park, with rooms ranging from the marshal's office and the jail to the blacksmith's shop. The ranch offers an archery and pistol range, horseback rides, evening entertainment, and an excellent restaurant that serves up three squares a day, included with lodging.

895 West Monument Rd. www.tombstonemonumentranch.com. ✆ **520/457-8707.** $280–$350 per person, discounts for couples and families staying in same room. Rates include 3 meals a day. **Amenities:** Bar; outdoor pool; free W-Fi.

Where to Eat in Tombstone

Unless you're absolutely famished, do not eat in Tombstone. Hold out for Bisbee or even Sierra Vista, either of which is only a half-hour's drive away. Restaurants in Tombstone cater exclusively to tourists, and both food and service are reliably disappointing—plastic chairs and burger baskets long ago supplanted historic character.

Big Nose Kate's Saloon ★ AMERICAN The food here isn't all that memorable, but the atmosphere sure is. Big Nose Kate's dates back to 1880 and is primarily a saloon. As such, it stays packed with visitors who have come to revel in Tombstone's outlaw past. While you sip your beer, why not order a sandwich and call it lunch? You might even catch some live country music.

417 E. Allen St. www.bignosekates.info. ✆ **520/457-3107.** No reservations. Sandwiches $7.50–$10; pizzas $13–$20. Daily 10am–midnight.

Crystal Palace ★ AMERICAN Okay, so the food here won't win any awards, but it's a fun setting. The bar is a fairly authentic reproduction of the original, and the wood floors have been pounded by countless cowboy boots. While you sip your beer and munch your buffalo burger, you can entertain yourself by trying to spot bullet holes in the pressed tin ceiling.

436 E. Allen St. www.crystalpalacesaloon.com. ✆ **520/457-3611.** No reservations. Main courses $9–$25. Daily 11am–8pm.

BISBEE ★★

94 miles SE of Tucson; 205 miles SE of Phoenix; 24 miles NW of Douglas

Arizona has a wealth of ghost towns that boomed on mining profits and then quickly went bust when the mines played out, but none is as impressive as Bisbee, which is built into the steep slopes of Tombstone Canyon on the south side of the Mule Mountains. Between 1880 and 1975, Bisbee's mines produced more than $6 billion worth of metals. When the Phelps Dodge Company shut down its copper mines here, Bisbee nearly went the way of other abandoned mining towns, but as the Cochise County seat, it was saved from disappearing into the desert dust.

Bisbee's glory days date from 100 years ago, and the town stopped growing in the early 20th century. As a result, it is now one of the best-preserved historic towns in the Southwest. Old brick buildings line narrow winding streets, and miners' shacks sprawl across the hillsides above downtown. Television and movie producers discovered these well-preserved streets years ago, and since then, Bisbee has doubled as New York, Spain, Greece, Italy, and, of course, the Old West.

Tucked into a narrow valley surrounded by red hills, Bisbee today has a funky cosmopolitan air. Many artists, musicians, and actors call the town home, and for years urban refugees have dropped out of the rat race to restore Bisbee's old buildings and open small inns, restaurants, and galleries in empty spaces in the once-thriving town. Between the rough edges left over from its mining days and this new fringe-culture atmosphere, Bisbee is one of Arizona's most interesting towns. However, be aware that Bisbee is not for every one. It appeals mostly to young, hip travelers in search of economical, and often somewhat eclectic, accommodations. On weekends, the rumble of motorcycles is a constant on Bisbee's streets, and there are a lot of people wandering the streets, visitor and resident, who can be politely described as permanently bewildered—which, by some lights, simply adds to the old city's charm.

Bisbee History 101

The rumor of silver in "them thar hills" first drew prospectors here in 1877, and within a few years the diggings attracted the interest of some San Francisco investors, among them Judge DeWitt Bisbee, for whom the town is named. However, it was copper and other less-than-precious metals that would make Bisbee's fortune. With the help of outside financing, large-scale mining operations were begun in 1881 by the Phelps Dodge Company. By 1910, the population had climbed to 25,000, and Bisbee was the largest city between New Orleans and San Francisco. The town boasted nearly 50 saloons and bordellos along the aptly named Brewery Gulch.

Essentials

ARRIVING Bisbee is on Ariz. 80, which begins at I-10 in the town of Benson, 45 miles east of Tucson.

SPECIAL EVENTS September's **Brewery Gulch Daze,** a celebration of Bisbee's bawdy past, includes live music, an art-car show, and a pet parade. In October, there is the **Bisbee 1000: The Great Stair Climb,** a race up and down the town's many public stairways.

VISITOR INFORMATION Contact the **Bisbee Visitor Center,** 2 Copper Queen Plaza (www.discoverbisbee.com; ✆ **866/224-7233** or 520/432-3554).

Exploring Bisbee

At the Bisbee Visitor Center, in the middle of town, pick up walking-tour brochures that guide you past the town's most important historic buildings and sites. On the second floor of the **Copper Queen Library,** 6 Main St. (✆ **520/432-4232**), the oldest public library in Arizona; old photographs give a good idea of what the town looked like in the past century.

Don't miss the **Bisbee Mining & Historical Museum** ★, 5 Copper Queen Plaza (www.bisbeemuseum.org; ✆ **520/432-7071**), housed in the 1897 Copper Queen Consolidated Mining Company office building. This small but com-

Artists and countercultural types have breathed new life into the Victorian downtown of Bisbee, a former copper-mining boomtown.

A Golfer's Nightmare

Beware the Bogeyman at the **Turquoise Valley Golf & RV Park,** 1794 W. Newell St. (www.turquoisevalley.com; ✆ **520/505-1642**) in nearby Naco. Dating to 1908, this little public course is the oldest golf course in Arizona, and boasts one of the few par-6 holes in the world. The hole, called the Rattler, stretches for 747 yards and is every golfer's nightmare. A round of golf here costs around $15 per player. The course is open daily from 7am to 7pm.

prehensive museum features exhibits on the history of Bisbee. It's open daily from 10am to 4pm; admission is $8 adults, $7 seniors, and $3 for kids 16 and under.

For another look at early life in Bisbee, walk up Brewery Gulch to the **Muheim Heritage House Museum,** 207 Youngblood Hill (www.bisbeemuseum.org; ✆ **520/432-4815**). Built between 1898 and 1915, the house has an unusual semicircular porch. The interior is decorated with period furniture. It's open daily from 10am to 2pm; admission is $4.

The **Southeastern Arizona Bird Observatory** (www.sabo.org; ✆ **520/432-1388**) has a public bird-viewing area at its headquarters 2 miles north of the Mule Mountain Tunnel on Ariz. 80 north of Bisbee (watch for Hidden Meadow Lane).

O.K. Street, which parallels Brewery Gulch but is high on the hill on the southern edge of town, is a good place to walk for views of Bisbee. At the top of O.K. Street a path leads up to a hill above town for an even better panorama of Bisbee's jumble of old buildings. Atop this hill, numerous small, colorfully painted shrines built into the rocks are filled with candles, plastic flowers, and pictures of the Virgin Mary. It's a steep climb on a rocky, very uneven path, but the views and the fascinating little shrines make it worth the effort. Tombstone Canyon Road, down below (comparatively, anyway), offers some of the same kind of street art with an easier walking course.

Mining made this town what it is, so be sure to take an underground mine tour to find out what it was like to be a miner here in Bisbee. **Queen Mine Tours ★** (www.queenminetour.com; ✆ **866/432-2071** or 520/432-2071;) takes visitors down into one of the town's old copper mines. Tours are offered daily between 9am and 3:30pm and cost $13 for adults, $5.50 for ages 4 to 12. The ticket office and mine are just south of the Old Bisbee business district at the Ariz. 80 interchange.

To explore some of the steeper and narrower streets of old Bisbee, take a 90-minute tour ($55) with **Lavender Jeep Tours** (www.lavenderjeeptours.com; ✆ **520/432-5369**). One of Lavender's most fun tours centers on the writing of local mystery author J. A. Jance; several other tours are also available. For a walk on the dark side, sign up for the 90-minute **Old Bisbee Ghost Tour** (www.oldbisbeeghosttour.com; ✆ **520/432-3308**), offered Friday through Sunday nights at 7pm; it costs $15, with a discount for booking online.

Bisbee Shopping

Bisbee has lots of interesting stores and galleries, and shopping is the main recreational activity here. Bisbee's mines once produced some of the most famous turquoise in the country, and you'll see quite a bit of turquoise jewelry around town. To see some quality jewelry created from minerals mined in the area, stop by **Czar Jewelry,** 13 Main St. (✆ **520/432-3027**). You'll find beautiful jewelry in a wide range of styles at **Jewelry Designs by Owen,** 45 Main St. (www.jewelrydesignsbyowen.com; (✆ **520/432-4400**). Across the street, at the **Gold Shop,** 67 Main St. (✆ **520/432-4557**), there's lots of turquoise set in gold instead of the more common silver settings. Another jewelry store worth checking out is **Uptown Tribal,** 39 Main St. (www.katedrew-wilkinson.com; ✆ **520/432-7818**), in the old J.C. Penney store near the library and post office.

In that same building, locally called the Mercantile after the old Phelps-Dodge company store, **Bisbee Books and Music** (www.bisbeebam.com; ✆ **520/353-4009**) has a wonderfully well-selected stock, mixing bestsellers with books of local interest. The music is just as interesting, including a constantly changing cast of guitars for sale.

If it's art you're after, you've got lots of good galleries to visit in Bisbee. You'll find fanciful kinetic sculptures and colorful paintings at **Sam Poe Gallery,** 33 Subway St. (www.sampoegallery.com; ✆ **520/432-5338**). **PanTerra Gallery,** 22 Main St. (www.panterragallery.com; ✆ **520/432-3320**) sells both the photographs of co-owner Charles Feil and gorgeous women's fashions and jewelry selected by his wife, co-owner Maralyce Ferree. At **Belleza Gallery,** 27 Main St. (www.bellezagallery.org; ✆ **520/432-5877**), your art purchase will go to a good cause—the gallery is operated by a not-for-profit organization that helps homeless women in a substance-abuse treatment program.

Bicyclists should be sure to drop by the **Bisbee Bicycle Brothel,** 43 Brewery Ave. (www.bisbeebicyclebrothel.com; ✆ **520/236-4855**), where cycling enthusiast Ken Wallace has a shop full of vintage road bikes, primarily from England and Italy, as well as some interesting modern bikes.

At **Optimo Custom Hat Works,** 47 Main St. (www.optimohatworks.com; ✆ **520/432-4544**), owner Grant Sergot will custom-fit your felt fedora, cowboy hat, or Panama straw hat. (By the way, Panama hats actually come from Ecuador, as author and part-time Bisbee resident Tom Miller documents in his book *The Panama Hat Trail.*)

If you're a chocolate lover, do not miss **Chocoláte,** 134 Tombstone Canyon Rd. (www.spiritedchocolate.com; ✆ **520/432-3011;** open only on weekends), a shop that makes chocolate bars and chocolate confections from cacao beans it roasts right here in Bisbee. Be sure to try the Madagascar chocolate; it has a unique flavor that may ruin you for any other chocolate. If chocolate isn't enough to satisfy your sweet tooth, how about some honey? The **Killer Bee**

Guy, 20 Main St. (www.killerbeeguy.com; ✆ **520/432-8016**), is full of honeys and honey products.

Where to Stay in Bisbee

MODERATE

Copper City Inn ★ Operated by Fred Miller (bartender at Bisbee's Cafe Roka since 1995) and his wife, Anita Fox, this inn boasts some of the most attractive rooms in Bisbee. One room is done up with French antiques; another, dedicated to early-20th-century hotel designer Mary Jane Colter, has Art Deco styling. A third has modern Mission-style furnishings and a full kitchen. All the rooms have balconies overlooking Bisbee. There's allergy-barrier bedding, and "green" cleaning products are used. Whichever room you reserve, you'll receive a complimentary bottle of wine upon check-in. The Copper City Inn is a "self-service" sort of place; when you make your reservation, you'll be given the key code for the door to your room.

99 Main St. www.coppercityinn.com. ✆ **520/432-1418** or 520/456-4254. 3 units. $125–$150 double. Rates include a voucher for off-site continental breakfast. No children under 16; no pets. **Amenities:** Access to nearby health club; free Wi-Fi.

Letson Loft Hotel ★★ Located up a flight of stairs, the Letson Loft Hotel feels a bit like an old Italian villa, and has some of the prettiest rooms in town. High ceilings, original wood floors, antique furnishings, and plush beds with great linens all add up to a level of comfort and class rarely seen in this funky town. Book one of the front rooms and you'll have a bay-window view of all the Main Street action. If you're a light sleeper, ask for a room at the back of the hotel or avail yourself of the bedside earplugs; Bisbee can be a bit noisy at times. One of my favorite rooms has a huge skylight and another has a claw-foot tub. There's even a suite with a kitchen.

26 Main St. www.letsonlofthotel.com. ✆ **877/432-3210** or 520/432-3210. 8 units. $175–$200 double. Rates include continental breakfast. No children under 12. **Amenities:** Concierge; free Wi-Fi.

INEXPENSIVE

Canyon Rose Suites ★ On the second floor of a commercial building just off Bisbee's main street, this property offers spacious suites with full kitchens, which makes it a good bet for longer stays. All units have hardwood floors and high ceilings. Works by local artists and a mix of contemporary and rustic furnishings give the place plenty of Bisbee character. Constructed on a steep, narrow street, the building has an unusual covered sidewalk, making it one of the more distinctive commercial buildings in town. The complimentary bottle of wine at check-in is a nice touch.

27 Subway at Shearer St. www.canyonrose.com. ✆ **520/432-5098.** 7 units. $123–$199 double. Children 12 and under stay free in parent's room. **Amenities:** Free Wi-Fi.

Copper Queen Hotel ★ Built in 1902 by the Copper Queen Mining Company right in the center of town, this is the oldest continuously operating hotel in Arizona. It has not had a thorough restoration, however; it feels more like an old hotel than a historic hotel. The atmosphere is casual yet quite authentic, with rooms opening off spacious hallways. Unfortunately, the rooms vary considerably in size, and the smallest are so cramped that they really aren't comfortable for two people. Rooms also vary considerably in the quality of the furnishings; be sure to ask for a renovated room. The restaurant's food can be uneven, but out front is a pleasant terrace for alfresco dining. And what would a mining-town hotel be without its ghosts? Yes, they say this place is haunted, as you'll discover on regular Thursday night ghost hunts.

11 Howell Ave. www.copperqueen.com. ✆ **520/432-2216.** 53 units. $89–$197 double. Children 17 and under stay free in parent's room. **Amenities:** Restaurant; lounge; small outdoor pool; free Wi-Fi.

Shady Dell Trailer Court ★ Yes, this really is a trailer court, but you'll find neither shade nor dell at the Shady Dell's roadside location just south of the Lavender Pit mine. What you will find are 10 vintage trailers, a 1947 Airporter bus done in retro-Tiki style, and a 1947 Chris Craft yacht, all of which have been lovingly restored. Although some of the trailers don't have their own private bathrooms (a bathhouse is in the middle of the property), they do have all kinds of vintage decor and furnishings—even tapes and records of period music and radio shows. In trailers that have vintage TVs, there are DVDs of old movies. Make reservations far in advance. There's also a 1957 vintage diner on-site.

1 Old Douglas Rd. www.theshadydell.com. ✆ **520/432-3567.** 11 units. $65–$125 per trailer (for 1–2 people). No children 15 or under. **Amenities:** Free Wi-Fi.

Where to Eat in Bisbee

Café Cornucopia, 14 Main St. (✆ **520/432-4820**) offers fresh juices, smoothies, and sandwiches, open Thursday through Tuesday from 11am to 4pm. For good coffee and a mining theme, check out the **Bisbee Coffee Co.,** Copper Queen Plaza, Main St. (www.bisbeecoffee.com; ✆ **520/432-7879**). For gourmet picnic supplies, stop by the **High Desert Market and Café,** 203 Tombstone Canyon Rd. (www.highdesertmarket.net; ✆ **520/432-6775**), which has organic produce, imported cheeses, wine, and other assorted goodies. The cafe here is a great place for breakfast or lunch.

Bisbee Breakfast Club ★ AMERICAN In the Lowell district on the far side of the Lavender Pit from old Bisbee, this huge diner is a local favorite. (So popular was this place with Tucson visitors, in fact, that four branch locations have opened in the Old Pueblo—and they're always crammed.) Big breakfasts (served all day) are the specialty here, and the cinnamon rolls are legendary around town. At lunch, try the coffee-charred breast of chicken salad; it'll really wake up your taste buds.

75 Erie St. www.bisbeebreakfastclub.com. ✆ **520/432-5885.** No reservations. Main courses $5.50–$10. Thurs–Mon 7am–3pm.

Bisbee's Table ★ REGIONAL AMERICAN Located in the Art Deco Copper Queen Plaza building at the bottom of Main Street, this is one of

Bisbee's best casual restaurants. Not only is the food decent, but there are also large photographs of old Bisbee that give the place a lot of historic character. At lunch or dinner, the buffalo burger is a good bet, as is the Caesar salad. Reliable dinner entrees include several steaks and a variety of pasta dishes. Grab a seat by the window for great people-watching.

2 Copper Queen Plaza. www.bisbeetable.com. ✆ **520/432-6788.** Reservations accepted for parties of 6 or more. Main courses $12–$36. Daily 11am–9pm.

Cafe Roka ★★ NEW AMERICAN The food at Cafe Roka is so good that it is reason enough for a visit to Bisbee. Casual and hip, this place is a real find in such an out-of-the-way town and offers good value as well as delicious and imaginatively prepared food. Chef Rod Kass, who opened Cafe Roka in 1992, takes pains to provide locally sourced products whenever possible, but he brings spectacular ingredients from all over the world, including a fine wine list. All meals include salad, soup, sorbet intermezzo, and your choice of entree (different entrees are priced differently). The grilled salmon with a Gorgonzola-dill crust and artichoke-and-portobello lasagna are two intriguing options. The flourless chocolate cake with raspberry sauce is an exquisite ending. Local artists display their works, and on Friday nights there is live jazz.

35 Main St. www.caferoka.com. ✆ **520/432-5153.** Reservations highly recommended. Main courses $16–$35. Fri–Sat 5–9pm.

Santiago's ★ MEXICAN For being so close—just 4 miles—from the international border, Bisbee doesn't have much to write home about by way of Mexican restaurants. Santiago's is a pleasing exception, with tasty concoctions that include one of the best fish tacos in all of Arizona. This is a casual place, but don't be surprised if, on a weekend night, someone sits down in the corner and starts playing classical guitar music. You'll find Santiago's a couple of doors down from the Copper Queen Hotel at the start of Brewery Gulch.

1 Howell Ave. www.santiagosmexican.com. ✆ **520/432-1910.** Reservations accepted for parties of 6 or more. Main courses $12–$17. Daily 11am–9pm.

Bisbee Entertainment & Nightlife

For more than a century, Bisbee's **Brewery Gulch** has been known for its many bars. Although there aren't nearly as many drinking establishments today as there were 100 years ago, a few dive bars remain especially popular with the weekend Harley-riding crowd from Tucson. For local microbrews, stop in at **Old Bisbee Brewing Company,** 200 Review Alley (www.oldbisbeebrewingcompany.com; ✆ **520/432-2739**), a tiny place wedged into a cramped little space in Brewery Gulch. They have a very good assortment of beers.

COCHISE COUNTY ★

Willcox: 81 miles E of Tucson; 192 miles SE of Phoenix; 74 miles N of Douglas

Bisbee, Tombstone, and Sierra Vista all lie within Cochise County, but much of the county is taken up by the vast Sulphur Springs Valley, bounded by several mountain ranges. Across this wide-open landscape, Apache chiefs Cochise and Geronimo once rode. Gazing out across this country today, it is easy to understand why the Apaches fought so hard to keep white settlers out.

Historians believe that the Apaches first moved into this region of southern Arizona sometime in the early 16th century. Their hunter-gatherer lifestyle was supplemented by raiding neighboring tribes for food and other booty. When the Spanish arrived in the area, the Apaches acquired horses and became even more efficient raiders. They attacked Spanish, Mexican, and eventually American settlers, and despite repeated attempts to convince them to give up their nomadic way of life, the Apaches declined the invitation. Not long after the Gadsden Purchase of 1848 made Arizona U.S. soil, more people than ever began settling in the region. The new settlers immediately became the object of Apache raids, and eventually the U.S. Army was called in to put an end to the attacks; by the mid-1880s, the army was embroiled in a war with Cochise, Geronimo, and the Chiricahua Apaches.

The Chiricahua and Dragoon mountains, which flank the Sulphur Springs Valley on the east and west, respectively, are relatively unknown outside the region. Arizonans and connoisseurs of wild, open country prize them, though, for they offer some of the Southwest's most spectacular scenery. Massive boulders litter the mountainsides, creating fascinating landscapes. The mountains abound with ringtail cats, black bears, and coatimundis, and the occasional jaguar comes calling there, too. The Chiricahua Mountains are also a favorite destination of bird-watchers, for it is here that the colorfully plumed elegant trogon reaches the northern limit of its range.

Willcox, which lies on I-10, is the region's main town and has lately become somewhat of a wine-touring destination. East of Willcox, the **Chiricahua National Monument** (p. 469) is perhaps the region's biggest draw. In the southern part of the region, the town of **Douglas** is an important gateway to Mexico. Across the border, Agua Prieta, Sonora, is worth a stop, if only for its many good restaurants and food stands. While in Douglas, be sure to stop at the historic Gadsden Hotel (p. 472); the Slaughter Ranch (p. 470) is also worth a visit.

If you're traveling I-10 between Benson and Willcox, by the way, be sure to stop in at **The Thing** (www.bowlintc.com/the-thing.html), announced by plenty of billboards along Arizona's highways. It's in the Shell station off Johnson Rd. (exit 322). I won't say what The Thing is—why spoil the fun?—but suffice it to say that the newly revamped roadside attraction, with jackalopes, dinosaurs, and space aliens leading up to it, is worth the $5 admission price. The gift shop is a hoot, too.

Essentials

ARRIVING Willcox is on I-10, with Ariz. 186 heading southeast toward Chiricahua National Monument.

SPECIAL EVENTS **Wings Over Willcox** (www.wingsoverwillcox.com; ✆ **800/200-2272**), a festival celebrating the annual return to the area of more than 40,000 sandhill cranes, takes place in January.

VISITOR INFORMATION The **Willcox Chamber of Commerce and Agriculture,** 1500 N. Circle I Rd. (www.willcoxchamber.com; ✆ **800/200-2272** or 520/384-2272), can provide information.

Exploring Willcox

Railroad Ave. in downtown Willcox is somewhat of a little historic district. Here you'll find the Rex Allen Museum (below), and the restored **Southern Pacific Willcox Train Depot,** 101 S. Railroad Ave., a redwood depot built in 1880. Inside the old depot is a small display of historical Willcox photos. Just north of it, **Railroad Avenue Park** is a congenial place to visit with locals and watch trains go rolling by (alas, they don't stop here anymore).

Downtown Willcox is also developing into a wine-touring destination. Currently, there are two tasting rooms in downtown Willcox, in addition to several wineries outside of town. The **Keeling-Schaefer Vineyards** tasting room, 154 N. Railroad Ave. (www.keelingschaefervineyards.com; ✆ **520/766-0600**) represents a winery southeast of town at the foot of the Chiricahua Mountains, which produces excellent syrah and grenache from estate-grown grapes, and also does chardonnay and a rosé. The tasting room is open Thursday through Sunday from 11am to 5pm, and the tasting fee is $7. Across the railroad tracks from the Keeling-Schaefer tasting room is the tasting room of **Carlson Creek Vineyard,** 115 Railview Ave. (www.carlsoncreek.com; ✆ **520/766-3000**), which produces primarily Rhone varietals. The tasting room is open Tuesday through Sunday from 11am to 5pm, and tastings cost $7.

Over in Portal, a 1½-hour drive southeast of Willcox, the **Colibri Vineyard,** 2825 W Hilltop Rd. (✆ **520/558-2401**) has been producing some truly excellent red and rosé blends in recent years. Call if you're in the vicinity.

Rex Allen Arizona Cowboy Museum ★ MUSEUM If you grew up in the days of the cowboy matinée idols, then you're probably familiar with Willcox's favorite hometown star: Rex Allen, the last of the singing cowboys, who made famous the song "Streets of Laredo." Allen died in 1999, but his legend lives on here in Willcox, so much so that one of the town's main streets is Rex Allen Drive. At the small museum dedicated to him, you'll find plenty of Allen memorabilia, as well as a Cowboy Hall of Fame exhibit. KoKo, Allen's beloved horse, is buried beneath a statue of Allen across the street, and some of Allen's ashes were scattered on KoKo's grave. The town celebrates Rex Allen Days every October. Next door to this museum, you'll find the small **Friends of Marty Robbins Museum,** 156 N. Railroad Ave. (✆ **520/766-1404**), open Monday through Saturday 10am to 4pm.

150 N. Railroad Ave. www.rexallenmuseum.org. ✆ **520/384-4583.** $2 adults, kids under 10 free. Tues–Sat 11am–3pm, Mon 10am–1pm. Closed New Year's Day, Thanksgiving, and Christmas.

Exploring Southwest of Willcox

While Chiricahua National Monument (p. 469) claims the most spectacular scenery in this corner of the state, a couple of areas southwest of Willcox in the Dragoon Mountains are almost as impressive. The first of these, **Texas Canyon,** lies right along I-10 between Benson and Willcox. Most people see it only through the window of a speeding car, but if you get off at the Dragoon Road exit and turn left instead of right toward the Amerind Foundation (below), you'll be able to park and walk among the huge boulders scattered across this rolling desert landscape.

South of the community of Dragoon, known for its pistachio farms, lies a rugged jumble of giant boulders known as **Cochise Stronghold** ★ (www.cochisestronghold.com). During the Apache uprisings of the late 19th century, the Apache leader Cochise used this rugged section of the Dragoon Mountains as his hideout and managed to elude capture for years. The granite boulders and pine forests made it impossible for the army to track him and his followers. Cochise eventually died and was buried at an unknown spot somewhere within the area (it's said that his warriors rode back and forth over the grave to trample any evidence of its existence). To reach Cochise Stronghold, take Ariz. 191 to Ironwood Rd. in Sunsites; follow it 9 miles to the campground entrance. Ironwood Rd. becomes a gravel road halfway there, but it should be manageable in a regular car, as long as there have been no heavy rains lately. For a short, easy walk, follow the .4-mile Nature Trail. For a longer and more strenuous hike, head up the Cochise Trail to the Stronghold Divide, a good destination for a 6-mile round-trip hike. For more info, contact the **Coronado National Forest Douglas Ranger District,** 1192 W. Saddleview Rd., Douglas (www.fs.usda.gov/Coronado; ✆ **520/364-3468**).

Amerind Foundation Museum ★★ MUSEUM Out of the way and difficult to find, this museum is well worth seeking out. Established in 1937, the Amerind Foundation is dedicated to the study, preservation, and interpretation of prehistoric and historical Indian cultures. To that end, the foundation has compiled the nation's finest private collection of archaeological artifacts and contemporary pieces. There are exhibits on the dances and religious ceremonies of the major southwestern tribes and cases full of archaeological artifacts amassed from numerous Amerind Foundation excavations over the years. Fascinating ethnological exhibits include amazingly intricate beadwork from the Plains tribes, old Zuni fetishes, Pima willow baskets, old kachina dolls, 100 years of southwestern tribal pottery, and Navajo weavings. The art gallery displays works by 19th- and 20th-century American artists such as Frederic Remington, whose paintings focused on the West. The small museum store has a surprisingly good selection of books and Native American crafts. Between Benson and Willcox, take the Dragoon Rd. exit (exit 318) from I-10 and continue 1 mile east.

2100 N. Amerind Rd., Dragoon. www.amerind.org. ✆ **520/586-3666.** $10 adults, $9 seniors, $8 college students, $7 kids 10–17, free for ages 10 and under. Tues–Sun 10am–4pm. Closed major holidays.

The extraordinary spires and balanced rocks of Chiricahua National Monument glow in the setting sun.

Exploring East of Willcox

Chiricahua National Monument ★★ NATURAL ATTRACTION Sea Captain, China Boy, Duck on a Rock, Punch and Judy—these may not seem like appropriate names for landscape features, but this is no ordinary landscape. These gravity-defying rock formations—called "the land of the standing-up rocks" by the Apache and the "wonderland of rocks" by the pioneers—are the equal of any of Arizona's many amazing rocky landmarks. Rank upon rank of monolithic giants seem to have been turned to stone as they marched across the forested Chiricahua Mountains. Some of these rocks, including Big Balanced Rock and Pinnacle Balanced Rock, seem ready to come crashing down at any moment. Formed about 25 million years ago by a massive volcanic eruption, these rhyolite badlands were once the stronghold of renegade Apaches. If you look closely at Cochise Head peak, you can even see the famous chief's profile. If you're in good physical condition, don't miss the chance to hike the 7.5-mile round-trip **Heart of Rocks Trail ★★**, which can be accessed from the visitor center or the Echo Canyon or Massai Point parking area. This trail leads through the most spectacular scenery in the monument. A shorter loop is also possible. Within the monument are a visitor center, a campground, a picnic area, miles of hiking trails, and a scenic drive with views of many of the most unusual rock formations. Campgrounds are available at $12 a night (see website for reservation information). If you spend the night, secure your food inside your vehicle—there are black bears about, and they love the same snacks we do, plus some.

12856 E. Rhyolite Creek Rd. (off Ariz. 186, 36 mi SE of Willcox). www.nps.gov/chir. ✆ **520/824-3560.** Free admission. Visitor center daily 8am–4:30pm. Closed Thanksgiving and Christmas.

Fort Bowie National Historic Site ★ HIKING TRAIL/HISTORIC SITE The Butterfield Stage, which carried mail, passengers, and freight across the Southwest in the mid-1800s, followed a route that climbed up and over Apache Pass, in the heart of the Chiricahua Mountains' Apache territory. In 1862, Fort Bowie was established near the mile-high pass to ensure the passage of the slow-moving stage as it traversed this difficult region. The fort was also used to protect the water source for cavalry going east to fight the Confederate army in New Mexico. Later, federal troops stationed at Fort Bowie battled Geronimo until, in 1886, the Apache chief finally surrendered. Today, little more than crumbling adobe walls remain, but the 1½-mile hike along the old stage route to the ruins conjures the ghosts of Geronimo and the Indian Wars, and the scenery is spectacular. Carry water and snacks. From Bowie, drive 13 miles south on Apache Pass Rd.; from Willcox, follow Ariz. 186 20 miles southeast, then go another 8 miles on a dirt road (E. Mogul Rd).

3203 S. Old Fort Bowie Rd. www.nps.gov/fobo. ✆ **520/847-2500.** Free admission. Visitor center daily 8am–4:30pm (closed Mon and Tues in summer); grounds daily dawn–dusk. Closed Thanksgiving and Christmas.

Exploring Douglas & Environs

The town of Douglas abounds in old buildings, and although not many are restored, they hint at the diverse character of this community. Just across the border from Douglas is Agua Prieta, in Sonora, Mexico, where Pancho Villa lost his first battle as Arizonans watched from across the line. In Agua Prieta, whitewashed adobe buildings, old churches, and sunny plazas give the place the delightful flavor of old Mexico. At the **Douglas Visitor Center,** 345 E. 16th St. (www.visitdouglas.com; ✆ **800/315-9999** or 520/364-2478), pick up a map to the town's historic buildings, as well as a rough map of Agua Prieta.

Slaughter Ranch Museum ★★ HISTORIC HOME Down a dusty gravel road outside Douglas lies a little-known southwestern landmark: the Slaughter Ranch. If you're old enough, you may remember a Walt Disney TV show called *Texas John Slaughter.* This was his spread. In 1884, former Texas Ranger John Slaughter bought the San Bernardino Valley and turned it into one

COCHISE COUNTY: birding HOTSPOT

To the east of Chiricahua National Monument, on the far side of the Chiricahuas, lies **Cave Creek Canyon,** one of the most important bird-watching spots in the United States. It's here that the colorful elegant trogon reaches the northern limit of its range. Other rare birds spotted here include sulfur-bellied flycatchers, and Lucy's, Virginia's, and black-throated gray warblers. Stop by the visitor center for tips on the best birding spots. Cave Creek Canyon is just outside the community of Portal. In summer, the canyon can be reached from the national monument by driving over the Chiricahuas on graded gravel roads. In winter, you'll likely have to drive around the mountains, which entails going south to Douglas and then 60 miles north on Ariz. 80 to Portal, or north to I-10, and then south 35 miles on Ariz. 80 to Portal.

The **Cochise Lakes** (actually, the Willcox water-treatment ponds) are another great bird-watching spot. Birders can see a wide variety of waterfowl and shorebirds, including avocets and ibises. To find the ponds, head south out of Willcox on Ariz. 186, turn right onto Rex Allen, Jr. Drive at the sign for the Twin Lakes golf course, and go past the golf course.

Between October and March, as many as 40,000 sandhill cranes gather in the Sulphur Springs Valley south of Willcox. In January, the town holds the **Wings Over Willcox** festival (www.wingsoverwillcox.com), a celebration of these majestic birds. To see sandhill cranes during the winter, head southwest of Willcox on U.S. 191; near the community of Cochise and the Apache Generating Station electricity plant, you'll find the **Apache Station Wildlife Viewing Area.** About 60 miles south of Willcox, off U.S. 191 near the town of Elfrida, there's the **Whitewater Draw Wildlife Area** (go south from Elfrida on Central Highway, turn right on Davis Road, and in another 2½ miles, turn left on Coffman Road and continue 2 miles on a dirt road that should be avoided after rainfall). The Sulphur Springs Valley is also well known for its large wintering population of raptors, including ferruginous hawks and prairie falcons.

Near Douglas, the large pond at **Slaughter Ranch** (above) and the adjacent **San Bernardino National Wildlife Refuge** are good birding spots in both summer and winter.

North of Willcox, at the end of a 30-mile gravel road, lies the **Muleshoe Ranch Cooperative Management Area** (www.nature.org; ✆ **520/212-4295**), a 49,000-acre Nature Conservancy preserve that contains seven perennial streams. These streams support endangered aquatic life as well as riparian zones that attract a large number of bird species—more than 180 species have been recorded here. To get here, take exit 340 off I-10 and go south; turn right on Bisbee Avenue and then right onto Airport Road. After 15 miles, at a fork in the road, take the right fork. If the road is dry, it is usually passable in a passenger car. In March and April, the headquarters and visitor center are open daily 8am to 5pm; in May and from September to February it's open Thursday through Monday; and in June and August it's open weekends only. From late September through May, overnight accommodations in casitas ($170–$225 double) are available by reservation (2-night minimum, 3-night minimum on holidays). Casita guests have access to hot springs on the grounds.

At the **Willcox Chamber of Commerce and Agriculture,** 1500 N. Circle I Rd. (www.willcoxchamber.com; ✆ **520/384-2272**), you can pick up several birding maps and checklists for the region. If you're in Tucson beforehand, stop in at the **Audubon Society bookstore** (300 E University Blvd # 120; ✆ **520/629-0510**) for information, as well as expert guidance about where to go and what to look for.

of the finest cattle ranches in the West. Slaughter later went on to become the sheriff of Cochise County and helped rid the region of the unsavory characters who had flocked to its many remote mining towns. Today, the ranch is a National Historic Landmark and has been restored to its late-19th-century appearance. Wide lawns surround the ranch buildings and a large pond attracts a variety of birds, making this a great winter birding spot. For the-way-it-was tranquility, this old ranch can't be beat. Even though half the road to the ranch headquarters is graded dirt and gravel, just about any car in good condition will make it without incident.

6153 Geronimo Trail, about 15 mi E of Douglas. www.slaughterranch.com. ✆ **520/558-2474.** $5 adults, free for kids 13 and under. Wed–Sun 9:30am–3:30pm. Closed New Year's Day and Christmas.

Where to Stay

IN & NEAR WILLCOX

Cochise Stronghold Retreat ★★★ Set on 5 acres of private land within Coronado National Forest's Cochise Stronghold area, this remote and beautiful B&B is one of my favorites in the state. The inn is an energy-efficient, passive solar home with two housekeeping suites. It makes a superb base for hikes amid the area's fascinating rock formations and for excursions farther afield in Cochise County. Innkeeper Nancy Yates is a great source of information both on solar-home design and on the preservation of desert. In-room breakfast options include Southwestern dishes such as mesquite-cornmeal pancakes made with flour produced by grinding mesquite-bean pods. For a luxury camping experience, stay in the inn's yurt. This inn is a great choice for bird-watching trips.

2126 W. Windancer Trail (P.O. Box 232), Pearce. www.cochisestrongholdretreat.com. ✆ **877/426-4141** or 520/826-4141. $189–$249 double; $149 yurt. Rates include full breakfast. 2-night minimum stay. **Amenities:** Jacuzzi; free Wi-Fi.

IN DOUGLAS

Gadsden Hotel ★ Built in 1907, the Gadsden is listed on the National Register of Historic Places. The marble lobby, though dark, is a classic. Vaulted stained-glass skylights run the length of the ceiling, and above the landing of the Italian marble stairway is a genuine Tiffany window. Although the carpets in the halls are well-worn and rooms aren't always spotless, many units have been renovated and refurnished; as of this writing, the suites were undergoing restoration. The lounge is a popular local hangout, with more than 200 cattle brands painted on the walls.

1046 G Ave. www.thegadsdenhotel.com. ✆ **520/364-4481.** 160 units. $99 double. Pets accepted ($15 per night). **Amenities:** Restaurant; lounge; room service; free Wi-Fi.

IN PORTAL

Portal Peak Lodge, Portal Store & Café ★ This motel-like lodge, located behind the general store/cafe in the hamlet of Portal, has fairly modern guest rooms that face one another across a wooden deck. Meals are available in the adjacent cafe. If you're seeking predictable accommodations in a remote location, you'll find them here.

2358 S. Rock House Rd. www.portalpeaklodge.com. ✆ **520/558-2223.** 16 units. $85–$120 double. **Amenities:** Restaurant.

Southwestern Research Station, The American Museum of Natural History ★ Located in Cave Creek Canyon, this field research station for New York's famed American Museum of Natural History welcomes guests when the accommodations are not filled by scientists doing research. As such, it is the best place in the area for serious bird-watchers, who will find the company of researchers a fascinating addition to a visit. Guests stay in simply furnished cabins scattered around the research center. Spring and fall are the easiest times to get reservations and the best times for bird-watching.

P.O. Box 16553, Portal. www.research.amnh.org/swrs. ✆ **520/558-2396.** 12 units. Mar–Oct $92 per person, double occupancy, plus $75 cleaning fee, all meals included; Nov–Feb $72 per person, double occupancy, no meals. Children 3 and under stay free in parent's room. **Amenities:** Dining room; outdoor pool; free Wi-Fi.

AREA GUEST RANCHES

Hideout Ranch ★ Nestled in the foothills of the Chiricahua Mountains, the Hideout Ranch offers rustic accommodations, delicious bunkhouse-style meals, and, best of all, unlimited access to a herd of horses to traverse the many mountain trails into that wonderland of rocks. The ranch is made up of a kind of petting zoo of cabins, cottages, and ranch buildings, with accommodations of various configurations, all of them cozy. There are no overnight stays; rooms are booked by the week.

Hideout Ranch Rd. (turn E off Ariz. 80 onto Sky Ranch Rd.) www.hideoutranch.com. ✆ **855/879-4433.** $275/day 1st wk, $247.50/day 2nd wk, $222.75/day 3rd wk. Rates include all meals. **Amenities:** Horseback riding; guest laundry; free Wi-Fi.

Sunglow Guest Ranch ★★ In the western foothills of the Chiricahua Mountains, roughly 40 miles southeast of Willcox, this remote 475-acre ranch surrounded by Coronado National Forest is one of the most idyllic spots in the state. Guests can ride mountain bikes, paddle a canoe on a small lake, fish, and hike the ranch's trails. There's also great bird-watching both on the ranch and in the nearby hills. Horseback riding can also be arranged for an additional charge. The guest rooms are quite large, with rustic Mexican furnishings. More than half the units have wood-burning fireplaces. The beautiful little dining hall/cafe, built in classic Western-ranch style, serves some of the best food in this corner of the state. The ranch has also made numerous changes in the past few years to be more eco-friendly.

14066 S. Sunglow Rd., Pearce. www.sunglowranch.com. ✆ **866/786-4569** or 520/824-3334. 9 units. $209–$389 double. Rates include breakfast and dinner. Children 5 and under stay free in parent's room. 2-night minimum. Pets accepted ($10 per night). **Amenities:** Dining room; babysitting; bikes; exercise room; Jacuzzi; outdoor pool; room service; free Wi-Fi.

CAMPGROUNDS

The 22-site Bonita Canyon Campground in **Chiricahua National Monument** (p. 469), on Ariz. 186 (✆ **520/824-3560**), charges $12 per night. Along the road to Portal not far from the national monument, there are several small national forest campgrounds. Some are free and some charge $10 for a site. At **Cochise Stronghold,** 35 miles southwest of Willcox off U.S. 191, a 10-site campground charges $10 per night. For info on the national forest campgrounds, contact the Coronado National Forest Douglas Ranger District (www.fs.usda.gov/coronado; ✆ **520/364-3468**). Reservations are not accepted for these campgrounds.

Where to Eat

IN WILLCOX

Right across the parking lot from the Willcox Chamber of Commerce (off I-10 at exit 340), you'll find **Stout's Cider Mill ★**, 1510 N. Circle I Rd. (www.cidermill.com; ✆ **520/384-3696**), which makes delicious concoctions with apples. You can get cider, cider floats, "cidersicles," apple cake, and the biggest apple pie in the world. It's open Monday through Saturday from 9am to 5pm and Sunday from 1 to 5pm.

Big Tex BBQ ★ BARBECUE Discerning barbecue lovers may prefer Rodney's (below), but Big Tex has it beat for ambience, located inside an old railroad car within whistle-blowing distance of the main tracks. The BBQ and burgers are fine, the fish dishes a little less inspired.

130 E Maley St. ✆ **520/384-4423.** Main courses $9–$17. Mon–Thurs 11am–8pm, Fri–Sat 11am–9pm.

Rodney's ★ BARBECUE Willcox doesn't have much in the way of good restaurants, but if you're a fan of barbecue, you'll want to schedule a stop at Rodney's. This hole in the wall near the Rex Allen Museum is so nondescript that you can easily miss it. Inside, you'll find Rodney Brown, beaming with personality and dishing up lip-smackin' barbecued pork sandwiches and plates of ribs, shrimp, and catfish. Be sure to ask Rodney about the park across the street, which he looked after for many years.

118 N. Railroad Ave. ✆ **520/507-1516.** Main courses $4–$12. No credit cards. Tues–Sun 11am–8pm.

En Route to Phoenix: The Safford Area & Mount Graham

Roughly 50 miles north of Willcox, off U.S. 191 in a unit of Coronado National Forest, rise the Pinaleño Mountains and 10,717-foot **Mount Graham,** a favorite summer-vacation spot for desert dwellers. Here you'll find campgrounds, hiking trails, and an astronomical observatory (see "Starry, Starry Nights" box, p. 437). This observatory, funded partly by the University of Arizona and partly by the Vatican, was built despite concerns that the mountaintop was the last remaining habitat of 400 endangered Mount Graham red squirrels.

Northwest of Mount Graham, at the end of a 45-mile gravel road, the perennial Aravaipa Creek flows through the **Aravaipa Canyon Wilderness.** This scenic canyon is bordered on both ends by the Nature Conservancy's **Aravaipa Canyon Preserve.** Together these natural areas protect Arizona's healthiest population of native desert fish species, as well as cougars, desert bighorn sheep, bobcats, and 200 species of birds. Permits, which are required for hiking in the canyon, can be requested from the **Bureau of Land Management,** Safford Field Office, 711 14th Ave., Safford, AZ 85546 (✆ **928/348-4400**) 13 weeks in advance of your visit (spring and fall are the most difficult times to get reservations). If you're an adventurous traveler with a four-wheel-drive vehicle, try the eastern approach to Aravaipa Canyon, by way of Willcox and a long graded (but occasionally bumpy and washed-out) dirt road through the tiny hamlet of Klondyke. There are numerous campsites along the way.

Not far from the turnoff for Mount Graham and just south of Safford, **Roper Lake State Park** (www.azstateparks.com; ✆ **928/428-6760**) has a hot spring, a campground, rustic rental cabins ($60–$70 per night), and a lake with a swimming beach. The day-use fee is $10 per car; camping costs $20 to $30. There's good bird-watching here and at the nearby Dankworth Pond (where you'll find a nature trail and an outdoor exhibit on the various Native American cultures that used this site in centuries past). The state park is off U.S. 191, about 6 miles south of Safford; the Dankworth Pond site is another 3 miles south.

At the **Kachina Hot Springs Mineral Spa,** 1155 W. Cactus Rd. (www.kachinamineralsprings.com; ✆ **928/428-7212**), 5 miles south of Safford, visitors can soak in hot mineral waters, enjoy a sweat wrap, and get a massage. Treatments range from $50 for a 15-minute soak, foot reflexology, and a 30-minute wrap, to $115 for a soak, wrap, foot reflexology, and 1-hour massage. Just around the corner, the more rustic **Essence of Tranquility,** 6074 S. Lebanon Loop (www.azhotmineralspring.com; ✆ **928/428-9312**) has cement-lined hot tubs and offers similar services. Use of tubs is $8 per person for 1 hour; 1-hour massages go for $65. Tubs are available Monday from 2 to 9pm, Tuesday through Saturday from 8am to 9pm, and Sunday from 8am to 7pm.

Just south of Safford off U.S. 191, **Eastern Arizona College's Discovery Park Campus,** 1651 W. Discovery Park Blvd. (www.eac.edu/discoverypark; ✆ **928/428-6260**) is an interesting stop for both kids and adults. This science park includes the Gov. Aker Observatory, which is home to one of the world's largest camera obscuras (a dark room inside of which views of the outdoors can be seen projected on a wall). The observatory also has a 20-inch telescope that is available for public use; a space-flight simulator ride is one of the park's top attractions. A marsh offers good birding opportunities. The park is open Monday through Friday from 8am to 5pm and Saturday from 4 to 9:30pm; admission is free.

Twenty miles northeast of Safford off U.S. 70, you'll come to the **Gila Box Riparian National Conservation Area** (www.blm.gov/visit/gilabox), a popular hiking area on BLM land. As at Aravaipa Canyon, this area preserves the landscape around a perennial stream; in this case, the upper reaches of the Gila River. There is no fee to hike the area.

For more information on the Safford area, contact the **Graham County Chamber of Commerce,** 1111 Thatcher Blvd., Safford (www.graham-chamber.com; ✆ **888/837-1841**), or the **Bureau of Land Management,** Safford Field Office, 711 14th Ave., Safford (www.blm.gov/office/safford-field-office; ✆ **928/348-4400**).

11

ARIZONA'S "WEST COAST"

Arizona's West Coast is formed not by the Pacific Ocean, but by the Colorado River. Separating Arizona from California and Nevada are 340 miles of Colorado River waters, most of which are impounded in three huge reservoirs—Lake Mead, Lake Mohave, and Lake Havasu—that provide water and electricity to such sprawling southwest metropolises as Phoenix and Las Vegas.

It's just a matter of time before the Big One hits and California goes tumbling into the churning waters of the Pacific Ocean. So went the popular thinking in the 1970s, when I moved to Arizona, with the logical conclusion that when that happened, our landlocked state would gain a whole bunch of beachfront property. Thus was the idea of Arizona's "West Coast" born, pitching the hot, dry, newly developing western corridor of the Grand Canyon State to retirees and entrepreneurs.

It worked. Bordering the Colorado River, Arizona's West Coast became a destination for winter visitors and college students on spring break. The historically important but quiet port of Yuma began to boom, while Parker and Quartzsite became prime destinations for RV-borne winter visitors and Lake Havasu City sprouted resort hotels. Those three huge manmade lakes with their thousands of miles of shoreline draw boaters, water-skiers, campers, birdwatchers, and anglers throughout the year—which explains why you see so many small boats parked in carports and backyards throughout Arizona.

Across the river from Bullhead City, Arizona, a miniature version of Las Vegas has grown up on the banks of the Colorado, in Laughlin, Nevada. An Indian casino downriver in Parker also does a thriving trade.

Arizona's West Coast is lined with lakefront resorts, hotels, RV parks, and campgrounds. It's a destination popular with Arizonans themselves, and the hotels or resorts are far less expensive than those in Phoenix, Tucson, or Sedona. People out this way prefer less elaborate lodgings, and especially rented houseboats, floating vacation homes that are immensely popular with families and groups. A fine getaway is to travel on the river to London Bridge, brought over stone by stone to Lake Havasu from England half a century ago and now one of Arizona's biggest tourist attractions.

Arriving

BY AIR Two airports serve western Arizona: **Las Vegas McCarran Airport** in Nevada, and the regional **Yuma International Airport** (www.yuma airport.com; ✆ **928/726-5882**), which is served from Phoenix by American Airlines. If you're flying into Las Vegas, **Tri-State Super Shuttle** (www.tristateshuttle.net; ✆ **800/801-8687** or 928/704-9000) operates to Laughlin, Nevada, just across the state border from Bullhead City; the fare is $50 each way ($60 without reservation) and $90 round-trip. The **Havasu/Vegas Express** (www.havasuvegasexpress.com; ✆ **800/459-4884** or 928/453-4884) operates a shuttle van between Lake Havasu City and Las Vegas. Fares are $62 one-way and $114 round-trip ($57 and $104 for seniors).

BY TRAIN **Amtrak** (www.amtrak.com; ✆ **800/872-7245**) runs passenger service to Yuma on its Sunset Limited route, which runs between Los Angeles and Orlando. The station is at 281 Gila St.

LAKE MEAD NATIONAL RECREATION AREA

70 miles NW of Kingman; 256 miles NW of Phoenix; 30 miles SE of Las Vegas, NV

Lake Mead National Recreation Area, which includes Lake Mead, Lake Mohave, and a scenic, free-flowing stretch of the Colorado River, straddles the border between Arizona and Nevada. Throughout the year, anglers fish for striped bass, rainbow trout, channel catfish, and other sport fish, while during the hot summer months, Lake Mead and Lake Mohave attract tens of thousands of water-skiers and personal watercraft riders. There are more facilities on the Nevada side of Lake Mead, close to Las Vegas, and so the recreation area tends to be more popular with Nevadans and Californians than with Arizonans.

Lake Mead, the larger of the two reservoirs, was created by Hoover Dam, the first major dam on the Colorado River, built between 1931 and 1935. By supplying huge amounts of electricity and water to Arizona and California, it set the stage for the phenomenal growth the region experienced in the latter half of the 20th century. Today, with water levels in a bathtub-ringed Lake Mead at all-time lows, the cities that depend on the lake's water have finally begun to address the issue of water conservation.

U.S. 93, which once ran across the top of Hoover Dam, connects Nevada and Arizona via the Mike O'Callaghan–Pat Tillman Memorial Bridge. (***Bridge buffs note:*** It's the highest concrete arch bridge in the world, at 900 feet.) The old road from Goldstrike Canyon to Hoover Dam makes for a twist-and-turn adventure. On either side of the river, secondary roads lead to various marinas on Lake Mead, and there are many miles of unpaved roads within the

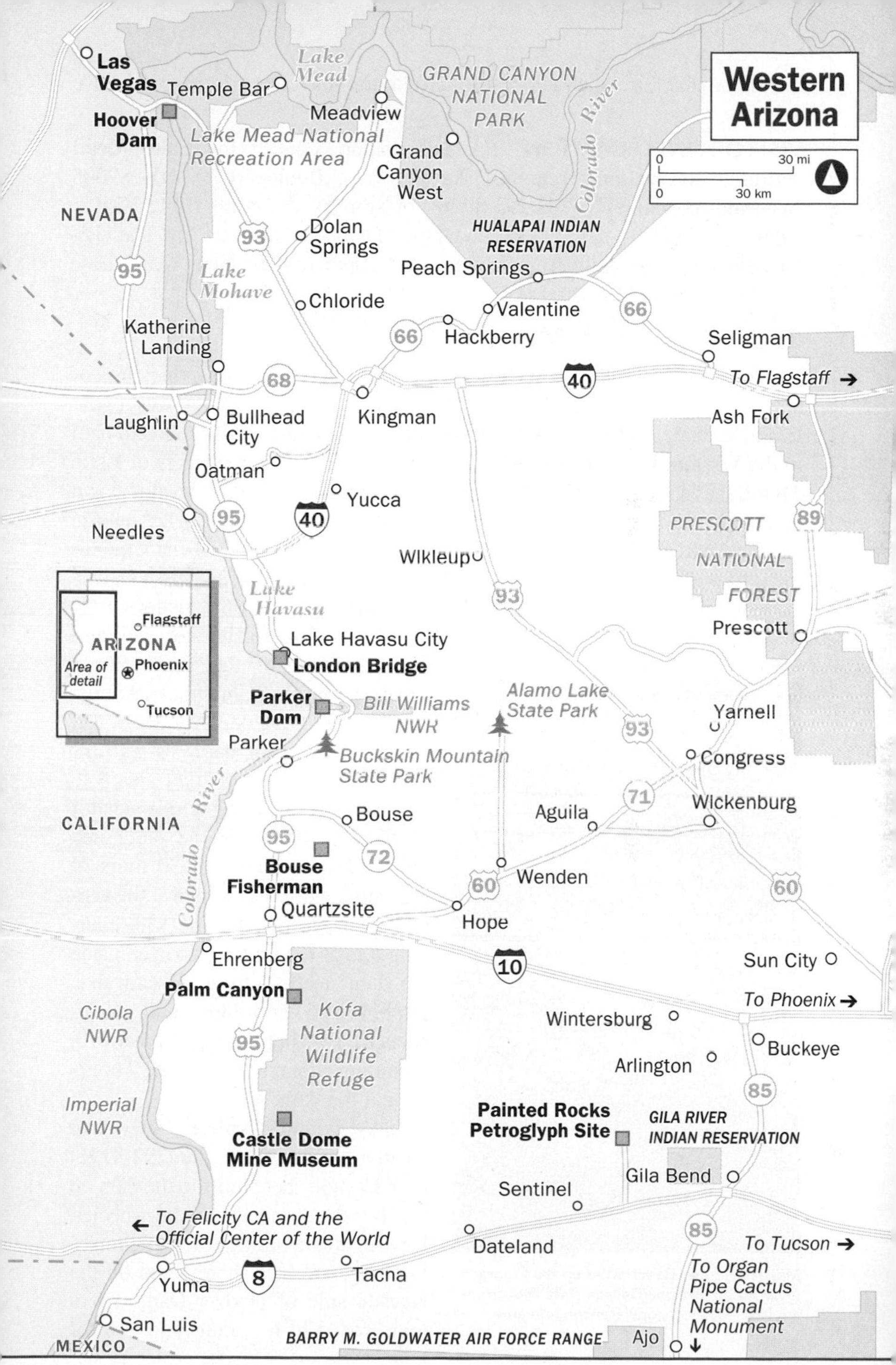
Western Arizona
0
30 mi
30 km
Las Vegas
Temple Bar
Lake Mead
GRAND CANYON NATIONAL PARK
Colorado River
Meadview
Hoover Dam
Lake Mead National Recreation Area
Grand Canyon West
NEVADA
93
Dolan Springs
HUALAPAI INDIAN RESERVATION
95
Lake Mohave
Peach Springs
Chloride
Valentine
66
Katherine Landing
Hackberry
Seligman
68
40
To Flagstaff
Ash Fork
Laughlin
Bullhead City
Kingman
Oatman
Yucca
Needles
PRESCOTT NATIONAL FOREST
89
Wikieup
Lake Havasu
Flagstaff
ARIZONA
Area of detail
Phoenix
Tucson
Lake Havasu City
London Bridge
Prescott
Parker Dam
Bill Williams NWR
Alamo Lake State Park
Yarnell
Parker
Buckskin Mountain State Park
Congress
71
CALIFORNIA
Bouse
Aguila
Wickenburg
72
Bouse Fisherman
60
Wenden
Quartzsite
Hope
10
Ehrenberg
Sun City
Palm Canyon
To Phoenix
Cibola NWR
Kofa National Wildlife Refuge
Wintersburg
Buckeye
Arlington
85
Imperial NWR
Painted Rocks Petroglyph Site
GILA RIVER INDIAN RESERVATION
Castle Dome Mine Museum
Gila Bend
Sentinel
To Felicity CA and the Official Center of the World
Dateland
To Tucson
Yuma
8
Tacna
To Organ Pipe Cactus National Monument
San Luis
MEXICO
BARRY M. GOLDWATER AIR FORCE RANGE
Ajo

recreation area for which it's best to have a high-clearance, four-wheel-drive vehicle.

VISITOR INFORMATION For information, contact the **Lake Mead National Recreation Area,** 601 Nevada Way, Boulder City, NV 89005 (www.nps.gov/lame; ✆ **702/293-8906**), or stop by the **Alan Bible Visitor Center** (✆ **702/293-8990**), between Hoover Dam and Boulder City. The visitor center is open daily from 8:30am to 4:30pm (closed New Year's Day, Thanksgiving, and Christmas).

Exploring Lake Mead

Standing 726 feet tall, from bedrock to top, and tapering from a thickness of 660 feet at its base to only 45 feet at the top, **Hoover Dam ★** (www.usbr.gov/lc/hooverdam; ✆ **866/730-9097** or 702/494-2517) is the tallest concrete dam in the Western Hemisphere. Behind this massive dam lie the waters of **Lake Mead,** the largest artificial lake in the United States. The water level is down so far that you can see a giant "bathtub ring" surrounding the lake, but the dam, built in better and wetter days, is still worth a visit, if only as a monument to our desire to control a drought-inclined nature that always bats last. To learn about the construction of Hoover Dam, stop in at the visitor center beside the dam on U.S. 93; it's open daily 9am to 6pm in summer, and until 5pm the rest of the year (closed Thanksgiving and Christmas). Admission is $10 for anyone over age 3, and guided tours of the dam cost $15 for adults, $12 for seniors and kids 4 to 16. Tickets, which include visitor center admission, can be purchased online. More extensive $30 tours of the dam are offered; stop in at the visitor center for tickets. The $30, hour-long tour is the only way to get inside the dam itself, a maze of catwalks, throbbing power turbines, and spooky silences. Parking is an additional $10. Including a tour, it takes about 2 hours to visit the dam.

Massive Hoover Dam bottles up the Colorado River on the Arizona-Nevada state line, creating Lake Mead, a popular recreation area.

Lake Mead Cruises (www.lakemeadcruises.com; ✆ **866/292-9191**) runs 1½-hour boat tours to the dam on the *Desert Princess* paddle-wheeler, leaving from Lake Mead Cruises Landing, off Lakeshore Road on the Nevada side of Hoover Dam. These tours cost $26 for adults and $13 for children 2 to 11. Other options include dinner cruises ($61.50 for adults, $25 for children) and brunch cruises ($45 for adults, $19.50 for kids).

One of the most interesting ways to see remote parts of Lake Mohave is by sea kayak. **Desert River Outfitters** (www.desertriveroutfitters.com; © **928/763-3033**) will rent you a boat and shuttle you and your gear to and from put-ins and take-outs. The trip through Black Canyon ($70 per person with a four-person minimum), starting at the base of Hoover Dam, is the most interesting route. (***Note:*** This trip requires advance planning because a permit is necessary.) You can also paddle past the casinos in Laughlin ($40), through the Topock Gorge ($60), or around Lake Mohave ($40). **Black Canyon River Adventures** (www.blackcanyonadventures.com; © **800/455-3490**) offers daylong raft trips through scenic Black Canyon on big motorized rafts, costing $99 per adult, $89 for kids 4 to 16. If you're not a paddler, this easy float is a great way to see this remote stretch of river—it's definitely a highlight of visiting this corner of the state.

Outdoor Activities

Swimming, fishing, water-skiing, sailing, windsurfing, and powerboating are the most popular activities in Lake Mead National Recreation Area. On Arizona shores, there are **swimming beaches** at Lake Mohave's Katherine Landing (outside Bullhead City) and Lake Mead's Temple Bar (north of Kingman off U.S. 93). Picnic areas can be found at these two areas, as well as at Willow Beach on Lake Mohave and at more than half a dozen spots on the Nevada side of Lake Mead.

BOATING

In Arizona, marinas can be found at **Katherine Landing** on Lake Mohave (just outside Bullhead City), near the north end of Lake Mohave at **Willow Beach** (best access for trout angling), and at **Temple Bar** on Lake Mead. There's also a boat ramp at **South Cove,** north of the community of Meadview at the east end of Lake Mead. This latter boat ramp is the closest to the Grand Canyon end of Lake Mead. On the Nevada side of Lake Mohave, there's a marina at **Cottonwood Cove,** and on the Nevada side of Lake Mead, you'll find marinas at **Boulder Beach, Las Vegas Bay, Callville Bay,** and **Echo Bay.** These marinas offer motels, restaurants, general stores, campgrounds, and boat rentals.

At **Temple Bar Resort & Marina** (p. 484) you can rent speedboats, fishing boats, and deck boats for $210 to $375 per day and a personal watercraft for $350 per day. At **Lake Mohave Marina** (p. 482) you can rent ski boats, fishing boats, and patio boats for between $120 and $585 per day and a personal watercraft for $360 per day.

Unlike these other two marinas, **Willow Beach Marina,** Willow Beach Rd. (www.willowbeachharbor.com; © **480-336-8601**), 14 miles south of Hoover Dam, is on a free-flowing stretch of the Colorado River downstream from Black Canyon. Bounded by rugged, rocky slopes and canyon walls, this is one of the prettiest stretches of the Colorado between Hoover Dam and Yuma. To explore this scenic stretch of river on your own, you can rent a canoe ($15 per hour), kayak ($10 to $20 per hour), or motorboat ($40 per hour) at the marina. ***Note:*** On Sundays and Mondays year-round, motorboats and personal watercraft are prohibited on this stretch of the river.

DESERT HIKING

Despite the area's decidedly watery orientation, there's quite a bit of mountainous desert here, home to bighorn sheep, roadrunners, and other wildlife. You'll also find petroglyphs scratched into rocks, relics of the people who lived here before European settlers arrived; the best place to see petroglyphs is **Grapevine Canyon,** due west of Laughlin, Nevada, in the southwest corner of the National Recreation Area. To reach Grapevine Canyon, take Nev. 163 west from Laughlin to milepost 13, turn right on the marked dirt road, and drive about 2 miles. From the trail head, it's less than a quarter-mile to the petroglyph-covered jumble of rocks at the mouth of Grapevine Canyon. Covering the boulders are thousands of cryptic symbols, as well as ancient illustrations of bighorn sheep. To see them, you'll have to do a lot of scrambling, so wear sturdy shoes (preferably hiking boots).

For information on other hikes, contact **Lake Mead National Recreation Area** (www.nps.gov/lame; ✆ **702/293-8990**).

FISHING

Fishing for monster striped bass (up to 50 lb.) is one of the most popular activities on Lake Mead, and while Lake Mohave's striped bass may not reach these awesome proportions, fish in the 25-pound range are not uncommon there. Largemouth bass, catfish, and even rainbow trout are plentiful in the national recreation area's waters. Try for big rainbows in the cold waters that flow out from Hoover Dam through Black Canyon and into Lake Mohave. (Please note that a five-trout limit is in force.) To fish from shore, you'll need a license from either Arizona or Nevada, depending on which shore you're fishing from. To fish from a boat, you'll need a license from one state and a special-use stamp from the other. Most Lake Mead marinas sell both licenses and stamps. You can also buy an Arizona fishing license online (https://license.azgfd.gov/home.xhtml).

If you don't have your own boat, try fishing from the shore of Lake Mohave near Davis Dam, where the water is deep. Anchovies and bloodworms work well as bait, with shot on your line to get it down to the depths where the fish are feeding. You can get bait, tackle, and fishing tips at the **Lake Mohave Marina,** 2690 E. Katherine Spur Rd. (www.katherinelanding.com; ✆ **928/754-3245**), at Katherine Landing, near Bullhead City.

Where to Stay Around Lake Mead

CAMPGROUNDS

In Arizona, there are campgrounds at **Katherine Landing** on Lake Mohave and at **Temple Bar** on Lake Mead. Both campgrounds have been heavily planted with trees, so they provide some semblance of shade during the hot, but popular, summer months. In Nevada, you'll find campgrounds at **Cottonwood Cove** on Lake Mohave and at **Boulder Beach, Las Vegas Bay, Callville Bay,** and **Echo Bay** on Lake Mead. Campsites at all campgrounds are $20 per night. For more information, contact **Lake Mead National Recreation Area** (www.nps.gov/lame; ✆ **702/293-8990**).

HOUSEBOATS

Callville Bay Resort & Marina ★ Why pay extra for a lakeview room when you can rent a houseboat that always has a 360-degree water view? There's no better way to explore Lake Mead than on one of these floating vacation homes. You can cruise for miles, tie up at a deserted cove, and enjoy a wilderness adventure with all the comforts of home. Houseboats come complete with full kitchens, air-conditioning, and space to sleep up to 13 people. Bear in mind that whoever's driving will have to have an Arizona boater card on the Arizona side, while a Nevada card is required for anyone born on or after January 1, 1983.

100 Callville Bay Rd., Overton, NV. www.callvillebay.com. ✆ **800/255-5561.** $2,100 and up per week. Pets accepted. **Amenities:** A/C; kitchen; no phones; no Wi-Fi.

Houseboats are a favorite lodging option with Lake Mead vacationers.

MOTELS

Katherine Landing Resort ★ Just up Lake Mohave from Davis Dam and only a few minutes outside Bullhead City, this older motel has huge rooms that are good for families. Most have some sort of view of the lake, which is across the road, and some have kitchenettes. Just across the road, the resort's nautical-theme restaurant and lounge overlook the marina. The newly renovated resort also has a convenience store and a bait-and-tackle store.

Katherine Landing, 2690 E. Katherine Spur Rd., Bullhead City. http://www.katherinelanding.com. ✆ **928/754-3245.** 51 units. $120–$135 double, $160 suite. Children 8 and under stay free in parent's room. No pets. **Amenities:** Restaurant; lounge; watersports equipment/rentals; free Wi-Fi.

Temple Bar Marina ★ Although basically just a motel, the Temple Bar Marina has a beach, great fishing nearby, and 40 miles of prime skiing waters extending from the resort. It makes a good budget getaway for anyone into watersports. A restaurant and lounge overlooking the lake provides economical meals. The resort also offers houseboat and powerboat rentals and has a convenience store.

1 Main St., Temple Bar. www.templebarlakemead.com. ✆ **800/255-5561** or 928/767-3211. 22 units. Apr–Oct $95–$120 double, $130 suite; Nov–Mar $77–$98 double, $111 suite. Pets accepted ($50 deposit plus $10 per night). **Amenities:** Restaurant; lounge; watersports equipment/rentals; free Wi-Fi.

BULLHEAD CITY & LAUGHLIN, NEVADA

30 miles W of Kingman; 60 miles N of Lake Havasu City; 216 miles NW of Phoenix

You may find it difficult at first to understand why anyone would ever want to live in Bullhead City. Established in the 1940s to house workers building the nearby Davis Dam, it's one of the hottest places in North America, with temperatures regularly topping 120°F (49°C) in summer. However, to understand the town's rapid growth in the last few years, you need only gaze across the Colorado River at the gambling mecca of Laughlin, Nevada, where the slot machines are always in action and the gaming tables are nearly as hot as the air outside. Before the advent of Indian casinos in Arizona, Laughlin, at Nevada's southernmost tip, was the closest place to Phoenix to do any gambling. The 10 large casino hotels across the river in Nevada still make Bullhead City one of Arizona's busiest little towns.

Laughlin is a perfect miniature Las Vegas, and much easier than Vegas to get around in. High-rise hotels loom above the desert like glass mesas, miles of neon lights turn night into day, and acres of asphalt are always covered with cars and RVs as crowds of hopeful gamblers go searching for Lady Luck. Cheap rooms and meals lure people into spending the money won downstairs in the casino.

GETTING AROUND The **Southern Nevada Transit Coalition** (www.sntc.net; ✆ **702/298-4435**) provides public bus service in Laughlin. The fare is $2 adults, $1 seniors and ages 6 to 17; one-day and 15-day passes are available. Free ferries shuttle to and from parking lots on the Arizona side of the river, and water taxis ($5 one-way, $20 day pass) go from casino to casino.

VISITOR INFORMATION For information on Bullhead City and Laughlin, contact the **Bullhead Area Chamber of Commerce,** 1251 Hwy. 95, Bullhead City (www.bullheadareachamber.com; ✆ **928/754-4121**). In Laughlin, stop by the **Laughlin Visitor Information Center,** 1555 Casino Dr. (www.visitlaughlin.com; ✆ **800/452-8445** or 702/298-3321).

Exploring Bullhead City & Laughlin

The casinos of Laughlin, Nevada, are known for having loose slots—that is, the slot machines pay off frequently. Consequently, Laughlin is a very popular weekend destination for Phoenicians and other Arizonans. In addition to the slot machines, there is keno, blackjack, poker, craps, off-track betting, and sports betting. All the hotels in Laughlin offer live entertainment of some sort, including an occasional headliner, but gambling is still the main event.

The casino town of Laughlin, Nevada, beckons Arizona-based visitors across the Colorado River.

WHERE TO STAY IN laughlin, nevada

Laughlin, Nevada, currently has 10 huge hotel-and-casino complexes, eight of which are on the west bank of the Colorado River (the ninth is across the street from the river, and the tenth is on the river but several miles south of town). All offer cheap rooms (often under $30 on weeknights) to lure potential gamblers. In addition to huge casinos with hundreds of slot machines and every sort of gaming table, these hotels all have several restaurants (think cheap steaks, prime rib, and all-you-can-eat buffets), bars and lounges (usually with live country or pop music), swimming pools, video arcades, ferry service to parking lots on the Arizona side of the river, valet parking, room service, car-rental desks, airport shuttles, gift shops, and gaming classes. The only real difference between most of these places is the theme each has adopted for its decor. Should you wish to stay at one of these hotels, here's the information you'll need:

- **Aquarius Casino Resort,** 1900 S. Casino Dr. (www.aquariuscasinoresort.com; ✆ **800/662-5825** or 702/298-5111)
- **Avi Resort & Casino ★**, 10000 Aha Macav Pkwy. (www.avicasino.com; ✆ **800/284-2946** or 702/535-5555)
- **Colorado Belle Hotel & Casino,** 2100 S. Casino Dr. (www.coloradobelle.com; ✆ **866/352-3553** or 702/298-4000)
- **Edgewater Hotel & Casino,** 2020 S. Casino Dr. (www.edgewater-casino.com; ✆ **866/352-3553** or 702/298-2453)
- **Golden Nugget Laughlin,** 2300 S. Casino Dr. (www.goldennugget.com/laughlin; ✆ **800/950-7700** or 702/298-7111)
- **Harrah's Laughlin ★**, 2900 S. Casino Dr. (www.harrahs.com; ✆ **800/221-1306** or 702/298-4600)
- **Pioneer Hotel & Gambling Hall,** 2200 S. Casino Dr. (www.pioneerlaughlin.com; ✆ **800/634-3469** or 702/298-2442)
- **River Palms Resort & Casino,** 2700 S. Casino Dr. (www.river-palms.com; ✆ **800/835-7904**)
- **Riverside Resort Hotel & Casino,** 1650 S. Casino Dr. (www.riversideresort.com; ✆ **800/227-3849,** 702/298-2535, or 928/763-7070)
- **Tropicana Express Hotel & Casino,** 2121 S. Casino Dr. (www.tropicanax.com; ✆ **800/243-6846** or 702/298-4200)

To learn about this area's history, visit the **Colorado River Museum,** 355 Hwy. 95, Bullhead City (http://coloradoriverhistoricalsociety.org/colorado-river-museum; ✆ **928/754-3399**), a half-mile north of the Laughlin Bridge. It's open Tuesday through Saturday 10am to 4pm (closed June–Aug). Admission is by $2 suggested donation.

BOAT TOURS

If you'd like to see a bit of the Colorado River, daily paddle-wheeler cruises are available through **Laughlin River Tours** (www.laughlinrivertours.com; ✆ **800/228-9825** or 702/298-1047) at the Aquarius Casino Resort. These cruises cost $12 for adults and $6 for children 4 to 10; dinner cruises ($45) are also available. At **Riverside Resort Hotel & Casino,** 1650 S. Casino Dr.,

Laughlin (www.riversideresort.com; ✆ **800/227-3849** or 702/298-2535), you can take a tour on the 65-foot USS *Riverside* to Davis Dam. These excursions last 80 minutes and cost $12 for adults and $6 for children 3 to 12.

If you'd rather look at natural surroundings than casino towers, consider booking a 6-hour jet-boat tour through scenic Topock Gorge, a 15-mile stretch of river bordered by multicolored cliffs, to the London Bridge (below) with **London Bridge Jet Boat Tours** (www.jetboattour.com; ✆ **888/505-3545** or 702/298-5498). Tours cost $70 for adults and $50 for children 12 and under. Tours don't operate in December or January.

Outdoor Activities

For information on **fishing** in nearby Lake Mohave, see p. 482.

Desert River Outfitters, 1034 U.S. 95, Bullhead City (www.desertriver-outfitters.com; ✆ **888/529-2533**) will rent you a kayak or canoe and shuttle you and your gear to and from put-ins and take-outs. The least expensive trip is down the Colorado River past the casinos in Laughlin ($40 for adults, $20 for children 6 to 15).

In Laughlin, golfers can play a round at the **Mojave Resort Golf Club,** 9905 Aha Macav Pkwy. (www.mojavegolf.com; ✆ **702/535-4653**), adjacent to the Avi Resort & Casino (see box, above). Carved out of dense thickets of desert vegetation, this course has wide, user-friendly fairways and charges greens fees of $89 to $109 during the cooler months (lower rates for Avi Resort guests). In Bullhead City, try the **Huukan Golf Course,** 5835 Desert Lakes Dr., Fort Mohave (www.mojavegolf.com; ✆ **928/768-1000**), 15 miles south of town off U.S. 95. Greens fees are around $39 in the cooler months. Rates after 1 or 2pm are usually lower at these courses.

Bird-watching is excellent in **Havasu National Wildlife Refuge** (www.fws.gov/refuge/Havasu; ✆ **760/326-3853**), a wintering area for many species of waterfowl. Much of this internationally renowned refuge lies within 15-mile-long Topock Gorge and can be reached only by boat. The most accessible birding areas are along the marshes near the communities of Golden Shores and Topock, both north of the I-40 bridge over the Colorado.

LAKE HAVASU & THE LONDON BRIDGE

60 miles S of Bullhead City; 150 miles S of Las Vegas, NV; 200 miles NW of Phoenix

"London Bridge is falling down, falling down, falling down." There once was a time when London Bridge really was falling down, the victim of age and deterioration. But that was before power-tool mogul Robert McCulloch, founder of Lake Havasu City, hit upon the brilliant idea of buying the bridge (not the long-demolished medieval version, but a granite bridge built in the 1820s) and having it shipped to his planned community in the Arizona desert.

That was half a century ago, and today London Bridge is still standing and still attracting tourists by the millions. An unlikely place for a bit of British heritage, true, but London Bridge has turned Lake Havasu City into one of Arizona's most popular tourist destinations, complete with uniformed beefeaters and Olde English theme attractions.

Lake Havasu was formed in 1938 by the building of the Parker Dam, but it wasn't until 1963 that McCulloch founded the town of Lake Havasu City. In the town's early years, not too many people were keen on spending time in this remote corner of the desert, where summer temperatures are often more than 110°F (43°C). Despite its name, Lake Havasu City at the time was little more than an expanse of desert with a few mobile homes on it. It was then that McCulloch began looking for ways to attract more people to his little "city" on the lake. His solution proved to be a stroke of genius.

Today, Lake Havasu City attracts an odd mix of visitors. In winter, the town is filled with retirees, and you'll rarely see anyone under the age of 60. On weekends, during the summer, and over spring break, however, Lake Havasu City is popular with Arizona and California college students, and many businesses and resorts now cater primarily to young partyers. Expect a lot of noise if you're here on a weekend or a holiday. Summers bring out the water-ski and personal-watercraft crowds.

VISITOR INFORMATION The **Lake Havasu Convention & Visitors Bureau,** 314 London Bridge Rd. (www.golakehavasu.com; © **800/242-8278** or 928/453-3444) has a visitor information center at 420 English Village, at the foot of the London Bridge. It's open daily from 9am to 5 pm.

Exploring London Bridge & Lake Havasu

Back in the mid-1960s, when London Bridge was indeed falling down—or, more correctly, sinking—into the Thames River due to heavy car and truck traffic, the British government decided to sell the bridge. Robert McCulloch and his partner paid nearly $2.5 million for the bridge, had it shipped 10,000 miles to California, and then trucked it to Lake Havasu City. Reconstruction began in 1968, and the grand reopening was held in 1971. Oddly enough, the 900-foot-long bridge was not built over water; it just connected desert to more desert on a peninsula jutting into Lake Havasu. It wasn't until after the bridge was rebuilt that a mile-long channel was dredged through the base of the

Seeing the Light

Lighthouses may seem as out of place in the desert as the London Bridge, but there are now 25 lighthouses along the shores of Lake Havasu, several of them in the parks flanking London Bridge. These replicas of famous navigation beacons from around the country, one-third the size of the originals, were built by the **Lake Havasu Lighthouse Club** (www.lh-lighthouseclub.org).

Like a mirage in the Arizona desert, the transplanted London Bridge and its faux-Tudor shopping-and-dining village.

peninsula, thus creating an island offshore from Lake Havasu City. At the base of the bridge, **English Village** is done up in proper English style and has a few shops, some casual restaurants, and Lake Havasu's main visitor center. There is also a waterfront promenade, along which you'll find several cruise boats and boat-rental docks.

Unfortunately, London Bridge is not very impressive as bridges go, and the commercialization of its surroundings makes it something of a letdown for some visitors. On top of that, over the years the jolly Olde England styling that once predominated around here has been supplanted by a Mexican beach-bar aesthetic designed to appeal to partying college students. However, in the last dozen years or so, Lake Havasu City has emerged as a vibrant Colorado River community, with a branch of Arizona State University, a good library, coffee shops, restaurants, and all the usual amenities on top of its tourist and party-destination role.

Just south of London Bridge on the "mainland" side, you'll find the large **Rotary Community Park,** which is connected to the bridge by a paved waterside path. Adjacent to the park, the **Lake Havasu Aquatic Center,** 100

Park Ave. (✆ **928/453-2687**) has an indoor wave pool, 254-foot water slide, and lots of other facilities.

ORGANIZED TOURS

Several companies offer different types of boat tours on Lake Havasu. **Bluewater Jet Boat Tours** (www.coloradoriverjetboattours.com; ✆ **928/855-7171**) runs 2½-hour jet-boat tours from the London Bridge up the Colorado River 25 miles to scenic Topock Gorge. The cost is $45 for adults, $42 for seniors, and $25 for children 5 to 12. Numerous other operators offer water tours, including a ferry ride across the river to the Chemehuevi Indian Reservation in California. For a listing, see **https://golakehavasu.com**.

In addition to tours on the water, there are tours *over* the water. **Havasu Parasail** (www.havasuparasail.com; ✆ **928/302-0683**) will strap you into a parasail and tow you behind a speedboat as you soar 600 to 800 feet over the lake. These short flights cost $69 to $79. Looking for something a bit quieter and slower paced? Between October and May, you can book a hot-air balloon ride with **Wanderlust Balloons** (www.wanderlustballoons.com; ✆ **928/486-1075**), which charges $200 per person ($210 with credit card) for an hour-long sunrise flight over the river.

Outdoor Activities

While the London Bridge is what made Lake Havasu City, these days watersports on 45-mile-long Lake Havasu are the area's real draw. Whether you want to go for a swim, take a leisurely pedal-boat ride, try parasailing, or spend the day water-skiing, there are plenty of places to get wet. Lake Havasu is known as the Jet Ski Capital of the World, so don't expect much peace and quiet when you're out on the water.

Canoeing the Colorado

Paddling down a desert river is a fascinating experience. Rugged rock walls, prickly cacti, and thickets of reeds drift by on shore as the cool water rushes past your boat. If you're interested in a scenic canoe tour, a couple of outfitters in the area provide boats, paddles, life jackets, maps, and shuttles to put-in and take-out points, though usually no guides. **Western Arizona Canoe and Kayak Outfitters** (www.azwacko.com; ✆ **888/881-5038** or 928/855-6414) offers self-guided kayak or canoe trips through beautiful rugged Topock Gorge, where you can see ancient petroglyphs and possibly bighorn sheep. Trips take 5 to 6 hours and the cost is $50 per person, which includes kayak/canoe rentals, paddles, life jackets, dry bags, coolers, and, most important, the shuttle service to the put-in point and back from the take-out point. **Jerkwater Canoe Company** (www.jerkwatercanoe.com; ✆ **800/421-7803** or 928/768-7753) offers a similar Topock Gorge excursion as well as other canoe and kayak trips of varying lengths. Jerkwater's Topock Gorge self-guided day-long trip is $51 per person. There is a two-person minimum.

BEACHES

The best in-town beach, **London Bridge Beach,** is located in a county park off West McCulloch Boulevard behind the Island Inn. This park has a sandy beach, lots of palm trees, and views of both the London Bridge and the distant desert mountains. There are also picnic tables and a snack bar. There are more beaches at **Lake Havasu State Park** (www.azstateparks.com; ✆ **928/855-2784**), 2 miles north of the London Bridge, and at **Cattail Cove State Park** (www.azstateparks.com; ✆ **928/855-1223**), 15 miles south of Lake Havasu City. Lake Havasu State Park charges a $15 day-use fee ($20 Friday–Sunday and state holidays); the fee for Cattail Cove is $10 weekdays and $15 weekends and holidays.

BOATING & WATERSPORTS

You can rent boats from **Arizona Water Sports,** 655 Kiowa Ave. (http://www.arizonawatersports.com; ✆ **800/393-5558** or 928/453-5558). Pontoon boats and ski boats equipped with water skis or knee boards are available; call for rates. If you're interested in kayaking or canoeing, numerous vendors located around London Bridge offer rental boats and lessons. Try **Southwest Kayaks** (www.southwestkayaks.com; ✆ **928/680-9257**) or **Rentals on the Beach** (www.londonbridgewatercraft.com; ✆ **928/453-8883**) for starters.

FISHING

Striped bass, also known as stripers, are the favorite quarry of anglers here. These fish have been known to weigh in at more than 60 pounds in these waters, so be sure to bring the heavy tackle. Largemouth bass in the 2- to 4-pound range are also fairly common, and giant channel catfish of up to 35 pounds have been caught in Topock Marsh. The best fishing starts in spring, when the water begins to warm up, but there is also good winter fishing.

GOLF

Lake Havasu Golf Club, 2400 Clubhouse Dr. (www.lakehavasugolfclub.com; ✆ **928/855-2719**), with two 18-hole courses, is the area's premier course. Seasonal and annual memberships are available, with a 1-month unlimited pass selling for $600. Greens fees for day visitors go for $69 to $74 before noon and $53 to $58 after noon, with substantial discounts for residents and for all comers in summer, when rates fall to $25–$39 for visitors. **Havasu Island Golf Club,** 1000 McCulloch Blvd. (www.nauticalbeachfrontresort.com; ✆ **928/855-5585**) is a 4,012-yard, par-61 executive course with lots of water hazards. Greens fees are $26 to $32 if you walk and $35 to $43 if you ride. The **Refuge Golf & Country Club,** 3275 N Latrobe Dr. (www.refugecountryclub.com; ✆ **928/764-1404**) offers memberships and day passes; call for rates. The 9-hole **Bridgewater Links,** 1477 Queens Bay Rd. (www.londonbridgeresort.com; ✆ **928/855-4777**), at the London Bridge Resort, is the most accessible and easiest of the area courses. Call for rates and tee times.

The most spectacular course in the region is the **Emerald Canyon Golf Course ★★**, 7351 Riverside Dr., Parker (www.emeraldcanyongolf.com; ✆ **928/667-3366**), about 30 miles south of Lake Havasu City. This municipal course plays through rugged canyons and past red-rock cliffs, where there are views of the Colorado River. One hole even has you hitting your ball off a cliff to a green 200 feet below! Greens fees are $65 to $75 in the cooler months ($49.75 after 1pm); tee-time reservations can be made a week in advance (further out if you pay $10 per player). Also in Parker, the 9-hole course at the **Havasu Springs Resort,** 2581 U.S. 95 (www.havasuspringsrvresort.com; ✆ **928/667-3361**) is said to be the hardest par-3 course in the state, set atop a rocky outcropping with steep drop-offs all around. Greens fees are only $12 for 9 holes, $18 for 18 holes.

Where to Stay Around Lake Havasu

Heat Hotel ★★ Located at the foot of the London Bridge, this surprisingly stylish boutique hotel is by far the hippest hotel between Scottsdale and Las Vegas. Guest rooms are reminiscent of those at W hotels, although here you get much more room at a much lower price. Rooms are large and have balconies, and most overlook the bridge or the water. Platform beds, stylish lamps, and a sort of Scandinavian-modern aesthetic make this the most distinctive hotel on this side of the state. The Inferno Suites, with their Tempur-Pedic beds and Jacuzzi tubs, are my favorite rooms here. ***One caveat:*** The open-air bar directly across the channels plays loud music until 2am on warm nights (especially during spring break).

1420 McCulloch Blvd. N., Lake Havasu City. www.heathotel.com. ✆ **888/898-4328.** 25 units. $169 double; $189–$429 suite. Pets accepted ($50 fee). **Amenities:** 2 bars; concierge; free Wi-Fi.

London Bridge Resort & Convention Center ★ Merry Olde England was once the theme at this timeshare resort, and Tudor half-timbers are jumbled up with towers, ramparts, and crenellations. However, England has given way to the tropics and the desert as the resort strives to please its young, partying clientele (who tend to make a lot of noise and leave the hotel looking much the worse for wear). Although the bridge is just out the hotel's back door, and a replica of Britain's gold state coach is inside the lobby, guests are more interested in the three pools and the tropical-theme outdoor nightclub. The one- and two-bedroom units are spacious, comfortable, and attractive, and those on the ground floor have double whirlpool tubs.

1477 Queens Bay, Lake Havasu City. www.londonbridgeresort.com. ✆ **866/331-9231** or 928/855-0888. 122 units. $184 1-bedroom; $224–$344 2-bedroom condo. **Amenities:** Restaurant; 2 lounges; 9-hole golf course; exercise room and access to nearby health club; Jacuzzi; 3 pools; spa; tennis court; watersports equipment/rentals; free Wi-Fi.

CAMPGROUNDS

There are campgrounds at both **Lake Havasu State Park** (www.azstateparks.com; ✆ **928/855-2784**), 2 miles north of the London Bridge on London Bridge Road, and **Cattail Cove State Park** (www.azstateparks.com; ✆ **928/855-1223**), 15 miles south of Lake Havasu City off U.S. 95. The former charges $35–40 per night per vehicle, the latter $30–35 per site. Reservations are available online.

Where to Eat in Lake Havasu City

Cha-Bones ★ AMERICAN A few blocks north of the London Bridge, this very stylish restaurant could hold its own in the big city, at least as far as the decor goes. The menu, on the other hand, sticks to familiar mesquite-grilled steaks, barbecued ribs, build-your-own burgers, a few designer pizzas, and, lately, a number of tapas. The menu doesn't break any new ground, but the setting is superb and the food good.

112 London Bridge Rd. www.chabones.com. ✆ **928/854-5554.** No reservations. Main courses $6–$13 lunch, $10–$40 dinner. Oct–Apr Sun–Thurs 11am–9pm, Fri–Sat 11am–10pm; May–Sept Sun–Thurs 11am–10pm, Fri–Sat 11am–11pm.

Javelina Cantina ★ MEXICAN Located at the foot of the London Bridge on the island side, this large, modern Mexican restaurant is affiliated with Shugrue's (below) on the other side of the street; like Shugrue's, it has a great view of the bridge, in this case from a large patio area that is heated during the cooler winter months. The bar has an excellent selection of tequilas, and margaritas are a specialty here. Accompany your libations with tortilla soup, fish tacos, or a salad made with blackened scallops, papaya, pecans, and blue cheese.

1420 McCulloch Blvd. www.javelinacantina.com. ✆ **928/855-8226.** Reservations recommended. Main courses $12–$35. Sun–Thurs 11am–9pm; Fri–Sat 11am–10pm.

Mudshark Brewery and Restaurant ★ SOUTHWESTERN/INTERNATIONAL At this big, boisterous brewpub a few blocks south of the London Bridge, you'll find excellent brews that go especially well with the pizzas, pastas, and other more substantial dishes on the menu. There's a movie theater right next door, which makes this a good spot for a night out.

210 Swanson Ave. www.mudsharkbeer.com. ✆ **928/453-2981.** Main courses $9–$23. Daily 11am–9pm.

Shugrue's ★ AMERICAN Just across the London Bridge from the English Village shopping complex, Shugrue's seems to be popular as much for its view of the bridge as for its food. Offerings include seafood, steaks, and prime rib at dinner, and burgers, sandwiches, and a short list of pastas at lunch. This place is a favorite of vacationing retirees and families. The adjacent affiliated **Barley Brothers Brewery** (below) has the same good view of the bridge and serves a menu calculated to appeal to a younger clientele.

At the Island Mall, 1425 McCulloch Blvd. www.shugrueslakehavasu.com. ✆ **928/453-1400.** Reservations recommended. Main courses $10–$17 lunch, $12–$36 dinner. Daily 11am–9pm.

Lake Havasu City Entertainment & Nightlife

Lake Havasu City has two brewpubs. **Mudshark Brewery** (above) is wildly popular, but if you want a brew with a view of the London Bridge, head to **Barley Brothers Brewery & Grill,** 1425 McCulloch Blvd. (www.barleybrothers.com; ✆ **928/505-7837**), which has a full menu as well as a long list of brews. Swanky **Martini Bay,** 1477 Queens Bay (www.londonbridgeresort.com; ✆ **928/855-0888**) is a stylish lounge at the London Bridge Resort. You can also do some gambling across Lake Havasu in California at the **Havasu Landing Resort and Casino** (www.havasulanding.com; ✆ **800/307-3610**), operated by the Chemehuevi Indian Tribe. To get there, catch a ferry from the Island Mall beside the London Bridge.

En Route to Yuma

THE PARKER DAM AREA

About 16 miles south of Lake Havasu City, the **Parker Dam** holds back the waters of Lake Havasu. (It's said to be the deepest dam in the world; 73% of its 320-foot height lies below the riverbed.) Beginning just above the dam and stretching south to the town of Parker is one of the most beautiful stretches of the lower Colorado River. Just before you reach the dam, you'll come to the **Bill Williams River National Wildlife Refuge** (www.fws.gov/refuge/bill_williams_river.html; ✆ **928/667-4144**), which preserves the lower reaches of the Bill Williams River and its cattail-choked confluence with the Colorado River. This refuge offers some of the best bird-watching in western Arizona. Keep your eyes open for vermilion flycatchers, Yuma clapper rails, soras, Swainson's hawks, and white-faced ibises.

Continuing south on U.S. 95, you'll reach a dam overlook and the Take-Off Point boat launch. Below the dam, the river becomes narrow and red-rock canyon walls close in. Although this narrow gorge is lined with mobile-home parks, the most beautiful sections have been preserved in two state parks:

The Desert Bar

Set on the site of an abandoned mine, the **Desert Bar** (www.thedesertbar.com), officially known as the **Nellie E Saloon,** makes use of salvaged parts and scrap metal left over from the mining days. A covered footbridge leads to the saloon, and in the parking lot, there's a steel "church" with a copper-roofed steeple. The bar is open from October through April, weekends only, from noon to 6pm. Expect live music and lots of retirees. From U.S. 95, turn east on Billy Mack Mine Rd. just north of Cienega Springs, fork right onto Cienega Springs Rd., and continue for 5 miles down a gravel road to the bar.

The Bouse Fisherman

If ancient rock art interests you, be sure to watch for Plomosa Road as you travel between Parker and Quartzsite. Off this road, you'll find a 30-foot carving (or geoglyph) known as the **Bouse Fisherman** or, more formally, the **Fisherman Intaglio.** This primitive image of a person spearing fish was formed by scratching away the rocky crust of the desert soil. Its origin and age are unknown, but it is believed to have been created centuries ago by native peoples and may depict the god Kumastamo, who is said to have created the Colorado River by thrusting a spear into the ground. Approximately 6 miles north of Quartzsite, turn off U.S. 95 onto Plomosa Road and drive 8 miles east. There's a quarter-mile trail to the site.

Buckskin Mountain State Park (www.azstateparks.com; ✆ **928/667-3231**) and **River Island State Park** (www.azstateparks.com; ✆ **928/667-3386**). Both parks have campgrounds ($35–$40 for campsites or cabanas at Buckskin Mountain; $30 for campsites at River Island); campsites can be reserved online. There are also day-use areas that include river beaches and hiking trails leading into the Buckskin Mountains. The day-use fee is $10 per vehicle at either park. In this area you'll also find the spectacular **Emerald Canyon Golf Course** (p. 492).

Where to Stay in Parker

Blue Water Resort and Casino ★★ Located 37 miles south of Lake Havasu City, this riverside casino resort is western Arizona's most impressive hotel. Even if you aren't interested in spending your time at the slot machines, you'll find something here that appeals to you. There's a marina, a mile of riverfront land, a miniature-golf course, a theater for live entertainment, a movie theater, and a big indoor pool complex (with water slide) that's designed to resemble ancient ruins. Guest rooms are all close to the water, which means nice river views but also traffic noise from the ski boats. Furnishings are standard motel modern.

11300 Resort Dr., Parker. www.bluewaterfun.com. ✆ **888/243-3360.** 200 units. $90–$164 double, $154–$250 suite. **Amenities:** 3 restaurants; snack bars; 2 lounges; theaters; exercise room; Jacuzzi; 4 pools; room service; free Wi-Fi.

QUARTZSITE

For much of the year, the community of **Quartzsite** is little more than a few truck stops at an interstate off-ramp, hot and dusty. But the population explodes with the annual influx of RV-dwelling winter visitors (also known as snowbirds), and from early January to mid-February, when the weather is downright perfect, warm during the day and mild at night, it's the site of numerous gem-and-mineral shows that together attract hordes of rockhounds on their way to and from the bigger show in Tucson. Among these shows, the

A Mining Ghost Town in the Desert

Back in the 19th century, the mountains of this region were pockmarked with mines. To get an idea of what life was like in the mining boomtowns, make a detour to **Castle Dome Mine Museum** (http://castledomemuseum.org; ✆ **928/920-3062**), a reconstructed mining town in the southern reaches of the Kofa National Wildlife Refuge. Take the Castle Dome turnoff near milepost 55 on U.S. 95 and drive east another 10 miles (only 3 miles are paved; the rest is graded gravel). From October through April, the museum/ghost town is open daily from 10am to 5pm; call for hours at other times of year. Admission is $15 for adults and $7 for children (free for children 6 and under).

QIA Pow Wow (www.qiaarizona.org; ✆ **928/927-6325**), held in late January, is one of the largest gem-and-mineral shows in the country. During the winter months, Quartzsite sprouts thousands of vendor stalls, as flea markets and the like are erected along the town's main streets. It's a paradise for thrift-hunters and fans of secondhand goods, antiques, and oddities alike. A variety of interesting food makes it a good place to stop for lunch or dinner. Be warned that from Quartzsite all the way up to Lake Havasu, accommodations in winter are scarce, so book as early as possible. When in Quartzsite, stop and pay your respects at a local landmark, the pyramid-shaped grave of a Syrian camel driver called Hadj Ali, or, as the locals called him, Hi Jolly.

For information on parking your RV in the desert outside Quartzsite, contact the **Bureau of Land Management,** Yuma Field Office, 2555 E. Gila Ridge Rd., Yuma (www.blm.gov/office/yuma-field-office; ✆ **928/317-3200**). Alternatively, you can get information and camping permits at the **La Posa Long-Term Visitor Area** (www.blm.gov/visit/la-posa-long-term-visitor-area), with entrance stations just south of Quartzsite on U.S. 95. The season runs from September 15 to April 15; a season permit costs $180 and a 14-day permit costs $40. Camping is free off-season.

KOFA NATIONAL WILDLIFE REFUGE

There are only a few places in Arizona where palm trees grow wild. One of them is 27 miles south of Quartzsite (turn off U.S. 95 18 miles south of Quartzsite). Palm Canyon lies within the boundaries of the 665,400-acre **Kofa National Wildlife Refuge,** which was formed primarily to protect the desert bighorn sheep that live in the rugged Kofa Mountains. At the end of a well-graded gravel road, it's a short walk to the narrow canyon. Although there are fewer than 100 palm trees, the hike there is a great way to experience these mountains up close. Keep your eyes peeled for desert bighorn sheep. Incidentally, the Kofa Mountains took their name from the King of Arizona Mine. For maps and more information, contact the Kofa National Wildlife Refuge, 9300 E. 28th St., Yuma (www.fws.gov/ refuge/kofa; ✆ **928/783-7861**).

YUMA

180 miles SW of Phoenix; 240 miles W of Tucson; 180 miles E of San Diego, CA

According to the *Guinness Book of World Records,* Yuma is the sunniest place on earth. Of the possible 4,456 hours of daylight each year, the sun shines in Yuma for roughly 4,050 hours, or about 90% of the time. Combine all that sunshine with the warmest winter weather in the country, and you've got a destination guaranteed to attract sun worshippers and other refugees from colder climes. In fact, each winter, tens of thousands of snowbirds (retired winter visitors) drive their RVs to Yuma from as far away as Canada. However, by late spring, all those RVers head north to escape the steadily rising temperatures, and by high summer, Yuma starts posting furnace-like high temperatures that make this one of the hottest cities in the country.

Way back in the middle of the 19th century, long before RVers discovered Yuma, this was one of the most important towns in the region, and known as the Rome of the Southwest because all roads led to Yuma Crossing—the shallow spot along the Colorado River where this town was founded. Despite its mid-desert location, Yuma became a busy port town in the 1850s as shallow-draft steamboats traveled up the Colorado River from the Gulf of California. In the 1870s, when the railroad pushed westward into California, it, too, passed through Yuma. Today, it is I-8, which connects San Diego with Tucson, that brings travelers to Yuma.

Yuma has more than a dozen golf courses and two important historic sites; it even has some claim to cinematic fame, with a range of movies from *Beau Geste* to *The Empire Strikes Back* having been filmed in the nearby sand dunes. Yet Yuma constantly struggles to attract visitors (blame it on the lure of San Diego, just a few hours away). It's still primarily a place to escape the cold and snows up north.

VISITOR INFORMATION The **Yuma Convention and Visitors Bureau,** 201 N. Fourth Ave. (www.visityuma.com; ✆ **800/293-0071** or 928/783-0071) operates a visitor center at the Yuma Quartermaster Depot State Historic Park, open daily 9am to 5pm (closed Mondays June–September).

Exploring Yuma

Historic downtown Yuma isn't exactly a bustling place, and it doesn't exactly abound in historical flavor. In the hope of drawing more visitors, Yuma has upgraded and restored some of its downtown historic buildings and spruced up its riverfront. A visual arts center downtown (p. 499) rivals galleries in Scottsdale, and an adjacent historic movie theater (p. 503), restored to its former glory, now serves as a performing arts center.

Arizona Historical Society Sanguinetti House Museum ★ HISTORIC HOME If you'd like to find out more about pioneer life in Yuma, stop by this territorial-period home, which is full of historical photographs

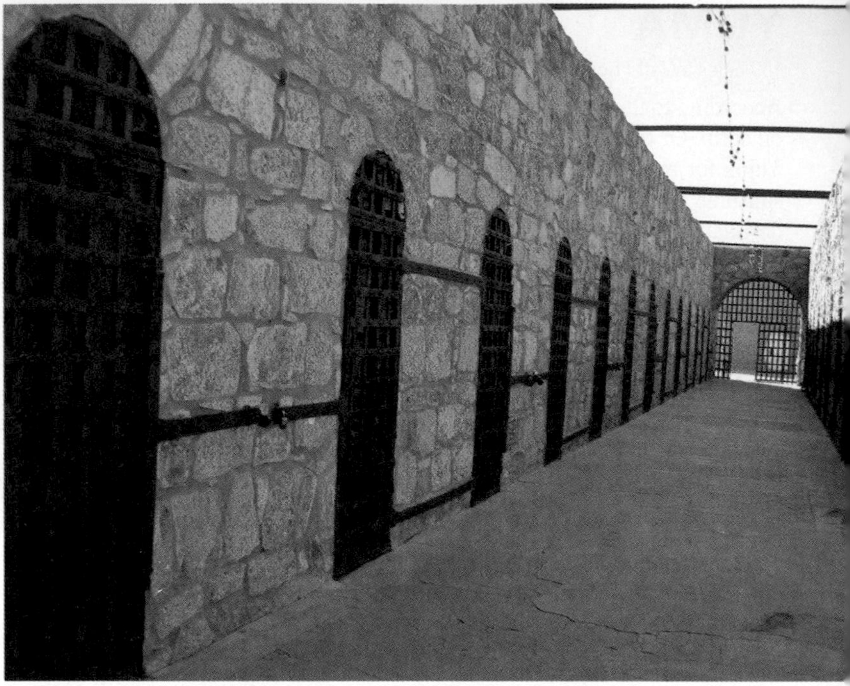

The restored Territorial Prison in downtown Yuma is a haunting relic of the town's Wild West past.

and artifacts and is surrounded by lush gardens and aviaries containing exotic birds. Adjacent to the museum is the **Garden Cafe,** a wonderful alfresco breakfast and lunch spot (p. 502).

240 S. Madison Ave. www.arizonahistoricalsociety.org. ✆ **928/782-1841.** $6 adults, $5 seniors and students 12–18, free for kids 12 and under; free 1st Sat of month. Tues–Sat 10am–3pm.

Colorado River State Historic Park ★ HISTORY PARK In 1865, Yuma Crossing, the narrow spot on the Colorado River where the town of Yuma sprang up, became the site of the military's Quartermaster Depot. Yuma was a busy river port back then, and supplies shipped from California were unloaded here and sent to military posts throughout the region. When the railroad arrived in Yuma in 1877, the Quartermaster Depot began to lose its importance in the regional supply network, and by 1883, the depot was closed. Today, the depot's large wooden buildings have been restored and exhibit everything from antique wagons to a replica telegraph office to officers' quarters furnished in period style. (It's no longer right on the Colorado River—the channel has shifted over the years.) Just imagine being stationed at this hot and dusty outpost in the days before air-conditioning. Exhibits tell the story of those who lived and worked at Yuma Crossing.

201 N. 4th Ave. (at the Colorado River). www.azstateparks.com. ✆ **928/783-0071.** Free admission. Daily 9am–5pm. Closed Christmas.

Yuma Territorial Prison State Historic Park ★ HISTORIC SITE If you've ever wondered where they really locked up the bad guys in the Wild West, check out this fortress-like prison on a bluff above the Colorado River. This prison opened for business in 1876 and, despite the thick stone walls and iron bars, was considered a model penal institution in its day. It even had its own electricity-generating plant and ventilation system. The prison museum has some interesting displays, including photos of many of the men and women who were incarcerated here.

220 N. Prison Hill Rd. www.yumaprison.org. ✆ **928/783-4771.** $8 adults, $6 seniors, $4 ages 7–13, free for kids 6 and under. Sept–May daily 9am–5pm; June–Aug Thurs–Mon 9am–5pm. Closed Christmas.

ORGANIZED TOURS

The Colorado River has been the lifeblood of the southwestern desert for centuries. **Yuma River Tours** (www.azbw.com/yumarivertours.php; ✆ **928/783-4400**) operates narrated jet-boat tours from Yuma to the **Imperial National Wildlife Refuge** (below), as well as a 48-mile trip upriver to Draper. Along the way, you'll learn about the homesteaders, boatmen, Native Americans, and miners who once relied on the Colorado River. Tours cost $38 to $89. This company also does tours in a paddle-wheeler.

Yuma Shopping

While Yuma may not seem at first like the sort of place to find cutting-edge contemporary art, that's just what you often find at the **Yuma Art Center and Galleries,** 254 S. Main St. (www.yumaaz.gov/parks-and-recreation/venues/art-center.html; ✆ **928/373-5202**), next door to the Historic Yuma Theatre. This gorgeous gallery could hold its own in Scottsdale—don't leave town without stopping by to see what's on view. It's open Tuesday through Saturday 10am to 6pm in summer, 10am to 8pm in winter. Admission is by donation. The **Yuma Symposium** (www.yumasymposium.org; ✆ **928/782-1934**), held here each year in late February, brings in talented artists from all over the country.

Down a landscaped alleyway off Main Street (at 224 Main St., across from Lutes Casino), there's a potpourri of small tourist-oriented stores. Just off Main Street, you'll also find two pottery studios/galleries: **Tomkins Pottery,** 78 W. Second St. (www.tomkinspottery.com; ✆ **928/782-1934**), and **Colorado River Pottery,** 67 W. Second St. (www.coloradoriverpottery.com; ✆ **888/410-2689** or 928/343-0413).

Outdoor Activities

If you're a bird-watcher, angler, or canoeist, you'll want to spend some time along the Colorado River north of Yuma. Here you'll find the **Imperial National Wildlife Refuge** (www.fws.gov/ /refuge/imperial; ✆ **928/783-3371**) and the **Cibola National Wildlife Refuge** (www.fws.gov/refuge/cibola; ✆ **928/857-3253**), which preserve marshes and shallow lakes along the river. One of the best ways to explore the Imperial National Wildlife Refuge is by kayak. You can rent one from **Jet Rent** (www.martinezlake.com; ✆ **928/314-4345**), which also rents jet skis and other watercraft. Multiday canoe trips are offered by **Yuma River Tours** (above) along this stretch of the lower Colorado, which features rugged, colorful mountains and quiet backwater areas.

Bird-watchers will also want to head out to **Betty's Kitchen Watchable Wildlife Viewing Area and National Recreation Trail** ($10 day-use fee per vehicle) and the adjacent **Mittry Lake Wildlife Area** (https://www.blm.gov/visit/mittry-lake). To get there, take U.S. 95 east out of town, turn north on Avenue 7E (Laguna Dam Rd.) and continue 9 miles. Shortly after the road turns to gravel, turn left to reach Betty's Kitchen; continue straight to reach Mittry Lake. Fall and spring migrations are some of the best times of year for birding at these spots; many waterfowl winter in the area as well. For information on both areas, contact the **Bureau of Land Management,** Yuma Field Office, 2555 E. Gila Ridge Rd. (www.blm.gov/office/yuma-field-office; ✆ **928/317-3200**).

During the warmer months (April through September), you can float a stretch of the Colorado River in an inner tube with **Yuma River Tubing** (www.yumarivertubing.com; ✆ **928/750-0247**), which rents inner tubes and operates a shuttle from West Wetlands Park, 350 N. 12th Ave. You can float the river for as little as an hour or as long as half a day, with prices ranging from $10 to $20.

GOLF

While Yuma's golf courses are not nearly as impressive as those at the resorts in Phoenix and Tucson, there are certainly plenty of them, and you can't beat the winter climate. The **Mesa del Sol Golf Club,** 12213 Calle del Cid (www.playmesadelsol.com; ✆ **928/342-1283**), off I-8 at the Fortuna Road exit, was designed by Arnold Palmer and is the most challenging local course open to the public. Greens fees are $50 during the cooler months ($41 for twilight play). The **Desert Hills Golf Course,** 1245 Desert Hills Dr. (www.deserthillsgc.com; ✆ **928/344-4653**) has been rated one of the best municipal courses in the state. Greens fees range from $35 to $48 during the cooler months, with a $10 discount if you walk.

Where to Stay in Yuma

Best Western Coronado Motor Hotel ★ With its red-tile roofs, whitewashed walls, and archways, this mission-revival building on the edge of downtown is the picture of a mid-20th-century motel—but rooms, all recently remodeled, are as up to date as you would expect from this worldwide franchise. The convenient location puts you within walking distance of a couple of good restaurants, Colorado River State Historic Park, and the Sanguinetti House Museum.

233 S. 4th Ave. http://besthotelinyuma.com. ✆ **877/234-5567** or 928/783-4453. 126 units. $93–$139 double; $119–$159 suite. Rates include full breakfast. Children 12 and under stay free in parent's room. Pets accepted ($50 deposit). **Amenities:** Restaurant; lounge; exercise room; Jacuzzi; 2 outdoor pools; free Wi-Fi.

Best Western InnSuites Yuma Mall ★ Located just off I-8 alongside the Yuma Palms Mall, this modern hotel offers an attractive setting and spacious accommodations at reasonable rates. Although not all the rooms are full suites, all are quite large and have loads of amenities—including a free happy hour—and nice decorative touches. The pool, though small, is in a pleasant courtyard.

1450 S. Castle Dome Ave. http://yuma.innsuites.com. ✆ **800/922-2034** or 928/783-8341. 166 units. $73–$153 double. Rates include full breakfast and evening social hour. Children 17 and under stay free in parent's room. Pets accepted ($25 fee). **Amenities:** Free airport transfers; exercise room; Jacuzzi; outdoor pool; 2 tennis courts; free Wi-Fi.

Hilton Garden Inn Yuma/Pivot Point ★★ The best new hotel in Yuma boasts the best location as well: The property backs up to both Colorado River State Historic Park and the city's downtown riverfront park. A paved walking and biking path also runs past the hotel. Rooms are large and have great beds and bathrooms with granite counters. While the hotel is designed primarily for business travelers (there's a small convention center across the parking lot), it also makes a good choice for vacationers looking to explore downtown Yuma.

310 N. Madison Ave. http://hiltongardeninn.hilton.com. ✆ **877/782-9444** or 928/783-1500. 150 units. $119–$159 double. Children 18 and under stay free in parent's room. **Amenities:** Restaurant; lounge; babysitting; exercise room; Jacuzzi; outdoor pool; room service; free Wi-Fi.

La Fuente Inn & Suites ★ Conveniently just off the interstate, this appealing hotel is done in Spanish colonial style with a red-tile roof, pink-stucco walls, and a fountain out front. Lush landscaping and a sort of tropical colonial decor in the lobby lend the hotel a somewhat exotic, tropical feel. Definitely not what you'd expect from a hotel just off the interstate. French doors open from the lobby onto the pool terrace and a large courtyard, around which the guest rooms are arranged. Standard units feature modern motel furnishings, while the well-designed suites offer much more space. The Spanish/tropical styling and pleasant courtyard pool area make this a good place for a sunny winter getaway.

1513 E. 16th St. www.lafuenteinn.com. ✆ **800/841-1814** or 928/329-1814. 96 units. $98–$119 double. Rates include full breakfast and evening happy hour. Children 9 and under stay free in parent's room. **Amenities:** Free airport transfers; exercise room and access to nearby health club; Jacuzzi; pool; free Wi-Fi.

Where to Eat in Yuma

Brownie's Café ★ AMERICAN Brownie's has been around forever—at least it's said to be Yuma's oldest restaurant, and it's a beloved breakfast and lunch venue for locals. The food is classic diner fare, from chicken-fried steak to omelets and pancakes, but with twists like homemade sausage and red Jell-O for dessert. It's a delicious blast from the past. If you want a taste of the real Arizona of ranchers, river rats, and prospectors, this is the place. I stop here nearly every time I'm in Yuma, and it's always a treat.

1145 S 4th Ave. ✆ **928/783-7911.** No reservations. Main courses $5–$10. Daily Sat–Thurs 5:45am–2pm; Fri 5:45 am–8pm.

The Garden Cafe ★★ LIGHT FARE In back of the Sanguinetti House Museum is Yuma's favorite breakfast and lunch spot (it's particularly popular with local retirees). Set amid quiet terraced gardens and large aviaries full of singing birds, the Garden Cafe provides a welcome respite from Yuma's heat. On the hottest days, misters spray the air with a gentle fog that keeps the gardens cool. There's also an indoor dining area. The menu consists of various delicious sandwiches, daily special quiches, salads, and rich desserts. Pancakes with lingonberry sauce are a breakfast specialty. On Sunday, there's a brunch buffet.

250 S. Madison Ave. www.gardencafeyuma.com. ✆ **928/783-1491.** Main courses $9–$12. Tues–Fri 9–10:45am and 11am–2:30pm; Sat 8–10:45am and 11am–2:30pm; Sun 8am–2:30pm. Closed June–Sept.

Lutes Casino ★ AMERICAN Lutes, in business since the 1920s, is a dark and cavernous restaurant known for serving the best hamburgers in town and for having the strangest decor, too—a misbegotten blend of neon signs, Old West paraphernalia, pop music posters, and international kitsch. You don't need to see a menu—just walk in and ask for a special. What you'll get is a cheeseburger/hot dog combo. Don't bother looking for slot machines or poker tables at Lutes Casino; they've been gone for years.

221 S. Main St. www.lutescasino.com. ✆ **928/782-2192.** No reservations. Sandwiches and burgers $2.50–$6.50. Mon–Thurs 10am–8pm; Fri–Sat 10am–9pm; Sun 10am–6pm.

River City Grill ★ INTERNATIONAL With its hip, big-city decor and innovative menu, this restaurant is something of a novelty in Yuma. Although you can get a steak at dinner and a burger at lunch, seafood dominates the menu. The crab-and-salmon cakes with spicy Thai peanut sauce are a must for a starter. Flavor combinations range all over the globe: Vietnamese spring rolls, Mediterranean salad, pad Thai, and Jamaican jerked chicken.

600 W. 3rd St. www.rivercitygrillyuma.com. ✆ **928/782-7988.** Reservations recommended. Main courses $8–$14 lunch, $14–$34 dinner. Mon–Sat 11am–2pm and 5–10pm; Sun 5–9pm.

Yuma Entertainment & Nightlife

In most small towns across Arizona, you'll find an old downtown movie theater. Most of them are boarded up and abandoned. Not so in Yuma. The renovated and updated **Historic Yuma Theatre,** 254 S. Main St. (http://www.yumaaz.gov/parks-and-recreation/venues/art-center.html; ✆ **928/373-5202**), the centerpiece of the Yuma Art Center, is now host to live theater productions and touring musical groups. Originally opened in 1912, the theater has been restored to its distinctive 1930s Art Deco decor.

Looking for something else to do after dark in Yuma? You can try your luck at the **Paradise Casinos,** 450 Quechan Dr. (www.paradise-casinos.com; ✆ **888/777-4946**), across the Colorado River on the Quechan Indian Reservation, or at the **Cocopah Casino,** 15318 S. Ave. B, Somerton (www.cocopahresort.com/gaming; ✆ **800/237-5687**), 15 minutes south of Yuma.

EAST TOWARD TUCSON

A long stretch of low scrub desert, dotted by ironwood trees and lava fields, rolls from Yuma east to Tucson. The view from Interstate 8 offers broad views of several craggy mountain ranges to the south that the Air Force uses for bombing practice, part of the vast Barry M. Goldwater Range; to the north runs the Gila River, at least when there's water in it. At exit 67, the **Dateland Date Gardens** (www.dateland.com; ✆ **928/454-2772**) is a place knowledgeable desert rats prize for its thick and creamy date shakes, a lifesaver on a hot afternoon.

The next exit to watch for is exit 102 (Painted Rock Dam Rd.), which will lead you north to an impressive collection of centuries-old petroglyphs and

The Center of the World

West of Yuma, I-8 heads out across the California desert toward San Diego, soon passing through barren, windswept sand dunes that Hollywood has long used to represent the Sahara. This region may seem like it's a long way from anywhere, but if you pull off the freeway 9 miles west of Yuma at exit 164 (Sidewinder Rd.), you'll find yourself in the "town" of **Felicity** (www.felicityusa.com; ✆ **760/572-0100**), which, according to town founder Jacques-Andres Istel, is the Official Center of the World. At this unusual attraction, based on Istel's children's book, *Coe The Good Dragon at the Center of the World,* you can stand inside a pyramid at the "exact" center of the world. As a bonus, you can admire Istel's monument to the history of French aviation and marvel at his granite remembrance walls. It's open for tours from Thanksgiving to Easter. I've long argued that the surrealism quotient is much higher in the desert states than elsewhere in America, and Istel's surreal concoction adds strength to my view. It's a lot of fun besides, and it's nowhere near the strangest thing you're likely to see out this way.

pictographs at the Bureau of Land Management's **Painted Rock Petroglyph Site ★**. (Head north 11 miles on Painted Rock Dam Rd., turn left onto dirt Rocky Point Rd., and continue another ½ mile to the parking area.) There is a $2 day-use fee here. For more information, contact the BLM Lower Sonoran Field Office, Rocky Point Rd., Gila Bend (https://www.blm.gov/visit/painted-rock-petroglyph-site; ✆ **623/580-5500**).

PLANNING YOUR TRIP TO ARIZONA

12

No matter what your plans are when you arrive in Arizona, you'll need to do some planning in advance to make the most of your visit. This chapter gives you the information to help plan your trip and point you toward some additional resources.

ARRIVING

By Plane

Most major U.S. airlines fly to both Phoenix/Scottsdale's **Sky Harbor** (p. 51) and **Tucson International** (p. 355). Phoenix is the more centrally located of the two airports and is about 2 hours closer to the Grand Canyon South Rim. If a trip to the Grand Canyon is your only reason for visiting Arizona, also consider flying into Las Vegas; it's a half-hour farther away but sometimes has lower airfares and better car-rental rates.

By Car

Arizona is bordered on the west by California and Nevada, on the north by Utah, on the east by New Mexico, and on the south by Mexico. **I-10**, which passes east-west through the state, runs from Los Angeles all the way to Jacksonville, Florida; both Phoenix and Tucson are directly on I-10, about 2 hours apart. **I-40** also runs east-west across the state, just south of the Grand Canyon, connecting to Albuquerque and to Los Angeles (via I-15). **I-8** leads west from Casa Grande, halfway between Phoenix and Tucson, to San Diego. There are two short north-south interstates in Arizona: **I-17** links Flagstaff with Phoenix, about a 2½-hour drive (add another 1½ hours to get to the Grand Canyon), and **I-19** runs south from Tucson to Nogales, on the Mexican border, about a 1-hour drive. For information on car rentals, gasoline, and driving rules in Arizona, see "By Car," below.

By Train

Amtrak (www.amtrak.com; ✆ **800/872-7245**) runs two trains through the state but neither stops in Phoenix. The **Sunset Limited** runs through Tucson on its route between Los Angeles and New Orleans, stopping also in San Antonio and Houston, Texas. The trip from Los Angeles to Tucson takes 10 hours and starts at $61. The **Southwest Chief** stops in Flagstaff and some smaller northern Arizona cities on its way from L.A. to Chicago.

By Bus

Greyhound (www.greyhound.com; ✆ **800/321-2222**) and **Trailways** (www.trailways.com; ✆ **877/467-3346**) serve several cities in Arizona. One Greyhound line runs across I-40 through Flagstaff, another from Flagstaff through Phoenix and Tucson to Nogales. You can easily get from Phoenix to L.A. or San Diego; Phoenix–L.A. fares start as low as $22.

GETTING AROUND

By Car

Arizona is a big state (the sixth largest), and because many of the state's top attractions are national parks, national monuments, and other natural areas, a car is almost a necessity for getting the most out of a visit to the state. As with airline fares and golf, car-rental fees vary wildly. They used to be quite high here, but now are generally in line with other Sun Belt cities, and, of course, prices spike during car shortages and the most crowded part of the tourist season.

Because Phoenix and Tucson are major resort destinations, both have numerous car-rental agencies. Rental rates in Tucson can be a bit lower than in Phoenix, and you'll save even more there on taxes and surcharges—in Phoenix, taxes and surcharges add more than 50% to rental car costs if you rent at the airport; in Tucson you'll probably pay $5 to $10 less per day. You can also often save money by renting at a non-airport location, which might be a smart option if, say, your resort will shuttle you from the airport.

If you're not a car-rental pro, try **www.autoslash.com**, which applies discounts from various institutions to your bill, or **www.priceline.com**, which I've always found reliable.

In Arizona, a right turn on a red light is permitted after a complete stop. Seat belts are required for the driver and for all passengers. Children 4 and under must be in a child's car seat, and ages 5 to 7 have to be in a booster seat. General speed limits are 25 to 40 mph in towns and cities, 15 mph in school zones, and 55 and 65 mph on highways in cities. On rural interstate highways, the speed limit can be as high as 75 mph.

If you're heading out of a city, keep your gas tank topped off. In many parts of the state, it's not unusual to drive 60 miles without seeing a gas station.

Note: Temps can reach 100 degrees as early as March and as late as October. Always carry drinking water with you while driving through the desert, and if you plan to head off on back roads, carry extra water for the car's radiator as well.

By Plane

Because Arizona is a big state, if your time is short, you may want to consider flying between cities. **Contour Airlines** (www.contourairlines.com; ✆ **888/322-6686**) will get you from Phoenix to Page, near Lake Mead. **American Airlines** (www.aa.com; ✆ **800/433-3200**) flies from Phoenix to Flagstaff.

By Train

The train is not really a viable way of getting around much of Arizona because there is no north-south Amtrak service.

By Bus

Greyhound (www.greyhound.com; ✆ **800/321-2222**) and **Trailways** (www.trailways.com; ✆ **877/467-3346**) run buses across the state. Shuttle bus service between most of the tourist cities in the vertical center of the state is available through **Arizona Shuttle** (www.arizonashuttle.com).

TIPS ON ACCOMMODATIONS

Hotel rates vary wildly across the year in different parts of the state. In the north, winter is cold and it's the slow season. In the south, summer is boiling and *that's* the slow season. If you're coming to Phoenix and have some leeway, aim for very early or very late summer, where there are good deals and the weather's still decent. The real deals at Phoenix resorts are in summer; if you can stand the heat, you can enjoy highly swanky environments for a fraction of the usual price.

Then there are **resort fees,** which start at $15 per night. These mandatory fees make posted room rates a fiction, but resorts continue to charge them. Definitely complain if the amenities included, from Wi-Fi to spas, aren't up to snuff. Otherwise, poke around for properties that don't have such fees—they deserve the business. You can get a bit more for your money in smaller towns off the interstates, where you'll find unfancy but clean, high-value lodgings. The farther you drive from resort areas, the more you'll save.

The new accommodation apps work here as they do elsewhere. Look to **Airbnb.com** and **VRBO.com** to see a wide range of options.

RV Camping

If you'll be traveling by RV or with a tent, you've got loads of camping options all across Arizona. However, be aware that campgrounds at and near Grand Canyon National Park fill up nightly during the summer and often in spring and fall as well. Make a campsite reservation as far in advance as

TURNING TO THE internet or apps FOR A HOTEL DISCOUNT

Before going online, it's important that you know what "flavor" of discount you're seeking. Currently, there are three types of online reductions:

1. **Extreme discounts on sites where you bid for lodgings without knowing which hotel you'll get.** You'll find these on such sites as **Priceline.com** and **Hotwire.com**, and they can be money-savers, particularly if you're booking within a week of travel (that's when hotels resort to deep discounts to get beds filled). As these companies use only major chains and depend on repeat business, you probably won't feel ripped off. My only caveat is that they work best with four-star hotels. The downside to cheaper rooms is that they are sometimes in a less-desirable corner of town; in Phoenix, for example, you might end up in a place along the somewhat grimy I-17 corridor.
2. **Discounts on chain hotel websites.** In 2016, all of the major chains began to reserve special discounts for travelers who book directly through the hotels' websites (usually in the portion of the site reserved for loyalty members). They weren't lying: These are always the lowest rates at these hotels, though discounts can range from as much as $50 to as little as $1. Our advice: Search for a hotel in your price range and ideal location (see the Note below for how to do that), and then, if it's a chain property, book directly through the online loyalty portal.
3. **Last-minute discounts.** Booking last minute can be a great savings strategy; prices sometimes drop in the week before travel, as hoteliers scramble to fill their rooms. But you won't necessarily find the best savings through companies that claim to specialize in last-minute bookings. Instead, use the sites recommended in the Note, below.

Note: Use the right hotel search engine. They're not all equal, as we at Frommers.com learned after putting the top 20 sites to the test in 20 cities around the globe. We discovered that Booking.com listed the lowest rates for centrally located hotels, and in the under $200 range, 16 out of 20 times—the best record, by far, of all the sites we tested. And Booking.com includes all taxes and fees in its results (not all do, which be frustrating). For top-end properties, both Priceline.com and HotelsCombined.com came up with the best rates, tying at 14 wins each.

It's a lot of surfing, I know, but in the hothouse world of AZ hotel pricing, this sort of diligence can pay off.

possible. To make campsite reservations at national park and national forest campgrounds, contact the **National Recreation Reservation Service** (www.recreation.gov; ✆ **877/444-6777** or 518/885-3639), where you can generally reserve a site 6 months in advance. To find out about campsites in state parks, contact **Arizona State Parks** (www.azstateparks.com; ✆ **602/679-2757**). If you're in the north Phoenix area, the state has a wonderful visitor's center just off I-17, at 23751 N. 23rd Ave. (✆ **602/542-4174**).

If you want to rent an RV, try **Cruise America** (www.cruiseamerica.com; © **800/671-8042**), which has offices in Mesa (a suburb of Phoenix), Tucson, and Flagstaff. Expect to pay between $300 and $1,300 per week (plus taxes) depending on the time of year (summer is higher) and size of the RV you rent. In central Phoenix, the family-owned **Elite RV Rentals,** 2204 W. Fillmore St. (www.elitervrentals.net; © **928/446-1833**) charges rental rates from around $660 to $1,200 per week.

TOURS & GUIDED TRIPS

Academic Trips

At the Grand Canyon, the **Grand Canyon Field Institute** (www.grandcanyon.org/fieldinstitute; © **800/858-2808** or 928/638-2481) offers a variety of educational programs throughout the year, primarily from early spring to late fall. Examples include guided hikes and backpacking trips (some for women only) with a natural-history or ecological slant, as well as photography classes, mule-assisted treks, rafting trips, and hands-on archaeology excursions.

Through its Ventures Trips, the **Museum of Northern Arizona** (www.musnav.org/ventures; © **928/774-5213**) offers educational camping, backpacking, and hotel-based tours primarily in the Colorado Plateau region of northern Arizona. Trips range in length from 1 to 6 days. The nonprofit **Old Pueblo Archaeology Center** organization (www.oldpueblo.org; © **520/798-1201**) leads numerous archaeology-oriented trips around Arizona. To learn more about the Native American cultures of Arizona, contact **Crossing Worlds Journeys & Retreats** (www.crossingworlds.com; © **800/350-2693** or 928/282-0846), which offers tours throughout the Four Corners region, visiting the Hopi mesas as well as the Navajo Reservation. Journeys of self-discovery are a specialty of this company.

Guided & Package Tours

If you want to see the best of Arizona but would rather not do all the logistical planning or driving, consider a guided tour. **Detours American West** (www.detoursamericanwest.com; © **866/438-6877**) specializes in small-group tours throughout Arizona and other parts of the Southwest. The British tour company **Trek America** (www.trekamerica.com; © **888/596-8719**), which specializes in off-the-beaten-path, small-group adventure travel, offers tours of the American Southwest; most include the Grand Canyon and other scenic Arizona locations. To tour the most spectacular sights in the state's Native American territory, including Monument Valley and Canyon de Chelly, try the Native Voices Tour offered by **High Point Tours** (www.ilivehistory.com; © **928/445-2639**). Company co-owner and guide Todd Weber, an experienced living-history presenter, highlights not only the area's fascinating geology, but also its colorful historical characters.

Volunteer & Working Trips

If you want to get more involved in wilderness preservation, consider a Sierra Club service trip, which lets you help build, restore, and maintain hiking trails in wilderness areas. Contact the **Sierra Club Outings Department** (www.sierraclub.org; © **415/977-5522**). The Sierra Club also offers hiking, camping, and other adventure trips to various Arizona destinations.

Thirty years or so ago, a Flagstaff school teacher dreamed of connecting various north-south trails in the state into a unified trail from Utah to the Mexico border. Those dreams are now a reality. You can join a work crew organized by the **Arizona Trail Association** (www.aztrail.org; © **602/252-4794**), spending 1 or 2 days building and maintaining various portions of the trail. The group also organizes a spectrum of runs, some of them up to 50 miles long!

OUTDOOR SPORTS

Thanks to the Grand Canyon—the most widely known white-water-rafting spot in the world and also one of the world's premier backpacking destinations—Arizona is known for active, adventure-oriented vacations. For others, it's synonymous with winter golf and tennis.

Bicycling

With its wide range of climates, Arizona offers good biking somewhere in the state every month of the year. In winter, there's road biking around Phoenix and Tucson, while from spring to fall, the southeastern corner of the state offers fun routes. In summer, mountain bikers head to the Sedona area, the White Mountains (in eastern Arizona), and Kaibab National Forest (between Flagstaff and Grand Canyon National Park). There's also excellent mountain biking at several Phoenix parks, and Tucson is one of the most bicycle-friendly cities in the country.

Backroads (www.backroads.com; © **800/462-2848** or 510/527-1555) offers a variety of multiday multisport trips visiting southern Utah and the Grand Canyon, Sedona, and the Tucson desert. **Sojourn Bicycling & Active Vacations** (www.gosojourn.com; © **800/730-4771**) offers weeklong bike tours of the Sonoran Desert near Tucson, Prescott, and Sedona. **Western Spirit Cycling Adventures** (www.westernspirit.com; © **800/845-2453**) has a number of interesting mountain-bike excursions, including trips to the North Rim of the Grand Canyon. **Arizona Outback Adventures** (www.aoa-adventures.com; © **866/455-1601**) does a variety of mountain-bike treks, including a 3-day trip in the Sonoran Desert.

Canoeing/Kayaking

By far the most memorable place for a flat-water kayak tour is Lake Powell, where **Hidden Canyon Kayak** (www.lakepowellhiddenkayak.com;

Casting a Line in Arizona

Large and small lakes around the state offer excellent fishing for warm-water game fish such as largemouth, smallmouth, and striped bass. There's good trout fishing in the lakes atop the Mogollon Rim and in the White Mountains; the easily accessible section of the Colorado River between Glen Canyon Dam and Lees Ferry, just upstream from the Grand Canyon, is among the country's most fabled stretches of trout water. To buy fishing licenses online, contact the **Arizona Game and Fish Department** (www.azgfd.com); the fee is $55 for non-residents. If you're planning to fish on an Indian reservation, you'll need to get a special permit from the reservation.

✆ **928/660-1836**) offers half-day to multiday tours. Guided kayak trips are also offered by **Kayak Powell** (www.kayaklakepowell.com; ✆ **928/660-0778**).

Golf

For many of Arizona's winter visitors, golf is the main attraction. The state's hundreds of golf courses range from easy public courses to PGA championship links. In Phoenix and Tucson, greens fees are higher in winter, generally ranging from about $150 to $250 for 18 holes at resort courses, including a golf cart. In summer, fees drop to less than half in some cases, a lot more in others. Almost all resorts offer special golf packages as well. If you're visiting in winter, reserve golf slots as far in advance as possible. You can book tee times online at your favorite course (see details in chapters 4 and 9), or poke around on **Golf Now** (www.golfnow.com) or **Tee Off** (www.teeoff.com) for deals. For municipal courses in Phoenix, which are quite good, go to www.phoenix.gov/parks/golf.

Hiking/Backpacking

Arizona offers some of the most fascinating and challenging hiking in the country. All across the state's lowland deserts, parks and other public lands are laced with trails that lead past saguaro cacti, to the tops of desert peaks, and deep into rugged canyons. The state also has vast forests, many in protected wilderness areas, with miles of hiking trails. See specific day-hike recommendations throughout this book.

The state's two most unforgettable overnight backpack trips are the hike down to Phantom Ranch at the bottom of the **Grand Canyon** (p. 235) and the hike into **Havasu Canyon** (p. 276), a side canyon of the Grand Canyon. A third popular backpacking trip is through **Paria Canyon,** a narrow slot canyon that originates in Utah and terminates in Arizona at Lees Ferry. There are also many overnight opportunities in the San Francisco Peaks north of Flagstaff and in the White Mountains of eastern Arizona. Guided backpacking trips of different durations and difficulty levels are offered by the **Grand Canyon Field Institute** (www.grandcanyon.org/fieldinstitute; ✆ **800/858-2808** or

928/638-2481) and by **Discovery Treks** (www.discoverytreks.com; © **480/247-9266**). Also check out multiday hiking and biking trips organized by **Backroads** (www.backroads.com; © **800/462-2848** or 510/527-1555).

Horseback Riding

All over Arizona there are stables where you can climb into the saddle of a sure-footed trail horse and ride off . . . well, if not into the sunset, certainly into some scenery you might never have seen before. Among the more scenic spots for riding are Grand Canyon National Park (p. 239), Monument Valley Navajo Tribal Park (p. 319), Canyon de Chelly National Monument (p. 314), the red-rock country around Sedona (p. 194), Phoenix's South Mountain Park and Superstition Mountains (p. 92), and the Santa Catalina foothills outside Tucson (p. 382). The famous mule rides down into the Grand Canyon require advance booking many months ahead. Both 1- and 2-day trips are offered; for reservations and information, contact **Grand Canyon National Park Lodges** (www.grandcanyonlodges.com; © **888/297-2757**). If you haven't booked ahead, it's worth calling the last-minute reservations phone number (© **928/638-2631**), or stopping by the transportation desk at **Bright Angel Lodge,** 9 Village Loop Dr. in Grand Canyon Village. Spaces sometimes open up with sudden cancellations.

Want to kick it up a notch? At **Arizona Cowboy College,** at Scottsdale's Lorill Equestrian Center, 30208 N. 152nd St. (www.cowboycollege.com; © **480/471-3151**), you can literally learn the ropes, as well as how to brand a calf and how to say "Git along little doggie!" like a real cowboy.

Hot-Air Ballooning

For much of the year, the desert has the perfect environment for hot-air ballooning—cool, still air and wide-open spaces. Dozens of ballooning companies operate across the state; most are in Phoenix and Tucson, but several others operate near Sedona, which is by far the most picturesque spot in the state for a balloon ride. See chapters 4, 5, and 9 for specific information.

Lodgings That Float

With the Colorado River turned into a string of long lakes, houseboat vacations are a natural in Arizona, allowing vacationers to move about the lake to fish, hike, and swim. Rentals are available on Lake Powell, Lake Mead, and Lake Mohave; the canyon scenery of Lake Powell makes it the hands-down best spot for a houseboat vacation. Make reservations well in advance for a summer trip. No prior experience (or license) is necessary, and plenty of hands-on instruction is provided before you leave the marina. See chapters 7 and 11 for more.

Skiing

Although Arizona is better known as a desert state, it also has snow-capped mountains and even a few ski areas. The biggest and best are **Arizona Snowbowl** (www.arizonasnowbowl.com; ✆ **928/779-1951**), outside Flagstaff, and **Sunrise Park Resort** (www.sunriseskipark.com; ✆ **855/735-7669**), on the White Mountain Apache Reservation in far east central Arizona, a good 3½ hours east of Phoenix. Snowbowl is more popular—it's easier to get there from Phoenix, and there are good restaurants and hotels in Flagstaff, a half-hour away. Snowbowl has more vertical feet of skiing, but Sunrise offers almost twice as many runs. Both ski areas offer rentals and lessons.

When it's a good snow year, Tucsonans head up to **Mount Lemmon Ski Valley** (www.skithelemmon.com; ✆ **520/576-1321**), the southernmost ski area in the U.S. Snows here aren't as reliable as they are farther north, so call first to make sure the ski area is operating.

During snow-blessed winters, **cross-country skiers** can find plenty of snow-covered forest roads outside Flagstaff, at the South Rim of the Grand Canyon, in the White Mountains around Greer and Alpine, and on Mount Lemmon outside Tucson.

Tennis

After golf, tennis is probably the most popular winter sport in the desert, and resorts all over Arizona have tennis courts. Keep in mind that some resorts require you to wear traditional tennis attire and don't include court time in the room rates. No courts anywhere in the state can match the views you'll have at Enchantment Resort, outside Sedona. Other tennis-oriented resorts include, in the Phoenix/Scottsdale area, the Phoenician, the Fairmont Scottsdale, the Arizona Grand Resort, and the Pointe Hilton Tapatio Cliffs Resort; and, in Tucson, the Lodge at Ventana Canyon, the Hilton Tucson El Conquistador Golf & Tennis Resort, the Westin La Paloma Resort & Spa, the Westward Look Resort, and the Omni Tucson National Resort.

White-Water Rafting

Rafting the Grand Canyon is the dream of nearly every white-water enthusiast—if it's one of yours as well, plan well ahead. Companies and trips are limited, and they tend to fill up early. For a discussion and list of companies that run trips down the Canyon, see p. 241. For 1-day rafting trips on the Colorado below the main section of the Grand Canyon, contact **Hualapai River Runners** (www.grandcanyonwest.com; ✆ **888/868-9378**). For rafting trips through the Grand Canyon lasting from 4 to 15 days, contact **Grand Canyon Whitewater** (www.grandcanyonwhitewater.com; ✆ **800/343-3121**).

Rafting trips are also available on the upper Salt River east of Phoenix, although some years there's just not enough water in the river to support them. If it's raftable, you can do trips of varying lengths with **Mild to Wild Rafting**

Staying Healthy in the Desert

If you've never been to the desert, be sure to prepare yourself for this harsh environment. No matter what time of year it is, the desert sun is strong and bright. Use sunscreen when outdoors, particularly up in the mountains, where the altitude makes sunburn more likely. But you can also get badly burned playing in the pool or tubing down the Salt River. The bright sun also makes sunglasses a necessity. In the desert, even when you don't feel hot, the dry air steals moisture from your body, so drink plenty of fluids. At the Grand Canyon, remember that a cool spring day at the rim can turn into three-digit temps at the bottom.

Bugs & Other Wildlife **Rattlesnakes** are common, but your chances of meeting one are slight—they tend not to come out in the heat of the day. Still, never stick your hand into holes among rocks in the desert, and keep an eye on where you're stepping when you're out tramping around. Everything from snakes to bobcats to coyotes have been seen in housing developments and resorts near the mountain parks, and even far into town. Arizona is also home to the **Gila monster,** a large black-and-orange poisonous lizard, but they are less common than rattlesnakes. The **tarantula** has developed a nasty reputation, but the tiny **black widow spider** is more likely to cause illness. **Scorpions** are another danger of the desert. Be extra careful when turning over rocks or logs that might harbor either black widows or scorpions, particularly at night.

Respiratory & Desert Illnesses
Valley fever, a fungal infection of the lungs, is common in the desert Southwest, although it generally affects only long-term residents. The fungus is carried by dust storms and winds blowing across farms and construction sites. Symptoms include fever, chest pain, fatigue, headaches, and rashes. If you plan to do any camping or backcountry travel in the Four Corners region, be aware of **hantavirus,** an often-fatal disease spread by mice. Symptoms include fatigue, fever, and muscle aches; if you develop any such symptoms within 1 to 5 weeks of traveling through the Four Corners, see a doctor.

High-Altitude Hazards Both the South Rim of the Grand Canyon and the canyon gateway city of Flagstaff are at around 7,000 feet (2,133 meters) in elevation; the North Rim of the Grand Canyon is at 8,000 feet (2,438 meters). While these elevations are generally not high enough to cause altitude sickness, they can cause shortness of breath after even moderate exercise. Take it slow, and remember that if you hike down into the Grand Canyon, you'll really feel the elevation when you start hiking back out.

(www.mild2wildrafting.com; (✆ **970/247-4789**), **Wilderness Aware Rafting** (www.inaraft.com; ✆ **800/462-7238**), and **Canyon Rio Rafting** (www.canyonrio.com; ✆ **800/272-3353**).

[FastFACTS] ARIZONA

Area Codes The area code in Phoenix is 602; in Scottsdale, Tempe, Mesa, and the east valley, it's 480; in Glendale and the west valley, it's 623. The area code for Tucson and southeastern Arizona is 520. The rest of the state is area code 928.

ATMs In Arizona, you'll find ATMs (cashpoints) just about everywhere. Fees tend to be higher at gas-station minimarts and most hotels and motels. To avoid fees, use your debit card in grocery stores and ask for cash back with your purchase.

Disabled Travelers Thanks to provisions in the Americans with Disabilities Act, most public places—hotels, restaurants, museums, public transit—are required to comply with accessibility regulations, although landmarked buildings are often exempt.

Arizona Raft Adventures (www.azraft.com; ✆ **800/786-7238**) offers Grand Canyon rafting trips for people with disabilities. In the northwest corner of the state, **Stagecoach Trails Guest Ranch** (www.stagecoachtrailsranch.com; ✆ **866/444-4471** or 928/727-8270) is a guest ranch designed to accommodate the needs of persons with disabilities. All the ranch buildings are accessible, and there are horseback-riding programs for persons with disabilities.

The **America the Beautiful Access Pass** gives travelers with visual impairments or those with permanent disabilities (regardless of age) free lifetime entrance to federal recreation sites administered by the National Park Service. You can apply for the Access Pass at any National Park Service facility that charges an entrance fee, or through the mail, with an application available online. You need to show proof of a medically determined disability. For more info, go to www.nps.gov/fees_passes.htm.

Drinking Laws The legal age for purchase and consumption of alcoholic beverages in Arizona is 21; proof of age is required, so it's a good idea to bring ID when you go out. In Arizona, liquor is sold at supermarkets and convenience stores. Do not carry open containers of alcohol in your car or any public area that isn't zoned for alcohol consumption. The police can fine you on the spot. The state aggressively prosecutes drunk drivers; don't even think about driving while intoxicated.

Electricity Like Canada, the United States uses 110 to 120 volts AC (60 cycles), compared to 220 to 240 volts AC (50 cycles) in most of Europe, Australia, and New Zealand.

Emergencies Call ✆ **911** to report a fire, call the police, or get an ambulance anywhere in the U.S. This is a toll-free call from public telephones. Be aware, however, that you may not always have cell phone service in remote locales, in mountainous areas, and sometimes even on highways.

Family Travel If you're planning to take in the sights in northern Arizona, keep in mind that distances are great out here. Don't expect to find someplace to eat whenever the kids are hungry; rest areas are few and far between. Pack food before heading out on a long drive. Also bring plenty to entertain the kids as you drive for hours through the same desert scenery.

Virtually all of the top resorts in Phoenix and Tucson offer children's programs, often elaborate ones.

Legal Aid While driving, if you are pulled over for a minor infraction (such as speeding), never attempt to pay the fine directly to a police officer; this could be construed as attempted bribery, a much more serious crime. You'll be given a ticket for which you can mail in a fine in lieu of appearing in court. If you are accused of a more serious offense, say and do nothing before consulting a lawyer. In the U.S., the burden is on the state to prove a person's guilt beyond a reasonable doubt, and everyone has the right to remain silent, whether he or she is suspected of a crime or actually arrested. Once arrested, a person can make one telephone call to a party of his or her choice. The international visitor should call his or her embassy or consulate.

LGBT Travelers Phoenix and Tucson have lively LGBT communities, focused in the downtown areas. See chapters 4 and 9 for local guides for gay doings. The rest of the state remains somewhat backward—most of the state's elected officials, for example, fought gay marriage until the bitter end. Tourist areas will be fine, but in out-of-the-way towns, overt same-sex couples might find themselves the object of comment or worse.

Mail At press time, domestic postage rates were 35¢ for a postcard, 50¢ for a letter. For international mail, a first-class letter or postcard of up to 1 ounce costs $1.15. For more info go to **www.usps.com**.

Marijuana Medical cannabis is legal, and there are dispensaries in even the state's smaller cities. You need a doctor's prescription and a state-issued ID to buy; these are not available to tourists. A provision in the state's law gives some cover to visitors with medical-marijuana certification from another state. That said, a vote for full legalization lost in 2016; possession of any non-prescription marijuana is a felony in Arizona. Phoenix, Tucson, Scottsdale, and Tempe don't engage in undue prosecutions, but I wouldn't take my chances in other jurisdictions. Travelers from states where cannabis is legal should not bring cannabis into Arizona if they don't have medical cards.

Money & Costs What will a vacation in Arizona cost? That depends on your comfort needs. If you drive an RV or carry a tent, you can get by very inexpensively and find a place to stay almost anywhere in the state. If you don't mind staying in motels that date from the 1940s, you can stay for less money in Arizona than almost anyplace else in the U.S., paying under $40 a night for a double in some off-the-beaten-track places; in southern Arizona in summer, even tony resorts may offer rooms for not much more. On the other hand, you can easily spend many hundreds of dollars a day on a room at a world-class resort in high season. Rooms in Sedona and at the Grand Canyon are at a premium; plan on spending between $150 and $200 for a mid-level room. In most places, clean, modern motels at interstate highway off-ramps charge $45 to $65 a night for a double room (a little bit more in Phoenix and Tucson).

Newspapers & Magazines The *Arizona Republic* (azcentral.com), published out of Phoenix, is Arizona's largest daily paper; the Tucson paper is the *Arizona Daily Star*, www.tucson.com. *Arizona Highways* is a beautiful and informative monthly magazine published by the Arizona Department of Transportation. The alternative paper in Phoenix is *New Times*, www.phoenixnewtimes.com. Tucson's Tucson Sentinel is a lively local news website, at www.tucsonsentinel.com.

Safety Arizona's violent crime rate ranks in the middle of U.S. states. Phoenix, like most other big cities, has seen murder rates on average go down from 20 years ago. Violent crime in tourist areas is fairly rare. You can expect to encounter U.S. Border Patrol checkpoints in the southern part of the state. Don't leave valuables, especially purses, wallets, or cameras, in view in your car when going for a

WHAT THINGS COST IN ARIZONA	$US
Taxi from the airport to downtown Scottsdale	21.00–36.00
Double room, moderate	150.00–200.00
Double room, inexpensive	65.00–100.00
Three-course dinner for one without wine, moderate	30.00–35.00
Bottle of beer	2.50–3.50
Cup of coffee	2.00–3.00
1 gallon of premium gas	3.30
Admission to most museums	10.00–15.00
Admission per vehicle to Grand Canyon National Park	30.00

hike or taking pictures at a scenic overlook. Rental cars are particular targets.

When driving long distances, always carry plenty of drinking water and, if you're heading off onto dirt roads, extra water for your car's radiator as well. When hiking or walking in the desert, keep an eye out for rattlesnakes; these poisonous snakes are not normally aggressive unless provoked, so give them a wide berth. Kids particularly should be warned about goofing around near cactus; an accidental fall on one can range from the painful (a prickly pear) to the agonizing (the mischievous cholla).

Senior Travel With its abundant sunshine, Arizona has long been a favorite vacation and retirement destination with seniors. The state goes out of its way to accommodate senior travelers with discounts on accommodations and attractions, discounted "early-bird" dinners at many restaurants, and economical places to park RVs. Seniors should get an **America the Beautiful Senior Pass,** issued by the U.S. National Park Service, which gives seniors 62 years or older lifetime entrance to all properties administered by the National Park Service for a one-time fee of $80. (A $20 annual pass is also available at any federal park site.) Besides free entry, the America the Beautiful Senior Pass also offers a 50% discount on some fees for camping, swimming, parking, boat launching, and tours. You can apply for the Access Pass at any National Park Service facility that charges an entrance fee, or go online to get an application to mail in. For more info, go to www.nps.gov/fees_passes.htm.

Smoking With the exception of buildings on tribal lands and at tobacco retailers, smoking is prohibited in public indoor spaces throughout Arizona. This regulation applies to restaurants and bars, although they can have outdoor patios where smoking is allowed. In my experience these are rare.

Speeding Most highway traffic in Arizona moves along at 9 or 10 miles over the posted speed limit, and the chance of being pulled over when you are moving along with normal traffic is nil. But be aware of Arizona's "felony speeding" law: You can be *arrested* for going more than 20 miles over the speed limit, or exceeding 85mph, which is 10 miles over the top state speed limit of 75mph. This law is selectively enforced, but a fun family vacation can turn into a major bummer if the cop who pulls you over for going 87mph is having a bad day.

Taxes In Arizona, the state, counties, and communities can all levy a sales tax (officially called a transaction privilege tax). In most places, you'll pay 9% or more. On car rentals at Phoenix Sky Harbor Airport, expect to pay 50% or more in taxes and surcharges; at Tucson Airport, you'll pay around 30%. You can sometimes save 10% or so on surcharges if you rent outside the airports, but sometimes the rental rates are higher outside of the airport, which cancels out the savings. Hotel room taxes range from around 9% to 17%. There is no sales tax at nonprofit gift shops, including those at museums.

Time The continental United States is divided into **four time zones:** Eastern Standard Time (EST), Central Standard Time (CST), Mountain Standard Time (MST), and Pacific Standard Time (PST). For example, when it's 5pm in London (GMT), it's noon in New York City (EST), 11am in Chicago (CST), 10am in Phoenix (MST), and 9am in Los Angeles (PST). **Daylight saving time** moves clocks ahead one hour at 1am on the second Sunday in March, and moves them back one hour at 1am the first Sunday in November. Here's the problem: **Arizona doesn't observe daylight saving time.** That means that Arizona is an hour *ahead* of L.A. in winter months but on the *same* time zone as the west coast during the summer. If you're traveling around the Southwest, remember that as you cross state lines in or out of Arizona you may or may not have to change the time on your watches and phones, depending on the season. And just to make things more complicated, in the northeastern corner of the state, you're technically in Navajo country—where daylight saving time *is* followed! This can trip you up on everything from hotel check-in or check-out times to tour reservations. Make a mental note of this if you're traveling in summer.

Tipping Foreign visitors might not realize that the custom of tipping is built into the U.S. service economy; most restaurant and hotel workers are paid low wages with the expectation that they'll make up for it in tips. Unless you're unhappy with the service, a tip is expected. In hotels, tip **bellhops** at least $1 per bag ($2–$3 if you have a lot of luggage) and tip the **maid staff** at least $1–$2 per day (more if you've left a big mess to be cleaned up). I personally put cash into the hands of the maid to make sure she gets it. Tip the **doorman** or **concierge** only if he or she has provided you with some specific service (for example, calling a cab for you or obtaining difficult-to-get theater tickets).

Tip a **valet-parking attendant** $2 every time you get your car.

In restaurants, bars, and nightclubs, tip **service staff** 15% to 20% of the check; **bartenders** $1 for a beer, $2 for a mixed drink; and **checkroom attendants** $1 or $2 per garment.

Tip **cab drivers** 15% of the fare; tip **skycaps** at airports at least $2 per bag; and tip **hairdressers** and **barbers** 15% to 20%.

Toilets You won't find public toilets or "restrooms" on the streets in most U.S. cities. Instead, use facilities in hotel lobbies, bars and restaurants, department stores, grocery and "big-box" stores, and service stations. Once in a while you'll find a restaurant with a "customers only" sign on the restrooms, but I'd be surprised if any would refuse a polite request. Hotels and fast-food restaurants are the best bet for clean facilities.

Visitor Information

For statewide travel information, contact the **Arizona Office of Tourism** (www.arizonaguide.com; ✆ **866/275-5816**). See the individual chapters for details on local tourist offices. For suggested driving tours along Arizona's scenic roads, check out **Arizona Scenic Roads** at www.arizonascenicroads.com.

Index

See also Accommodations and Restaurant indexes, below.

General Index

C

D

H

I

J

K

L

M

N

Q

R

S

Y

Z

Accommodations

Restaurants

Photo Credits

Cover, © beboy/Shutterstock.com; p. i, © Irene Pearcey; p. 2, © Zhukova Valentyna; p. 4, © donvictorio/Shutterstock.com; p. 7, © Adriana Sta. Rosa; p. 9, © reisegraf.ch; p. 10, © Roderick Eime; p. 14, © MattLphotography; p. 16, © Chris Curtis/Shutterstock.com; p. 22, © Brent Hofacker; p. 26, © Scott Proko; p. 55, © Sean Pavone; p. 62, © Joseph Sohm/Shutterstock.com; p. 64, © EQRoy/Shutterstock.com; p. 66, © Manuela Durson/Shutterstock.com; p. 69, © Gregory E. Clifford; p. 70, © LunaseeStudios/Shutterstock.com; p. 74, © ShutterDivision/Shutterstock.com; p. 86, © Christopher Halloran/Shutterstock.com; p. 89, © Gregory E. Clifford/Shutterstock.com; p. 116, © BCFC/Shutterstock.com; p. 136, © Mark Skalny/Shutterstock.com; p. 145, © BCFC/Shutterstock.com; p. 157, © tishomir/Shutterstock.com; p. 159, © Thomas Trompeter/Shutterstock.com; p. 161, © Paul R. Jones; p. 167, © FiledIMAGE/Shutterstock.com; p. 172, © Chris Curtis; p. 181, © Sue Stokes; p. 182, © randy andy/Shutterstock.com; p. 186, © Joseph Sohm; p. 195, © Edwin Verin; p. 199, © Autumn Sky Photography/Shutterstock.com; p. 201, © reisegraf.ch; p. 203, © Wollertz/Shutterstock.com; p. 224, © Galyna Andrushko; p. 234, © John Gress Media Inc/Shutterstock.com; p. 239, © Mark Baldwin/Shutterstock.com; p. 244, © Paul R. Jones/Shutterstock.com; p. 252, © Tom Grundy; p. 260, © Nick Fox/Shutterstock.com; p. 263, © Zack Frank; p. 264, © Paul R. Jones/Shutterstock.com; p. 265, © Coconino National Forest; p. 273, © Ingus Kruklitis/Shutterstock.com; p. 277, © Ryan Kelehar; p. 279, © Hayk Shalunts/Shutterstock.com; p. 286, © Jon Chica/Shutterstock.com; p. 289, © melissamn/Shutterstock.com; p. 296, © Joseph Sohm; p. 303, © Avi Drori; p. 304, © Genevieve_Einzig; p. 308, © Judith Lienert; p. 313, © Zack Frank; p. 319, © JeniFoto; p. 323, © Staci Lichterman/Shutterstock.com; p. 325, © Nathan B Dappen; p. 327, © Chris Baltazar; p. 335, © Tom Roche; p. 337 top, © Peggy Hazelwood/Shutterstock.com; p. 337 bottom, © Zero Degrees Photography; p. 341, © TygerGilbert; p. 346, © Aaron Fortin; p. 351, © Tom Tietz; p. 357, © Sean Pavone; p. 361, © CatonPhoto; p. 364, © Jon Manjeo; p. 365, © meunierd/Shutterstock.com; p. 373, © Joseph Sohm; p. 374, © woodsnorthphoto/Shutterstock.com; p. 378, © travelview/Shutterstock.com; p. 381, © hessianmercenary; p. 415, © Ken Bosma; p. 419, © tishomir/Shutterstock.com; p. 427, © Anton Foltin; p. 432, © Thomas Trompeter/Shutterstock.com; p. 433, © Thomas Trompeter/Shutterstock.com; p. 442, © jpeterson; p. 449, © Takahashi Photography; p. 456, © Atomazul/Shutterstock.com; p. 460, © Barna Tanko/Shutterstock.com; p.469, © Paul B. Moore; p. 480, © Joseph Sohm; p. 483, © MattLphotography; p. 485, © Andrew Zarivny/Shutterstock.com; p. 489, © Prayitno/Thank you for (12 millions +) view; p. 498, © Paul R. Jones; Back cover, © tonda/iStock.

NOTES

NOTES